Leaving Iberia

Islamic Law and Christian Conquest in North West Africa

Jocelyn Hendrickson

In memory of my grandmother
Gladys Granlund Hendrickson
June 10, 1921–June 27, 2020

Library of Congress Control Number:
2021908030

This book was published with the generous assistance of a
Book Subvention Award from the Medieval Academy of America.

Printed in the United States of America
978-0-674-24820-5

Contents

APPENDICES

ACKNOWLEDGMENTS

If this book were to have a soundtrack, one song would stand out. In Bob Dylan's "When I Paint My Masterpiece," a young man laments the "long, hard drive" of far-flung travels and longs for that future day when his masterpiece is complete, when everything "is gonna be different." I can relate wholeheartedly to that long-anticipated moment when a labor of love is finally brought to fruition. Yet I look back on this journey with joy and gratitude, not melancholy. The years and miles that I have traveled in the service of this project have been thoroughly enjoyable, and an immense privilege. I am honored to have this opportunity to thank those who were "there with me" as I dreamed of painting this particular "masterpiece."

So many kind and thoughtful people have supported and inspired me that I must make only a humble attempt to thank them all here. I owe my most substantial debt to the graduate school mentors whose brilliant guidance, steady encouragement, and astonishing generosity made this work possible: the late Richard Martin, Gordon Newby, Joyce Burkhalter Flueckiger, Carl Ernst, Kristen Brustad, and especially my advisor, Devin Stewart, who first sparked my interest in the *fatwās* considered here. In Cairo, I am grateful to Emad Abou Ghazi for an invaluable seminar in Arabic paleography and in Fez, to Muhammad Wassu and Ali Fellali for countless hours spent unravelling the complexities of medieval Arabic legalese. Long before I could have contemplated those complexities, my initial forays into Arabic and Islamic law were encouraged by my undergraduate mentors, Terri DeYoung and Brannon Wheeler.

Colleagues near and far have provided insightful comments on versions of this work. I am especially grateful to Amira Bennison, Mohammad Fadel, Maribel Fierro, David Powers, Gerard Wiegers, and the late L.P. Harvey for suggestions that helped reshape my doctoral dissertation into this book. At conferences and workshops, scholars who have made valuable suggestions and pointed me toward important resources include Ellen Amster, Abigail Krasner Balbale, M'Hamad Benaboud, Mohamad Ballan, Ziad Bentahar, Eric Calderwood, Vincent Cornell, Hussein Fancy, Allen Fromherz, Barbara Fuchs, Katie Harris, Seth Kimmel, Libby Nutting, Etty Terem, Paul Powers, Janina Safran, Justin Stearns, John Tolan and Natalie Zemon Davis. At my home institutions, I thank my colleagues for fostering a supportive intellectual community; special thanks are due to Siobhan Byrne, John Cotts, Ehud Ben Zvi, Ryan Dunch, Courtney Fitzsimmons, Louise Harrington, Jaymie Patricia Heilman, Kristy King, Francis Landy, Felice Lifshitz, Ann McDougall, Rogers Miles, Ken Mouré, James Muir, Steve Patten, Sharon Romeo, David Sulz, Jonathan Walters, Melissa Wilcox, and Walt Wyman. At Whitman College and the University of Alberta, students in my advanced seminars have engaged with and critiqued my work, pushing me to new insights. I am especially grateful to Cassandra Baker, Eleanor Ellis, Brynne Healy, Emily Kumpf, and Nakita Valerio. Thanks also to Axel Perez Trujillo, who provided valuable research assistance for part 2.

For critical moral support and guidance at the earliest stages of this project, I am indebted to my cohort at Emory, Duke, and the University of North Carolina-Chapel Hill, including Amy Allocco, Supriya Gandhi, Melanie Magidow, Robert Moore, Youshaa Patel, María del Mar Rosa-Rodríguez, Karen Ruffle, Peter Valdina, David Vishanoff, Luke Whitmore, and Brett Wilson. For assistance in navigating the libraries, streets, and rooftops of Cairo, Fez, Rabat, Madrid, Barcelona, Tunis, Oran, and Nouakchott, I am sincerely grateful to Rani Abdellatif, Sabahat Adil, Rose Aslan, Karen Bauer, Cassie Chambliss, Julie Coons, Carl Davila, Thomas DeGeorges, Camilo Gómez-Rivas, Hamid Lahmer, Yuen-Gen (Toby) Liang, Matthew Melvin-Koushki, Reem Morsi, Yahya ould El-Bara, Sayeed Rahman, Amanda Rogers, Adriana Valencia, and James Wheeler.

I am particularly indebted to the librarians, archivists, copyists, and shopkeepers whose assistance, patience, trust, and good humor facilitated many years of searching through catalogues, poring over manuscripts, and hunting down essential resources, from out-of-print single volumes to shiny new editions. I owe a special thanks to the staff and directors who granted me permission to obtain copies of manuscripts, lithographs, and rare books at the following libraries: the Ḥasaniyya (Royal) Library in Rabat (especially Chouqui Binebine and Mohammed Said Hinchi), the Moroccan National Library (especially Shafiq and Nozha Ben Saadoun), the King ʿAbd al-ʿAzīz Āl Saʿūd Foundation in Casablanca, the Qarawiyyīn Library in Fez, the General Library and Archives in Tetouan, the Tunisian National Library, the Algerian National Library, the El Escorial Monastery library, and the Library of Alexandria. My fond gratitude also goes to the helpful staff at Dār al-Amān, Maktabat al-Ṭālib, and Maktabat ʿĀlam al-Fikr in Rabat; Maktabat al-Turāth (Maktabat Sī Bennanī) in Fez; and Dar Attakafa in Casablanca. Special thanks are also due to Sjoerd van Koningsveld, Gerard Wiegers, and Umar Ryad for sharing with me their unpublished edition of a key text. Without their generosity, I could not have accomplished some of this book's primary aims.

I am honored and humbled to have received the material and financial support of numerous institutions. My research abroad was supported by a Fulbright Islamic Civilization fellowship; a fellowship from the Center for Arabic Study Abroad II; the Social Science Research Council's International Dissertation Research Fellowship; a Fulbright-Hays Doctoral Dissertation Research Abroad Fellowship; and a travel grant from the American Institute for Maghrib Studies. I am grateful to the Charlotte W. Newcombe Foundation for a year of writing supported by a Doctoral Dissertation Fellowship. Additional trips were supported by Whitman College, a National Endowment for the Humanities Summer Institute, and the University of Alberta. I also thank James Wellman at the Jackson School of International Studies and Clark Lombardi at the University of Washington Law School for helping me obtain Visiting Scholar status while writing on Bainbridge Island, Washington. Generous grants from the University of Alberta and the Medieval Academy of America supported the publication of this book.

Abroad, this research was also facilitated by the support of several research centers. I gratefully acknowledge the assistance of the Moroccan-American Commission for Educational and Cultural Exchange, the Centre d'Etudes Maghrébines à Tunis, the Centre d'Etudes Maghrébines en Algérie, and the Consejo Superior de Investigaciones Científicas. In particular, I thank Daoud Casewit, Saadia Maski, James Miller, Larry Michalak, Riadh Saadaoui, Robert Parks, and Maribel Fierro.

One previously published journal article draws on portions of part 1: "Muslim Legal Responses to Portuguese Occupation in Late Fifteenth-Century North Africa," *Journal of Spanish Cultural Studies* 12.3 (2011). I thank Taylor & Francis for permission to include that material here.

At the Program in Islamic Law at Harvard Law School, I thank Intisar Rabb, Kathi Ivanyi, Mona Rahmani, and Sharon Tai for shepherding this book through to publication and overseeing the creation of its Online Companion. The insightful comments and criticism of four anonymous reviewers improved this book immensely. Thanks also Valerie Joy Turner, who prepared the indexes and whose expert copyediting has improved nearly every page of this book.

Completing this project would not have been possible without professional childcare, one of the most critical forms of research support for parents of small children. I am especially grateful to the staff at Hospitals and Community Day Care Centre and at the University Infant Toddler Centre, both in Edmonton, and at Jardín de Infancia El Alhelí in Rabat. The excellent care they provided my children afforded me precious time and peace of mind.

My warmest gratitude goes to friends and family whose persistent encouragement, companionship, and moral support have sustained me throughout this project: my father Loel and mother Karen, my brother Aquila and sister-in-law Nichole; my late grandmother Gladys, aunt Dawn, cousin Dakota, and cousin-in-law Becca; and my in-laws Vickie, Jon, Reen, Crystal, Graeme, and Janna. Thank you also to Tannis, David, Ann, Mary, Phil, Eleanor, Kären, and Larry for cheering me on at various stages of this journey. Finally, I am grateful to my husband Ashley for joining me on this journey, and to our daughters, Raven and Peregrine, for truly making everything different, in wondrous and unexpected ways.

Note on Transliteration, Dates, and Online Resources

This book follows the guidelines of the *Chicago Manual of Style*, 17th edition, and the system of Arabic transliteration adopted by the *International Journal of Middle East Studies*, with a few exceptions. Most notably, in accordance with the style guide for the Harvard Series in Islamic Law, the initial definite article (*al-*) is omitted from proper names when mentioned alone, after the first appearance (al-Wansharīsī becomes Wansharīsī). Arabic names of people, places, and dynasties are normally transliterated with diacritics, except those with commonly recognized English renderings (Fez not Fās, Almoravids not al-Murābiṭūn). Commonly used Spanish and French spellings are occasionally preferred over both English and Arabic transliteration (Córdoba not Cordoba or Qurṭuba). If the Arabic title of a work has become well known, I refer to the work by that title (*Asnā al-matājir*). For other works that appear frequently, I translate the title into English and thereafter refer to the work primarily by its translated title (*al-Jawāhir al-mukhtāra* becomes *Selected Jewels*). I use italics and headline-style capitalization for translated titles (*Prohibition on Plundering*), instead of reserving this style for published translations; the majority of works cited have not been translated and many of them remain unpublished even in the original Arabic. Where an author has published in multiple languages, I give priority to that author's preferred or predominant spelling, but include additional forms of the name in the bibliography. Arabic terms in the singular are frequently made plural with the addition of "s" (*fatwā* becomes *fatwās* not *fatāwā*). Translations from the Qur'ān are based on those published by M.A.S. Abdel Haleem, A.J. Arberry, Muhammad Marmaduke Pickthall, and ʿAbdullah Yūsuf ʿAlī, with slight modifications. All other translations from Arabic, French, and Spanish are my own, unless otherwise indicated. Where two dates or centuries appear, they are given in the AH/CE format, with the Islamic (*hijrī*) date (Anno Hegirae or After Hijra) preceding the Common Era date. Where dates appear alone, they refer to the Common Era.

SHARIAsource, the online portal of the Program in Islamic Law at Harvard Law School, will publish an Online Companion for *Leaving Iberia* containing additional material and resources. These materials include my Arabic editions of two key texts, copies of many of the primary sources referred to in the printed book, short bibliographies, maps, and a digital copy of the book.

INTRODUCTION

CHAPTER 1

Leaving Iberia

The Holy Virgin . . . freed Her church from them, for in that way She banishes those She despises. Therefore, Her church is now free, for never can Muḥammad hold power there [in Murcia] because She conquered it, and furthermore, She will conquer Spain and Morocco, and Ceuta and Asilah.[1]

In 1491, or shortly prior, an obscure North African jurist named Abū ʿAbd Allāh b. Qaṭiyya wrote to the leading jurist in Fez, the capital of the Waṭṭāsid state, with a request for counsel regarding a local case. A group of Andalusī Muslims (from al-Andalus, or Islamic Iberia) had abandoned their homes, property, and former lives in the Iberian Peninsula. Fleeing with their religion and children, they managed to escape infidel rule and resettle in the land of Islam. Ibn Qaṭiyya does not say where their journey began, but we can deduce that the emigrants must have been residents of the Naṣrid Kingdom of Granada, the last Iberian Muslim kingdom. If so, they would have found themselves subjects of the Crown of Castile as the Christian "Reconquest"[2] of Iberia neared completion and the Christian-Muslim frontier moved ever closer to the city of Granada, which soon surrendered to Ferdinand of Aragon and Isabella of Castile. Fearing their future as Muslims in a Christian land, and mindful of their Islamic legal obligation to emigrate to Muslim territory rather than remain

---

1 Number 169 from the *Cantigas de Santa María*, a collection of songs in praise of Mary, commissioned or written by Alfonso X of Castile in the third quarter of the thirteenth century. Translated from the Galician-Portuguese by Kathleen Kulp-Hill and quoted in "Tales of Marian Miracles," *Medieval Iberia: Readings from Christian, Muslim, and Jewish Sources*, ed. Olivia Remie Constable, 2nd ed. (Philadelphia: University of Pennsylvania Press, 2012), 367.

2 The term "Reconquest" (or *reconquista*) is used for convenience, but reflects a Christian perspective. Muslim sources usually refer to the Christian conquest of Muslim territory in Iberia as "the fall of al-Andalus." On the concept of "Reconquest," see Alejandro García Sanjuán, "Rejecting al-Andalus, Exalting the Reconquista: Historical Memory in Contemporary Spain," *Journal of Medieval Iberian Studies* 10, no. 1 (2018): 127–45; and Francisco García Fitz, *La Reconquista* (Granada: University of Granada, 2010), 11–33.

under Christian rule, they had taken what they could carry, crossed the Mediterranean, and landed somewhere in the Maghrib (North Africa), most likely in present-day Morocco.

After successfully completing their obligatory emigration, or *hijra*, these Andalusī Muslims were dismayed that they could not find any replacement for the security, prosperity, or community they had left behind. They changed their minds, regretted their decision to emigrate, and wanted to return to Iberia.

Thus far the story of these unfortunate emigrants is remarkable but not unique; waves of refugees fled or were expelled from Iberia during and after the Reconquest, and some of them later returned home.[3] These particular Andalusīs caught the attention of the authorities and historians when they allegedly began to mock the Maghrib and the very idea of *hijra*, and to conspicuously broadcast their hopes that the ruler of Castile would allow their return to an "infidel" kingdom. Ibn Qaṭiyya complains that the emigrants "openly derided the land of Islam" while praising the land of unbelief, that they actively sought any possible means to return to Castile, and that they were overheard making such comments as "Emigrate from there to here? Rather, it is from here to there that emigration should be required!"

Ibn Qaṭiyya's query bristles with offense at this bold reversal, this declaration that the Maghrib is so inferior to Castile that native North Africans ought to abandon *their* homeland and seek Christian rule on the other side of the Strait of Gibraltar. His angry missive catalogues the emigrants' offenses, requests guidance as to the punishments they deserve, and feigns the need for clarification as to whether or not a true *hijra*, for the sake of God, should be undertaken under whatever conditions He wills—or if the journey is only necessary when material comfort and convenience are assured.

Aḥmad b. Yaḥyā al-Wansharīsī (d. 914/1508), the leading jurist of Fez, wrote two lengthy *fatwā*s, or legal opinions, confirming the obligation of these and other Muslims to migrate to Muslim territory, prohibiting their voluntary residence under non-Muslim rule, and recommending a severe, exemplary punishment for these emigrants. Their insults against Islam and offenses against the public order constituted *fitna*, or the spread of corrupt ideas. Wansharīsī is even less sympathetic than Ibn Qaṭiyya to the emigrants' plight, and describes these Andalusīs as vile, contemptible people whose repugnant actions nearly amount to infidelity. Worse yet are those who choose to live under infidel rule without emigrating, a condition Wansharīsī stresses is not permitted "for even one hour of one day, because

3 For an overview of population movements in medieval and early modern Iberia, see Mercedes García-Arenal, *La Diaspora des Andalousiens*, L'Encyclopédie de la Méditerrané 13 (Aix-en-Provence, France: Édisud, 2003).

of the pollution, the filth, and the religious and worldly corruptions to which this gives rise."[4]

After Muslims had coexisted with Christians and Jews for nearly eight centuries in the Iberian Peninsula, why was Wansharīsī so convinced that grievous injury would result if Muslims remained even one hour in the same company, but under Christian rather than Muslim rule? Why were he and Ibn Qaṭiyya so quick to condemn these Andalusīs who had endured and sacrificed so much, and who insisted they had emigrated in pious fulfillment of their religious obligations? Were these jurists just applying inherited doctrines, or did other factors shape their rendering of the law?

In *Leaving Iberia* I offer the first sustained analysis of Islamic legal responses to Christian conquests in both Iberia and North Africa in the late fifteenth and early sixteenth centuries. The fall of al-Andalus from the twelfth to the fifteenth century (as the "Reconquest" was known to Muslims) has been seen as a major turning point for Islamic history, when the first substantial Muslim populations fell under permanent Christian rule. This reversal of fortunes has inspired a substantial scholarly literature addressing the Islamic legal status of Muslims under Christian rule, but scholars have focused almost exclusively on conquered Muslims in Iberia. *Leaving Iberia* shifts our attention toward an overlooked body of *fatwās* addressing the status of Muslims living under Portuguese and Spanish control in North Africa itself, beginning in the fifteenth century. By moving beyond the shores of the Iberian Peninsula and following Christian conquerors into North Africa, in this book I add a significant chapter to the story of Christian-Muslim relations in the medieval Mediterranean. In light of this new material, this work also dramatically reinterprets the most prominent legal texts concerning the obligation of Iberian Muslims to migrate to Muslim territory.

In this introduction I explain briefly how Christian conquests challenged Muslim jurists and situate the book's arguments in the two primary academic fields to which they contribute. In North African and Iberian historiography, *Leaving Iberia* challenges the continued perception of Iberian exceptionalism, a perception that has outlasted older debates regarding *convivencia*, or interreligious coexistence. In Islamic legal historiography, this book rethinks our approach to the study of Islamic legal adaptation and authority, now that the theory of the "closing of the gate of *ijtihād*," which posits medieval intellectual stagnation, has been discredited

4 Aḥmad b. Yaḥyā al-Wansharīsī, *al-Miʿyār al-muʿrib waʾl-jāmiʿ al-mughrib ʿan fatāwī ahl Ifrīqiyā waʾl-Andalus waʾl-Maghrib*, ed. Muḥammad Ḥajjī, et al., 13 vols. (Rabat: Wizārat al-Awqāf waʾl-Shuʾūn al-Islāmiyya, 1981–83), 2:138. I have translated this *fatwā* in full in appendix B.

and discarded. In the conclusion I step beyond these two fields to consider this project's contribution to the study of Islam in North and West Africa.

The Tide Turns

When Ṭāriq b. Ziyād first led a Muslim army across the Strait of Gibraltar[5] from North Africa to Iberia in 711, the invading force formed the western edge of a rapidly expanding Islamic empire. Within one century of Muḥammad's death in 632, Muslim territory stretched across North Africa into the Iberian Peninsula in the west, and into parts of Central Asia and the Indus River Valley in the east. While an initial foray across the Pyrenees was repulsed, by the mid-eighth century, Muslims established lasting control over most of the Iberian Peninsula. Following the Abbasid defeat of the Umayyad dynasty in the east in 750, a surviving member of the Umayyad family established a new emirate in Iberia, one that later became the independent Umayyad caliphate of Córdoba (929–1031). Although the caliphate disintegrated into rival Muslim states (*ṭāʾifas*) in the early eleventh century, together the caliphal and Ṭāʾifa periods have been praised as the Golden Age of al-Andalus, as a time of intellectual and artistic florescence enjoyed by Jews, Christians, and Muslims alike.[6]

The tide began to turn in the late eleventh century, beginning with King Alfonso VI of Castile's 1085 conquest of Toledo, the former Visigothic capital. Iberia's Christian kingdoms began to make permanent territorial gains at the expense of the Muslim *ṭāʾifa* ("party") states. Two successive Berber dynasties from the Far Maghrib (present-day Morocco), the Almoravids and the Almohads, attempted to reunite Muslim Iberia in the twelfth century.[7] They were ultimately unsuccessful and the Christian kingdoms steadily advanced, conquering most of the peninsula by the mid-thirteenth century.

From roughly 1260 until 1492, Muslims in al-Andalus fell into two major groups: those who lived under Christian rule and those who lived in, or migrated to, Naṣrid Granada, which survived as the last Muslim kingdom in Iberia. The former, who lived under Christian rule, were known as Mudéjars;[8] they were allowed to continue practicing Islam, subject to

5 Gibraltar ("Jabal Ṭāriq") and the strait were named after this commander, Ṭāriq b. Ziyād.

6 For a popular articulation of this view, see, for example, María Rosa Menocal's *The Ornament of the World: How Muslims, Jews, and Christians Created a Culture of Tolerance in Medieval Spain* (Boston: Back Bay Books, 2002).

7 I have retained the term "Berber" for convenience, but note that originally, this was a derogatory term applied by foreigners to indigenous North Africans. The many "Berber" tribes gathered under this umbrella term are linguistically and ethnically distinct.

8 The Arabic term *mudajjanūn* or *ahl al-dajn* means 'domesticated' for animals and indicates submissiveness for humans. For a discussion of the term, see Gerard Wiegers, *Islamic Literature in Spanish and Aljamiado: Yça of Segovia (fl. 1450), His Antecedents and Successors* (Leiden: Brill, 1994), 3.

certain restrictions that varied over time and by region. The fall of Granada in 1492 marks the end of independent Muslim rule in the peninsula and the expulsion of the Jews.[9] At that point, all Iberian Muslims became Mudéjars until forced conversions and regional expulsions began at the turn of the sixteenth century.[10] By 1526, all Muslims remaining in the Iberian Peninsula had been converted, nominally at least, to Christianity. These converts, who became known as Moriscos, were subject to a number of royal decrees, missionary campaigns, and relocations aimed at ensuring their sincere conversion to Christianity and full assimilation into Christian society. Between 1609 and 1614, when these efforts were deemed unsuccessful, the Moriscos were expelled from Iberia.

While Muslims had fallen under non-Muslim rule in parts of India and China as early as the eighth century, and in the Levant during the crusades, these cases involved smaller populations, or were temporary, and appear to have had little impact on Islamic legal thought.[11] Christian conquests in the medieval western Mediterranean, including Sicily (1061–1091) and especially Iberia (1085–1492) were of far greater consequence for Muslim jurists. In Iberia, Muslims had ruled over Jews and Christians who for centuries had accepted a subordinate, *dhimmī* status, until Christian advances permanently inverted this hierarchy and brought large and long-established Muslim populations under Christian rule. As a center of Islamic learning, al-Andalus was also important symbolically, although it was not yet cast as the "lost paradise" that it later became in Muslim thought.[12]

---

9 In March 1492 Ferdinand and Isabella decreed the expulsion of Jews from their realms (Castile, Aragon, and newly conquered Granada), and made their daughter's marriage to King Manuel of Portugal conditional upon the expulsion of Jews and Muslims from his realm; King Manuel complied by issuing a decree in 1496 that took effect in 1497. Lastly, Navarre expelled its Jews in 1498, also as a result of pressure from the Catholic Monarchs.

10 Muslims were expelled from Portugal in 1497. In Granada and then in Castile more broadly, Muslims were subject to mass conversions from 1499 to 1501; this was followed by an edict in 1502 requiring the conversion or emigration of all Muslims in Castile. This policy requiring conversion or expulsion was extended to Navarre upon the territory's incorporation into the Spanish Crown in 1515. In Aragon, a large number of Muslims were forcibly baptized from 1520 to 1522, and in 1525 the conversions were confirmed as valid. In 1525, Charles V (as Holy Roman Emperor and King of Spain) decreed that Muslims in Catalonia, Aragon, and Valencia must choose conversion or expulsion. By 1526, when the last of these decrees took effect, all Muslims in Spain had become Moriscos, or "crypto-Muslims." For these dates, see L. P. Harvey, *Muslims in Spain: 1500–1614* (Chicago: University of Chicago Press, 2005).

11 For an overview of Muslim legal responses to Christian conquest across legal schools, see Khaled Abou El Fadl, "Islamic Law and Muslim Minorities: The Juristic Discourse on Muslim Minorities from the Second/Eighth to the Eleventh/Seventeenth Centuries," *Islamic Law and Society* 1, no. 2 (1994): 154–56.

12 On the development of al-Andalus as a lost paradise, see Justin Stearns, "Representing and Remembering al-Andalus: Some Historical Considerations Regarding the End of Time and the Making of Nostalgia," *Medieval Encounters* 15, nos. 2–4 (2009): 355–74.

The persistence of substantial Mudéjar communities in Iberia challenged three closely related theoretical assumptions for jurists working in the Mālikī school of law, the dominant legal school in the Islamic West (Northwest Africa, Sicily, and Iberia). First, the Mudéjars' long-standing presence in Iberia and ability to practice Islam under Christian rule problematized the classical legal dichotomy dividing the world between *dār al-Islām* ("the land of Islam") and *dār al-ḥarb* ("the land of war"). The jurists who elaborated the Islamic legal tradition assumed that Muslims inhabited *dār al-Islām*, where Islamic ethical and legal norms prevailed, though they might travel to *dār al-ḥarb* for purposes such as trade. Rather than an arena of active combat, as the name might suggest, *dār al-ḥarb* denoted territory beyond the frontiers of Islam, where non-Muslim laws governed the population and those who entered the area. If conquered Muslims could still practice Islam, did their territory merit a new, third designation? Or did they now inhabit *dār al-ḥarb*, but as a new category of Muslim, subject to different legal considerations from those of temporary travelers?

Second, by this period, jurists in all four Sunnī schools of law, not just Mālikīs, were expected to ground their opinions in the established doctrines of their schools, rather than to derive new legal rules directly from the Qurʾān and Ḥadīth.[13] Yet the available corpus of Mālikī texts provided little applicable material for Muslims living under non-Muslim rule. The formative period of Islamic law (roughly the seventh through the ninth centuries) was a time in which dramatic conquests took place and Muslims gained immense political power. As new territories and diverse populations were incorporated into the Islamic empire, early jurists formulated a basic code governing the relationships between the Muslim ruling elite and their non-Muslim subjects, primarily Christians and Jews. *Dhimmīs* were free to practice their own religions in exchange for payment of a special tax (the *jizya*) and acknowledgment of their inferior status.

The context of rapid Islamic expansion meant that these early jurists had little reason to ponder the status of Muslims living under non-Muslim rule; rather, it was a priority to establish the status of non-Muslim minorities living in Muslim territory. Their discussions regarding Muslims in *dār al-ḥarb* were limited, for example, to cases of traders, pilgrims, and other travelers, or individual converts to Islam. Wansharīsī protests that the early jurists to whom one should look for guidance did not address the case of a territory changing from *dār al-Islām* to *dār al-ḥarb*, as this was unheard

13 Adherence to school doctrine is known as *taqlīd*, as opposed to *ijtihād*, the independent derivation of new law. Western scholarship on Islamic law long held that the four primary Sunnī schools of law agreed to close the "gate of *ijtihād*" in the mid-ninth century; see below for a discussion of this theory. Muslim tradition also laments a lapse in the practice of *ijtihād*, and calls for its renewal are an integral component of both conservative and liberal modern Islamic reform movements.

of in their time; it had simply not happened. He dates the first such change to the loss of Sicily and parts of al-Andalus in the eleventh century.[14] How would medieval, self-described *muqallid* ("follower") jurists leverage the resources of their legal heritage to address the novel but critical set of legal issues arising from this unprecedented new reality?[15]

Third, although Mālikī jurists found a partial solution to these first two challenges (conquered Muslims and the lack of precedent) in the doctrine of *hijra*, which required Muslims who found themselves in *dār al-ḥarb* to migrate to *dār al-Islām*, many Mudéjars proved unable or unwilling to comply. This obligation to migrate from lands of unbelief and oppression was modeled on Muḥammad's original *hijra* from polytheist Mecca, where he faced persecution, to Medina, where he established the first Muslim polity in 622; this event marks the beginning of the Islamic calendar. The earliest Muslims were required to leave everything and follow Muḥammad in order to strengthen the nascent Muslim community, escape persecution, and avoid contributing to the strength of the enemy in Mecca. From the vantage point of *dār al-Islām*, the case of al-Andalus seemed to fit this model quite well: Muslims who remained under Christian rule would become a persecuted minority, practice a compromised version of Islam, and all the while contribute to Christian power by constituting a vital part of the Christian workforce. The emigration of the Mudéjars meant they could maintain their religious integrity, avoid becoming subordinate (in addition to losing their land), harness their talents for the Muslim world, and earn a heavenly reward for emulating the Prophet's example.

From the Mudéjars' perspective, the situation was far more complex. Although many did emigrate from conquered territories, either to Granada prior to 1492, or to North African cities such as Tetouan and Fez, a substantial number remained in the Iberian Peninsula. Among their compelling reasons to stay was their reluctance to abandon property or family, and the expense and physical risks of the journey itself, including potential enslavement if caught violating a royal ban on emigration.[16] A better life in *dār al-Islām* was also far from guaranteed, as Wansharīsī's unhappy emigrants discovered.

---

14 Wansharīsī, *al-Mi'yār* 2:124–25. Mālikī jurists appear to be unaware of any legal precedents from the eastern Islamic lands that might have resulted from Muslims living under non-Muslim rule.

15 A *muqallid* practices *taqlīd*, or emulation and application of school doctrine. In contrast, a *mujtahid* is capable of *ijtihād*, the independent derivation of new rules from the Qur'ān and Ḥadīth.

16 Policies on emigration varied by Christian kingdom. In Valencia, where a large Muslim minority provided essential labor, emigration without a royal license was prohibited for much of the late fourteenth and fifteenth centuries, and punishable by enslavement. See Mark D. Meyerson, *The Muslims of Valencia in the Age of Fernando and Isabel: Between Coexistence and Crusade* (Berkeley: University of California Press, 1991), 15, 30–31, 223–24.

Beyond the Reconquest

The regretful Andalusīs with whom I opened this chapter were not the first Muslims to complicate the theoretically straightforward obligation to perform *hijra*, nor was Wansharīsī the first or only jurist to address these issues. Yet scholarship on Islamic legal responses to medieval Christian conquests in the Mediterranean has centered primarily on the opinions of just two jurists, Wansharīsī and his fellow resident of Fez (or Fāsī) Ibn Abī Jumʿa al-Wahrānī (d. 917/1511). Often viewed as the epitome of all that ailed Islamic law in the post-formative period (after the ninth century), Wansharīsī's two 1491 *fatwās* on the obligation to emigrate (*Asnā al-matājir* and the "Marbella *fatwā*") have been described as unimaginative and strict at best, and blamed for the "destruction of Spanish Islam" at worst.[17] Wahrānī's text, known as his "1504 *fatwā*" advised the first Granadan Moriscos as to how they might maintain adherence to Islam without being detected and despite being forced to perform such acts as praying in church or drinking wine. Scholars have often described Wahrānī as a voice of openness, compassion, and creativity in the face of Wansharīsī's rigidity and authoritarian orthodoxy. The opinions of these two jurists are among the most widely discussed premodern *fatwās* on any subject.

By focusing on a handful of *fatwās* concerning Iberian Muslims and—to a much lesser extent—Sicilian Muslims, scholars have treated the phenomenon of Muslims living under Christian rule as a European issue. Yet both Portugal and Spain expanded into North Africa in the fifteenth century, beginning with Portugal's 1415 conquest of Ceuta and Spain's 1497 conquest of Melilla. By the early sixteenth century, Portugal controlled most of North Africa's Atlantic port cities and commanded tribute from vast hinterlands in what is now southern Morocco. By 1511, Spain had captured a series of southern Mediterranean ports that stretched to Tripoli. Portugal only withdrew from its final Maghribī holding at Mazagan in 1769, while Ceuta and Melilla remain in Spanish hands today.

In part 1 of this book I introduce this neglected chapter of Iberian-North African history (chapter 2) and the fascinating but equally neglected Islamic legal responses to which it gave rise (chapter 3). In his compilation entitled *al-Jawāhir al-mukhtāra* (*Selected Jewels*),[18] which until now remains in manuscript form, Maghribī jurist ʿAbd al-ʿAzīz al-Zayyātī (d. 1055/1645) preserved a significant corpus of *fatwās* issued in response to

---

17 For "destruction," see Felipe Maíllo Salgado, "Consideraciones acerca de una fatwà de al-Wanšarīšī," *Studia Historica* 3, no. 2 (1985): 185; and Maíllo Salgado, "Del Islam residual," in *España, al-Andalus, Sefarad: Síntesis y nuevas perspectivas*, 134 (Salamanca: Universidad de Salamanca, 1988): 137.

18 Hereafter, I refer to Zayyātī's work as *Selected Jewels*.

Portuguese occupation of parts of the Far Maghrib[19] in the late fifteenth and early sixteenth centuries. These texts, largely unknown and unexplored, are particularly important as they enable us to compare legal responses to Christian conquest in both Iberia and North Africa. Whereas combat is not countenanced in the texts that focus on Iberia, those that focus on the Maghrib, for example, encourage active *jihād* against the Portuguese; in fact, these *fatwās* constitute a rare instance of recorded indigenous resistance to the expansion of Iberian empire in the fifteenth century. The definition of what constitutes submission to Christian authority is also much less clear in the *fatwās* (or "jewels") preserved by Zayyātī.

Yet we find significant commonalities in the *fatwās* addressing Mudéjars and Maghribīs, and these challenge the presumption that the Iberian Muslim predicament was exceptional. These legal opinions share a set of concerns and legal categories, including the obligation to emigrate and the legal consequences of specific Muslim-Christian relationships. A little-known *fatwā* by Wansharīsī provides a particularly compelling link between opinions focused on Iberian Muslims, versus those related to North African Muslims. Zayyātī's compilation shows that Wansharīsī was among a group of Fāsī jurists who responded to a similar set of questions regarding the status of Muslims in Portuguese-controlled Morocco shortly prior to Wansharīsī's late-1491 composition of *Asnā al-matājir* and the Marbella *fatwā*. The "Berber *fatwā*," Wansharīsī's contribution to this lively juristic discourse, reads like a rough draft of *Asnā al-matājir*. This explicit textual overlap demonstrates that Zayyātī's "jewels" (as I refer to the opinions he preserved on this issue) and Wansharīsī's two well-known opinions all formed part of a larger discourse on the status of conquered Muslims on both sides of the Mediterranean in the late fifteenth and early sixteenth centuries.

In part 2 of this book I dramatically reinterpret *Asnā al-matājir* and the Marbella *fatwā* in light of the juristic discourse of the time. Previous studies of these two prominent texts have emphasized their impact on Iberian Muslims. These opinions are assumed to have circulated in Iberia, where they encouraged Muslim elites to emigrate and thus left the poor vulnerable to exploitation and conversion. In contrast, I argue that Wansharīsī's infamous

19 In Arabic, *al-Maghrib al-aqṣā*, or the Far Maghrib, is used to mean the western portion of North Africa that is now Morocco. In general usage, the term "Maghrib" can mean the area that is modern-day Morocco (the country name is al-Maghrib in Arabic), but it can also mean North Africa more broadly, stretching from modern-day Morocco to Libya. When it is clear that a reference concerns Morocco only (and "Morocco" would be anachronistic), I often use the more specific term the "Far Maghrib." Likewise, I employ "Ifrīqiyā" for the territory roughly corresponding to modern-day Tunisia. I have included a glossary of terms following the appendices and chronology.

texts concern the Portuguese occupation of Maghribī ports as much as they do Iberia. We have no evidence of their contemporary circulation outside the Maghrib.

Asnā al-matājir in particular is best understood as a product of, and contribution to, the Maghribī discourse on Muslim-Christian relations in Morocco itself. I maintain that Wansharīsī advanced his most powerful arguments against residence under non-Muslim rule in the framework of his ostensibly Mudéjar-focused *fatwās* not because he viewed the Iberian Muslim predicament as distinct, but because he considered the fate of Iberia's Muslims to be a conclusive historical precedent. The loss of al-Andalus provided Wansharīsī with a powerful rhetorical platform to encourage active resistance against the Portuguese, warn Maghribīs against collaboration with the enemy, and articulate a veiled critique of the Waṭṭāsid sultan's treaties with Portugal.

By reading *Asnā al-matājir* in its North African context and reassessing its relationship to new and familiar texts regarding Mudéjars and Maghribīs we can obtain a richer, more nuanced understanding of Muslim responses to Christian conquest. Only by linking the legal discourses regarding conquered Muslims on both sides of the Mediterranean can we gain a fuller picture of Mālikī legal thought on this issue, of the impact of shifting frontiers on normative religious discourse, and of the functions of legal opinions in conditions of political upheaval. A primary goal of this book is thus to challenge the entrenched perceptions of Iberian exceptionalism that have often obscured meaningful continuities between historical processes in the Iberian Peninsula and elsewhere. Through a detailed case study of Islamic legal responses to Christian conquest, in this book I broaden the frame of reference we use to imagine interreligious relations in the medieval and early modern western Mediterranean.

The story of Muslim, Christian, and Jewish interaction in Iberia is often portrayed as distinctive and self-contained, bounded geographically by the confines of the peninsula and temporally by the 1492 conquest of Granada and expulsion of the Jews, if not by the 1609–14 expulsion of the Moriscos. Yet, it was only in hindsight that Christian Iberia's vision of *the* Reconquest settled on these borders and claimed 1492 as a victorious conclusion. The same ideologies of reconquest and crusade that were mobilized in Iberia were used to justify Portugal and Spain's ultimately unsuccessful expansion into the Maghrib, and Iberia's Christian-Muslim frontier straddled the Strait of Gibraltar for over seventy-five years (1415–92). The fall of Granada simply shifted that frontier fully into North Africa.[20]

20 In the chronology that follows the appendices, I have split events in Africa and Europe into two columns, in order to provide a visual representation of their temporal overlap.

The influx of Iberian Christians, Jews, and Muslims into the Maghrib fostered a variety of economic, social, and political relationships that crossed religious lines. We know about some of these relationships because they were prominent enough to provoke complaints and prohibitions by legal and political authorities. Portugal, for example, banned maritime trade with Azemmour for two years when cooperation between the city's Jewish and Muslim merchants was deemed detrimental to the Crown's commercial interests.[21] Many of the *fatwās* preserved by Zayyātī target Muslim-Christian trade or partnerships; fishing with the enemy emerges as a provocative and especially treacherous violation of communal boundaries for Maghribī Muslims. These interreligious interactions mirrored the complexity, if not the stability, of cohabitation among the religious communities in medieval Iberia. Moreover, peoples and processes in the Maghrib were integrally connected to those in Iberia.

The modern sense of medieval Iberia as a unique world stems primarily from a twentieth-century historiographical debate over Spain's national identity.[22] The concept most often associated with Spain's distinctiveness is *convivencia* (coexistence), a term first developed by linguist Ramón Menéndez Pidal (1869–1968) to describe competing dialectical norms. Historian Américo Castro (1885–1972) adapted this concept to signify the symbiotic cohabitation of Christians, Muslims, and Jews in the Iberian Peninsula in the medieval period. Against then-dominant notions of Spain and Spanish identity as eternal, fixed entities, Castro argued in *España en su historia: cristianos, moros, y judíos* (1948) that Spanish identity or "Spanishness" (*Hispanidad*) arose from the centuries-long *convivencia* of Spain's "three castes." For Castro, Christian society assimilated elements of Muslim and Jewish culture, including Islam's system of religious tolerance. In *España: un enigma histórico* (1956), Claudio Sánchez-Albornoz (1893–1984)

21 Vincent Cornell, "Socioeconomic Dimensions of Reconquista and Jihad in Morocco: Portuguese Dukkala and the Saʿdid Sus, 1450–1557," *International Journal of Middle East Studies* 22 (1990), 385.

22 For summaries of this debate and analysis of the historiography of interreligious relations in medieval Iberia more broadly, see Thomas Glick, "Convivencia: An Introductory Note," in *Convivencia: Jews, Muslims, and Christians in Medieval Spain*, ed. Vivian Mann, Thomas Glick, and Jerrilynn Dodds (New York: George Braziller, 1992), 1–9; Alex Novikoff, "Between Tolerance and Intolerance in Medieval Spain: An Historiographic Enigma," *Medieval Encounters* 11, nos. 1–2 (2005): 7–36; Maya Soifer, "Beyond *convivencia*: Critical Reflections on the Historiography of Interfaith Relations in Christian Spain," *Journal of Medieval Iberian Studies* 1, no. 1 (2009): 19–35; Anna Akasoy, "*Convivencia* and Its Discontents: Interfaith Life in al-Andalus," *International Journal of Middle East Studies* 42 (2010): 489–99; and Hisham Aidi, "The Interference of al-Andalus: Spain, Islam, and the West," *Social Text* 24, no. 2 (2006): 67–88. On the premodern antecedents to this modern debate, see Ross Brann, "Andalusi Exceptionalism," in *A Sea of Languages: Rethinking the Arabic Role in Medieval Literary History*, ed. Suzanne Conklin Akbari and Karla Mallette (Toronto: University of Toronto Press, 2013), 119–34.

forcefully rejected Castro's favorable assessment of Spain's multireligious past. Sánchez-Albornoz insisted that medieval interreligious relations were conflictual rather than creative, and that Muslim and Jewish society had no formative impact on Spanish identity, which predated the Muslim invasion. He saw the essential Spanish character reflected in the centuries-long struggle to eliminate Islam and restore a purely Christian religious identity. Thus, for Sánchez-Albornoz, *reconquista* rather than *convivencia* defined the medieval period, but this, too, distanced Spain from the rest of Europe: "Slow-witted, barbaric Africa . . . twisted and distorted the future fate of Iberia, and took it down a path, which cost Spain dear."[23] According to Sánchez-Albornoz, Muslims arrested Spanish history; they did not enrich the nation's economic and cultural development. Both historians agreed that Spain's past distinguished it from the rest of Europe.

The conviction that *convivencia* was a distinctive feature of medieval Iberian history long outlasted this debate over Spanish national identity. The concept, ranging in meaning from simple coexistence to an idyllic state of enlightened harmony and cultural fluorescence, has appealed to myriad groups. Many Jews and Muslims look back with nostalgia to the lost "Golden Age" of Sepharad (as the peninsula was known to Jews) or al-Andalus, respectively. The period of Muslim rule offered hope and historical evidence to those wishing to challenge the "Clash of Civilizations" perception that Islam is inherently incompatible with Christianity, Judaism, or the West.[24] Continued coexistence under Christian rule helped combat negative portrayals of Spanish intolerance and cruelty that resulted from the Inquisition and conquest of the Americas. For some champions of European secularism, religious tolerance under both Muslim and Christian rule were Spain's contribution to the modern development of pluralism. Spain's otherness has also been used to promote tourism, from the Franco-era slogan "¡España es diferente!" to today's festivals of "three cultures."

Historians of medieval Iberia have now moved away from approaches to interreligious relations that reduce those interactions to a simplistic model of peaceful tolerance or endemic violence. Historiography post-*convivencia* focuses on detailed archival studies, grounded in particular regions and time periods, that offer nuanced views of the interactions between individuals or different religious groups. Concepts with greater analytical utility like acculturation, cultural diffusion, and social and economic integration,

23 Claudio Sánchez-Albornoz, *"España y el Islam," Revista de Occidente*, VII (1929), 27. As quoted in Luce López-Baralt, *Islam in Spanish Literature From the Middle Ages to the Present*, trans. Andrew Hurley (Leiden: Brill, 1992), 28.

24 See Bernard Lewis, "The Roots of Muslim Rage," *Atlantic Monthly* 266, no. 3 (Sept 1990): 47–60; Samuel Huntington, "The Clash of Civilizations?" *Foreign Affairs* 72, no. 3 (1993): 22–49. Huntington expanded this article into a book, published in 1996.

have displaced *convivencia*, and new models for understanding Iberia's interreligious relations have emerged.[25]

While the demise of *convivencia* has eroded some of the foundations of Iberian exceptionalism, a sense of fundamental difference between Iberia and North Africa has persisted. Despite centuries of mutual entanglement, from the Muslim invasion of 711 to Spain's continued sovereignty over Ceuta and Melilla, Iberia and North Africa have generally been studied in isolation from one another. The constraints of national and academic boundaries, as well as of geographic and linguistic divides, have impeded the production of research that does justice to the commonalities and interconnections shared by these two regions.

A number of scholars, especially those working in the Spanish academy, have overcome these divides.[26] Their early efforts paved the way for the formation, in 2010, of the Spain-North Africa Project (SNAP), an interdisciplinary academic organization promoting the study of North Africa and Iberia as a unified region.[27] In their introduction to a 2013 special issue of *Medieval Encounters*, the organization's first executive board assessed the barriers to scholarship in the field, reviewed a substantial body of existing scholarship linking Iberia and North Africa, and introduced a body of new work in this area, placing this work in the broad geographical frame of the western Mediterranean.[28] Over the last decade, an explosion of new

25 For example, Thomas Glick distinguished between acculturation and assimilation, arguing that cultural diffusion could coexist with social distance and with ethnic conflict; see Glick, *Islamic and Christian Spain in the Early Middle Ages: Comparative Perspectives on Social and Cultural Formation* (Leiden: Brill, 1979), 165; available online through the Library of Iberian Resources Online (https://libro.uca.edu). David Nirenberg's argument for the interdependence of violence and tolerance in sustaining balanced intergroup relations has been particularly influential; see Nirenberg, *Communities of Violence: Persecution of Minorities in the Middle Ages* (Princeton: Princeton University Press, 1996). Brian Catlos has introduced a "Principle of Convenience" (*conveniencia*), holding that pragmatic self-interests and mutual dependence trumped sectarian, ideological commitments; see Catlos, *Muslims of Medieval Latin Christendom, c. 1050–1614* (Cambridge: Cambridge University Press, 2014), esp. 515–35. These models and others are discussed in the historiographical analyses of *convivencia* noted above (n. 19), which remain excellent overviews for the study of interreligious relations in Iberia. On interreligious relations in the medieval and early modern Mediterranean more broadly, see Adnan A. Husain and K. E. Fleming, eds., *A Faithful Sea: The Religious Cultures of the Mediterranean, 1200–1700* (Oxford: Oneworld, 2007).

26 Of particular note are Maribel Fierro, Mercedes García-Arenal, Miguel Manzano, María Jesús Viguera Molins, Delfina Serrano, and Francisco Vidal Castro, whose works appear below and throughout this book.

27 The Spain-North Africa Project was founded by participants in the 2010 National Endowment for the Humanities Summer Institute on "Cultural Hybridities: Christians, Muslims, and Jews in the Medieval Mediterranean." I am honored to have been a founding member of SNAP and am grateful to Brian Catlos and Sharon Kinoshita for organizing this Institute, one of many NEH Summer Institutes they have held together in Barcelona.

28 See Yuen-Gen Liang, Abigail Krasner Balbale, Andrew Devereux, and Camilo Gómez-Rivas, "Unity and Disunity across the Strait of Gibraltar," *Medieval Encounters* 19, nos. 1–2 (2013).

research has "spanned the Strait"; this work is largely framed as contributing to the study of the medieval and early modern western Mediterranean.[29]

In *Leaving Iberia* I contribute to this growing body of work by approaching Iberia and North Africa as integrally connected. Yet my aim is not to move seamlessly between Iberian and Maghribī sources, nor is the work fully contained in a Mediterranean framework.[30] Instead, I place the Maghrib at the center of analysis, in two senses. Geographically, I place the Maghrib in the middle, situated between al-Andalus (and France) to the north and West Africa to the south; this placement is most pertinent to part 4. Meanwhile, throughout the core of this book I assert the centrality of the Maghrib to the question of Muslims living under Iberian Christian rule, by shifting our attention from the Iberian to the Maghribī dimensions of this shared, interconnected phenomenon.

The presumption of essential difference between Iberia and the Maghrib has persisted with regard to the treatment of religious minorities. Until recently, the Almoravid and Almohad empires were routinely depicted as "fundamentalist," intolerant forces bent on destroying Iberia's more

---

The authors trace the beginnings of scholarship on an "interconnected Mediterranean world" to French historian Fernand Braudel. They provide helpful bibliographic footnotes throughout their article. Of particular relevance are their references to institutions fostering trans-Strait research (4–5 n. 9), research on Spanish involvement in North Africa (11 n. 24), research on the Almoravids and Almohads (13 n. 29), and European research on North Africa, including work that spans the North Africa-Iberia divide, in the French academy (19 n. 41), the Spanish academy (26–27 n. 57), and the Portuguese academy (29–30 n. 63).

29 "Spanning the Strait" refers to the title of a 2011 SNAP Symposium. A sampling of work from the past decade includes Beatriz Alonso Acero, *España y el Norte de África en los Siglos XVI y XVII* (Madrid: Editorial Síntesis, 2017); Eric Calderwood, *Colonial al-Andalus: Spain and the Making of Modern Moroccan Culture* (Cambridge: Belknap Press, 2018); Julia Clancy-Smith, *Mediterraneans: North Africa and Europe in an Age of Migration, c. 1800–1900* (Berkeley: University of California Press, 2012); Daniel Hershenzon, *The Captive Sea: Slavery, Communication, and Commerce in Early Modern Spain and the Mediterranean* (Philadelphia: University of Pennsylvania Press, 2018); and Miguel Manzano, "La Península Ibérica y el Norte de África en los Inicios del bajo Medievo: Relaciones políticas y apuntes historiográficos," in *711–1616: De Árabes a Moriscos: Una Parte de la Historia de España*, ed. M. Fierro, J. Martos, J.P. Monferrer, and M.J. Viguera (Córdoba, Al-Babtain Foundation, 2012), 67–86.

30 An excellent recent work that bridges the Iberian-North African divide by weaving together insights gleaned from Latin, Romance, and Arabic primary sources is Hussein Fancy, *The Mercenary Mediterranean: Sovereignty, Religion, and Violence in the Medieval Crown of Aragon* (Chicago: University of Chicago Press, 2016). As the title suggests, Fancy joins much recent work in this area by adopting a "Mediterranean approach" (12). In contrast, *Leaving Iberia* draws on Iberian, Maghribī, and Mauritanian sources primarily in Arabic and, while contributing to the study of each of these regions and the western Mediterranean, ultimately centers itself on the Maghrib rather than the Mediterranean. Nonetheless, *Leaving Iberia* shares and affirms Fancy's approach to religion by treating religious motivations as sincere and religious texts as socially and politically relevant. Fancy's research on Muslim soldiers serving in the Aragonese army leads him to critique Catlos's principle of convenience (noted above) as overly dismissive of religion (Fancy, *Mercenary*, 103–10).

enlightened, multi-confessional society.[31] With regard to the status of Muslim minorities, Iberia has occasionally shared the spotlight with Sicily, but almost never with the Maghrib, despite Iberian expansion there in the fifteenth century.[32] The case of *Asnā al-matājir* alone shows that a text once thought to be of crucial importance for Iberian Muslims was likely written by, for, and about Maghribī Muslims. This text thus serves as a powerful example of the need to widen our focus beyond the artificial boundaries of nationalist historiographies and academic disciplines. To better understand Muslim responses to Christian conquest, we must leave behind an almost exclusive focus on Iberia's conquered Muslims as uniquely worthy of study.

Adaptation and Authority in Islamic Law

Ever since Ayatollah Ruhollah Khomeini's 1989 issuance of a *fatwā* calling on Muslims to kill British author Salmon Rushdie for his insults to Islam and Muḥammad in *The Satanic Verses*, the Arabic term for a legal opinion has been erroneously conflated, in the West, with a "death sentence."[33] Ironically, this conflation only began to erode in the wake of the terrorist attacks of September 11, 2001, as Muslims were pressed to denounce each new act of terror or extremism. Since then, *fatwās* have become the recognizable currency of official Muslim repudiation of violence committed by Muslims in the name of Islam. Issued by learned religious authorities, including many appointed by governments of Muslim majority countries, these statements have the power to represent and to shape the values of lay Muslims. *Fatwās* of denunciation are increasingly authored in groups and transmitted through the mass media for consumption by Muslims and

31 As noted by Liang, et al. ("Unity and Disunity," 13), this treatment of the Almoravids and Almohads meant that "even in periods when the Maghrib and Iberia constituted a political unity, nineteenth- and twentieth-century scholarship emphasized distinctions between the two sides of the Strait." Important works challenging this perspective include Maribel Fierro, *The Almohad Revolution: Politics and Religion in the Islamic West during the Twelfth-Thirteenth Centuries* (Farnham: Ashgate, 2013); Fierro, "Alfonso X 'The Wise': The Last Almohad Caliph?" *Medieval Encounters* 15, no. 2 (2009): 175–98; and Amira K. Bennison, *The Almoravid and Almohad Empires* (Edinburgh: Edinburgh University Press, 2016).

32 For a notable exception, see Amira Bennison, "Liminal States: Morocco and the Iberian Frontier between the Twelfth and Nineteenth Centuries," in *North Africa, Islam and the Mediterranean World: From the Almoravids to the Algerian War*, ed. Julia Clancy-Smith (London: Frank Cass, 2001), 11–28. For an overview and sources on Muslims under Norman rule in Ifrīqiyā (modern-day Tunisia) in the mid-twelfth century, see Catlos, *Muslims*, 102–12.

33 Islamophobic groups have sought to perpetuate this conflation. In New York City in 2010 and in Edmonton in 2013, bus advertisements asked, "Is There a Fatwa on Your Head?" Ostensibly offering help to Muslim women fearful of their murderous relatives, these ads promoted anti-Muslim sentiment by associating Islamic law with domestic violence. See *NBC News*, "Bus Ads Target Muslims 'Leaving Islam'," May 27, 2010; and *CBC News*, "ETS Pulls Controversial 'Honour Killings' Advertisements," October 29, 2013.

non-Muslims alike.[34] More recently, the alarming spread and brutality of the Islamic State (formerly the Islamic State of Iraq and Syria, or ISIS)[35] was met with formal *fatwās* by prominent British, Saudi, Mauritanian, and Australian clerics.[36] In an effort to reduce community susceptibility to radical ideas, Muslim clerics advanced scriptural proof texts and legal arguments condemning the Islamic State and prohibiting Muslims from joining their cause. Government officials, who welcomed these *fatwās* on behalf of the broader public, contributed to the construction of these texts' authority, suggested that an obligation to condemn such atrocities had been met, and sought to protect ordinary Muslims from a backlash of Islamophobia.[37]

Likewise, when Wansharīsī and his peers authored *fatwās* on Muslims submitting to Portuguese authority, they were intervening in an ongoing military conflict and its accompanying war of ideas. They resisted Christian territorial expansion by working to render unacceptable the actions of fellow Muslims whose submission to Christian authority undermined these jurists' normative vision of Muslim society. Unlike today's public *fatwās*, these fifteenth- and sixteenth-century opinions were individually composed and circulated primarily among legal professionals. The Fāsī jurists featured in part 1 likely shared their oral or written opinions with one another, in addition to providing formal responses to their questioners, who may have been regional jurists seeking the advice of more learned or influential jurists in the capital. Before reaching lay audiences, these responses were likely reformulated as sermons, lessons, or private counsel.

34 In 2014, Sheila Musaji published a blog post with links to collective condemnations of violence by Muslim religious scholars. See Sheila Musaji, "Muslim Voices—Part I—Fatwas & Statements by Muslim Scholars & Organizations," *American Muslim*, July 20, 2014, http://theamericanmuslim.org/tam.php/features/articles/muslim_voices_against_extremism_and_terrorism_part_i_fatwas/.

35 At the time of writing, this largely defeated jihadist group was still known by a number of names, including the Islamic State of Iraq and Syria (ISIS), the Islamic State of Iraq and the Levant (ISIL), and Daesh (the Arabic acronym for al-Dawla al-Islāmiyya fī al-ʿIrāq wa'l-Shām, "the Islamic State of Iraq and the Levant"). At its height in 2015, the Islamic State controlled large parts of Syria and Iraq, with an estimated population of eight million people; most of this territory was recovered by late 2019. See *BBC News*, "IS 'Caliphate' Defeated but Jihadist Group Remains a Threat," March 23, 2019.

36 See Zachary Davies Boren, "ISIS Terror Threat: Leading British Muslims Issue Fatwa Condemning Terror Group," *Independent*, October 30, 2014; Ian Black, "Saudi Clerics Declare ISIS Terrorism a 'Heinous Crime' under Sharia Law," *Guardian*, September 17, 2014; Dina Temple-Raston, "Prominent Muslim Sheik Issues Fatwa Against ISIS Violence," *NPR Morning Edition*, September 25, 2014; and Paul Farrell, "Grand Mufti of Australia Condemns ISIS 'Horrors Conducted Overseas,'" *Guardian*, September 24, 2014.

37 For example, US President Barack Obama referred to Mauritanian scholar Abdullah bin Bayyah's statement in a speech before the UN General Assembly (see Temple-Raston, "Prominent Muslim Sheik"), while two British politicians spoke approvingly of the British leaders' *fatwā*. Richard Kerbaj, Tim Shipman, and Marie Woolf, "UK Imams put Fatwa on Jihadists," *Sunday Times*, August 31, 2014.

Many of these jurists also hoped their responses would influence state policy regarding its subjects' interactions with foreign occupiers; ideally, where the jurists' moral authority ended, the state's coercive power began.

While we cannot know how lay Muslims or the state responded to most of these texts, we can learn from jurists' attempts to shape their views. This is not a book about the lives of Mudéjars or conquered Maghribī Muslims, nor is it about Waṭṭāsid-Portuguese relations, though there are glimpses of each. It is a work of legal history, concerned with understanding how jurists composed their opinions, to whom they circulated the finished products, and what they hoped to achieve by doing so. Legal discourse, grounded in the community's foundational sources of religious authority, is a primary medium through which Muslim identity is constructed and legitimate Muslim-Other relationships prescribed. Thus, Islamic legal literature concerning the treatment of *dhimmīs* has long been exploited; legal discourses on Muslims under Christian rule represent an equally rich, but relatively neglected, resource for analyzing interreligious hierarchies and articulations of distinct religious identities.

Investigating Muslim-Christian relations also involves interrogating Muslim-Muslim relations and competing configurations of Muslim identity. Many of the legal texts I analyze in this study assert a vital link between Muslim religious identity, territory, and power. When territorial losses brought substantial Muslim populations under Christian control, the legal discourse concerning these populations focused not only on their ability to fulfill their religious obligations, but also on the nature of the relationships between Muslims living under Muslim rule and those in Christian territory. By analyzing jurists' rhetoric regarding these conquered Muslims—often focused on their incapacities, transgressions, subversive relationships with Others, and forfeited rights—we can better understand how political crisis shaped medieval constructions of the ideal, virtuous Muslim subject.

In *Leaving Iberia* I proceed chronologically through five case studies, all of which focus on legal opinions regarding Muslims living under Christian rule. Three medieval cases, concentrated in a fifteen to twenty-five-year period before and after the fall of Granada, form the core of the book. As noted above, part 1 treats Zayyātī's "jewels," my term for the body of *fatwā*s in *Selected Jewels* that addresses Iberian conquests in North Africa. While the full range of opinions I consider stretches from the 1480s to the 1520s, most of these opinions likely date between the mid-1480s and 1491. In part 2, I address Wansharīsī's two 1491 *fatwā*s obligating Mudéjar emigration; these are his *Asnā al-matājir* and his Marbella *fatwā*. I devote part 3 to Wahrānī's 1504 *fatwā* to Granadan Moriscos. While all of these texts were composed by Maghribī jurists over a relatively short period of time and in response to Christian Iberian conquests, they differ substantially in terms of form, function, arguments, and audience.

The final two cases, in part 4, are legal arguments for and against Muslims' obligation to emigrate from French-controlled territory in colonial Algeria (1830–1960) and Mauritania (1903–60). These texts affirm that this earlier period was pivotal and continued to resonate for Muslims facing similar legal questions centuries later. They also reveal a provocative divergence in the fates of the medieval opinions considered in parts 1–3. While the opinions preserved in Zayyātī's *Selected Jewels* leave barely a trace in these colonial-era *fatwās* and Wahrānī goes entirely without mention, Wansharīsī's *Asnā al-matājir* and the Marbella *fatwā* became the Mālikī school's most important authoritative precedents on the permissibility of Muslims maintaining their residences under Christian rule. In contrast, of the many voices in the late fifteenth century, only that of Wahrānī clearly went on to be copied and valued by generations of lay Muslims living under Christian rule in Iberia. Why did Wansharīsī's and Wahrānī's opinions enjoy such disparate legacies, and why were all of the *fatwās* preserved by Zayyātī seemingly forgotten?

Interrogating the long-term impact of these opinions represents a departure from existing scholarship, which focuses more narrowly on jurists' capacity to adapt Islamic law to the current needs of Muslim populations. When judged by their responsiveness to the needs of Mudéjars, Wansharīsī's 1491 *fatwās* have not fared well. Some scholars blamed Wansharīsī for willfully refusing to embrace necessary adaptations that would legitimize Mudéjar communities; others suggested that his opinions reflect an Islamic legal orthodoxy that was, in the fifteenth century, simply too rigid to accommodate Muslims living under non-Muslim rule. In contrast, scholarly treatments of Wahrānī's sympathetic advice to the Moriscos have praised its practicality and the originality of his opinion.

These approaches are clear demonstrations of two trends in Islamic legal historiography. Critiques of Wansharīsī have often perpetuated the now-discredited theory of medieval stagnancy (i.e., the "closing of the gate of *ijtihād*"), while appreciation for Wahrānī has aligned with a more current trend that identifies *fatwās* as the primary locus of adaptation and continued development in Islamic law. A brief review of these approaches helps clarify my own perspective.

Building on the work of Joseph Schacht, Western and Muslim scholars alike have long held that following the consolidation of the four existing Sunnī schools of law in the tenth century, the "gate of *ijtihād*," or independent legal reasoning, had closed. According to this theory, jurists no longer had interpretive freedom, Islamic law then steadily ossified, and, unable to adapt to new historical realities, the outmoded legal system became increasingly irrelevant to the changing needs of society.[38] In 1984, Wael Hallaq published a seminal article discrediting the primary tenets of this theory.[39] Over the past thirty years, a number of scholars have joined him, and argued convincingly, in large part through the analysis of *fatwās*, that Muslim jurists continued to engage in independent reasoning (*ijtihād*) and to contribute to the development of legal thought and practice in the post-formative period (i.e., beyond the consolidation of the major legal schools).[40] Sherman Jackson has suggested that some later jurists exhibited more advanced intellectual achievements than their predecessors, as evidenced by their novel opinions based on an ever-growing body of school literature.[41]

Fatwās were central to refuting the "closing of the gate" theory because they serve as sites for the active negotiation of moral boundaries and accommodation of legal and ritual change.[42] As opposed to works of legal theory (*uṣūl al-fiqh*), which treat the principles governing the derivation of law from the revealed sources (the Qurʾān and Ḥadīth), or manuals of substantive law (*mutūn* and *mukhtaṣars*), which set forth the basic, agreed-upon rules in a given school of law, *fatwās* treat actual personal or public concerns that arise in specific historical and geographic contexts. *Fatwās* consist of two parts, the *istiftāʾ* (question) posed by a *mustaftī*

38 Joseph Schacht, *An Introduction to Islamic Law* (Oxford: Clarendon Press, 1964), esp. 69–75. The most succinct and oft-quoted statement of Schacht's thesis is found on 70–71.

39 Wael Hallaq, "Was the Gate of Ijtihad Closed?" *International Journal of Middle East Studies* 16 (1984): 3–41. See also Hallaq, "From *Fatwās* to *Furūʿ*: Growth and Change in Islamic Substantive Law," *Islamic Law and Society* 1, no. 1 (1994): 29–65; Hallaq, "Murder in Cordoba: *Ijtihâd, Iftâ'*, and the Evolution of Substantive Law in Medieval Islam," *Acta Orientalia* 55 (1994): 55–83; Hallaq, *Authority, Continuity, and Change in Islamic Law* (Cambridge: Cambridge University Press, 2001), esp. ch. 6.

40 For examples, see Baber Johansen, *Contingency in a Sacred Law: Legal and Ethical Norms in the Muslim* Fiqh (Leiden: Brill, 1999), esp. ch. 8; Sherman Jackson, *Islamic Law and the State: The Constitutional Jurisprudence of Shihāb al-Dīn al-Qarāfī* (Leiden: Brill, 1996); and Haim Gerber, *State, Society, and Law in Islam: Ottoman Law in Comparative Perspective* (Albany, NY: State University of New York Press, 1994), esp. ch. 4.

41 Jackson, *Islamic Law and the State*, 227.

42 On the importance of *fatwās* for historical research, as well as overviews of their form and functions, see David S. Powers, *Law, Society, and Culture in the Maghrib, 1300–1500* (Cambridge: Cambridge University Press, 2002); Powers, "*Fatwās* as Sources for Legal and Social History: A Dispute over Endowment Revenues from Fourteenth-Century Fez," *Al-Qanṭara* 11, no. 2 (1990): 295–341; Brinkley Messick, *The Calligraphic State: Textual Domination and History in a Muslim Society* (Berkeley: University of California Press, 1993), esp. ch. 7; Muhammad Khalid Masud, Brinkley Messick, and David Powers, "Muftis, Fatwas, and Islamic Legal Interpretation," in *Islamic Legal Interpretation: Muftis and Their Fatwas*, ed. Masud, et al. (Cambridge: Harvard University Press, 1996), 3–32; Mohammad Fadel, "Rules, Judicial Discretion, and the Rule of Law in Naṣrid Granada: An Analysis of *al-Ḥadīqa al-mustaqilla al-naḍra fī al-fatāwā al-ṣādira ʿan ʿulamāʾ al-ḥadra*," in *Islamic Law: Theory and Practice*, ed. R. Gleave and E. Kermeli (London: I.B. Tauris, 1997), 49–86; and Jakob Skovgaard-Petersen, *Defining Islam for the Egyptian State: Muftīs and Fatwas of the Dār al-Iftā* (Leiden: Brill, 1997), esp. 1–35.

(questioner), and the jurist's response. The questions (if they have been preserved—oftentimes they are not) reveal the types of legal issues that led to interpersonal conflicts or weighed on an individual's conscience; thus, they provide fertile material for the study of social and economic history as well as religious practices. The *muftīs*' answers help us to understand the procedures by which a given corpus of legal texts was applied to specific cases; this material is particularly important to the exploration of the ongoing development of legal thought, the functions and discretionary powers of jurists, and the interrelationships of religious scholars, society, and the state.

While scholars now agree that jurists continued to exercise individual discretion in their work as *muftīs*, they disagree as to the long-term impact of innovative *fatwās* on the working doctrine of a given school of law. Hallaq saw the incorporation of select *fatwās* into legal manuals as the primary process by which evolving social realities effected doctrinal change.[43] Against this now-dominant position in Islamic legal studies, Norman Calder drew a distinction between flexibility in the law as practiced and appreciable change in the law as preserved. Calder believed that jurists chose how to apply the universals of their tradition to the particulars of the cases before them, but those acts of discretion did not amount to significant change in the "inherited literary expression of the law" as recorded in legal manuals.[44]

In *Leaving Iberia* I adopt a new approach to the evaluation of both legal adaptation and the long-term impact of individual *fatwās*. In broad terms, I am interested in the construction and maintenance of authoritative legal precedents. This involves analyzing how jurists craft texts that become authoritative for their intended audiences in the present as well as identifying factors that position some opinions over others to remain compelling for later jurists confronted with similar legal issues.

With regard to juristic discretion, my approach includes scrutinizing the active work required to sustain seemingly conservative norms, especially in the face of rapidly changing circumstances. Because of their efforts to demonstrate the continued intellectual vitality of medieval legal thought, scholars have overemphasized *fatwās* that deviate clearly from accepted school doctrine or that offer explicitly innovative solutions to novel cases. Yet we can find substantial adaptation in far less obvious places, including opinions that support "illiberal" or established doctrines. Medieval jurists often masked their own innovations in order to maintain the appearance of

43 Hallaq, *Authority*, 166–235.

44 Norman Calder, *Islamic Jurisprudence in the Classical Era*, ed. Colin Imber (Cambridge: Cambridge University Press, 2010), 161. In this posthumous book, Calder argues that the expression of legal norms in *mukhtaṣars* became more concise, refined, and organized over time, but that the actual norms remained largely unchanged.

continuity with accepted precedents. As concealing novelty was a primary means of establishing authority, we must pay as much attention to jurists' omissions and subtle manipulations as we do to their explicit protests and assurances.

I have laid the foundations for my approach in a pair of articles for *Islamic Law and Society*. In two broadly diachronic case studies using Mālikī *fatwā*s, I have argued for the importance of at least three underexplored modalities of juristic discretion involving misrepresentation or deception: manipulation of precedents, unacknowledged borrowing (plagiarism), and dissemblance. My first case study, treating opinions on trading with the enemy, highlights jurists' manipulation of precedents and demonstrates that the "mere" application of existing school doctrine to a recurring case may involve considerable juristic flexibility.[45] For example, the well-known Granadan jurist Abū Isḥāq al-Shāṭibī (d. 790/1388) mischaracterized a key precedent in order to better support a prohibition on selling weapons to Christians, even though this was the standard position, and he was denying that local circumstances had in fact produced a novel legal question. The second case study, regarding opinions prohibiting the pilgrimage to Mecca, focuses primarily on politically motivated dissemblance. In this case, the legal justifications offered for an opinion are a fiction that masks the underlying political imperatives informing a particular policy.[46] For nearly eight centuries Mālikī jurists proclaimed, for example, that any Andalusī or Maghribī Muslim who might miss one or more of their daily prayers during the journey to and from Mecca is prohibited from setting forth. The unstated political motives behind this exaggerated concern for prayer included retaining human and financial resources and guarding against the spread of infectious diseases. Dissemblance, manipulation of precedent, and unacknowledged borrowing all feature in *Leaving Iberia*.

With regard to the long-term impact of *fatwā*s, I do not judge the impact of a given *fatwā* on "the law" by its incorporation into legal manuals or textbooks. Instead, I consider an opinion to have enduring relevance to the extent that it continues to be deployed, favorably or unfavorably, in later legal texts of any genre. *Fatwā*s are routinely cited in later *fatwā*s as authoritative precedents capable of bolstering legal arguments; they do not need to be endorsed or included by the authors of legal manuals in order to impact the legal thought and practice of later jurists. For example, in the case noted above, these *fatwā*s did not lead to a blanket prohibition of the

45 See Jocelyn Hendrickson, "Is al-Andalus Different? Continuity as Contested, Constructed, and Performed across Three Mālikī Fatwās," *Islamic Law and Society* 20, no. 4 (2013): 371–424.

46 See Jocelyn Hendrickson, "Prohibiting the Pilgrimage: Politics and Fiction in Mālikī *Fatwās*," *Islamic Law and Society* 23, no. 3 (2016): 161–238.

pilgrimage—this did not become *the* Mālikī doctrine; but precedents from eleventh- and twelfth-century *fatwās* were deployed periodically to justify travel bans well into the modern period. Moreover, from the early modern period onward Wansharīsī's vast *fatwā* compilation, *al-Miʿyār al-muʿrib*, arguably superseded the Mālikī school's most important legal textbook, the *Mukhtaṣar Khalīl*, as an arbiter of school doctrine.[47] For example, in one of his famous responses to the Algerian resistance leader Amīr ʿAbd al-Qādir (d. 1883) regarding *jihād* against the French, ʿAlī b. ʿAbd al-Salām al-Tasūlī (d. 1842) confirms that a prohibition on selling weapons to the enemy is "the [Mālikī] school doctrine as stated in the *Miʿyār*."[48]

The Maghribī opinions on Muslim submission to Christian rule that remain extant from the turn of the sixteenth century present a fruitful set of cases by which to consider both juristic discretion and the long-term impact of rulings. By comparing the enduring relevance or obscurity of these opinions, we can ask better questions regarding their various forms, functions, and intended audiences at the time they were issued. Conversely, by analyzing how these jurists crafted and circulated their opinions at the time, we can better understand why some texts remained meaningful for later Muslims or authoritative for later jurists confronted with similar legal problems. Specifically, I argue that while Zayyātī's "jewels," Wansharīsī's 1491 *fatwās*, and Wahrānī's advice to the Moriscos were all well adapted to their present contexts, Wansharīsī's *Asnā al-matājir* and the Marbella *fatwā* were far better positioned to serve as the opinion of record for future generations of Mālikī jurists—and we can identify the reasons for this.

Many of the *fatwās* preserved by Zayyātī, including Wansharīsī's lesser-known Berber *fatwā*, convey an expectation that jurists have an immediate role to play in encouraging armed resistance and in condemning Muslim collaboration with the enemy. Some were written hastily, many are fairly short, and many are tied to particular localities. As a set they offer practical, relatively tailored responses not overburdened with proof texts. Their short-term practicality is not matched by long-term influence.

If one of these jurists had not responded quite so urgently—but had instead crafted a more substantial, formal work meant to last the test of time, would the result have been different? This is essentially what

47 David Powers estimates that the *Miʿyār*, the most prominent Mālikī *fatwā* compilation, contains at least 5,000 *fatwās* issued between 1000 and 1500 by hundreds of *muftīs* in North Africa and al-Andalus. Its full name is *al-Miʿyār al-muʿrib wa'l-jāmiʿ al-mughrib ʿan fatāwī ahl Ifrīqiyā wa'l-Andalus wa'l-Maghrib* (*The Clear Standard and Extraordinary Collection of the Legal Opinions of the Scholars of Ifrīqiyā, al-Andalus, and the Maghrib*). Powers, *Law, Society, and Culture*, 4–9; Powers, "Aḥmad al-Wansharīsī (d. 914/1509)," in *Islamic Legal Thought: A Compendium of Muslim Jurists*, ed. Oussama Arabi, David S. Powers, and Susan A. Spectorsky (Leiden: Brill, 2013), 378–82.

48 Hendrickson, "Is al-Andalus Different?," 420.

Wansharīsī did, although he too drafted an initial, unpolished opinion regarding Maghribī cooperation with the Portuguese. The composition of *Asnā al-matājir* and the Marbella *fatwā* did not just follow on the heels of a shared Maghribī discourse regarding Muslim submission to foreign authority—it was meant to replace that discourse with a single authoritative text. Wansharīsī crafted his two 1491 opinions to be the final word in his own time and to become, together, the authoritative Mālikī precedent for later jurists on the obligation to emigrate. Ibn Qaṭiyya's timely questions regarding Mudéjars provided a compelling frame story for Wansharīsī's improved responses, while his inclusion of only these two opinions in his *Miʿyār* ensured that they would have a far broader professional readership than those *fatwās* Zayyātī later preserved in his *Selected Jewels* (an appropriate title, considering the rarity with which these "jewels" are later cited).

The enduring relevance of Wansharīsī's 1491 opinions challenges the notion that *Asnā al-matājir* and the Marbella *fatwā* represent a legal orthodoxy so stagnant that it was already "unresponsive" in the late fifteenth century. "Orthodoxy" is a problematic term especially ill-suited to describe any *fatwā*, which is essentially an ad hoc and non-binding opinion issued by one jurist, who is normally acting as a private individual, in response to a question that may treat an unprecedented set of circumstances.[49] Wansharīsī did not have at his disposal a fixed set of established rules that he could apply to a recurring case, although he worked hard to maintain the impression that he did. His claims to continuity with school consensus are contrived, a way to mask his own interpretive work and bolster the authority of his opinion.

Because of the complexity of this central case study, part 2 consists of two chapters devoted to Wansharīsī's 1491 opinions. Chapter 4 addresses Ibn Qaṭiyya's questions as well as the dating, circulation, intended audiences, and framing of Wansharīsī's responses. Here I make my primary argument for reading these *fatwās* in their North African context, as a veiled commentary on Portuguese occupation of parts of the Far Maghrib. Chapter 5 moves into a technical discussion of Wansharīsī's legal arguments. I demonstrate that Wansharīsī strategically selected and rearranged existing precedents, proof texts, and new legal arguments in order to design an opinion in response to two contexts (Muslims living under Christian rule in Iberia and North Africa) and likely to resonate with future jurists. Chief among these existing materials is an earlier *fatwā* by Andalusī jurist Muḥammad b. Rabīʿ (d. 719/1319); from it, Wansharīsī borrowed extensively and

49 On the uses and abuses of this concept in Islamic Studies, see M. Brett Wilson, "The Failure of Nomenclature: The Concept of 'Orthodoxy' in the Study of Islam," *Comparative Islamic Studies* 3, no. 2 (2007): 169–94.

without acknowledgment. I argue that Wansharīsī's original sections of *Asnā al-matājir* and the Marbella *fatwā*—distinguished clearly from the "plagiarized" material in this book's appendices—are adaptations of his opinions to the active military context of fifteenth-century Morocco.

Part 3 consists of a single chapter reinterpreting Wahrānī's 1504 *fatwā* to the Moriscos, in which he advises them as to the clandestine practice of Islam. Historian L. P. Harvey called this text the "key theological document for the study of Spanish Islam" in the Morisco period, for good reason.[50] Because lay Iberian "crypto-Muslims" continued to copy Wahrānī's text as late as 1609, presumably at great risk, it has been reasonable to assume that his advice offered valuable solutions to real problems. By sanctioning precautionary dissimulation (*taqiyya*), Wahrānī offered a superb adaptation of "the law" to meet the needs of Moriscos.

Yet Wahrānī was not responding, as scholars have argued, to the same legal predicament as did Wansharīsī, only with compassion instead of cruelty and with rebellious originality instead of reactionary inflexibility. These texts are responses to fundamentally different legal issues and serve fundamentally different purposes, for distinct audiences. In his argumentative treatise meant to influence legal professionals, Wansharīsī confirms that capable Mudéjars are obligated to emigrate; while Wahrānī offered heartfelt guidance to those lay Moriscos who were fundamentally unable to migrate.

These texts diverge so strikingly because Wahrānī's 1504 *fatwā* is not, in fact, a *fatwā*. While scholars have assumed that his text answers a long-lost question, I argue that, after he encountered the 1501 Morisco appeal to Ottoman Sultan Bāyazīd II (an understudied text), Wahrānī was moved to offer Moriscos his unsolicited advice. In chapter 6, I make the case for a direct relationship between these two texts and explore the implications of reading Wahrānī's "*fatwā*" as a response to a formal poem meant to move a sultan, not to a practical question posed to a jurist.

In part 4 I conclude the book with two chapters analyzing Islamic legal responses to European colonization in nineteenth-century Algeria and early twentieth-century Mauritania. Generous documentation allows for the analysis of complete *fatwās* and letters written by Mālikī scholars arguing both in support of, and against, Muslims' obligation to emigrate from French-controlled territory in each country. These chapters confirm the lasting force and appeal of *Asnā al-matājir* and the Marbella *fatwā*; even those jurists who disagreed with Wansharīsī were compelled to grapple with his opinions.

50 Harvey, *Muslims in Spain*, 60.

The focal point of these closing chapters is a lengthy *fatwā* by Mauritanian jurist Muḥammad ʿAbd Allāh al-Buṣādī (d. 1933 or 1934), whose devastating critique of Wansharīsī's central legal analogy demonstrates that unassailable legal reasoning was not a reason for the success of Wansharīsī's opinions. For Algerians and Mauritanians, these texts evoked the tragedy of al-Andalus and allowed them to translate this powerful communal memory into a functional legal argument. The colonial-era cases suggest that historical and political events contribute as much to the construction and maintenance of authoritative legal precedents as does sound legal reasoning or continuity with school doctrine.

Legal discourse is a realm of competing ideas, and those that "win out" do so for myriad reasons. In tracing the circumstances and legacies of the medieval texts I analyze, I propose a method for understanding which legal opinions succeed and which fail to become authoritative opinions for later jurists. Central to this endeavor is the recognition that legal texts—especially *fatwās* on matters of urgent political concern—are strategically constructed, persuasive, and prescriptive. Moreover, they are shaped by a set of legal, political, generic, professional, and material constraints and imperatives that work to amplify or obscure certain types of arguments, concerns, and real-world details.[51] Working to identify a given jurist's particular constraints is crucial to understanding his opinions. In other words, we must not approach politically sensitive opinions as we would a tax code, consulting a dry reference work to retrieve information. These opinions have far more in common with the lawyers' closing arguments in popular crime dramas—in both instances, jurists shape events and arguments into compelling stories, grounded as much in emotional appeal as in rational evidence.

Reading legal texts with greater attention to contextual pressures and silences first requires access to those texts. In three appendices, I provide annotated translations of most of the medieval texts under discussion. The book's Online Companion will include my Arabic editions of additional legal opinions.

51 See Hendrickson, "Prohibiting the Pilgrimage," 204–6.

PART 1

Fishing with the Enemy: Zayyātī's *Selected Jewels*, ca. 1480s to 1520s

CHAPTER 2

Iberian Reconquest and Crusade in North Africa

The relationships between Jews, Christians, and Muslims in medieval and early modern Iberia have long fascinated scholars and non-specialists alike. Much of this fascination is focused on aspects of Iberian history thought to be exceptional or exemplary as compared with European and Islamic history elsewhere. The coexistence of these three religious communities on European soil for nearly a millennium, under both Muslim and Christian rule, raises provocative questions: What does it mean to say that medieval Iberians, unique among Europeans, "nourished a complex culture of tolerance"?[1] Why have so many Jews and Muslims remembered Sepharad or al-Andalus as a Golden Age or lost paradise? Did Iberian Muslim rulers embrace an extraordinary model of pluralism? If so, is that precedent a challenge to modern-day claims regarding Muslims' inherent incompatibility with Christians, Jews, or European civilization more generally? Or was medieval Iberia distinguished by an epic, centuries-long Christian struggle to reclaim Iberia from Muslim invaders, one that culminated in the "last crusade in the West"?[2] How should we account for the Spanish Inquisition's singular preoccupation with religious and ethnic purity, with forcible conversions of Muslims to Christianity, and the expulsion of Jews and Muslims from Iberia?

Each of these persistent questions reflects an underlying assumption that the Iberian Peninsula hosted a distinctive, self-contained, and extraordinary complex of interreligious relations in the period between the early eighth-century Muslim invasion and 1492, marking Granada's surrender and the expulsion of the Jews, or the early seventeenth-century expulsion of the Moriscos. This assumption is not entirely wrong, but it is greatly exaggerated. The Reconquest was not considered complete in 1492, nor was Castile's war for Granada the last crusade in the West. Granada's surrender did not establish a neat southwest border between European Christendom and Islamic empires. Most importantly, the expulsions of Jews

1 Menocal, *Ornament of the World*, 11.

2 Joseph O'Callaghan, *The Last Crusade in the West: Castile and the Conquest of Granada* (Philadelphia: University of Pennsylvania Press, 2014).

and Muslims from Iberia did not bring the story of Iberia's Christian-Muslim-Jewish relations to an end.

By the early fifteenth century, Christian Iberia's conquests extended to North Africa, motivated in part by the same ideologies of reconquest and crusade current in the peninsula. These conquests linked the two regions politically and reproduced in North Africa some of the elements considered unique to Iberia. For over a century, a mix of Iberian Christian nobles, soldiers, administrators, merchants, and sailors sought their fortunes in what is now Morocco. Joining these Christians were Muslims and Jews who left Iberia as a result of voluntary emigration, Castile's expulsion of the Jews in 1492, or Portugal's expulsion of both Muslims and Jews in 1497. With this influx came new patterns of interreligious relations and conversions in North Africa that were integrally related to, but often fundamentally different from, the Christian-Muslim-Jewish dynamics of the Iberian Peninsula.

By following the stories of these Iberians to the Maghrib, we can explore in more detail, with new data, some of the questions so often presumed to relate only to Iberian history. Here we investigate one such area of inquiry: How did Muslim jurists respond to Christian conquests? This question has been associated overwhelmingly with Iberia, and not entirely without cause. The gradual fall of al-Andalus has been considered a pivotal moment in Islamic history, when some of the first substantial Muslim populations came under permanent non-Muslim rule. Prior periods of Christian conquest elsewhere involved fewer Muslims or were of shorter duration, and led to the production of fewer legal texts (that are extant). While we have only a dozen or so opinions treating the legal status of Muslims under Christian rule in Iberia, this constitutes a treasure trove as compared with Muslims in such regions as India, China, the Levant, or the Balkans. A rich scholarly literature is devoted to *fatwās* assessing the legal status of Mudéjars, especially concerning their obligation to emigrate.[3]

Yet a nearly exclusive focus on conquered Iberian Muslims has led scholars to overlook a significant legal discourse that arose in the southern Mediterranean context in the fifteenth century. While historian Vincent Cornell argues that "even the fall of Granada in 1492 failed to provoke the same level of outrage and despair" among Maghribīs as the Portuguese conquest of Ceuta in 1415, Muslim responses to Christian rule in North Africa in general, and legal responses in particular, remain understudied.[4]

3 The scholarly literature on Mudéjars' obligation to emigrate is addressed further in part 2. The best overviews of these opinions are P. S. van Koningsveld and Gerard Wiegers "The Islamic Statute of the Mudejars in the Light of a New Source," *Al-Qanṭara* 17, no. 1 (1996): 19–58 and Kathryn Miller, *Guardians of Islam: Religious Authority and Muslim Communities in Late Medieval Spain* (New York: Columbia University Press, 2008), ch. 1, 20–43.

4 Vincent Cornell, *Realm of the Saint: Power and Authority in Moroccan Sufism* (Austin: University of Texas Press, 1998), 164.

This neglect is all the more glaring considering that ʿAbd al-ʿAzīz al-Zayyātī's *Selected Jewels* preserves nearly as many opinions addressing Muslim submission to Christian rule in the Maghrib as scholars have identified in relation to a four-hundred-year Mudéjar period in Iberia.

Mālikī legal opinions grappling with fifteenth- and sixteenth-century conquests in North Africa are so little known, and the Portuguese and Spanish presence had such a limited long-term cultural impact, that one might assume that these events were of minor importance. On the contrary, the Portuguese conquests in particular had serious social, economic, and political consequences for Maghribī Muslims. Divisions between Maghribīs who facilitated or resisted the Portuguese compounded the social and psychological disruptions that came along with captive-taking, slave raids, active warfare, and the depopulation of cities such as Ceuta. The loss of Muslim political autonomy in the Far Maghrib, coupled with the loss of revenues from overseas trade and the costs of war, served as a catalyst for a major shift in the configuration of political authority in Morocco that has lasted to the present day.

While the legal opinions treated in the next chapter date from roughly the 1480s to the 1520s, in this chapter I provide a broad overview of fifteenth- and sixteenth-century Portuguese and Spanish conquests in parts of North Africa. This larger historical context demonstrates the long-term impact of the events to which Zayyātī's "jewels" respond. It also complicates the Ibero-centric narrative that adopted the 1492 fall of Granada as the natural culmination of Christian Iberia's aspirations for reconquest and that claimed the shores of the Iberian Peninsula as the geographic limits of notable Christian-Muslim-Jewish interrelations in the medieval western Mediterranean.

Portugal: Conquest, Crusade, and Contraction

For over a century Portugal expanded its holdings in Morocco, until, from the 1540s onward, a series of withdrawals signaled its permanent contraction.[5] Although the coastal fortress of Mazagan (Mazagão) remained in Portuguese hands until 1769—over 350 years after the initial conquest of Ceuta—Portugal's greatest aspiration, to establish a contiguous coastal

5 The best short overview of the Portuguese in North Africa is A. R. Disney, *A History of Portugal and the Portuguese Empire, Volume Two: The Portuguese Empire* (Cambridge: Cambridge University Press, 2009), 1–26. Weston Cook Jr. provides a comprehensive military history of Portuguese-Maghribī engagements in *The Hundred Years War for Morocco: Gunpowder and the Military Revolution in the Early Modern Muslim World* (Boulder: Westview Press, 1994). On fifteenth- and sixteenth-century Morocco, especially the southern region in the sixteenth century, see Cornell, *Realm of the Saint*; Matthew Racine, *A Most Opulent Iliad: Expansion, Confrontation & Cooperation on the Southern Moroccan Frontier, 1505–1542* (San Diego: Lake George Press, 2012) and Aḥmad Būsharb, *Dukkāla wa'l-istiʿmār al-Burtughālī ilā sanat ikhlā' Āsafī wa-Āzammūr, 1481–1541* (Casablanca: Dār al-Thaqāfa, 1984).

territory extending to the power centers of Fez and Marrakesh, was never realized. One historian has suggested that Portugal's contraction and ultimate defeat in Morocco represents "the first and perhaps only European colonial 'failure' of the sixteenth century."[6] This failure helps explain Western historians' neglect of the Iberian ventures in North Africa and their focus on the overwhelming success of the Spanish and Portuguese in India and the Americas. For our purposes, however, Portugal's ultimate defeat in Morocco makes it even more important to understand Muslim responses to Christian conquest in this period.

Both ideological and practical motivations drove Portugal's expansion into North Africa. Portuguese kings were granted five papal bulls in the mid-fourteenth century authorizing crusades against Granada or North Africa, but until the early fifteenth century, these were deterred by the Black Death and war with Castile.[7] King João I (r. 1385–1433) then left the conquest of Granada to Castile, but crossed the Strait of Gibraltar and in 1415 captured the Mediterranean port of Ceuta (Sabta). The victory was not only a symbolic reversal of the 711 Muslim invasion of Iberia from Ceuta but was also of considerable strategic and economic import. The city's proximity to the strait granted Portugal greater leverage against Muslim pirates and Castilian advances, as well as access to Saharan trade caravans bringing gold from West Africa. The Maghrib also provided a nearby theatre of war, in which royals and nobility could earn honor and booty. Three of João's sons received their knighthoods after the Portuguese held a Mass in Ceuta's primary mosque, which had been cleansed and converted into a church promptly after the conquest.

Over the next century, through a combination of warfare and political and economic incentives offered to nobles or to whole populations willing to subordinate themselves to Portuguese rule, Portugal assumed control of most of Morocco's Mediterranean and Atlantic ports. Internal rivalries for control of the Marīnid state that had dominated Morocco since the late thirteenth century weakened official resistance to Portuguese expansion, increased local autonomy, and encouraged coastal populations to seek the protection and trade opportunities afforded by Lisbon to *mouros de paz* ("peaceful Moors").

The first stage of Portuguese conquests, concentrated in northern Morocco, enhanced Portugal's trade networks and reputation for crusading. They also exacted a heavy toll on the Portuguese Crown, the political and economic viability of the Marīnid state, and the coastal population of Morocco. While a number of port cities, including Salé, Anfa (now Casablanca), Safi, and

6 Racine, *Opulent*, 8.
7 Disney, *History of Portugal*, 2

Azemmour forged peaceful commercial agreements with Lisbon beginning in the 1450s, this period was marked by costly warfare and raiding. Portuguese Ceuta faced substantial counter-attacks from 1419 onward. King Duarte's (r. 1433–38) unsuccessful crusade to capture Tangier in 1437 ended in surrender, a promise to relinquish Ceuta, and his brother Fernando's eventual death in captivity when that promise proved false. King Afonso V (r. 1438–81), who was granted another crusade bull 1443, conquered al-Qaṣr al-Ṣaghīr (Alcácer-Ceguer), between Tangier and Ceuta in 1458; a siege to recover the town was unsuccessful. Two years later, Safi formally seceded from Morocco and allied with Portugal. In contrast, Anfa embargoed Portuguese grain purchases and was destroyed in retaliation (1468–69). Afonso V launched the first of several unsuccessful attempts to take Tangier in 1460 and authorized raids against several ports, including Asilah (Aṣīla, Arzila), al-ʿArāʾish (Larache), and Tetouan. Portugal's northern Moroccan conquests culminated in the 1471 capture of both Asilah and Tangier. Afonso V, who was rewarded with lower tithes by the papacy, commissioned a series of monumental tapestries commemorating the battles and adopted a new title: Rei de Portugal e dos Algarves d'aquem e d'alem mar ("King of Portugal and the Algarves, both here and across the sea").[8]

Portugal's conquests were facilitated by, and helped to accelerate, a tumultuous transition from Marīnid to Waṭṭāsid rule in Fez. The failure of Marīnid sultan Abū Saʿīd ʿUthmān III (r. 800–823/1398–1420) to recover Ceuta contributed to widespread dissatisfaction with the Marīnid state and possibly to his assassination in 823/1420. Abū Zakariyyāʾ Yaḥyā I, the Waṭṭāsid governor of Salé, became the regent for ʿAbd al-Ḥaqq II, the one-year-old heir to the Marīnid throne. The successful defense of Tangier in 1437 helped keep Abū Zakariyyāʾ in power until his death in 1448. Although ʿAbd al-Ḥaqq II had in the meantime come of age, two more Waṭṭāsids acted as viziers and de facto rulers until this last Marīnid sultan established direct rule from 1459 to 1465.

After seizing control from his Waṭṭāsid vizier in 1459, ʿAbd al-Ḥaqq ordered most of the Banū Waṭṭās in Fez killed. According to the traditional account, ʿAbd al-Ḥaqq then appointed a Jew, Hārūn, as vizier. This deeply unpopular move was exacerbated when Hārūn, the Jewish vizier, extended taxation to two traditionally exempt groups, the *sharīf*s ("nobles") who could claim prophetic lineage, and the *ʿulamāʾ* (scholars). While aspects of this account are legendary, it is clear that the people of Fez were burdened

8 Racine, *Opulent*, 15. On the tapestries, see Fundación Carlos de Amberes, *The Invention of Glory: Afonso V and the Pastrana Tapestries* (Madrid: Ediciones El Viso, [2011]). The cover image for *Leaving Iberia* is a detail from "Landing at Asilah," one of the four tapestries commissioned by Afonso V.

heavily by the taxes required to support ʿAbd al-Ḥaqq's campaigns against the Portuguese, the Castilians (who reclaimed Gibraltar in 1462), and the Waṭṭāsids who controlled cities outside Fez.[9] In 1465, ʿAbd al-ʿAzīz al-Waryāglī, a preacher at the Qarawiyyīn mosque, led a general revolt in Fez which resulted in the proclamation of the Idrīsid Muḥammad al-Ḥafīd al-ʿImrānī al-Jūṭī, the leader of the *sharīf* community in Fez, as the new ruler. When ʿAbd al-Ḥaqq was assassinated upon return from a military campaign, the Marīnid line came to an end.

Muḥammad al-Shaykh (r. 1472–1504) overthrew Jūṭī and established himself as the first independent Waṭṭāsid sultan after a short-lived period of Idrīsid rule that was restricted to Fez.[10] He pursued rule at the expense of his own city (Asilah) and failed to make any commitment to regain Portuguese-held territory, a choice that proved disastrous for many of his subjects. While besieging Fez in 1471, Muḥammad al-Shaykh ceded Asilah to Portugal and signed a twenty-year peace treaty with Afonso V; in it, Muḥammad al-Shaykh recognized Afonso's sovereignty over all Portuguese-held territories as well as Tangier. Tangier was taken without a fight after its inhabitants, and those of al-ʿArāʾish, abandoned their cities with the knowledge that no military would defend them. Afonso occupied al-ʿArāʾish in 1473.

The Maghribī counterpart to Afonso's lavish tapestries commemorating his dual victories in 1471 is perhaps the *Kitāb al-jihād* (*Book of Jihād*) by Muḥammad b. Yaggabsh al-Tāzī (d. 920/1514), a Berber Sufi and jurist. Tāzī's influential treatise was inspired by the devastating battle for Asilah, in which two thousand Maghribīs were killed and over five thousand were taken captive. He offered this poetic lament for the captives:

> If your eyes had seen how they left, you would have wept blood
> Mothers were separated from their children, and husband from wife
> Their tears streamed down their cheeks, for the loss of those they loved
> The veil was taken away from the virgin, revealing all her beauty and charm
> And the enemy stared at her beauty, while her tears accompanied her moans . . .
> O you people, the best in the world, nation of the Great Guide
> Don't you, O people, have any pity? Your brothers and sisters are helpless
> And are enduring humiliation and insult, despair and suffering, fear and hatred

9 Mercedes García-Arenal, "The Revolution of Fās in 869/1465 and the Death of Sultan ʿAbd al-Ḥaqq al-Marīnī," *Bulletin of the School of Oriental and African Studies* 41, no. 1 (1978): 65.

10 Cook, *Hundred Years War*, 98.

> Think on the condition of those chained captives, poor and degraded in dire hardship
> Yesterday, they were like kings in their land, and this morning they are humiliated slaves.[11]

Tāzī invokes the tragic fate of Asilah, especially that of the city's women, and urges them not to mourn but to mobilize Maghribīs in defense of Muslims and Muslim territory. In his treatise on *jihād*, Tāzī reminds his fellow scholars (*ʿulamāʾ*) of the suffering and shame inflicted on the Maghrib by foreign conquests, he exhorts them to pursue internal reform and armed resistance, and he warns them of the "grievous torment" awaiting Maghribīs if they fail to act.[12]

Indeed, following the initial loss of Ceuta, armed resistance to foreign occupation was organized both with and without the sanction of the central state. Abū Zakariyyāʾ successfully defended Tangier in 1437 by depending on the help of Berber and Arab groups from the south and southeast that were led into combat by *sharīf*s. In the 1470s, Idrīsid *sharīf* ʿAlī b. Rashīd founded the town of Chefchaouen, the most important of four centers of resistance against Portuguese holdings in northern Morocco; yet Ibn Rashīd's successful recruitment of *mujāhidūn* (warriors) from among Berber tribesmen and Andalusī emigrants and prosecution of the *jihād* led to confrontation rather than collaboration with the state.[13] In 1495, Muḥammad al-Shaykh even sought military assistance from Portuguese-held Ceuta to force Ibn Rashīd to recognize Waṭṭāsid authority, a move that suggests that the king was more concerned with retaining power than defending Muslim lands from Christian expansion.

In the fifteenth century, the second stage of the Portuguese expansion featured a relatively peaceful series of treaties between the Crown and Morocco's southern Atlantic ports, but in the early sixteenth century the expansion devolved into direct conquests, increasingly aggressive exploitation inland, and war with the newly-formed Saʿdian dynasty. Three of the treaties issued under kings João II (r. 1481–95) and Manuel I (1495–1521) have been preserved, and offer a striking image of Portugal's expectations of these towns' *mouros de paz*.[14] In 1497, Manuel

11 Translation by Nabil Matar in *Europe Through Arab Eyes, 1578–1727* (New York: Columbia University Press, 2009), 61. The original Arabic is included in Abū Bakr al-Būkhuṣaybī, *Aḍwāʾ ʿalā Ibn Yaggabsh al-Tāzī* (Casablanca: Maṭbaʿat al-Najāḥ al-Jadīda, 1976), 146–47.

12 Cornell, *Realm of the Saint*, 238.

13 Other tribal and Sufi leaders founded centers of armed resistance in the south.

14 These treaties are available in Pierre de Cenival, ed., *Les Sources Inédites de L'Histoire du Maroc. Première Série—Dynastie Saʿdienne, Archives et Bibliothèques de Portugal*, vol. 1, *Juillet 1486–Avril 1516* (Paris: Paul Geuthner, 1934), 1–35, hereafter, *SIHMP*. The documents from Azemmour and Safi represent renewals or renegotiations of previously existing agreements.

I stipulated the following conditions of vassalage to the inhabitants of Massa, an Atlantic port city south of what is now Agadir: the "Moors" are to provide an annual tribute of two horses; Portuguese vessels are exempted from the duties imposed on other ships; all merchants and vessels must be accorded safe passage; the locals are to receive and obey Portuguese agents and to sell them horses; they are to allow the construction of a fortress wherever the Portuguese desire and are to sell to the craftsmen anything they require; they may conduct trade through the port only with the permission of the Portuguese factor who will reside in the fort; and they are to house him until its completion. In exchange, the king assures them that "we will receive you and treat you as our own, and from now on we will command that you be under our protection and be treated, guarded, and defended as our natural subjects and vassals."[15] This protection extended to the seas and to Portugal itself, where these Maghribī subjects would be welcome to travel without cost on Portuguese ships, for the purpose of trade. Finally, fifteen children from Massa's notable families were to be held as hostages to ensure the security of Portuguese agents during the construction of the fortress.

The two documents from Azemmour (1486) and Safi (1488) are composed in the first-person plural voice of their Maghribī signatories, but were likewise drawn up by Portuguese officials. The provisions are quite similar to the Massa agreement, although abbreviated, and include a few notable exceptions. The inhabitants of Azemmour agreed to provide 10,000 shad (a type of fish) in annual tribute, loaded onto Portuguese ships free of duty, while Safi agreed to pay 300 *mithqals* of gold in cash or kind annually, along with two good horses. Only the Azemmour treaty concludes with an assurance that all of the city's inhabitants, including its *shaykhs*, jurists, and students, agree to the conditions, and that the document has been endorsed by Azemmour's *qāḍī* (judge) and *khaṭīb* (preacher) as conforming with "our law," presumably meaning Islamic law.[16]

The conditions of these treaties do not, of course, conform to Islamic law; João II's chancellery would have included this clause as a means of enhancing the legitimacy of the Azemmour document and facilitating its enforcement. All three treaties reflect aspects of Portuguese-Moroccan relationships in and around the tributary port cities that other Muslims

All volumes in the *Les Sources Inédites de L'Histoire du Maroc* series are available online through the Centro de História d'Aquém e d'Além-Mar: http://www.cham.fcsh.unl.pt/ext/portugalemarrocos/portugalemarrocos.html.

15 Translation by Malyn Newitt in Newitt, ed., *The Portuguese in West Africa, 1415–1670: A Documentary History* (Cambridge: Cambridge University Press, 2010), 33. Newitt translates the Massa document in full.

16 *SIHMP*, 1:14 (Arabic version), 1:22–23 (French translation from the original Portuguese).

residing elsewhere found religiously objectionable and traitorous. They objected to the willingness of Muslims to live under Christian rule, their payment of tribute to Christian overlords, and their provision of livestock and other necessary supplies to an enemy power. The Azemmour treaty's claim that religious authorities sanctioned it likely incensed Muslim jurists like Tāzī and the authors of the *fatwās* examined below, if they were aware of the specific conditions of this document. While jurists in Fez were unlikely to have seen the actual treaties, knowledge of their general provisions would have circulated among the political and religious elite in the Waṭṭāsid capital.

In addition to these activities, Moroccan mercenaries also fought and spied for Portugal under tribal leaders, or *qāʾids* (*alcaides dos mouros*), who served as regional rulers and assisted the Portuguese in the economic exploitation of inland areas. The most prominent among such *qāʾids* was Yaḥyā-u-Taʿfuft (d. 1518), whom Manuel I invested as *alcaide dos mouros* for Safi and the surrounding Dukkāla region in 1516. Yaḥyā-u-Taʿfuft was paid a generous salary, received bribes from regional merchants in exchange for favors, and supervised troops who collected taxes from the willing *mouros de paz* while raiding those areas beyond Portuguese control. Submission to Portuguese authority offered a measure of stability, protection, and profit in an otherwise "anarchic" political landscape that featured self-governing tribes, towns, and territories alongside four distinct dynasties competing for power in southern Morocco: the Portuguese, the Waṭṭāsids, the Hintātī (rulers of Marrakesh until 1524), and, after 1510, the Saʿdians.[17]

Under João II, Portugal attempted only one major military advance in northern Morocco. The construction of Graciosa, a fortress to be situated on the Lukkus River near al-ʿArāʾish, was supported by a 1486 papal crusading bull promising a plenary remission of sins and indulgence to all who fought against the "infidels."[18] Muḥammad al-Shaykh's forces successfully thwarted the project in 1489, but only in exchange for a ten-year extension of the Luso-Waṭṭāsid peace treaty set to expire in 1491.

Manuel I, the last Portuguese king to pursue extensive territorial expansion in Morocco, was driven by a deep commitment to crusade against Islam and a desire to be respected as a great champion of Christendom.[19] While his reign is best remembered for Vasco de Gama's discovery of a maritime route to India in 1497–99, Manuel's primary aspiration abroad was the

17 Cook, *Hundred Years War*, 137. According to Cook, both contemporaries and modern historians characterize this period of Moroccan history as "anarchic."

18 Racine, *Opulent*, 17.

19 On Manuel's ideological motivations, see François Soyer, *The Persecution of the Jews and Muslims of Portugal: King Manuel I and the End of Religious Tolerance (1496–7)* (Leiden: Brill, 2011), 161, and 273–79.

successful prosecution of military campaigns against "the infidels in Africa."[20] Manuel hoped to conquer all of Morocco's coastal lowlands, followed by the two major power centers of Fez and Marrakesh, and finally to lead a crusade to recapture Jerusalem and the Holy Land. To this end, he obtained two papal bulls in 1496, one in 1497, and another in 1514—well after the "last crusade" in Iberia. Pope Alexander VI granted Manuel two years' worth of church tithes collected in Portugal to finance his North African crusade and granted plenary indulgences to those fighting or contributing financially to the cause.[21] Manuel ordered both Jews and Muslims expelled from Portugal in 1497, although in practice this resulted in forced conversion for Jews. In 1505, Manuel circulated a tract in Europe, ostensibly addressed to the Pope, that reiterated his dedication to crusading, criticized the failure of other European kings to act, claimed that Portuguese armies would soon destroy Mecca, and even took credit for Castile's decision to forcibly convert its Muslims in 1502.

Despite his ideological passion and fanciful rhetoric, Manuel's military campaigns in Morocco, conducted primarily between 1505 and 1515, fell far short of his aspirations. Portugal succeeded in constructing several new fortresses, including Santa Cruz do Cabo de Gué (near Agadir), Mazagan (now El Jadida, near Azemmour), and Castelo do Mar (at Safi). Both Safi and Azemmour, previously under treaty, were brought under direct Portuguese rule; Azemmour, accused of multiple treaty violations, was conquered in a bloody battle that prompted the inhabitants of several nearby towns to first evacuate their cities in fear, then return to negotiate tributary agreements.[22] As late as 1514, Manuel boasted that the conquest of all Morocco was at hand, but two major failures in 1515 signaled the end of his expansionist ambitions: a direct attack on Marrakesh was repulsed, as was an attempt to build a fortress on the Sibu River at Maʿmūra (near Kenitra) that would have supplied an assault on Fez.[23] From the 1520s, the Portuguese adopted a defensive posture and began to contract their holdings from the 1540s onward.

Even as the Portuguese suffered key military defeats, their destructive policies under Manuel seriously compromised the stability and profitability of Portugal's Moroccan venture, as Vincent Cornell has shown.[24] By the late fifteenth century, the Maghrib had become a keystone in Portugal's imperial economy: grains, leather, fish, and other goods from southern Morocco's

20 Soyer, *Persecution*, 166. Soyer argues that this aspect of Manuel's reign has been neglected by historians committed to portraying him as a "modern" ruler. Soyer, *Persecution*, 161.
21 Soyer, *Persecution*, 165 (1496 bulls) and 277 (1497 bull); Racine, *Opulent*, (1514 bull).
22 Racine, *Opulent*, 20–21.
23 Racine, *Opulent*, 20.
24 Cornell, "Socioeconomic Dimensions," 387–88.

coastal plains were shipped north to be exchanged for European goods, while textiles, horses, and wheat were shipped south to be traded for slaves and gold in West Africa. Most of the cereals were collected as tribute, gathered from the productive agricultural hinterlands surrounding Portuguese-held ports, or from all the territory that could be brought into submission with the help of local leaders and *qāʾids* (as noted above). Yet in the early sixteenth century, agricultural production and local trade both deteriorated as a result of instability and lawlessness among Portugal's tribal allies and the Crown's increasingly predatory, short-term methods of resource extraction. Devastating slave raids into territories beyond Portuguese control led Berber populations to emigrate from the Dukkāla region. Even *mouros de paz* were raided for slaves and their crops were plundered and destroyed if they failed to deliver the annual tribute expected from them; these measures only exacerbated the situation by reducing both the labor force and the productive capacity of the land.[25] During a famine in 1521–22, many Moroccans sold themselves into indentured servitude to prevent starvation, and even converted to Christianity in the hopes of receiving better treatment.[26] Others sold their daughters into slavery; according to one report, in 1522 alone, 60,000 Moroccan women were sold in Spain.

These figures make the devastation, if not the shock, of Asilah's 1471 captive haul seem relatively minor, and the earlier words of Tāzī, prophetic:

> [The people of this land] will be shackled with chains and irons and every day they will suffer grievous torment; they will become like chattel and slaves and those who only yesterday were rich and secure will tomorrow be poor and afraid. They will be robbed of their possessions, their material conditions will be upset, their women will be separated from them, their daughters will be taken from them, and the unbelievers will compete over the prices at which they will purchase them. Then they will be separated from each other and sent to every land and [the unbelievers] will seduce them away from their religion and will undermine the strength of their convictions.[27]

While critics like Tāzī and the jurists considered below obliquely targeted the inaction of the Waṭṭāsids, official armed resistance to the Portuguese also took its toll on the Maghribī population.[28] The inhabitants of Tit, who fled during Portugal's 1513 conquest of Azemmour, returned and negotiated

25 Cornell, "Socioeconomic Dimensions," 393–94.

26 Cornell, "Socioeconomic Dimensions," 394. See also Cook, *Hundred Years War*, 117.

27 Translation by Cornell, *Realm of the Saint*, 238. For the Arabic original, see Būkhuṣaybī, *Aḍwāʾ*, 126.

28 On Tāzī's oblique critique of the sultan, see Scott Kugle, *Rebel Between Spirit and Law: Ahmad Zarruq, Sainthood, and Authority in Islam* (Bloomington: Indiana University Press, 2006), 81–82; Cornell, *Realm of the Saint*, 237–40.

tributary status, only to have their town destroyed by the Waṭṭāsids in retaliation. The Waṭṭāsids forcefully evacuated several towns near Safi and Azemmour in 1514, and relocated tribes suspected of disloyalty near Maʿmūra in 1515.[29] It is difficult to overstate the misery endured by ordinary Maghribīs in the early sixteenth century as a result of war, enslavement, dislocation, deprivation, and famine.

Spain's Unfinished Reconquest

In thirteenth-century Iberia, it would have been difficult to predict that Portugal would cross the strait into North Africa long before Castile or Aragon. In 1291, the Castilian and Aragonese kings signed a treaty affirming Castile's right to conquer North African territory west of the Muluia River—near what is now the Moroccan-Algerian border—and Aragon's right to conquer lands to the east.[30] These kings hoped to advance their kingdoms' strategic and commercial interests through these acquisitions on the Mediterranean's southern shore. In the early fourteenth century, James II of Aragon (r. 1291–1327) also advocated a crusading agenda proposed by Ramón Llull, according to which the conquests of Granada and then the Maghrib would facilitate the establishment of a southern Mediterranean crusading route that would lead, via Alexandria, all the way to Jerusalem. By the time of Granada's surrender nearly two centuries later, Portugal's already established foothold in Morocco only increased the Spanish monarchs' commitment to a program of North African conquests.

In 1492, Ferdinand of Aragon and Isabella of Castile celebrated their "reconquest" of Granada, a victory made all the more momentous because it was the last Muslim kingdom in Iberia. Yet they did not celebrate the end of the broader Reconquest, an as-yet-unfinished project to "reclaim" the formerly Christian territory held by the Visigothic kings prior to the 711 Muslim invasion of Iberia. Castilian chroniclers, jurists, and rulers asserted that the ancient Roman province of Mauretania Tingitana, including northern Morocco and the Canary Islands, had formed part of the Visigothic realm and was therefore the rightful inheritance of the Crown of Castile.[31]

Castile thus viewed Portugal's designs on Morocco as a usurpation of these rights as well as a strategic threat. When Pope Eugenius IV issued the 1436 crusading bull *Reg Regnum* to the Portuguese Crown, just before the failed assault on Tangier, Castile protested the provision granting Portugal

29 Cook, *Hundred Years War*, 153–54.
30 Soyer, *Persecution*, 274.
31 Soyer, *Persecution*, 274; Andrew Devereux, "North Africa in Early Modern Spanish Political Thought," *Journal of Spanish Cultural Studies* 12, no. 3 (2011): 277–78; *SIHMP*, 1:204.

the right to conquer "all infidels in Africa."[32] Once Isabella secured the Castilian throne, a series of Luso-Castilian agreements and papal bulls demarcated the two Crowns' spheres of influence and conquest in North Africa.

In the 1479 Treaty of Alcáçovas, which ended the War of the Castilian Succession, Portugal relinquished its claim to the Canary Islands (and to the Castilian throne), while Castile recognized Portugal's right to the "Kingdom of Fez," or most of modern Morocco; the agreement was given papal sanction in the 1481 bull *Aeterni Regis*. The 1494 Treaty of Tordesillas, while primarily concerned with the partition of newly-discovered lands in the Americas, reconfirmed most of Portugal's claims in North Africa and granted Castile lands to the east of Melilla.[33] Isabella and Ferdinand, who had turned their attention toward the southern Mediterranean following the conquest of Granada, secured a crusading bull in 1494 (*Redemptor Noster*) and another bull in 1495 (*Ineffabilis et Summi*) recognizing their right to any lands they conquered in Africa—as long as they did not interfere with lands already conquered by a Christian power. When Pope Alexander V (1492–1503) bestowed the title of the "Catholic Monarchs" on Ferdinand and Isabella in 1496, he reminded them of their promise "to carry the war to the Africans, enemies of the Christian name."[34] Manuel complained in vain that *Ineffabilis et Summi* failed to recognize explicitly Portugal's own prior right to African conquests. Yet in 1497, he was granted his own papal bull of the same name and terms, confirming Portuguese possession of any current and future conquests at the expense of infidels in Africa. Finally, the Luso-Castilian Treaty of Sintra in 1509 granted Castile rights to the Mediterranean coast stretching eastward from Peñón de Vélez de la Gomera, a small island off Badis, while Portugal was granted the territory west of Vélez as well as the entire Atlantic coast of North Africa, except the Castilian fortress of Santa-Cruz de Mar Pequeña, constructed in 1477–78 on the mainland opposite the Canary Islands.

These territorial agreements, as well as Castile's preoccupation with the war for Granada, meant that, during the late fifteenth and early sixteenth centuries, Spain's presence in Morocco had less devastating consequences

32 On the treaties and papal bulls discussed here, see Soyer, *Persecution*, 273–77; *SIHMP*, 1:203–20.

33 *SIHMP*, 1:209. In order to secure southern Mediterranean ports from which to combat Muslim pirates, Castile claimed the existence of a "Kingdom of Vélez" that included Melilla and Caçaça and was distinct from the Kingdom of Fez, which remained in Portugal's sphere of conquests.

34 O'Callaghan, *The Last Crusade*, 193. Pope Alexander praised the newly minted Catholic Monarchs for conquering Granada, fighting heresy in their realms, and expelling the Jews—but not for completing *the* Reconquest as we know it now, the "recovery" of the Iberian Peninsula for Christendom.

than that of Portugal.[35] After the conquests of Melilla (1497) and Peñón de Vélez de la Gomera (1508), Ferdinand directed his forces eastward, capturing a series of strategically located "plazas" along the southern Mediterranean coast, including Oran (1509), Algiers (1510), Bijāya (1510), and Tripoli (1511).[36] Unlike Portugal's policy of inland commercial penetration, Spain focused largely on controlling maritime shipping lanes and establishing a supply chain stretching ever closer to Jerusalem. The plazas were emptied of Muslim inhabitants and replaced with Christian settlers, but the hinterlands were left under local leadership. Like Portugal, Spain's greatest aspirations in North Africa ultimately went unfulfilled: Mauretania Tingitana was not fully "recovered," nor was a southern Mediterranean route to the Holy Land ever completed. After Ferdinand's death in 1516, the Ottoman Empire's ascendancy in the eastern Mediterranean deterred Ferdinand's successors from the continued pursuit of his crusading agenda.

Spain's conquests in Morocco are important for two reasons: they placed additional political and economic pressure on the Maghrib and they incited competition with the Portuguese over territory, religious prestige, and favor with the papacy. The achievement of political and religious goals was closely intertwined for both Crowns, as the Pope held the authority to allocate possession rights to all non-Christian territories, and domestic political legitimacy depended on the ruler's image as a devout Christian defender of the faith. Ferdinand and Isabella's strong rhetoric designating the Maghrib as a vital zone for crusades and reconquest was echoed by Manuel's pronounced embrace of a religious imperative to conquer Fez and Marrakesh in the same period, and certainly increased Maghribī Muslims' sense that their territorial and religious integrity were both under siege.[37]

The impact of the rivalry between Castile and Portugal in the late fifteenth century is perhaps best illustrated by Manuel's decision to expel Portugal's Muslim population. Scholars have long assumed that Manuel agreed to expel Jews and Muslims from his realm in 1497 in fulfillment of the conditions imposed by Ferdinand and Isabella for Manuel to marry

35 Although Isabella and Ferdinand administered their respective kingdoms (Castile and Aragon) separately, I use the term Spain for their joint conquests and aspirations in the Maghrib after 1492, and for Ferdinand's conquests following Isabella's death in 1504. Ferdinand ruled as regent of Castile from 1504 until his death in 1516, at which point his grandson Charles I (later Charles V, the Holy Roman Emperor) inherited both kingdoms and ruled Castile and Aragon as the king of Spain.

36 Isabella only lived to see the Moroccan conquests, but urged her successors in her 1504 will not "to cease from the conquest of Africa and to fight for the faith against the infidels." O'Callaghan, *The Last Crusade*, 248.

37 On the political theory underpinning Spain's African conquests, see Devereux, "North Africa." See also Andrew Devereux's *The Other Side of Empire: Just War in the Mediterranean and the Rise of Early Modern Spain* (Ithaca: Cornell University Press, 2020). I regret that this book arrived too late for me to make use of it here.

their eldest daughter. Many have further suggested that Manuel acquiesced because he hoped the marriage might position him to inherit the Castilian and Aragonese thrones, and to rule, one day, over all of Iberia. Historian François Soyer has now argued convincingly that Manuel's actions are better explained by his commitment to crusading in Morocco than a desire to unify Iberia.[38] While Manuel did agree to expel Jews and *converso*s (Jewish converts to Christianity) in order to complete the marriage and secure peace with Castile and Aragon, we have no concrete evidence that the Spanish demanded that he also expel Portugal's Muslims. For Soyer, the unexpected expulsion of the Muslims, the first of its kind in Iberia, was meant to impress the Pope. In the wake of the Catholic Monarchs' new title and papal bull authorizing African conquests, Manuel needed to enhance his credentials as a Christian king and devoted crusader. Six months after promulgating his edict of expulsion, Manuel was rewarded with an equivalent bull validating his own African conquests. At that point, his peace with Castile allowed him to focus on his overseas ambitions in Morocco and India. Soyer's innovative research shows that greater attention to Portuguese and Spanish interests in North Africa promises to improve our understanding of peninsular politics.

The Reconfiguration of Power in Morocco

The Iberian conquests reduced Muslims' political autonomy, placed nearly all of Morocco's Mediterranean and Atlantic ports and overseas trade revenues in foreign hands, burdened Maghribīs with the costs of war, and led to significant demographic attrition and social fragmentation in the form of casualties, captivity, dislocations (flight and forced migrations), and divided loyalties. While many of these impacts dissipated in the mid-sixteenth century as Portugal's North African holdings diminished, Iberian occupation contributed decisively to a long-term shift in the configuration of political authority in Morocco.

Following the Almoravids and the Almohads, the Marīnids (r. 1244–1465) were the third Berber dynasty to rule the Far Maghrib. Like their predecessors, the Marīnids sought to bolster their religio-political authority by providing patronage and privileges to *sharīf* families, those who claimed descent from the Prophet Muḥammad. By the fifteenth century, these families (the *shurafāʾ*) had become a prominent class whose religious and political influence was further enhanced by their active involvement in

38 François Soyer, "King Manuel I and the Expulsion of the Castilian *Conversos* and Muslims from Portugal in 1497: New Perspectives," *Cadernos de Estudos Sefarditas* 8 (2008): 33–62; Soyer, *Persecution*, 278–84. Portugal's Jewish population was not actually expelled from Portugal; they were prevented from leaving and forcibly converted to Christianity.

jihād against the Portuguese. As noted, the *sharīfs*' mobilization of irregular warriors was crucial to the successful defense of Tangier in 1437.[39] Just months after that victory, the tomb of Mūlay Idrīs II was "rediscovered" in the heart of Fez; this led to the establishment of a sanctuary that conferred substantial economic benefits and political power on the Idrīsid *sharīfs*. Thus, the Idrīsids were well positioned to assume power in the wake of the 1465 popular revolt that ended the Marīnid dynasty.

While the Idrīsids only retained control of Fez for six years, the Far Maghrib was moving decisively away from a model of political legitimacy that vested authority in tribal dynasties and toward a *sharīf*ian model that combined religious and political legitimacy, a model that has prevailed through to the present-day ʿAlawite monarchy. This shift was solidified with the rise of the Saʿdian dynasty, founded in the Sūs region of southern Morocco in the early sixteenth century. The Saʿdians' political appeal rested on three foundations: their claim to prophetic lineage; their devotion to *jihād* against the Portuguese and their tribal allies (after several key victories, it was the Saʿdians rather than the Waṭṭāsids that forced Portugal to withdraw from southern Morocco beginning in 1541); and finally, the Saʿdians benefitted from the direct support and ideology of the Jazūliyya Sufi order. The order's founder and enduring exemplar, Muḥammad b. Sulaymān al-Jazūlī (d. 869/1465), promoted a model of saintly authority in which spiritual masters serve as successors to the Prophet in all his dimensions—religious, political, and military. In accordance with this vision, the Saʿdians eagerly promoted themselves as just *imāms* capable of religious and military leadership.

The Saʿdians' compelling new model of religio-political legitimacy, a modern army equipped with European weapons technology, and their substantial organizational and administrative acumen propelled this new dynasty to victory over the Waṭṭāsids and the Portuguese.[40] By 1536 the Waṭṭāsids were forced to recognize Saʿdian sovereignty in southern Morocco, and in 1554 they were fully defeated by the new *sharīf*ian state. For the Portuguese, the deathblow came in 1578, at the Battle of Wādī al-Makhāzin. King Sebastião I (r. 1554–78), who had hoped to revive a Portuguese offensive in Morocco, was killed in what one scholar has described as "the greatest military disaster the Portuguese ever suffered in the course of their overseas expansion."[41] In Portugal, the repercussions

39 On the roles of *sharīfs* and Sufi orders in organizing resistance against foreign expansion, see Cornell, *Realm of the Saint*, esp. ch. 6 (155–95) and ch. 8 (230–71).

40 On the rise and success of the Saʿdians, see Cornell, "Socioeconomic Dimensions," and Cook, *Hundred Years War*.

41 Disney, *History of Portugal*, 19. This battle is also known as the Battle of the Three Kings, or the Battle of Ksar al-Kabir. Two rival Saʿdian kings, Muḥammad al-Mutawwakkil (r. 981–83/1574–76) and his uncle ʿAbd al-Mālik (r. 983–86/1576–78), were also killed.

of this defeat contributed to the kingdom's absorption into the empire of the Spanish Habsburgs two years later. The Saʿdian dynasty remained in power until 1659, when they were succeeded by the ʿAlawite monarchy still in power today.

Iberian Empires

In this historical overview I have approached the Iberian conquests in North Africa as a regional phenomenon, as an extension of peninsular politics and ideologies. A broader view is also instructive. The 1415 conquest of Ceuta, noted here for its impact on Maghribī Muslims, also marks the inception of the Portuguese Empire, which is considered the first modern colonial empire and the first global power. The Portuguese Empire, in one form or another, lasted nearly six centuries, from Ceuta until the handover of Macau to China in 1999. With regard to Spain, many readers primarily think of 1492 not for the fall of Granada or the expulsion of Iberian Jews, but for Christopher Columbus's Castilian-backed voyages of discovery to the Americas. Two years after Columbus "sailed the ocean blue," these two Iberian powers signed the first of two major treaties tasked with no less than the division of the entire non-Christian world into Spanish and Portuguese spheres of conquest. In the 1494 Treaty of Tordesillas, the finer details of Spain's and Portugal's competing claims in North Africa were negotiated even as vast swaths of the earth yet to be "discovered," exploited, settled, and converted were partitioned.

How did conquered peoples view the advent of the Portuguese and Spanish empires? Miguel León-Portilla's 1959 *Visión de los vencidos* (*Vision of the Vanquished*) (translated into English in 1962 as *The Broken Spears: The Aztec Account of the Conquest of Mexico*), first introduced popular audiences to indigenous accounts of the Spaniards' arrival in Mexico and their conquest of Tenochtitlan (1519–21), the capital of the Aztec empire.[42] This now-classic, "revolutionary" book, which has sold hundreds of thousands of copies, became a staple for generations of university students and indigenous rights activists. The accounts that León-Portilla rendered accessible challenged long-dominant triumphalist Spanish narratives, including such myths as the easy defeat of the Aztecs by a handful of men and the widespread native adoration of the Spaniards as superior, even divine.

42 Miguel León-Portilla, ed. and introd., *The Broken Spears: The Aztec Account of the Conquest of Mexico*, trans. Lysander Kemp, expanded ed. (Boston: Beacon Press, 2006). On the text's "revolutionary" impact, see J. Jorge Klor de Alva's foreword, *Broken Spears*, xi. I am grateful to Julie Charlip at Whitman College for introducing me to this text.

The access to indigenous voices offered by León-Portilla's sources, while incredibly important, comes with considerable caveats.[43] Our central source for native views of the conquest of Tenochtitlan is a vast ethnographic work compiled by the Spanish Franciscan missionary Fray Bernardino de Sahagún beginning around 1547. The accounts preserved by Sahagún were recorded at least thirty years after the conquest, with the aid of local Nahua graduates of missionary-run schools. The native informants' memories would not only have been shaped by their subject status at the time of collection, but also by their post-conquest conversion to Christianity. Sahagún retained editorial control over the final text. A final complication worth noting is that Nahuatl, the oral language of Sahagún's informants, was adapted to the Spanish alphabet only after the conquest. Sahagún's team recorded these memories in this new written form of the Nahuatl, alongside Spanish translations.

By contrast, we have a variety of texts written by and for North Africans through which we can explore native responses to Portuguese conquests in Morocco. We might suspect Tāzī of dramatic flourishes in his poetic lament for the 1471 fall of Asilah, but we do not have any reason to doubt that he wrote soon after the city's defeat, in his own voice, as part of a well-established literary tradition, for fellow Maghribī Muslims. Tāzī's poem even parallels in some ways the famous semi-poetic Nahua lament for Tlatelolco captured by the English title *The Broken Spears*: "Broken spears lie in the roads / We have torn our hair in our grief / The houses are roofless now, and their walls / Are red with blood."[44] While this translation is contested—it may be broken bones, rather than spears—readers eager to celebrate evidence of indigenous resistance have nonetheless made these lines the "most famous in Nahuatl."[45] Tāzī's lament, meant to mobilize *jihād*, is evidence not just of a valiant defeat but of ongoing resistance.

The legal texts I examine in the following chapter likewise constitute a clear form of resistance against Portuguese domination. They were written by and for Maghribī Muslims in direct response to ongoing Moroccan engagement with the Portuguese. These jurists were steeped in a centuries-old legal tradition, one that was well adapted to the written composition and circulation of their views. If we are eager to do the difficult work of rehabilitating the native voices conveyed by Sahagún and others,

43 Stuart B. Schwartz, ed. and introd., *Victors and Vanquished: Spanish and Nahua Views of the Conquest of Mexico* (Boston: Bedford/St. Martin's, 2000), 20–28.

44 The translation of this line, as well as its prosaic or poetic nature, has been debated. See John F. Schwaller, "Broken Spears or Broken Bones: Evolution of the Most Famous Line in Nahuatl," *The Americas* 66, no. 2 (2009): 241–52 and Miguel León-Portilla, "A Reply to John F. Schwaller," in the same issue, 252–54.

45 Schwaller, "Broken Spears," 241.

why have we neglected the written record left to us by Maghribī Muslims, in their own voices?

It will strike many readers as incongruous to compare the Portuguese conquests in Morocco with the Spanish conquests in the Americas. Portugal's investment in Morocco appears minor, and the damage to Maghribī lives and fortunes slight, when compared with Spain's impact on the Americas. Yet if dissimilarities can teach us as much as similarities, comparing the popularity of *The Broken Spears* to the near-complete obscurity of Zayyātī's *Selected Jewels* is defensible, and even beneficial. These legal opinions do not help us recover the voices of a population once assumed to have disappeared. Nor do they shed light on events considered central to American or European history. Perhaps most importantly, they do not depict the earliest encounters between two civilizations truly foreign to one another, so foreign that the diseases carried by one devastated the other.

With this last point, we have returned to where we started: Iberia and North Africa formed part of one intimately connected region in the medieval and early modern periods. Centuries before they ever discussed the status of Muslims under Portuguese rule in North Africa, Mālikī jurists helped delimit the roles of Jews and Christians living under Muslim rule in Iberia. By the late fifteenth century, Iberians and Maghribīs were known to each other, had ruled one another, and shared a shifting population that had criss-crossed the Strait of Gibraltar for one reason, then another. The texts that follow shed light on one part of this evolving story, when Christian Iberian conquerors met Muslim Maghribī resistance on the southern shores of the Mediterranean.

CHAPTER 3

Islamic Legal Resistance to Christian Conquest

This chapter explores an important but overlooked aspect of indigenous resistance to Iberian conquest in northern Morocco; namely, legal opinions issued by Muslim jurists in the late fifteenth and early sixteenth centuries. A set of *fatwās* preserved by ʿAbd al-ʿAzīz b. al-Ḥasan al-Zayyātī (d. 1055/1645)[1] addresses the status of Muslims in "enemy" territory as well as the permissibility of waging *jihād* against foreign occupiers absent the Muslim ruler's permission. While some of these opinions sanction irregular *jihād*, their primary aim is the deterrence of collaboration with foreign powers. The jurists likely wrote in opposition to Waṭṭāsid inaction and the Maghribī *mouros de paz* who concluded treaties with the Portuguese.

Muslim jurists resisted foreign dominance not by deriding or directly attacking the Christian enemy, but by assigning religious consequences to specific social, economic, and political behaviors deemed threatening to Muslims' communal identity, political autonomy, and territorial integrity. These texts show that in the context of increasing and seemingly voluntary Muslim submission to an expanding Christian occupation, jurists sought to maintain the territorial and political integrity of Muslims by safeguarding their religious and communal identity. Boundary crossings and political treachery were seen as religious disobedience, as individual Muslims' religious transgressions could have grave political ramifications.

---

1 Zayyātī was likely born in Fez, traveled as far as Egypt to study Qurʾān recitation and the legal sciences, then settled in Tetouan, where he devoted himself to teaching, writing, and serving as *imām* in a local mosque until his death in 1055/1645. For his biography, see the notices for Zayyātī and his father in Muḥammad al-Qādirī, *Nashr al-Mathānī li-ahl al-qarn al-ḥādī ʿashar waʾl-thānī*, ed. Muḥammad Ḥajjī and Aḥmad al-Tawfīq, 4 vols. (Rabat: Dār al-Maghrib lil-Taʾlīf waʾl-Tarjama waʾl-Nashr, 1977–82), 2:30 and 1:198–99). Qādirī's notices are reproduced in Muḥammad Ḥajjī, ed., *Mawsūʿat aʿlām al-Maghrib* (Beirut: Dār al-Gharb al-Islāmī, 1996), 4:1421 and 3:1218–19. For later composite notices, see Ḥajjī, *al-Ḥaraka al-fikriyya biʾl-Maghrib fī ʿahd al-Saʿdiyyīn* (Rabat: Dār al-Maghrib lil-Taʾlīf waʾl-Tarjama waʾl-Nashr, 1977–78), 2:421; Muḥammad Dāwūd, *Mukhtaṣar Tārīkh Tiṭwān* (Tetouan: Maʿhad Mawlāy al-Ḥasan, 1953), 279–80; Khayr al-Dīn al-Ziriklī, *al-Aʿlām: qāmūs tarājim li-ashhar al-rijāl waʾl-nisāʾ min al-ʿarab waʾl-mustaʿribīn waʾl-mustashriqīn*, 14th ed. (Beirut: Dār al-ʿIlm lil-Malāyīn, 1999), 4:16; and ʿUmar Riḍā Kaḥḥāla, *Muʿjam al-muʾallifīn* (Beirut: Muʾassasat al-Risāla, 1993), 2:159.

The *fatwās* preserved in Zayyātī's *Selected Jewels* are also significant because they broaden our understanding of Muslim legal thought regarding Muslims living under non-Muslim rule. As noted, opinions on this issue have attracted ample attention in the scholarly literature, much of it focused on two 1491 *fatwās* (*Asnā al-matājir* and the Marbella *fatwā*) issued by Fez's chief *muftī* Aḥmad b. Yaḥyā al-Wansharīsī (d. 914/1508) and included in his monumental work *al-Miʿyār al-muʿrib*. An important subset of the *fatwās* preserved by Zayyātī were authored by Wansharīsī and several of his contemporaries; thus, we have a valuable opportunity to compare Mālikī rulings on Muslims living under Christian rule in Iberia and North Africa. Placing these opinions in comparative perspective suggests that, while modern scholars have focused overwhelmingly on Christian-Muslim relations in Iberia, Muslim jurists in the late fifteenth century did not view the predicament of Muslims living under Christian rule in Iberia as exceptional. Rather, voluntary Muslim residence in Christian territory raised similar concerns in both Iberia and North Africa even before their fates diverged in the early sixteenth century, when forced conversions marked the start of the Morisco period in Iberia. We still have much to learn by examining the case of North Africa, where Muslims continued to develop a variety of relationships with Christians, one of which was voluntary conversion to Christianity (and thus inclusion in the Christian community).

Zayyātī's set of *fatwās* addressing Muslim-Christian relations in and around Portuguese-occupied territory appears in the chapter on *jihād* in his compilation, whose full title is *al-Jawāhir al-mukhtāra fīmā waqaftu ʿalayh min al-nawāzil bi-Jibāl Ghumāra* (*Selected Jewels: Legal Cases I Encountered in the Ghumāra Mountains*). Despite its title, the compilation includes opinions from rural and urban areas of northern Morocco; that is, Zayyātī interprets the area broadly, and includes more than the narrow mountainous area once affiliated with the Ghumāra Berber tribes. Most of the opinions date from the fifteenth and sixteenth centuries. Although *Selected Jewels* remains unedited and little-studied, the numerous copies preserved in Moroccan manuscript libraries attest to its importance, as do the later jurists who used Zayyātī's work as a primary source for their own compilations. Such works include ʿAlī b. ʿAbd al-Salām al-Tasūlī's nineteenth-century *al-Jawāhir al-nafīsa*, still in manuscript form, and Muḥammad al-Mahdī al-Wazzānī's two twentieth-century collections *al-Miʿyār al-jadīd* and *al-Nawāzil al-ṣughrā*, both published.[2]

2 At least sixteen partial or complete manuscript copies of *al-Jawāhir al-mukhtāra* are held in Morocco by the General Library and Archives in Tetouan, the Ḥasaniyya Library (Rabat), the Moroccan National Library (Rabat), the ʿAllāl al-Fāsī Institute (Rabat), the Muʾassasat al-Malik ʿAbd al-ʿAzīz Āl Saʿūd (Casablanca), and the Dāwūdiyya Library (Tetouan). I used three of these copies to produce the first partial Arabic edition of Zayyātī's chapter on *jihād*:

The *fatwās* I analyze here were issued by eight jurists, six writing in the late fifteenth century and two in the early sixteenth century.[3] The texts are undated, the questioners are not named, and most of the locations and specifics are vague; even the Portuguese are simply referred to as enemies or Christians. Yet some of these details may be inferred from contextual factors, and part of what makes *Selected Jewels* such a promising source for future study is the fact that Zayyātī retained many of the contextual details and textual ambiguities that other compilers may have edited out.[4] For ease of comparison, the *fatwās* are divided into three groups below.

Fishing with the Enemy: Ibn Barṭāl, Māwāsī, and Wansharīsī

This first group of opinions was issued by ʿĪsā b. Aḥmad al-Māwāsī (d. 896/1491), ʿAlī b. ʿAbd Allāh al-Aghsāwī, known as Ibn Barṭāl (d. ca. 901/1495), and Wansharīsī. All three jurists were active in Fez in the last quarter of the fifteenth century and appear to have been presented with the same or a similar set of questions regarding Muslim cooperation with the Portuguese. These *fatwās* are the most easily comparable to one another and to Wansharīsī's well-known opinions. Whereas *Asnā al-matājir* and the Marbella *fatwā*, treated in the next two chapters, engage more narrowly with the obligation to perform *hijra* (emigrate from non-Muslim to Muslim territory), these *fatwās* respond to a broad range of issues related to Muslim relationships with Christian authorities in and around Christian-controlled territory.

Jocelyn Hendrickson, "The Islamic Obligation to Emigrate: Al-Wansharīsī's *Asnā al-matājir* Reconsidered" (PhD dissertation, Emory University, 2009), 411–36. I also consulted two manuscript copies of Tasūlī's *al-Jawāhir al-nafīsa*, which are available at the Ḥasaniyya Library in Rabat (MS 12575) and the Tunisian National Library (MS 5354). At least one additional copy of *Selected Jewels* is held by the library of Amīr ʿAbd al-Qādir University of Islamic Sciences in Constantine, Algeria. On the basis of this Algerian copy and two Moroccan ones, Ghaniya Aṭwī produced a partial edition of this text as an MA thesis; see Ghaniya Aṭwī, *al-Jawāhir al-mukhtāra mimmā waqaftu ʿalayh min al-nawāzil bi-jibāl Ghumāra*, MA thesis, University of Constantine 2, Algeria (2013). Wazzānī's two compilations have been published as Muḥammad al-Wazzānī, *al-Nawāzil al-jadīda al-kubrā fīmā li-ahl Fās wa-ghayrihim min al-badw wa'l-qurā, al-musammā bi-: Al-Miʿyār al-jadīd al-jāmiʿ al-muʿrib ʿan fatāwī al-mutaʾakhkhirīn min ʿulamāʾ al-Maghrib*, ed. ʿUmar b. ʿAbbād, 12 vols. ([Rabat]: Wizārat al-Awqāf wa'l-Shuʾūn al-Islāmiyya, 1996–2000) [henceforth referred to as *al-Miʿyār al-jadīd*]; Wazzānī, *al-Nawāzil al-ṣughrā, al-musammā: Al-Minaḥ al-sāmiya fī al-nawāzil al-fiqhiyya*, ed. Wizārat al-Awqāf wa'l-Shuʾūn al-Islāmiyya, 4 vols. ([Rabat]: Wizārat al-Awqāf wa'l-Shuʾūn al-Islāmiyya, 1992–93).

3 For translations of most of these texts, see appendix A.

4 In his two *fatwā* compilations Wazzānī includes versions of many of the opinions preserved by Zayyātī, but they have been heavily edited and some jurists' names are misspelled.

Ibn Barṭāl

Zayyātī includes three *fatwā*s by Abū al-Ḥasan ʿAlī al-Aghsāwī, known as Ibn Barṭāl,[5] who weighs in on the legal statuses of five categories of

5 As this jurist's identity has been the subject of confusion and is central to my argument, a discussion of the sources is necessary. Zayyātī offers the fullest version of his name in the third *fatwā* attributed to him: "Abū al-Ḥasan ʿAlī b. ʿAbd Allāh b. ʿAlī al-Aghsāwī, who I believe is the one known as Ibn Barṭāl." Zayyātī signals this same uncertainty regarding the jurist's *ism shuhra* (name by which he is known) in all three *fatwās*, indicating that this jurist was not well known. Ibn Barṭāl's name appears in the same form in Tasūlī's *al-Jawāhir al-nafīsa*, but Wazzānī mistakes "al-Aghsāwī" for "al-Anṣārī" in his *al-Nawāzil al-ṣughrā* (1:419); this mistake is repeated by Laḥsan al-Yūbī, who further misidentifies the jurist as "Ibn Qarṭāl" (Yūbī, *al-Fatāwā al-fiqhiyya fī ahamm al-qaḍāyā min ʿahd al-Saʿdiyyīn ilā mā qabl al-ḥimāya* [(Rabat): Wizārat al-Awqāf wa'l-Shu'ūn al-Islāmiyya, 1998], 212). While I have not located a dedicated biographical entry for Ibn Barṭāl, he appears in *Dawḥat al-nāshir*, Ibn ʿAskar's biographical work devoted to scholars active in the sixteenth century. In his entry for the Fāsī jurist Mūsā b. al-ʿUqda al-Aghsāwī (d. 911/1506), Ibn ʿAskar states that Mūsā studied with ʿAbdūsī (d. 849/1446) and Māwāsī (d. 896/1491) and that he was a contemporary of Waryāglī (d. 894/1488–9) and Ibn Barṭāl. See Muḥammad Ibn ʿAskar, *Dawḥat al-nāshir li-maḥāsin man kāna bi'l-Maghrib min mashāyikh al-qarn al-ʿāshir*, ed. Muḥammad Ḥajjī, 3rd ed. (Casablanca: Manshūrāt Markaz al-Tūrāth al-Thaqāfī al-Maghribī, 2003), 37. The same details are reproduced in Muḥammad b. Jaʿfar al-Kattānī, *Salwat al-anfās wa-muḥādathat al-akyās bi-man uqbira min al-ʿulamā' wa'l-ṣulaḥā' bi-Fās*, ed. ʿAbd Allāh al-Kāmil al-Kattānī, et al. (Casablanca: Dār al-Thaqāfa, 2004), 3:109. On this basis, I believe Ibn Barṭāl was from Fez and died around 901/1495, at the opening of the sixteenth century and between the dates for his contemporaries Waryāglī and Mūsā b. al-ʿUqda. By contrast, van Koningsveld and Wiegers ("Islamic Statute," 38) identify the Ibn Barṭāl whose *fatwās* appear in *Jawāhir al-mukhtāra* with another Ibn Barṭāl who shared some students with the Andalusī scholar Ibn Rabīʿ (d. 719/1319). Yet Zayyātī's Ibn Barṭāl cannot be the same as this earlier Andalusī scholar, for at least six reasons: (1) The full name ("Abū ʿAbd Allāh Muḥammad b. ʿAlī b. Muḥammad b. Barṭāl") offered in van Koningsveld and Wiegers' source, Ibn al-Khaṭīb's *al-Iḥāṭa fī akhbār Gharnāṭa*, does not match that given by Zayyātī; (2) the *nisba* al-Aghsāwī, recorded by Zayyātī, refers to a tribe known to inhabit the Ghumāra mountain range in northern Morocco (al-Kattānī, *Salwat al-anfās*, 1:299). In fact, Zayyātī's Ibn Barṭāl is likely a corruption of "al-Baqqāl," a family of Aghsāwīs known for their resistance to the Portuguese, whose descendants include the "patron saint" of Tangier, Muḥammad al-Ḥājj al-Baqqāl (d. 1130/1718); (3) We would expect Zayyātī to focus on jurists who trace their ancestry to this very region, after which his *fatwā* compilation is named; (4) Ibn al-Khaṭīb's association of the Andalusī Ibn Barṭāl with Ibn Rabīʿ is no stronger than Ibn ʿAskar's association of an Ibn Barṭāl with the four Fāsī scholars noted above; (5) Ibn Barṭāl's *fatwās* include two explicit references to events in the Maghrib: he answers a question from (Portuguese-) occupied Asilah and praises the inhabitants of Mount Ḥabīb (in the Ghumāra range) for fighting the infidels; and (6) most importantly, the questions Zayyātī's Ibn Barṭāl answers are very similar to those directed to Māwāsī and Wansharīsī. Van Koningsveld's and Wiegers' note regarding Ibn Barṭāl was tangential to their argument and based on two fleeting references in Lisān al-Dīn b. al-Khaṭīb, *al-Iḥāṭa fī akhbār Gharnāṭa*, ed. Yūsuf ʿAlī Ṭawīl (Beirut: Dār al-Kutub al-ʿIlmiyya, 2003), 4:4 and 4:332. Nonetheless, Alan Verskin has recently endorsed their conflation of these two Ibn Barṭāls, based on one additional consideration: a portion of Ibn Barṭāl's third *fatwā* seems to mention a hoped-for victory by Marīnid ruler Abū al-Ḥasan ʿAlī b. ʿUthmān II (r. 731–49/1331–48); see Verskin, *Islamic Law and the Crisis of the Reconquista: The Debate on the Status of Muslim Communities in Christendom* (Leiden: Brill, 2015), 22 n. 83. Here Verskin appears to endorse my own emendation of this text, suggested in my Arabic edition of this *fatwā* (Hendrickson, "The Islamic Obligation," 419–21). All of the manuscripts read "ʿImād al-Marīnī"; I have suggested that we read this as ʿUthmān al-Marīnī, and noted that parts of this anomalous passage are corrupted and it appears out of place (as

Muslims who live under Christian rule and three other groups living on the Christian-Muslim frontier. His *fatwās* are apparently all responses to the same impatient questioner, who had re-submitted his questions, despite Ibn Barṭāl's protest (in the third *fatwā*) that he had responded immediately, when they first arrived. This set of *fatwās* offers a fascinating glimpse into a rather messy process of legal advice, hastily composed in response to an urgent but complicated and ever-changing set of questions.

In the first *fatwā*, an unknown questioner asks Ibn Barṭāl about a group of Muslims whose territory the Christians have conquered, and who have agreed to a pact requiring them to pay tribute to their new overlords. The questioner divides these Muslims into five groups based on their relationship with the Christians: (1) those who only pay them tribute, (2) those who trade among them, (3) those who spy for them, (4) those who fight for them against other Muslims, and (5) those whom the Christians have exempted from paying tribute, a group that includes prayer leaders and those who perform the call to prayer. The questioner wishes to know the legal statuses of these groups with respect to the inviolability of their lives and property, the validity of their leading prayer, and the admissibility of their testimony (in court cases, giving evidence, etc.).

Ibn Barṭāl's response begins with an overall assessment of those who have agreed to pay tribute to the Christians; he describes them as "a depraved people, disobedient to God, and in violation of the *sunna* [exemplary behavior] of His Prophet."[6] He then addresses each of the five groups, beginning with those who only pay the tribute. These Muslims are disobedient to God because of their submission and their payments to Christians. They may not testify or lead prayer, but as Muslims their lives and property remain inviolable. Those who also trade with the Christians, apparently in the market squares of the Portuguese fortresses, share this status but sin more gravely than the first group.[7]

As for those who spy for the Christians, Ibn Barṭāl states "the commonly accepted view is that [taking] the life of a spy is licit, that he should be killed, and that his killer should be rewarded."[8] This opinion renders any

we might expect in this set of three garbled *fatwās*); see the notes in appendix A as well as the Arabic edition. As "ʿUthmān al-Marīnī," this figure must refer to Abū Saʿīd ʿUthman II (r. 710–31/1310–31) or more likely Abū Saʿīd ʿUthman III (r. 800–823/1398–1420); Verskin's Ibn ʿUthman is neither supported by the one manuscript of *al-Jawāhir al-mukhtāra* that he consulted, nor by any of the additional copies I consulted. Further, the Ibn Barṭāl who shared students with Ibn Rabīʿ is likely to have died prior to the reign of ʿUthmān II. Finally, it is worth noting that Algerian jurist al-Sharīf al-Tilimsānī (d. 1264/1848), discussed in part 4, understands Ibn Barṭāl to be a fifteenth-century contemporary of Māwāsī and Ibn Zakrī.

6 Appendix A, 268.

7 On these markets, see Racine, *Opulent*, 97–98.

8 Appendix A, 268.

mention of property, testimony, or prayer unnecessary; a group whose lives are forfeit clearly cannot lead prayer or offer testimony. The status of those who fight for and sell weapons to the enemy is similarly straightforward: they have "deviated from the religion, and their status is [like] that of the Christians."[9] The implication is that this group has committed apostasy and that their lives and property are forfeit.

Finally, Ibn Barṭāl states that the prayer leaders and callers to prayer likewise sin more gravely than the others, presumably in comparison with the first group of Muslims who pay tribute only. The sin of this fifth group is greater because they are exemplars, to whom lay Muslims look for guidance. Although they do not pay tribute, they lose their probity and may not testify or lead prayer. They must relocate and repent.

In the second and third *fatwās*, Ibn Barṭāl is asked to differentiate between the legal statuses of Muslim groups who are living near, rather than under the direct control of, the Christians. The first group is engaged in some form of resistance against the Christians; in the first version of this three-part question, this initial group is described as waging war "like the people of Jabal (Mount) Ḥabīb,"[10] while in the second version, the group merely cultivates land that belongs to the Christians, and steals the yield without the enemy's knowledge.

The second group of Muslims has signed a treaty with the Christians, but has vowed not to pay them any tribute. As described in the third *fatwā*, the treaty obligates the Muslims to pay a regular tribute to the Christians beginning in October, presumably of the year the question was posed. A rapidly approaching deadline helps explain the urgency that resulted in the resubmission of this question. In the second *fatwā*, the questioner states that this group's plan is to flee if and when they are asked for the payment. In the third *fatwā*, the group also plans to flee rather than pay, and they are described as being well disposed to serve at the frontlines of a *jihād* if other Muslims come to their aid. The third group also signed this treaty, but is content to remain and pay the required tribute "for as long as the world remains."[11]

---

9 Appendix A, 268.

10 Appendix A, 271. According to al-Ḥasan al-Wazzān (Leo Africanus), this is one of the mountains of the al-Ḥabt region of northwestern Morocco, inhabited by the Ghumāra and other tribes. After the Portuguese seizure of Tangier in 1471, many Tangerines moved to this mountain, but remained poorly protected and were often raided by the Portuguese. Jean-Léon L'Africain, *Description de l'Afrique*, ed. and trans. E. Épaulard, et al. (Paris: Adrien-Maisonneuve, 1956), 1:268–70. Jabal Ḥabīb may be a mistake for Jabal Zabīb, which Kattānī (*Salwat al-anfās*, 1:299) associates with the Ghumāra range, as do the editors of Nāṣirī's history of the Maghrib. Aḥmad al-Nāṣirī, *Kitāb al-Istiqṣā li-akhbār duwal al-Maghrib al-Aqṣā*, ed. Muḥammad Ḥajjī, et al. (Casablanca: Manshūrāt Wizārat al-Thaqāfa wa'l-Ittiṣāl, 2001), 5:266.

11 Appendix A, 271–72.

Ibn Barṭāl opens each of the two responses by describing this situation as a "horrifying affair that has threatened the pillars of Islam and blotted out the very days and nights."[12] He then responds to both versions of this three-part question as though they consisted of the three categories set forth in the second *fatwā:* a first group engaged in *jihād*, a second group that has signed a treaty but will leave if necessary rather than pay tribute, and a third group that is content to remain where they are and pay the tribute. Ibn Barṭāl praises the first group:

> The [first] third [i.e., first of three groups] who remain in a state of war with the enemy and [in a state] of preparation for *jihād* against them, and who lie in wait to attack them—they are the Muslims whose intercession is accepted because of [the strength of] their Islam, and from the dust of whose footsteps we must seek a blessing; for they are engaged in the greatest act of devotion to God. I only wish I were with them, so that I could attain a great victory.[13]

The second group—reduced in both versions of the answer to those who will flee rather than pay—is neither completely praiseworthy nor completely blameworthy. Ibn Barṭāl writes that they have committed a reprehensible act by "residing in a territory in which the infidel has established his control, supremacy, and dominance" over their families and property, but that they still have the opportunity to be among the saved, as long as they fulfill their intention by fleeing as soon as the tribute is imposed.[14] While the questioner describes these Muslims as living in the immediate vicinity of Christians, rather than directly under their control, Ibn Barṭāl's response suggests that he considers this land, now under treaty to pay tribute to Christians, equivalent in status to Christian territory. He focuses on the group's residence in Christian-dominated lands as their primary transgression, and endorses the group's intention to relocate as the appropriate solution.

While the third of these three groups (the "third third" below) is wholly blameworthy, Ibn Barṭāl considers that lay Muslims on the frontier who pay tribute to the enemy, but commit no additional offenses such as trading with them, may be unaware of the implications of their actions or may be led astray by their local leaders:

> As for the third third, they are a truly vile third, because they have lost their religion and their [standing in this] world . . . for it is not permissible for a Muslim to conclude a treaty with the infidels which stipulates that

12 Appendix A, 272 and 273.
13 Appendix A, 273; see also 272.
14 Appendix A, 273; see also 272.

> he must pay them a tribute . . . What is obligatory upon you and upon our masters who reside there is to inform this third of their error and to rebuke, as much as they can, those among this third who have power and authority. Then if they disobey, they should be renounced; and it will not be permissible for you to act as their guardians or executors, nor for you to witness for them, nor to pray the funeral prayer for their dead, nor to attend to their [legal] affairs, unless they turn back from their sinful action and their contemptible depravity.[15]

Ibn Barṭāl demands that his questioner and honorable peers residing in this area do all they can to inform these people of their sins and guide them from error, and prohibits his addressees from offering religious and legal services to those residents who persist in their ways. These instructions make it clear that Ibn Barṭāl's questioner and fellow addressees are legal professionals or other religious leaders whose knowledge and responsibilities include informing the population of their religious obligations and attending to their legal affairs. The questioner's repeated request for a *fatwā* from Fez thus suggests that the issue of what exactly constituted living under Christian authority was not clear-cut even to many jurists in this period. As noted, Ibn Barṭāl classifies this region as being under Christian rule, whereas the questioner may have been unsure of the territory's legal status and the inhabitants are either unaware or unconcerned that they are violating a religious prohibition against living under non-Muslim rule. Ibn Barṭāl's directive that this third group be informed of their sins and guided from error thus tasks the local religious leaders with convincing these residents not only to refuse to pay the tribute, but also to move to a region not subject to a treaty with the Christians.

For those residents who persist in their ways after receiving guidance and counsel, that is, those who remain and intend to pay the tribute, Ibn Barṭāl implies that their membership in the Muslim community must be suspended. Local religious leaders should not recognize their requests for the services they would normally offer fellow Muslims, such as performing funeral prayers or witnessing their marriages and other contracts. This loss of status is not permanent, but should be enforced until and unless the population returns to the fold.

15 Appendix A, 274. This passage appears only in Ibn Barṭāl's third *fatwā*. The corresponding section of the second *fatwā* must be considered corrupted. In the second *fatwā*, Ibn Barṭāl assigns the death penalty to those who merely pay tribute, whereas in the first and third *fatwās*, the punishment for spies is death. See appendix A, 272. At the end of Wansharīsī's Berber *fatwā*, Zayyātī admits that his source for these opinions contains many mistakes.

The urgency of Ibn Barṭāl's *fatwās* is a result of the state of active warfare that informs most of the opinions preserved by Zayyātī and marks a clear point of divergence between Muslims living under Christian rule in Iberia and Muslims in the Maghrib. While *jihād* to regain territory in Iberia was no longer an option for Andalusī Muslims, it was still a viable and meritorious activity in Morocco. Not only does Ibn Barṭāl praise those engaged in physical resistance and condemn spying or fighting for the enemy, he also stresses the importance of not engaging in any trade that would empower or enrich the Christians against their Muslim adversaries. He appends this expectation of economic boycott to the second and third *fatwās*, even though trade is not mentioned in these questions. Furthermore, he laments that Muslims in "these lands" engaged in such detrimental trade instead of enduring patiently while awaiting assistance from fellow Muslims.[16]

Ibn Barṭāl's *fatwās* are undated, but must post-date the 1471 conquests of Asilah and Tangier. In the third *fatwā*, Ibn Barṭāl answers an unrelated question regarding a man from Asilah who was taken captive by the enemy; the questioner also prays for the city's return to Muslim rule. The regions that Ibn Barṭāl renounces for trading voluntarily with the Portuguese may include Salé, Safi, and Azemmour.

Māwāsī

Zayyati includes one *fatwā* by ʿĪsā b. Aḥmad al-Māwāsī (d. 896/1491),[17] who at one point served as the chief *muftī* of Fez.[18] Like his Fāsī peers, Māwāsī is asked about a group of Muslims who reside in areas that have fallen to infidel rule. The questioner asks if it is permissible for these Muslims to remain where they are, despite the fact that they could easily move. As in the questions posed to Ibn Barṭāl, these Muslims are then divided into several groups based

16 Appendix A, 272 and 274–75.

17 On Māwāsī, whose full name is Abū Mahdī ʿĪsā b. Aḥmad b. Muḥammad al-Māwāsī al-Baṭṭū'ī, see Kaḥḥāla, *Muʿjam al-mu'allifīn*, 2:796; Badr al-Dīn al-Qarāfī, *Tawshīḥ al-Dībāj wa-ḥilyat al-ibtihāj*, ed. Aḥmad al-Shatīwī (Beirut: Dār al-Gharb al-Islāmī, 1983), 270; Aḥmad b. al-Qāḍī al-Miknāsī, *Durrat al-ḥijāl fī ghurrat asmā' al-rijāl*, ed. Muṣṭafā ʿAbd al-Qādir ʿAṭā (Beirut: Dār al-Kutub al-ʿIlmiyya, 2002), 378; Ibn al-Qāḍī al-Miknāsī, *Jadhwat al-iqtibās fī dhikr man ḥalla min al-aʿlām bi-madīnat Fās* (Rabat: Dār al-Manṣūr lil-Ṭibāʿa wa'l-Wirāqa, 1973–74), 2:502–3; Aḥmad Bābā al-Tinbuktī, *Kifāyat al-muḥtāj li-maʿrifat man laysa fī al-Dībāj*, ed. Muḥammad Muṭīʿ (Rabat: Wizārat al-Awqāf wa'l-Shu'ūn al-Islāmiyya, 2000), 1:320–21; al-Tinbuktī, *Nayl al-ibtihāj bi-taṭrīz al-Dībāj*, ed. ʿAlī ʿUmar (Cairo: Maktabat al-Thaqāfa al-Dīniyya, 2004), 1:335; Muḥammad Ḥajjī, ed., *Alf sana min al-wafayāt* (Rabat: Maṭbūʿāt Dār al-Maghrib lil-Ta'līf wa'l-Tarjama wa'l-Nashr, 1976), 152 and 272.

18 Māwāsī must have been chief *muftī* after his teacher Muḥammad al-Qawrī (d. 872/1468) and before Ibn al-Qāḍī al-Miknāsī (d. 917/1511). Wansharīsī refers to him as *the faqīh* and *muftī* of Fez in the *Miʿyār* (4:485–86). On the chief *muftīs* of Fez in this period, see Devin Stewart, "The Identity of 'The *Muftī* of Oran,' Abū l-ʿAbbās Aḥmad b. Abī Jumʿah al-Maghrāwī al-Wahrānī (d. 917/1511)," *Al-Qanṭara* 27, no. 2 (2006): 297–98.

on their relationship to Christian authority: those who live under infidel rule under a treaty that requires the payment of tribute; those who trade with the enemy; those who provide the enemy with information about the Muslims; and those who not only fish with the enemy, but who voice contentment with their arrangement. Māwāsī notes that these fishermen say to their enemy partners, "may God prolong this period."[19]

Māwāsī prohibits these Muslims from remaining under infidel rule, from paying tribute to a non-Muslim ruler, and from interacting with them for the purpose of trade. Māwāsī, like Ibn Barṭāl, states that Muslims who remain under Christian rule may not give testimony or lead prayer, but as Muslims, their lives remain inviolable. While the two jurists' *fatwās* are nearly identical on these points, Māwāsī's response departs from that of Ibn Barṭāl in that Māwāsī conflates the status of spies with those who fish contentedly with the enemy.[20] While these were distinct categories in the question, Māwāsī ends his *fatwā* with a statement describing both groups as "closer to the infidels than to the believers, because love for the infidel and praying for his strength and power over the Muslims are among the signs of unbelief."[21] Māwāsī thus implies that those who openly desire infidel rule and prefer it to Muslim rule are like apostates, and apostates' lives and property are forfeit.

Aḥmad b. Yaḥyā al-Wansharīsī

Abū al-ʿAbbās Aḥmad b. Yaḥyā al-Wansharīsī spent the first half of his life in Tlemcen, where he studied with many of the Zayyānid capital's most distinguished scholars and began his legal career as a teacher, *muftī*, and author. In 1469, he fled to Fez after his home was ransacked on the orders of Sultan Muḥammad IV, for what offense we do not know. Wansharīsī, forced to abandon his books and other possessions, arrived in Fez during the brief period of Idrīsid rule that preceded the Waṭṭāsids' independent reign. Despite these circumstances he quickly re-established himself as a leading scholar of Mālikī law and Arabic linguistics, earned a prominent teaching position, gained access to an extensive private library, and served as the city's chief *muftī*. Wansharīsī authored most of his nearly thirty works in Fez, where he remained until his death in 914/1508.[22]

19 Appendix A, 270.

20 Māwāsī's first paragraph, which treats the permissibility of living under non-Muslim rule in general and those who pay tribute, resembles the equivalent passage in Ibn Barṭāl's third *fatwā*, while Māwāsī's second paragraph, concerning those who trade with the enemy, is nearly identical to Ibn Barṭāl's treatment of the same group in his first *fatwā*.

21 Appendix A, 271.

22 The most recent biography of Wansharīsī, with an up-to-date list of his published works, may be found in Powers, "al-Wansharīsī," 375–82. Francisco Vidal Castro provides a more

In the *fatwā* preserved by Zayyātī, Wansharīsī is asked about a group of Berbers who failed to relocate when their territory became subject to Christian rule, despite being able to. The question is nearly identical to the one posed to Māwāsī, complete with a category of Muslims who fish with the enemy and pray for continued infidel rule.[23] In his response, Wansharīsī largely agrees with Ibn Barṭāl and Māwāsī but places greater emphasis on the obligation to emigrate and on the prohibition on trading with the enemy. He states that for those capable of emigrating, submission to infidel rule is not permissible even "for one instant or one hour of one day."[24] Wansharīsī supports his statement with a much abbreviated version of the evidence he later presents in *Asnā al-matājir*, including Qur'ān 4:97–99 that enjoins *hijra*; a *ḥadīth* report in which Muḥammad denounces Muslims living among infidels; a scholarly consensus that requires the emigration of new converts from infidel to Muslim territory; and the disapproval of Mālik, the school's eponymous founder, of any Muslim's residence in non-Muslim territory.

Concerning trade, Wansharīsī states that it is prohibited to enter enemy territory for any reason other than the ransoming of prisoners and doing so results in a loss of legal probity, that is, the ability to give testimony and lead prayer. He links trading with the enemy to providing them with war materiel, and calls for public action to prevent such treachery:

> It is obligatory upon the leaders of the Muslims and upon the community (may God provide for and assist them) to prevent entry into *dār al-ḥarb* [the land of war] for trade, and to place observation posts along the route for this [purpose], such that no one finds a way [to enter]. This is especially [necessary] if it is feared that something will be brought to them for use in their wars (something that [would increase their] power over the Muslims and whose sale to [the enemy] is prohibited).[25]

This is a bold statement. While Māwāsī and Ibn Barṭāl addressed the responsibilities of lay Muslims and, in addition, Ibn Barṭāl tasked religious leaders with rebuking and renouncing offending Muslims, Wansharīsī goes

---

comprehensive account of his life and works in Vidal Castro, "Aḥmad al-Wanšarīsī (m. 914/1508): Principales aspectos de su vida," *Al-Qanṭara* 12, no. 2 (1991): 315–52; Vidal Castro, "Las obras de Aḥmad al-Wanšarīsī (m. 914/1508): Inventario analítico," *Anaquel de Estudios Árabes* 3 (1992): 73–112; Vidal Castro, "El *Mi'yār* de al-Wanšarīsī (m. 914/1508). I: Fuentes, manuscritos, ediciones, traducciones," *Miscelánea de Estudios Árabes y Hebráicos* 42–43, no. 1 (1993–94): 317–61; Vidal Castro, "El *Mi'yār* de al-Wanšarīsī (m. 914/1508). II: Contenido," *Miscelánea de Estudios Árabes y Hebráicos* 44, no. 1 (1995): 213–46.

23 In the question posed to Wansharīsī, this group is conflated with spies; this conflation also occurs in Māwāsī's answer (though not in the question posed to him).

24 Appendix A, 276.

25 Appendix A, 278. Wansharīsī goes on to list a number of items whose sale to non-Muslims living outside Muslim territory (*ḥarbīs*) is prohibited. On Mālikī law regarding trading with the enemy, see Hendrickson, "Is al-Andalus Different?"

further, by placing demands on the political authorities. Surveillance and the denial of passage into foreign-occupied territory would normally be associated with the coercive powers of a governing authority. Yet he implies that these governing authorities are failing to meet their obligations, and he calls on the public to use coercion to prevent treachery. This short passage may be read as an implicit, oblique critique of the state as well as an authorization for the irregular use of force.

Like Māwāsī, Wansharīsī offers a range of opinions as to the punishment for spying, but leads with the opinion that spies should be killed without an opportunity to repent. He then addresses Muslims' use of the enemy's courts, fishing with the enemy, and praying for the continuation of infidel rule. While Māwāsī conflated the latter two categories with spying and judged all such offenders as apostates, Wansharīsī is far more lenient with regard to fishing with the enemy and using their courts; he views these actions as reprehensible rather than prohibited.

Wansharīsī reserves his severest judgment for those who pray for the continuation of enemy rule. He writes, "It is evident that this is a sign of the supplicant's apostasy and deviation from right belief, and of the corruption of his heart and of his convictions . . . this [prayer] indicates contentment with unbelief; and contentment with unbelief is unbelief."[26] The best possible outcome for these apostates, according to Wansharīsī, is that they be beaten severely enough to inspire their repentance. He implies that they should be killed if repentance is not forthcoming.

The Berber *fatwā* ends with Wansharīsī's answer to an additional question posed only to him, on the permissibility of buying property that belonged to Muslims but was seized by the "infidel enemy." The questioner is particularly concerned about the recovery of Arabic books. Wansharīsī reviews some precedents regarding the purchase of Muslim property in *dār al-ḥarb* and concludes that entering enemy territory to purchase these books is permissible, although the buyer should proceed in order of priority, beginning with the Qur'ān and the most important religious sciences. This response creates room for the ransom-like recovery of objects that Wansharīsī and others clearly felt should not be in infidel hands, while reinforcing the very narrow scope of legitimate trade with anyone residing in Christian-occupied territories, here clearly classified as *dār al-ḥarb*.

The *fatwā*s of Ibn Barṭāl, Māwāsī, and Wansharīsī all clearly point to an ongoing state of foreign occupation and resistance in the Maghrib. Ibn Barṭāl offers high praise for those ready to wage *jihād* against the enemy, while all three jurists render verdicts on several offenses clearly related to war: paying tribute to the enemy, enriching or empowering the enemy

26 Appendix A, 280.

through trade, spying for the enemy, and fighting on the enemy's behalf. In this context, fishing with the enemy might seem an odd category of offense, and leads us to wonder why it features in the questions posed to Māwāsī and Wansharīsī.

The case of the fishermen suggests that seemingly pragmatic, everyday partnerships with the Portuguese could be the most dangerous threats to Muslim sovereignty. The intimacy fostered by working together in a risky, potentially lucrative, and essential venture would further ordinary Muslims' reliance upon and trust in Christians. In the questions posed to these jurists, fishing with the enemy is associated with those who ask God to prolong the times under Christian rule; and in both answers, those who express this affection for the enemy are condemned as apostates. In his answer, Māwāsī conflates contented fishermen with spies, which is understandable—intimate partnerships could readily lead Muslims to transmit sensitive information to the Christians. For his part, Wansharīsī decouples fishing and praying for the continuation of enemy rule, and focuses instead on what he considers a greater form of treachery than intimacy or spying: the public expression of contentment with Christian rule and its material benefits. He also addresses this offense in the abstract instead of retaining the fishermen as an illustrative case. That is, he states that any Muslims who express contentment with enemy rule might undermine resistance to foreign occupation and weaken the Muslim cause, a danger Wansharīsī returns to address in *Asnā al-matājir*.[27]

Fishing was also a vital source of food and royal revenue for the Portuguese fortresses. Among the first personnel King Manuel requested for the new fortress at Santa Cruz in 1513 were a translator, a doctor, and two fishermen to provide sustenance. Over a year later, the *feitor* (factor) complained that the residents were starving because there were still no fishermen.[28] Perhaps by that point, a targeted campaign by resistance forces, including jurists, had rendered Maghribīs particularly reluctant to fish for the Portuguese.

---

27 In Ibn Barṭāl's second *fatwā*, there may be an equivalent to those who express contentment with subordination to Christian authority. In this text, the "third third," those Muslims whose offenses are most severe, have said they intend to remain in their lands and pay tribute "for as long as the world remains." Ibn Barṭāl charges them with apostasy and suggests that they should be killed. If this second *fatwā* is not the result of textual corruption—as suggested above—then Ibn Barṭāl's severity with regard to this group might be considered a reaction to their expression of contentment, rather than just their payment of tribute or refusal to migrate.

28 This example, based on Portuguese correspondence, is found in Racine, *Opulent*, 93–95.

Scholars and Soldiers: Bijāʾī, Waryāglī, and Ibn Zakrī

The questions posed to Ibn Barṭāl, Māwāsī, and Wansharīsī, and their responses, share enough common elements to suggest that a loosely defined set of questions circulated among a specific group of Fāsī jurists at a given point in time. Their answers may have been drafted over several months, and likely varied in response to newly arising cases, more nuanced questions, and engagement with other jurists' opinions. This formal discourse on Muslims living under non-Muslim authority in Morocco must have taken place in the twenty-year period following the 1471 capture of Asilah and before Māwāsī's death in Rajab 896/May 1491. It is quite possible that these opinions were composed in the mid to late 1480s, if the terms of Portugal's treaties with ports such as Safi and Azemmour became widely known at this time.

Zayyātī includes four additional *fatwās* by Waryāglī, Bijāʾī, and Ibn Zakrī that would have been written in late fifteenth-century Fez and Tlemcen. This group of four opinions also treats Muslim cooperation with and conflict in Portuguese occupied territories, but shows a greater variance in both questions and answers than do the opinions of Ibn Barṭāl, Māwāsī, and Wansharīsī. This set of questions employs a less fixed and abstract typology of Muslim actions and may be inspired by more specific circumstances, although two of these four *fatwās* remain oblique with regard to their subjects' identities and locations. Ibn Zakrī's *fatwās* provide greater context, as they mention four Portuguese-occupied cities by name.

Bijāʾī

Zayyātī preserves one *fatwā* by Aḥmad al-Bijāʾī (d. ca. 901/1495). While his biographers describe Bijāʾī as being "from Bijāya, then Tlemcen," in fact he spent at least part of his career in Fez, where he may well have composed this *fatwā* in the same time period as the three jurists treated above.[29] Unlike his contemporaries, Bijāʾī answers a question posed by an

29 Abū al-ʿAbbās Aḥmad b. Muḥammad al-Ḥājj al-Bijāʾī, *thumma* al-Tilimsānī (of Bijāya, then Tlemcen; d. ca. 901/1495) Bijāya, also spelled Bougie, Bejaïa or Bugia, is a Mediterranean port city located in modern-day Algeria, to the east of Algiers. Ibn ʿAskar, who reproduces the answer component of this *fatwā*, states that Bijāʾī died at the beginning of the tenth (/ sixteenth) century (*Dawḥat al-nāshir*, 114–15). Muḥammad Ḥajjī thus assigns Bijāʾī the approximate death date of 901/1495 (*Mawsūʿat aʿlām al-Maghrib*, 2:807–8). One manuscript of *al-Jawāhir al-mukhtāra* records al-Lajāʾī instead of al-Bijāʾī; biographical notices for al-Bijāʾī under the name Abū al-ʿAbbās Aḥmad b. Muḥammad b. ʿĪsā al-Lajāʾī may be found in Muḥammad Makhlūf, *Shajarat al-nūr al-zakiyya fī ṭabaqāt al-Mālikiyya*, ed. ʿAbd al-Majīd Khayālī (Beirut: Dār al-Kutub al-ʿIlmiyya, 2003), 1:345; Ibn al-Qāḍī al-Miknāsī, *Jadhwat al-iqtibās*, 1:122; and Tinbuktī, *Nayl al-ibtihāj*, 1:121. While none offer a death date, other details place Bijāʾī in Fez in the late fifteenth century. He studied with such Fāsī jurists as ʿAbd Allāh al-ʿAbdūsī (d. 849/1446) and answered at least one question posed to the scholars of Fez (Wansharīsī, *al-Miʿyār*, 7:305).

individual who appears to reside in Portuguese-controlled territory and who seeks sincere advice as to his own circumstances (not a set of rules to be applied to others). Bijāʾī's advice is the most nuanced and permissive of the responses featured in this section of *Selected Jewels*.

The questioner describes a region populated by oppressors and evildoers, in which unlawful acts and taxes are widespread, in which Muslims are debased and infidels glorified, in which oppressors hold themselves high while the learned humble themselves, and in which Muslims pay taxes on all purchased goods. As a student of the religious sciences, he is concerned that none of the region's virtuous men, including his master, openly condemn the reprehensible acts with which they are surrounded. Is it permissible to remain in such a place, or must he migrate in order to avoid continued exposure to negative influences? If he stays, is it permissible to buy taxed goods?

Initially, Bijāʾī states that a true believer is obligated to "flee with his religion" (in pious defense of his faith) from *fitna* (corrupting influences) and to settle only where traditional religious practices are upheld. Religious knowledge should be obtained only from worthy masters, even if one must travel to find them. He cites the familiar verse enjoining emigration, Qurʾān 4:97 ("Was God's earth not spacious enough for you to have migrated therein?"), but notes that the obligation to emigrate only applies to the questioner if he is able to move and to find the instruction he seeks elsewhere. If emigration is too difficult or the man cannot find a more virtuous land or worthier master, Bijāʾī recommends staying in place and cultivating patience. By citing two additional verses of support for the weak and oppressed, he provides the man with a Qurʾānic framework within which to view his situation and justify his continued residence in the territory described.[30]

In the remainder of the *fatwā*, Bijāʾī counsels his questioner to adhere to the law to the extent possible; while he may avail himself of the legal dispensations (relaxations of the law) that become permissible in times of necessity, he must exercise discretion in doing so. The man should study what he needs to and learn what he can from anyone with knowledge; Bijāʾī even notes that many have profited from the skills and knowledge of infidels and sinners. Likewise, the man should buy what clothing and food he requires, but without living recklessly. Bijāʾī's advice to avoid indulging in too many 'permitted' actions suggests that his questioner is already an advanced student capable of judging the legal status of his own actions.

30 Bijāʾī refers to Qurʾān 4:98, which exempts the weak from the obligation to emigrate, and Qurʾān 4:75, in which an oppressed people pray for a protector.

In comparison with the other surviving *fatwās* from this period, Bijāʾī's opinion is more personal, sympathetic, and permissive. Instead of a third party presenting jurists with a typology of Muslims exhibiting certain behaviors, in this case we hear the personal appeal of a concerned Muslim seeking advice as to his course of action. Bijāʾī's *mustaftī* (questioner) portrays himself as a devout religious student who is far from content with his current teachers and surroundings, who hopes to better his situation by seeking sincere advice from a qualified jurist, and who has presumably not yet sinned by engaging in prohibited acts or by disregarding professional legal advice that suggests that he is able and obligated to emigrate. Bijāʾī accepts the man's motivations as pious and trusts in his ability to assess his own actions. While he addresses the obligation to emigrate, Bijāʾī is not insistent that his *mustaftī* do everything in his power to move.

Perhaps most striking, in comparison to the *fatwās* above, Bijāʾī does not unambiguously insist that Muslim-ruled areas of the Maghrib are always preferable to foreign-dominated regions. While the *mustaftī* and Bijāʾī are cautious and only subtly refer to the predicament of a Muslim living under Christian rule, the region in question must be a tribute-paying hinterland under Portuguese domination, if not a port city under direct Portuguese rule. By linking his questioner's obligation to emigrate to the existence of a more suitable destination, and then advising the man as to how he can make the best of his current situation, Bijāʾī implies that no more virtuous or worthy region is available to him.

Waryāglī

If Bijāʾī's text is the most sympathetic opinion to appear in the chapter on *jihād* in *Selected Jewels*, the single *fatwā* that Zayyātī preserves by ʿAbd Allāh al-Waryāglī (d. 894/1488–9)[31] is the least forgiving toward Muslims who chose to reside under Christian authority. Waryāglī, who returned from studying law in Tlemcen to find Tangier and Asilah beset by Christians, pursued a legal career even as he engaged in armed resistance against Portuguese encroachment. He lived in a defensive outpost in

31 The most substantial biographical notices for Abū Muḥammad ʿAbd Allāh b. ʿAbd al-Wāḥid al-Waryāglī (d. 894/1488–9) appear in Ibn ʿAskar's *Dawḥat al-nāshir* (34–37) and in Ibn al-Qāḍī al-Miknāsī's *Jadhwat al-iqtibās* (2:439–40); the death date given by Ibn ʿAskar is incorrect. While in most notices Waryāglī's name is spelled with a *jīm*, in *Jadhwat al-iqtibās* this letter is replaced with a three-pointed *kāf*. These two variants, as well as a *ghayn* or a *kāf* with a second upper slash, are used interchangeably in Maghribī orthography to represent the hard 'g' found in many Berber names. Note that this jurist is distinct from the ʿAbd al-ʿAzīz al-Waryāglī noted above, who led the 1465 revolt in Fez. On ʿAbd Allāh al-Waryāglī, see also Makhlūf, *Shajarat al-nūr*, 1:384; Tinbuktī, *Nayl al-ibtihāj*, 1:251–52; Ibn al-Qāḍī al-Miknāsī, *Durrat al-ḥijāl*, 317; Kattānī, *Salwat al-anfās*, 3:386–87; and Qarāfī, *Tawshīḥ al-Dībāj*, 111 (spelled al-Wazyāḥī).

Morocco's northwestern al-Habṭ region, where he devoted each winter and spring to teaching, serving as a judge, and issuing *fatwās*; and each summer and fall, he engaged in *jihād*. Waryāglī eventually settled in Fez, where his biographers note that he assumed a position of leadership in the scholarly community and was asked to respond to the most difficult and important legal issues.

The question posed to Waryāglī concerns "our Muslim brothers" who remained in their own lands despite becoming subject to infidel laws and influences and despite the opportunity to move to Muslim-ruled territory nearby. While this basic problem is similar to the one presented to Ibn Barṭāl, Māwāsī, and Wansharīsī, the question posed to Waryāglī is unambiguous regarding the legal status of the territory in question and treats all of the Muslims residing there voluntarily under infidel laws as a single category. The questioner asks if these Muslims' lives, families, and property are forfeit and if their prayers, giving of alms, and fasting are valid.

Waryāglī's response is uncompromising. He declares these Muslims to be a vile and contemptible group whom God has led astray "through the spread of unbelief into their hearts," and immediately establishes that they should be considered apostates. Their offenses include contentment with living under "the impure infidels," strengthening the enemy, and exposing Islam to scorn. In Waryāglī's opinion, this group must be killed, their property taken as booty, and their wives seized so that they may be remarried to other (Muslim) men in Muslim territory. The *fatwā* closes as follows:

> Oh questioner, you have committed a serious error by calling them "our Muslim brothers." Rather, they are our enemies and the enemies of the religion (may God frustrate their efforts and block their good fortune). They are the brothers and supporters of the infidels (may God strengthen the Muslims against them and enable their swords to [strike] their necks and the necks of the infidels) whose group they have joined and to whose side they have gone. Peace be upon you, oh questioner, but not upon them.[32]

Here Waryāglī reiterates that Muslims who voluntarily remain under Christian rule not only *may* be killed, but that they *must* be killed. He chastises his questioner for even referring to these people as Muslims and prays for God to guide the fighters' swords to the necks of both the Christians and the apostates who live in their midst.

The severity of Waryāglī's opinion likely reflects his experiences as a warrior as well as a jurist. Muslims who remained in Portuguese territory would have hampered the ability of warriors to conduct raids and attacks

32 Appendix A, 269–70.

without the possibly of harming fellow Muslims. Solutions to this ethical and logistical obstacle included convincing those resident Muslims to separate themselves from the enemy targets of attack by moving to Muslim territory, or removing the distinction between these two groups by denying the inviolability of those Muslims who chose to remain amidst the enemy. While emigration has the added benefit (from a military standpoint) of increasing the ranks of those able to fight, it is a far more complex and time-consuming solution. Waryāglī was probably quite aware, from his experience fighting, of the importance of alleviating concerns regarding the wrongful killing of fellow Muslims; thus, his *fatwā* emphasizes the prohibition of living under Christian rule, but wastes no time praising or encouraging emigration. It was most likely meant to assist warriors in the successful prosecution of *jihād*.

Ibn Zakrī

Aḥmad b. Zakrī (d. 899–900/1493–4) is the sixth and final fifteenth-century jurist whose opinions on Maghribī-Portuguese relations appear in this section of *Selected Jewels*.[33] Ibn Zakrī was a contemporary of the five jurists treated above, but wrote from Tlemcen, where he served as chief *muftī*, rather than from Fez. A number of his other opinions—though not these two—are featured in Wansharīsī's *Miʿyār*.[34] The two short opinions preserved by Zayyātī share Waryāglī's concern for *jihād*, but explicitly address both the conduct of war and the specific regions in question.

The first question concerns a *sharīf* engaged in *jihād* in the environs of Ceuta and "her sisters," presumably other Portuguese-controlled cities. The questioner wishes to know if this man's actions are permissible considering that the sultan, whose area of control extends to this region, has signed a treaty with the polytheists. He also asks if the treaty itself, which was signed for a term of over twenty years, is legitimate. Ibn Zakrī responds that the *sharīf* may continue to fight the enemy if he believes the enemy to be fighting Muslims elsewhere, and as long as he will not suffer harm "at the hands of those who would prevent him from combating the enemy,"[35] presumably agents of the ruler. The jurist also declares that the treaty in question is void because such treaties may only be signed for two or three years, and because the terms of the treaty are too favorable to the enemy.

33 Abū al-ʿAbbās Aḥmad b. Muḥammad b. Zakrī al-Tilimsānī (d. 899–900/1493–4). On him, see Ibn ʿAskar, *Dawḥat al-nāshir*, 108–9; Makhlūf, *Shajarat al-nūr*, 1:386; Tinbuktī, *Nayl al-ibtihāj*, 1:136–37; Tinbuktī, *Kifāyat al-muḥtāj*, 1:125–26; Ibn al-Qāḍī al-Miknāsī, *Durrat al-ḥijāl*, 48; Ḥajjī, *Mawsūʿat aʿlām al-Maghrib*, 2:798; *EI*², s.v. "Ibn Zakrī" (M. Hadj-Sadok).

34 Ibn Zakrī appears to have answered a number of questions of mutual interest posed to the jurists of Fez and Tlemcen. For example, Wansharīsī preserves the opinions of eight jurists, including Ibn Zakrī, on the demolition of a synagogue in Tamanṭīṭ. See Powers, "al-Wansharīsī," for an analysis of these opinions and of Wansharīsī's commentary.

35 Appendix A, 285.

In the second question, Ibn Zakrī is asked to assess those tribes of the Far Maghrib near Ceuta, Tangier, Asilah, and al-Qaṣr al-Ṣaghīr "that have intermingled their affairs with [those of] the Christians."[36] The questioner notes that friendship has developed between these tribes and the enemy. The tribes inform the Christians of impending attacks by Muslims, and the Muslims thus find the enemy prepared for them. The Muslims must pass through these tribes' lands in order to fight the Christians, and often the tribes fight the Muslims alongside the Christians. What is the status of these tribes' lives, property, women, and children? Should these tribes be exiled, and if they refuse, may they be fought? In response, Ibn Zakrī asserts simply that these people should be fought and killed like the infidels with whom they have allied. He refers briefly to Qurʾān 5:51, which commands believers not to ally with Jews and Christians and warns that any believer who does so will be considered one of them.

Like Waryāglī, Ibn Zakrī thus presumes a state of open warfare in the Maghrib, warfare in which some Muslims are complicating the efforts of others to forcibly resist Portuguese occupation. In Waryāglī's case, the problematic Muslims are content to live under direct Portuguese authority, while in Ibn Zakrī's case they are actively spying and fighting for the enemy. While Waryāglī's opinion is severe, Ibn Zakrī's is arguably bolder and more sensitive politically. Both jurists condemn these Muslims and support irregular Maghribī warriors, but Ibn Zakrī is far less oblique regarding the specific Muslims in question. More strikingly, Ibn Zakrī clearly challenges Waṭṭāsid authority by declaring the "sultan's" treaty—which must be the Luso-Waṭṭāsid agreement signed in 1471—to be invalid and harmful to the Muslim cause.[37]

Crossing Borders: Musfir and Ibn Hārūn

The foregoing *fatwās*, all issued in the late fifteenth-century Maghrib, constitute the earliest extant opinions regarding Iberian conquests in North Africa. The six jurists above employ at least two distinct but overlapping legal models for assessing the inviolability, probity, and religious identity of Muslims whose illegitimate relations with Christians undermine resistance to Portuguese expansion. In the first model, a Muslim's status is determined by such actions as spying or fighting for the enemy, while in the second model, his status hinges on whether or not he voluntarily—or even contentedly—resides in Christian territory.

36 Appendix A, 285. The Portuguese conquered al-Qaṣr al-Ṣaghīr (Ksar es-Seghir, Alcácer-Ceguer), on Morocco's Mediterranean coast, in 1458.

37 The issue of conducting war without approval of the *imām*, or reigning political authority, also features in a number of sixteenth- and seventeenth-century Maghribī opinions. See Yūbī, *Ahamm al-qaḍāyā*, 190–98. Yūbī misidentifies Ibn Zakrī.

Were these technical legal classifications solely the concern of jurists and their presumably elite questioners? Did these opinions have any effect on popular attitudes and behaviors? I consider two additional *fatwās* from the early sixteenth century that suggest that this formal juristic discourse had a popular counterpart and that shifts in legal status resulting from improper relationships with Christians had practical consequences for ordinary Maghribīs. In addition, these two cases, both based on the legal rule that apostasy invalidates a man's marriage to his Muslim wife, offer us a rare window into the experiences of Muslim women in this period.

In the first question, Muḥammad al-Nālī, known as Musfir (d. 928/1521–2), is asked about a thief who fled to ʿAyn Shams "with the other apostates" while his wife stayed in *dār al-Islām*.[38] She had been remarried to a Muslim for a couple of years when her ex-husband returned to Islamic territory from the "land of the apostates" (*arḍ al-murtaddīn*). The man wanted his wife back and claimed to have fled from unjust laws, while the woman's agent countered that it was the man's choice to flee to that land and if one spouse commits apostasy, the marriage is, as a consequence, invalid, and divorce is automatic. Musfir responds that the people of ʿAyn Shams and similar areas surrounding Tangier and al-Qaṣr—presumably al-Qaṣr al-Ṣaghīr—should not be referred to as apostates. Instead, such people should be referred to as disobedient to God; only those who do not understand the meaning of apostasy would use this term. If it cannot be proven that the man in question has become an infidel voluntarily, with conviction and contentment, then according to Musfir, his wife should be returned to him despite her subsequent remarriage. Even if this man settled in the land of unbelief (*dār al-kufr*) for an extended period, as long as he remained Muslim, his matrimonial authority over his wife would not be revoked; such a revocation may only take place if it is proven that he has left the religion of Islam.

The tone of Musfir's response is one of chastisement, and suggests that he is frustrated by a common assumption among Maghribīs that any Muslim who moves to or even seeks temporary refuge in certain areas is automatically rendered an apostate. In this case, if the ex-wife and her new husband had harbored any doubts regarding the legal consequences of this man's actions, they presumably would not have risked committing adultery

38 Abū ʿAbd Allāh Muḥammad b. Aḥmad al-Nālī, known as Musfir (d. 928/1521–2), was a prominent *muftī* from the Ghumāra region. On him, see Ibn ʿAskar, *Dawḥat al-nāshir*, 37; Ḥajjī, *Mawsūʿat aʿlām al-Maghrib*, 2:844. Wazzānī includes this text in *al-Miʿyār al-jadīd*, 3:49–50. In the manuscripts of *Selected Jewels*, see Moroccan National Library (BNRM) MS 1698, 2:50; Ḥasaniyya Library (Ḥ) MS 5862, 253–54; General Library and Archives of Tetouan (T) MS 178, 268. Manuscript page numbers are given here because Nālī's opinion is not included in appendix A.

by marrying one another. These assumptions demonstrate that by the early sixteenth century, the relationship between territory and religious identity was not merely an academic concern of jurists, but was also a matter about which the court of popular opinion could be quick to condemn Muslims residing in the orbit of Portuguese-controlled ports.

A second *fatwā* issued by ʿAlī al-Maṭgharī al-Fāsī, known as Ibn Hārūn (d. 951/1545), reinforces the conclusion that a popular conflation between territorial and religious boundary crossing was of practical consequence for Maghribī marriages.[39] In this case, Ibn Hārūn is asked about a Christian prisoner of war who converted to Islam while captive, married a Muslim woman and had a child with her, fled to enemy territory (*dār al-ḥarb*) for a year or so, then returned to find his wife remarried on account of his apostasy. This man then married another Muslim woman, had a child with her, and returned to *dār al-ḥarb* for ten months while she was pregnant with their second child. Upon his return, he found her, too, engaged to another man; she stated that her first husband had made his apostasy apparent, that she would not return to him, and that he had gone to *dār al-ḥarb* without cause. Unlike Musfir, Ibn Hārūn sided with the wives by agreeing that if the case was as described, the man was an apostate who must repent or be killed, and the second wife was free to marry whomever she wished. At the conclusion of this *fatwā*, Zayyātī includes an endorsement of Ibn Hārūn's opinion by Abū al-Qāsim b. Khajjū (d. 956/1549).[40]

A 1517 letter sent to Lisbon by Yaḥyā-u-Taʿfuft, Portugal's *alcaide dos mouros* for the Dukkāla region, shows that these accusations of apostasy extended to the south. Yaḥyā-u-Taʿfuft complained that the Muslims considered him a Christian, while the Christians considered him a Muslim; when he walked in the streets of Safi, everyone called him a traitor.[41] As

39 Ibn ʿAskar, *Dawḥat al-nāshir*, 51; Tinbuktī, *Kifāyat al-muḥtāj*, 1:368–69; Ibn al-Qāḍī al-Miknāsī, *Durrat al-ḥijāl*, 408. According to Ibn ʿAskar, Ibn Hārūn was a teacher and *muftī* in Fez whose funeral was attended by the Sultan Abū al-ʿAbbās Aḥmad b. Muḥammad al-Waṭṭās (r. 935–52/1526–45 and 954–6/1547–9). Wazzānī includes this text in *al-Miʿyār al-jadīd*, 3:50. In the manuscripts of *Selected Jewels*, see Moroccan National Library (BNRM) MS 1698, 2:39; Ḥasaniyya Library (Ḥ) MS 5862, 246; General Library and Archives of Tetouan (T) MS 178, 261. Manuscript page numbers are given here because Ibn Hārūn's opinion is not included in appendix A.

40 Abū al-Qāsim b. ʿAlī b. Khajjū (d. 956/1549), a Mālikī jurist who studied in Fez and was active in northern Morocco. On him, see Cornell, *Realm of the Saint*, 266–67.

41 *SIHMP*, 2:106–110 (French summary and Portuguese translation of the original). On Yaḥyā-u-Taʿfuft, see Matthew Racine, "Service and Honor in Sixteenth-Century Portuguese North Africa: Yahya-u-Taʿfuft and Portuguese Noble Culture," *Sixteenth Century Journal* 32, no. 1 (2001): 67–90. I follow Racine and Cornell in the spelling of "Yaḥyā-u-Taʿfuft," with the exception that I add diacritics to "Yaḥyā." This name appears in various forms in primary and secondary sources, including as "Abū Zakariyā Yaḥyā b. Muḥammad ū Taʿfūft" (*SIHMP*, 1:326), "Yaḥyā Ou Taʿfouft (*SIHMP*, 2:106), "cide Iahia" (*SIHMP*, 2:111), "Yhea Tafuu" (*SIHMP*, 2:112), "Yaḥyā ū Taʿfūft" (Būsharb, *Dukkāla*, 13 ff.), Yahya ibn Tafuft (Disney, *History of Portugal*, 10),

a servant of Portugal tasked with collecting tribute from the *mouros de paz* and protecting these "peaceful Moors" from both Christian and Muslim predation, Yaḥyā-u-Taʿfuft occupied a precarious position and was vulnerable to malicious rumors regarding his true loyalties. Less than a year after this appeal to King Manuel to restore his reputation, Yaḥyā-u-Taʿfuft was stabbed fatally in the back by members of a Maghribī tribe allied with the Portuguese.

These final texts point to a culture of fluid conversions, border crossings, and unstable identities and loyalties in and around Portuguese-occupied Morocco. In his discussions of the close of the fifteenth century and beginning of the sixteenth, historian Weston Cook writes that "Religious line-crossing occurred everywhere, and persons might change faiths or sects several times en route to the Beyond. Christianity and Islam ordered death for apostasy, but fluid borders and the excuse of forced conversion gave maneuver room to the quick and the deft."[42] Alongside prisoners of war, those with incentives to maintain flexible loyalties included local Muslim leaders or merchants who allied with the Portuguese, European converts to Islam (*ʿulūj*) conducting trade in Morocco, and Andalusī refugees—some of whom had already been forcibly converted to Christianity—in pursuit of new lives. Unfortunately, those in pursuit of profit and power also used this "maneuver room" to ascribe false identities to others they wished to enslave, ransom, or kill. In the same letter noted above, for example, Yaḥyā-u-Taʿfuft complains that the local Portuguese authorities conspire to capture or kill Maghribīs (who came to Safi to trade or to supply provisions) by misidentifying them as members of unallied tribes from the Shāwiyya region.[43]

Are these early sixteenth-century cases evidence that the fifteenth-century juristic discourse condemning submission to Christian authority effectively shaped popular attitudes? We cannot be sure. At the very least, these legal texts were one facet of a broader current of resistance against the Portuguese, a resistance in which Maghribīs sought to discourage cooperation with Christians by conflating religious identity with both territory and political loyalty. The ongoing state of war in Morocco, the influx of foreign merchants and refugees, and the phenomenon of shifting loyalties must have made the establishment of clear, even stark, legal formulas an appealing solution.

---

and "Yaḥyā u Tāʿfuft," in Bernard Rosenberger, "Yaḥyā u Tāʿfuft (1506–1518): des amibitions déçues," *Hespéris-Tamuda* 31 (1993): 21–59.

42 Cook, *Hundred Years War*, 142–43.

43 Racine, "Service and Honor," 86.

Modern commentators often speak of the "light" of medieval Iberia.[44] It is seen as a technologically advanced, intellectually curious society flourishing in the midst of an otherwise bleak period of European history. In it, we find an instructive beacon of interreligious hope, alerting the modern world to the precedents and possibilities of Christian-Muslim-Jewish pluralism. While scholars are rightly fascinated by myriad aspects of medieval Iberian history, we must be careful not to exaggerate the singularity of the Iberian experience.

Studies regarding Muslims living under Christian rule in the premodern period focus overwhelmingly on Iberia. Factors justifying this attention include the novelty of such sizable and well-established Muslim populations living under Christian rule; the successful transition of these populations to a stable Mudéjar status that in some cases lasted for centuries; the cultural impact of the Muslims on their Christian conquerors; the interesting diversity of Mudéjar experiences across multiple Christian kingdoms; and the ample documentation available for some of these regions, particularly for those living under the Crown of Aragon. Just as importantly, Iberia's Muslims constituted one of only a few Muslim populations living in Europe. The story of these Muslims' defeat and the (re-)establishment of Christian rule throughout Iberia looms large in Christian triumphalist and Spanish nationalist narratives, neither of which is served by following the story of Iberia's Muslim-Christian relations into North Africa.

The history of Portuguese and Spanish expansion into North Africa has been sorely neglected, such that it has been possible for a robust scholarly discourse on Islamic legal responses to Muslims living under Christian rule during and after the Reconquest to make almost no mention of Zayyātī's collection or the *fatwās* examined here.[45] In his recent monograph devoted

44 Examples include Robert Gardner, et al., *Cities of Light: The Rise and Fall of Islamic Spain* (Unity Productions Foundation and Gardner Films, 2007), and Simon R. Doubleday and David Coleman, eds., *In the Light of Medieval Spain: Islam, the West, and the Relevance of the Past* (New York: Palgrave, 2008).

45 Hossain Buzineb, citing *al-Jawāhir al-mukhtāra*, introduced the opinions of Ibn Barṭāl, Māwāsī, and Waryāglī in his 1989 article on the obligation to emigrate. Unfortunately, he assumed these jurists were writing about Iberian Muslims and he offered only partial names without dates. Buzineb, "Respuestas de Jurisconsultos Maghrebies en Torno a la Inmigración de Musulmanes Hispánicos," *Hespéris Tamuda* 16–17 (1988–89): 53–67. Two articles by Mohammed Mezzine treat Zayyātī's chapter on *jihād*, but are more focused on warfare and diplomacy than the Islamic legal issue of submission to Christian rule. See Mezzine, "Jihād au pays Jbala (XVIème et XVIIème siècles): Effervescence et regulation," in *Jbala: histoire et société: études sur le Maroc du Nord-ouest*, ed. Ahmed Zouggari, et al., 61–87 (Paris: Editions du CNRS, 1991); Mezzine, "Les relations entre les places occupées et les localités de la region de Fès aux XViéme et XVIiéme siècles, a partir de documents locaux inédits: Les Nawāzil," in *Relaciones de la Peninsula Ibérica con el Magreb, siglos XIII-XVI: Actas del coloquio celebrado en Madrid, 17–18 de diciembre de 1987*, ed. Mercedes García-Arenal and Maria Viguera (Madrid: Consejo Superior de Investigaciones Científicas, 1988), 539–60. Yūbī addresses these *fatwās* in his *Ahamm al-qaḍāyā* (esp. 199–245), but unlike Buzineb and Mezzine, he relies on the heavily edited and error-prone versions preserved by Wazzānī.

to this legal issue, historian Alan Verskin assures readers that Wansharīsī's contemporaries must have been writing about Iberia, not North Africa. The Portuguese presence was of such negligible impact on Maghribī lives, Verskin suggests, that it was unlikely to have inspired legal responses on the topic of Muslim submission to Christian governance.[46] He prefaces a discussion that includes Māwāsī, Waryāglī, and Ibn Zakrī with the observation that these jurists, "no doubt responding to greater Christian control over the Iberian Peninsula, thought that a harsher stand against the Mudéjars was necessary."[47] He does not mention the Maghribī identity of these three jurists, or the Moroccan cities mentioned in both of Ibn Zakrī's opinions. Elsewhere, Verskin also reassigns Ibn Barṭāl to fourteenth-century al-Andalus despite his response regarding occupied Asilah.

To strip these opinions of their Maghribī context and assimilate them to the better-known debate over Muslim minorities in Iberia is to be blinded by the light of al-Andalus, to maintain a narrow focus on European Muslim history to the exclusion of North African Muslim experiences. We have much to gain from considering Muslim legal responses to Christian conquests in North Africa, especially before the temporal and geographic boundaries of the Reconquest became fixed and before Wansharīsī's *Asnā al-matājir* and Marbella *fatwās* became the Mālikī opinions of record on this issue. The eight jurists treated in this chapter are not the only voices in *Selected Jewels* to address Portuguese and Spanish conquests in the Maghrib, but they are the earliest such opinions; they show Islamic law functioning as a means of indigenous resistance to Iberian empire as early as the fifteenth century, and they broaden our understanding of Islamic legal discourse on Muslim submission to non-Muslim authorities.[48]

In this discourse, opinions focused on Mudéjars and Maghribīs share a common set of legal categories, concerns, and rules, including the obligation to emigrate (*hijra*) and the legal consequences of specific Muslim-Christian relationships for a Muslim's probity, inviolability of life and property, family status, and religious identity. Yet the Maghribī-focused opinions are distinctive for their prominent concerns related to active warfare, including collaboration with the enemy and the conduct of *jihād*. The set of *fatwās* preserved in Zayyātī's work also indicates a formal but urgent process

46 Verskin, *Islamic Law*, 22.

47 Verskin, *Islamic Law*, 103–4. As noted above, Verskin misidentifies Ibn Barṭāl as an Andalusī. He does not address Bijāʾī, Musfir, or Ibn Hārūn. While he mentions Wansharīsī's Berber *fatwā* briefly in another chapter (*Islamic Law*, 101–102), he refers to its subjects as Bedouin rather than adopting the specifically North African term "Berbers" used in the *fatwā*.

48 Some of these other opinions are treated in Yūbī and Mezzine's works noted above. See also Hendrickson, "Prohibiting the Pilgrimage," 186–90, for analysis of a mid-sixteenth-century opinion related to Portuguese occupation preserved in Tasūlī's *al-Jawāhir al-nafīsa*.

by which multiple contemporary jurists (Ibn Barṭāl, Māwāsī, Wansharīsī, and possibly Waryāglī) answered the same or similar questions, with the clear expectation that these jurists' opinions would have a real impact on matters of widespread public concern. Further, perhaps unsurprisingly for matters of public import in a time of war, at least two of the *fatwās* studied here (Wansharīsī and Ibn Zakrī) feature an oblique political critique of the Waṭṭāsid regime.

Modern scholars' neglect of these opinions is thus regrettable, but it is also understandable. The most prominent Mālikī *fatwā* collection, Wansharīsī's *Miʿyār*, does not include these opinions, nor are most of them cited in later texts related to Muslims under non-Muslim rule. In the following chapters, I explore the reasons for this obscurity in contrast with the prominence of Wansharīsī's *Asnā al-matājir* and his Marbella *fatwā*, composed shortly after most of the "jewels" analyzed here.

PART 2

Andalusīs in Africa and the Man from Marbella (*Asnā al-matājir* and the Marbella *Fatwā*), 1491

CHAPTER 4

Ibn Qaṭiyya's Questions: "Emigrate from There to Here?"

As we have seen, Wansharīsī and at least five of his peers in Fez and Tlemcen wrote *fatwā*s on Muslims living under Portuguese authority in the Maghrib in the late fifteenth century. Therefore, we would expect Wansharīsī to include in *al-Miʿyār al-muʿrib* at least one of these important opinions, which were composed by some of the Waṭṭāsid state's most illustrious jurists. Yet Wansharīsī excluded all of them, even his own Berber *fatwā*, from this monumental *fatwā* compilation. Instead, he wrote and preserved lengthy responses to two new questions posed by an obscure jurist named Ibn Qaṭiyya, responses related to Iberian Muslims whose homelands had fallen under Christian rule. What made these new questions, regarding unhappy Andalusī emigrants to North Africa and a man who stayed in Marbella, more compelling?

Wansharīsī's exclusion from the *Miʿyār* of the opinions Zayyātī later included in his much smaller, far less influential *al-Jawāhir al-mukhtāra* offers us a rare opportunity to explore the process by which a given set of historical texts was favored for preservation at the expense of other, seemingly worthy candidates. The *Miʿyār* quickly became an essential textbook and reference work for Mālikī jurists, and centuries later it was still viewed as an arbiter of school doctrine. In choosing what to include and what to leave out, Wansharīsī became one of history's "winners," shaping the body of opinions that would be studied, debated, and implemented by future generations of jurists. Knowing which texts Wansharīsī read (and wrote), but ultimately rejected, allows us to explore his decisions in curating the *Miʿyār*'s section on the obligation to emigrate.

Our first conclusion may be that for Wansharīsī, the *fatwā*s that focused on the Portuguese occupation, and his own two *fatwā*s featuring Andalusīs all grapple with the same basic legal issue: the prohibition on submitting to a non-Muslim political authority. If these opinions treated separate and distinct legal issues, it would have been reasonable for Wansharīsī to preserve all of them. The fact that he did not include all of them suggests that Wansharīsī considered *Asnā al-matājir* and the Marbella *fatwā* to be sufficiently instructive for his readership on this legal issue; his inclusion of these two opinions rendered the *fatwā*s on the Portuguese redundant. This redundancy is further indicated by the content of *Asnā al-matājir*, which overlaps significantly with these earlier *fatwā*s. As we see below, aspects of Ibn Qaṭiyya's question echo key components of Māwāsī's *fatwā* and the Berber *fatwā*. Even more strikingly, the Berber *fatwā* appears to be a rough draft of those parts of *Asnā al-matājir* that Wansharīsī composed himself. Thus, presumably Wansharīsī faced at least two choices in crafting this section of the *Miʿyār*. First, he could preserve an array of *fatwā*s all related to the issue of Muslims living under Christian rule, or he could focus his readers' attention exclusively on his own opinions as the correct ones; he chose the latter option, elaborating and preserving for posterity only his own opinions. Second, he could have crafted his most compelling statement on the obligation to emigrate as an answer to either the Berber question or Ibn Qaṭiyya's questions. He could not do both, because he would need to repeat too much of the same material.

I argue that it was answers to Ibn Qaṭiyya's questions that Wansharīsī developed most fully and for broad dissemination because they offered (in comparison to the questions that focused on the Maghrib) a far better rhetorical platform for the construction of authoritative arguments regarding the Islamic obligation to emigrate. These Iberian cases were not more urgent, important, or exceptional. Yet their narrative appeal, lack of complexity, reduced political sensitivity, and reference to the loss of al-Andalus made them strategic choices for development into legal opinions that could persuade both contemporary and future readers of the evils of Muslim subjection to non-Muslim rule.

This chapter, the first of two in which I analyze *Asnā al-matājir* and the Marbella *fatwā*, thus begins with the question components of these influential texts. The questions not only provide the rhetorical framework and mandate for the responses; they are also essential for understanding the immediate audience of the *fatwā*. While ostensibly concerned with Iberian Muslims, these questions make clear that fellow Maghribī jurists were the primary audiences for Wansharīsī's opinions, and that *Asnā al-matājir*, in particular, was intended to serve as a commentary on Muslim cooperation with Portuguese occupiers. As I show in the next two chapters, *Asnā al-matājir* and the Marbella *fatwā* are best understood in their North African context, as an extension of the contemporary legal discourse on Muslim-Portuguese relations.

Overview of *Asnā al-matājir* and the Marbella *Fatwā*

Wansharīsī's two well-known *fatwās* on the obligation to emigrate appear together in the *Miʿyār*. Each *fatwā* opens with the text of a question sent to him by a jurist named Ibn Qaṭiyya, whom Wansharīsī praises as an accomplished preacher and master jurist. In the first question, Ibn Qaṭiyya describes a group of conquered Andalusīs who abandoned their homes and possessions, and went to great lengths to emigrate to North Africa. Once they arrived, the emigrants found themselves penniless, unprotected, and longing for home. They mocked the idea of obligatory migration to North Africa and publicly expressed their preference for Castile and its inhabitants. Ibn Qaṭiyya solicits Wansharīsī's opinion as to the punishment they deserve, and requests confirmation that the obligation to emigrate is not contingent on guarantees of material comfort.

In his response, Wansharīsī cites over a dozen Qurʾānic verses and *ḥadīth* reports, and the unanimous consensus of jurists, in support of an Islamic legal prohibition on voluntary residence in infidel territory. Just as Muḥammad emigrated from Mecca to Medina in order to escape persecution and to found the first Islamic community, so, too, Iberian Muslims must refuse the multiple humiliations of subjection to Christian rule and show their solidarity with Muslims by immigrating to Muslim territory. Fearing that these Andalusīs could create serious communal discord, or *fitna*, Wansharīsī urges their severe punishment in this world, and predicts hellfire for them in the next.

In the Marbella *fatwā*, Ibn Qaṭiyya asks if a man from the Iberian town of Marbella might remain there in order to help others deal with the Christian authorities. Ibn Qaṭiyya notes that this man and most of those around him are capable of emigrating and have been granted permission to do so. As in *Asnā al-matājir*, Wansharīsī strongly argues against the permissibility of this man voluntarily residing under Christian rule.

These Andalusī emigrants and the man from Marbella have captured the imaginations and sympathies of modern commentators sensitive to the plight of religious minorities in post-Reconquest Spain and Portugal. By contrast, Wansharīsī has inspired anger and scorn for what many view as deliberate cruelty in the name of strict adherence to an outmoded system of law. Although a substantial scholarly literature now treats both of these *fatwās*, misunderstandings have persisted regarding such key aspects of the texts as their audience, circulation, and even purpose. I address each of these in turn, beginning with a preliminary discussion of the available editions and composition dates of *Asnā al-matājir* and the Marbella *fatwā*.

Editions and Translations

Asnā al-matājir, one of the lengthiest single Mālikī *fatwās*, is distinguished by the presence of a colophon giving the text a formal title and composition date. Wansharīsī's full title is *Asnā al-matājir fī bayān aḥkām man ghalaba ʿalā waṭanih al-Naṣārā wa-lam yuhājir, wa-mā yatarattabu ʿalayh min al-ʿuqūbāt wa'l-zawājir* (*The Most Noble Commerce: An Exposition of the Legal Rulings Governing One Whose Homeland Has Been Conquered by the Christians and Who Has Not Emigrated, and the Punishments and Admonishments Accruing to Him*). This *fatwā* appears in the *Miʿyār*'s chapter on *jihād*, where opinions related to *dhimmī*s and to Muslims traveling or trading in non-Muslim territory are found alongside those more directly concerned with the conduct of war.[1] *Asnā al-matājir* also circulated as an independent treatise, of which there are at least two extant manuscripts.[2] The Marbella *fatwā* immediately follows *Asnā al-matājir* in the *Miʿyār*, but is not included in independent manuscripts of *Asnā al-matājir*, nor does the Marbella *fatwā* have a title or date. While modern scholars are not necessarily wrong to consider these texts together as one long exposition on the status of Muslims under non-Muslim rule, *Asnā al-matājir*'s colophon and independent circulation suggest that Wansharīsī presented this longer text as his primary composition on the obligation to emigrate.

The fact that the first partial Arabic edition of Wansharīsī's opinions was produced a century and a half ago, and multiple full editions have been produced in the past twenty years, is a testament to the scholarly value of these texts and to their continued relevance for modern Muslims. Joseph Müller published an edition of the question component (only) of *Asnā al-matājir* in 1866,[3] and thirty years later the two opinions appeared together in the 1896–97 lithograph printing of the *Miʿyār*.[4] Egyptian historian Ḥusayn Muʾnis published the first, and still the best-known, modern printed edition of both opinions in his seminal 1957 study published in the *Revista*

1 Wansharīsī, *al-Miʿyār*, 2:119–41.

2 El Escorial MS 1758, fols. 83b–94a; Muʾassasat al-Malik ʿAbd al-ʿAzīz Āl Saʿūd MS 10–164. Moroccan National Library MS 1071K, fols. 161a–171a, labeled in the card catalogue as "*fatwā* by al-Wansharīsī on *hijra*," also appears to be a partial copy of *Asnā al-matājir*.

3 Marcus Joseph Müller, *Beiträge zur Geschichte der westlichen Araber*. 2 vols. (Munich: G. Franz, 1866–78), as cited in Ḥusayn Muʾnis, ed., *Asnā al-matājir fī bayān aḥkām man ghalaba ʿalā waṭanih al-Naṣārā wa-lam yuhājir, wa-mā yatarattabu ʿalayh min al-ʿuqūbāt wa'l-zawājir*, Aḥmad b. Yaḥyā al-Wansharīsī (al-Ẓāhir [Cairo]: Maktabat al-Thaqāfa al-Dīniyya, 1996), originally published in *Revista del Instituto Egipcio de Estudios Islámicos en Madrid* 5 (1957): 1–63 (also numbered 129–91), 1. All references are to the original article (henceforth Muʾnis, "Asnā al-matājir"); the pagination of the article differs slightly from the book.

4 Aḥmad al-Wansharīsī, *al-Miʿyār al-muʿrib wa'l-jāmiʿ al-mughrib ʿan fatāwī ahl Ifrīqiyā wa'l-Andalus wa'l-Maghrib*, ed. Ibn al-ʿAbbās al-Būʿazzāwī, et al., 12 vols. (Fez lithograph, 1897–98), 2:90–110.

del Instituto Egipcio de Estudios Islámicos en Madrid. Muʾnis's article, in which the Marbella *fatwā* appears as an appendix of *Asnā al-matājir*, was republished in book form in 1996.[5] An Algerian edition[6] comparing Wansharīsī's opinions to two nineteenth-century treatises debating emigration as a means of resistance to French colonization appeared in 1981, the same year that the modern edition of the *Miʿyār* was published in Rabat and Beirut.[7] A 2005 edition (available online) appends four Saudi Arabian *fatwās* affirming the obligation of contemporary Muslims to immigrate to Muslim countries, including a *fatwā* issued by Saudi Arabia's Permanent Committee for Research and Iftāʾ.[8] Finally, in 2006, Dublin-based Syrian scholar Aḥmad b. ʿAbd al-Karīm Najīb published the first thoroughly annotated critical editions of *Asnā al-matājir* and the Marbella *fatwā*.[9]

Despite the importance of these texts, their first full translations into Western languages did not appear until the 1980s.[10] Felipe Maíllo Salgado

5 The article is Muʾnis, "Asnā al-matājir," 1–63. See note above for the book. Muʾnis bases his edition of *Asnā al-matājir* primarily on the El Escorial manuscript noted above, and secondarily on the Fez lithograph of the *Miʿyār*. His edition of the Marbella *fatwā* is based solely on the lithograph. Muʾnis's edition remains popular in part because the book version has been included in a number of electronic databases of Islamic texts.

6 Muḥammad b. ʿAbd al-Karīm, *Ḥukm al-hijra min khilāl thalāth rasāʾil Jazāʾiriyya* (Algiers: al-Sharika al-Waṭaniyya lil-Nashr waʾl-Tawzīʿ, 1981). The Algerian opinions are those of Algerian leader ʿAbd al-Qādir (d. 1883), who advocated emigration, and Muḥammad b. al-Shāhid al-Jazāʾirī (d. 1836–7), who advocated remaining in French territory. See chapter 7 for a discussion of these opinions. Ibn ʿAbd al-Karīm's edition of Wansharīsī's two opinions (pp. 67–103) are based on the Fez lithograph.

7 Unless otherwise noted, all references to the *Miʿyār* are to the modern edition published in Rabat, noted earlier. In 1981–83, the Beirut publisher Dār al-Gharb al-Islāmī produced a parallel edition with identical pagination; a list of errata was appended, but only to the Beirut edition, and it captures an insignificant number of the errors in these volumes. *Asnā al-matājir* and the Marbella *fatwā* appear in volume 2, pp. 119–41. In 2012, Beirut publisher Dār al-Kutub al-Islāmī published a new eight-volume version of the *Miʿyār*, edited by Muḥammad ʿUthmān.

8 Abū Yaʿlā al-Bayḍāwī, ed., *Asnā al-matājir fī bayān aḥkām man ghalaba ʿalā waṭanih al-Naṣārā wa lam yuhājir, wa-mā yatarattabu ʿalayh min al-ʿuqūbāt waʾl-zawājir*, by Aḥmad b. Yaḥyā al-Wansharīsī (n.p., 2005). The document may be downloaded from multiple websites, including (www.ahlalhdeeth.com). This edition of *Asnā al-matājir* is based on Muʾnis's edition, the Rabat edition of the *Miʿyār*, and the version reproduced by the Egyptian Mālikī jurist Muḥammad ʿIllaysh (d. 1299/1882) in his own *fatwā* collection, *Fatḥ al-ʿAlī al-mālik fī al-fatwā ʿalā madhhab al-Imām Mālik*, discussed in chapter 7. Of the four contemporary *fatwās*, one was issued by Saudi Arabia's Permanent Committee for Research and Iftāʾ and three were issued by individual *muftīs*: former Grand Muftī of Saudi Arabia Shaykh ʿAbd al-ʿAzīz b. ʿAbd Allāh b. Bāz, known as Bin Bāz (d. 1999), Shaykh Muḥammad b. Ṣāliḥ b. ʿUthaymīn (d. 2001), and Shaykh Ṣāliḥ b. Fawzān (1933–).

9 Aḥmad Najīb, ed., *Asnā al-matājir fī bayān aḥkām man ghalaba ʿalā waṭanih al-Naṣārā wa-lam yuhājir, wa-mā yatarattabu ʿalayh min al-ʿuqūbāt waʾl-zawājir*, by Abū al-ʿAbbās Aḥmad b. Yaḥyā al-Wansharīsī (n.p.: al-Markaz al-Iʿlāmī lil-Dirāsāt waʾl-Nashr, 2006). Also published online at (www.saaid.net). Najīb's edition is based on the El Escorial and Casablanca manuscripts of *Asnā al-matājir*, a manuscript of the *Miʿyār* held in the Moroccan National Library (MS 6002, 2:88–92), and on the lithograph and Rabat editions of the *Miʿyār*.

10 Emile Amar published a partial French paraphrase of al-Wansharīsī's texts in 1908, while Vincent Lagardère provided brief summaries, also in French, in 1995. Emile Amar, "La

published the first translation of the Marbella *fatwā* into Spanish in 1985, while Aboobaker Asmal's 1998 doctoral dissertation included the first English translations of both *fatwās*; unfortunately, Asmal's dissertation remained inaccessible until recently.[11] A more accessible, but non-academic and incomplete English translation of the two texts appeared in a 2006 anthology for a contemporary Muslim audience, designed to promote *hijra*.[12] My appended translations of *Asnā al-matājir* and the Marbella *fatwā*, based on Najīb's 2006 critical edition, are the most thoroughly annotated translations of these texts to date and the first to distinguish Wansharīsī's original work from the material he borrowed from Andalusī jurist Ibn Rabīʿ (d. 719/1319).[13]

Composition Dates

While Ibn Qaṭiyya's questions are not dated, their content and Wansharīsī's colophon to *Asnā al-matājir* allow us to place these legal documents and their subjects in historical context. Most scholars agree that *Asnā al-matājir* bears a composition date of 19 Dhū al-Qaʿda 896/22 September 1491, just a few months before the surrender of the city of Granada. Before emigrating, the Andalusīs described in the question resided outside the capital, but somewhere in the recently conquered kingdom of Granada.

The surrender of Granada came at the end of a decade-long war (1482 to 1492) that gradually brought the whole of the former Naṣrid kingdom under Castilian control. Unfortunately, Ibn Qaṭiyya does not offer us sufficient details to determine precisely where these emigrants lived, when their region was conquered, or whether or not they lived as Mudéjars prior

---

pierre de touche des Fétwas de Aḥmad al-Wanscharîsî: Choix de consultations des faqîhs du Maghreb," *Archives Marocaines* 12 (1908): 192–200; Vincent Lagardère, *Histoire et Société en Occident Musulman au Moyen Âge: Analyse du Miʿyār d'al-Wanšarīsī* (Madrid: Consejo Superior de Investigaciones Científicas, 1995), 48. L.P. Harvey included a partial English translation of the Marbella *fatwā* in *Islamic Spain, 1250 to 1500* (Chicago: University of Chicago Press, 1990), 56–58.

11 Felipe Maíllo Salgado "Consideraciones," 186–91; Aboobaker M. Asmal, "Muslims under Non-Muslim Rule: The *Fiqhi* (Legal) Views of Ibn Nujaym and al-Wansharisi," PhD dissertation (University of Manchester, 1998), 150–81. As of 2015, the dissertation may be downloaded freely from the British Library's E-Theses Online Service (EThOS): http://ethos.bl.uk/OrderDetails.do?uin=uk.bl.ethos.496372.

12 Husayn bin ʿAwdah al-ʿAwaayishah, ed., *A Conclusive Study on the Issue of Hijra and Separating from the Polytheists*, trans. Abu Maryam Ismaʿeel Alarcon (n.p., NY: Al-Ibaanah Book Publishing, 2006), 51–77.

13 The translations included here as appendices B and C, now revised, first appeared in my dissertation, "The Islamic Obligation," 340–94. Alan Verskin offers an additional English translation of the Marbella *fatwā* in his anthology *Oppressed in the Land? Fatwās on Muslims Living under Non-Muslim Rule from the Middle Ages to the Present* (Princeton: Markus Wiener, 2013), 21–32, and of both texts in *Islamic Law*, 137–73.

to emigrating.[14] If they arrived in the Maghrib the year before Wansharīsī's formal response to their case, then we can assume that these Andalusīs left home in 895/1490 or 896/1491.

Despite the presence of a composition date at the close of *Asnā al-matājir*, one persistent error and an alternative to 896/1491 appear in the scholarly literature. In the introduction to his edition, Mu'nis states that Wansharīsī composed *Asnā al-matājir* on 19 Dhū al-Qaʿda 890.[15] This is clearly a mistake, as his edition itself gives the correct year of 896 [/1491].[16] Nonetheless, at least five later authors relied on Muʾnis's study and adopted the erroneous date.[17] Van Koningsveld and Wiegers argued for an alternative date of 898/1493, based on three considerations: the year printed in the Rabat edition of the *Miʿyār* is unclear; 19 Dhū al-Qaʿda 896 appears to be a Friday, but Wansharīsī specifies that he finished on a Sunday, a day of the week consistent with 19 Dhū al-Qaʿda 898/9 September 1493; and Wansharīsī fails to mention the possibility that the regretful emigrants could return to a part of Granada still under Muslim rule, an omission that for these scholars is best explained by a post-1492 composition.[18]

The dominant reading, 19 Dhū al-Qaʿda 896 (corresponding to 22 September 1491), may be corroborated even given these three considerations. The most relevant manuscripts and the lithograph edition of the *Miʿyār* must be privileged over the Rabat edition, which is a slightly revised but error-ridden copy of the lithograph edition. The El Escorial and Muʾassasat al-Malik ʿAbd al-ʿAzīz Āl Saʿūd manuscripts of *Asnā al-matājir*, the Moroccan National Library manuscript of the *Miʿyār* consulted by Najīb, and, we assume, the unspecified manuscripts of the *Miʿyār* consulted by the

---

14 Neither Ibn Qaṭiyya nor Wansharīsī employs the term "Mudéjar" or any other technical term for Muslims living under non-Muslim rule. The term *ahl al-dajn* (Mudéjars) appears in *Asnā al-matājir* once, when Wansharīsī cites the work of another jurist. In the question component of the Marbella *fatwā*, Ibn Qaṭiyya describes Iberian Muslims as *Muslimūn dhimmiyyūn*, or Muslim *dhimmīs*, using the term (*dhimmīs*) normally associated with Jews and Christians living under Muslim rule.

15 This date corresponds to 27 November 1485. Mu'nis, "Asnā al-matājir," 2.

16 Ibid., 54.

17 Asmal, "Muslims under Non-Muslim Rule," 176; Leila Sabbagh, "La Religion des Moriscos entre Deux Fatwas," in *Les Morisques et leur Temps: Table Ronde Internationale, 4–7 Juillet 1981, Montpellier*, 45–56 (Paris: Éditions due Centre Nationale de la Recherche Scientifique, 1983), 46; Muḥammad Razūq, *Al-Andalusiyyūn wa-hijrātuhum ilā al-Maghrib khilāl al-qarnayn 16–17* (Rabat: Ifrīqiyā al-Sharq, 1998), 148 n. 43; Míkel de Epalza, "La voz official de los musulmanes hispanos mudéjares y moriscos, a sus autoridades cristianas: cuatro textos, en árabe, en castellano y en catalán-valenciano," *Sharq al-Andalus* 12 (1995), 293; and María Jesús Rubiera Mata, "Los moriscos como criptomusulmanes y la taqiyya," in *Mudéjares y moriscos: cambios socials y culturales: Actas de IX Simposio Internacional de Mudejarismo* (Teruel, Spain: Centro de Estudios Mudéjares, 2004), 541.

18 Van Koningsveld and Wiegers, "Islamic Statute," 53–55. The Rabat printed edition of the *Miʿyār* records *s.n.h* (*sīn.nūn.tāʾ marbūṭa*) for the year of composition, rather than *s.t.h.* (*sīn. tāʾ.tāʾ marbūṭa*), or six.

eight editors of the Fez lithograph edition, all attest to a composition year of 896.[19] The Rabat edition of the *Miʿyār* records *s.n.h.* (*sīn.nūn.tāʾ marbūṭa*) as the final word in the composition date (following "eight hundred ninety"), which is indeed unclear and nonsensical. Yet this word is a mere dot away from *s.t.h.* (*sīn.tāʾ.tāʾ marbūṭa*), or the "six" in 896. While Van Koningsveld and Wiegers note that Michael Casiri's catalogue of the El Escorial's Arabic manuscripts gives 898 as the composition date of the monastery's *Asnā al-matājir* manuscript, the manuscript itself reads 896.[20] A subsequent version of the El Escorial catalogue, begun by Hartwig Derenbourg and completed by E. Lévi-Provençal and H. P. J. Renaud (1884–1941), corrects Casiri's error.[21]

The discrepancy between Wansharīsī's specification of Sunday and the Friday given by contemporary date converters is also within the margin of error for these conversions. Dhū al-Qaʿda would have begun at sunset the night that a new moon was sighted, an event that could differ by one or two days from the fixed estimation of a mathematic converter. Finally, Wansharīsī's omission of the city of Granada as an acceptable destination is compatible with a composition date just four months prior to that city's surrender. By the time *Asnā al-matājir* was composed, the fall of Granada would have been foreseeable, even inevitable. Ibn Qaṭiyya and Wansharīsī were concerned about the legal consequences of the emigrants' actions rather than the possibilities of their satisfactory resettlement, and the emigrants themselves aspired to return to Castile, presumably to their own abandoned homes. The desire for security and stability driving these emigrants' rejection of the obligation to live in *dār al-Islām* further suggests that they would have been equally disinclined to live in the threatened city of Granada as they were in the fragmented Maghrib.

While the Marbella *fatwā* is not dated, I argue that we have sufficient textual and historical evidence to place its composition in 1491 or 1492.

---

19 Escorial MS 1758, fol. 94a; Muʾassasat al-Malik ʿAbd al-ʿAzīz Āl Saʿūd MS 10–164, page 17 (unnumbered). Najīb lists his manuscript and printed sources in the introduction to his edition, but does not note any variants on the date of composition (896) given in the text. Najīb, *Asnā al-matājir*, 20–21, 110. For the date in the lithograph edition, see Wansharīsī, *al-Miʿyār* (ed. al-Būʾazzāwī, et al.), 2:106.

20 Van Koningsveld and Wiegers mention Casiri's catalogue in "Islamic Statute," 53. Although Vidal Castro favors sources that give the date of the *fatwā* as 896, he also notes Casiri's date and quotes from his catalogue. Vidal Castro shows an internal inconsistency in Casiri's date, which is given as 898/1492 (it should be 896/1491 or 898/1493). Vidal Castro, "Las obras," 81 n. 17.

21 The descriptive table of contents prefacing the El Escorial's microfilm copy of this manuscript (MS 1758) gives the date of *Asnā al-matājir* as 896/1491 and refers to Casiri's old number for the manuscript (1753) and Derenbourg's new number (1758). The table of contents appears to be a copy of the relevant page in Derenbourg's catalogue, which I have not consulted directly.

As Van Koningsveld and Wiegers have demonstrated, Wansharīsī's two opinions draw heavily on a previous *fatwā* by Ibn Rabīʿ.[22] A textual comparison of Ibn Rabīʿ's text with *Asnā al-matājir* and the Marbella *fatwā* suggests that Wansharīsī considered Ibn Qaṭiyya's two questions together; Wansharīsī appears to have carefully divided the arguments and proof texts he found in Ibn Rabīʿ's opinion, incorporating some of these arguments into *Asnā al-matājir* and apportioning others to his Marbella *fatwā*. The result is that each of Wansharīsī's two opinions have a coherent logic and distinct set of proof texts.[23] It is also possible that Wansharīsī completed *Asnā al-matājir* using those arguments from Ibn Rabīʿ's *fatwā* that appealed to him most, and then received the Marbella question. In that case, he would have answered the latter with the remaining portions of Ibn Rabīʿ's text that he found compelling, careful to avoid redundancy with the material he had already borrowed for *Asnā al-matājir*. While this scenario is less likely, a delayed response to the Marbella question would help explain the circulation of *Asnā al-matājir* alone, as an independent manuscript. If Ibn Qaṭiyya sent his two questions to Wansharīsī separately, it is not likely that the Marbella *fatwā* could have preceded *Asnā al-matājir*. If Wansharīsī had begun working from Ibn Rabīʿ's text much earlier than 1491, we would expect some of its language and ideas to appear in the Berber *fatwā*. Yet the Berber *fatwā* reflects none of the extensive borrowing from Ibn Rabīʿ that we see in Wansharīsī's later answers.

On the basis of historical events, many scholars have concluded only that the Marbella *fatwā* must post-date that city's 1485 conquest.[24] Only Abdelkhalek Cheddadi has advanced a concise date range for the text, arguing that the situation described in the question is most consistent with the period between 1492 and 1495.[25] He interprets Ibn Qaṭiyya's insistence

---

22 Van Koningsveld and Wiegers, "Islamic Statute," 22–38 (summary of Ibn Rabīʿ's text), 52 (relationship with Wansharīsī's *fatwās*).

23 My comparison is based on an unpublished Arabic edition of Ibn Rabīʿ's text produced by Van Koningsveld, Wiegers, and Umar Ryad. I am very grateful to these scholars for generously sharing their work with me.

24 Harvey, *Islamic Spain*, 56–57; Verskin, *Islamic Law*, 15. Four earlier scholars also recorded an erroneous date of 901/1495 for the Marbella *fatwā*, apparently based on Muʾnis's date for Wansharīsī's completion of the *Miʿyār*. The connection between these two events is not compelling, and the *hijrī*/Gregorian correspondence for this date is not internally consistent. See Sabbagh, "La religion," 46; Razūq, *al-Andalusiyyūn*, 149; Epalza, "La voz official," 293; Rubiera Mata, "Los moriscos," 541; and Muʾnis, "Asnā al-matājir," 2. In the colophon of *al-Miʿyār* (12:395), the date of completion for the full work is given as 28 Shawwāl 901, corresponding to 10 July 1496 (as noted in Powers, *Law, Society, and Culture*, 5).

25 Abdelkhalek Cheddadi, "Émigrer ou rester? Le dilemma des morisques entre les fatwas et les contraintes du vécu," *Cahiers de la Méditerranée* 79 (2009), 4. In the Rabat edition of *al-Miʿyār* (2:137), the editors title this *fatwā* "The author's insistence on the necessity of emigration for the Andalusīs after the fall of Granada." In their assumption that the Marbella *fatwā* was issued after the surrender of the city of Granada they likely followed the same logic as Cheddadi.

that the Marbellans were given permission to emigrate at any time as a reference to the provisions of the Capitulations of Granada. Muslims were not only granted the freedom to emigrate, but were promised free passage in Christian ships for the first three years after Granada's surrender; after that point, they were required to pay a tax and to arrange their own travel.[26] Yet these particular capitulations applied only to the city of Granada.

The Marbellans had negotiated their terms of surrender in 1485, at which point the town's urban population was expelled and replaced by Christian settlers.[27] The rural population requested, and was granted, Mudéjar status. As may have been typical for the agreements negotiated during Castile's 1484–87 city-by-city conquest of western Granada, the Capitulations of Marbella did not grant the rural population an explicit right to emigrate.[28] Furthermore, from January 1488 to February 1490, Marbellans were confined to their residences, on penalty of forfeiting their property and being enslaved.[29] It was only at this point that the region's Mudéjar population, including that of Marbella, was explicitly granted permission to purchase an emigration license and to embark at Málaga for passage to North Africa. Given that the "man from Marbella" had remained in the region for some time after others had emigrated, it was likely 1491 by the time his case reached Wansharīsī via Ibn Qaṭiyya. Thus, both textual and historical considerations support a late 1491 or early 1492 composition date for Wansharīsī's response to the Marbella question.

Reading the Questions

The question components of *Asnā al-matājir* and the Marbella *fatwā* are strikingly long and rich in detail in comparison with most preserved *fatwās*, which briefly summarize the nature of the query. Generous narratives about the lay Muslim subjects of the questions precede Ibn Qaṭiyya's specific appeals for legal advice. Thus, historians interested in the social, economic,

26 L. P. Harvey provides a partial translation of the Capitulations of Granada in *Islamic Spain*, 314–21.

27 Ángel Galán Sánchez and Rafael Peinado Santaella, *La repoblación de la costa malagueña: Los repartimientos de Marbella y Estepona* (Málaga: Centrode Ediciones de la Diputación de Málaga, 2007), 30–45, 252–57.

28 Miguel Angel Ladero Quesada provides an overview of capitulation agreements during the conquest of Granada in "Mudéjares y repobladores en el Reino de Granada (1485–1501)," *Cuadernos de Historia Moderna* 13 (1992): 47–71. Following the 2007 publication of the Capitulations of Granada, Jesús Suberbiola Martínez challenged an earlier assumption that emigration was permitted for all conquered Mudéjars in this period, and argued that only the urban populations were given this option. Suberbiola Martínez, "Primeros Encabezamientos del Reino de Granada: El Secretario Real, Hernando de Zafra, y las rentas de los mudéjares de Ronda, Marbella y la Garbía," *Baetica: Estudios de Arte, Geografía e Historia* 30 (2007): 269–71.

29 Suberbiola Martínez, "Primeros Encabezamientos," 259.

and political realities of the Mudéjars in the wake of Christian conquests have focused primarily on the first portion of each question. Their reading of these texts privileges the experiences of Iberians and has led to conclusions that differ significantly from my own regarding the audience, circulation, and purpose of Wansharīsī's responses. While scholars have long assumed that these works were meant to circulate among an Iberian audience in order to encourage emigration or to chastise non-emigrant Muslims, I argue that one of the primary purposes of *Asnā al-matājir*, and possibly the Marbella *fatwā*, was to condemn collaboration with Portuguese occupiers in the Maghrib.

Ibero-Centric Reading

To explain how such disparate conclusions might be reached, I explore two ways of reading the questions, beginning with what I will call an Ibero-centric reading. First, consider the initial portion of the question in *Asnā al-matājir*:

> The honorable master jurist, the accomplished preacher, the enduring virtuous exemplar, the pure sum of excellence, the man most admired for his moral rectitude, Abū ʿAbd Allāh b. Qaṭiyya (may God perpetuate his noble achievement and reputation) sent me the following text:
>
> "Praise be to God alone. Your answer [is requested], my master (may God be pleased with you and [may He] benefit the Muslims by means of your life) regarding a legal case that has arisen (*nāzila*). This [concerns] a group among those Andalusīs who emigrated from al-Andalus, who left behind their houses, property, orchards, vineyards, and other types of immovable property; who spent in addition to this a large sum of their available money, and who escaped from under the rule of the infidel community; and who allege that they fled for the sake of God, taking with them [only] their religion, their lives, their families, their offspring, and whatever money they had left, or that some of them had left; and who (praise be to God the exalted) settled in the land of Islam (*dār al-Islām*), in obedience to God and His Prophet and under the authority of Muslim rule.
>
> "After having reached the land of Islam they regretted their emigration (*hijra*). They became angry and alleged that they found their condition difficult and impoverished. They alleged that they did not find in the land of Islam, which is this land of the Maghrib (may God preserve it, safeguard its lands, and aid its ruler) any kindness, ease, or support, nor did they find sufficient security with respect to their ability to move throughout the region. They made this clear in a variety of ugly statements that demonstrated their weakness in religion, their

> lack of true certainty in their beliefs, and the fact that their emigration was not for God and His messenger as alleged. Rather, it was only for worldly gain[30] that they hoped to attain immediately upon their arrival, in convenient accordance with their desires. When they found that [emigration to the Maghrib] was not amenable to their interests, they openly derided the land of Islam and its state of affairs, cursing and defaming that which had prompted their emigration. They openly praised the land of unbelief (*dār al-kufr*) and its inhabitants, and (openly expressed) regret at having left it.
>
> "It is [even] occasionally reported that one of them, in rejecting emigration to the land of Islam, which is this land (may God protect it), said, 'Emigrate from there to here? Rather, it is from here to there that emigration should be required!' And that another of them said, 'If the ruler of Castile came to these parts, we would go to him requesting that he send us back there,' meaning to the land of unbelief. [It is reported] also that some of them are looking for any kind of scheme by which they may return to the land of unbelief, thereby reverting, by any means possible, to [living] under infidel rule."[31]

These Andalusīs' incredible sacrifices, their expression of pious motives, the desperation and cruelty they encountered in the Maghrib, and their fervent desire to return home have, for a long time, struck readers as the most important aspects of this moving narrative. The plight of these emigrants exemplified the tremendous difficulties facing many Mudéjars and evoked sympathy for their condition in general. As Muslim populations fell under Christian rule from the late eleventh century onwards, their fates varied considerably by region and time period. For the most part, Mudéjars were guaranteed the safety of their lives and property, granted freedom of religious practice, and given substantial communal autonomy.[32] They constituted a deep-rooted, integrated, and legitimate, if second-class, presence in Iberian Christian societies and economies. They were often granted the freedom to remain on their lands, to relocate within the kingdom, or to migrate to Muslim

---

30 *Li-dunyā yuṣībūnahā*. This language appears in a popular *ḥadīth*, according to which actions are rewarded according to their intentions; those who emigrate for God and His messenger are thus rewarded, whereas a *hijra* motivated by worldly gain or marriage is assessed accordingly. See, for example, *Ṣaḥīḥ al-Bukhārī, Kitāb Badʾ al-waḥy, bāb kayfa kāna badʾ al-waḥy* . . . , *ḥadīth* 1, in Muḥammad b. Ismāʿīl al-Bukhārī, *Ṣaḥīḥ al-Bukhārī*, ed. Muṣṭafā al-Bughā (Damascus: Dār Ibn Kathīr, 1993), 1:3. The same phrase appears in additional *ḥadīth* reports in *Ṣaḥīḥ al-Bukhārī* and in other collections. For *ḥadīth* citations, I give the name of the collection, the title of the book (*kitāb*), and the full name or first words of the chapter (*bāb*), followed by the number of the *ḥadīth* as it appears in the print edition that I consulted.

31 Wansharīsī, *al-Miʿyār*, 2:119–20; appendix B, 288–89. A full translation and discussion of sources is available in appendix B.

32 For an overview of Mudéjar communities, see Harvey, *Islamic Spain*, or Catlos, *Muslims*.

territory. Exceptions included Muslims in larger cities, who were forced to move outside the city walls within a year or two of that city's conquest. In some cases, especially where sustained resistance inflicted significant damage on the Christian army, the Muslim population of a city was killed or enslaved en masse. Over time, Mudéjar rights were often curtailed, taxes became more burdensome, and their freedom of movement was further restricted. From the late fourteenth century in Valencia, where Mudéjars provided crucial agricultural labor, emigration was prohibited and unlicensed travelers risked capture and enslavement.[33]

As the Andalusīs in Ibn Qaṭiyya's question appear to have emigrated voluntarily rather than by compulsion, their moving narrative brings into sharp relief the dilemma faced by those Muslims who were able to choose between living as Mudéjars or abandoning their homelands. This group is described as having left behind houses and agricultural properties, and only some of them were able to retain any money. This suggests that the group lived in the countryside in western Granada, where they would have received permission to emigrate after 1490, but not the right to sell their real estate; Muslims conquered in the eastern part of the kingdom retained this right.[34] The "large sum" of money they spent may refer to the purchase of expensive licenses to emigrate, as well as travel costs. They likely booked passage to North Africa from Málaga, following the same route to Ibn Qaṭiyya's unnamed town as that taken by the compatriots of the man from Marbella, one of whom probably conveyed the man's query at a slightly later date.

Why did these Andalusīs sacrifice their property and livelihoods? In describing their motivations to a religious authority (Ibn Qaṭiyya), they cited their pious desire to preserve their religion and live under Muslim rule. Although Mudéjars retained a general freedom of religion, their practices were subject to varying constraints, including prohibitions on the public display of religion and the loss of urban congregational mosques. Submission to Christian authority violated the Islamic obligation to emigrate, and incurred both the sin and the scorn of Muslim authorities in *dār al-Islām*. Yet these emigrants were undoubtedly motivated by practical concerns as well. They left Granada during a time of active warfare, when Christian settlers were replacing Muslims inside the city walls, and increasingly oppressive taxes were being collected, often by corrupt officials.

---

33 Catlos, *Muslims*, 174.

34 Muslims in eastern Granada, which was conquered from 1488 to 1489, were permitted to sell their real estate and relocate, until a revolt in 1490 resulted in a revocation of this privilege. Had *Asnā al-matājir*'s Andalusīs lived in the east, they likely would have emigrated earlier and with the proceeds of their properties. Suberbiola Martínez, "Primeros Encabezamientos," 271; Ladero Quesada, "Mudéjares," 48.

The situation of Muslims in western Granada had become increasingly difficult, and movement was restricted, in the wake of two events in 1487: the murder of sixteen tax collectors by a frustrated populace in Benadalid, near Ronda, and the protracted siege of Málaga, during which Isabella and Ferdinand narrowly escaped an assassination attempt in their own tent. Almost all Málagans who were not killed were taken captive, including 6,000 who could not buy their own freedom and were distributed as slaves.[35] In the same year, the last Naṣrid ruler Abū ʿAbd Allāh Muḥammad XII (r. 887–88/1482–83 and 891–97/1486–92), known as Boabdil, sent envoys to the Mamluk and Ottoman rulers in an unsuccessful attempt to secure aid, even as the outcome of the final war for Granada was increasingly clear. Many Granadan Muslims resorted to legal or clandestine emigration in the hopes of a better future. Between 1482 and the 1500–1502 forced conversions of Mudéjars, the kingdom of Granada's Muslim population was reduced by nearly forty percent by emigration, war casualties, and enslavement.[36]

Unfortunately, as Ibn Qaṭiyya's question illustrates so vividly, emigration failed to guarantee a better life. While many Andalusī emigrants thrived in North Africa, particularly in Ifrīqiyā, others fell victim to plunder or struggled to support themselves in a foreign economy.[37] The anonymous author of *Nubdhat al-ʿaṣr*, our only contemporary Arabic chronicle of the fall of Granada, confirms that conditions in the Maghrib were severe at the time of Boabdil's arrival, in approximately 898/1493.[38] Fez in particular was rendered so inhospitable by famine, elevated prices, and plague that many Andalusī emigrants returned to Granada, presumably taking advantage of a right of return promised in the city's capitulations.[39] Curiously, the anonymous chronicler blames these returnees for the rapidity with which the capitulations were revoked and Granadan Muslims forcibly converted to Christianity. He explains that their devastating descriptions of North Africa

35 Suberbiola Martínez, "Primeros Encabezamientos," 256–59 (Benadalid); Harvey, *Islamic Spain*, 300 (Málaga); Isabel Montes Romero-Camacho, "Judíos y Mudéjares," *Medievalismo* 13/14 (2004): 263–64 (Málaga).

36 Montes Romero-Camacho, "Judíos y Mudéjares," 262.

37 On the success of Andalusī emigrants in Ifrīqiyā, see Ramzi Rouighi, *The Making of a Mediterranean Emirate: Ifrīqiyā and Its Andalusis, 1200–1400* (Philadelphia: University of Pennsylvania Press, 2011).

38 After the surrender of Granada, Boabdil repaired briefly to the Alpujarras prior to arriving in Fez. Anonymous, *Ākhir ayyām Gharnāṭa: Nubdhat al-ʿaṣr fī akhbār mulūk Banī Naṣr*, ed. Muḥammad Riḍwān al-Dāya, 2nd ed. (Beirut: Dār al-Fikr al-Muʿāṣir, 2002), 108–9. I address this chronicle further in chapter 6. On Boabdil's life following the surrender of Granada, see Harvey, *Islamic Spain*, 327–28.

39 Harvey, *Islamic Spain*, 318 (right of return). The phenomenon of emigrants returning to Iberia is attested elsewhere. On an Andalusī who was accused of being a spy in Fez and who later returned to Iberia, see Kugle, *Rebel between Spirit and Law*, 82–83. On Valencian Muslims returning after emigration, see Meyerson, *Muslims of Valencia*, 97. Rubiera Mata notes several other instances of return in "Los moriscos," 546–47.

sharply curtailed emigration, encouraged submission to Christian rule, and accelerated the oppression and exploitation of Granadan Muslims. While other contemporary accounts attribute the violation of the capitulations to Cardinal Francisco Jiménez de Cisneros's aggressive conversion tactics, some later Maghribī authors repeat and embellish *Nubdhat al-ʿaṣr's* account blaming Muslim returnees for the ultimate fate of Granada's Muslims.[40]

While *Asnā al-matājir* focuses on emigrants, the Marbella *fatwā* highlights some of the difficulties facing Muslims who remained in the kingdom of Granada. Castile deliberately encouraged Muslim elites, especially the military aristocracy, to emigrate, and leave behind a more manageable and docile population of agricultural workers, craftspeople, and lower-level administrators.[41] Throughout the Mudéjar period, elites with the means to emigrate were the most likely to do so, along with religious scholars, whose livelihoods often depended on the patronage available in *dār al-Islām*. While some scholars remained and rose to greater prominence as they replaced their defeated political and military leaders as sources of cohesion and authority, many communities experienced an acute loss of leadership.[42] Such a predicament is suggested by the first half of Ibn Qaṭiyya's question in the Marbella case:

> This [concerns] a man from Marbella who is known for his virtue and piety, and who, when the people from his area emigrated, stayed behind in order to search for his brother who had gone missing while fighting the enemy in enemy territory (*dār al-ḥarb*). He searched for any news of him up until now, but did not find him and has lost hope. So he wanted to emigrate but another reason arose [that caused him to remain behind], namely, that he is a spokesman and support for the subject Muslims (*al-Muslimīn al-dhimmiyyīn*) where he resides, as well as for those like them who live in the neighboring areas of western al-Andalus. When difficult situations arise for them with the [Christians], he speaks with the Christian officials, argues on their behalf, and saves many of them

40 North African historian al-Maqqarī al-Tilimsānī (d. 1041/1632) repeats *Nubdhat al-ʿaṣr*'s version of events (without attribution) in *Azhār al-riyāḍ fī akhbār ʿIyāḍ*, while Moroccan author Muḥammad al-Ṭālib b. al-Ḥājj al-Sulamī (d. 1857) embellishes the story in his *Riyāḍ al-ward fīmā intamā ilayh hādhā al-jawhar al-fard*. See al-Maqqarī al-Tilimsānī, *Azhār al-riyāḍ fī akhbār ʿIyāḍ*, ed. Muṣṭafā al-Saqqā, et al., 5 vols. ([Rabat]: Ṣundūq Iḥyāʾ al-Turāth al-Islāmī, 1978), 1:67–8. On Sulamī, see P. S. van Koningsveld and G. A. Wiegers, "An Appeal of the Moriscos to the Mamluk Sultan and Its Counterpart to the Ottoman Court: Textual Analysis, Context, and Wider Historical Background," *Al-Qanṭara* 20, no. 1 (1999): 162–63. Harvey provides a summary of the account related to Cisneros in *Islamic Spain*, 328–39.

41 Harvey, *Islamic Spain*, 328; Catlos, *Muslims*, 213.

42 Manuela Marín, "Des migrations forcées: Les 'Ulema d'Al-Andalus face à la conquête chrétienne," in *L'Occident musulman et l'Occident chrétien au Moyen Âge*, ed. Mohammed Hammam (Rabat: Faculté des Lettres, 1995), 55.

> from serious predicaments. Most of them are incapable of taking on this [role] for them; in fact, if he emigrated they would hardly be able to find his equal in this skill. Great harm would befall them in his absence, if they were to lose him.[43]

This description suggests that the man from Marbella was one of a few educated and articulate community leaders remaining in western al-Andalus after the Castilian conquests in the mid-1480s. Without his diplomatic prowess and diligence, we are told, the Muslims of an entire region would be subject to untold injustices and exploitation. This portion of the question emphasizes the character and virtuous intentions of the man from Marbella, but also the precarious status of Mudéjar communities that remain without leadership. Thousands of Muslims appear to be dependent upon the skills of just one man—one who remained in the region only by his own misfortune.

Many readers of these two *fatwās* not only sympathized with the Andalusīs in question, but drew a direct link between the destruction of Islam in Iberia and the Islamic obligation to emigrate, especially as articulated by Wansharīsī. The argument is that Mudéjar communities were weakened by depopulation, especially of the wealthy and powerful, and by the alienation that resulted from the rejection by their own religious authorities of their attempts to live as Muslims under Christian rule. This vulnerability facilitated the Mudéjars' tragic decline, from tolerable or even favorable treaties of surrender, to heavy taxation and increased restrictions and relocations, to forced conversion, and eventually to the final expulsions of 1609–14.

Ḥusayn Muʾnis forcefully articulated this perspective in a 1957 study that set the tone for decades of subsequent scholarship on these texts.[44] He suggests that most of what befell the Mudéjars may be attributable to the loss of their political and religious leadership. In contrast, he suggests that the Mozarabs (Christians living under Muslim rule in Iberia) were able to maintain their Christian identity precisely because their leaders, clerics, and wealthiest members stayed with them. Because these Christian spokesmen were ready and able to engage the Muslim authorities, Mozarab communities endured rather disintegrated. For Muʾnis, the Marbella *fatwā* demonstrates that jurists who required Mudéjar leaders to emigrate were complicit in abandoning their weakest coreligionists to the mercy of the enemy. The rulings of Wansharīsī "and his like" that condemned these weak Muslims as *kuffār* (infidels), had the "worst possible effect" on those

43 Wansharīsī, *al-Miʿyār*, 2:137; appendix C, 323. For a full translation of this *fatwā*, see appendix C.

44 Muʾnis, "Asnā al-matājir," 15.

Muslims who remained in Iberia.[45] Mu'nis asks why these abandoned, oppressed communities should suffer torment on earth as well as in the afterlife. What could have been easier for them than to commit apostasy and convert to Christianity, thereby at least sparing themselves some of their earthly suffering? By posing these questions, Mu'nis implies that Wansharīsī's insistence on the obligation to emigrate encouraged apostasy instead; for Mudéjars who were unable to migrate or to negotiate a better position for themselves as Muslims under Christian rule, and who were already considered sinners or even apostates by Muslim jurists, conversion to Christianity might have seemed a compelling option.

While I investigate Wansharīsī's answers to Ibn Qaṭiyya's questions in the next chapter, I note here a few problems with Mu'nis's assessment. In *Asnā al-matājir*, Wansharīsī stopped short of calling the regretful Andalusīs unbelievers; Mu'nis appears to be making generalizations on the basis of Wansharīsī's texts alone, as he does not refer to the other *fatwā*s he views as equivalent; and relatively few Muslims in the late Mudéjar and Morisco periods appear to have converted willingly or genuinely to Christianity. In an overlooked 1975 article, ʿAbd al-Qādir al-ʿĀfiyya further argued that Mu'nis's comparison between Mozarabs and Mudéjars is unconvincing, as Muslim rulers' tolerance of Christian communities was not fully reciprocated by Christian rulers.[46] ʿĀfiyya attributes the disparate fates of these two minority communities primarily to the policies and intentions of the ruling power, arguing that Mozarabs never faced a choice between expulsion and conversion. He notes that a *fatwā* by the prominent Tunisian jurist Abū ʿAbd Allāh Muḥammad al-Māzarī (d. 536/1141) permitting Muslim judges to reside in Christian Sicily made no difference in the ultimate fate of the island's Muslim population, and he finds Wansharīsī's insistence on emigration a reasonable position by which to safeguard Muslim identity.

Mu'nis's argument regarding the negative impact of *Asnā al-matājir* and the Marbella *fatwā* proved far more influential than ʿĀfiyya's critique.[47] Historian Abdel-Majid Turki approvingly cited Mu'nis's conclusion that, in contrast to Māzarī's generosity, Wansharīsī's *fatwā*s were nothing but "grievous and fateful" for the Muslims he condemned.[48] Felipe Maíllo Salgado agreed that Muslim jurists like Wansharīsī "contributed to the

45 Mu'nis, "Asnā al-matājir," 18.

46 ʿAbd al-Qādir al-ʿĀfiyya, "al-Hijra min al-Firdaws al-Mafqūd wa-fatwā wa-taʿlīq," *al-Manāhil* 3, no. 4 (1975): 316–28.

47 Despite Vidal Castro's inclusion of ʿĀfiyya's article in a bibliography of works on the *Miʿyār*, the piece appears to have gone unnoticed by all other scholars writing on Wansharīsī's *fatwā*s. Vidal Castro, "El Miʿyār I," 352.

48 Abdel-Majid Turki, "Consultation Juridique d'al-Imam al-Mazari sur le Cas des Musulmans Vivant en Sicile sous l'Autorité des Normands," *Mélanges de l'Université Saint-Joseph* 50 (1984), 696 n. 22.

destruction of Spanish Islam," and took the argument a step further, stating that "it was not Christian intolerance which did away with the Spanish Muslims in the Middle Ages, [this] was merely the final deathblow of a process in which the Muslims themselves did everything possible for it to end this way."[49] In an article describing Wansharīsī as a "fanatic obsessed by his intransigence" Alejandro García Sanjuán concurred with Maíllo Salgado that Muslim jurists were as much to blame for the fate of Iberian Islam as were Christians.[50]

These claims regarding the impact of Wansharīsī's texts reveal an assumption that these *fatwās* were circulated widely in Iberia and were meant to encourage Mudéjar emigration. Asmal even theorized that Wansharīsī employed more accessible arguments in the Marbella *fatwā* as a second attempt to encourage Iberian Muslims to emigrate, after *Asnā al-matājir* did not yield sufficient emigration.[51] Because readers sympathized with the Andalusīs in both texts, it has been easy to imagine that ordinary Muslims had a direct role in the process of posing the questions, receiving the jurist's answers, and even circulating the *fatwās*. Several scholars have erroneously asserted that in *Asnā al-matājir* and the Marbella *fatwā*, Wansharīsī was responding directly to questions posed by the emigrants or by the man from Marbella.[52] For example, Kathryn Miller writes that in *Asnā al-matājir* "al-Wansharīsī, in fact, was asked by recent emigrants to the Maghrib whether they might be permitted to return to Christian Spain"; she makes a similar claim regarding the Marbella *fatwā*.[53] García Sanjuán is one of a few authors to mention Ibn Qaṭiyya, but he conflates him with the man from Marbella, suggesting that Ibn Qaṭiyya asked Wansharīsī, on his own behalf, whether or not he could remain in his conquered city in order to assist other Muslims.[54]

---

49 Maíllo Salgado, "Consideraciones," 185; Maíllo Salgado, "Del Islam residual," 137. My translations from the Spanish.

50 Alejandro García Sanjuán, "Del *Dār al-Islām* al *Dār al-Ḥarb*: La Cuestión Mudéjar y La Legalidad Islámica," in *Actas del I Congreso de Historia de Carmona: Edad Media* (Carmona: Diputacion de Sevilla, 1997), 181, 185.

51 Asmal, "Muslims under Non-Muslim Rule," 222–23, and also 189, 198, 211, 217. Asmal believed *Asnā al-matājir* dated to 891/1486.

52 See Louis Cardaillac, *Morisques et Chrétiens: Un affrontement polèmique (1492–1640)*, 2nd ed. (Zaghouan, Tunisia: Centre d'Etudes et de Recherches Ottomanes, Morisques, de Documentation et d'Information, 1995), 80; Sabbagh, "La Religion," 46.

53 Kathryn Miller, "Muslim Minorities and the Obligation to Emigrate to Islamic Territory: Two *Fatwās* from Fifteenth Century Granada," *Islamic Law and Society* 7, no. 2 (2000), 264 (*Asnā al-matājir*), 264–65 and 275 n. 58 (Marbella). Miller also mistakenly describes the man from Marbella as a recent emigrant.

54 García Sanjuán, "La Cuestión Mudéjar," 180.

The Ibero-centric reading of *Asnā al-matājir* and the Marbella *fatwā* may be summarized as follows: Wansharīsī received two distinct questions regarding the obligation for Mudéjars to leave their conquered Iberian homelands. The questions were either posed by these Mudéjars or by an intermediary who is not mentioned in most of the scholarly literature. Recognizing the importance of this issue for Iberian Muslims in general, Wansharīsī chose to compose elaborate answers to both questions, answers suitable for a wide distribution. He then delivered the texts to the regretful Andalusī emigrants and the man from Marbella—possibly via the intermediary. He may also have circulated additional copies of the two texts in order to increase the impact of his opinions on those Mudéjars who had not yet emigrated.

Wansharīsī in the North African Context

In contrast to the assumption that Wansharīsī wrote to persuade a lay Iberian audience, I argue that he wrote primarily for Maghribī audiences, that these *fatwās* did not necessarily circulate in Iberia, and that even if they did, it is anachronistic to attribute significant Mudéjar emigration to Wansharīsī's opinions. To understand why I place these *fatwās* in a predominantly North African context, consider the following lines from the question component of *Asnā al-matājir*:

> "The honorable master jurist . . . Abū ʿAbd Allāh b. Qaṭiyya . . . wrote to me with the following . . ."
>
> ". . . they did not find in the land of Islam, which is this land of the Maghrib . . ."

In focusing on the plight of the Mudéjars, scholars have neglected important aspects of the questions posed to Wansharīsī. In this legal genre, the content of the question and the identity of the questioner (*mustaftī*), who is the immediate audience for the *fatwā*, set the parameters for the tone and content of the response. We know from the text of the question that the *mustaftī*, Ibn Qaṭiyya, is a jurist located somewhere in the Maghrib. Unfortunately, there appears to be no record of him in the biographical dictionaries and historical chronicles that cover this period.[55] As most

55 Ibn Qaṭiyya's name is unusual and may have been corrupted. A few scholars have vocalized the name as "Ibn Quṭiyya," meaning "son of a Gothic woman." This rendering is plausible, but lacks the expected definite article and a long "u," and seems out of place for fifteenth-century North Africa. The famous Ibn al-Qūṭiyya (d. Córdoba, 367/977) was a historian of early Islamic Spain who claimed to descend from the Visigothic king Wittiza through his granddaughter Sara the Goth. The vocalization "Ibn Qaṭiyya" is likewise a conjecture, but fits better with the rhyming pattern in the question's formal prose. Given that "Qaṭiyya" should rhyme

Muslims emigrating from western Granada after 1490 embarked at Málaga, our regretful Andalusīs and someone conveying the man from Marbella's query likely sailed south from there to a Mediterranean port (in modern-day Morocco).[56] One possible destination is Badis, a port mid-way between Tetouan and Melilla that the anonymous chronicler of *Nubdhat al-ʿaṣr* associates with departures from Málaga in the aftermath of 1492.[57] Ibn Qaṭiyya might have been located in Badis or in another town near the Mediterranean coast that was under Waṭṭāsid authority.

With regard to Ibn Qaṭīyya's audience, that is, his own *mustaftī* (questioner), we can rule out the Andalusīs described in *Asnā al-matājir*. Even a cursory reading of the *istiftāʾ* suggests that for the group that wishes to return to Iberia, the only person whose permission they desired was the King of Castile. The regretful Andalusīs are described as "looking for any kind of scheme by which they may return to the land of unbelief, thereby returning, by any means possible, to life under infidel rule."[58] Presumably, they stopped asking *muftīs* for advice after arriving in the Maghrib and commencing their "cursing and defaming [of] that which had prompted their emigration," i.e., of those *muftīs* who had ruled that they were obliged to emigrate.[59] These emigrants, at least as they are portrayed in *Asnā al-matājir*, would not have sought Ibn Qaṭiyya's advice politely or voluntarily, nor would they have sent a direct petition to Wansharīsī.

I suggest that Ibn Qaṭiyya's original *mustaftī* was a judge or other representative of the state. In the first half of the question component in *Asnā al-matājir*, Ibn Qaṭiyya describes a number of offenses committed by the emigrants after arriving in the Maghrib: they openly derided *dār al-Islām*, openly praised infidels and the land of unbelief (*dār al-kufr*), expressed regret at having left *dār al-kufr*, mocked the obligation to emigrate, suggested that all Muslims should emigrate to infidel territory, sought privileges from the ruler of Castile, and actively sought a way to return to infidel rule. In the next part of the question, Ibn Qaṭiyya asks Wansharīsī's opinion as to the appropriate punishment for these transgressions:

> What manner of sin, diminished religious standing, and loss of credibility accrues to them for this? Are they committing the very act of disobedience [to God] from which they were fleeing, if they persist

with *baqiyya*, "enduring," the name may be corrupted from *?.q.y* rather than *q.ṭ.y*. I am grateful to Devin Stewart for this insight.

56 Suberbiola Martínez, "Primeros Encabezamientos," 271.

57 Anon., *Nubdhat al-ʿaṣr*, 119. In the 1509 Treaty of Sintra, Portugal confirmed Spain's right to the territory east of Peñón de Vélez de la Gomera, a small island off Badis. Spain has held Vélez de la Gomera, now a peninsula, from 1508 to the present. Badis remained loyal to the Waṭṭāsids while local rulers in Tetouan and Chefchaouen maintained their autonomy.

58 Wansharīsī, *al-Miʿyār*, 2:120.

59 Wansharīsī, *al-Miʿyār*, 2:120.

> in this behavior without repenting and returning to God (may He be exalted)? What of those among them who—God forbid!—return to the land of unbelief after having reached the land of Islam? Is it obligatory to punish those among them who have been witnessed making these statements, or the likes of them? Or should there be no [punishment] until they have been admonished and warned concerning this matter? Then whoever repents to God (may He be exalted) would be left alone, with the hope that his repentance would be accepted, and [only] those who persist in this [behavior] would be punished?
>
> Or, should they all be ignored, leaving each one to whatever he has chosen? [Should we assume] that for those God establishes contentedly in the land of Islam, their intention is valid and God (glory be to Him) will reward them for it, while whoever chooses to return to the land of unbelief and resume [submission] to infidel rule invites God's wrath? [In this case] should those who malign the land of Islam, whether explicitly or implicitly, be left alone without lament?[60]

Here Ibn Qaṭiyya seeks a second opinion as to the nature of the emigrants' transgressions: Are they sins for which God will hold them to account? Are they also offenses against the public order, for which they should be punished in the here and now? In the first paragraph, his questions for Wansharīsī seem to be rhetorical; Ibn Qaṭiyya suggests that the emigrants have at the very least sinned, that their sins may be as grave as the failure to emigrate, and that they have lost their credibility, rendering them unfit to serve as legal witnesses or to assume positions of religious leadership. In the second paragraph, Ibn Qaṭiyya presents a range of approaches to the problem posed by the Andalusīs, including social avoidance, sincere counsel, and punishment. Here he appears genuinely unsure of the correct course of action.

Wansharīsī's response to this set of questions regarding the nature of the Andalusīs' offenses and the appropriate course of action is quite certain. Even before confirming the emigrants' sins and their loss of credibility, Wansharīsī emphasizes that they must be punished, in this world, for their crimes:

> [As for] the ugly language, the cursing of the land of Islam (*dār al-Islām*), the desire to return to the land of polytheism and idols, and other detestable monstrosities which could only be uttered by the depraved, that you report coming from those emigrants—disgrace is required for them in this world and the next, and they must be lowered to the worst of positions. It is obligatory for whomever God has empowered in the land and enabled to prosper to seize these people.

60 Wansharīsī, *al-Miʿyār*, 2:120; appendix B, 289.

> He must inflict upon them a severe penalty and an intense, exemplary punishment, through beating and imprisonment, so that they do not transgress the bounds of God. This is because their corrupting ideas (*fitna*) are more severely damaging than the trials of hunger, fear, or the taking of people and property . . . Fondness for submission to polytheist rule, living among Christians, the determination to reject emigration, [the] reliance upon infidels, contentment with paying them the poll tax (*jizya*),[61] renouncing the honor of Islam, [the] obedience to the *imām* (ruler), and allegiance to the sultan, [contentment with] the Christian sultan's triumph over, and degradation of, [Islamic power and honor]—[these are] serious, perilous abominations, mortal blows that verge on unbelief (*kufr*)—may God protect us.[62]

This passage reveals two major implications in relation to the audience of *Asnā al-matājir*. First, Ibn Qaṭiyya raises the possibility that the emigrants' statements constitute criminally prosecutable offenses, and Wansharīsī insists that the authorities must inflict corporal punishment and imprisonment on those responsible. This appeal to the coercive power of the state indicates that Ibn Qaṭiyya might have been in a position to advise a court where the offending Andalusīs awaited judgment. Maghribī and Andalusī judges were often required to consult *muftī*s on points of law after establishing the facts of a case.[63] The glowing epithets with which Wansharīsī praises Ibn Qaṭiyya, despite his obscurity, might then be understood as respect for his office as a court *mushāwar* (advisor).[64] Alternatively, Ibn Qaṭiyya might have been outraged at the behavior of these emigrants and wished to gather support for his views prior to requesting that a formal case be pressed against them. In both cases, his primary audience would be a local judge. Ibn Qaṭiyya would have written to Wansharīsī as the leading jurist of Waṭṭāsid Fez for a supporting opinion and received *Asnā al-matājir*, but we cannot know whether or not he shared Wansharīsī's response directly with the judge. Ibn Qaṭiyya might have drafted a fresh document for submission to his own *mustaftī* after consulting Wansharīsī.

---

61 Often translated as "poll tax," this is the term for the tax paid by *dhimmī*s, Christians and Jews living under Muslim rule; the term also came to signify monies paid by Muslim subjects to their Christian rulers.

62 Wansharīsī, *al-Miʿyār*, 2:132; appendix B, 314.

63 On *muftī*s as advisors to courts in al-Andalus and the Maghrib, see Manuela Marín, "*Shūra* et *ahl al-Shūra* dans al-Andalus," *Studia Islamica* 62 (1985): 25–51; David Powers, *Law, Society, and Culture*, 17–22. Powers suggests that most of the *fatwā*s preserved in the *Miʿyār* may have been issued at the request of judges.

64 If Ibn Qaṭiyya was a *mushāwar*, his position may explain why he did not produce any works of his own, at least that we are aware of; his *fatwā*s would have been seen primarily by the judge of the court he advised, and may not have circulated among a community of jurists.

Second, Wansharīsī's call for an *exemplary* punishment indicates that he believed that it was necessary for a North African public to see the beating being inflicted upon the slanderous emigrants. In composing *Asnā al-matājir*, Wansharīsī must have been trying to convince the Maghribī authorities to implement a punishment of sufficient severity and publicity to counteract the *fitna*, or damage to the social fabric, that he identifies as the emigrants' primary offense. While we might be tempted to read the emigrants' public statements sympathetically, as evidence of their despair and hardship, it is clear that for Ibn Qaṭiyya and Wansharīsī, these declarations constituted a serious threat to the public order.

When we place these emigrants in their North African context, what is most striking is their resemblance to those (mentioned in Māwāsī's *fatwā* and the Berber *fatwā*) fishing contentedly with the enemy and praying for the continuation of the times. In the earlier *fatwā*s, these emigrants' basic offenses—contentment with infidel rule and their public expression of a desire for the continuance of that rule—are the crimes for which Māwāsī and Wansharīsī reserved their gravest assessment, apostasy. The foregrounding of these crimes in *Asnā al-matājir* renders the regretful Andalusīs players on a Maghribī stage, while the exemplary punishment Wansharīsī prescribes for them must be interpreted as a lesson for Maghribī Muslims still in the process of negotiating their complex relationships with Christian authorities.

The portion of *Asnā al-matājir*'s question and response considered thus far strongly suggests that this text must be viewed as part of a larger discourse on the status of conquered Muslims on both sides of the Mediterranean in the late fifteenth and early sixteenth centuries. Rather than viewing the Iberian Muslim predicament as exceptional, Wansharīsī and his peers had every reason to believe that Christian Iberia's aspirations were to extend their permanent conquest to North Africa. These jurists must have been particularly alarmed to find a group of Iberian Muslims spreading the idea among Maghribīs that Christian rule is *not* a threat to be combated, rather it is to be preferred over Muslim rule.

While Wansharīsī was concerned with public order, we cannot assume that the Andalusīs in question or the lay public ever saw the *fatwā* itself. *Asnā al-matājir* is a technical legal treatise full of the proof texts and rationales required to convince professional jurists of a nuanced argument. When writing for commoners, professional etiquette required *muftī*s to present simple, straightforward answers. We can assume only two immediate audiences for this text: Ibn Qaṭiyya, as the *mustaftī*, and the wider community of Mālikī legal professionals who would have consulted the *Miʿyār* once it was completed, copied, and circulated throughout North

Africa. In addition, those copies of *Asnā al-matājir* that have survived as independent treatises suggest that Wansharīsī circulated this text among his peers in Fez, as a contribution to their discourse on the obligation to emigrate.

Ibn Qaṭiyya's questions in *Asnā al-matājir* and the Marbella *fatwā* provide Wansharīsī with a broad mandate to compose formal, treatise-length opinions that would offer the final word in the contemporary juristic discourse on Muslim submission to "infidel" authority and serve as an authoritative precedent for future generations that would read the *Miʿyār*. In the question portion of *Asnā al-matājir* cited above, Ibn Qaṭiyya's questions position Wansharīsī to establish the worldly consequences of Muslims' open expression of a preference for infidel rule and of a voluntary return to *dār al-ḥarb* following emigration. The final portion of Ibn Qaṭiyya's question in *Asnā al-matājir* offers Wansharīsī a platform for a more general statement on the obligation to emigrate:

> Clarify for us, by means of a comprehensive, general, explicit, and sufficient statement, the judgment of God (may He be exalted) concerning all of this. Is it a condition of [the obligation to] emigrate that no one has to emigrate other than to a standard of living guaranteed to be in accordance with his desires, immediately upon arrival and in whatever region of the Islamic world he has alighted? Or is this not a condition? Instead, is emigration obligatory from the land of unbelief to the land of Islam [no matter if] that entails sweetness or bitterness, abundance or poverty, or hardship or ease, with regard to conditions in this world? Surely its purpose is the protection of religion, family, and offspring,[65] for example, and escape from the infidel community's rule to that of the Muslim community, and to whatever God wills by way of sweetness or bitterness, poverty or wealth, and so on, with respect to worldly conditions.[66]

Here Ibn Qaṭiyya specifically requests an exposition that will be applicable to a wide range of cases. Unlike his questions regarding the emigrants' punishment, in which Ibn Qaṭiyya appears to genuinely entertain a range of possible approaches (though he is clear on the fact of their sin), this set of questions leaves no doubt as to his position on their obligation to emigrate. His exaggerated straw man version of the emigrants implies that they felt entitled to instant comfort and wealth wherever they happened to

65 These are three of the five essential human interests (religion, life, intellect, lineage, and property) that the law is designed to protect according to the theory of *maqāṣid al-sharīʿa* (objectives of the law), elaborated by jurists such as Ghazālī and Shāṭibī.

66 Wansharīsī, *al-Miʿyār*, 2:120; appendix B, 290.

land in *dār al-Islām*. Ibn Qaṭiyya feigns the need to inquire whether or not the obligation to emigrate is conditional upon material comfort, then closes with a succinct declaration of the position for which he is asking Wansharīsī to furnish support: any Muslim truly devoted to the protection of his religion and family would suffer whatever hardship and loss was necessary to leave infidel territory and resettle under Muslim rule.

Ibn Qaṭiyya's *istiftāʾ* in the Marbella *fatwā* presents Wansharīsī with the opportunity to comment on another aspect of the obligation to emigrate. After describing the current situation of the man in question, Ibn Qaṭiyya asks:

> Is residing with them under infidel rule permitted for him, on account of the benefit (*maṣlaḥa*) his residence entails for those unfortunate [Muslim] *dhimmīs*, even though he is capable of emigration anytime he wishes? Or is this [residence] not permitted for him, as they also have no dispensation for their residence there subject to infidel laws, especially considering that they have been granted permission to emigrate and that most of them are capable of doing so whenever they wish? Presuming that this were permitted to him, would he thus also be granted a dispensation to pray in his garments [as they are], in accordance with whatever ability he has [to keep them pure]? For they [his garments] generally would not be free from major ritual impurities (*najāsa*) as a result of his frequent interactions with the Christians, his dealings with them, and his sleeping and arising in their homes while serving these subject Muslims in the manner stated?[67]

Although Ibn Qaṭiyya allows the Marbellan to appear sympathetic in the first half of his *istiftāʾ*, in the second half, he critiques the man sharply. Ibn Qaṭiyya stresses that both the man and the Mudéjars for whom he advocates are capable of emigrating at any time, implying that this population is neither as helpless nor as worthy of assistance as they may seem; rather, they are voluntarily subjecting themselves to harm by remaining under Christian authority. Ibn Qaṭiyya then presents the specter of a slippery slope of dispensations that would be required to accommodate this man's (and by extension all Mudéjars') inability to perform his ritual obligations properly if he fails to emigrate.

The Marbellan *istiftāʾ*, like that of *Asnā al-matājir*, is designed to elicit from Wansharīsī a compelling response that prohibits voluntary residence under Christian rule and overcomes distinct objections to the obligation to emigrate. In *Asnā al-matājir*, Wansharīsī is asked to elaborate on the general rules and conditions pertaining to this obligation while demonstrating that

67 Wansharīsī, *al-Miʿyār*, 2:137; appendix C, 323–24.

the hardships of relocation or unfavorable conditions in *dār al-Islām* do not justify remaining in Christian territory. The Marbella *fatwā* focuses on the consequences of remaining under Christian rule. Instead of maligning Muslim territory, the man in question acknowledges the precariousness of the Mudéjars' situation in *dār al-ḥarb*, where they are continually threatened with injustice. In this case, Wansharīsī must defeat the notion that a Muslim might legitimately remain under Christian rule in order to assist others in their interactions with the authorities. In effect, Ibn Qaṭiyya is asking two broad questions in the Marbella question: Is remaining in *dār al-ḥarb* ever meritorious? What possible harm could result if one remains for seemingly pious purposes? Wansharīsī's mandate is to identify and condemn the ways in which Muslims who choose to remain under Christian rule are compromising their religion and enabling their communities' suffering and deterioration. Ibn Qaṭiyya conveniently elides any mention of Mudéjars who are truly unable to emigrate, and does not ask Wansharīsī to grapple with a case in which a capable Muslim remains to aid a population who cannot emigrate, whose only option is submission to their new Christian overlords.

Who did Wansharīsī write the Marbella *fatwā* for? As with *Asnā al-matājir*, we can only be certain that he wrote for Ibn Qaṭiyya and for the professionals who would read the *Miʿyār*. But in this case it is plausible that Ibn Qaṭiyya's own *mustaftī* was the man from Marbella himself, who may have sent a letter to the Maghrib asking for a dispensation from the obligation to emigrate. The first portion of the *istiftāʾ*, which may reflect the man's self-presentation, carefully presents his current status as legitimate—until now he has remained in *dār al-ḥarb* in search of a brother who had gone missing in battle, as he is presumably aware that ransoming a captive is one of the few permitted reasons for remaining in enemy territory.[68] Ibn Qaṭiyya may have intended to send a copy of Wansharīsī's response to the Marbellan; this text is much shorter than *Asnā al-matājir* (although still quite long for a *fatwā* to a lay Muslim), is based largely on rational arguments rather than legal precedents, includes few technical terms, and relates primarily to the basic obligations of Islam with which any Muslim should have been familiar. Alternatively, Ibn Qaṭiyya may have consulted the Marbella *fatwā* but composed a more succinct version to return to his *mustaftī*. In either case, we cannot know if Ibn Qaṭiyya's response reached the Marbellan.

---

68 For example, Ibn Rushd al-Jadd ("the grandfather," d. 520/1126) states, "It is not permissible for any Muslim to enter the land of polytheism for trade or any other reason, except to ransom a Muslim." Abū al-Walīd Muḥammad b. Aḥmad b. Rushd, *al-Muqaddimāt al-mumahhidāt li-bayān mā iqtaḍathu rusūm al-Mudawwana min al-aḥkām al-sharʿiyyāt waʾl-taḥṣīlāt al-muḥkamāt li-ummahāt masāʾilihā al-mushkilāt*, ed. Saʿīd Aḥmad Aʿrāb (Beirut: Dār al-Gharb al-Islāmī, 1988), 2:153.

We have no material evidence regarding the circulation of Wansharīsī's *fatwās* in Mudéjar communities. Although one manuscript copy of *Asnā al-matājir* is now held by the El Escorial monastery library outside Madrid, the text is undated and does not bear a copyist's name. The *fatwā* is bound together in one volume with several other texts, but none of them reveals the provenance of the volume. We have no compelling reason to believe that this copy of *Asnā al-matājir* was produced or circulated in al-Andalus, as many of the Arabic manuscripts held by the Escorial were acquired by the Spanish Crown directly from Morocco at the close of the Morisco period.[69] Madrid's Biblioteca Nacional likewise contains one copy of the *Miʿyār* that includes Wansharīsī's chapter on *jihād*, and therefore both of Wansharīsī's "Iberian" *fatwās*; but this copy of the *Miʿyār* is undated and may have entered Spain after the Mudéjar and Morisco periods.[70] No individual copies of the Marbella *fatwā* are mentioned in the scholarly literature or in the relevant manuscript catalogues, nor is this text preserved in any North African *fatwā* collections beyond the *Miʿyār*.[71] Finally, neither these *fatwās* nor the *Miʿyār* are included in the lists gathered by L. P. Harvey and Gerard Wiegers of materials known to have survived and circulated in Iberia during the Morisco period.[72]

Even if *Asnā al-matājir* or the Marbella *fatwā* had circulated in Iberia, these opinions could not be considered a major reason for Mudéjar emigration or Islam's decline in Iberia. By his own count, Wansharīsī was writing four hundred years after the start of the Mudéjar period, which he dates to the eleventh-century fall of Sicily and parts of al-Andalus.[73]

69 For example, roughly 4,000 Arabic manuscripts were seized from a ship carrying the private library of Saʿdian sultan Mawlāy Zaydān (r. 1012–36/1603–27) and sent to El Escorial in 1614, the final year of the Morisco expulsions. See Daniel Hershenzon, "Traveling Libraries: The Arabic Manuscripts of Muley Zidan and the Escorial Library," *Journal of Early Modern History* 18 (2014): 535–58.

70 Vidal Castro, "El-Miʿyār I," 336–37. Vidal Castro lists a number of partial copies of the *Miʿyār* held by the Biblioteca Nacional. Only MS 4883 contains the first and second parts of the work, which presumably correspond to the first four volumes of the modern edition.

71 For the list of manuscript libraries that I consulted in person, see Libraries and Archives Consulted, which directly precedes the bibliography. I also consulted the printed catalogues (only) for a number of smaller libraries. On all of these libraries, see also Jocelyn Hendrickson and Sabahat Adil, "A Guide to Arabic Manuscript Libraries in Morocco: Further Developments," *MELA Notes: Journal of Middle Eastern Librarianship* 86 (2013): 1–19; Hendrickson, "A Guide to Arabic Manuscript Libraries in Morocco, with Notes on Tunisia, Algeria, Egypt, and Spain," *MELA Notes: Journal of Middle Eastern Librarianship* 81 (2008): 15–88.

72 Harvey, *Muslims in Spain*, 142–203, esp. 154–56 (legal works); Wiegers, *Islamic Literature*, 223–29. The Morisco period began in Castile with forced conversions to Christianity in 1500–1502. I am unaware of any studies that determine when and where the *Miʿyār* first circulated, but it is unlikely to have been prior to Wansharīsī's death in 914/1508. As noted, Powers estimates that Wansharīsī continued to modify the compilation until his death.

73 In *Asnā al-matājir* (2:125, appendix B, 298–99), Wansharīsī states that the phenomenon of Muslims living under non-Muslim rule began in the fifth/eleventh century with the fall of

The Islamic obligation to emigrate was already well known among Mudéjar communities, as jurists began discussing the status of Muslims who remained in conquered territory as early as the 185/801 conquest of Barcelona. The biographical account of a Valencian *imām* reports that he and his fellow townspeople emigrated around 488/1095, "fleeing with their religion." And, for example, the Naṣrid king Yūsuf III of Granada (r. 1408?–17) sent a circular to all Mudéjars urging them to fulfill their religious duty to emigrate by moving to Granada and joining the *jihād* against Christians.[74] Even the subjects of Wansharīsī's two *fatwās* were well aware of their doctrinal obligation to emigrate—the Andalusīs had fulfilled this obligation at great personal cost while the Marbellan was hoping for a special dispensation (*rukhṣa*) from an acknowledged general rule requiring emigration. The discovery that Wansharīsī copied most of his material from an earlier *fatwā* by Ibn Rabīʿ also demonstrates that most of the ideas found in these two texts had already been articulated by the early fourteenth century, rather than the late fifteenth century.

Not only was Wansharīsī unlikely to have been a prime resource for Mudéjars contemplating emigration, but religio-legal considerations were also not the only factors that influenced Muslim migrations within and from Iberia. The Mudéjar period witnessed large-scale population transfers as Muslims left conquered areas and resettled in still-Muslim territories, and as Christians relocated from previously-held areas to settle in newly-conquered territories.[75] Where emigration was voluntary, both religious scholars and lay Muslims chose to relocate for a variety of economic, political, social, and religious reasons.

The obligation to emigrate was well known in Iberia on the eve of Granada's surrender. Iberian Muslims had been weighing the established doctrine of *hijra* alongside other considerations for generations when Wansharīsī composed these texts, whose circulation among lay Iberian Muslims has not been documented and, especially in the case of *Asnā al-matājir*, may never have taken place. While the fall of Granada brought

---

Sicily and parts of al-Andalus (Toledo fell in 1085). In a text that Wansharīsī places immediately after *Asnā al-matājir* and the Marbella *fatwā* in the *Miʿyār*, Ibn ʿĀṣim (d. ca. 857/1453) similarly states that *tadajjun*, living as Mudéjars, had begun four hundred years previously, or in the fifth/eleventh century (2:151). On the term "Mudéjar" and jurists' selection of this date as the beginning of Mudéjar Islam, see Wiegers, *Islamic Literature*, 2–6.

74 Marín, "Des migrations forcées," 49 (Valencian *imām*); Harvey, *Islamic Spain*, 59–60 (Naṣrid circular). On Barcelona, see Wansharīsī, *al-Miʿyār*, 2:129–30, appendix B, 309–11; van Koningsveld and Wiegers, "Islamic Statute," 49; Jean-Pierre Molénat, "Le problème de la permanence des musulmans dans les territoires conquis par les chrétiens, du point de vue de la loi islamique," *Arabica* 48, no. 3 (2001), 396–97.

75 On Iberian migrations from the time of the Muslim conquest through the Morisco period and beyond, see García-Arenal, *La Diaspora des Andalousiens*.

a new wave of emigrants to North African shores, it is unlikely that Wansharīsī composed his two "Iberian" *fatwās* primarily to encourage Mudéjar emigration.

Verskin has recently puzzled over the timing of Wansharīsī's *fatwās*. Why did Wansharīsī devote such lengthy responses to the status of Mudéjars just as this population ceased to exist as such? Assuming that the applicability of these texts was "sharply limited in time" and that jurists had little to gain from addressing the "anomalous legal situation" of the Mudéjars after most Iberian Muslims had emigrated, Verskin concludes that these texts are, at the very least, "an important example of the culmination of much legal reflection" on Muslims living under non-Muslim rule.[76]

In response to such questions, I suggest that, once we place Wansharīsī's *fatwās* in their North African context, it becomes clear that there is nothing anachronistic about these texts. The problem of voluntary Muslim submission to Christian authority was deeply relevant in the Maghribī landscape, where Portugal controlled most major Atlantic ports and many Muslims willingly collaborated with their Christian overlords, while other Maghribīs engaged in an active *jihād* against the occupiers. Maghribī Muslims had been paying tribute to Portuguese overlords, serving in their armies, spying for them, and trading with them for the better part of a century when Wansharīsī wrote *Asnā al-matājir* and the Marbella *fatwā*. Castile captured Melilla a few years later (1497), and Portugal continued to expand its holdings in Morocco until 1541.

While Wansharīsī was not writing for Iberian Muslims, the imminent cessation of Muslim Iberian rule was precisely what made it so important for him to respond to Ibn Qaṭiyya's "Iberian" questions. These questions provided a more compelling framework for the development of a comprehensive, authoritative statement on the obligation to emigrate than the questions recorded by Zayyātī, for at least four reasons. First, for Wansharīsī, the fate of Iberia's Muslims represented a conclusive precedent. The loss of al-Andalus served as a warning for his contemporary Maghribī audience of the consequences of complacency in the face of unchecked Christian advances, and for later generations who would read the *Miʿyār*, it provided a more concrete historical precedent than the still-unfolding situation in Morocco.

The relative simplicity of the Mudéjar context allowed Wansharīsī to present his North African audiences with one type of Muslim submission to Christian authority, and its tragic outcome. Whereas the questions Wansharīsī and his peers faced about relations with the Portuguese were complex and nuanced, Ibn Qaṭiyya's questions were simplified into a single

76 Verskin, *Islamic Law*, 11.

vision of Mudéjar existence, namely, what to do with those who chose to reside under Christian rule despite the ability to emigrate. The Marbella question adds the continuous threat of exploitation and injustice to this basic image of Mudéjar life, while *Asnā al-matājir* denigrates the character of Mudéjars by suggesting that they would risk an arduous reverse migration in order to embrace enemy rule even after reaching *dār al-Islām*.

In reality, of course, Mudéjar existence was far from uniform. In his original *fatwā*, Ibn Rabīʿ acknowledges this diversity by employing a three-part typology of Mudéjar communities based on their demographic strength relative to the enemy (Christians) and the Mudéjars' degree of integration into Christian society.[77] Yet, in his own compositions, Wansharīsī omits this section of Ibn Rabīʿ's *fatwā*, thereby rendering the Andalusī case as straightforward and unambiguous as possible. He elides the complexities of real Muslim-Christian relations, in both Iberia and the Maghrib, in order to advance one definitive doctrinal position applicable to all cases of Muslims living under non-Muslim authority.

While Ibn Qaṭiyya and Wansharīsī reduce the Mudéjars in *Asnā al-matājir* and the Marbella *fatwā* to a single unambiguous model, their stories also had a narrative appeal that represented a third advantage over the opinions preserved by Zayyātī. The primary questions in *Selected Jewels* (those posed to Ibn Barṭāl, Māwāsī, and Wansharīsī) shared a list of typologies abstracted from actual Muslim-Christian relations in the Maghrib and largely stripped of contextual detail. The typologies are dry and forgettable, aside from the odd remark about fishing or rogue harvesting. By contrast, Ibn Qaṭiyya's vivid narratives bring to life the experiences and attitudes of individual characters. For modern scholars, these gripping stories evoke sympathy for the Mudéjars, though Ibn Qaṭiyya's tone in each question shows that he anticipates a very different reaction from his own audience. The voices of the regretful Andalusīs are meant to shock and offend, while the Marbellan case presents a dramatic irony—readers are meant to understand what the well-meaning but naïve Marbellan does not, which is that his efforts only enable the unnecessary humiliation and exploitation of the Muslim population, whose lives are already precarious. Together, these narratives make Wansharīsī's *fatwās* far more compelling and memorable than Zayyātī's "jewels."[78]

Finally, Ibn Qaṭiyya's questions allowed Wansharīsī to craft a powerful but veiled commentary on the foreign occupation of the Maghrib in his time. In his Berber *fatwā*, Wansharīsī called upon the "leaders of the Muslims," as well as the community, to prevent any interaction with Portuguese-occupied

77 Van Koningsveld and Wiegers, "Islamic Statute," 34–35.
78 On the use of narrative in *fatwās*, see Hendrickson, "Prohibiting the Pilgrimage."

areas. By the time Wansharīsī wrote *Asnā al-matājir*, the Waṭṭāsid sultan Muḥammad al-Shaykh had renewed a long-term peace treaty with Portugal. As a result, Wansharīsī suppressed the more overt political critique found in his Berber *fatwā* and in Ibn Zakrī's *fatwā*s by excluding them from the *Miʿyār* and instead including *Asnā al-matājir*, which places the blame for Muslim defeat safely in distant Iberia. After fleeing the wrath of one sultan in Tlemcen and finding refuge in Fez, Wansharīsī likely found it expedient not to disseminate a treatise openly combating the Portuguese presence in the Maghrib, implicitly condemning the Waṭṭāsid treaty, and undermining Waṭṭāsid authority to set the terms of warfare. *Asnā al-matājir* and the Marbella *fatwā* also cast Andalusīs as the lay Muslim antagonists rather than fellow Maghribīs, another deflection of overt blame that may have increased the resonance of these texts with those Maghribīs who were growing increasingly resentful of Andalusī immigrants. Wansharīsī's exclusion of Waryāglī's *fatwā* from the *Miʿyār* likely also reflects Wansharīsī's aversion to Waryāglī's harsh condemnation of fellow Maghribīs.[79]

In this chapter, I have argued that Wansharīsī seized the opportunity provided by Ibn Qaṭiyya's questions to write the final word on the contemporary juristic debate on Muslim submission to non-Muslim rule. Excluding his own Berber *fatwā* and the opinions of his contemporaries, which all focused on Portuguese occupation of the Maghrib, in the *Miʿyār* he preserved only *Asnā al-matājir* and the Marbella *fatwā*, both ostensibly concerned with Iberian Muslims. I have explained *why* we should consider the primary audiences for these ostensibly Iberian-focused texts to be North African, and *why* we should view the condemnation of Maghribī-Portuguese collaboration as one of their principal messages. In the following chapter, I analyze Wansharīsī's responses, in order to demonstrate *how* he crafted opinions that not only addressed both the Iberian and Maghribī contexts, but that would also continue to be adaptable to future manifestations of the same legal issue.

79 Wansharīsī and Waryāglī were also involved in an acrimonious dispute over a teaching position in Fez. On the dispute and related *fatwā*s, see Ibn al-Qāḍī al-Miknāsī, *Jadhwat al-iqtibās*, 2:439–40; Vidal Castro, "Principales aspectos," 330–31; Wansharīsī, *al-Miʿyār*, 7:347–54.

CHAPTER 5

Wansharīsī's Answers: Authority and Adaptation

In Wansharīsī's time, jurists were expected to avoid the appearance of exercising *ijtihād*, of deriving new legal rules through direct engagement with the Qur'ān and Ḥadīth. Instead, they valued *taqlīd* (lit., "imitation"), or fidelity to the rules and methods attributed to their schools' eponymous founders and earliest disciples. Later jurists like Wansharīsī built carefully upon the foundations established by these earlier authorities, strove to maintain consistency with established school doctrine, and to exhibit a pious deference to the scholarly achievements of earlier generations.[1] Later jurists—defined by Mālikīs as all those following Ibn Abī Zayd al-Qayrawānī (d. 386/996)—cited scriptural proof texts and advanced new solutions to evolving legal problems, though their opinions were accepted more readily the more they conformed to existing tradition. This conformity to a set of doctrinal foundations, alongside a scholarly consensus regarding the accepted parameters for disagreement, produced the predictable legal outcomes we now associate with the rule of law.[2]

Wansharīsī's answers to Ibn Qaṭiyya's questions reflect the authority that fellow Mālikīs assigned to inherited school doctrines. He works hard to convince his readers that his responses consist of nothing more daring or innovative than the application of existing doctrine to a recurring, settled case. Wansharīsī so successfully maintains this impression of continuity with received tradition that Mu'nis presents his *fatwā*s as the epitome of *taqlīd*, which, by Mu'nis's time, was denigrated as slavish obedience to outdated norms. In reading *Asnā al-matājir* and the Marbella *fatwā*, Mu'nis laments:

> We get a picture of the level and type of knowledge in the Far Maghrib during the ninth century AH [/fifteenth century CE]; we see that knowledge at that time reached no farther than the level of collection,

1 Mālikīs consider Ibn Abī Zayd to be the school's first "later" jurist. Maryam Muḥammad Ṣāliḥ al-Ẓufayrī, *Muṣṭalaḥāt al-madhāhib al-fiqhiyya wa-asrār al-fiqh al-marmūz fī al-aʿlām wa'l-kutub wa'l-ārā' wa'l-tarjīḥāt* (Beirut: Dār Ibn Ḥazm, 2002), 156.

2 On *taqlīd*, see Mohammad Fadel, "The Social Logic of *Taqlīd* and the Rise of the *Mukhtaṣar*," *Islamic Law and Society* 3, no. 2 (1996): 193–233; Gerber, *State, Society, and Law*, esp. ch. 4.

> memorization, and repetition, just as was the case in the East at the time. The days of creative scholars capable of *ijtihād* had vanished . . . all that remains before us are *muqallidūn* [those who practice *taqlīd*] in the derivative branches of *fiqh*, or collators and compilers, who take from here and put there . . . they make mistakes or are reckless in *qiyās* [analogical reasoning]. They apply rulings haphazardly without analyzing the contingent circumstances or changing conditions. They are convinced of a resemblance of sources without bothering to study the current conditions . . . all this, while the *sharīʿa* before them is lenient, with ample room for consideration.
>
> This *shaykh* who undertook to produce an opinion regarding the fate of the Muslims remaining in al-Andalus did not go to the trouble, while sitting and writing this *fatwā*, of researching the conditions of those upon whose affairs he was ruling. [Nor did he bother to] thoroughly investigate their history or to acquaint himself with the reasons which compelled them to stay in al-Andalus and which prevented them from emigration to the Maghrib. He did not mention that they are, first and foremost, weak humans, for whom it is difficult to leave their lands and the places familiar [to them] throughout a long life, those places where their fathers and grandfathers spent long centuries . . . but our *shaykh* memorizes rather than investigates, and treats with severity our brothers in religion whose situation, the misfortunes of the times, is between two millstones grinding without mercy.[3]

In this second paragraph, Muʾnis's appeal for sympathy with the Mudéjars resonated with many scholars, and laid the foundations for the Ibero-centric approaches to these texts discussed in the previous chapter. Yet the primary thrust of this passage is his argument that Islamic law is fundamentally lenient and adaptable to changing circumstances. For Muʾnis, Wansharīsī's senseless, inhumane cruelty in *Asnā al-matājir* and the Marbella *fatwā* does not just reflect his personal failing, rather it typifies the harm done by centuries of *muqallidūn* who were unable and unwilling to reinterpret revelation to meet the needs of a changing society.

While Muʾnis and Wansharīsī thus agree on the latter's lack of innovation, we should not accept this narrative too quickly. In this chapter

3 Muʾnis, "Asnā al-matājir," 5–6. My translation from the Arabic. On Wansharīsī's *fatwās* as evidence of the lack of *ijtihād* in his time, see also Maíllo Salgado, "Consideraciones," 181–82; Emilio Molina López, "Algunas consideraciones sobre los emigrados andalusíes," in *Homenaje al prof. Darío Cabanelas Rodríguez, O.F.M., con motivo de su LXX aniversario* (Granada: Universidad de Granada, 1987), 429; Abdel-Majid Turki, "Pour ou contre la légalité du séjour des musulmans en territoire reconquis par les chrétiens: Justification doctrinale et réalité historique," in *Religionsgespräche im Mittelalter*, ed. Bernard Lewis and Friedrich Niewöhner (Wiesbaden: Harrassowitz, 1992), 323.

I offer concrete examples of Wansharīsī's efforts to avoid the appearance of innovation. Here, it is worth placing Muʾnis's influential views in historical context. As an Egyptian historian, Muʾnis's forceful critique of Wansharīsī, published just one year into Gamal Abdel-Nasser's presidency (1956–70), reflected the intellectual and political currents of his time. In the late nineteenth and early twentieth centuries, such thinkers as Jamāl al-Dīn al-Afghānī (1838–97), Muḥammad ʿAbdūh (1849–1905), and Rashīd Riḍāʾ (1865–1935) established the modernist Islamic movement.[4] Modernists called for fresh interpretations of the Qurʾān and Ḥadīth through *ijtihād*, but unlike many Salafis, they did not aim for the restoration of a pure, original Islam purged of syncretic accretions. Instead, they sought to demonstrate the compatibility of Islam with human reason, modern technology, and certain Western values. To justify selective adoptions from the West and circumvent countervailing legal rules, modernists presented the Islamic schools of law (*madhhabs*) as rigid and outdated, preserved in time by conservative jurists invested in the status quo.

By Muʾnis's time, this modernist critique of inherited law and established legal authorities dovetailed with a historiographical tradition that characterized the Ottoman period as one of prolonged stagnation. Both trends helped justify the modernizing reforms imposed by Nasser, who brought Egypt's Islamic institutions under state control in an effort to counter the Muslim Brotherhood, give his nationalist projects Islamic legitimacy, and assert Egypt's primacy among Arab and Islamic states. Nasser wrote a preface to Muʾnis's 1956 *Miṣr wa-risālatuhā* (Egypt's mission) in which he credits ancient Egypt with the qualities and achievements he hoped to foster in the modern state: ingenuity in science and engineering, advances in medicine, a flourishing artistic culture, the defense and enrichment of Islamic civilization, and "scholars who developed new ideas and interpretations concerning the law of Islam."[5]

Muʾnis participated in a modernizing discourse that was eager to condemn centuries of inherited legal traditions as ossified and unusable, and ready to replace these with fresh interpretations suitable for the modern world. In his scathing critique of *Asnā al-matājir* and the Marbella *fatwā*, Muʾnis promotes a vision of Islamic legal reasoning as a once-great craft that could be restored to relevance and excellence if only scholars discarded existing doctrines and revisited the original sources with a

---

4 On modernist Islam, see Charles Kurzman, "Introduction: The Modernist Islamic Movement," in *Modernist Islam, 1840–1940: A Sourcebook*, ed. Kurzman (Oxford: Oxford University Press, 2002), 3–27.

5 Amos Perlmutter translates an excerpt from Nasser's preface in *Egypt: The Praetorian State* (New Brunswick, NJ: Transaction Books, 1974), 69–70. For the original preface, see Ḥusayn Muʾnis, *Miṣr wa-risālatuhā* (Cairo: Dār al-Maʿārif, 1956), 5–8.

modern scientific mindset, one that prioritizes ingenuity, practicality, and the common good.

Yet the modernists' call to reopen the "gate of *ijtihād*" to allow direct engagement with the Qurʾān and Ḥadīth rested on the presumption that this gate had been closed in the first place. Now, this theory, according to which jurists were restricted to implementing their predecessors' opinions following the consolidation of the major law schools in the fourth/tenth century, has been disproven and discarded in most academic scholarship on Islamic law.[6] We know that after the establishment of the *madhhabs*, jurists continued to support the use of *ijtihād* in theory and to exercise it in practice. Even if most jurists presented themselves as humble *muqallids*, they nonetheless continued to adapt and expand the law, and they continued to honor elite jurists by ascribing to them the level of *ijtihād*.

Here I argue that even Wansharīsī, who has been viewed as the model *muftī* who perfectly represented the presumed stagnation of Islamic law in the fifteenth century, exercised considerable juristic discretion and innovation in crafting *Asnā al-matājir* and the Marbella *fatwā*. As much as it may appear that Wansharīsī strictly applied an "orthodox" Mālikī doctrine on Muslim residence under non-Muslim rule, in fact, he employed a range of subtle tactics, including the manipulation and elision of past precedents, unacknowledged borrowing (in modern parlance, plagiarism), and oblique references in order to accomplish several aims. These aims include a straightforward response to Ibn Qaṭiyya's questions regarding Andalusīs, an oblique condemnation of Muslim cooperation with foreign occupiers in the Maghrib, a veiled critique of the Waṭṭāsids, and the composition of a forceful treatise meant to be preserved for future generations as the Mālikī school's authoritative statement on living under Christian rule.

In the remainder of this chapter I delve into the specifics of Wansharīsī's responses to Ibn Qaṭiyya's questions. While I offer full translations in the appendices, in this chapter I give concrete examples illustrating Wansharīsī's methods, aims, and strategic choices. Most of my analysis focuses on *Asnā al-matājir*, which is more substantial and more clearly adapted to Wansharīsī's context.

6 See the introduction for a discussion of this theory and its refutation.

Wansharīsī's Adaptation of Ibn Rabīʿ's *Fatwā*

Van Koningsveld and Wiegers' discovery that Wansharīsī relied extensively on a *fatwā* issued by Andalusī jurist Ibn Rabīʿ (d. 719/1319)[7] presents a remarkable opportunity. We can identify each section of Ibn Rabīʿ's text, first issued in late thirteenth- or early fourteenth-century Màlaga, that Wansharīsī chose to reproduce, omit, re-arrange, or augment with new text in order to adapt it to his own context in the late fifteenth-century Maghrib. By analyzing each of these adaptations, we can better understand Wansharīsī's motives and priorities in crafting his own opinions. Furthermore, the ability to isolate those sections of *Asnā al-matājir* and the Marbella *fatwā* original to Wansharīsī allows us to productively compare it with the Berber *fatwā* discussed in part 1. In addition to the adaptations I address below, throughout the text, Wansharīsī makes minor stylistic changes to his predecessor's *fatwā*, transforming Ibn Rabīʿ's ordinary prose into rhyming prose, or *sajʿ*.

In appropriating Ibn Rabīʿs *fatwā* for his own purposes, one of Wansharīsī's first decisions must have been to not acknowledge his source, or in modern terms, to plagiarize. Beyond simply omitting Ibn Rabīʿ's name, Wansharīsī offers no indication that the bulk of these two *fatwā*s consist of borrowed material. There are at least three possible reasons for this. Wansharīsī may have wanted to bolster his own authority by taking credit for the superior work of another jurist. Or he may have thought it would strengthen the authority of his opinions to restrict his citations to older, more respected legal masters such as Mālik (d. 179/795), Ibn Rushd al-Jadd (d. 520/1126), and Ibn al-ʿArabī (d. 543/1148).

Most importantly, Wanhsarīsī's elision of this source allowed him to conceal the circumstances under which Ibn Rabīʿ's *fatwā* was produced.[8] In the question component of Ibn Rabīʿ's text, a student asks for the legal argument prohibiting residence under Christian rule. The student conveys the opinion of another jurist, one who supported the permissibility of Muslims' continuing to live in their conquered homelands. The unnamed jurist's arguments include these Muslims' ability to manifest their religion (that is, to practice their religion overtly) and live in safety under the terms of their treaty. The student conveys two *ḥadīth*s as evidence that it would be unnecessary to emigrate under these conditions: "Whoever believes in God and his messenger, performs the prayer, pays *zakāt*, fasts Ramadan,

7 This jurist, whose full name is Muḥammad b. Yaḥyā b. ʿAbd al-Rahmān b. Aḥmad b. Rabīʿ al-Qurṭubī al-Mālikī al-Ashʿarī, was born in Córdoba but spent much of his career in Málaga. Ibn Ḥajar al-ʿAsqalānī (d. 852/1449), *al-Durar al-kāmina fī aʿyān al-mi'a al-thāmina*, ed. ʿAbd al-Wārith Muḥammad ʿAlī, 4 vols. in 2 (Beirut: Dār al-Kutub al-ʿIlmiyya, 1997), 4:173–74 (no. 4772).

8 See van Koningsveld and Wiegers, "Islamic Statute," for a full, detailed summary of Ibn Rabīʿ's text.

and performs the pilgrimage to the House [of God], it is incumbent upon God to allow him to enter Paradise whether he has emigrated in the way of God or remained in land of his birth" and "There is no *hijra* after the conquest [of Mecca]."[9] While Wansharīsī refutes these arguments over the course of his two texts, the suppression of this unnamed jurist's considered, evidence-based argument against emigration serves to maintain the fiction of a definitive juristic consensus on the prohibition of residence under non-Muslim rule. He further avoids reminding his audience of the first of these two *ḥadīth* reports, or acknowledging that in other circumstances a Muslim population had lived contentedly and securely under Christian rule.

Introduction to *Asnā al-matājir*: Destinations

Wansharīsī's first notable departure from Ibn Rabīʿ is his new introduction for *Asnā al-matājir*. While both jurists open with an unequivocal declaration that emigration from non-Muslim to Muslim territory is obligatory, Wansharīsī immediately complicates this obligation. Not content with "Muslim territory" as a single undifferentiated destination, he argues that Muslims are also obligated to emigrate from lands of oppression, *fitna*, injustice, and sin. Among the evidence he presents is a passage by Andalusī jurist Ibn al-ʿArabī,[10] who poses and then responds to the objection that there may be no land free from these vices:

> If one were to object, "What if no place can be found other than one like that [where truth does not prevail]?" We would respond that one should choose the least sinful place. For example, if a region contains unbelief, then a region containing injustice is better than that. Or if a region contains justice along with the forbidden (*al-ḥarām*), then a region containing injustice along with the permitted (*al-ḥalāl*) is better than that for residence. Or, if there are transgressions of God's rights in one region, then that is preferable to a region with transgressions against men . . . ʿUmar b. ʿAbd al-ʿAzīz [r. 99–101/717–20] (may God be pleased with him) has said, "So-and-so is in Medina, so-and-so is in Mecca, so-and-so is in Yemen, and so-and-so is in Syria; by God, the earth is filled with injustice and oppression."[11]

9 The first *ḥadīth* ("whoever believes") can be found in *Ṣaḥīḥ al-Bukhārī*, *Kitāb al-Tawḥīd*, *bāb* "*wa-kāna ʿarshuh ʿalā al-māʾ*," *ḥadīth* 6987 (Bukhārī, *Ṣaḥīḥ al-Bukhārī*, 6:2700). The second *ḥadīth* ("no *hijra*") will be discussed below.

10 Abū Bakr Muḥammad b. ʿAbd Allāh b. Muḥammad, known as Ibn al-ʿArabī (d. 543/1148), was a prominent Mālikī jurist from Seville. See *EI*², s.v. "Ibn al-ʿArabī" (J. Robson); Muṣṭafā Ibrāhīm al-Mashannī, *Ibn al-ʿArabī al-Mālikī al-Ishbīlī (468–543 AH) wa-tafsīruh Aḥkām al-Qurʾān* (Jordan: Dār ʿAmmār, 1990), 13–40.

11 See appendix B, 291–92, for notes. Wansharīsī, *al-Miʿyār*, 2:121; Ibn al-ʿArabī, *ʿĀriḍat al-aḥwadhī bi-sharḥ Ṣaḥīḥ al-Tirmidhī*, ed. Jamāl Marʿashlī, 13 vols. in 8 (Beirut: Dār al-Kutub al-ʿIlmiyya, 1997), 7:66 (vol. 7 is in physical vol. 4).

Why would Wansharīsī complicate matters with this classification of destinations based on the degree of sinfulness, so early in his *fatwā*? He likely did so in order to respond to both the specifics of Ibn Qaṭiyya's question and to the broader political context in Morocco. The regretful emigrants claimed that the Maghrib was an unworthy destination, one lacking in justice, security, hospitality, and prosperity. While later in his response Wansharīsī vigorously defends his homeland, here he seems to acknowledge its imperfections in order to stress that these material conditions are irrelevant to the obligation to emigrate. Even if the emigrants encountered rampant injustice and insecurity in the Maghrib, this would not diminish its superiority over Christian Iberia or their own legal obligations to leave Iberia.

Wansharīsī's introduction also reflects the uncertainty in Zayyātī's "jewels" regarding the legal designation of particular regions in Morocco. Regions under nominal Muslim control that paid tribute to Portugal, for example, might have been considered particularly corrupt Muslim territory rather than non-Muslim territory. Ibn al-ʿArabī's distinctions set a higher standard for emigration than just settling in a region that is convenient, but whose designation as Muslim territory is tenuous. In his formulation, a resident of a region clearly more corrupt and sinful than its neighbors must move to a more just—or, in Wansharīsī's context—a less ambiguously Muslim-controlled region.

Evidence from the Qurʾān

Following his introduction, Wansharīsī presents a dozen passages from the Qurʾān that command emigration or prohibit Muslims from forming alliances with Jews, Christians, or infidels. This section is largely taken from Ibn Rabīʿ's *fatwā*, although Wansharīsī rearranges the verses in order to foreground a passage addressing exemptions from the obligation to emigrate. He likely does this because of the questions at hand.

As noted in chapter 3, the people whose cases Ibn Qaṭiyya presents in his two questions challenge the obligation to emigrate in different ways. The man from Marbella acknowledges this obligation but desires a personal dispensation in order to mediate on behalf of a Mudéjar community. The regretful emigrants suggest that the obligation should be disregarded entirely if Muslims might experience greater material comfort and security in their conquered homelands than they would in *dār al-Islām*. Thus, in *Asnā al-matājir*, Wansharīsī refutes these claims at the outset, making clear that there is a single legitimate reason for a conquered Muslim not to emigrate: namely, his "total incapacity" to do so "by any means."[12]

12 Wansharīsī, *al-Miʿyār*, 2:121; appendix B, 292.

In support of his assertion that concern for one's homeland and material comfort are not valid considerations with regard to emigration, Wansharīsī cites Qur'ān 4:97–99:

> "Those whom the angels take in death while they are wronging themselves, the angels will say to them: 'In what circumstances were you?' They will say, 'We were abased in the earth.' The angels will say, 'Was God's earth not spacious enough for you to have migrated therein?' Hell will be the refuge for such men—a wretched end! [97] Except for the weak among men, women, and children, who are unable to devise a plan and are not shown a way; [98] as for these, perhaps God will pardon them. God is Most Clement, Oft Forgiving." [99]

This is the passage most often cited as evidence for the obligation to emigrate. In the long first verse, angels interrogate a number of people who claim to have been oppressed by the conditions in which they lived. The angels, who rebuff their claims to passive victimhood, chastise them for persisting under such conditions their whole lives instead of migrating elsewhere. We are told that their failure to acknowledge the earth's bounty and to improve their own conditions in this world will compound their misery in hell.

At this juncture in *Asnā al-matājir* Wansharīsī's task is to explain the legal import of the next two verses, which promise divine forgiveness to those who are truly incapable of emigrating. The Qur'ān contrasts those who falsely claim to be abased (*mustaḍʿafīn*) with those who are genuinely weak (also *mustaḍʿafīn*). For Wansharīsī, this latter category includes those who are very sick or very weak, captive or disabled, or simply powerless to find any means to emigrate. Their actions will be excused, as their legal status is equivalent to someone who is coerced into pronouncing words of unbelief. Later in *Asnā al-matājir*, Wansharīsī adds to this brief discussion on inability by clarifying that people who face substantial hardship at any stage of the journey, from finding the means of travel to experiencing poverty in a new land, remain capable of emigration.[13] In his Berber *fatwā*, Wansharīsī notes that those who would likely perish if they attempted the journey are among those excused from the obligation.[14]

Wansharīsī thus views *hijra* as an obligation of the utmost importance and urgency, one that requires more serious sacrifices and admits fewer exemptions than religious obligations such as the pilgrimage to Mecca or fasting in Ramadan. Yet his position is not as uncompromising as it has

13 Wansharīsī, *al-Miʿyār*, 2:132; appendix B, 313.
14 Appendix A, 277.

seemed to many observers.[15] He does not condemn or even disparage Muslims that he deems truly unable to leave their conquered homelands, and he notes their excused status very early in *Asnā al-matājir*.

Nonetheless, it is true that Wansharīsī dispatches the question of "ability" quickly, without dwelling on possible scenarios meriting exemption or grappling with the specifics of difficult cases. He does this by design; by presenting only capable Muslims, Ibn Qaṭiyya's questions conveniently relieve Wansharīsī of such a burden. We are told that the man from Marbella and most of those around him may emigrate anytime they wish, while the regretful emigrants noted in *Asnā al-matājir* appear unafraid of the enemy and quite capable of emigrating, such that they are eager to emigrate a second time, in reverse. Wansharīsī avoids more complicated cases, for example: what if the man from Marbella wanted to remain there in order care for his elderly parents, who were truly unable to leave Marbella? What if some of the regretful emigrants left wives and children at home, and they now wished to return to them? These are more difficult questions. As it is, Wansharīsī responded to a carefully curated set of circumstances that allowed him to focus almost entirely on the obligation for *capable* Muslims to emigrate.

The Qur'ānic verses cited in the remainder of this section of *Asnā al-matājir* are striking, because none of them, beyond Qur'ān 4:97–100, mention *hijra*. Instead, they prohibit alliances with "unbelievers," the "enemy," or "Jews and Christians."[16] The premise that these verses prohibit "harmonious coexistence" among Muslims and Christians is a misconception; in this instance, the word for "allies" (*awliyā'*) connotes political loyalty and military allegiance, not friendship or shared residence.[17] In this section, Wansharīsī argues that submission to non-Muslim political authority is the primary evil that renders it imperative to emigrate and makes his argument applicable to the Muslims he is addressing. While in Zayyātī's "jewels," political submission is associated with collaboration and treachery, in Wansharīsī's Iberian *fatwās* it is associated instead with disobedience to God and the disgrace of Islam; he avoids an overt political critique.

If there were any doubt that Wansharīsī is arguing specifically against Muslim submission to Christian rule, and not against all forms of shared

15 Abdel-Majid Turki, for example, described Wansharīsī as issuing a "fatwā pour taxer d'infidélité, de la manière la plus catégorique et dogmatique, tout musulman persistant à demeurer en Espagne après la chute de ce qui restait de l'Andalus entre les main des chrétiens." Turki, "Consultation," 6.

16 Aboobaker Asmal first made this point in "Muslims under Non-Muslim Rule," 203 and 213–14.

17 Kathryn Miller suggests that these verses, especially Qur'ān 5:51–52, "condemn harmonious coexistence—very much what some Spanish historians would idealize as *convivencia*—as an illness of the heart." Miller, *Guardians of Islam*, 39. Some English translations of the Qur'ān translate *awliyā'* (allies) as "friends."

residence or coexistence, his opening to the Marbella answer is clear and forceful in this regard:[18]

> Our one almighty God placed the poll tax (*jizya*) and abasement around the necks of the cursed infidels, as chains and shackles which they must drag about across the lands and in the major cities and towns, demonstrating the power of Islam and honoring its chosen prophet. Thus any Muslim . . . who attempts to invert these chains and fetters [by placing them] on his [own] neck has contravened God and His messenger . . . Living with infidels, without [their being] subject tributaries (*ahl al-dhimma*), is not permitted or allowed for even one hour of one day because of the pollution, the filth, and the religious and worldly corruptions to which this gives rise, throughout their lives.[19]

Wansharīsī describes Muslim political supremacy as the divinely ordained "natural order," one that is essential for Muslims to practice Islam properly. In the remainder of the Marbella *fatwā,* he seeks to demonstrate that Christian power pervades and corrupts every important aspect of Muslim life and practice. At the same time, Wansharīsī affirms the well-known and established Islamic legal principle that allows Jews and Christians to live as *dhimmī*s in submission to Muslim authority. As the tone of this passage suggests, his opinions regarding the implementation of the *dhimmī* pact appear to have been uncharitable and cruel, even for his time—but he does not challenge the theological or legal underpinnings of the general doctrine allowing Christians and Jews to live among Muslims as *dhimmīs*.[20]

Linking Lone Converts to Conquered Muslims

In a typical Islamic legal argument, Qur'ānic verses are followed directly by the relevant Ḥadīth reports, which are second only to the Qur'ān as the strongest textual evidence for juridical claims. While Ibn Rabīʿ adopts the expected order, Wansharīsī instead inserts a key precedent, one that concerns converts to Islam in *dār al-ḥarb*, between the evidence from the Qur'ān and Ḥadīth. The positioning of this precedent reflects its crucial importance to the logic and authority of Wansharīsī's overall argument.

---

18 Scholars have not always been careful to distinguish between Islamic doctrines regarding coexistence with Christians in general, and Muslims living under Christian rule specifically. Referring to the legal obligation to emigrate, María Jesús Rubiera Mata argued that Islam's prohibition on coexistence with Christians was one of the earliest Moriscos' most fundamental problems. Rubiera Mata, "Los moriscos," 537.

19 Wansharīsī, *al-Miʿyār*, 2:137–38; appendix C, 324–25.

20 Against many of his contemporary peers, Wansharīsī advocated the destruction of a synagogue in Tamanṭīṭ that he claimed violated a prohibition on constructing new *dhimmī* houses of worship. See Powers, "al-Wansharīsī," 382–99.

Wansharīsī relies on the testimony of Ibn Rushd al-Jadd, one of the most prominent jurists in the Mālikī tradition, to establish what I call the "lone convert" precedent.[21] Early Mālikī jurists considered the case of someone who converted to Islam in *dār al-ḥarb* and they determined that he must live in Muslim territory rather than remain among non-Muslims. Ibn Rushd al-Jadd asserts that "Emigration remains obligatory until the day of judgment" for these converts, "by virtue of the Book, the Sunna, and the consensus of the community."[22] A primary element of this scholarly consensus, grounded in views attributed to Mālik, is the conviction that Muslims must not be subject to non-Muslim laws. In the context of his work, Ibn Rushd al-Jadd builds on this precedent to argue that Muslims must not travel (even temporarily) to non-Muslim territory for the purpose of trade.[23] With regard to residing in a non-Muslim land for the long term, he remarks that only a Muslim diseased in faith could be content with this.

In *Asnā al-matājir*, Wansharīsī's first step toward claiming a scholarly consensus for the obligation of conquered Muslims to emigrate involves presenting the lone convert's obligation to emigrate as an unassailable precedent. Simply stated, he draws an analogy between these two cases, arguing that the same rule should be applied to both because they share a key element; namely, Muslims who find themselves living under non-Muslim rule. In reality, Wansharīsī works hard to avoid the appearance of using analogical reasoning, or *qiyās*, to extend the rule established for the lone covert to the case of conquered Muslims. *Qiyās* is the technical legal term for a form of independent reasoning (*ijtihād*) subject to particular constraints. One such constraint relates to which rules can be extended to new cases—only rules that have been established and explained in clear scriptural proof texts or, more rarely, through scholarly consensus, can be used. Thus, a rule derived through juristic reasoning—such as the rule for the lone convert—may not be extended to a new case by means of *qiyās*.

Wansharīsī is at pains to present the lone convert and the conquered Muslim not as two different cases, but as two "manifestations" of a single case: that of Muslims who willingly remain under non-Muslim rule. He states that the earliest jurists chose to use only one of these two manifestations as an illustrative example in their discussions, but adds that their conclusions

21 Abū al-Walīd Muḥammad Ibn Rushd al-Jadd, grandfather ("*al-jadd*") of the Ibn Rushd known to the West as Averroes, served as chief judge of Córdoba under Almoravid ruler ʿAlī b. Yūsuf b. Tāshufīn (r. 500–537/1106–43). See Delfina Serrano Ruano, "Ibn Rushd al-Jadd (d. 520/1126)," in *Islamic Legal Thought*, ed. Oussama Arabi, 295–322 (Leiden: Brill, 2013).

22 Wansharīsī, *al-Miʿyār*, 2:124; appendix B, 296–97. Wansharīsī is quoting from *al-Muqaddimāt al-mumahhidāt*, Ibn Rushd al-Jadd's commentary on *al-Mudawwana*.

23 See Hendrickson, "Is al-Andalus Different?," for the views of Mālikī scholars, including Ibn Rushd al-Jadd, on trading with the enemy.

nonetheless apply to all instances of the general case. Wansharīsī argues that those early masters could not have been expected to address conquered Muslims explicitly, because this scenario arose for the first time after the conquests of Sicily and parts of al-Andalus in the fifth century (eleventh century CE). When they needed a rule for conquered Muslims, jurists at that time assimilated this new question to the case of the lone converts, as they considered the new case to be completely equivalent, in the eyes of the law, to the existing case.

Wansharīsī does not offer names, but assures readers that these eleventh-century jurists exerted a minimum of independent intellectual effort (*ijtihād*) and exhibited a maximum of deference for precedent. He thus projects his desired rule for conquered Muslims onto the earliest plausible jurists, while simultaneously eliding their identities in order to trace the real origins of this rule back to the "great masters," the founding figures of the major legal schools. Wansharīsī avoids having to defend an illegitimate form of *qiyās*, and further denies conducting any new legal thinking, regardless of whether or not it was performed legitimately.

By introducing passages from Ibn Rushd al-Jadd that are not present in Ibn Rabīʿ's *fatwa*, Wansharīsī may have intended to make two additional points that are specifically relevant to his contemporary Maghribī context. First, Ibn Rushd al-Jadd's condemnation of trading in *dār al-ḥarb* aligns well with the concerns articulated in most of Zayyātī's "jewels." In his Berber *fatwā*, Wansharīsī was so concerned with trade that he called for manned roadblocks to prevent access to Christian-controlled territories. Second, perhaps to soften the impact of Ibn Rushd al-Jadd's forceful rhetoric, Wansharīsī notes that emigrants may return to their homelands if, or when, these lands revert to Muslim territory. This possibility was not worth mentioning in relation to al-Andalus just before the fall of Granada, but Maghribīs who were waging regular campaigns to recover territory conquered by the Portuguese harbored realistic hopes of returning home.

Evidence from the *Ḥadīth*

Wansharīsī treats only four *ḥadīth* reports, one of which appears to nullify the obligation to emigrate and which therefore makes this section of *Asnā al-matājir* much more complex. Ibn Rabīʿ addressed only two of these *ḥadīths*, and omitted mention of the "no *hijra* after the conquest [of Mecca]" tradition even though his questioner, as noted, asked him directly about its relevance to Mudéjars. While Wansharīsī's maneuvering is far from transparent, I suggest that his introduction of substantial new material in this section is meant to further three goals: to reconcile the "no *hijra*" *ḥadīth* with the continued obligation to emigrate; to address the Companions' *hijra* to Christian-ruled Abyssinia; and to emphasize the importance of *jihād*. Wansharīsī accomplishes these aims by juxtaposing key passages from two earlier authorities.

The initial portion of Wansharīsī's *ḥadīth* section, borrowed from Ibn Rabīʿ, presents two *ḥadīths* to support the obligation to emigrate. In the first report, a group of converts were killed by a Muslim raiding expedition. Although the converts prostrated in an attempt to indicate that they had converted and protect their lives, the attacking party did not understand the meaning of their actions. Muḥammad ordered that only half the customary blood money be paid as compensation for the accidental killing of Muslims, and explained "I am not responsible for any Muslim who lives among the polytheists."[24] In the second *ḥadīth*, which closely resembles Qurʾān 5:51, Muḥammad instructs his followers not to live among polytheists, for "whoever lives among them or associates with them, is one of them."[25] For Ibn Rabīʿ and Wansharīsī, these two *ḥadīths* establish a clear and obvious obligation for Muslims to live among Muslims, clearly separate from polytheists.

Wansharīsī then cites a pair of *ḥadīth* reports that appear to be contradictory, and along with them he offers two explanations, which are also somewhat contradictory, of how to reconcile the *ḥadīths*. In the first *ḥadīth*, Muḥammad proclaims "the duty to emigrate will not cease until repentance ceases; and repentance will not cease until the sun rises in the West."[26] In the second, he states, "there is no *hijra* after the conquest [of Mecca], but there [remains the obligation of] *jihād* and [correct] intention; so if you are summoned to battle, then go forth."[27]

---

24 *Sunan al-Tirmidhī, Abwāb al-Siyar, bāb mā jāʾa fī karāhiyyat al-muqām bayna aẓhur al-mushrikīn, ḥadīth* 1709, in Muḥammad b. ʿĪsā al-Tirmidhī, *Sunan al-Tirmidhī wa-huwa al-Jāmiʿ al-Kabīr*, ed. Markaz al-Buḥūth wa-Taqniyat al-Maʿlūmāt (Cairo: Dār al-Taʾṣīl, 2016), 2:601; *Sunan Abī Dāwūd, Kitāb al-Jihād, bāb al-nahy ʿan qatl man iʿtaṣama biʾl-sujūd, ḥadīth* 2645, in Sulaymān al-Azdī al-Sijistānī Abū Dāwūd, *Sunan Abī Dāwūd*, ed. Shuʿayb al-Arnaʾūṭ and Muḥammad Kāmil Qurrah Balalī (Damascus: Dār al-Risāla al-ʿĀlamiyya, 2009), 4:280–83; *Nasāʾī (Kitāb al-Sunan al-Kubrā), Kitāb al-Qasāma, bāb al-qawd bi-ghayr ḥadīda, ḥadīth* 6956, in Aḥmad b. Shuʿayb al-Nasāʾī, *Kitāb al-Sunan al-Kubrā*, ed. Ḥasan ʿAbd al-Munʿim Shalabī and Shuʿayb al-Arnaʾūṭ (Beirut: Muʾassasat al-Risāla, 2001), 6:347–48. Ibn al-ʿArabī discusses this *ḥadīth* in *ʿĀriḍat al-aḥwadhī*, 7:78–79.

25 *Sunan al-Tirmidhī, Abwāb al-Siyar, bāb mā jāʾa fī karāhiyyat al-muqām bayna aẓhur al-mushrikīn, ḥadīth* 1710 (Tirmidhī, *Sunan al-Tirmidhī*, 2:602); *Sunan Abī Dāwūd, Kitāb al-Jihād, bāb fī al-iqāma bi-arḍ al-shirk, ḥadīth* 2787 (Abū Dāwūd, *Sunan Abī Dāwūd*, 4:413–14).

26 *Sunan Abī Dāwūd, Kitāb al-Jihād, bāb fī al-hijra, hal inqaṭaʿat?, ḥadīth* 2479 (Abū Dāwūd, *Sunan Abī Dāwūd*, 4:136).

27 *Ṣaḥīḥ al-Bukhārī, Kitāb al-Jihād waʾl-siyar, bāb faḍl al-jihād waʾl-siyar, ḥadīth* 2631 (Bukhārī, *Ṣaḥīḥ al-Bukhārī*, 3:1025); *Ṣaḥīḥ al-Bukhārī, Kitāb al-Jihād waʾl-siyar, bāb wujūb al-nafīr . . . , ḥadīth* 2670 (Bukhārī, *Ṣaḥīḥ al-Bukhārī*, 3:1040); *Ṣaḥīḥ Muslim, Kitāb al-Imāra, bāb al-mubāyaʿa baʿd fatḥ Makka . . . , ḥadīth* 86, in Muslim b. al-Ḥajjāj al-Qushayrī al-Nīsābūrī, *Ṣaḥīḥ Muslim*, ed. Muḥammad Fuʾād ʿAbd al-Bāqī (Beirut: Dār Iḥyāʾ al-Kutub al-ʿArabiyya,

This section of Wansharīsī's text presents a number of puzzles, including: Why introduce these two *ḥadīths* at all? The most straightforward explanation is that Wansharīsī felt compelled to repudiate the use of the "no *hijra*" *ḥadīth* as counter-evidence against the obligation to emigrate. Although Wansharīsī does not mention a contemporary adversary akin to the anonymous jurist in Ibn Rabīʿ's question, similar arguments may well have been circulating in his time. To admit that such arguments had currency would undermine Wansharīsī's claim of scholarly consensus regarding emigration; instead, he treats the problem of the "no *hijra*" *ḥadīth* by explaining its relationship to the "does not cease" *ḥadīth*.

The first method of reconciling these two *ḥadīths* is that of Abū Sulaymān al-Khaṭṭābī (d. 386/996 or 388/998), who assigns them to two distinct *hijras*. The *hijra* that "does not cease" is the one enjoined by Qurʾān 4:100, revealed when polytheist Meccan persecution of the earliest Muslims had begun to intensify. In this period, a number of Companions took refuge in Christian-ruled Abyssinia, although Khaṭṭābī does not refer explicitly to this event. This first *hijra* was recommended only, but after Muḥammad performed his own *hijra* from Mecca to Medina (in 622 CE), all Muslims were required to join him in Medina. This obligatory *hijra*, the one addressed in the "no *hijra*" *ḥadīth*, ceased to be compulsory following the conquest of Mecca (630 CE). According to Khaṭṭābī, the first *hijra* endures as a recommended or desirable duty.

Wansharīsī partially undermines this explanation by introducing a second method of reconciling the "no *hijra*" *ḥadīth* with the *ḥadīth* of the enduring obligation to emigrate. Adapting a commentary on this *ḥadīth* by Ibn al-ʿArabī (also quoted above), Wansharīsī presents not two, but three forms of *hijra*: that of the Prophet and his Companions, motivated by fear for their religion and lives; the *hijra* of the Companions to join Muḥammad in Medina; and emigration from *dār al-ḥarb* to *dār al-Islām*. In this formulation the first two *hijra*s were obligatory, and came to an end with the conquest of Mecca. The third type endures and "remains obligatory until the day of judgment."[28]

Of these two approaches, Ibn al-ʿArabī's typology was clearly better suited to Wansharīsī's argument. Only this third type of *hijra* assigns conquered Muslims an enduring obligation to leave their homelands for Muslim territory. Why, then, does Wansharīsī devote substantial space to Khaṭṭābī's interpretation? He must have intended to use Ibn al-ʿArabī's

---

1991), 3:1488; *Sunan al-Tirmidhī, Abwāb al-Siyar, bāb mā jāʾa fī al-hijra, ḥadīth* 1693 (Tirmidhī, *Sunan al-Tirmidhī*, 2:595). On these traditions and others related to *hijra* in early Islam, see Patricia Crone, "The First-Century Concept of Hijra," *Arabica* 41, no. 3 (1994): 352–87.

28 Appendix B, 302. Wansharīsī is quoting Ibn al-ʿArabī in this passage.

commentary to refute aspects of Khaṭṭābī's presentation, which might have been a well-known or attractive way of reconciling these two *ḥadīths*. Beyond confirming the *hijra* from infidel to Muslim territory as both obligatory and enduring, two additional arguments are implicit in Wansharīsī's endorsement of Ibn al-ʿArabī's model over that of Khaṭṭābī.

First, Khaṭṭābī's enduring form of *hijra* was not just recommended, but characterized by fear for one's religion and one's life. By rejecting this type of enduring *hijra* in favor of one based on territorial affiliation, Wansharīsī effectively asserts that the *hijra* based on territorial affiliation is not conditional upon threats to religion or life. Such threats, while important to Wansharīsī, are relegated to the Marbella *fatwā*; the message in *Asnā al-matājir* is that emigration from infidel to Muslim territory is an independent obligation in and of itself. Conquered Muslims may not protest emigration on account of their perceived security or ability to openly practice their religion. Their obligation is not conditional on insecurity at home any more than it is on the promise of security or wealth in *dār al-Islām*.

Second, the rejection of Khaṭṭābī's account places the Abyssinian model of emigration firmly in the past. This model, according to which prominent Companions were granted asylum and were respected by the Christian king of Abyssinia (modern-day Ethiopia) in the years prior to Muḥammad's *hijra*, is now commonly used by those seeking early Islamic sanction for Muslims to reside in Christian-majority countries. Indeed, Muʾnis finds Wansharīsī's later invocation of this precedent hypocritical, given that it casts Muslim residence under Christian rule in a favorable light.[29] Yet here Wansharīsī appears to leverage Ibn al-ʿArabī's typology to argue that this type of *hijra* only existed prior to the conquest of Mecca and the rise of Muslim power in 630. Wansharīsī is free to praise the sacrifices and correct intentions of these early Companions while confining the inconvenient aspects of their precedent to a bygone era under the authority of the "no *hijra*" *ḥadīth*.

Wansharīsī's decision to quote this *ḥadīth* in full is the final notable element of his *ḥadīth* section. The second half of the "no *hijra*" *ḥadīth*, which emphasizes *jihād* as a continuing obligation, does not appear in Ibn Rabīʿ's *fatwā*, even in the question component. Yet this is Wansharīsī's second citation of the full *ḥadīth*; the first appeared in Ibn al-ʿArabī's passage ranking emigrants' destinations. Wansharīsī does not elaborate on the importance of *jihād* here, but even these brief mentions reinforce a recurring theme in *Asnā al-matājir*, a theme that likely had a far greater resonance in his contemporary Maghribī context than in the Mudéjar context.

29 Muʾnis, "Asnā al-matājir," 8.

Inviolability of Muslims' Lives and Property

The added emphasis on *jihād* in *Asnā al-matājir*, in comparison with Ibn Rabīʿ's *fatwā*, is the most striking feature of Wansharīsī's next section, which is a review of legal opinions regarding the lives and property of Muslims residing in *dār al-ḥarb*. In this section he addresses a well-known point of disagreement between the major law schools as well as within the Mālikī school: Is it the profession of Islam or one's presence in Muslim territory that guarantees the inviolability of a person's life and property? In Ibn Rabīʿ's *fatwā*, this discussion ultimately reinforces the obligation to emigrate by showing that residence in enemy territory is not only sinful, but also carries substantial legal repercussions that may extend to the forfeiture of one's most basic entitlements as a member of the *umma* (Muslim community). In *Asnā al-matājir*, Wansharīsī's enhanced version of this section adapts the material to the Maghribī context by emphasizing the consequences of Muslims living in enemy territory during periods of active or potential armed conflict.

In the portion of this section largely shared with Ibn Rabīʿ, Wansharīsī reviews the positions of Mālik, Shāfiʿī, Abū Ḥanīfa, and several Mālikī scholars. In brief, Mālik and Abū Ḥanīfa held that Islam guarantees the inviolability of a Muslim's life, but not his property, which is only protected if he brings it to *dār al-Islām* and establishes ownership of it there.[30] Abū Ḥanīfa qualified this position with the caveat that the accidental killing of a Muslim in *dār al-ḥarb* necessitates atonement rather than the payment of blood money. Among Mālikī jurists, Ashhab (d. 204/819), Saḥnūn (d. 240/854), and Ibn al-ʿArabī all agreed with Shāfiʿī, who held that a Muslim's life and property are both inviolable, even in *dār al-ḥarb*. In contrast, Aṣbagh b. al-Faraj (d. 225/840) and Ibn Rushd al-Jadd agreed with the position attributed to Mālik.

These early jurists (with the exception of Ibn al-ʿArabī) presumed that the Muslim under discussion was a lone convert to Islam residing outside Muslim territory, or perhaps a Muslim who had entered *dār al-ḥarb* temporarily. As earlier in *Asnā al-matājir*, Wansharīsī states that later jurists—those who first encountered the problem of conquered Muslims—applied these rules and points of legitimate disagreement first articulated with regard to lone Muslims, to the case of conquered Muslims, with one notable exception. Abū ʿAbd Allāh b. al-Ḥājj (d. 529/1134), a Mālikī judge in Córdoba, recognized a legally significant distinction between lone converts and conquered Muslims with regard to property rights. He

30 Here and elsewhere, my use of the male pronoun reflects the usage of my source materials. The default subject of premodern Islamic legal texts is the healthy, sane, adult, free male Muslim. Rules and considerations that apply to other groups, including women, are specifically noted as such.

held that conquered Muslims should retain the full property rights they enjoyed prior to conquest, because they had always been Muslims resident in Muslim territory. In contrast, for lone converts a period of unbelief had once rendered their property licit to Muslims.

Wansharīsī's inclusion of Ibn al-Ḥājj's opinion is somewhat surprising, as it challenges his earlier suggestion that later Mālikī jurists were unanimous in conflating the case of conquered Muslims with that of lone converts. Yet Wansharīsī not only identifies Ibn al-Ḥājj (while Ibn Rabīʿ had not), but he also introduces a key precedent used by Ibn al-Ḥājj as evidence for his views. Wansharīsī conveys the opinion offered by Mālik's most prominent Egyptian disciple, Ibn al-Qāsim (d. 191/806–7), in response to a question posed by Córdoban jurist Yaḥyā b. Yaḥyā al-Laythī (d. 234/848) regarding the status of the Muslims who remained in Barcelona following its conquest in 185/801.[31] These Muslims failed to emigrate during the one-year grace period set by their conquerors, then joined their Christian overlords and fought other Muslims, out of fear that they would be killed if Muslims recovered the city. According to Ibn al-Qāsim, these Muslims are equivalent in status to bandits or rebels, because they remain Muslim; they should be referred to the ruler for punishment, and their property is not licit. For Ibn al-Ḥājj, if property rights are retained even by conquered Muslims who fight for the enemy, then surely those whose only offense is residing under Christian rule retain their property rights as well.

This position is clearly at odds with those of Wansharīsī and his contemporaries with regard to Muslims who fight with the enemy against fellow Muslims in Portuguese-occupied Morocco. It quickly becomes clear that Wansharīsī presents Ibn al-Ḥājj's divergent opinion in order to refute it, and to exploit the case of Barcelona as an example of the problems posed by and for Muslims who remain commingled with the enemy. As a counter to Ibn al-Ḥājj, Wansharīsī cites Ibn Rushd al-Jadd's commentary on the exchange above. According to Ibn Rushd al-Jadd, Ibn al-Qāsim's position regarding the Barcelonan Muslims' property "is in clear contradiction to Mālik's opinion," which is that a lone convert's property and family are legitimate booty for an invading Muslim army.

Nearly all of the new material in the section on inviolability in *Asnā al-matājir* shares this emphasis on the consequences of remaining in *dār al-ḥarb* during a time of conflict. The Barcelona example serves as a bookend to a section that opens with two new passages from the works of Ibn al-ʿArabī that address two *ḥadīth*s related to the inviolability of converts. In both cases (that of the Banū Jadhīma—mentioned here for the second time—and that of Khathʿam), converts remaining among non-Muslims were killed accidentally

31 For notes on these figures and the source, see appendix B, 309–11.

by invading Muslims. Together, these passages must have served as a warning to Wansharīsī's Moroccan audiences (the jurists and the lay communities they advised) that fighters are not necessarily responsible for distinguishing Muslims from non-Muslims in the heat of battle.

Wansharīsī's conclusion to this section is also well adapted to his context of foreign occupation of parts of the Maghrib. He first reasserts the equivalence between lone converts and conquered Muslims, and then reaffirms the existence of legitimate scholarly disagreements regarding the inviolability of these Muslims' lives and property. While these first two points might make sense for the Iberian context, with his final points Wansharīsī moves decisively toward the rhetoric associated with contemporary *fatwās* on Muslim cooperation with the Portuguese. If converted or conquered Muslims fight for the enemy, he notes, the scope of juristic discretion related to the issue of their residence no longer applies—at that point, jurists must agree with the preponderant opinion that the lives of these Muslims are licit. Likewise, if these Muslims render material aid to the enemy, the opinion that their property is licit must be considered preponderant. Wansharīsī's most definitive and severe conclusion is that the preponderant opinion regarding these Muslims' children, even in cases of residence and not physical support of enemies, is that they should be captured and raised among Muslims, "safe from religious corruption and protected from the sin of abandoning emigration."[32] This last position is reminiscent of Waryāglī's views concerning the wives of Muslims living under non-Muslim rule. The prospect of Muslim fighters capturing the wives or children of Muslims who reside in enemy territory and returning with them to *dār al-Islām* may have been seen as an idle threat, but surely one that was more plausible in the Maghrib than in Iberia in the late fifteenth century.

It is worth noting that ultimately, Wansharīsī does not endorse a position on the property rights of Muslims whose only offense is residence in non-Muslim territory. While he appears to lean toward Ibn Rushd al-Jadd, who held that their property is licit, Wansharīsī also relies heavily on the opinions of Ibn al-ʿArabī, who disagreed. Wansharīsī instructs his readers to consider the various opinions adopted by past authorities. For his purposes, this is sufficient. To bolster the case for emigration, Wansharīsī only needs to demonstrate that the legitimate range of scholarly opinions on this issue includes the position that Muslims in *dār al-ḥarb* have no established property rights.[33] Leaving these rights as an open question

32 Wansharīsī, *al-Miʿyār*, 2:130; appendix B, 310–12.

33 Some scholars have assumed that Wansharīsī endorsed Mālik's position unequivocally, or that the loss of property rights for Muslims in enemy territory was meant as a form of punishment, or both. See, for example, Maíllo Salgado, "Del Islam residual," 136. In discussing property rights, Wansharīsī does not employ the language of punishment. Fritz Meier's

further allows Wansharīsī to distinguish between an area of legitimate debate and those matters that are *not* open to debate. And among those not open to debate, he includes the obligation to emigrate, the forfeiture of inviolability for Muslims who actively assist the enemy in fighting Muslims, and the recognition that Muslim invaders cannot be expected to protect Muslims living in enemy territory. Wansharīsī's adaptations to this section of Ibn Rabī'ʿs *fatwā* suggest that he found these latter concerns, all relevant to the active military conflict, both serious and pressing.

Andalusī Emigrants: Worldly Punishment

In the final third of *Asnā al-matājir*, Wansharīsī turns to the specifics of the case at hand. He denounces the claims of the regretful Andalusīs, identifies their offenses, and addresses the consequences of their actions in this life and the next. Wansharīsī devotes two distinct sections to these consequences, the first one devoted to the emigrants' worldly punishments and changes to their legal status, and the second devoted to their probable fate in the hereafter. As Wansharīsī's comments in the first of these two sections (on worldly punishments) have been crucial to understanding his motives and intended audiences, I have addressed much of this material above, and therefore only summarize it here.

Wansharīsī adopted a three-pronged approach to denouncing the emigrants' claim that they should have been exempt from the obligation to emigrate and should be allowed to return to Castile under Christian rule because of their impoverished condition in the Maghrib. He emphasizes that poverty has no legal relevance to the obligation to emigrate. Here he revisits the Qur'ānic exemption for those truly incapable of emigration and reiterates the failure of these Andalusīs to qualify for such a dispensation (*rukhṣa*). Wansharīsī further stresses the necessity of prioritizing religious matters over worldly concerns. And he praises the sacrifices made by those early Companions who fled to Abyssinia prior to Muḥammad's *hijra*. Lastly, he invokes the Qur'ānic assertion that the earth is spacious and vigorously defends the Maghrib in particular as a land of plenty. This passage, following an assertion that emigrants in general will find bounty and sustenance, is striking for what we might call its patriotism, which he presents by personifying the Maghrib:

> [This is] especially [true] in this devout Maghribī region (may God preserve it, increase its honor and nobility, and protect it from the

suggestion that these deliberations reflect practical military concerns is more accurate. See Meier, "Über die umstrittene Pflicht des Muslims, bei nichtmuslimischer Besetzung seines Landes auszuwandern," *Der Islam* 68 (1991), 70.

> vicissitudes of fortune and sorrow, from its center to its frontier), for its soil is among the most fertile on God's earth, and its lands among the most spacious in length and breadth, especially the city of Fez and its jurisdiction, its districts, and the regions surrounding it in every direction.[34]

Although we normally find praise and supplications for a ruler or patron in the opening or colophon to a legal text, Wansharīsī inserts his effusive praise for his adopted homeland in a rather unusual place, in the midst of a legal argument. This sentiment is part of Wansharīsī's overall strategy to suppress the more overt political critique of Zayyātī's "jewels" and replace it with the more subtle, veiled criticism we find in *Asnā al-matājir* and the Marbella *fatwā*. While he seems unable to muster any kind words for Waṭṭāsid sultan Muḥammad al-Shaykh, who had just renewed a long-term treaty with Portugal, here Wansharīsī nonetheless does not criticize his ruler and appears grateful for the refuge and status granted to him in the Waṭṭāsid capital. Moreover, his personification of and supplications for the "devout" Maghrib from "center to frontier" offer no hint of the apostasy and treachery with which Wansharīsī had recently charged his fellow Maghribīs in the Berber *fatwā*. Instead, Wansharīsī's criticism is deflected toward the Andalusīs, who serve as the only Muslim agents of corruption and treachery in these two later *fatwās*.

As elaborated in chapter 3, the spread of dangerous, corrupting ideas (*fitna*) is foremost among the offenses of the Andalusīs in *Asnā al-matājir*. In addition to the disparaging public statements noted earlier, their transgressions (against God and the public order) include the prioritization of worldly concerns over religion, their preference to submit to infidels, their rejection of *hijra*, reliance on infidels, willingness to pay the *jizya* to non-Muslims, and as a result of all this, the degradation of Islam. As many of these trangressions are mental dispositions or attitudes, this list indicates what Wansharīsī feared might seduce a Maghribī audience and threaten Muslim sovereignty in Morocco, if the emigrants' actions were left unchecked and unpunished.

For Wansharīsī, the most important worldly consequence of the offenses of the regretful Andalusīs is the exemplary, severe physical punishment and imprisonment he prescribes for them. As I argued in chapter 4, in the emigrants' Moroccan context, this exemplary punishment was meant as a deterrent to any Maghribīs who might be susceptible to these Andalusīs' ideas, especially their preference for Christian rule. Furthermore, it was meant as a warning to those Maghribīs already cooperating with the

34 Wansharīsī, *al-Mi'yār*, 2:131; appendix B, 312.

Portuguese. In addition to recommending punishment for these specific Andalusīs, Wansharīsī also notes that Muslims who refuse to emigrate, return to live under infidel rule, or desire such a return, thereby lose their legal credibility. These Muslims may not serve as judges, witnesses, or prayer leaders, nor may they occupy any other religious offices requiring probity and credibility.

Mudéjar Judges and Māzarī

Near the end of his section on the worldly consequences of the Andalusī emigrants' actions, Wansharīsī turns his attention to an additional legal issue, namely, whether or not legal documents certified by judges serving under non-Muslim rule are admissible or valid in the land of Islam (*dār al-Islām*).[35] In the academic literature on *Asnā al-matājir*, this has been one of the most discussed, but least understood, portions of the text. Though it is not long, this section is important for a number of reasons. With regard to this matter, Wansharīsī departs completely from Ibn Rabī''s template, rejects his predecessor's section on lay Muslims' probity, and composes a new section focused instead on the validity of the attestations of judges with Mudéjar or equivalent status. Given that neither Ibn Rabī' nor Ibn Qaṭiyya mentions this issue, we can conclude that Wansharīsī's independent, unsolicited foray into this subject means that the question of whether or not to honor these documents as legally valid within *dār al-Islām* was of special concern and relevance in his time. Further, this section's central precedent, a *fatwā* issued by (Imām) Abū ʿAbd Allāh Muḥammad al-Māzarī (d. 536/1141), is the longest acknowledged citation in *Asnā al-matājir*. Despite the clear importance Wansharīsī attached to it, modern commentators have often construed Māzarī's *fatwā* as a foreign element in *Asnā al-matājir*, a lenient voice at odds with the remainder of the text.

Here I argue that it is necessary to read this section on judges in general, and Māzarī's *fatwā* in particular, in the same manner that we should read *Asnā al-matājir*: in its North African context. Scholars have seen Māzarī's *fatwā* as opposed to that of Wansharīsī because they approach it as a text fundamentally concerned with Muslims living under Christian rule in Europe. That is, modern scholars have read this text through the same Euro- and Ibero-centric lenses that have dominated scholarship on *Asnā al-matājir* and the Marbella *fatwā*. If, instead, we read Māzarī's opinion in its North African context, as I show below, it becomes evident that this text

35 The expression used most often here and elsewhere is *khiṭāb al-qāḍī*. The editor of Wazzānī's *al-Miʿyār al-jadīd* (3:32 n. 1) defines this as a written document sent by a judge in one region to a judge in another region, attesting to the validity of notarized documents or of

is fundamentally concerned with the adjudication of the rights of Muslims in North Africa, especially with regard to immigrants. This approach allows us to understand why Wansharīsī chose to showcase Māzarī's opinion to the exclusion of other available precedents. I argue that both jurists ultimately believe that the attestations of judges serving under Christian rule should be accepted in North Africa; yet, they do so reluctantly, as a necessary practical accommodation of legal realities that are at odds with their ideals concerning Muslim-Christian relationships.

In this section, Wansharīsī cites five precedents related to judges, three that directly address the validity of their attestations in *dār al-Islām*, followed by two that concern judges' acceptance of appointments by unjust rulers. Taken together, this collection of precedents presents us with another of *Asnā al-matājir*'s many puzzles, as each one pulls us in a different direction from the last. For example, the two final precedents that relate to appointments by unjust rulers are at odds with one another. In the first, Mālik resolves a dispute by confirming that judges must not accept appointments made by unjust rulers. In the second, the Tunisian jurist Ibn ʿArafa (d. 803/1401) states that if a judge is appointed by a usurper, Mālikī jurists should not hold this against him, because judicial affairs must not be disrupted.[36] Wansharīsī does not attempt to reconcile these two precedents, although we are clearly meant to understand that the category of "unjust" rulers includes all non-Muslim rulers, even if it is not limited to them.

One key to solving this particular puzzle, I argue, is to recognize two basic problems that underlie Māzarī's *fatwā* and this section of *Asnā al-matājir* as a whole. The first, larger problem exists between the ideal that all Muslims should live under Muslim rule (and that any conquered Muslims would be able and willing to emigrate) and the reality of continued Muslim residence in *dār al-ḥarb*. The second problem exists between the general rule that voluntary residence or travel in *dār al-ḥarb* renders a Muslim's testimony and judgments invalid and the imperative to maintain the rule of law and administration of justice. In the case of the two precedents just cited, I suggest that Wansharīsī is not just pointing to an area of legitimate scholarly disagreement, but that he is also affirming the ideal position (that Muslim judges should never have to accept appointments from unjust rulers), while

individuals' rights that have been verified before the first judge and that require recognition in the recipient judge's jurisdiction. Wiegers (*Islamic Literature*, 86–87) translates the same term as "homologation," or a court's confirmation or ratification of a document. Wansharīsī devotes a lengthy section of the *Miʿyār* (10:60–76) to the various conventions according to which judges sent opinions and documents to one another. A section on *khiṭāb al-qāḍī* is also normally treated in works of *adab al-qāḍī* (or *adab al-qaḍāʾ*), which treat the professional standards and practices of judging.

36 Wansharīsī, *al-Miʿyār*, 2:134; appendix B, 319.

simultaneously acknowledging the reality (that the continuance of justice requires that some judges to do just that).

The three conflicting precedents that Wansharīsī cites regarding the admissibility of judges' attestations may be explained with reference to these same problems. The first and third statements, both short, support the view that attestations provided by judges in non-Muslim or rebel territory are not admissible. Curiously, the first is by Ibn ʿArafa, the same jurist whom Wansharīsī subsequently cites as recognizing the need for judges to accept appointments from unjust rulers. In this case, Ibn ʿArafa offers the general rule that "the acceptance of a judge's attestation is conditional upon the validity of his appointment by someone who is demonstrably entitled to appoint him."[37] Jurists in Ifrīqiyā (modern-day Tunisia), he states, should therefore treat any written communications coming from Mudéjar judges cautiously. The other precedent favoring the rejection of attestations consists of a *fatwā* issued by some Andalusī jurists regarding those Muslims living under the authority of ʿUmar b. Ḥafṣūn (d. 305/918), an accused apostate who led a rebellion against the Umayyads of Córdoba in 267/880. These unnamed jurists rejected the testimony of such Muslims and the attestations of their judges.

Wansharīsī presents these two precedents before and after Māzarī's *fatwā*, which supports the general rule that voluntary residence under Christian rule invalidates both the testimony of Muslim witnesses and the attestations of their judges. Yet the question posed to Māzarī was designed to elicit need-based exceptions and pragmatic qualifications to this general rule, and he obliged in this. The broad historical context for this undated question is the Norman conquest of Sicily, which took place during the first thirty years (453–483/1061–91) of Māzarī's life (453–536/1061–1141). Muslims ruled Sicily for about two centuries (ca. 212–453/827–1061); this was followed by a gradual conquest that brought substantial Muslim communities under Christian rule, and also meant that close familial and trade relationships with Zīrid Ifrīqiyā continued. Māzarī, the leading jurist of his time, left a sizeable body of *fatwā*s that sheds light on these relationships and on the political and economic circumstances of Muslims in Norman Sicily and Zīrid Ifrīqiyā (362–543/973–1148).[38]

---

37 Wansharīsī, *al-Miʿyār*, 2:133; appendix B, 315.

38 On Māzarī, see Ḥasan Ḥusnī ʿAbd al-Wahhāb, *Kitāb al-ʿUmr fī al-muṣannifāt waʾl-muʾallifīn al-Tūnisiyyīn*, ed. Muḥammad al-ʿArūsī al-Maṭwī and Bashīr al-Bakkūsh (Beirut: Dār al-Gharb al-Islāmī, 1990), 1:696–704; Ibn Farḥūn, *al-Dībāj al-mudhahhab fī maʿrifat aʿyān ʿulamāʾ al-madhhab*, ed. Maʿmūn b. Muḥyī al-Dīn al-Jannān (Beirut: Dār al-Kutub al-ʿIlmiyya, 1996), 374–75; Makhlūf, *Shajarat al-nūr*, 1:186–88. Over two hundred of Māzarī's *fatwās* are preserved in Wansharīsī's *Miʿyār* and in Abu al-Qāsim al-Burzulī's (d. 841/1438) *Jāmiʿ masāʾil al-aḥkām*. These are the primary sources for an edition of Māzarī's *fatwās* edited by al-Ṭāhir al-Maʿmūrī. See Burzulī, *Fatāwā al-Burzulī: Jāmiʿ masāʾil al-aḥkām li-mā nazala*

Māzarī's unnamed questioner asked him "about rulings from the judge of Sicily, as well as [the testimony] of their professional witnesses. Should these be accepted [in Ifrīqiyā] or not—considering the necessity [of these offices], and given that it is not known whether their residence there under the infidels is by compulsion or by choice?"[39] Notably, the question focuses entirely on court practice. The questioner does not raise the issue of whether or not Sicilian Muslims may lead the prayer or witness a marriage contract in their home communities; rather, he is solely concerned with the reception in North Africa of legal communications "coming from" the chief judge or professional witnesses in Sicily. This is a leading question meant to elicit a positive response, as the questioner offers two reasons these communications should be accepted: the administration of justice is a communal necessity, and these officials may be residing in Sicily by compulsion, not by choice.

In his response, Māzarī reviews two factors that might impugn a judge's credibility and therefore invalidate his pronouncements: his residence under infidel rule, and his appointment to office by infidels. As noted, Māzarī confirms that residence under non-Muslim rule is prohibited and, if done willfully and without a valid reason, results in a loss of probity. Yet this general rule is not Māzarī's prime focus. Instead, he emphasizes the need to give Muslims the benefit of the doubt if the reasons for their residence are unknown. These Muslims enjoy the presumption of probity until and unless proven otherwise. Even in the case of willful residence, according to Māzarī, a Muslim's probity is not compromised if his reason for remaining is sound. Māzarī states that valid reasons to remain include the hope of converting infidels and the ransom of Muslim prisoners.[40] As for his appointment by an infidel ruler, Māzarī does not see this as something that compromises the Sicilian judge's integrity, nor that of any similarly appointed officials. He not only confirms that the role of judges is a communal necessity, but further states that if the Muslim community requests the appointment (from a Christian ruler), "it is just as though a Muslim sultan had appointed him."[41]

Māzarī's *fatwā* lacks a precise conclusion, but the clear policy implication of his statements is that the pronouncements of Sicily's chief judge may

---

min al-qaḍāyā bi'l-muftīn wa'l-ḥukkām, ed. Muḥammad al-Ḥabīb al-Hīla, 7 vols. (Beirut: Dār al-Gharb al-Islāmī, 2002); Māzarī, *Fatāwā al-Māzarī*, ed. al-Ṭāhir al-Maʿmūrī (Tunis: al-Dār al-Tūnisiyya lil-Nashr, 1994). Hady Roger Idris draws extensively on Māzarī's opinions in his history of the Zīrid state, *La Berbérie Orientale sous les Zīrīds: Xe-XIIe siècles*, 2 vols. (Paris: Adrien-Maisonneuve, 1962). Sarah Davis Secord analyzes Māzarī's opinions related to Sicily in Davis Secord, "Muslims in Norman Sicily: The Evidence of Imām al-Māzarī's Fatwās," *Mediterranean Studies*, 16, no. 1 (2007): 46–66.

39 Wansharīsī, *al-Miʿyār*, 2:133; appendix B, 315.

40 In another version of Māzarī's *fatwā*, he includes the hope of recovering territory for Islam as an acceptable reason to remain in non-Muslim territory. See notes in appendix B.

41 Wansharīsī, *al-Miʿyār*, 2:134; appendix B, 317–18.

be accepted in the courts of Ifrīqiyā, as should documents attested to by professional Sicilian witnesses. Why was this important? We would expect that Muslims emigrating from Sicily to Ifrīqiyā during and after the Norman conquest would have brought an array of legal documents with them. There must have been emigrants who needed to prove the validity of a will, bequest, marriage, or divorce, and whose documents would have been notarized in Sicily prior to their departure. We have at least one case in the *Miʿyār* in which a Tunisian man hoping to collect his inheritance had to convince a skeptical judge of the validity of the death certificate, because his relative had died in Sicily and the certificate was certified there.[42] We would also expect merchants in Ifrīqiyā to have been handling (and possibly contesting) contracts for goods and services involving Sicilian Muslim partners. Some merchants may have been eager to consider contracts concluded or testimony given in Sicily to be null and void.

In one of Māzarī's many *fatwās* related to trade with Sicily, we find reason to believe that indeed, such contracts were disputed.[43] Māzarī recalls that during a famine in Mahdiyya, people resorted to buying food in Sicily. A legal dispute arose between two men at the time, most likely in the late 1080s. One man sought to invalidate the testimony offered by a witness for his adversary, because the witness had traveled to Sicily and this impugned his probity. This case eventually reached the sultan, who convened the region's scholars to debate a need-based dispensation from the Mālikī prohibition on travel to enemy territory for trade. If mere travel to Sicily was considered in this case a potential reason to reject a man's testimony, even when many jurists approved of such travel, then we would expect that Tunisians bringing claims against current or former Sicilians would have exploited their rivals' residence under Christian rule in order to discredit their documents and testimony.

It is important to note that while Māzarī supported the acceptance of legal documents certified in Sicily, during the aforementioned debate he rejected the proposed dispensation to allow Muslims from Ifrīqiyā to travel to Sicily to buy much-needed wheat. On the basis of his *fatwā* on probity, some commentators hailed Māzarī as a sympathetic, lenient jurist who justified Muslim residence in Christian Sicily. Both Mu'nis and Turki found Māzarī's liberal approach to be at such odds with the rest of *Asnā al-matājir* that they seemed to think that Wansharīsī must not have considered this opinion carefully, or must have disagreed with it.[44] Yet Māzarī had a reputation

42 See the *fatwā* issued by Ibn al-Ḍābiṭ, most likely in the early eleventh century (*al-Miʿyār*, 10:113). Elsewhere in the *Miʿyār* (2:273), Wansharīsī describes Ibn al-Ḍābiṭ as a student of Abū al-Ḥasan al-Lakhmī (d. 478/1085–6), as was Māzarī.

43 I analyze and translate two versions of this *fatwā* in Hendrickson, "Is al-Andalus Different?"

44 Mu'nis, "Asnā al-matājir," 17–18; Turki, "Consultation," 694; Turki, "Pour ou contre," 318.

in the Mālikī school of strictly adhering to school doctrine and refusing to bend the rules for the sake of convenience. He held fast to the prohibition on travel to Sicily for trade, even in the face of famine, and to the principle that Muslims must not be subject to non-Muslim laws. While Māzarī's statements on residence in Sicily are relatively generous, I argue that his position was not likely driven by sympathy for the predicament of Muslims remaining under Christian rule. Instead, Māzarī's *fatwā* was based on the importance of facilitating the administration of justice in *dār al-Islām*. In giving the Sicilian judge and witnesses the benefit of the doubt as to their probity, Māzarī was not endorsing their residence under Christian rule, nor that of any other Muslim; he was finding a way to justify honoring legal documents of Sicilian origin in the courts of Ifrīqiyā. This pragmatic solution to a practical problem would have allowed Tunisian judges to verify the rights of Sicilian emigrants and to adjudicate disputes between parties in North Africa, even when some or all of them had business or family ties to Sicily. The alternative—a sweeping rejection of every legal document brought to Ifrīqiyā from Christian Sicily, or signed in Ifrīqiyā by a Sicilian—would have undermined the rule of law in North Africa and discouraged new emigration from Sicily.

Wansharīsī, I argue, found himself in a similar situation, with similar motives. We cannot reasonably assume that he disagreed with Māzarī's opinion. He granted Māzarī's opinion more space than any other citation in *Asnā al-matājir*, and he chose this opinion over possible alternatives, most notably those of Ibn Rabīʿ and ʿAbdūsī (discussed below), and he did this to address a topic he was not asked about. Nor does Wansharīsī introduce this opinion in order to refute it, as was the case with Ibn al-Ḥājj's opinion on inviolability. In this section on probity, the opinions supporting the rejection of attestations from Muslim judges under Christian rule are insufficiently developed to serve as a refutation, as those opinions are not reinforced by any commentary from Wansharīsī. Thus, we must assume that Wansharīsī featured Māzarī's *fatwā* because he found it to be a valuable and relevant precedent, and because it was issued by one of the Mālikī school's most revered jurists.

The issue of accepting legal documents that originated in *dār al-ḥarb* in the courts of *dār al-Islām* is the central reason for Wansharīsī's inclusion of Māzarī's opinion in *Asnā al-matājir*. This must have been a pressing matter in Wansharīsī's time, as former Mudéjars still had to administer to their interpersonal affairs, even in the Maghrib. Documents certified by judges serving in Portuguese-controlled areas of the Maghrib would have raised similar concerns for other jurists in *dār al-Islām*; we know that the authority of these judges' was questioned and often flouted.[45] By allowing the contracts

45 See Cornell, "Socioeconomic Dimensions," 386–87.

and other documents of emigrants to be reviewed in Maghribī courts rather than dismissed out of hand for bearing the attestation or witness of a judge or notary under Christian authority, Wansharīsī might have intended to further any, and most likely all, of the following aims: (1) to encourage more emigration from Portuguese-controlled territories; (2) to extend support and legal recognition to existing Iberian emigrants, in order to facilitate their integration into Maghribī society; and (3) to bolster the rule of law in the Maghrib in general, including in Portuguese-controlled areas.

Here we may ask, why did Wansharīsī not state his case more clearly, why did he rely on a somewhat conflicting set of precedents to convey his policy? I suggest that while both Māzarī and Wansharīsī endorsed a pragmatic compromise in favor of emigration and the rule of law, that compromise was perhaps quite uncomfortable for Wansharīsī. Writing after four centuries of territorial losses in al-Andalus and while the Portuguese were actively encroaching on Maghribī soil, Wansharīsī was even less inclined than Māzarī to embrace exceptions to the Mālikī prohibition on residence under non-Muslim rule, or to the consequences for violating this rule. Yet if he refused to compromise he would be asking emigrants to risk invalidating all of their existing marriage contracts, wills, partnerships, and other credentials. Thus, Wansharīsī endorsed the acceptance of these documents, but only by prominently citing a formidable early authority, Māzarī, and without including any direct commentary of his own.

To gain additional perspective on the role of Māzarī's opinion in *Asnā al-matājir*, it is worth reviewing two alternative *fatwā*s that Wansharīsī might have cited instead. The most immediate alternative is the language in Ibn Rabīʿ's *fatwā*.[46] If Wansharīsī had been concerned primarily or exclusively with the legal status of Mudéjars, the scope of this opinion should have fit his purposes. Ibn Rabīʿ addresses the validity of Mudéjars' testimony in the abstract, as Mudéjars; that is, in their normal lives at home in *dār al-ḥarb*. He does not mention judges, attestations, or the acceptance of Mudéjar testimony in Muslim territory. If Wansharīsī had only wanted to harshly criticize these Muslims, Ibn Rabīʿ's text should have been suitable, as Ibn Rabīʿ offered fewer reasons than Māzarī did to accept the probity of conquered Muslims. In choosing Māzarī's *fatwā* over this section of Ibn Rabīʿ's *fatwā*, Wansharīsī shifted the focus of this section to events in North Africa, adopted a practical compromise that facilitates migration into *dār al-Islām*, and grounded his position on an authoritative precedent set by an earlier, well-respected master of Mālikī law.

The second alternative *fatwā* that merits review is one issued by ʿAbd Allāh al-ʿAbdūsī (d. 849/1446), who served as the chief *muftī* of Fez and the

46 See van Koningsveld and Wiegers, "Islamic Statute," 33–34.

imām of the Qarawiyyīn mosque.[47] ʿAbdūsī's opinion offers an important point of comparison with *Asnā al-matājir* because it covers much of the same ground as Māzarī's *fatwā*. Many scholars considered ʿAbdūsī more pragmatic and moderate than Wansharīsī with regard to the legal status of Mudéjars, even suggesting that Wansharīsī excluded this *fatwā* from the *Miʿyār* because of its leniency.[48] I argue that ʿAbdūsī's opinion is important, but not because of its "leniency" toward Mudéjars. Instead, it is significant because it demonstrates that the acceptance of legal documents originating in *dār al-ḥarb* was an issue of concern in Fez in the generation or two prior to Wansharīsī. As with Māzarī's *fatwā*, ʿAbdūsī's opinion offers a pragmatic compromise that might appear sympathetic to continued Muslim residence in *dār al-ḥarb*, but ultimately supports emigration to *dār al-Islām*.

The question posed to ʿAbdūsī explicitly concerns legal affairs in North Africa. The text opens as follows:

> the *muftī* of Fez was asked about a document from the lands of the Christians that is [verified] by the testimony of professional Mudéjar witnesses and requires a judgment in Muslim territory. May [a judgment] proceed on the basis of this [document] if the handwriting of the aforementioned witnesses is verified, or not?[49]

The remainder of the question asks if these witnesses lose their probity on account of their residence (in *dār al-ḥarb)*, whether or not their ability or inability to emigrate is pertinent in this regard, if the rulings issued by a Mudéjar should be considered valid, and if it matters whether these judges were appointed by the Muslim community or by the Christian ruler.

---

47 ʿAbd Allāh b. Muḥammad b. Mūsā al-ʿAbdūsī was also one of Waryāglī's teachers, as noted in part 2. Makhlūf, *Shajarat al-nūr*, 1:367; Tinbuktī, *Nayl al-ibtihāj*, 1:249–50; Qarāfī, *Tawshīḥ al-Dībāj*, 114.

48 On ʿAbdūsī as pragmatic or moderate, see Molina López, "Algunas consideraciones," 428; van Koningsveld and Wiegers, "Islamic Statute," 50; and Rubiera Mata, "Los Moriscos," 541. On Wansharīsī's possible omission of ʿAbdūsī's *fatwā* because of its leniency, see Jean-Pierre Molénat, "Le problème," 395; Wiegers, *Islamic Literature*, 87 n. 77; and Miller, "Muslim Minorities," 259 n. 9.

49 The full version of this *fatwā* is included in two fifteenth-century Granadan *fatwā* collections: one by an unknown author, Anon., *al-Ḥadīqa al-mustaqilla al-naḍra fī al-fatāwā al-ṣādira ʿan ʿulamāʾ al-ḥaḍra*, ed. Jalāl ʿAlī al-Qadhdhāfī al-Juhānī (Beirut: Dār Ibn Ḥazm, 2003), 144–45 (partial edition of El-Escorial MS 1096); and Abū al-Faḍl (or Abū al-Qāsim) b. Ṭarkāṭ (d. after 854/1450), *al-Nawāzil*, BN Madrid MS 5135, fols. 72v–72r. Wazzānī includes an abridged version in both *al-Miʿyār al-jadīd* (3:35) and *al-Nawāzil al-ṣughrā* (4:299–300). Wiegers offers a full English translation of Wazzānī's version (*Islamic Literature*, 86–87), while Etty Terem (*New Texts, Old Practices: Islamic Reforms in Modern Morocco* [Stanford: Stanford University Press, 2014], 106–7) offers a partial translation of the same. In his new edition of ʿAbdūsī's *fatwās*, Hishām al-Muḥammadī includes both the original and abridged versions of this text: ʿAbd Allāh al-ʿAbdūsī, *Ajwibat al-ʿAbdūsī*, ed. Hishām al-Muḥammadī (Rabat: Wizārat al-Awqāf wa'l-Shuʾūn al-Islāmiyya, 2015), 423–25.

ʿAbdūsī's answer begins with a condemnation of voluntary residence under Christian rule. He declares that such residence is a major sin and claims that there is a scholarly consensus rejecting the testimony of any Muslim who is capable of emigrating but does not do so. As further evidence, ʿAbdūsī cites the *ḥadīth* in which Muḥammad denies responsibility for any Muslim residing among the polytheists, and Mālik's assertion that only the soul of a Muslim whose faith is diseased could be content to live in a land of unbelief and idol worship. ʿAbdūsī's position is that Mudéjars are obligated to emigrate even if they must relinquish all of their property and expend all of their resources just to reach *dār al-Islām*. Yet, they are not required to risk their lives; if they fear for themselves or for their families, they may remain where they are without compromising their probity.

If a Mudéjar community has appointed its own judge, ʿAbdūsī affirms the validity of his rulings in that community. Documents certified by the judge are also admissible in other jurisdictions, provided that his appointment by the community can be confirmed and his handwriting verified. If the Christian king appoints a judge, the rulings of that judge are invalid unless the Muslim community willingly accepts his judgeship. In that case, according to ʿAbdūsī, it is the same as if they had appointed him in the first place. If this judge appoints professional witnesses to serve as notaries, their signed testimony is also admissible—presumably in other courts—according to the conditions for verifying the testimony of those not present at court.[50] Lastly, ʿAbdūsī notes that some jurists disallow documents certified by Mudéjar judges because the Christian ruler appointed them to preside over the Muslims, and the Muslims were compelled to accept them.

Does this opinion offer a stark contrast to *Asnā al-matājir*? Scholars have argued that ʿAbdūsī is more pragmatic and sympathetic to Mudéjars because he grants these Muslims the "right" to remain under Christian rule, he does not require them to risk their lives to emigrate, he accepts their testimony, and he recognizes their approval of the judges appointed for them as meaningful. None of these points is convincing. The first part of ʿAbdūsī's *fatwā*, as summarized above, quite forcefully upholds the obligation to emigrate and condemns Muslims who voluntarily remain under Christian rule. He is explicit that Muslims must ruin themselves financially, if necessary, in order to reach Muslim territory. While he exempts Muslims who fear for their lives and families, it is fair to conclude

50 These conditions are discussed in judges' manuals (*adab al-qāḍī*) and in the section of the *Miʿyār* that Wansharīsī devotes to correspondence between judges (10:60–76, as noted above). Normally, two witnesses were to accompany a document in order to attest to its authorship and the identity of any signatories, including lay Muslims and judges. In practice, a receiving judge would often accept a document based on his own recognition of the other judge's handwriting.

that Wansharīsī does, too. In *Asnā al-matājir*, Wansharīsī repeatedly notes that those who are too weak to emigrate are exempt from the obligation. In the Berber *fatwā*, his list of exempted individuals includes those who would perish if they set forth.[51]

The second part of ʿAbdūsī's *fatwā* is best compared with Māzarī's parallel opinion, as the centerpiece of the section on judges and testimony in *Asnā al-matājir*. Both jurists honor legal documents produced by Muslims in Christian territory in Muslim territory, subject to specific conditions. For ʿAbdūsī, the acceptance of these documents is conditional upon the Muslim community's proven and voluntary approval of the judge. For Māzarī, the nature of the judge's appointment is irrelevant; while the people's approval of their judge reinforces his authority, his rulings must be considered valid even if he is appointed by an "infidel," because the judiciary is a necessary element of society. Māzarī's condition for honoring a judge's certifications in Muslim territory is that his residence under Christian rule be excusable. As noted, Māzarī not only excuses involuntary residence but also gives Muslims the benefit of the doubt if the circumstances of their residence are unknown, and he further advances several justifications for voluntary residence under Christian rule. In contrast to ʿAbdūsī's narrow exception allowing Muslims who fear for their lives to remain where they are and retain their probity, Māzarī's approach is far more generous; in his formulation, blameworthy residence and the loss of probity is the exception to the rule, as this only occurs if there is solid proof that a Muslim has remained under Christian rule voluntarily and without good cause.

If we consider these two points of comparison—Wansharīsī and ʿAbdūsī on the obligation to emigrate, and Māzarī and ʿAbdūsī on the acceptance of legal documents certified by judges in Christian territory—it is hard to see ʿAbdūsī as more lenient and pragmatic. How could Wansharīsī record Māzarī's more generous *fatwā* twice in the *Miʿyār*, including quite prominently in *Asnā al-matājir*, and suppress ʿAbdūsī's opinion for greater leniency?[52] It is more likely that Wansharīsī knew of this opinion but excluded it as redundant and far less authoritative than Māzarī's opinion.[53]

Two factors have contributed to a misunderstanding of the relationship between ʿAbdūsī's opinion and Wansharīsī's *Asnā al-matājir*. The first is the persistent assumption that Māzarī's *fatwā* cannot be reconciled with Wansharīsī's aims, and thus that we may consider it a foreign element that should be separated from those parts of *Asnā al-matājir* that must represent Wansharīsī's *real* opinion; scholars have characterized ʿAbdūsī's *fatwā* as

51 Appendix A, 277.
52 Māzarī's *fatwā* also appears in the *Miʿyār*'s section on judging (10:107–8).
53 Wansharīsī included many of ʿAbdūsī's other opinions in the *Miʿyār*.

more pragmatic and lenient than that of Wansharīsī because they have disregarded Wansharīsī's favorable inclusion of Māzarī's *fatwā*. Even more incongruously, *Asnā al-matājir* has often been characterized as the (cruel, strict) opposite or inverse of Māzarī's (lenient, compassionate) *fatwā*, as though this opinion were not an integral part of *Asnā al-matājir*.[54] Scholars also encountered ʿAbdūsī's *fatwā* through Wazzānī's abridged summary and commentary in *al-Miʿyār al-jadīd*.[55] Wazzānī's most significant edit to ʿAbdūsī's opinion involves his removal of the final line, which notes that many jurists refuse to accept documents from Mudéjar judges because they were appointed by a Christian ruler without the consent of the Muslim community.[56] Given that ʿAbdūsī views the admissibility of documents as conditional upon the Muslim community's consent to the appointment of the judge, this last line renders his position somewhat ambiguous.[57] Wazzānī's abridgement effectively strengthens ʿAbdūsī's endorsement of these judges' authority.

More significantly, Wazzānī structures the relevant section of *al-Miʿyār al-jadīd* as an argument against Wansharīsī's position on Muslims living under non-Muslim rule, and instead favors what he perceived to be ʿAbdūsī's

54 In addition to the above references, see A. L. Udovitch, "Muslims and Jews in the World of Frederic II: Boundaries and Communication," *Princeton Papers in Near Eastern Studies* 2 (1993): 83–104; Farhat Dachraoui, "Integration ou exclusion des minorités religieuses: La concepcion islamique traditionnelle," in *L'expulsió dels moriscos: conseqüències en el món Islàmic i el món cristià* (Barcelona: Generalitat de Catalunya, 1994), 195–203; García Sanjuán, "La Cuestión Mudéjar," 180–83. The first section of Udovitch's article, titled "Can Muslims Live Under Infidel Rule? A Tale of Two Fatwas," contrasts Wansharīsī's severe opinion denying Muslims the right to live in Christian Spain with Māzarī's pragmatic, accommodating response that "fully legitimizes all of Muslim institutional life in Christian Sicily" (Udovitch, 83–84). Dachraoui refers to Māzarī's compassionate *fatwā* as the inverse of Wansharīsī's (201). García Sanjuán quotes Udovitch approvingly and states that Māzarī's *fatwā* is far less "intransigent and dogmatic" than those of Wansharīsī (*Asnā al-matājir* and the Marbella *fatwā*), without addressing Wansharīsī's inclusion of the former.

55 On Wazzānī and his crafting of *al-Miʿyār al-jadīd* in general, see Terem's *New Texts, Old Practices*. On Wazzānī's treatment of *fatwā*s related to Muslims under non-Muslim rule, including those of Wansharīsī and ʿAbdūsī, see ch. 4, esp. 91–110.

56 This line is present in Ibn Ṭarkāṭ's *al-Nawāzil*, Wazzānī's stated source for this text. BN Madrid MS 5135, fol. 72r. Ibn Ṭarkāṭ's version is also identical to the one preserved in Anon., *al-Ḥadīqa al-mustaqilla*, which has been published. Wazzānī's other significant edit is replacing Ibn Ṭarkāṭ's references to Mudéjars with more general language regarding believers living in Christian lands. On Ibn Ṭarkāṭ, see M. Isabel Calero Secall, "Una aproximación al studio de las fatwas granadinas: Los temas de las fatwas de Ibn Sirāŷ en los Nawāzil de Ibn Ṭarkāṭ," in *Homenaje a Prof. Darío Cabanelas Rodrígeuz, O.F.M., Con Motivo de su LXX Aniversario* (Granada: Universidad de Granada, 1987), 1:189–202.

57 ʿAbdūsī's *fatwā* reflects his own understanding of judicial appointments in Iberia. Two articles by Ana Echevarría Arsuaga shed light on the actual process of judicial appointments in fifteenth-century Mudéjar Castile: Echevarría Arsuaga, "De Cadí a Alcalde Mayor: La Élite Judicial Mudéjar en el Siglo XV (I)," *Al-Qanṭara* 24, no. 1 (2003): 139–68; Echevarría Arsuaga, "De Cadí a Alcalde Mayor: La Élite Judicial Mudéjar en el Siglo XV (II)," *Al-Qanṭara* 24, no. 2 (2003): 273–90.

more sound position. Wazzānī first presents the Berber *fatwā*, followed by his own comment that Wansharīsī went too far by completely rejecting these Muslims' testimony and the documents certified by their judges.[58] Wazzānī then reproduces the full section on probity from *Asnā al-matājir*, attributing it to the *Miʿyār* in general (rather than to *Asnā al-matājir* specifically), and appends to it several opinions favoring the validity and necessity of Muslim judges in Christian territory. The last of these opinions is that of ʿAbdūsī, which Wāzzanī follows with a second comment rejecting Wansharīsī's position:

> This (discussion) is better than the preceding response by the author of the *Miʿyār*, in which he did not allow the testimony of their witnesses or the attestations of their judges under any circumstances. [This is better] because of the opinion held by some scholars that Islamic territory does not become *dār al-ḥarb* merely because infidels take control of it, but rather [it becomes *dār al-ḥarb*] when the rites of Islam are no longer performed there. As long as the rites of Islam, or most of them, are still performed in that [territory], it is not *dār al-ḥarb*.[59]

Wazzānī, who witnessed the establishment of the French Protectorate during the last decade of his life, chose to defend the ethical character of Muslims living under Christian authority.[60] He rejected Wansharīsī's views on the subject and instead advocated a model in which a territory remains Muslim as long as its inhabitants are able to perform Islamic rituals and practices.

To strengthen his case, Wazzānī distorts the opinion of his famous predecessors. Even in the Berber *fatwā*, Wansharīsī (like Māzarī and ʿAbdūsī) only rejects the testimony of lay Muslims who live voluntarily under non-Muslim rule and of Muslims who enter *dār al-ḥarb* for trade, an act that he associates in that *fatwā* with providing materiel to the enemy. Although he also quotes Ibn ʿArafa's statement that the Mālikīs refused to accept the pronouncements of Mudéjar judges, this too is in relation to voluntary residence and without further comment from Wansharīsī. Wazzānī does not link Māzarī's *fatwā* explicitly to *Asnā al-matājir*, nor does he grapple with the implications of Wansharīsī's reliance on this opinion. In failing to take Wansharīsī's endorsement of Māzarī seriously, and in exaggerating the contrast between Wansharīsī's opinion in *Asnā al-matājir* and ʿAbdūsī's opinion, Wazzānī appears to have had a formative impact on the way modern scholars approached these opinions.

58 Wazzānī, *al-Miʿyār al-jadīd*, 3:31–32.
59 Wazzānī, *al-Miʿyār al-jadīd*, 3:35.
60 Terem first made this point in *New Texts, Old Practices*, 107.

ʿAbdūsī may well have had an impact on Wansharīsī's thinking, as well. This earlier *fatwā* suggests that judges in Fez were concerned with the admissibility of Mudéjar legal documents in the early fifteenth century, at least fifty years prior to the composition of *Asnā al-matājir*. ʿAbdūsī's pragmatism in this opinion can be seen less in his presumed acceptance of Muslim life in Iberia, and more in his conditional support for recognizing Mudéjar-attested legal documents in Maghribī courts. This opinion provides a solution to a North African problem, one that likely involved former Mudéjars who had already emigrated to the Maghrib. ʿAbdūsī might have paved the way for Wansharīsī to adopt a similar compromise between condemning voluntary residence under Muslim rule, while advocating the acceptance of these legal documents in order to uphold justice in Maghribī courts and remove an obstacle to immigration from Portuguese-held territory. Yet, in Wansharīsī's milieu (as opposed to Muʾnis's modernist Egypt) the prevailing logic regarding legal authority would have led him to seek out the oldest, most authoritative opinion available with which to make this point, this concession to reality—that of Māzarī, an *imām* or master jurist known for his refusal to bend rules.[61]

Andalusī Emigrants: The Hereafter

In the final section of *Asnā al-matājir*, Wansharīsī addresses the fate of the regretful Andalusī emigrants in the hereafter. An initial portion of this section, borrowed from Ibn Rabīʿ, addresses those who refuse to emigrate or who return to enemy territory after emigrating. According to the majority of scholars, these Muslims will face a "severe torment" for committing a major sin, but they will not suffer eternally.

The remainder of this section, which is Wansharīsī's original material, specifically addresses the Andalusīs who were overheard mocking the obligation to emigrate and expressing a desire to return to Castile. One paragraph in particular is noteworthy:

> Whoever commits and is ensnared in this [behavior] has hastened disgrace for his wicked soul, [disgrace which is] guaranteed in this world and the next. Yet in terms of [his] disobedience, sin, injurious conduct, vileness, odiousness, distance from God, diminished [religious

61 Wansharīsī includes in the *Miʿyār* several other opinions on the validity of judges' rulings outside Muslim territory and the acceptance of their documents in *dār al-ḥarb*. See the opinions associated with Ibn ʿArafa (10:66–67), Abū al-Ḥasan al-Qābisī (10:135), Burzulī (2:438–39 and 6:156–57), various jurists (2:439 and 6:95), and Abū al-Faḍl al-ʿUqbānī (4:294). These precedents do not present a uniformly favorable or unfavorable position as to the probity of Muslims and their judges outside Muslim territory, or the admissibility of the judges' documents.

> standing], blameworthy [status], and [his being] deserving of the greatest condemnation, he does not equal someone who abandons emigration completely, by submitting to the enemy and by living among those who are far [from God].[62]

This passage is striking, as Wansharīsī shifts from condemning the behavior of these Andalusīs to using their case as a means to emphasize the magnitude of the sin of those who have not yet emigrated. He indicates that as grave as these Andalusīs' sins may be, and as deserving as they may be of the exemplary punishments that he has just prescribed, the sins of those content to remain under infidel rule are far more heinous, and their fate is even more grievous. This pivot at the end of the *fatwā* supports the notion that Wansharīsī has been providing answers relevant to two distinct contexts in *Asnā al-matājir*: the one provided by Ibn Qaṭiyya's questions, in which the Muslims in question have already emigrated, and a second context for which jurists were still actively encouraging emigration, and which I argue must be Muslim submission to Portuguese authority in the Maghrib. Here Wansharīsī appears to issue one last warning to his fellow Maghribīs about the consequences of remaining under Christian rule.

It is also worth noting that these consequences, however dire, are muted in comparison to those Wansharīsī alludes to in the Berber *fatwā*. In *Asnā al-matājir*, he considers those who fail to emigrate major sinners, but still Muslims. Their worst offenses, including submission to infidel rule and contentment with the degradation of Islam, are "serious, perilous abominations, mortal blows that verge on unbelief (*kufr*)."[63] By contrast, in the Berber *fatwā* Wansharīsī not only charges those who pray for the continuance of infidel rule with outright apostasy, but he also further reinforces the severity of this condemnation with several precedents to the effect that "contentment with unbelief is unbelief."[64] He ends the passage by implying that it would be charitable to beat these offenders as severely as possible, in the hopes they might turn toward repentance.

In *Asnā al-matājir* Wansharīsī shifts his tone and target. Rather than accusing his fellow Maghribīs of apostasy, he warns that the foreign Andalusīs who have so failed to appreciate the Maghrib are *close* to infidelity. We might have viewed these as two unrelated opinions if Zayyātī's still-obscure *fatwā* collection had not alerted us to the fact that Wansharīsī suppressed the Berber *fatwā* in favor of circulating and preserving *Asnā al-matājir*, and if we could not place these two *fatwā*s in chronological

62 Appendix B, 320.
63 Appendix B, 314.
64 Appendix A, 280.

order, noting that the Waṭṭāsid sultan renewed a peace treaty with Portugal in the period between Wansharīsī's composition of the Berber *fatwā* and *Asnā al-matājir*. In light of this changed political context, Wansharīsī appears to have deliberately moderated his criticism (that appears in the Berber *fatwā*) and deflected explicit blame from his compatriots and his ruler (in *Asnā al-matājir*), exercising the restraint and caution we might expect of a treatise meant for a broad audience in a politically sensitive atmosphere.

The Marbella *Fatwā*

The Marbella *fatwā*, roughly one-quarter the length of *Asnā al-matājir*, is a far more accessible, less technical document. It contains a minimum of scriptural proof texts and authoritative precedents and is free of divergent opinions or discussions of legal methodology. Instead, the text appeals to basic Islamic principles and to logical reasoning. In an introductory section that is original to Wansharīsī (and noted above), he emphasizes that the natural order requires the dominance of Islam and Muslims over Jews and Christians who live in their midst. The remainder of the answer, which consists primarily of one continuous excerpt from Ibn Rabīʿ's *fatwā*, is an inventory of the corruptions and dangers that result from inverting this hierarchy. These include rendering Muslims unable to perform the five pillars properly, and unable to pursue *jihād* despite an obligation to do so; degrading Islam and holding Muslims in contempt; causing Muslims to fear that their lives, families, and property might be seized and exploited, especially if Christians break their treaties; luring Muslim women into illicit relationships with infidel men; and causing Muslims, over time, to adopt the language, culture, and even religion of those in power.

As the Marbella *fatwā* contains relatively little material original to Wansharīsī and scant engagement with legal precedents, in this chapter I have focused primarily on *Asnā al-matājir*. For the present purposes, with regard to the Marbella *fatwā*, Wansharīsī's primary decision was to preserve this question and reply to it with a portion of Ibn Rabīʿ's text. As suggested, the Marbella question is memorable and relatable, as it adds narrative appeal to Wansharīsī's dual statements on the obligation to emigrate. It also allows him to refute at least two arguments that might have gained currency in his time: that remaining in Christian-controlled territory could be meritorious, and that doing so might not cause much harm. In effect, Wansharīsī counters the proposition that Muslims may remain under non-Muslim rule as long as they can still manifest their religion (the position held by the unnamed jurist mentioned in Ibn Rabīʿ's question) by arguing that this was an impossibility, a contradiction in terms.[65] For Wansharīsī, even the most basic religious obligations, such as prayer and fasting, cannot be properly fulfilled in the absence of Muslim dominance and a legitimate Muslim ruler. The practice of Islam is inseparable from Muslim power.

Preserving the Marbella *fatwā* also allowed Wansharīsī to advance substantial arguments grounded in logical reasoning and current and historical events. He was able to argue that every kind of reasoning one might employ produces the same result—an absolute prohibition on voluntary residence under non-Muslim rule. At the same time, he maintained a separation between these forms of argumentation and the technical legal reasoning and textual precedents of *Asnā al-matājir*. It may be that Wansharīsī intended the Marbella *fatwā* to be accessible and compelling for lay Muslims, although we have no evidence that it circulated independently of the *Miʿyār*.

Although Wansharīsī is often characterized as inflexible and unable to adapt to changing circumstances, the strict fidelity to the past that he appears to maintain in these two texts is a strategic illusion, not the shackles of a stagnant orthodoxy. He supports this illusion through a range of tactics: he claims that a scholarly consensus regarding lone converts extends to conquered Muslims; he claims that the equivalence between these two groups was established by the earliest possible legal authorities; he conveniently neglects to name those authorities; he denies that he utilized any analogical reasoning or that there is anything novel in linking these two cases; he juxtaposes *ḥadīths* and commentary to support one of many possible interpretations (that *hijra* from *dār al-ḥarb* has always been an enduring obligation); and he cites the opinions of respected Mālikī jurists like Ibn Rushd al-Jadd, Ibn al-ʿArabī, and Māzarī, while concealing his extensive reliance on at least one later jurist, namely Ibn Rabīʿ. All of these strategies mask the considerable interpretive work Wansharīsī engages in to create the impression that a long-standing, unassailable Mālikī consensus prohibits Muslims from remaining in conquered territories. In reality, he actively constructs that precedent, and works to assert its prior existence and continued dominance over competing understandings of Islamic law and Muslim identity.

It is difficult to determine what those understandings might have been. Aside from the opinions noted here in the course of parts 1 and 2, scholars

65 This position that Muslims who can practice their religion may remain in non-Muslim territory was endorsed by Shāfiʿī jurists and others. See Abou El Fadl, "Islamic Law and Muslim Minorities."

have located only three additional premodern Mālikī *fatwās* from Iberia and North Africa that address the obligation of conquered Muslims to emigrate.[66] All three of these *fatwās* require emigration. ʿAbd al-Raḥmān "Ibn Miqlāsh," writing from Oran in 794/1397, excoriated Muslims for remaining in conquered Iberia. While he accused them of self-deception for thinking that they would earn a better living in infidel territory, we do not have a sense of their reasons for not emigrating.[67] Granadan *muftī* Muḥammad al-Ḥaffār (d. 811/1408) was asked if Mudéjars in general must emigrate, if one spouse may emigrate without the other, and if so, if a husband must first pay his wife's dower. Ḥaffār evidently found the framing of this query disingenuous, as he responded that one spouse's refusal to emigrate is no excuse for the other to stay. He stressed that emigration is obligatory even if a man must leave his wife, or vice versa, as religious welfare supersedes worldly interests.[68] In the third *fatwā*, Granadan chief judge Muḥammad al-Mawwāq (d. 897/1492) holds that a man may not even visit his parents in *dār al-ḥarb*—let alone honor their request to live nearby—unless he has the means to bring them back to *dār al-Islām*.[69]

These last two *fatwās* that prioritize emigration over marriage and filial piety suggest that family ties contributed significantly to the conflicts of interest and obligation facing potential emigrants. Mawwāq hints that

---

66 In addition to Abou El Fadl's article ("Islamic Law and Muslim Minorities") covering all major legal schools, several scholars have provided overviews of the known Mālikī *fatwās* on the obligation to emigrate. See van Koningsveld and Wiegers, "Islamic Statute"; Muhammad Khalid Masud, "The Obligation to Migrate: The Doctrine of *Hijra* in Islamic Law," in *Muslim Travellers: Pilgrimage, Migration, and the Religious Imagination*, ed. Dale F. Eickelman and James Piscatori (Berkeley: University of California Press, 1990), 29–49; and Maribel Fierro, "La Emigración en el Islam: Conceptos Antiguos, Nuevos Problemas," *Awrāq* 12 (1991): 11–41. In addition to North African and Andalusī jurists, a few Egyptian Mālikīs issued relevant opinions; see van Koningsveld and Wiegers, "Islamic Statute," 19–22 and 38–49; and Verskin, *Islamic Law*, 48–52. I do not review them here because they post-date Wansharīsī and we do not know when they might have circulated in the Islamic West.

67 The text describes its author as Abū Zayd ʿAbd al-Raḥmān, son of the late *shaykh* Abū ʿAbd Allāh Muḥammad b. Yūsuf al-Sinhājī, known as Ibn Miqlāsh. While this *muftī* is referred to as Ibn Miqlāsh in academic literature, this *ism shuhra* may belong to his father instead; neither one has been located in biographical dictionaries. The *fatwā* is preserved in a single manuscript copy at the Biblioteca Nacional de España (BN Madrid MS 4950, fols. 226r–231v), now available digitally on the library's website (www.bne.es). Hossain Buzineb includes a partial transcription of this *fatwā* in "Respuestas," 61–66. See also Miller, *Guardians of Islam*, 32–37.

68 Miller includes an edition and translation of this *fatwā*, by Muḥammad b. ʿAlī al-Anṣarī al-Ḥaffār, in "Muslim Minorities," 278–80. The text is preserved in a single manuscript copy at the Biblioteca Nacional de España (BN Madrid MS 5324, fols. 47r–48r). Miller describes this *fatwā* as measured and pragmatic (in comparison with Wansharīsī's opinions) because Ḥaffār requires that the dower and any other debts be paid prior to separation. I am not convinced that he meant to endorse non-payment of debts as a loophole allowing Mudéjars to avoid emigration, nor does this insistence on family separation strike me as particularly accommodating.

69 Miller edits and translates this *fatwā*, by Muḥammad b. Yūsuf b. Abī al-Qāsim al-ʿAdārī al-Mawwāq, in "Muslim Minorities," 284–8. The text is preserved in a single manuscript copy at the Biblioteca Nacional de España (BN Madrid MS 5324, fols. 135v–136r).

there were legal opinions favoring alternative solutions to these conflicts and includes a summary of a *fatwā* issued by his contemporary, al-Faraj b. Ibrahīm al-Basṭī. According to Basṭī, someone choosing to enter enemy territory must weigh the harm and benefits of the journey, and search within himself to identify the lesser of two evils. For those already resident in *dār al-ḥarb*, Basṭī offers hope that they may be of service to others while awaiting an opportunity to leave.[70] Although Basṭī's *fatwā* is no longer extant, this summary raises the possibility that he and other jurists sanctioned the choice to defer emigration or to visit Christian territory under certain circumstances, including a compelling conflict of legal obligations.

Because *fatwās* like that of Basṭī have not survived, our best evidence for the legal ideas Wansharīsī disagreed with are in his own texts. Ibn Rabīʿ's unnamed Andalusī adversary offered four justifications for residence under Christian rule: (1) the Mudéjars' ability to manifest their religion, (2) the "no *hijra* after the conquest [of Mecca]" *ḥadīth* suggesting that emigration is no longer obligatory, (3) Mudéjars' potential to spread the word of God among non-Muslims, and (4) their confidence in the treaties protecting their rights. Wansharīsī suppresses any mention of this jurist or his reasoning, yet addresses each of his arguments, primarily through the Marbella *fatwā*. This suggests not only that Wansharīsī felt the need to refute these ideas, but also that he and other jurists succeeded in actively suppressing such alternative opinions; we now know Ibn Rabīʿ's text only through a single, unpublished, privately-held manuscript near Tetouan. In addition to the arguments of this unnamed adversary, we know from *Asnā al-matājir* that Ibn al-Ḥājj found that the analogy between lone converts and conquered Muslims was flawed and that Māzarī countenanced a variety of reasons for remaining in Norman Sicily, including the hope of converting Christians to Islam. It is also possible that the ideas voiced by lay Muslims in Ibn Qaṭiyya's questions were in fact held by some jurists: that Muslims may remain in Christian territory if they are helping those less fortunate, or if they are earning a good livelihood but would be impoverished by emigration.

In part 4 of this book I argue that Wansharīsī succeeded in positioning his texts to become the Mālikī school's precedents of record on the obligation to emigrate. Yet *Asnā al-matājir* and the Marbella *fatwā* ultimately prevailed not because they represent a uniform party line among jurists in the Islamic West during and after the Reconquest, nor because they employ an irreproachable set of proof texts and legal arguments. In fact, as the opinions produced in colonial Algeria and Mauritania also show, many later

70 On Basṭī, see Miller, "Muslim Minorities," 273. The summary of Basṭī's *fatwā* is written in the first person (by Basṭī), without an introduction by Mawwāq, and does not fit well in the larger text. See BN Madrid MS 5324, fol. 136r, lines 4–11; Miller, "Muslim Minorities," 285–86, 288.

jurists found Wansharīsī's claims tenuous and debatable, including his core assertion of equivalence between lone converts and conquered Muslims.

A number of specific factors contributed to the success of these opinions, including Wansharīsī's strategic choices in crafting his own *fatwā*s and in curating the contents of the *Miʿyār*. As I argued in chapter 3, Wansharīsī made a crucial choice to frame his master statement against submission to Christian rule as a pair of responses to Ibn Qaṭiyya's questions related to Iberia, and to omit his own and his peers' responses to the Portuguese occupation of parts of the Maghrib, for at least four reasons: he could (1) present the Iberian case as a tragic warning for Maghribīs, (2) claim to apply unambiguous legal rules to a clear and simple problem, (3) engage his audience through the narrative appeal of Ibn Qaṭiyya's stories, and (4) protect himself by critiquing his ruler and countrymen implicitly rather than explicitly. In this chapter I have focused on how Wansharīsī took advantage of the platform provided by these questions, and Ibn Rabīʿ's existing *fatwā*, in order to craft an authoritative treatise for future generations, all while addressing his contemporary Iberian and Maghribī contexts. A comparison between *Asnā al-matājir* and Ibn Rabīʿ's text reveals that each of Wansharīsī's major departures from Ibn Rabīʿ's *fatwā* was done in order to adapt his responses to the specifics of Ibn Qaṭiyya's questions, or to the historical context of Portuguese occupation of parts of the Maghrib, or to both. By comparing *Asnā al-matājir* and the Berber *fatwā*, we see a distinct softening of tone; this deliberate move broadened the appeal of Wansharīsī's major statement on emigration and reduced the risk that he might face repercussions for critiquing his ruler.

At this point, it is worth returning full circle, to the questions that offered Wansharīsī such a convenient and effective mandate to compose *Asnā al-matājir* and the Marbella *fatwā*. Was Wansharīsī just fortunate that Ibn Qaṭiyya's questions appeared in the years following his peers' shared discourse on Portuguese occupation, and before he finished the *Miʿyār*? Or are these questions as carefully manufactured as the answers? In other words, are the questions "true"? While scholars of Islamic law generally assume that the *istiftāʾ* component of a *fatwā* is historically reliable, in this case we have ample reason to be skeptical.[71] We know that *muftī*s themselves

71 Wael Hallaq devotes the first ten pages of his 1994 article "From *Fatwā*s to *Furūʿ*" (29–38) to establishing that *fatwā*s reflect real-world situations, not purely theoretical, academic exercises. Writing about the Marbella *fatwā* in particular, Alejandro García Sanjuán argues that while Wansharīsī "detaches himself from reality" in the answer, we can nonetheless rely on the question, the origins of which are "hardly speculative or hypothetical but, in fact, absolutely real and genuine." Alejandro García Sanjuán, *Till God Inherits the Earth: Islamic Pious Endowments in al-Andalus, 9–15th Centuries* (Leiden: Brill, 2007), 29. These positions represent a reasonable academic consensus, one that made sense in the context of refuting the older thesis that medieval Islamic legal texts were too theoretical and too

are cautious with regard to the facts presented to them by their petitioners, and that compilers often stripped queries of personal details in order to record cases that are more general and therefore more widely applicable. It is not unreasonable to suppose that when their work was recorded for posterity, *muftī*s likewise modified the actual questions posed to them or invented new ones in order to preserve more important, more convenient, or simply more polished *fatwā*s. Ibn Qaṭiyya's questions represent plausible scenarios and they certainly convey real legal concerns, but it is not improbable that Wansharīsī himself rendered those concerns into a textual form as the two questions attributed to Ibn Qaṭiyya. He was clearly comfortable borrowing the bulk of his answers without acknowledging his source (Ibn Rabīʿ), and there may be good reason for our inability to locate Ibn Qaṭiyya in the relevant biographical literature. Plausibility also does not render a story true, but it does make that story far more compelling.

Finally, we must address the question of whether or not a *muftī* can say one thing and mean another.[72] We accept that allegory and veiled political critique play important roles in other literary genres. For example, Shel Silverstein's *The Giving Tree* is about more than a tree, and George Orwell's *Animal Farm* is about the Russian Revolution of 1917, not farm animals. Is legal literature too pious, dry, or simple to contain multiple meanings or convey indirect messages? I argue that it is not. On the contrary, real-life problems and desires are distorted and obscured when they are translated into legal discourse. Most obviously, they must be expressed in conformity with the existing parameters of what constitutes a legally valid argument or a relevant fact. A noise complaint might be motivated purely by racial bias, for example, or a company might cite minor, documented offenses in order to fire an employee for reasons that are illegal (such as discrimination) or unproven (such as sexual harassment). As I have argued elsewhere, complex *fatwā*s are shaped not only by the existing legal framework, but also by political pressures, generic conventions, professional etiquette, and material constraints. Moreover, in crafting persuasive responses, jurists

stagnant to meet the needs of changing societies. My hope is that the continuing adaptability and responsiveness of this tradition has now been sufficiently established to withstand the suggestion that *some* jurists, *sometimes* entertained hypotheticals, created a composite question from more than one petitioner's concern, or invented a question entirely to justify a particular response.

72 In rejecting my argument that Wansharīsī's opinions include a veiled commentary on the Portuguese occupation, Alan Verskin insists that the most logical approach is to view these texts "as being fundamentally about what he says that they are about, that is, Iberian Muslims." Verskin, *Islamic Law*, 22. He also states that Wansharīsī was writing at a time when the Waṭṭāsids were openly at war with the Portuguese, and thus, had little to hide: this is incorrect. The Waṭṭāsid sultan Muḥammad al-Shaykh signed a twenty-year peace treaty with Portugal's Afonso V in 1471, then renewed it for an additional ten years. The Maghribīs fighting against the Portuguese during this time did so without official sanction, or as rivals to the Waṭṭāsids. See chapter 2 on the political history of this period.

often employ such "fictional" devices as unacknowledged borrowing, dissemblance, misrepresentations of precedent, oblique references, and imaginative stories.[73]

For example, over the course of eight centuries, prominent Mālikī jurists employed what I call politically motivated dissemblance in a series of *fatwā*s discouraging or prohibiting Andalusīs and Maghribīs from performing the pilgrimage to Mecca. While these *muftī*s' stated rationales included the possibility that a pilgrim might miss a single prayer on the way to Mecca and back, the most compelling motivations behind these opinions were clearly political, not religious. Many of these opinions concerning the pilgrimage to Mecca were requested by rulers who wanted religious justifications to issue public policies designed to increase their control over their subjects, especially during military campaigns or widespread epidemics.

In another vein entirely, anthropologist Hussein Ali Agrama found that contemporary Egyptian *muftī*s carefully curated the advice they offer their petitioners, in order to provide them with legal answers most conducive to personal improvement, rather than bringing the most relevant points of doctrine immediately or fully to bear on each case.[74] It is often said that Islamic law governs every aspect of life; if so, then vice versa many of life's complexities have an impact on the law. We must read carefully between the lines of legal texts to identify the particular constraints and imperatives at work in any given case. The unstated factors influencing the production of a text may be of paramount importance—as when ʿAbd al-Hādī al-Ṣiqillī (d. 1311/1893) provided Morocco's king Ḥasan I (r. 1873–94) with a lengthy *fatwā* justifying a ban on the pilgrimage, seemingly based on every possible rationale *except* public health. In the same era, France banned the pilgrimage to Mecca from neighboring Tunisia and Algeria because of the recurring cholera epidemics that had been ravaging Mecca and Medina; indeed, cholera claimed Ṣiqillī's own life, and that of 33,000 fellow pilgrims, in the pilgrimage of 1893.[75] Ṣiqillī's *fatwā* said one thing (Maghribīs must not attempt the pilgrimage if they fear they might miss any prayers as a result of their journey), but meant another (because of the cholera epidemic and other dangers, pilgrims were a threat to Morocco's public health and national security), in the sense that he obscured the motivations for his opinion.[76]

---

73 See Hendrickson, "Prohibiting the Pilgrimage," esp. 203–9.

74 Hussein Ali Agrama, "Ethics, Tradition, Authority: Toward an Anthropology of the Fatwa," *American Ethnologist*, 37.1 (2010), 2–18.

75 On this *fatwā*, see Hendrickson, "Prohibiting the Pilgrimage," 198–203 (discussion) and 223–38 (translation).

76 Note that even if we believe a jurist said what he meant, we can still legitimately disagree as to the meaning of the resulting legal text or what its author intended to communicate; thus, for example, there are several different, well-defined modes of judicial interpretation in contemporary United States law.

PART 3

Wahrānī's "*Fatwā*" to the Moriscos, 1504

CHAPTER 6

Unsolicited Advice

In 910/1504, North African jurist Aḥmad b. Abī Jumʿa al-Wahrānī (d. 917/1511) authored a remarkable document, known simply as his "1504 *fatwā*." In the text, Wahrānī praises a group of Muslims for their steadfast faith and offers them practical advice as to how they might adhere to Islam without being detected by Christian authorities, and despite being forced to perform such forbidden acts as praying in church or drinking wine. Scholars have agreed that he must have been writing in response to a legal question, now lost, sent to him at the turn of the sixteenth century by Granadan Muslims, the first Iberian Muslims to be forcibly converted to Christianity. Wahrānī assures them that as long as their intentions are pure, their actions, that is, doing what is necessary to avoid persecution, will not be considered sins.

At least three aspects of Wahrānī's text have made it one of the most widely discussed documents related to Muslims living under Christian rule in the medieval and early modern Mediterranean. First, because the "1504 *fatwā*" provides encouragement and practical advice without mentioning emigration, scholars have seen this text as a welcome departure from, and possible rebuttal of, Wansharīsī's two opinions requiring emigration. Second, we also know that Wahrānī's text was important to the lay Muslims to whom it was addressed. Despite repeated prohibitions of the use of Arabic and the confiscation and burning of Arabic texts, Moriscos continued to copy this text, presumably at great risk, until as late as 1609. L. P. Harvey has even called this text "the key theological document for the study of Spanish Islam" in the Morisco period.[1] Third, scholars have seen Wahrānī's advice, together with the Moriscos' seemingly enthusiastic reception of it, as a significant instance of Sunnī recourse to *taqiyya*. This doctrine, which allows for precautionary dissimulation in the face of danger, is usually associated exclusively with Shīʿī Islam.[2]

---

1 Harvey, *Muslims in Spain*, 60.

2 On the question of Morisco *taqiyya*, especially as relates to Wahrānī's text, see L. P. Harvey, "Crypto-Islam in Sixteenth-Century Spain," in *Actas del Primer Congreso de Estudios Árabes e Islámicos, Córdoba, 1962*, ed. F.M. Pareja (Madrid: Comité Permanente del Congreso de

Despite over a century of scholarship on Wahranī's "1504 *fatwā*," central aspects of the text have remained obscure. The author was known only as the "Muftī of Oran" until 2006, when Devin Stewart identified him and clarified that he probably authored this text in Fez, where he had settled, not in Oran, his childhood home.[3] In this chapter, I argue that the so-called "1504 *fatwā*" was not a *fatwā*. Wahrānī most likely composed this text as an unsolicited letter of support and guidance, not a formal legal opinion issued in response to a petitioner's now-lost question.

It would appear that only one scholar, Abdelkhalek Cheddadi, has raised this possibility—that it was not a *fatwā*. In 2009, he noted that Wahrānī's text lacks two expected elements of a *fatwā*: a succinct reference to a concern or question submitted to the jurist, if not a full record of the question itself; and a robust set of scriptural and legal proof texts to justify Wahrānī's unconventional opinion.[4] Wahrānī alludes to a few Qur'ānic verses and *ḥadīth* reports, but cites only one prior legal authority.

Neither of these problems is definitive proof that this text was not a *fatwā*. We might continue to assume that the question to which Wahrānī responded is lost, and that a lack of proof texts only indicates that he was addressing a lay audience rather than fellow legal professionals. Concision would also have been crucial for a text that was meant to be smuggled into Granada and read clandestinely in the wake of that city's forcible conversions in 1500 and public burning of Arabic books in 1499 and 1501.[5]

Yet, I agree with Cheddadi's doubts and argue that we can make a stronger case for an alternative reading of this text. We have a more plausible reason for Wahrānī's letter than a now-lost question: the 1501 Morisco Appeal to the Ottoman sultan Bāyazīd II. The striking correspondence between Wahrānī's advice and the specific hardships described by the Moriscos in this earlier

---

Estudios Árabes e Islámicos, 1964), 163–64, 170–71; Cardaillac, *Morisques et Chrétiens*; Sabbagh, "La Religion," 53–55; Míkel de Epalza, "L'Identité onomastique et linguistique des morisques," in *Actes du II symposium international du C.I.E.M. sur religion, identité et sources documentaries sur les morisques andalous*, ed. Abdeljelil Temimi (Tunis: Institut Supérieur de Documentation, 1984), 269–79; Fierro, "La Emigración," 21–22; de Epalza, "La voz oficial," 290–95; Rubiera Mata, "Los moriscos," 545–47; Cheddadi, "Émigrer ou rester?" 8–9; María del Mar Rosa-Rodríguez, "Simulation and Dissimulation: Religious Hybridity in a Morisco Fatwa," *Medieval Encounters* 16 (2010), 143–58; Luis F. Bernabé-Pons, "*Taqiyya, niyya* y el islam de los moriscos," *Al-Qanṭara* 34, no. 2 (2013): 491–500; Devin Stewart, "Dissimulation in Sunni Islam and Morisco *Taqiyya*," *Al-Qanṭara* 34, no. 2 (2013): 439–90; Patrick J. O'Banion, "'They Will Know Our Hearts': Practicing the Art of Dissimulation on the Islamic Periphery," *Journal of Early Modern History* 20 (2016): 193–217.

3 See Stewart, "Identity," esp. 295–300.

4 Cheddadi, "Émigrer ou rester?" 7–8.

5 On book burning and additional legislation against the use of Arabic, see van Koningsveld and Wiegers, "Appeal of the Moriscos," 172–73; Mercedes García-Arenal and Fernando Rodríguez Mediano, *The Orient in Spain: Converted Muslims, the Forged Lead Books of Granada, and the Rise of Orientalism*, trans. Consuelo López-Morillas (Leiden: Brill, 2013), 41–42; 47–56.

appeal, composed in the formal Arabic verse of a *qaṣīda*, suggests a direct textual relationship. Despite continued interest in both of these texts, the connections between them have remained unnoticed and unexplored. In this chapter I advance a tentative case for their interconnection and explore the implications of reading Wahrānī's text as a response to a formal poem meant to move a sultan, not a practical question posed to a jurist.

The First Moriscos

Wahrānī composed his letter just fifteen years after *Asnā al-matājir* and the Marbella *fatwā*, a short span of time in which the fortunes of Granada's Muslims changed dramatically. When Ferdinand and Isabella took control of Granada in January 1492, Iberia's last independent Muslims became Mudéjars. Initially, their legal status was not novel; Muslims had been living under Christian rule in Iberia for four centuries, since the 1085 fall of Toledo. The Capitulations of Granada, signed on 25 November 1491, were considered quite generous.[6] Muslims retained ownership of their homes and mosques, were not to be disturbed in their religious practices and customs, were to be judged by their own laws and judges, and were not only permitted to immigrate to North Africa if they preferred, but would be assisted in doing so. In return, they only had to give up any Christian captives,[7] pay their customary taxes for the first three years (to be adjusted thereafter), and agree to be faithful subjects to their new monarchs.

The protections promised by this treaty of surrender lasted less than a decade.[8] While Christian immigration to Granada was initially limited because Christians had agreed to respect Muslim property rights, in 1498 the city was split into two residential zones. Muslims agreed to live in the hilly Albaicín district, to make way for an influx of Christian settlers who were recruited, in part, through royal tax incentives. The following year, Cardinal Francisco Jiménez de Cisneros, the Archbishop of Toledo and Queen Isabella's confessor, arrived in Granada and launched an aggressive campaign to convert the city's Muslims. Cisneros convinced Isabella and Ferdinand that the efforts of Granada's own archbishop, Hernando de

6 Harvey provides a partial translation of the Capitulations of Granada in *Islamic Spain*, 314–21.

7 Christian captives are mentioned in at least four of this treaty's 48 provisions (numbers 15, 37, 38, and 42, as listed in Harvey's translation noted above). These were captives taken during the ten-year war for Granada (1482–92) or in the course of frontier-raiding expeditions between Granada and Castile, then held for ransom or sold into slavery. In provision no. 26, the capitulations mention Christian slaves taken to North Africa.

8 On this period from 1492 to 1502, see Harvey, *Islamic Spain*, 324–39; Harvey, *Muslims in Spain*, 14–58; García-Arenal and Rodríguez Mediano, *The Orient in Spain*, 35–63; David Coleman, *Creating Christian Granada: Society and Religious Culture in an Old-World Frontier City, 1492–1600* (Ithaca, NY: Cornell University Press, 2003), 1–20.

Talavera, were producing too few converts. Whereas Talavera respected the capitulations and advocated the use of Arabic in preaching and persuasion, Cisneros turned to physical force, bribery, and publicly burning Arabic books. His initial targets consisted of Christian converts to Islam ("renegades" or *elches*) and their families, a group that had been explicitly protected by the treaty of surrender.

The tensions fostered by Cisneros's new tactics came to a head in December 1499, when residents of the Albaicín killed an officer of justice who had been sent to question the daughter of a renegade. Muslims sealed off their quarter in a short-lived uprising that the Crown quickly put down, but with severe consequences. The capitulations were annulled and Granada's Muslims were forced to choose between conversion or expulsion from the kingdom, in exchange for a royal pardon for rebellion. The mass conversions, carried out between December 1499 and February 1500, sparked a wave of revolts in the Alpujarras and the mountains near Ronda. These revolts were suppressed militarily, with considerable violence and additional mass conversions, over the course of approximately one year (1500–1501). In their wake, Isabella issued an edict in July 1501 prohibiting all unconverted Muslims from remaining in, or entering, the former Kingdom of Granada; the rationale was that these free Muslims would disrupt the Christianization of the new converts.[9] A *pragmática* proclaimed in Seville in 1502 extended this policy requiring emigration or conversion to the remainder of Castile and León. As emigration was subject to nearly insurmountable restrictions, the vast majority of Muslims converted to Christianity. By 1526, the same policy was extended throughout Spain, bringing the Mudéjar period to an end.

The 1501 Morisco Appeal

An introduction to the Morisco Appeal and to Wahrānī's text is necessary, prior to making a case for their connection. The Morisco Appeal is undated and anonymous; it comes to us through *Azhār al-riyāḍ fī akhbār ʿIyāḍ*, a biographical work by the seventeenth-century Maghribī historian Aḥmad al-Maqqarī (d. 1041/1632).[10] Maqqarī explains that an Iberian Muslim composed this poem for Ottoman sultan Abī Yazīd (Bāyazīd II, r. 1481–1512) after the "infidels" (as he refers to the Christians) had gained full control of the peninsula. Based on the events described in the text, James

9 Meyerson, *Muslims of Valencia*, 53–56.

10 Maqqarī, *Azhār al-riyāḍ*, 1:108–15. This work is far broader than the biography of Andalusī judge al-Qāḍī ʿIyāḍ (d. 544/1149) for which it is named. On Maqqarī, see *EI*², s.v. "Al-Maḳḳarī" (E. Lévi-Provençal and Ch. Pellat); Sabahat Adil, "Memorializing al-Maqqarī: The Life, Work, and Worlds of a Muslim Scholar," PhD dissertation, University of Chicago, 2015.

Monroe has argued convincingly that a Morisco must have composed the text in 1501.[11] These events include the forced conversions of Granada's Muslims, the annulment of the Capitulations of Granada, and the brutal suppression of rebellions in several villages of the Alpujarras, all of which occurred between late 1499 and early 1501. The poem opens and closes with praise of the recipient and appeals for aid, while the body of the *qaṣīda* is devoted to three themes: the indignities suffered by the Muslims following the Christians' violation of the treaty of surrender; the forced nature of the Muslims' conversion to Christianity, and the Muslims' desire to publicly profess their continued adherence to Islam, an ambition that required the sultan's aid to achieve.

The appeal begins with a prose introduction addressed to the Ottoman court, praising Bāyazīd II and praying for the expansion of his realm.[12] The author refers to "Our Lord Abū Yazīd" as the "Sultan of Islam and the Muslims," who is king of the Arabs, Turks, and others across two seas and two continents. This flattering and strategic recognition of Bāyazīd's authority over, and thus responsibility to protect all Muslims is reinforced in the first line of the poem, which is addressed to "the best of caliphs." Both the introduction and poem's invocation (verses 1–18) emphasize the Ottoman emperor's role as the conqueror of infidels and the defender of the faith, whose victories have been aided by God and, it is hoped, will make Bāyazīd "king over every nation" (line 6). Here the poet refers to military conquest as one of the primary bases of the emperor's legitimacy, perhaps to remind any unintended Christian readers of the Ottomans' growing power.

The second half of the poem's invocation (lines 9–18) introduces the community of Granadan Muslims in need of aid. The appeal is sent "on behalf of some slaves who have remained in a land of exile, in Andalus in the West (*ʿabīd takhallafū bi-Andalus biʾl-gharb fī arḍ ghurba*)" (line 9). At the outset, the poet establishes two important terms of identification. This is the first of three instances in which the poet refers to his community as slaves (*ʿabīd*) instead of worshipers (*ʿibād*),[13] to emphasize the violence done to them and their situation of powerlessness. He also indicates that their geographic location, formerly at the western edge (*al-gharb*) of Islamdom, has become an isolated land of exile (*arḍ ghurba*). While this

11 James T. Monroe, "A Curious Morisco Appeal to the Ottoman Empire," *Al-Andalus* 31, nos. 1–2 (1966): 282–83. Monroe provides the full Arabic text (289–93) and an English translation of the *qaṣīda* (294–303), but omits the prose introduction. All English translations and line numbers below are based on Monroe, with minor adjustments.

12 Maqqarī, *Azhār al-riyāḍ*, 108–9. Van Koningsveld and Wiegers provide an English translation of the introduction, omitted by Monroe, in van Koningsveld and Wiegers, "Appeal of the Moriscos," 166–67.

13 In the singular, *ʿabd* can mean either slave or servant, but the plurals are distinct: *ʿabīd* generally means slaves, whereas *ʿibād* means servants of God, or Muslims.

is the poet's only reference to *ghurba*, it may be the basis for Wahrānī's repeated use of this important concept, as seen below.

The remainder of the invocation lists some of the calamities that have stricken this community. Old men have been reduced to tearing out their hair, women have been made to unveil their faces, priests have forced young women into secluded places, and old women have been compelled to eat pork and carrion.[14] These afflictions build toward the two central complaints of the poem: their forcible conversion to Christianity and betrayal by the Christian authorities (line 20). The following section of the poem accounts for this tragic turn of affairs, justifies the Muslims' actions, and stresses that they did everything in their power to retain their autonomy and religious identity. The Muslims fought with all their might until their armies were devastated, their walls were destroyed by cannon fire, and their food stores diminished (lines 21–31). It was also clear, notes the poet, that "no rescue was forthcoming from our brethren" (line 30). Still, they surrendered only to spare their children's lives, and because the terms of their victors appeared acceptable: they would be allowed to live like Mudéjars, with the freedom to practice their religion and to remain in their homes if they liked, or to immigrate across the sea if they preferred (lines 32–39). After defeat came treachery: the Christian ruler broke the treaties that he had guaranteed to uphold and "converted us to Christianity by force, with harshness and severity" (lines 37–41).

A list of grievances inflicted upon the Moriscos in the wake of their forced conversions follows (lines 42–64). All Arabic books of religion were burned with scorn; those who were discovered to have fasted or prayed were also cast into the fire; those who refused to attend church were imprisoned and their property was seized; food and drink were forced upon them during Ramadan; they were ordered to curse the Prophet Muḥammad; those overheard chanting Muḥammad's name were beaten and imprisoned; the dead were refused burial unless a priest could administer to them; and Muslims' names were changed against their will. The poet places equal emphasis on the dire conditions of the Moriscos and the severe consequences they faced for

14 I translate "*khalwa*" here as "secluded places" rather than Monroe's "bed of shame"; I believe Wahrānī is referring to the prohibition of a woman of marriageable age being alone with an unrelated man in a private place where illegitimate physical contact could occur. Qualified support for these complaints (or fears?) can be found in the new capitulation agreements drawn up between 1499 and 1501 for several towns in the former Kingdom of Granada. As an example of these Morisco-period agreements, Harvey summarizes the 1501 capitulations for Vélez Rubio in *Muslims in Spain*, 45–48. The provisions stipulate that meat must be slaughtered in the Christian manner, that clergy will be appointed to instruct the townspeople in the Catholic faith, and that they will be allowed to wear their current clothes (only) until they wear out. Van Koningsveld and Wiegers point to Angel Gálan Sánchez's finding that this otherwise common stipulation regarding clothing is missing for the towns that participated in the Alpujarras revolts; thus, they may have been forced to abandon their dress upon surrender and conversion. Van Koningsveld and Wiegers, "Appeal of the Moriscos," 171.

resistance or persevering in the practice of Islam, underscoring at every turn that they were powerless to prevent this oppression on their own. The final part of this section shifts into a present-tense lament rather than a historical account; in it, the poet deplores the Moriscos' new Christian identities, the idolatry with which priests indoctrinate their defenseless children every day, their former mosques that have been turned into dungheaps, minarets that have been transformed into belltowers, and their towns that protect only Christians. "We have become slaves," reiterates the poet, "not captives who may be ransomed, nor even Muslims who pronounce their declaration of faith" (line 64).

The poet's singular focus on religious concerns is striking. In *Asnā al-matājir*, Wansharīsī rejected the unhappy Andalusīs' claims that they had emigrated with a valid religious intention, because their complaints focused on material concerns and physical safety. In contrast, the appeal presents the Moriscos as wholly focused on religious identity and practice. Any pressing concerns related to their livelihoods, living quarters, safety, food supplies, or health were strategically omitted. The poet instead addresses three of the five "pillars" of Islam (the testament of faith, prayer, and fasting) along with categorically prohibited acts (cursing the Prophet, eating pork), the erasure of Islam from public recognition (burnt books, changed names, the violation of the sanctity of mosques and minarets), and the threat that Muslim children will be raised as Christians. This carefully curated set of complaints, emphasizing the Moriscos' threatened but persistent identity as Muslims, is restricted to the most salient grounds for appeal to the Ottoman emperor as caliph and defender of the faith.

The final third of the *qaṣīda* (lines 65–105) lists the Moriscos' specific requests and stresses even more forcefully that the Moriscos' conversion to Christianity is forced and not sincere. Their primary request is for Bāyazīd to intercede with the Pope (line 76), and force him to account for the treachery of the Catholic Monarchs (i.e., the title given to Ferdinand and Isabella). The bases of this challenge are the two key principles of reciprocity and fidelity. The poet notes that when Muslim kings had power (presumably in Iberia), they protected the Christians, who retained their religion and their homes (lines 78–79). The Muslims were faithful to their word, as breaking treaties is against every faith and is especially disgraceful on the part of a king (lines 78, 80–81). The poet also points to Ottoman control of Christianity's place of origin (line 73), implying that Bāyazīd should threaten reprisals if the Moriscos' right to practice Islam was not restored.[15] This principle of

15 Van Koningsveld and Wiegers note that this "place of origin" may refer to Asia Minor broadly. If it refers to Jerusalem specifically, which remained under Mamluk control until 1517, this line would represent a mistake in the revision of this appeal from an earlier version directed to the Mamluk sultan in Cairo ("Appeal of the Moriscos, 175"). Van Koningsveld and Wiegers,

reciprocity and retaliation in the treatment of religious minorities was an established component of Muslim-Christian international relations in the Mediterranean since at least the early fourteenth century.[16]

Not only had prior embassies been unsuccessful in convincing Ferdinand and Isabella to change their policies, but the poet further indicates that the Catholic Monarchs lied to a recent Egyptian delegation, claiming that the Muslims of Granada had chosen conversion of their own free will (lines 84–87).[17] This report underscores the Moriscos' desperation, after an initial appeal to Mamluk Egypt failed, and then introduces one of the most emotionally charged sections of the poem. The poet reiterates that it was only "fear of death and being burned" that impelled them to convert and assures his audience that "in every glance our recognition of God's monotheism can be observed" (lines 88–89). If the Christian rulers persist in claiming that these conversions were obtained without violence, the sultan is challenged to "ask Huéjar about its inhabitants: how they became captives and slaughterlings under [the burden] of humiliation and misfortune . . . Ask Belefique . . . As for Andarax, its people were consumed by fire. It was in their mosque that they all became like charcoal" (lines 92 and 95). Other historical sources corroborate the events cited and help us date the poem. Christian chroniclers Luis del Mármol Carvajal and Alonso de Santa Cruz reported that in early 1500, soldiers killed 3,000 Muslim prisoners in Andarax, and the explosion of a nearby mosque killed an additional 600 women and children who had taken refuge inside.[18] The

---

who discovered the Mamluk version in a privately-held Moroccan manuscript, compare the two in "Appeal of the Moriscos." They suggest that the Mamluk version was composed in early 1500 and the Ottoman version about a year later, in early 1501. They place the Ottoman version after the Egyptian delegation came to Granada, which indicated the failure of the Mamluk Appeal, and before the conversion edict of July 1501. I do not find it necessary for the text to have been composed prior to this edict, but there is also no reason to assume that it was composed much later than the events cited in the text. The poet's repeated complaint that his community has been forcibly converted may refer to the conversions that followed the Albaicín and Alpujarras revolts only, or may include the 1501 edict.

16 For example, in 1302 King James II of Aragon convinced Mamluk sultan al-Nāṣir Muḥammad to re-open some Christian churches in Egypt that had been closed, arguing that Muslims in Aragon would receive treatment comparable to that of Christians under the sultan's rule. See van Koningsveld and Weigers, "Appeal of the Moriscos," 179–86, for further details on this and other diplomatic negotiations between the thirteenth and fifteenth centuries.

17 José Enrique López de Coca Castañer argues that the Egyptian delegation to Ferdinand and Isabella, which is only mentioned in the Ottoman version, can be dated to April 1501. López de Coca Castañer, "Mamelucos, otomanos y caída del reino de Granada," *En la España Medieval* 25 (2008): 246.

18 On Andarax, Huéjar, and Belefique, see the sources quoted in van Koningsveld and Wiegers, "An Appeal of the Moriscos," 177–78; Monroe, "Curious Morisco Appeal," 301–2; Harvey, *Muslims in Spain*, 42–43; L. P. Harvey, "The Political, Social, and Cultural History of the Moriscos," in *The Legacy of Muslim Spain*, ed. Salma Khadra Jayyusi, 2nd ed., 2 vols. (Leiden: Brill, 1994), 1:207–8.

1499 Huéjar uprising resulted in the slaughter of its inhabitants in January 1500, and in early 1501 the men of Belefique were killed or imprisoned for their revolt, while the women were taken captive. In a version of the appeal preserved in a nineteenth-century Moroccan biography, this section of the poem is extended to include the 1501 suppression of a revolt in Málaga.[19] As the poem cites these particular historical incidents but does not mention any events beyond early 1501, it is reasonable to assume that it was composed in mid-1501.

Following this list of atrocities, the poet returns to the Moriscos' specific requests:

> Could our religion not be left to us as well as our ritual prayer, as they swore to do before the agreement was broken? If not, let them allow us to emigrate from their land to North Africa, the homeland of our dear ones, with our belongings. For emigration is better for us than remaining in unbelief, enjoying power but having no religion (lines 97–99).

Notably, the Moriscos' first choice is to remain where they are, but to return to the Mudéjar status that they were promised initially and that their fellow Muslims enjoyed for such a long time. Only in the event that this is impossible would they like to emigrate to North Africa, a fate the poet seems to find so unpleasant that he must clarify that this would at least be better than apostasy. It is also significant that these two options should be pursued diplomatically, presumably as part of Bāyazīd's negotiations via the Pope. While the appeal hints at the threat of retaliation against Christians living under Ottoman rule, there is no suggestion or hope that the sultan might rescue the Moriscos through force of arms. This diplomatic approach was realistic, as the Ottomans (and the Mamluks before them) were fully occupied elsewhere, and this would have served as a precaution lest the appeal was intercepted in Iberia. Fears that the Moriscos would serve as a "fifth column" for invading Muslims persisted throughout the sixteenth century and were a major factor in the expulsion of the Moriscos from 1609 to 1614.

---

19 Ibn al-Ḥājj al-Sulamī's biography, also mentioned in chapter 4, contains four additional lines not included in Maqqarī's version. Beyond mentioning Málaga, they reiterate the Moriscos' status as "slaves unable to practice their religion" and stress the severity with which the Christians punished those who refused to convert. It is unclear whether or not these lines should be accepted as part of the original poem sent to Bāyazīd II. It is likely that Maqqarī's version is abridged or was based on a deficient manuscript (as van Koningsveld and Wiegers suggest), but it is also possible that Sulamī's version represents a later embellishment. Sulamī's commentary before and after the poem is based on unacknowledged passages in the anonymous Arabic chronicle *Akhbār al-ʿaṣr*, with some significant changes. See Ibn al-Ḥājj al-Sulamī, *Riyāḍ al-ward fīmā intamā ilayh hādhā al-jawhar al-fard*, ed. Jaʿfar b. al-Ḥājj al-Sulamī (Damascus: Maṭbaʿat al-Kātib al-ʿArabī, 1993), 1:195–201; Anon., *Akhbār al-ʿaṣr fī inqiḍāʾ dawlat Banī Naṣr*, ed. Ḥusayn Muʾnis (Cairo: al-Zahrāʾ lil-Iʿlām al-ʿArabī, 1991), 117–19; Anon., *Nubdhat al-ʿaṣr*, 108–11; van Koningsveld and Wiegers, "Appeal of the Moriscos," 162–63, 177–78.

We know little about the circulation of the appeal, but can surmise that at least one copy was brought to Morocco, possibly not long after its composition. This is where we find the only extant copy of the earlier 1500 Morisco appeal to the Mamluks. And this is also where Maqqarī would have encountered the 1501 version sent to the Ottomans. While he composed his more famous *Nafḥ al-ṭīb* in Cairo, Maqqarī gathered his biographical and historical materials in the Maghrib and wrote *Azhār al-riyāḍ* in Fez, where he established an independent legal career after serving in the court of Saʿdian Sultan Aḥmad al-Manṣūr (r. 986–1012/1578–1603).[20] If the version of the 1501 appeal that Ibn al-Ḥājj al-Sulamī (d. 1857) includes in his biographical work *Riyāḍ al-ward* was not adapted from *Azhār al-riyāḍ*, it is possible that he too relied on a version of the text found in Morocco.[21]

Our anonymous Morisco poet, who presumably composed both the Mamluk and Ottoman versions of the appeal, may have emigrated to Morocco with copies of both texts, or they may have been carried by a close associate. Van Koningsveld and Wiegers have suggested that the poet, who likely belonged to an elite class of Granadan Muslims, may have accepted administrative responsibilities under Christian rule in post-1492 Granada.[22] This status would explain his knowledge of past diplomatic exchanges and might have allowed him the resources and connections to immigrate to North Africa even after the forced conversions. Alternatively, the appeal sent to Bāyazīd might have traveled through the Maghrib and been copied on its way to Istanbul.

The "1504 *Fatwā*"

It is quite plausible that a copy of the 1501 Appeal found its way to Morocco before the end of the year, and to Fez within the next two years. There it might have come to the attention of another recent emigrant to the Waṭṭāsid capital, Aḥmad b. Abī Jumʿa al-Wahrānī.[23] After spending his childhood in Oran (thus the *nisba* "al-Wahrānī"), Ibn Abī Jumʿa—much like his contemporary Wansharīsī—completed his legal education in Tlemcen, where he remained

20 Maqqarī was born in Tlemcen in approximately 1577 and received his formative training there, then spent most of the period between 1600 and 1618 in Fez and Marrakesh. He traveled east in 1618, initially to perform the pilgrimage, but never returned. He composed *Nafḥ al-ṭīb*, his famous history of Muslim Iberia and biography of Granadan polymath Lisān al-Dīn b. al-Khaṭīb (d. 776/1374–5), in Cairo, where he died in 1041/1632. See Adil, "Memorializing al-Maqqarī," for details on his life and works.

21 Sulamī may have relied on the same copy of the 1501 appeal as did Maqqarī, with Maqqarī omitting the four lines noted above. Alternatively, Maqqarī and Sulamī may have worked from different copies of the appeal; or Sulamī's version may represent a later embellishment (his own or someone else's) of the original.

22 Van Koningsveld and Wiegers, "Appeal of the Moriscos," 185.

23 On the identity, life, and works of Abū al-ʿAbbās Aḥmad b. Abī Jumʿa al-Maghrāwī al-Wahrānī, see Stewart, "Identity"; on the likely date of his move to Fez, see p. 296.

for the early part of his career. Stewart suggests that Wahrānī then moved to Fez sometime after 1493, but well before his death there in 917/1511. In Fez, he became a prominent jurist, teaching in one of the city's many colleges of law. It was here that he would have composed his "1504 *fatwā*"—which I refer to as "Wahrānī's letter" or "the 1504 Letter" from this point on—and would have encountered the Moriscos who prompted his missive.

We do not have the original of Wahrānī's text, but four extant versions offer clues as to its dating and contents. The copy known as "V" (for Vatican) is the only one in Arabic; in 1951, historian Muḥammad ʿAbd Allāh ʿInān discovered that it had been copied into the initial folios of an unrelated manuscript volume now preserved in the Vatican library.[24] This copy offers a clear date for the text's original composition, which is confirmed in copies "M" (for Madrid) and "X" (for unknown location): 1 Rajab 910/8 December 1504. The copy date for V is unknown, but must post-date the volume itself, which was copied in Paterna, Valencia, in 1519.[25] As suggested by Harvey and seemingly confirmed by the other copies, V may be partially abridged because of space constraints; for example, it omits a number of pious phrases present in "A" (for Aix-en-Provence). Nonetheless, this version remains the most reliable, as it is likely the earliest copy and the only one in Arabic, the original language of the text.

The versions known as M and A are Wahrānī's Arabic text translated into *aljamiado*, or Spanish written in a modified Arabic script.[26] Copy M confirms the composition date of 1 Rajab 910 (in Hijrī only) and adds a copy date of 3

24 Copy V is MS Vatican, Borgiano arabo 171, fols. 2–4. Harvey provides a full Arabic edition of V, establishes the four abbreviations used here, and reproduces images of the manuscript folios containing V in "Crypto-Islam," 174–78; the folios appear on five unnumbered plates between pp. 178 and 179. Harvey also offers a near-complete English translation of V in *Muslims in Spain*, 61–63. Stewart offers a partial English translation in "Dissimulation," 476–77. Rubiera Mata provides a nearly complete Spanish translation in "Los moriscos," 541–54. Copy V was first discovered by Muḥammad ʿAbd Allāh ʿInān, who published his Arabic edition three times between 1952 and 1966; for publication details see Stewart, "Identity," 266–67, n. 3.

25 On the date and provenance of this volume, see Rubiera Mata, "Los moriscos," 545–46; Pieter Sjoerd van Koningsveld and Gerard Wiegers, "Marcos Dobelio's Polemics against the Authenticity of the Granadan Lead Books in Light of the Original Arabic Sources," in *Polemical Encounters: Christians, Jews, and Muslims in Iberia and Beyond*, ed. Mercedes García-Arenal and Gerard Wiegers (University Park, PA: Pennsylvania State University Press, 2019), 264–65 n. 26 and n. 37.

26 Version M is MS Madrid, Library of the Real Academia de la Historia, 280.13 (T-13 of the Gayangos collection), fols. 28r–32r. Pedro Longás first published a partial, modernized transcription of M in his *Vida religiosa de los moriscos* (Madrid, 1915), 305–7; Harvey offers a complete transcription in "Crypto-Islam," 171–74. Version A is Bibliothèque Méjanes MS 1223, fols. 130r–139r (also numbered MS 1367). Jean Cantineau published a transcription of the *aljamiado* along with a French translation in his "Lettre du Moufti d'Oran aux Musulmans d'Andalousie," *Journal Asiatique*, 210 (1927), 1–17 (Cantineau incorrectly records the folios as 130v–138v). Rubiera Mata has published a modernized Spanish translation of A online through the Fundación Biblioteca Virtual Miguel de Cervantes: http://www.cervantesvirtual.com/nd/ark:/59851/bmcdz066. Accessed February 9, 2018.

May 1563 (in Gregorian only). This copy is shorter than V, as the translator omitted some passages that were difficult to understand or translate. Only copy A gives the original composition date as the beginning of Rajab 909 (or December 1503), likely the error of a translator who may have been working from an intermediary copy with only a Christian date.[27] We have no copy date for A, but it appears to be an integral part of a coherent volume that has been dated to 1609. The volume, containing texts in both Arabic and *aljamiado*, is largely concerned with Islamic worship, especially prayer and purity. Scholars have concurred that both A and M were produced by and for Aragonese Moriscos, whose primary language had shifted from Arabic to Romance long before their legal status changed from Mudéjar to Morisco.[28] If A was indeed copied in 1609, the same year as the Edict of Expulsion, Wahrānī's text would be one of the first written for Moriscos and one of the last to be copied by them, over a century later.

Manuscripts of Wahrānī's Text
Original composed in Arabic in Fez in 910/1504

Version (named for current location)	**Presumed copy date and place**	**Language**	**Notes**
V (for Vatican)	1519 or later, Valencia	Arabic	Potentially abridged; found in Pastrana (Castile) in 1622, later sent to the Vatican
M (for Madrid)	3 May 1563, Aragon	*aljamiado*	Omits some passages
A (for Aix-en-Provence)	1609, Aragon	*aljamiado*	
X (for location unkown; now found in Madrid)	1633, Madrid	Spanish in Latin letters	Translation of V by Marcos Dobelio, with added commentary

27 This is the explanation offered by Cantineau, "Lettre du Moufti," 15–16. On this date, see also Harvey, "Crypto-Islam," 165–66.

28 On the provenance of the manuscript volume containing A, see Jean-Pierre Molénat, "Le manuscript *aljamiado* Méjannes 1367 (1223): Un itinéraire entre l'Aragon et la Provence," in *Tercera Primavera del Manuscrito Andalusi: Viajes y viajeros*, ed. Mostafa Ammadi, 99–105 (Casablanca: Universidad Hassan II, Facultad de Letras y Ciencias Humanas, 2011).

Copy X is a 1633 Spanish translation of V, composed in Latin letters.[29] Unlike the *aljamiado* versions A and M, it was produced by and for Christians after the 1609–14 expulsion of the Moriscos. Scholarship on X, which was assumed lost until María del Mar Rosa-Rodríguez located it in Madrid in 2006, has advanced considerably in recent years. Mercedes García-Arenal and Fernando Rodríguez Mediano identified the translator as Marcos Dobelio (ca. 1572–1654), an Arabophone eastern Christian of Kurdish origin who worked as a professor of Arabic in Rome before moving to Spain in 1610.[30] A committee assembled by King Philip III (r. 1598–1621) appears to have recruited Dobelio that year to assist the Archbishop of Granada and Seville, Pedro Vaca de Castro y Quiñones (1534–1623) with his ongoing efforts to translate the "Lead Books of the Sacromonte." These cryptic texts were discovered buried in a hillside near Granada between 1594 and 1599, and were purported to be ancient Christian writings, composed in Arabic by two Arab Christian saints who arrived in Iberia during the first Christian century. The discovery was accompanied by newly unearthed saints' relics, stories of miraculous healing, and a great enthusiasm among the clergy and populace for what these texts had to offer: a sacred Christian past for a newly Christianized city, and a preeminent place for Spain in the stories of Christianity's first saints and martyrs. Eventually, the texts turned out to be elaborate forgeries, likely produced by Moriscos in a last-ditch attempt to forge common theological ground between Muslims and Christians in Iberia, to revalorize Arabic, and to preserve a tolerable space for Moriscos in Spain.

Pieter Sjoerd van Koningsveld and Gerard Wiegers have recently argued that Dobelio's translation of Wahrānī's letter forms part of a treatise Dobelio authored in 1633 titled *Discurso sobre el libro que se hallo en el monte de Valparayso entitulado uida y milagros de Xro nuestro señor* (Discourse on the Book Which Was Found on Mount Valparaíso Entitled *Life and Miracles of Christ Our Lord*).[31] Dobelio also mentions Wahrānī's text in the

29 Copy X is MS BRAH Gayangos n. 1922/36 (antiguo 28), fols. 343r–346r. In 2006, María del Mar Rosa-Rodríguez located this version, long assumed lost, at the Real Academia de la Historia in Madrid. She subsequently published the first transcription and translation of X. See Rosa-Rodríguez, "Simulation and Dissimulation," esp. 158–65 (discussion), 165–74 (transcription), and 174–80 (English translation).

30 On Marcus Dobelio and his relationship to the Lead Books and copy X of Wahrānī's text, see García-Arenal and Rodríguez Mediano, *The Orient in Spain*, chapters 11–12, 245–94; van Koningsveld and Wiegers, "Marcos Dobelio's Polemics," 203–21, 263–65. García-Arenal and Rodríguez Mediano provide an overview of the Lead Books affair in *The Orient in Spain*, chapter 1, 13–33.

31 Van Koningsveld and Wiegers locate the *Dirscurso* in fols. 269r–387v of Royal Academia de la Historia MS 19-2-2 36 (a slightly different rendering of this MS number than the one offered by Rosa-Rodríguez, above). Dobelio's title refers to the *Vita Jesu* (for short), which is Lead Book no. 7 (of 21). See Van Koningsveld and Wiegers, "Marcos Dobelio's Polemics," 206–7,

introduction to his 1638 *Nuevo descubrimiento de la falsedad del metal* (*The New Unveiling of the Falseness of Metal*), a work in which he argued that the Lead Books were a Morisco forgery.[32] In the *Nuevo descubrimiento*, Dobelio grounded his controversial arguments for Morisco authorship in the Arabic style of the Lead Books and in their content, in which Christian characters populate the narratives and are infused with qualities adapted from Islamic and Arabic sources. Thanks to a cache of Morisco texts placed at his disposal by the Inquisitor General, Don Pedro Pacheco, Dobelio was able to trace this Christianized content to its origins in specific Arabic texts known to have circulated in Morisco communities. This cache, which appears to have contained copy V of the 1504 *fatwā*, was found abandoned in a house in Pastrana, in the province of Guadalajara in New Castile.[33] When Granada's Moriscos were forcibly relocated in the wake of the Second Alpujarras Rebellion in 1568–70, a substantial number settled in Pastrana, where they continued to speak Arabic up until—and even after—their expulsion in 1610.[34] At least two sets of abandoned Arabic books were discovered in Pastrana in 1615 and 1622, many of which were forwarded to the Inquisitor General. Dobelio appears to have consulted these texts between 1622 and the drafting of his two treatises in 1633 and 1638; thereafter, the volume containing V would have been forwarded to its present location in the Vatican.

Prior to the most recent research linking Dobelio to V, scholars raised the possibility that Dobelio was working from an Arabic version of Wahrānī's original letter that may have preserved more of Wahrānī's original text than does V. This speculation arose because X is much longer than V; could Dobelio have had access to an unabridged, but now lost, Arabic version of Wahrānī's letter? This now seems unlikely, but we must nonetheless account for the additional material present in X, and articulate why it is that we should not attribute that additional material to Wahrānī.

Dobelio was writing for a Christian audience, in support of a highly controversial position, and over a century after Wahrānī's original

---

210. These authors also offer the first Arabic edition and English translation of this Lead Book, which was only made available to researchers in 2010. See "Marcos Dobelio's Polemics," 222–63.

32 Only the introduction to the *Nuevo descubrimiento* is extant, in three copies, but van Koningsveld and Wiegers characterize this introduction as a full treatise. Van Koningsveld and Wiegers, "Marcos Dobelio's Polemics," 207.

33 Researchers initially believed that this cache must have contained an Arabic copy of Wahrānī's letter, possibly a longer version than V. Van Koningsveld and Wiegers now argue that Dobelio was working specifically with V, not another Arabic version of the letter. Van Koningsveld and Wiegers, "Marcos Dobelio's Polemics," 264–65, nn. 26 and 37.

34 On Pastrana's Morisco community and this cache of books, see García-Arenal and Rodríguez Mediano, *The Orient in Spain*, 275–85. A 1631 report suggests that fifteen Morisco families still lived in Pastrana.

composition. I argue that he added the material unique to version X in order to explain points of doctrine unfamiliar to his audience, "translate" concepts into Christian terms, or bolster his own arguments regarding this text and its relationship to the Lead Books. The preamble to X, for example, expresses hope that the Moriscos will receive forgiveness for their sins and that they will be counted among those who have confessed and received grace. This language has no equivalent in the other versions and must represent Dobelio's attempt to render the text more intelligible to a Christian audience, rather than material original to Wahrānī that is missing from version V.[35] A postscript pertaining to prayer and purity, the most notable section that is unique to X, cannot be a faithful rendition of Wahrānī's original. It refers to Muḥammad as the "false prophet," replaces the Qur'ānic address "Oh you who believe!" with "Oh you who have fallen," and refers to the fifth *sūra* (chapter) of the Qur'ān as the fourth. This postscript further notes that "they" (Muslims) are confused about the true meaning of "the table" mentioned in Qur'ān 5:112–14, which "we" (Christians) understand as a reference to "the supper of Our Lord or the miracle by which he [Jesus] fed . . . twelve thousand people with five fish and two loaves of bread."[36] In addition to these polemical references, the style of the postscript is markedly different from the main text. The postscript refers to two earlier jurists and a *ḥadīth*, in addition to quoting a long Qur'ān verse (5:6) in full; this constitutes a greater reliance on proof texts than in the remainder of the text, which is devoted to practical advice rather than explanations of doctrine.

Not only does X reflect Dobelio's Christian biases, but we must also bear in mind the larger polemical environment in which this translation was produced. García-Arenal and Rodríguez Mediano contend that Wahrānī's letter was foundational in shaping Dobelio's *Nuevo descubrimiento* into "what it really is, a polemical, anti-Islamic treatise."[37] In the 1504 Letter, Dobelio found evidence that the deceit and subterfuge wrought by the Morisco authors of the Lead Books was justified in Islamic theological terms. Contrary to what their ardent defenders, including Pedro de Castro, wanted to believe, Dobelio argued that these Books were "secret Islamizing

35 Rosa-Rodríguez, "Simulation and Dissimulation," 166–67 (transcription of "X"), 175 (translation, which I have modified slightly). García-Arenal and Rodríguez Mediano (*The Orient in Spain,* 40) note that Christian clergy who instructed new converts in Arabic faced a problem with regard to the lack of an Arabic word or Islamic concept for the confession of sins.

36 Rosa-Rodríguez, "Simulation and Dissimulation," 172–74 (transcription of postscript), 179–80 (translation). Dobelio cites Qur'ān 5:6, a verse related to purification, but his argument with Muslims' understanding of the table reference pertains to 5:112–14, in which a disciple asks Jesus to have the Lord send down a table spread with food. The *sūra* title ("al-Mā'ida") is taken from these verses.

37 García-Arenal and Rodríguez Mediano, *The Orient in Spain*, 291.

literature" legitimized by the same principles that guided the Moriscos' clandestine practice of Islam.[38] Dobelio was quickly dismissed from the Lead Books translation project and was later subjected to personal attacks, including the claim that he was a Muslim convert to Christianity, who reverted to Islam prior to his death.[39]

Each version of Wahrānī's text contributes to our understanding of the Moriscos' changing historical and linguistic circumstances, and to the importance these communities attached to this document. A substantial scholarly literature has summarized and explored various aspects of this text; for the present purposes, I present the 1504 Letter in comparison with the Morisco Appeal. Here I privilege version V, as it is directly comparable to the Arabic in the appeal, and is likely the earliest copy and the most faithful to Wahrānī's original. I also note some elements from version X that are not present in V, along with important discrepancies in the other versions.

The Case for a Textual Relationship

Three elements of Wahrānī's letter bear a compelling resemblance to the Morisco Appeal, and suggest that Wahrānī may have composed his missive in response to the appeal. Two of these shared elements pertain to the two most central aspects of Wahrānī's letter: his validation of the Moriscos' identity as Muslims, and the practical recommendations that he offers this community on how to practice Islam in secret. The third shared element relates to his hope that an Ottoman victory will soon restore these Muslims' freedom to worship publicly.

The Ghurabā'

As noted earlier, the appeal's anonymous poet describes his community as one of slaves and exiles, beyond Islamic territory or power; unable to practice their religion, they inhabit an *arḍ ghurba*, a foreign land or place of exile. This concept is echoed four times in Wahrānī's letter, three times in the preamble and once in the closing:

> "May God grant our brothers, who are holding fast to their religion as one holds fast to a burning ember, abundant rewards . . . Though they are far now, they will be close (*al-ghurabāʾ al-qurabāʾ*), God willing, to the vicinity of His Prophet in the highest garden of paradise . . ."

38 García-Arenal and Rodríguez Mediano, *The Orient in Spain*, 290.

39 García-Arenal and Rodríguez Mediano, *The Orient in Spain*, 250 (dismissal), 265, 266 (examples of personal attacks). Pedro de Castro was particularly invested in the notion that the Lead Books supported the belief in the Immaculate Conception of Mary, which at the time was not yet an official Catholic doctrine. See also van Koningsveld and Wiegers, "Marcos Dobelio's Polemics," 205–6.

> "[The author is] . . . asking you, out of your loyalty in your exile (*ghurbatikum*), to pray assiduously . . ."
>
> "Blessed are those in exile (*al-ghurabāʾ*), who are upright while those around them are corrupt."[40]
>
> "May this message reach those in exile (*al-ghurabāʾ*), God willing."[41]

I argue that Wahrānī adopted a term of self-reference found in the *qaṣīda* that affirms the poet's allusion to a prominent *ḥadīth* stating, "Islam began as a stranger (*gharīb*^{an}) and it will return as a stranger (*gharīb*^{an}), as it began. Therefore, blessed are the strangers (*al-ghurabāʾ*)."[42] Ḥadīth commentators interpreted these "strangers" as a small group of believers who clung to their faith despite considerable suffering at the hands of a non-Muslim majority—like the earliest Muslims in Mecca suffered and persevered. For example, Shāfiʿī scholar Ibn al-Athīr (d. 606/1210) explains,

> the blessing on strangers refers to Paradise (destined) for those Muslims who lived at the beginning of Islam and those who will live at the end. God gave Paradise especially to them, because they bore patiently the harm done to them first and last and adhered steadfastly to the religion of Islam.[43]

Wahrānī's repetition of this heavily symbolic term thus likens his addressees to an embattled remnant of righteous believers surrounded by unbelievers at the end of time. This sense is further heightened by a second *ḥadīth* invoked in Wahrānī's preamble, one that foresees a time when maintaining piety will be as difficult as grasping a live coal.[44]

---

40 The Arabic text of these first three passages may be found in Harvey, "Crypto-Islam," 174–75. All English translations of V are based on an unpublished draft translation by Devin Stewart, with slight modifications and added emphases. I am very grateful to Stewart for permission to cite this work. Harvey's translation of this text in *Muslims in Spain* omits Wahrānī's preamble, where these three passages appear.

41 This line appears in Wahrānī's closing. Harvey, "Crypto-Islam," 178 (Arabic text).

42 *Ṣaḥīḥ Muslim, Kitāb al-Īmān, bāb bayān anna al-Islām badaʾa gharīban . . .* , *ḥadīth* 232 (Muslim b. al-Ḥajjāj, *Ṣaḥīḥ Muslim*, 1:130–31). This *ḥadīth* is recorded in several major collections, with some variants. On this report, see Franz Rosenthal, "The Stranger in Medieval Islam," *Arabica* 44 (1997): 59–63. While it is possible that the poet used *arḍ ghurba* merely as a play on *al-gharb*, the West, this is unlikely. As Harvey notes (*Muslims in Spain*, 63 n. 8) multiple *ḥadīth* reports popular in Iberia envisioned a special role for the *ghurabāʾ* of al-Andalus at the end of time.

43 Majd al-Dīn b. al-Athīr (d. 606/1210), *al-Nihāya fī gharīb al-ḥadīth waʾl-athar*, as quoted in Rosenthal, "The Stranger," 63.

44 This *ḥadīth* states "There will come upon the people a time in which someone who is steadfast in his religion will be like someone who is holding fast to a burning ember." *Sunan al-Tirmidhī, Abwāb al-Fitan, bāb al-ṣābir fīhim . . .* , *ḥadīth* 2426 (Tirmidhī, *Sunan al-Tirmidhī*, 3:330).

Wahrānī's affirmation of the Moriscos' Muslim identity may be read as a response to the poet's clear concern that Muslims in Islamic territory might perceive his community as apostates who are undeserving of rescue. While his letter does not directly address the poet's primary term of self-reference, that of slaves—other than perhaps to replace it with *ghurabāʾ*—Wahrānī appears to respond to the lament that the Moriscos have become "slaves, not captives who may be ransomed, nor even Muslims who pronounce their declaration of faith (*wa-lā muslimīn nuṭquhum biʾl-shahāda*)." In his closing, Wahrānī assures his readers that "We—*we* will witness on your behalf (*wa-naḥnu nashhadu la-kum*) in front of God that you believed in God and accepted Him."[45] It is because the Moriscos cannot bear witness themselves that Wahrānī offers to witness on their behalf, that they were indeed among the faithful.

In X, each of the four passages that read "*ghurabāʾ*" or "*ghurba*" in V are translated into Spanish as *captivos y peregrinos* ("captives and pilgrims").[46] If X is translated from an Arabic copy that contained material not present in the other three versions, as some scholars have suggested, these passages may indicate that Wahrānī (in his original text) also responded to the reference to captivity (cited above). In that case, these puzzling references to captivity could be a rejoinder to the appeal, and meant to confirm that the Moriscos are indeed worthy of ransom; the references to "pilgrims" might be meant to elevate the Moriscos' status as devout Muslims. However, it is far more likely that Dobelio either misunderstood the reference to *ghurabāʾ* himself, or chose to translate this concept into terms that would make more sense for his Christian audience—thus the familiar "pilgrims" instead of "exiles" and his use of two terms (captives and pilgrims) instead of one (exiles) because he was uncertain of the translation.[47]

Here it is worth distinguishing Wahrānī's characterizations of both his intended audience and himself from those added by the translators or editors of A, M, and X. Despite the appeal's reference to al-Andalus, in V, Wahrānī's only reference to the physical location of his addressees is his use

45 Harvey, "Crypto-Islam," 178 (Arabic text).

46 Only the closing instance also preserves a sense of exile, as Wahrānī prays that his letter will "get to the hands of the captives and pilgrims in foreign lands." Rosa-Rodríguez, "Simulation and Dissimulation," 172 (transcription), 179 (translation).

47 Version A retains all four references to this concept in modified Arabic, as *loš algariboš* for *al-ghurabāʾ* and *vueštra algaribeza* for *ghurbatikum* (Cantineau, "Lettre du Moufti," 7 and 10). Version M is similar for the first three references, but omits the fourth (Harvey, "Crypto-Islam," 171–72). Both Morisco translators appear to have understood the reference and retained the Arabic terms as more meaningful than a translation, just as they retained words like "Allāh" and "aṣṣala." Cantineau, who did not understand the reference, errs in translating all four instances of this concept. In the closing instance, he replaces "*loš algariboš*" with "Arabes (d'Espagne)." Cantineau, "Lettre du Moufti," 10–11, 14.

of term exile or *ghurba*. He also relies on *ghurabāʾ* to the exclusion of such terms as "believers" or "Muslims," a choice that heightens his identification of this group as an embattled remnant and resonates with one of the few indicators of identity offered in the appeal. An introduction describing the text as a response provided by the "Muftī of Buhran" to certain requests made by those in "Andalusiya" has been added to version M.[48] Version A opens and closes with editorial remarks describing this text as the translation of a judgment and response sent by the Muftī of Wahrān to those Andalusīs who had been forcibly converted to Christianity. Curiously, A then clarifies that a *muftī* is the major religious authority in Islam.[49]

The "Muftī of Oran," the title by which Wahrānī was long known in the scholarly literature on this text, thus reflects the name given to him by the translators of versions A and M. For his part, in the preamble to the text Wahrānī introduces himself only as a humble servant of God; at no point does he refer to himself as a jurist or *muftī*, nor to his text as a *fatwā* or as a response to a missive he received. In his closing, Wahrānī instructs his addressees to write to him concerning difficult matters, so that he may guide them.[50] Along with the practical advice he offers, this may be the reason the Moriscos were confident that he was writing to them in his capacity as a *muftī*; like modern commentators, they were guessing at the origins of this text. By the time A was translated, this title of "*muftī*" was, paradoxically, foreign enough to require definition and yet revered enough to greatly exaggerate the importance of its holder. This exaggeration was one strategy by which the Moriscos would have reassured themselves of the legitimacy and authority of Wahrānī's advice.

Dobelio's introduction to X mirrors V in not referring to Wahrānī as a *muftī*, or to his letter as a response to the Andalusīs' requests. Instead, Dobelio gives the author's name ("Obaydala Ahmed Abcinabigiomoa, originally from Almagro . . .") followed by a description of the text as a letter sent to "all Moriscos in general, and other captives who keep to the sect of Mahoma in Spain and elsewhere."[51] This short introduction reflects

---

48 Harvey, "Crypto-Islam," 171.

49 This final phrase is: "*Muftī quiere đezir el mayor đel ad-dīn đel al-islām.*" Cantineau, "Lettre du Moufti," 6 and 10. As noted above, Cantineau also inserted a reference to the Arabs of Spain into his translation; there is no parallel in the original.

50 Later in the closing section, Wahrānī further remarks "*wa-lā budda min jawābikum.*" Wahrānī may mean "I had to respond to you," in which case my interpretation would be that the appeal moved him to send an unsolicited response to the poet's community. Yet the passage is ambiguous. The Morisco translator of M omits the phrase, while the translator of A interprets Wahrānī to mean, "it is necessary for you to answer me." Wahrānī may also mean "you will surely receive a (favorable) response" from God, to whom he has just promised to witness on the Moriscos' behalf. Cantineau, "Lettre du Moufti," 9; Harvey, "Crypto-Islam," 178.

51 Rosa-Rodríguez, "Simulation and Dissimulation," 165–66 (transcription); 174–75 (translation; modified here).

its time and author, and, like the editorial additions to A and M, must not be confused with Wahrānī's own composition. The reference to Islam as the "sect of Muḥammad" is polemical, while the term "Moriscos" would have been anachronistic in Wahrānī's time.[52] Dobelio also misinterprets "al-Maghrāwī," a reference to Wahrānī's North African tribe, as indicating the Castilian town of Almagro, and takes the humble formula *ʿubayd Allāh* ("the insignificant servant of God") as part of Wahrānī's name. Even the catalogue entry for this manuscript, "Epístola Mahomética del Apóstata" (Muḥammadan Letter from the Apostate), is polemical and presumably reflects language found elsewhere in Dobelio's draft.

Practical Advice

The provisions found in the body of Wahrānī's letter constitute the second and primary point of correspondence between this text and the Morisco Appeal. Wahrānī's advice is not a perfect match for the poet's complaints. For example, his letter does not address veiling, burial, or fasting, and he offers advice concerning usury and marriage, matters that do not correspond to parallel grievances in the appeal. Yet the majority of his advice provides practical solutions to problems noted explicitly in the *qaṣīda*.

Two central concerns, the performance of prayer and the avoidance of blasphemy, dominate Wahrānī's 1504 Letter. Along with fasting, these are the two concerns that are explicitly linked to severe punishments, including death, in the Morisco Appeal. The poet complains that those discovered fasting or praying have been thrown into the fire (verse 45), those who refused to attend church were beaten and imprisoned and their property confiscated (verse 46), and those found chanting the Prophet's name were beaten, fined, imprisoned, and humiliated (verses 50–51); instead, they were ordered to curse the Prophet and refrain from invoking him (verse 49). Arguably, these are also the two issues cited in the appeal that would most concern Wahrānī from a legal standpoint: prayer, including the testimony of faith, is the core daily ritual practice of Islam, while cursing the Prophet is one of the few capital crimes in Islamic law.[53]

With regard to prayer, Wahrānī offers alternatives and dispensations for both purification and prayer, along with strategies for coping with forced

52 It was not until the middle of the sixteenth century that "Morisco," formerly an adjective similar to "Moorish," was used widely to refer to Muslims who had been converted to Christianity, and their descendants. Harvey, *Muslims in Spain*, 2–4. My use of this term in this chapter and elsewhere reflects current scholarly terminology, not the actual terms used by the early sixteenth-century authors under consideration.

53 While scholars of the appeal have noted that the appearance of apostasy would pose a serious problem for the Moriscos, the gravity of cursing the prophet has not received sufficient attention. This capital offense might have loomed especially large in Iberia because of the mid ninth-century movement in Córdoba in which nearly fifty Christians were executed for apostasy and blasphemy, including many who sought martyrdom by publicly cursing the Prophet.

church attendance. He encourages the Moriscos to pray without risking detection by using gestures, by making up the day's prayers at night, if possible, and by reducing *tayammum*, already a symbolic form of ablution, to little more than a glance:

> You should pray, even if by a gesture... You should wash away pollutions, even by swimming in rivers... You should perform *tayammum*, even by wiping your hands on the walls. If you are unable to do even this... you may point with your hands and your face to pure earth or stone or trees which are suitable for *tayammum*.[54]

Here, it is clear that Wahrānī takes both the dangers faced by the Moriscos and their desire to express tangibly their commitment to Islam quite seriously. These recommendations balance safety with the reassurance that one is performing a minimal set of physical actions linked to Islam's ritual obligations.

Nonetheless, Wahrānī also affirms that his audience is exempt from their usual obligations and that it is their inward intentions that matter most. When forced to attend church, for example, he suggests:

> If, at the time of prayer, they force you to prostrate yourself to idols, or to attend their prayers, then make firm your intention, and intend your legally required prayer. Face the idol they face, while focusing on God, even if it is not in the direction of the *qiblah* [i.e., toward Mecca], for the obligation to pray in this direction is dropped with respect to you.[55]

Proper intention, or *niyya*, is essential to the legitimacy of any ritual act, even when that act is performed fully and correctly. Wansharīsī's assertion that the unhappy Andalusīs did not leave Iberia with the correct intention, therefore, implied that their emigration, regardless of the sacrifices they made to complete it, might be illegitimate in the eyes of God. Conversely, Wahrānī assures his audience that their intentions alone will be sufficient to satisfy God, even if they cannot perform the required actions—or indeed, even while they are being forced to enact Christian practices or utter blasphemies.

Wahrānī's section on blasphemy imagines that the Moriscos might be forced to express such creedal statements such "Jesus is the son of God" and "Jesus died on the Cross" in addition to insulting Muḥammad. While these specific statements do not appear in the appeal, I suggest Wahrānī may be responding to the verses regarding forced church attendance and mandatory daily religious instruction for children. The poet laments that the priests teach their children "unbelief, idolatry, and falsehood,

54 Harvey, "Crypto-Islam," 175–76 (Arabic of V); unpublished English translation by Stewart.
55 Harvey, "Crypto-Islam," 176 (Arabic of V); unpublished English translation by Stewart.

while they are entirely unable to circumvent [the Christians] by any trick (*ḥīla*) . . ." (verse 59). Working from his own sense of what these falsehoods might entail, Wahrānī provides a repertoire of verbal strategies, specifically equivocations and allusions (*tawriya* and *alghāz*), by which the Moriscos may thwart the intentions of the priests.[56] If made to curse Muḥammad, for example, they should pronounce the name "Mamad" instead, intending thereby to curse someone other than the Prophet. This advice allows the Moriscos to protect themselves and their communities by appearing to comply with their oppressors' demands, while simultaneously avoiding the utterance of blasphemies. However, if it is not possible to employ these strategies, Wahrānī counsels his audience to "be at peace in your hearts in faith," a reference to Qur'ān 16:106, and to repeat the required statements while rejecting them inwardly.[57]

Beyond prayer and blasphemy, Wahrānī briefly addresses a handful of other potential concerns: drinking wine, eating pork, intermarriage, usury, and almsgiving. In the case of each prohibited action, Wahrānī advises the Moriscos to perform the required act while maintaining the belief that this would be forbidden if they were not under duress. They must also resolve to change the situation if they find the power to do so. Wahrānī notes that this principle of outward conformity and inward rejection extends to any other forbidden actions forced upon the community.

Of these potential concerns, only the consumption of pork is mentioned explicitly in the appeal. Yet we can account for the additional problems included in the letter in at least two ways. The first and most obvious explanation is that Wahrānī is guessing. Instead of responding to a question enumerating the Moriscos' specific legal dilemmas, he is trying to imagine what those dilemmas might be, based on the contents of a document written for another purpose entirely. The appeal is often more dramatic than detailed. For example, it refers to some faces that have been bared—does this complaint reflect an isolated act of aggression toward individual women, or the enforcement of a new law systematically applied to all women? Without a clear sense of the specifics, I suggest that Wahrānī responded to the clearest and most important legal problems evident in the appeal—prayer, blasphemy, and the consumption of forbidden foods—while doing his best to offer useful but succinct advice that would cover other potential concerns. This proposition is supported by the letter's extensive reliance on the conditional tense—"*if* they ask you to X, *then* do Y"—and the fact that

56 On this section of Wahrānī's text, see Stewart, "Dissimulation," esp. 465–80.

57 Qur'ān 16:106 reads "Anyone who disbelieves in God after he has believed—not one who is compelled, while his heart is at peace in faith, but those who open their breast to unbelief—on them is the wrath of God. Theirs will be a great torment."

some of Wahrānī's guesses miss the mark.[58] For example, it is improbable that a Morisco request for advice would have complained of intermarriage between Morisco men and Christian women, or the requirement to state that Mary is God's wife.[59]

Some of the incongruities between the appeal and letter may also be explained by Wahrānī's secondary reliance on the testimony of Iberians who immigrated to Morocco in the wake of Granada's forced conversions. In particular, it is possible that he encountered a copy of *Akhbār al-ʿaṣr fī inqiḍāʾ dawlat Banī Naṣr* (*The News from the Period: The End of the Naṣrid Dynasty*).[60] This anonymous chronicle, which appears to be a soldier's eyewitness account of the 1482–92 war for the kingdom of Granada, concludes with a brief summary of the city of Granada's surrender and the subsequent fate of its Muslims. For the period beginning with Boabdil's 1491 negotiations for surrender through to the forced conversions and rebellions of 1499–1501, *Akhbār al-ʿaṣr* (hereafter, *The News*) exhibits some striking similarities to the appeal in tone and content. The chronicle stresses that surrender came only as a last resort, after Muslim fighters had died and food supplies had dwindled, the people had become weak with hunger,

58 Jurists often use the conditional in *fatwās*, but this is normally used to indicate a range of possibilities based on the questioner's ability, as Wahrānī does with purification, or to distinguish between different cases mentioned in the question, as seen in the multi-part answers offered by Wansharīsī and his peers in chapter 3. In contrast, Wahrānī's frequent use of the conditional often indicates solutions to potential problems that may not be clear or known.

59 The statement regarding Mary appears in Wahrānī's section on blasphemy. Harvey notes the incongruity of Wahrānī's advice on intermarriage and the Christians' concern with *limpieza de sangre* (purity of blood). See Harvey, "Crypto-Islam," 166–67.

60 *Akhbār al-ʿaṣr* is the original chronicle on which the later, slightly revised *Nubdhat al-ʿaṣr fī akhbār mulūk Banī Naṣr* (*Short Treatise from the Period: The History of the Naṣrid Kings*) is based. Both versions of the text are undated and anonymous. In the interest of accessibility, I cite the best editions of both versions, that of Ḥusayn Mu'nis for *Akhbār al-ʿaṣr* and Muḥammad Riḍwān al-Dāya for *Nubdhat al-ʿaṣr* (mentioned in chapter 4). *Akhbār al-ʿaṣr* was first edited by Marcus Joseph Müller in Munich in 1863 as *Die letzten Zeiten von Granada*, with an accompanying German translation. *Nubdhat al-ʿaṣr* was first edited by Alfredo Bustani in Larache in 1940, as *Nubdhat al-ʿaṣr fī akhbār mulūk Banī Naṣr*, and was accompanied by a Spanish translation by D. Carlos Qirós, titled *Fragmento de la época sobre noticias de los Reyes Nazaritas o Capitulación de Granada y Emigración de los andaluces a Marruecos*. Bustani's Arabic edition only (without translation) has been reprinted by several publishers, most recently by Alwarrak Publishing (London, 2017). On the two versions of this chronicle, see the articles "Ajbār al-ʿAṣr" (1:55–57) and "Nubḏat al-ʿAṣr" (6:621–22) both by A. C. López y López and F. N. Velázquez Basanta, in *Biblioteca de al-Andalus*, ed. Jorge Lirola Delgado and José Miguel Puerta Vílchez, 7 vols. and 2 appendix vols. (Almería: Fundación Ibn Tufayl de Estudios Árabes, 2004–13); Ryan Szpiech, "Conversion as a Historiographical Problem: The Case of Zoraya/Isabel de Solís," in *Contesting Inter-Religious Conversion in the Medieval World*, ed. Yaniv Fox and Yosi Yisraeli (New York: Routledge, 2016), 26 and 34–35, n. 4 and 7. On the relationship between Maqqarī's *Azhār al-riyāḍ* and this chronicle, see Velázquez Basanta, "La relación histórica sobre las postrimerías del Reino de Granada, según Aḥmad al-Maqqarī (s. XVII)," in *El Epílogo del Islam Andalusí: La Granada del Siglo XV*, ed. Celia del Moral (Granada: Universidad de Granada, 2002), 481–554.

and their requests for aid from the Maghrib had gone unanswered.[61] Like the appeal, *The News* states that the Christians initially promised generous terms, but their displays of justice and generosity turned out to be deceit and trickery. The terms of the capitulations were violated one by one until they were no more, according to the chronicle, at which point the Granadan Muslims were forced to convert to Christianity.

The unknown author of *The News* identifies less with this converted population than does the poet who wrote the appeal, and he offers fewer details as to their specific grievances. Nonetheless, his lament regarding their plight, as follows, offers additional insight into Wahrānī's advice to these Moriscos:

> They entered their religion unwillingly and all of al-Andalus became [a] Christian [land]. No one remained there who proclaimed "There is no god but God, and Muḥammad is the messenger of God" . . . Church bells were placed in the minarets, where before had been the call to prayer, and in the mosques were [hung] images and crosses, where before there had been the remembrance of God and recitation of the Qurʾān. Alas, how many weeping eyes and mournful hearts are in [that land now], and how many of them [are] weak and abased, who were unable to emigrate to join their Muslim brethren. Their hearts are inflamed and their tears flow copiously as they watch their children worship crosses, as they prostrate before idols, consume pork and carrion, and drink wine . . . while they are unable to circumvent [the Christians], nor to restrain or to rebuke them [in any way]. Anyone who does so is made to suffer the most severe punishment and torment.[62]

This passage may well have inspired Wahrānī to address the forced consumption of wine, especially as its refusal is linked to severe punishment. The language of his letter regarding prostration before idols also closely resembles that of *The News*, while this section of the chronicle as a whole confirms the Moriscos' inability to escape their dire predicament.

61 Harvey translates this portion of *Nubdhat al-ʿaṣr* in *Islamic Spain*, 310–11, and in Harvey, "Chronicling the Fall of Nasrid Granada: *Kitāb nubdhat al-ʿaṣr fī akhbār mulūk Banī Naṣr*," in *Historical Literature in Medieval Iberia*, ed. Alan Deyermond (London: Department of Hispanic Studies, Queen Mary and Westfield College, 1996), 110–11.

62 Anon., *Akhbār al-ʿaṣr*, 118. See also Anon., *Nubdhat al-ʿaṣr*, 109–10. My translation from the Arabic. Mohamad Ballan previously translated most of this passage in his thesis on the appeal, and noted the similarity between the appeal and the chronicle. See Ballan, "Between Castilian *Reconquista* and Ottoman *Jihād*: An Analysis of the 1501 Hispano-Muslim *Qaṣīda* to Bayezid II," MA thesis (University of Chicago, 2010), 25. This passage uses the Qurʾānic term for those too weak to emigrate.

Could Wahrānī have seen a copy of *The News*, in addition to the appeal? We know little about these three texts—the appeal, *The News*, and the letter, and any relationship between them is not only plausible, but has implications for dating *The News*. Historians Angel Custodio López y López and Fernando Nicolás Velázquez Basanta posit that *The News* was composed in Fez in the early sixteenth century, shortly after the events described.[63] Like the appeal, *The News* is undated but must have been written after mid-1501, as the chronicler mentions the suppression of revolts in Huéjar, Alpujarras, Andarax, and Belefique. Based on the possibility that Wahrānī was partially inspired by this text, I propose that *The News* was drafted between late 1501 and late 1504 and that it circulated to some extent in Fez, alongside the appeal. While *The News* could have been composed as late as 1530, based on the probable lifespan of a soldier old enough to fight in the early 1480s, there is no compelling evidence to explain why he would wait so long after 1501 to compose his account.

It is worth noting that it is unlikely that our anonymous poet and chronicler are the same person. The appeal is written from the perspective of a Muslim forcibly converted to Christianity, who strongly identifies with the collective plight of this group and defends their continued commitment to Islam. By contrast, the chronicler who composed *The News* divides the last Granadan Muslims into three groups: those who accepted forcible conversion, those who refused and were all killed (this is the context in which he mentions the suppressed rebellions), and those who retreated to a high mountain and resisted until they were granted passage to North Africa. The chronicler, who implicitly places himself in this third group, does not ascribe any remaining trace of Islam to the first, forcibly converted group. Instead, he declares that upon the departure of the mountain group, the light of Islam was extinguished in al-Andalus.[64] Therefore, while Wahrānī

63 See López y López and Velázquez Basanta, "Ajbār al-ʿAṣr," 55–56. I am grateful to Dr. López y López for confirming (in a private communication) that the composition date of 1540 often associated with this chronicle was based on an error in reading the El Escorial manuscript of *The News*. The error first appeared in Müller's edition of the text and has been repeated since, despite its improbability; a soldier who was twenty years old in 1482 would be seventy-eight in 1540, meaning that he waited forty years to record his experiences.

64 Anon., *Akhbār al-ʿaṣr*, 119; Anon., *Nubdhat al-ʿaṣr*, 111. In Ibn al-Ḥājj al-Sulamī's later adaptation of this story, he credits the mountain group with sending the appeal to Bāyazīd and claims that the sultan responded with threats that successfully secured this group's freedom to emigrate. This speculation enhances the legacy of Ibn al-Ḥājj al-Sulamī's ancestors and provides an explanation for their ability to emigrate, but we have no evidence that the appeal prompted such a response from Bāyazīd (and we do know that Ferdinand allowed a group of rebels to emigrate in early 1501 following the defeat of Alonso de Aguilar in Rio Verde). Furthermore, Ibn al-Ḥājj al-Sulamī's account is even less charitable toward the converted group than is *The News*, and therefore even farther from the poet's perspective. Ibn al-Ḥājj al-Sulamī allows that the converted Muslims hid their faith until their deaths, but states that their children grew up as unbelievers. A clear hierarchy thus emerges between the superior

may have been inspired in part by *The News*, his sympathies clearly lie with the people represented by the poet's appeal. The 1504 Letter takes the Moriscos' continued faith seriously, provides them with practical guidance, and reassures them—perhaps in light of such attitudes as those of the chronicler—that there are indeed fellow Muslims willing to acknowledge their faith.

The Hope of Ottoman Intervention

The third element common to both the appeal and Wahrānī's letter is their shared hope that the Ottomans will come to the Moriscos' aid. In the closing section of his letter, Wahrānī prays that God will "turn the wheel of fortune to Islam's favor, so that you may worship God in the open, by the power of God, without trials or tribulations, indeed through the victory of the noble Turks."[65] While a prayer asking God to restore lost territory to Islam would be expected here, the specificity of Wahrānī's hope for a Turkish victory has struck observers as a curious addition to his *fatwā*.[66] But as an affirmation of the Moriscos' fervent request for Ottoman intervention, as expressed in the appeal, the reference makes perfect sense.

What is more curious than Wahrānī's prayer for Ottoman aid is the disparity between his vision of what that aid would achieve, on the one hand, and the Moriscos' desired outcomes, on the other. According to the appeal, the Moriscos want to be Mudéjars, to live under the terms of their original capitulations. If, and only if, a return to their prior status is impossible, their second choice would be the right to immigrate from Iberia to North Africa. While the Moriscos request diplomacy, Wahrānī prays for war; he envisions a military intervention that restores Muslim rule to Iberia. If the letter is indeed a response to the appeal, Wahrānī misunderstood, rejected, or attempted to reorient the Moriscos' desires.

Implications

In this chapter I have advanced the plausible, rather than definitive, case that Wahrānī's so-called 1504 *Fatwā* is in reality an unsolicited response to the 1501 Morisco Appeal. This alternative reading of Wahrānī's 1504 Letter has two primary implications. First, we must reconsider the relationship between Wahrānī and his original addressees. If the earliest Moriscos never asked

mountain group, who never agreed to convert, and the Moriscos, who doomed their children to infidelity. Ibn al-Ḥājj al-Sulamī, *Riyāḍ al-ward*, 196. On rebel emigration, see López de Coca Castañer, "Mamelucos," 245.

65 Harvey, "Crypto-Islam," 178 (Arabic of "V"); unpublished English translation by Stewart. This passage is similar in versions A (Cantineau, "Lettre du Moufti," 9) and X (Rosa-Rodríguez, "Simulation and Dissimulation," 172 and 179), but omitted from M.

66 Cantineau, "Lettre du Moufti," 15.

him a question, then this particular text no longer constitutes evidence that these Muslims perceived a need for legal advice, or that they assigned greater authority to North African jurists. We would not be justified in imagining that Wahrānī received a confused plea from Moriscos vexed by their own lack of religious authorities. Instead, the jurist was responding to a formally composed *qaṣīda*, authored by a well-educated member of an elite class, and intended for the ruler of the most powerful empire in Islamdom. The poem is assertive, not confused, and it defends the Moriscos' bravery and piety while leaving the character of North Africans in doubt; the poet states that Iberian Muslims had no choice but to submit to Christian rule when their own forces were destroyed and no rescue was forthcoming from their "brethren." Although the Maghrib is the poet's desired destination if his community must emigrate, he refers to past embassies sent to the Mamluks and Ottomans—the inability of North Africans to render meaningful assistance is unstated. Viewed in this way, Wahrānī's response is somewhat presumptuous and defensive, but thus even more remarkable. Wahrānī must have been moved by a sense of moral obligation to offer what advice he could, even though he was not asked to do so.

Reading Wahrānī's letter as unsolicited advice also helps to explain the disparity between this text and Wansharīsī's two 1491 *fatwās* on emigration. While Wahrānī and Wansharīsī were long assumed to have written *fatwās* on the same general topic—conquered Muslims living under Christian rule in Iberia—the relationship between their opinions has been a subject of debate.

Leila Sabbagh argued that these *fatwās* were complementary: Wansharīsī addressed Muslims who were capable of emigrating, while Wahrānī addressed those incapable of doing so.[67] Hossain Buzineb countered that the two jurists' opinions were not only opposed to one another, but moreover that Wahrānī should be distinguished from all other Mālikī jurists as the only one to propose a "revolutionary," "original" solution to the problem of Christian conquest.[68] Later scholars not only agreed with Buzineb, but the contrast itself further sharpened the rhetorical divide between Wansharīsī's "fanatical intransigence" and Wahrānī's "acute sympathy" toward conquered Iberian Muslims.[69] Devin Stewart then posited a direct relationship between the texts, arguing that Wahrānī likely intended his

67 Sabbagh, "La Religion," 52–55. See also Fierro, "La Emigración," 20–22.

68 Buzineb, "Respuestas," 53–54; 59–60. See also Epalza, "La voz oficial," 293; Razūq, *Al-Andalusiyyūn*, 151–52; Rubiera Mata, "Los moriscos," 541–47.

69 García Sanjuán "La Cuestión Mudéjar," 185 (fanatical intransigence); Harvey, *Muslims in Spain*, 60 (acute sympathy). García Sanjuán cites Buzineb approvingly; Harvey's evaluation of Wahrānī involves a less direct comparison with the "older, unbending," and "orthodox" view of the law (64–65).

fatwā as a rebuttal of Wansharīsī's opinions.[70] More recently, Cheddadi suggested that these texts might not be comparable after all, as Wahrānī's *fatwā* clearly assumes that emigration was impossible.[71]

I argue that the texts of Wansharīsī and Wahrānī are neither complementary nor opposed. It is certainly fruitful to compare them, but this comparison only reveals that *Asnā al-matājir* and the Marbella *fatwā* differ in almost every respect from the 1504 Letter. These texts treat distinct legal issues and are addressed to different audiences for distinct purposes. Wansharīsī responds to two questions that directly concern the obligation for capable Mudéjars to emigrate. Together, his two formal legal opinions constitute a two-part, argumentative treatise supported with proof texts and legal precedents. This technical treatise was likely meant to meet the immediate needs of Ibn Qaṭiyya as a court advisor and to inform and persuade the professional legal audience of the *Miʿyār*. This wider audience ultimately included Wansharīsī's own colleagues and students as well as future generations of jurists throughout the Mālikī world, or most of Muslim Africa.

In contrast, Wahrānī's letter is a heartfelt, practical guide composed to help a lay Morisco community approximate adherence to Islamic law under the gravest circumstances of fear and oppression. Wahrānī does not mention emigration, not even to clarify these Muslims' exemption from the obligation. He likely saw little point in stating the obvious: a group that is forced to curse the Prophet and drink wine, and that is incapable of praying except with the barest of gestures, would be incapable of the infinitely more difficult task of an overseas migration en masse. If Wahrānī was reading *The News* in addition to the appeal, he also would have noted the explicit identification of those were converted by force with those who were too weak to emigrate. *Asnā al-matājir*'s technical discussions and proof texts would have been inappropriate for this lay audience, and also would have been an unnecessary hindrance to smuggling the text into Granada and transmitting it to future generations of clandestine Muslims. Wahrānī provides only enough legal evidence—one authoritative precedent and a few Qurʾānic verses and allusions to *ḥadīths*—to give the Moriscos confidence in the legitimacy of his opinions. He does not use any of Wansharīsī's arguments and seems to be concerned solely with inspiring the Moriscos to remain steadfast in their faith, not with convincing other jurists of the validity of their struggle. Wahrānī likely did not intend any further audience beyond this lay community, and probably made no attempt to distribute the

70 Stewart, "Identity," 298–300. García-Arenal and Rodríguez Mediano agree with this perspective in *The Orient in Spain*, 290.

71 Cheddadi, "Émigrer ou rester?" 6–9. See also Bernabé-Pons, "*Taqiyya*" 497–99.

letter among his peers in Fez for the purposes of scholarly debate. Thus, we should not be surprised to find (in part 4) that Wahrānī's text had no appreciable impact on later Mālikī thought on the obligation to emigrate.

Another notable implication arises from reading Wahrānī's letter as a response to the Morisco Appeal. Scholars have continually remarked on Wahrānī's silence on the issue of emigration. This silence is indeed puzzling, not because we should assume that Wahrānī rejected the cruel imposition of this obligation on conquered Muslims. Instead, it is puzzling because Wahrānī fails to acknowledge or support the *Moriscos' own stated desire* to join their coreligionists in the Maghrib if they cannot live at home as Mudéjars. Was he simply powerless to help them emigrate? Or did he imagine a glorious Ottoman victory in Iberia as preferable to the arrival of yet more Iberian refugees on the shores of North Africa? While we have ample indication that Wahrānī's advice served the Moriscos well, and for far longer than he could have intended or anticipated, this element of disjunction is the reason that I have called Wahrānī's letter "unsolicited advice," despite this term's usual negative connotations.

PART 4

Christian Conquest Revisited: French Algeria and Mauritania, Nineteenth and Twentieth Centuries

CHAPTER 7

Algeria: Hearing the News of al-Andalus

The Ottoman Empire did not come to the aid of those first Moriscos. They did not fulfill the anonymous poet's 1501 request for diplomatic assistance, nor did they answer Wahrānī's 1504 prayers for military aid. Instead, the Ottomans expanded southward into the Levant and Egypt, defeating the Mamluks in 1517; they then moved westward into the Mediterranean, where they established a powerful naval force. As part of this expansion, they incorporated Algeria into the Ottoman Empire in 1525, followed by Tunisia in 1574. While Christian rule was solidly established in Iberia, the Ottoman Regency of Algiers kept most of the central Maghrib under Muslim rule for three centuries, until the 1830 French occupation of Algiers.[1]

With the advent of the modern colonial period, the Islamic legal doctrine of *hijra* regained religious and political relevance. Like their fifteenth- and sixteenth-century forbears, North and West African jurists turned to legal precedents for guidance in addressing Christian conquests in Muslim Africa. Unlike their predecessors, these colonial-era jurists had recourse to a robust body of opinions that dealt directly with such conquests; they were not forced to extrapolate from the cases of lone converts or traders traveling to *dār al-ḥarb*. Sufficient precedents were available that, in fact, these nineteenth- and twentieth-century jurists needed to make choices. Which opinions did they find most compelling: Zayyātī's "jewels," composed in response to European conquests on North African soil, Wansharīsī's more elaborate *fatwās* evoking the fall of al-Andalus, or Wahrānī's heartfelt letter reassuring conquered Muslims that they can survive oppression?

In the next two chapters I explore this question by analyzing legal discourses on the obligation to emigrate, as they relate to two colonial contexts: nineteenth-century Algeria and twentieth-century Mauritania. There are certainly other cases available for comparative analysis. Many

1 On the sixteenth-century Mediterranean, see Andrew C. Hess, *The Forgotten Frontier: A History of the Sixteenth-Century Ibero-African Frontier* (Chicago: University of Chicago Press, 1978). After the establishment of the Ottoman Regency, Spain retained key coastal possessions in what is now Algeria. Most notably, the Spanish captured Oran in 1509 and did not fully withdraw until 1792.

West African *jihād* movements in this period featured calls to perform *hijra*, to leave territory controlled by European powers or by nominally Muslim rulers. Yet the Algerian and Mauritanian cases are instructive because in each case, we have complete extant texts composed by Mālikī jurists who argued both for and against the obligation to emigrate. Both cases also involve the same colonizer, France, although the different geographical and temporal contexts provide some useful contrasts.

In this chapter I treat the legal debate regarding *hijra* in colonial Algeria. The central figure in the debate is ʿAbd al-Qādir al-Jazāʾirī (1808–83), who led an armed resistance movement against the French between 1832 and 1847. Of the nine legal texts I review, at least six were composed at ʿAbd al-Qādir's request or under his supervision. All appear to have been composed during his *jihād*, between the mid-1830s and the mid-1840s. Thus, these opinions share with Zayyātī's "jewels" a context of active military resistance to European encroachment on Maghribī soil. Yet the colonial-era texts cite Zayyātī's "jewels" only occasionally. We also find no mention, explicit or implicit, of Wahrānī's 1504 Letter to the Moriscos.

Asnā al-matājir and the Marbella *fatwā* clearly dominate the Algerian *hijra* debate. In one instance (that of Muḥammad ʿIllaysh), these two texts are reproduced in full, almost without additional commentary. Even Ibn al-Shāhid, who rejects *hijra*, devotes substantial effort to refuting Wansharīsī's arguments. The Algerian texts clearly demonstrate that Wansharīsī succeeded in producing authoritative precedents that continued, centuries later, to shape Mālikī thought on Muslim submission to Christian rule. The reasons for that success, which I proposed in part 2, are worth bearing in mind as we consider this first set of colonial-era texts. First, Wansharīsī included his own opinions on emigration in the *Miʿyār*, which achieved a broad circulation and enhanced his scholarly reputation; second, he used Ibn Qaṭiyya's memorable questions to frame a thoroughly argued yet simple, relatively straightforward case for obligatory emigration; and third, he downplayed his concerns regarding the Portuguese in Morocco, in order to focus fully on the loss of al-Andalus as an indisputable historical precedent in support of his argument.

Algerian *Hijra* and *Jihād*

France conquered Algiers in 1830, followed closely by the Mediterranean ports of Oran, to the west of the capital, and ʿAnnāba, to the east. Refugees from the Algerian coast sailed to Morocco, where they were resettled in Tetouan and Fez, with generous assistance from the ʿAlawī sultan of Morocco, Mawlāy ʿAbd al-Raḥmān b. Hishām (r. 1822–59). Mawlāy ʿAbd al-Raḥmān, who referred to these newcomers as *muhājirūn* (emigrants), praised their refusal to live under infidel rule, and cited this refusal as a testament to their strong faith. As historian Amira Bennison notes, the sultan's remarks invoked both the original Muhājirūn of the prophetic era and those Andalusīs who performed *hijra* from Iberia to North Africa during and after the Reconquest.[2]

Over the next half century, a substantial number of Algerians who found themselves under French rule opted to emigrate in response to their new circumstances.[3] Many left for neighboring Morocco and Tunisia, while others traveled to Libya, the Hijaz, or Syria. As in Iberia, these emigrants were not motivated solely by religious obligation. They also left to escape violence and oppression; to protest increasing French control over religious and educational institutions; to avoid cholera, famine, or military conscription; and to join religious and political movements elsewhere.

A brief overview of these developments is useful at the outset. France's 1830 conquests were initially confined to the central coast of Algeria; it remained unclear who would establish sovereignty over the western province of Oran. Morocco's Mawlāy ʿAbd al-Raḥmān accepted an oath of allegiance (*bayʿa*) from the residents of Tlemcen later that year and sent an expedition to assume control of the city. He further coordinated a *jihād* against French-occupied Oran in the hope of unifying the region's tribes behind ʿAlawī rule and gaining prestige as a defender of the faith. By late 1831 both the Tlemcen and Oran initiatives had failed, leading to serious domestic unrest in Morocco and threats of French retribution. In response, Mawlāy ʿAbd al-Raḥmān withdrew his governor from western Algeria in 1832. The tribal alliance he had fostered floundered, leading some factions to consider an alliance with the French. Power in western Algeria was split between rival tribes, the religious brotherhoods, and the local elites who had occupied positions of influence under Turkish rule.[4]

The *jihād* against the French continued, but its leadership was transferred to Muḥyī al-Dīn al-Jazāʾirī, leader of the Qādiriyya Sufi order, who had the blessing and patronage of Mawlāy ʿAbd al-Raḥmān. Muḥyī al-Dīn in turn delegated this military role to his younger son ʿAbd al-Qādir, and several regional tribes offered their allegiance to him in 1832. ʿAbd al-Qādir, now recognized as an *amīr* (commander), established a base of power at Mascara. His legitimacy was grounded in the religious authority of the Qādiriyya order, his own *sharīf* lineage, his command of a *jihād* against infidel rule, and his status as the deputy of ʿAbd al-Raḥmān, formalized in 1834.

2 Amira Bennison, *Jihad and its Interpretations in Pre-Colonial Morocco: State-Society Relations during the French Conquest of Algeria* (London: RoutledgeCurzon, 2002), 47–48.

3 On Algerian emigration from 1830 to 1911, see Allan Christelow, *Algerians without Borders: The Making of a Global Frontier Society* (Gainesville: University Press of Florida, 2012), 50–81.

4 Bennison, *Jihad*, 48–74.

ʿAbd al-Qādir signed the first of two treaties with the French in 1834. The governor of Oran agreed to recognize ʿAbd al-Qādir's sovereignty in the interior of the province, south of a French coastal zone. This treaty gave the *amīr* time to build an organized army, appoint local officials who could administer justice and collect taxes, and establish a consultative assembly to advise his new government.[5]

Yet, in the absence of an active *jihād*, ʿAbd al-Qādir's support among regional tribes declined. When the Dawāʾir and Zmāla tribes broke with him in 1835 and sided with the French, hostilities erupted between ʿAbd al-Qādir and the French governor of Oran. At the outset, this resumption of ʿAbd al-Qādir's campaign bolstered his religious and political legitimacy among his Algerian and Moroccan supporters, but he soon suffered a major defeat. The French gained control of Mascara and Tlemcen, the two most important cities in western Algeria. ʿAbd al-Qādir's prestige and tribal support deteriorated, while Mawlāy ʿAbd al-Raḥmān grew alarmed by the French proximity to Fez. As refugees from Tlemcen arrived in Fez, the ʿAlawī sultan renewed his commitment to ʿAbd al-Qādir's *jihād* and provided him with substantial military and financial assistance.[6]

ʿAbd al-Qādir signed a second agreement with the French in 1837.[7] The Treaty of Tafna allowed the French to concentrate on taking control of the eastern province of Constantine. In exchange, they withdrew from Tlemcen, recognized ʿAbd al-Qādir's authority in the provinces of Oran and Titteri, and promised to terminate relations with the Dawāʾir and Zmāla tribes. Yet ʿAbd al-Qādir still struggled to maintain sufficient support for his rule among the tribes and religious brotherhoods of western Algeria. In late 1838, the leaders of the rival Tijāniyya Sufi order denied him entry to their center at ʿAyn Mādī, an oasis town at the edge of the Sahara. ʿAbd al-Qādir responded with a protracted siege that succeeded in forcing the Tijānī leadership out of ʿAyn Mādī in early 1839, but failed to win him their recognition of his authority. The Tijāniyya, whose affiliated tribes controlled much of western Algeria as far as the Sahara, instead formed closer relations with the French.[8]

Also in 1839, ʿAbd al-Qādir again resumed active *jihād* against the French, claiming that they had violated the terms of the Tafna treaty by encroaching

---

5 Bennison, *Jihad*, 82–84; Rudolph Peters, *Islam and Colonialism: The Doctrine of Jihad in Modern History* (The Hague: Mouton Publishers, 1979), 53–55.

6 Bennison, *Jihad*, 84–93.

7 Bennison, *Jihad*, 93–98.

8 Tom Woerner-Powell, *Another Road to Damascus: An Integrative Approach to ʿAbd al-Qādir al-Jazāʾirī (1808–1883)* (Berlin: De Gruyter, 2017), 31–32; Raphael Danziger, *Abd al-Qadir and the Algerians: Resistance to the French and Internal Consolidation* (New York: Holmes & Meier, 1977), 161–63.

on his territory.[9] This new round of hostilities prompted the French to launch a systematic conquest of Algeria; this was completed in 1857. ʿAbd al-Qādir sought refuge in Morocco in 1843, but in 1844 a subsequent French attack forced ʿAbd al-Raḥmān to sign a treaty agreeing to treat the Algerian resistance leader as an outlaw. In the years that followed, ʿAbd al-Qādir moved between Algeria and Morocco, until he was finally forced to surrender to the French in 1847. He was held in France until 1852, then allowed to resettle in Damascus, where he died in 1883.[10]

It was imperative for ʿAbd al-Qādir to demonstrate the religious legitimacy of his *jihād* and state-building efforts. He sought religious justifications for his leadership of a lawful *jihād*, his right to collect taxes, and his use of force against fellow Muslims who were collaborating with the enemy. As the legal opinions I review here show, *hijra* proved to be one of the most important doctrines at his disposal. Throughout his *jihād*, ʿAbd al-Qādir and his supporters continued to emphasize that it was obligatory to emigrate in order to bolster resistance to the French, undermine the credibility of those Muslims who submitted to foreign rule, and heighten the urgency and legitimacy of their own cause.

Ibn Ruwīla's Letter to Ibn al-Kabābṭī

The title page to a curious manuscript in the Algerian National Library contains three colophons, each in a different hand.[11] The first, in a neat red Maghribī script, is a provocative challenge to the addressees of the letter:

> this is what Qaddūr b. Ruwīla has written to the jurists of the Muslim *dhimmī*s of Algiers. Read it! Understand it! If you find any refutation, then provide it in response. If not, then repent and return to God (may He be exalted) and emerge from [your] subjection [to the infidel]! Peace.

Just under this first colophon, in larger red print, a second note informs readers that the marginal commentary was added by ʿAlī b. al-Ḥaffāf. Finally, on the side, a note scrawled in black exclaims that this Ibn al-Ḥaffāf has clearly lost his mind. This third contributor invites us to marvel at the oddity of this document, as Ibn al-Ḥaffāf insulted the people of Algiers and

9 Peters, *Islam and Colonialism*, 55.

10 Bennison, *Jihad*, 97–157.

11 This letter is extant in two undated manuscript copies, Algerian National Library MSS 1304 and 2083. MS 1304 contains the three original colophons, which are combined into one note in MS 2083. The latter, a copy of MS 1304, must have been produced sometime after 1890, as the combined note mentions Ibn al-Ḥaffāf's death. Jamāl Ganān published Ibn Ruwīla's letter only, without the title page or marginal commentary, in his anthology *Nuṣūṣ siyāsiyya Jazāʾiriyya fī al-qarn al-tāsiʿ ʿashar, 1830–1914* (Algiers: Dīwān al-Maṭbūʿāt al-Jāmiʿiyya, 2009), 119–21. This published version is based on MS 2083, and has minor errors.

issued a *fatwā* as to their apostasy, then he accepted an appointment as *muftī* of Blida, under French rule.

This is an introduction to a type of legal discourse that differs from the one preserved from the late fifteenth and early sixteenth centuries. In the Algerian case, we can observe jurists arguing directly with their peers, who were fellow Algerian jurists faced with personal decisions regarding their Islamic legal obligations and relationships with the French. Alongside sophisticated legal arguments, we also see raw, personal attacks that indicate the high stakes each side attached to the question of emigration as a religious obligation. Those remaining under French rule were defending their homes, livelihoods, and right to be recognized as Muslims; those who held emigration to be an immediate imperative were defending Muslim sovereignty in Algeria and trying to deter fellow Muslims from cooperating or collaborating with the French.

Qaddūr b. Muḥammad b. Ruwīla (d. 1272/1855–6),[12] who was born and educated in Algiers, left the capital after the French conquest and went on to serve as ʿAbd al-Qādir's counselor and chief secretary. He addresses this letter primarily to Muṣṭafā b. al-Kabābṭī (d. 1277/1860–1),[13] who held an appointment as the official Mālikī *muftī* of Algiers from 1831 to 1843.[14] While undated, the letter must have been composed between 1835 and

12 Ibn Ruwīla, referred to as Kaddour ben Mohammed ben Rouila or Berrouila in French sources, served as ʿAbd al-Qādir's deputy in Miliana prior to joining and serving him directly. Ibn Ruwīla was taken prisoner by the French and ultimately allowed to emigrate east, where he performed the *ḥajj* (pilgrimage to Mecca) and rejoined ʿAbd al-Qādir briefly before he died in Beirut. On Ibn Ruwīla, see ʿAbd al-Raḥmān al-Jīlālī, *Tārīkh al-Jazāʾir al-ʿāmm*, 7th ed., 4 vols. (Algiers: Dīwān al-Maṭbūʿāt al-Jāmiʿiyya, 1994), 4:144–47; Muḥammad b. al-Amīr ʿAbd al-Qādir al-Jazāʾirī, *Tuḥfat al-zāʾir fī tārīkh al-Jazāʾir waʾl-Amīr ʿAbd al-Qādir*, ed. Mamduḥ Ḥaqqī, 2nd ed., 2 vols. (Beirut: Dār al-Yaqaẓa al-ʿArabiyya, 1964), 2:594; ʿĀdil Nuwayhiḍ, *Muʿjam aʿlām al-Jazāʾir min ṣadr al-Islām ḥattā muntaṣaf al-qarn al-ʿishrīn* (Beirut: Manshūrāt al-Maktab al-Tijārī lil-Ṭibāʿa waʾl-Nashr waʾl-Tawzīʿ, 1971), 131–32; Muṣṭafā b. Tuhāmī, *Sīrat al-Amīr ʿAbd al-Qādir*, ed. Yaḥyā Buʿazīz (Beirut: Dār al-Gharb al-Islāmī, 1995), 153.

13 Muṣṭafā b. Muḥammad, known as Ibn al-Kabābṭī (d. 1277/1860–1), was born in Algiers, completed his legal education in 1812, and taught law until his appointment as Mālikī judge of Algiers in 1243/1827–8. He remained in this position during the first year of French occupation; in 1831, he was promoted to chief Mālikī *muftī*. He held this office until 1843, when a dispute with the French authorities resulted in his exile. He settled in Alexandria, where he died. On his career and dispute with the French, see Abū al-Qāsim Saʿd Allāh, *Abḥāth wa-ārāʾ fī tārīkh al-Jazāʾir*, 4th ed., 5 vols. (Beirut: Dār al-Gharb al-Islāmī, 2005), 2:11–48, esp. 2:14–33.

14 Under Ottoman and then French rule, *muftī*s and judges were appointed from both the Mālikī and Ḥanafī schools of law. On the Mālikī *muftī*s of Algiers, see Nūr al-Dīn ʿAbd al-Qādir, *Ṣafaḥāt min tārīkh madīnat al-Jazāʾir min aqdam ʿuṣūrihā ilā intihāʾ al-ʿahd al-Turkī* ([Algiers]: n.p., 1965), 183–85; Muḥammad al-Ḥafnāwī, *Taʿrīf al-khalaf bi-rijāl al-salaf*, ed. Muḥammad Abū al-Ajfān and ʿUthmān Baṭṭīkh (Beirut: Muʾassasat al-Risāla, 1982), 2:480–81.

1843.[15] In it, Ibn Ruwīla is responding to a personal attack by Ibn al-Kabābṭī; apparently, the latter had accused Ibn Ruwīla of hypocrisy when he found Ibn Ruwīla's written communications with the French too reverential. Ibn Ruwīla explains that he ceased using the reverential language in question four years prior, and repented of having done so. He proceeds to list ten acts of loyalty to the French committed by Ibn al-Kabābṭī and his peers, each of which he finds more serious than his own past offense. Those who have chosen to remain in Algiers are in the exact position described and denounced in the Marbella *fatwā*, according to Ibn Ruwīla, who then copies Wansharīsī's text in full and directs his readers to study it carefully.[16]

Ibn al-Ḥaffāf's Commentary on Ibn Ruwīla's Letter

In the margins of Ibn Ruwīla's letter, ʿAlī b. al-Ḥaffāf (d. 1307/1890)[17] comments on both the introduction and the text of the Marbella *fatwā*. He frequently addresses Ibn al-Kabābṭī and several of his peers in Algiers by name, comparing them to the man from Marbella and forcefully accusing them of the same violations detailed in Wansharīsī's *fatwā*. Through these pointed accusations, Ibn al-Ḥaffāf suggests that the jurists of Algiers are doing more harm than good to their communities, though they might think they are providing desperately needed services. The jurists are leaders who should model correct behavior, but instead of emigrating they model subservience to infidels and expose themselves to filth through their regular contact with Christians, who engage in all manner of impurities and uncleanliness. These remarks, particularly those related to the degradation of Islam, are peppered with provocative interrogatives: "With God [as your witness], oh people of Algiers: Which rites are dominant in Algiers, the rites of Islam or the rites of the infidel?" "Are these matters a debasement

15 While several sources suggest that Ibn al-Kabābṭī authored a *fatwā* in defense of remaining in Algiers, none refer to a specific primary source, and Ibn Ruwīlā makes no reference to such a *fatwā* in this letter. Saʿd Allāh (*Abḥāth*, 2:20 n. 10) suggests that Ibn Ruwīla composed this letter in 1834. This conjecture may be based on Ibn Ruwīla's comment that ʿAbd al-Qādir had prohibited his use of certain phrases four years earlier, which would make 1834 the earliest possible year of composition. Yet Ibn Ruwīla also refers to the reverential reception given to Ferdinand Philippe, Duke of Orléans and heir apparent to the French throne, when he visited Algiers. As the duke's first visit was in 1835, the letter must have been composed in 1835 or later (the duke's last visit was in 1840). The latest possible date for the letter is 1843, the last year in which Ibn al-Kabābṭī remained in his post.

16 Ibn Ruwīla mistakenly refers to this text as *Asnā al-matājir* (the title of which he offers in full), but he copies only the Marbella *fatwā*.

17 On ʿAlī b. ʿAbd al-Raḥmān b. Muḥammad al-Ḥaffāf, known as Ibn al-Ḥaffāf (d. 1307/1890), see Nuwayhiḍ, *Muʿjam*, 115; Ḥafnāwī, *Taʿrīf al-khalaf*, 2:269–70. Ibn al-Ḥaffāf served as the Mālikī *muftī* of Blida, a town south of Algiers that was occupied by the French in 1839, and later of Algiers, from 1290/1873–4 until his death there in 1890.

and mockery of the noble word or not, you *dhimmīs*?"[18] The word *dhimmīs* appears throughout as a term of insult.

This commentary is remarkable for our purposes, not because of Ibn al-Ḥaffāf's later reversal, but because of his complete confidence in Wansharīsī's text as an authoritative statement of doctrine. Even more so than Ibn Ruwīla, Ibn al-Ḥaffāf assumes that his readers will accept the validity of the arguments and evidence presented in the Marbella *fatwā*. He makes no attempt to establish Wansharīsī's credentials. Instead, Ibn al-Ḥaffāf only shows that the Marbella *fatwā* applies to his peers' present situation in Algiers; he systematically links their names and actions to the attitudes and violations described by Ibn Qaṭiyya and Wansharīsī. For Ibn al-Ḥaffāf, the Marbella *fatwā* is not just a piece of evidence or one argument among others, but the dominant lens through which he views, and condemns, the *muftīs* of French Algiers.

Ibn al-Shāhid's Letter from Algiers

Muḥammad b. al-Shāhid al-Jazā'irī (d. 1253/1836–7),[19] who served as Mālikī *muftī* of Algiers for much of the period between 1778 and 1792, composed a letter (undated) justifying his decision not to emigrate after the French conquest.[20] Ibn al-Shāhid indicates that he is responding directly to the unnamed author of a hate-filled letter slandering him and his peers and accusing him of apostasy for remaining in Algiers under French rule. While Ibn al-Ḥaffāf may come to mind as the author of the letter, his accusations in the above commentary do not extend to apostasy; Ibn al-Shāhid's response must be to another text.

---

18 Algerian National Library MS 1304, 4v; MS 2083 4r. Both examples appear on the same page. Among the "matters" referred to in the second interrogative is the placing of a cross on the Ketchaoua Mosque, seized by force in late 1831 in violation of the treaty of surrender of Algiers. Thoroughly renovated under French rule, the former mosque became the Cathedral of Saint Philippe until Algerian independence in 1962, when the crosses and other symbols were removed.

19 This is the death date given by the copyist at the close of Ibn al-Shāhid's letter. See also Abū al-Qāsim Sa'd Allāh, *Tārīkh al-Jazā'ir al-thaqāfī min al-qarn al-'āshir ilā al-rābi' 'āshar al-Hijrī (16–20 m.)*, 2nd ed. (Algiers: al-Mu'assasa al-Waṭaniyya lil-Kutub, 1985), 2:284–85. Ibn al-Shāhid's terms as *muftī* appear in 'Abd al-Qādir, *Ṣafaḥāt*, 184, 208–9; Ḥafnāwī, *Ta'rīf al-khalaf*, 2:481. Sa'd Allāh suggests that Ibn al-Shāhid was still alive in 1839, but this conjecture is based on a possibly erroneous present-tense reference to the jurist published that year. See B. Vincent, "Vers sur la conquête d'Alger," *Journal Asiatique* (December 1839): 503–7.

20 This letter, preserved in Algerian National Library MS 1305, has been published: Ibn 'Abd al-Karīm, *Ḥukm al-hijra*, 105–24. Ganān includes an abridged version of the letter in *Nuṣūṣ siyāsiyya*, 136–41. Verskin has translated a short excerpt from this letter in his *Oppressed in the Land*, 96–99.

Although Ibn al-Shāhid does not mention Wansharīsī's *fatwās*, the arguments to which he responds clearly reveal his opponent's reliance on *Asnā al-matājir* and the Marbella *fatwā*. In constructing his defense, Ibn al-Shāhid employs three main strategies. First, he concedes the validity of some of the precedents cited by his opponent, but contests their applicability to the Algerian context. For example, Ibn al-Shāhid agrees that Qurʾān 4:97–99 indicates an obligation to emigrate in the absolute sense, but he argues that this passage "concerns only those capable of emigrating . . . as for those who are incapable—like us—you establish no evidence against them with this."[21] He suggests that those Algiers residents who have not yet emigrated are exempted by Qurʾān 4:98–99 because of their poverty, the insecurity of the routes, or their need to await more opportune conditions. Curiously, Ibn al-Shāhid also accepts the Mālikī position that travel to enemy territory for trade is reprehensible. He argues that this opinion—presumably that of Ibn Rushd al-Jadd—supports his own position that residence among infidels is at worst a sinful act of disobedience. If remaining under infidel rule is reprehensible, but not prohibited, he argues, then it cannot constitute apostasy.

Ibn al-Shāhid's second strategy is to reject the validity of his opponent's (and Wansharīsī's) legal arguments. He cites a number of exegetes, primarily adherents of the Shafiʿī and Ḥanafī legal schools, who held that emigration is only obligatory if Muslims cannot practice their religion. Ibn al-Shāhid asserts that the Muslims in the capital remain practicing Muslims, contrary to his opponent's uninformed and inappropriate speculations—his opponent had suggested that the destruction of several mosques indicated that Muslims were unable to pray and were content with unbelief. Ibn al-Shāhid even turns the tables on his interlocutor in response to an insinuation that the Muslim women of Algiers were "with the infidels." Rather than entertain the possibility that sexual relations between Christian men and Muslim women were taking place (a spectre raised in the Marbella *fatwā*), Ibn al-Shāhid accuses his opponent of *qadhf*, or false accusation of adultery, and reminds him of the Qurʾānic punishment for this crime. Ibn al-Shāhid further rejects the basic premise of Wansharīsī's Marbella response by proposing that many jurists in Algiers have remained there for the laudable cause of guiding the commoners, who might otherwise fall into unbelief.

Ibn al-Shāhid's third defensive strategy is an appeal to the doctrine of compulsion. In response to the suggestion that his peers interact too closely with the French and are obsequious, Ibn al-Shāhid protests "they are compelled in this, and God has made compulsion a reason to forgive those

21 Ibn ʿAbd al-Karīm, *Ḥukm al-hijra*, 107–8.

who utter words of unbelief, as long as their hearts remain secure in faith."[22] He cites Qur'ān 16:106 (one of the verses to which Wahrānī had alluded) in support of this assertion. Ibn al-Shāhid further adduces Qur'ān 3:28, which instructs Muslims not to ally with unbelievers but excuses those who do so as a precaution, in order to protect themselves.[23] While 3:28 appears in *Asnā al-matājir* as a warning against such alliances, Ibn al-Shāhid instead highlights the fear-based exception to this prohibition.

Here, we may wonder if Ibn al-Shāhid had Wahrānī's letter to the Moriscos in mind. While it is possible that he did, it is very unlikely. Only Qur'ān 16:106 and the principle of compulsion link these two letters, and they are employed to justify rather different behaviors. Whereas Wahrānī invoked the principle of compulsion to excuse such acts as drinking wine, blasphemy, and missing prayers, Ibn al-Shāhid claims that Algerian Muslims face no such constraints. Instead, his appeal to compulsion is meant to justify flattery of the French and cooperation with them. This recourse to the principle of compulsion is the closest any of the Algerian texts come to mentioning Wahrānī's text or ideas.

Tasūlī's First Response to ʿAbd al-Qādir

In February 1837 ʿAbd al-Qādir wrote to the Moroccan sultan requesting a *fatwā* from the scholars of Fez. As part of his continued efforts to secure the military and financial support of the tribes in western Algeria, he posed several questions related to *jihād*. Are the lives and property of those who join the enemy, provide them with horses, or inform them of the Muslims' weaknesses forfeit? Can those who refuse to help defend their religion and territory be punished, and can their property be seized? For those who refuse to pay alms or the war tax, can they be considered rebels and treated accordingly?[24] With this set of questions, ʿAbd al-Qādir was seeking both religious justification and official ʿAlawī sanction to condemn as rebels those tribes that refused to support his *jihād* against the French and to use force against them, where necessary, to secure needed resources.[25] When he wrote this, ʿAbd al-Qādir was serving as ʿAbd al-Raḥmān's deputy and had not yet signed the Treaty of Tafna, concluded on 30 May 1837.

---

22 Ibn ʿAbd al-Karīm, *Ḥukm al-hijra*, 113.

23 Qur'ān 3:28, one of the primary proof texts for the doctrine of *taqiyya*, reads "Let not the believers take unbelievers for their allies in preference to believers. Whoever does this has no connection with God, unless you but guard yourselves against them as a precaution . . ." This is Devin Stewart's translation, which appears in Stewart, "Dissimulation," 452.

24 An annotated translation of this question, along with an evaluation of the Arabic sources and prior translations can be found in Hendrickson, "Is al-Andalus Different?," 417–19.

25 On ʿAbd al-Qādir's embassy to Mawlāy ʿAbd al-Raḥmān, see Bennison, *Jihad*, 91–93.

ʿAbd al-Raḥmān conveyed this request to the chief judge of Fez, ʿAlī b. ʿAbd al-Salām al-Tasūlī (d. 1258/1842), a prolific Mālikī scholar and active proponent of *jihād*.[26] In a five-part treatise dated June 1837, Tasūlī sanctions the use of force against rebels and enemy collaborators, as well as the seizure of their wealth. He further devotes a section of this lengthy *fatwā* to an unsolicited question on emigration, and in it he confirms the obligation to emigrate from conquered territory.[27] Much of this section consists of excerpts, which he acknowledges, from *Asnā al-matājir*. To this material Tasūlī adds his own commentary, in which he adapts Wansharīsī's *fatwā* to the current situation in Algeria.

It is worth noting that many of Tasūlī's comments render his own statement on *hijra* stricter than those of Wansharīsī, in keeping with the harsher, more urgent, and more personal tone of much of the Algerian debate. For example, Tasūlī asserts that because all those who live in infidel territory must contribute financially to the enemy, seizure of their property is licit.[28] He also supports Ibn Rushd al-Jadd's opposition to entering *dār al-ḥarb* for trade, and cites Māzarī's prohibition of the same (not included in *Asnā al-matājir*); he further suggests that these opinions may imply that it is not permissible to cross infidel territory, even en route to the pilgrimage.[29] This was the first of two *fatwās* that Tāsulī composed for ʿAbd al-Qādir.

ʿIllaysh's Response to ʿAbd al-Qādir

In an effort to bolster the religious legitimacy of his positions, ʿAbd al-Qādir also solicited two *fatwās* from the prominent Egyptian Mālikī jurist Muḥammad ʿIllaysh (d. 1299/1882).[30] In contrast to his first question to Tasūlī, ʿAbd al-Qādir's initial request to ʿIllaysh addresses the question of emigration.[31] Without providing details or names, ʿAbd al-Qādir states that

26 On him, see Tasūlī, *Ajwibat al-Tasūlī ʿan masāʾil al-amīr ʿAbd al-Qādir fī al-jihād*, ed. ʿAbd al-Laṭīf Ṣāliḥ (Beirut: Dār al-Gharb al-Islāmī, 1996), 36–60; Muḥammad al-Manūnī, *Maẓāhir yaqẓat al-Maghrib al-ḥadīth*, 2nd ed., 2 vols. (Beirut: Dār al-Gharb al-Islāmī, 1985), 27–30; Makhlūf, *Shajarat al-nūr*, 1:567–68; Kattānī, *Salwat al-anfās*, 1:266.

27 The section of this treatise devoted to *hijra* can be found in Tasūlī, *Ajwibat al-Tasūlī*, 301–10; Jazāʾirī, *Tuḥfat al-zāʾir*, 1:326–28.

28 Tasūlī, *Ajwibat al-Tasūlī*, 310.

29 Tasūlī, *Ajwibat al-Tasūlī*, 305.

30 Abū ʿAbd Allāh Muḥammad b. Aḥmad ʿIllaysh (d. 1299/1882) was born in Cairo to a family of Maghribī origin, educated at al-Azhar, and served as Egypt's head Mālikī *muftī* from 1854 until his 1882 imprisonment for supporting the ʿUrābī movement; he died in prison. On him, see Muḥammad ʿIllaysh, *Fatḥ al-ʿalī al-mālik fī al-fatwā ʿalā madhhab al-Imām Mālik*, 2 vols. (Cairo: Muṣṭafā al-Bābī al-Ḥalabī, 1958), 1:2–4; Makhlūf, *Shajarat al-nūr*, 1:551–52; Ziriklī, *Al-Aʿlām*, 6:19–20.

31 For the question, see ʿIllaysh, *Fatḥ al-ʿalī*, 1:375. Wazzānī also includes the question and part of ʿIllaysh's response in *al-Miʿyār al-jadīd* (3:81–90), but does not identify the questioner and attributes the answer only to "a later scholar." The question has been translated into English by at least three scholars: Peters, *Islam and Colonialism*, 58; Muhammad Umar, "Islamic Discourses

the infidels conquered "a Muslim region." Some of the inhabitants emigrated while others remained, subjecting themselves to infidel rule and paying taxes to the enemy. Jurists from each group then issued *fatwās* supporting their own positions. Those jurists in favor of obligatory emigration accused those who remained of strengthening the enemy, and they consider these Muslims' lives and property to be forfeit. Those who remained insist that they are not obligated to emigrate, because Qurʾān 3:28 allows those who are afraid to maintain otherwise prohibited relations with unbelievers, and because the *ḥadīth* that states there is "no *hijra* after the conquest" means that emigration is no longer obligatory.

ʿIllaysh's response demonstrates his complete dependence on Wansharīsī (even more than Ibn Ruwīla, who offered a short introduction of his own prior to copying the full Marbella *fatwā*). ʿIllaysh merely reproduces the full texts of both *Asnā al-matājir* and the Marbella *fatwā*, without substantial comments or modifications.[32] By doing this, he fails to address directly the argument of those Algerian jurists (such as Ibn al-Shāhid) who appealed to Qurʾān 3:28 to justify remaining under infidel rule. While Wansharīsī tackles the problem of the "no *hijra*" *ḥadīth* in *Asnā al-matājir*, he discusses exemptions from obligatory emigration only in relation to weakness and incapacity, as mentioned in Qurʾān 4:98, not in relation to the danger alluded to in Qurʾān 3:28. In relying wholly on Wansharīsī's *fatwās* despite this lacuna, ʿIllaysh seems to suggest that his predecessor's texts resolved the question of *hijra* definitively, and that no further questions or arguments are worth addressing. ʿIllaysh's second exchange with ʿAbd al-Qādir, in 1846, does not relate to *hijra*.[33]

---

on European Visitors to Sokoto Caliphate in the Nineteenth Century," *Studia Islamica* 95 (2002): 140–41; Verskin, *Oppressed in the Land*, 100–101; Verskin, *Islamic Law*, 111–12. The question is undated and does not identify ʿAbd al-Qādir, but his authorship can be presumed on at least three grounds. ʿAbd al-Qādir's son states that his father requested *fatwās* from Fez and Egypt simultaneously (Jazāʾirī, *Tuḥfat al-zāʾir*, 1:316), although the son notes that he did not see the Egyptian response (Jazāʾirī, *Tuḥfat al-zāʾir*, 1:329). The editor of *Fatḥ al-ʿalī* follows this exchange, in which ʿIllaysh's questioner is not named, with another exchange between the two in which ʿAbd al-Qādir is indeed named. Finally, in the Tunisian National Library MS 2418 (fols. 1b–17a), ʿIllaysh's response regarding *hijra* is followed by ʿAbd al-Qādir's own treatise on *hijra*, another response by Tasūlī, and a later Egyptian response to ʿAbd al-Qādir's questions. These associations strongly suggest that ʿIllaysh directed his *fatwā* on *hijra* to ʿAbd al-Qādir.

32 ʿIllaysh, *Fatḥ al-ʿalī*, 1:375–87. ʿIllaysh's version of *Asnā al-matājir* contains a few minor discrepancies as compared with the *Miʿyār*; these are noted in Abū Yaʿla al-Bayḍāwī's 2005 edition of *Asnā al-matājir* (see chapter 4, n. 8). The most significant difference between the two versions is simply that ʿIllaysh places the response portion of *Asnā al-matājir* before the question.

33 ʿAbd al-Qādir's second query to ʿIllaysh accuses Mawlāy ʿAbd al-Raḥmān of assisting the French, signing an illegitimate treaty with them, and betraying those who are waging *jihād* to preserve Muslim territory. Jazāʾirī, *Tuḥfat al-zāʾir*, 1:471–80; ʿIllaysh, *Fatḥ al-ʿalī*, 1:387–92. See also Peters, *Islam and Colonialism*, 60–61.

Tasūlī's Second Response to ʿAbd al-Qādir

In 1839, ʿAbd al-Qādir sent a second *istiftāʾ* (question) to Fez, this time forwarded to Fez's chief judge ʿAbd al-Hādī al-ʿAlawī (d. 1271/1854–5);[34] this was answered by both ʿAbd al-Hādī and Tasūlī.[35] According to ʿAbd al-Qādir's son and chronicler Muḥammad, this new query was occasioned when several coastal tribes chose infidel protection.[36] After warning them of their grave sin and entreating them to join their brethren in the interior (presumably, to fight the French), ʿAbd al-Qādir felt that his only recourse was to attack them. Prior to taking this step, he consulted the scholars: are those who submit to the infidel, ally with them, and fight for them against Muslims considered apostates? Does the duty to defend Muslim territory extend to Muslim residents of territories adjacent to those where there is fighting?

In his response, dated March 1840, ʿAbd al-Hādī refuses to call these Muslims apostates and cautions ʿAbd al-Qādir against leveling such accusations too readily. Yet he confirms that if a particular region is conquered and cannot defend itself, *jihād* becomes the individual responsibility of all those nearby, including women. If they cannot participate by fighting, then they must do so financially. ʿAbd al-Hādī does not address emigration directly, nor does he cite the opinions of Wansharīsī or his contemporaries.

Tasūlī adopts a far more antagonistic tone than does ʿAbd al-Hādī with regard to ʿAbd al-Qādir's adversaries. He first points his readers to the section on *hijra* in his 1837 treatise, then offers a second response to ʿAbd al-Qādir, as a supplement to the earlier text.[37] Tasūlī explains that he

34 Abū Muḥammad ʿAbd al-Hādī b. ʿAbd Allāh b. al-Tuhāmī al-Ḥusaynī al-ʿAlawī (d. 1271/1854–5) served as the chief judge of Fez for twenty years. Makhlūf, *Shajarat al-nūr*, 1:572.

35 ʿAbd al-Qādir's full question and ʿAbd al-Hādī's response appear in Jazāʾirī, *Tuḥfat al-zāʾir*, 1:384–89; Wazzānī, *al-Nawāzil al-ṣughrā*, 1:414–17; and Wazzānī, *al-Miʿyār al-jadīd*, 10:291–97. Peters (*Islam and Colonialism*, 59–60) translates part of the question into English. ʿAbd al-Qādir's full question also concerns the status of a group of Ibāḍīs known as the Banī Mzāb. The first part of the question and Tasūlī's response appear in Tunisian National Library MS 2418, fols. 13b–16a. Only ʿAbd al-Hādī's response is dated (March 1840), but Tasūlī's response was presumably issued the same year. Wazzānī confuses aspects of ʿAbd al-Qādir's 1837 and 1840 exchanges in both of his *fatwā* compilations. In *al-Miʿyār al-jadīd*, where he includes a condensed version of Tasūlī's first response (3:61–63), Wazzānī erroneously states that ʿAbd al-Hādī's response to the same question is included in *al-Nawāzil al-ṣughrā*. What we find in *al-Nawāzil al-ṣughrā* is actually ʿAbd al-Hādī's 1840 response to this second *istiftāʾ*, rather than a response to the 1837 question answered by Tasūlī. In another section of *al-Miʿyār al-jadīd*, Wazzānī follows ʿAbd al-Hādī's 1840 response (10:291–97) with another condensed version of Tasūlī's 1837 treatise (10:297–304), as though both texts were answers to the same question. Tasūlī's second response to ʿAbd al-Qādir remains unpublished.

36 Jazāʾirī, *Tuḥfat al-zāʾir*, 1:384.

37 Tunisian National Library MS 2418 consists of the following *fatwās*: (1) ʿIllaysh's two responses to ʿAbd al-Qādir, together with the questions, as they also appear in *Fatḥ al-ʿalī* (fols. 1a–10a); (2) ʿAbd al-Qādir's treatise *Ḥusām al-dīn* (fols. 10a–13b), discussed below; (3) Tasūlī's second

will elaborate on three offenses committed by Muslims in this new query: informing the enemy of the Muslims' weaknesses, fighting for the enemy, and living with them under their rule. With regard to those who commit either of the first two offenses, Tasūlī's position is that once the enemy is defeated, these people may be killed without offering them an opportunity to repent.[38]

Tasūlī's response to those who commit only the third offense (living under enemy rule) is worth quoting at length (my emphases):

> With regard to those who are living among the Christians, the master Zayyātī states in his *fatwā* compilation, [*al-Jawāhir*] *al-mukhtāra*: [According to] the *fatwās* that our learned masters have issued concerning them [Muslims], it is necessary to kill them and take their property as *fay'*, meaning booty (*ghanīma*), because the land [they are in] is infidel territory and their property is under infidel control, not under their own control. This is because they can take it from them [i.e., the infidels can seize the Muslims' property] whenever they wish, given that the territory is theirs and they have authority over it [the land and everything in it].
>
> Likewise, their [Muslim] wives should be captured and taken from them until they reach Muslim territory, [where] they should be divorced by a judge. These [women] should be prevented from [remarrying] their spouses, and they should be married off [to other men]. It is not permissible for the wives [of men living among Christians] to remain with them.
>
> [Wansharīsī] states in the *Miʿyār*, [and this is] the gist of it: *Any Muslim who has continued living with them and has not emigrated to us after the tyrant's seizure of his land, or who flees from us to them,* does not have [valid possession of his] property or children, because the infidels have possession [of them], just as the territory is in their possession. [This legal assessment is derived] through an analogy with [the case of] one who was originally an infidel, converted to

response, together with ʿAbd al-Qādir's second question to Fez (fols. 13b–16a). Tasūlī is misidentified as ʿAlī al-Rasūl at the beginning of this text and as al-Rasūlī at the end; (4) a *fatwā* issued by Egyptian jurist Muṣṭafā al-Būlāqī in response to Tasūlī's *fatwā* (fols. 16a–17a); (5) the anonymous compiler's statement (in 1268/1852) that he has copied these *fatwās* on the obligation to emigrate; and (6) a closing prayer in verse. The entire manuscript is listed in the library's catalogue as *Risāla fī wujūb al-hijra wa'l-jihād* (*Treatise on the Obligatory Status of Emigration and Jihād*) by Muḥammad ʿIllaysh al-Azharī. While I have not seen any reference to this manuscript in the relevant scholarly literature, it may contain the only extant copy of Tasūlī's second response to ʿAbd al-Qādir and Būlāqī's response to Tasūlī.

38 Tasūlī distinguishes between those fighting for the enemy, who must be killed, and those fighting against other Muslims as a group of illegitimate rebels (*muḥāribūn*), whose punishment should be determined by the ruler.

> Islam, and remained with them; for he possesses neither property nor children, by agreement of Mālik and Abū Ḥanīfa (may God, the exalted, have mercy upon both of them).
>
> Then [Wansharīsī] states: *One who is originally Muslim and remains in their land, or who flees from us to them*, is analogous to one who was originally an infidel and converted to Islam, and remained in their territory, until [Muslims from *dār al-Islām*] raided [the territory]; [the case of the original Muslim] is assimilated to [the case of the convert] with respect to all [of these] legal assessments. This is by agreement of the later jurists, because [the original Muslim] is their equivalent in all meaningful respects. This analogy [that the later jurists agreed upon] was of the utmost excellence.
>
> Furthermore, [Wansharīsī] states: *If these Muslims who have fled from us to them, or who have continued living with them from the beginning*, fight against us, the opinion that their lives are licit must be [chosen as] the preponderant [opinion] at that point. If they support [their allies] materially in their battle against us, the opinion that their property is licit must be preponderant. Capturing their children has been determined [already] as the preponderant opinion.[39]

This section of Tasūlī's response is remarkable for two reasons: the first is his use of Waryāglī (d. 894/1488–9), whose *fatwā* on emigration was the most uncompromising opinion that Zayyātī included in his *Selected Jewels*; the second is Tasūlī's re-interpretation of *Asnā al-matājir*. While Tāsulī credits the first two paragraphs here only to Zayyātī as the compiler of *al-Jawāhir al-mukhtāra* (*Selected Jewels*), he is quoting from Waryāglī's *fatwā*. We know that Tasūlī was intimately familiar with the full set of late fifteenth-century *fatwā*s issued in response to Portuguese occupation, as he included them in his own unpublished *fatwā* compilation, *al-Jawāhir al-nafīsa* (*Precious Jewels*). Thus, his choice to apply that earlier era's most unforgiving opinion to the Algerian context is calculated. Tasūlī may have felt that ʿAbd al-Qādir's second request for a *fatwā* regarding those tribes loyal to France merited a more strongly worded response than he had offered in his original treatise, or he may have introduced Waryāglī's text to counter ʿAbd al-Hādī's more reserved opinion. This appears to be the only time Waryāglī's *fatwā* is quoted in the Algerian *hijra* debate.[40]

While he quotes faithfully from Waryāglī, Tasūlī takes some liberties in this summary of *Asnā al-matājir*. Whereas Wansharīsī addressed Muslims who failed to emigrate, who returned to their homelands after emigrating,

---

39 Tunisian National Library MS 2418, fol. 14a–14b.

40 This part of Waryāglī's *fatwā* later appears in a Mauritanian *fatwā*, as we see in the next chapter, but only through a citation of Tasūlī's response to ʿAbd al-Qādir.

or who desired to return, Tasūlī renders these categories as Muslims who have failed to emigrate or who "flee from us to them." In this new formulation, there is still a category of Muslims who emigrate in the wrong direction (that is, from Muslim to Christian territory), but in this case, they are not returning to their own homelands after successfully emigrating, as the Andalusīs of *Asnā al-matājir* hoped to do. Instead, for Tasūlī, this group consists of traitors who voluntarily defect from the Muslim side to join the infidels. Further in Tasūlī's *fatwā*, this group is mentioned first, as the primary category of Muslims who have failed to emigrate from infidel to Muslim territory. Tasūlī thus adapts the authoritative precedent of *Asnā al-matājir* to support his own opinion, but not just by arguing that Wansharīsī's *fatwā* is applicable to the Algerian context; rather, he reformulates his predecessor's categories such that Wansharīsī appears to have been writing directly about this new type of case. The fact that Tasūlī felt a need to claim that he was relying on the *Miʿyār* when in fact he altered Wansharīsī's text is confirmation, albeit in a different fashion than the *fatwā*s of Ibn Ruwīla and ʿIllaysh, of the unparalleled authority of this source in colonial-era Algeria.

The remainder of Tasūlī's *fatwā* is concerned primarily with the evidence necessary to declare that a Muslim is an apostate and with an apostate's legal status with regard to his property, wives, and children. Unlike ʿAbd al-Hādī, Tasūlī is quite willing to consider ʿAbd al-Qādir's enemies apostates. He considers fighting and spying for the enemy to be strong evidence of apostasy, in part because those who commit these offenses "know that if the infidel enemy takes control of the country, Islam will be extinguished there . . . thus they are fighting to elevate the word of the infidels [above that of Islam]."[41] In ʿAbd al-Qādir's own treatise on these issues, discussed below, the Algerian leader makes a similar statement that suggests that he, like Tasūlī, considers it inevitable that the French will attempt to eradicate Islam from the areas under their control. With respect to the tribes mentioned in ʿAbd al-Qādir's *istiftāʾ*, Tasūlī states that if they glorify the infidel's religion, according to the criteria set forth in his *fatwā*, they are indeed apostates. In the event that it cannot be proven that a particular group has glorified unbelief or committed another act necessarily indicative of apostasy, then their status accords with the analogy presented in the *Miʿyār*; that is, they are equivalent to converts to Islam who fail to emigrate from *dār al-ḥarb* to *dār al-Islām*. If their only offense is subjecting themselves to infidel authority, Tasūlī states that their property is forfeit and their wives and children should be taken from them, but that their lives remain inviolable.[42]

41 Tunisian National Library, MS 2418, fol. 14b.
42 Tunisian National Library, MS 2418, fols. 15b–16a.

Following Tasūlī's response is a *fatwā* issued by Egyptian Mālikī jurist Muṣṭafā al-Būlāqī (d. 1263/1847).[43] After reading ʿAbd al-Qādir's question and Tasūlī's response, Būlāqī issued a *fatwā* in which he states even more forcefully than Tasūlī that there is no doubt that the actions described by ʿAbd al-Qādir constitute apostasy. Būlāqī does not address emigration or those subject to non-Muslim rule.

Fatwā of al-Sharīf al-Tilimsānī

We know of one final *fatwā* that we can assume was solicited by ʿAbd al-Qādir in an effort to bolster support for the *jihād* against the French, in this case by securing religious sanction to attack Muslims who were affiliated with the French.[44] The February 1841 *fatwā* was issued by Muḥammad b. Saʿd al-Sharīf al-Tilimsānī (d. 1264/1848),[45] who was at the time serving as *khaṭīb* of the Great Mosque of Taza. It concerns some factions of the Banū ʿĀmir tribe[46] who had placed themselves under Christian protection voluntarily and in the absence of any compulsion, in order to transit to a place of safety. The question is, should their property, like that of the unbelievers, be considered booty?

In his response, al-Sharīf al-Tilimsānī stresses that they should rely on the many *fatwā*s that Maghribī scholars have issued in relation to similar concerns beginning in the fifteenth century. He advises that these jurists must be our exemplars, because of their superior knowledge in religion. Al-Sharīf al-Tilimsānī offers three *fatwā*s as instructive examples of this genre; all of these were treated in part 1 of this book: Māwāsī's *fatwā* and one composite version of Ibn Barṭāl's *fatwā*, each of which address categories of interaction with the Christians, and Ibn Zakrī's second *fatwā*, the one regarding "tribes of the Far Maghrib" who intermingle with and aid the Christians.

43 This jurist's name is spelled Muṣṭafā al-Bulāqī in the manuscript (fol. 16b), but likely refers to Muṣṭafā al-Būlāqī, an Egyptian Mālikī jurist. At least one of his *fatwā*s appears in Muḥammad ʿIllaysh's *Fatḥ al-ʿalī*.

44 The questioner is identified only as *amīr al-muʾminīn* (Commander of the Faithful), a title used by both ʿAbd al-Qādir and the Moroccan sultan, Mawlāy ʿAbd al-Raḥmān. ʿAbd al-Qādir is the far more likely candidate, especially as the question resembles other requests that have been identified as his. It is also possible that ʿAbd al-Qādir sent the question to the Moroccan sultan, who forwarded it to al-Sharīf al-Tilimsānī.

45 Muḥammad b. Saʿd b. al-Ḥājj al-Ḥasanī al-Baydarī al-Tilimsānī (d. 1264/1848), known as al-Sharīf al-Tilimsānī, was a judge in Ottoman Tlemcen who moved to Fez, returned briefly to Tlemcen during Mawlāy ʿAbd al-Raḥmān's attempt to incorporate the city into the Moroccan sultanate, and then fled to Fez when the French captured Tlemcen in 1835. Al-Sharīf al-Tilimsānī, who had left behind all his books and money, soon found Fez too expensive and settled in Taza, where he likely composed this opinion. He returned to Fez in 1262/1846, for the last two years of his life. See Kattānī, *Salwat al-anfās*, 3:97–98; Ḥajjī, *Mawsūʿat aʿlām al-Maghrib*, 7:2581.

46 On the Banū ʿĀmir, see Bennison, *Jihad*, 140–151. This *fatwā*, dated 30 Dhū al-Ḥijja 1256/22 February 1841, appears in Wazzānī, *al-Nawāzil al-ṣughrā*, 1:417–20.

Curiously, al-Sharīf al-Tilimsānī notes that these and other opinions are recorded in the *Miʿyār* and should be consulted there.[47] This misattribution suggests that the *Miʿyār* so dominated Mālikī jurisprudence in this period that all important precedents were assumed to be found in its many volumes. In reality, al-Sharīf al-Tilimsānī would have found these *fatwās* in a copy of Zayyātī's *Selected Jewels* or possibly Tasūlī's *al-Jawāhir al-nafīsa*. Either he failed to realize that these were not in the *Miʿyār* or, less likely, he hoped to bolster the authority of the precedents he was citing by falsely asserting their inclusion in Wansharīsī's prestigious compilation.

While al-Sharīf al-Tilimsānī's failure to recognize Zayyātī's *Selected Jewels* as his source confirms the relative obscurity of that compilation, his *fatwā* nonetheless reaffirms that many nineteenth-century Maghribī jurists were in fact aware of this body of opinions on cooperation with the Portuguese. Notably, the three "jewels" that al-Sharīf al-Tilimsānī finds particularly applicable to the Algerian case differ from the one *fatwā*—that of Waryāglī—that Tasūlī features in his second response to ʿAbd al-Qādir. Here we might ask why these seemingly apt precedents were so infrequently cited. Surely Tasūlī, for example, would have agreed with Ibn Zakrī's assessment that tribespeople who affiliate with the enemy should be fought and killed "like the infidels with whom they have allied."[48] Why, then, does Tasūlī overlook that *fatwā* in favor of a text like *Asnā al-matājir*, one he needed to manipulate in order to increase its relevance to the Algerian context? ʿAbd al-Qādir's own contribution to the Algerian debate, below, may provide some clues.

The Tijāniyya

By 1841, the French sought to undermine Algerian calls for *hijra* by soliciting a *fatwā* permitting Muslims to accept Christian rule. The plan was proposed to Governor-General Thomas Robert Bugeaud by Léon Roches, a French convert to Islam who had worked as ʿAbd al-Qādir's secretary from 1837 until 1840. In August 1841 Roches traveled to Qayrawān, where he obtained the desired *fatwā* from a council of religious authorities of the Tijāniyya, a Sufi order hostile to ʿAbd al-Qādir. The *fatwā* affirmed that a Muslim people may submit to infidel rule on the following conditions: that further combat would bring only misery and death without hope of victory; that the Muslims would be granted freedom to exercise their religion; and

47 It is by virtue of reproducing al-Sharīf al-Tilimsānī's *fatwā* in his *al-Nawāzil al-ṣughrā* that Wāzzānī includes these three earlier *fatwās* in his compilation. See part 1 and appendix A for details.

48 See appendix A, 286.

that Muslim women and children would be respected.[49] Unfortunately, Roches's brief summary of this response offers no indication of the legal reasoning or textual evidence employed.

This *fatwā*, solicited by the French in exchange for gifts and status, apparently had little impact. In his memoir, Roches claims to have had this document ratified by scholarly councils in both Cairo and Mecca. These additional efforts might have bolstered the authority of the Tijānī *fatwā*, but they ultimately proved fictional.[50] Governor-General Jules Cambon revisited the idea of Meccan endorsement over fifty years later, as France prepared a new military campaign to annex the Touat region. In order to prevent the renewed calls for *hijra* that Cambon anticipated in response to this campaign, he commissioned an Algerian pilgrim to obtain a *fatwā* during the 1893 pilgrimage. The text, composed by the *muftī* of Mecca and ratified by his Shāfiʿī and Mālikī counterparts, stressed the obligation to emigrate for those capable, but permitted residence in any territory where Muslim judges upheld Islamic law.[51]

ʿAbd al-Qādir's Treatise

In January 1843, ʿAbd al-Qādir produced his own treatise-length *fatwā* titled *Ḥusām al-dīn li-qaṭʿ shabah al-murtaddīn* (*The Sword of Religion that Severs [Muslims'] Resemblance to Apostates*), in which he argues for obligatory emigration.[52] While his fifteenth-century counterpart Waryāglī is said to have split the year between waging *jihād* and offering religious guidance, in this text ʿAbd al-Qādir seems to have performed these meritorious acts simultaneously. He claims to have composed this text only in order to assist certain individuals who want to better understand the law as it regards submission to infidel rule or reliance on the enemy. He further states that he undertook this task while guarding the frontier, with no recourse to his books or other resources.[53] It is equally likely that

49 Léon Roches, *Dix ans à travers l'Islam: 1834–1844*, new ed. (Paris: Librairie Académique Didier, n.d.), 241.

50 Marcel Émerit, "La Légende de Léon Roches," quoted in Jamil Abun-Nasr, *The Tijaniyya: A Sufi Order in the Modern World* (New York: Oxford University Press, 1965), 70.

51 Ganān, *Nuṣūṣ siyāsiyya*, 262–64.

52 Ibn ʿAbd al-Karīm published an edition of this treatise; it is based on two manuscripts held by the Moroccan National Library (Ibn ʿAbd al-Karīm, *Ḥukm al-hijra*, 43–66). ʿAbd al-Qādir's son Muḥammad offers a longer version of the text in his chronicle of his father's life (Jazāʾirī, *Tuḥfat al-zāʾir*, 1:411–23). The title of this treatise does not appear explicitly in the text but is based on elements of ʿAbd al-Qādir's colophon (Jazāʾirī, *Tuḥfat al-zāʾir*, 1:411). One of the two Moroccan manuscripts Ibn ʿAbd al-Karīm consulted bears the title offered above, as does Tunisian National Library MS 2418 (fols. 10a–10b). The other Moroccan manuscript Ibn ʿAbd al-Karim consulted bears the title, *Ḥusām al-dīn: Sayf al-dīn al-qāṭiʿ li-shabah al-murtaddīn*, which is identical in meaning (Ibn ʿAbd al-Karīm, *Ḥukm al-hijra*, 45).

53 Jazāʾirī, *Tuḥfat al-zāʾir*, 1:422; Ibn ʿAbd al-Karīm, *Ḥukm al-hijra*, 66.

ʿAbd al-Qādir was prompted solely by his own desire to circulate the most compelling possible argument against submission to French rule. *Ḥusām al-dīn* (*Sword of Religion*), the most extensive of the Algerian writings on emigration, appears to be fully informed by ʿAbd al-Qādir's own legal research, the Egyptian and Moroccan opinions addressed above, and the arguments advanced by Algerian jurists who remained in French territory.

Over the course of his treatise, ʿAbd al-Qādir deploys most of the reasoning and proof texts found in *Asnā al-matājir* and the Marbella *fatwā*, weaving them together with a variety of new arguments, counter-arguments, and historical examples. Yet despite the length and complexity of this treatise, *Sword of Religion* does not refer to the precedents preserved by Zayyātī, or to Wahrānī's 1504 Letter. As we can be sure that ʿAbd al-Qādir was at least familiar with those "jewels" cited by Tasūlī and al-Sharīf al-Tilimsānī, his choice to exclude these precedents from *Sword of Religion* again raises the question of why Wansharīsī's two *fatwā*s that ostensibly focus on Andalusīs predominated over these alternatives from the same period.

A key passage in ʿAbd al-Qādir's treatise may provide some answers. In this passage, which appears in the final third of *Sword of Religion*, ʿAbd al-Qādir refutes the claim that Muslim lives and religious practices are protected by French guarantees. He asserts that only a feeble-minded idiot would place his trust in the infidels or their treaties, for "we do not accept their testimony [as legally valid] with regard to themselves, let alone with regard to ourselves!"[54] This unacknowledged quote from the Marbella *fatwā* is reinforced with an appeal to the historical precedent of al-Andalus:

> It is as though the news of al-Andalus has not reached this idiot! Especially [regarding] the people of Córdoba who, when the infidels conquered them, came to an agreement with them as to sixty-some provisions that the [Muslims] stipulated as the terms [of their surrender]. These did not last a year before they violated them, one after another. In the end the infidel began to approach the Muslim and say to him: "Your father, or your grandfather, or your grandfather's grandfather, was an infidel, so return to unbelief and leave the religion of Islam!"[55]

Two elements of this passage are at once characteristic of ʿAbd al-Qādir's treatise and also help to explain why Wansharīsī's precedents proved so influential in the Algerian context. First, the fall of al-Andalus was treated as an instructive historical precedent with the power to corroborate the

54 Jazāʾirī, *Tuḥfat al-zāʾir*, 1:418; Ibn ʿAbd al-Karīm, *Ḥukm al-hijra*, 59.

55 Jazāʾirī, *Tuḥfat al-zāʾir*, 1:418; Ibn ʿAbd al-Karīm, *Ḥukm al-hijra*, 59. My translation is based on a composite of these two sources, which differ slightly.

textual precedents conveyed by *Asnā al-matājir* and the Marbella *fatwā*. In this passage, a broken surrender treaty in Córdoba validates and illustrates Wansharīsī's argument that Christian promises cannot be considered legitimate or trustworthy. For those in the larger Algerian debate advocating emigration, the "news of al-Andalus"—that accepting military defeat ultimately leads to the end of Islam, not just the end of Muslim rule—would have confirmed Wansharīsī's most dire warnings and assessments of sin.

While the forced conversions and expulsions of the Morisco period enhanced the authority of Wansharīsī's Iberian *fatwā*s, ʿAbd al-Qādir made his own contribution to the debate on *hijra*: he granted these historical events further legal authority of their own. According to ʿAbd al-Qādir, he and his fellow jurists were not just encouraged, but required to heed the lessons of the past. He noted that many legal rules in the Mālikī school are based on the principle that what is expected is akin to reality; for example, the dispensation that allows prayers to be combined on account of rain may be invoked if rain is merely anticipated. In response to those "feeble in intellect and religion" who protest (as does Ibn al-Shāhid) that the French have not ordered Algerian Muslims to convert, ʿAbd al-Qādir argues that such an order must be anticipated:

> The infidels will most likely order [Muslims to convert]. For if they had not ordered this, then all trace of Islam would not have been obliterated from the [Iberian] Peninsula, from Sicily, and from the other places seized by the infidels, such that not one Muslim remains in them. According to the principles [of Mālikī law], is the most likely [scenario] similar [in legal weight] to that which has been realized, or not? The correct opinion is that it is.[56]

Here ʿAbd al-Qādir asserts that it is of no consequence whether or not the French have attempted to curtail Algerians' religious practices or other rights. Nor does he claim that it can be known with certainty that they will do so; rather, the strong probability that they will use their power to restrict these practices in the future constitutes a valid legal argument for the obligation to emigrate.

In making this argument, ʿAbd al-Qādir chooses to assert the post-1500 fate of Iberia's Muslims as the inevitable consequence of Christian conquest and as the relevant past most predictive of Algerians' future under French rule. He assimilates the fate of Sicily's Muslims to the forced conversions of the Morisco period, and glosses over four centuries of Mudéjar life in Iberia. ʿAbd al-Qādir did not consider it useful for Algerian Muslims to identify with (as legally binding history) the period of Portuguese encroachment in the

56 Ibn ʿAbd al-Karīm, *Ḥukm al-hijra*, 61.

Maghrib, presumably because this ended with Islam in Morocco intact. ʿAbd al-Qādir thus had little incentive to cite Zayyātī's "jewels," as they invoke the wrong past—a past with an outcome that did not accord with his vision of the future.

While ʿAbd al-Qādir might have pointed to Wahrānī's 1504 Letter as an example of the legal advice Algerians might soon need if they do not heed his own, we have no reason to believe he knew of this text. The letter also would have done little to counter the argument that Algerians under French rule are free to practice Islam; ʿAbd al-Qādir's opponents could readily have dismissed the circumstances addressed by Wahrānī as irrelevant to their own condition. In contrast, *Asnā al-matājir* and the Marbella *fatwā* address the claims of those Muslims who, like ʿAbd al-Qādir's opponents, were free to practice Islam under Christian rule, or who argued that emigration was not an immediate priority.

This attention to counter-arguments is the second element of ʿAbd al-Qādir's "news of al-Andalus" passage above that is at the heart of both his treatise and the importance of Wansharīsī's precedents for the Algerian *hijra* debate as a whole. Nearly half of *Sword of Religion* is devoted to refuting the claims of rival jurists like the "idiot" ʿAbd al-Qādir berates in this passage. As we have seen above, the Algerian debate featured heated exchanges and personal attacks between jurists arguing for and against the necessity of emigration. While ʿAbd al-Qādir does not name his adversaries, it is clear that he was contending seriously with contemporary jurists who had issued legal opinions opposed to his own. For example, he describes those who use the "no *hijra*" *ḥadīth* to excuse submission to Christian rule as ignorant, would-be jurists who issue *fatwās* without knowledge. They err and mislead others, seemingly fulfilling Muḥammad's statement that "a time will come for the people when their scholars have a worse stench than a donkey's corpse."[57] In contrast, it would seem that Zayyātī's "jewels" do not refute serious, competing legal opinions that legitimize cooperation with the Portuguese. Instead, the *fatwās* of Ibn Barṭāl, Māwāsī, and Waryāglī were devoted primarily to prescriptive statements of rules and consequences.

Wansharīsī's *Asnā al-matājir* and the Marbella *fatwā* provide compelling precedents for ʿAbd al-Qādir and his peers in part because they were designed to address counter-arguments. While Wansharīsī refuses to acknowledge a scholarly rival, Ibn Rabīʿ's *fatwā* was framed as a response to an Iberian jurist who approved of Muslims residing under Christian rule. Thus, the extensive material that Wansharīsī borrows from Ibn Rabīʿ is oriented toward the refutation of professional and popular arguments

57 Jazāʾirī, *Tuḥfat al-zāʾir*, 1:416; Ibn ʿAbd al-Karīm, *Ḥukm al-hijra*, 56. I have been unable to locate this *ḥadīth*.

against emigration. Moreover, Ibn Qaṭiyya's questions offered rationales for continued residence in the voices of lay Muslims, affording Wansharīsī an opportunity to refute these ideas using a memorable story and without admitting scholarly dissent.

In the remainder of his treatise, ʿAbd al-Qādir mixes Wansharīsī's arguments and proof texts with original arguments in order to meet the needs of his nineteenth-century Algerian audience. Many of the ideas he counters are familiar from earlier texts on *hijra*. For example, he argues that concern for one's property is not a valid excuse to remain in conquered territory (as "stipulated" by Wansharīsī), and that Muslims cannot perform their religious obligations correctly under Christian rule (he refers readers to the Marbella *fatwā*). He mocks the idea that Christian treaties provide sufficient protections (by drawing on both Wansharīsī and historical precedent, as above), and refutes unfavorable interpretations of the "no *hijra*" *ḥadīth* (by drawing extensively on *Asnā al-matājir*).[58] ʿAbd al-Qādir also questions the sincerity of those who claim to be too weak to emigrate. If they are truly constrained like captives, he argues, they must not marry or engage in sexual relations, lest any resulting children be seized from them and raised as infidels.[59]

Sword of Religion also addresses some less familiar—and mutually inconsistent—arguments against *hijra*. According to one argument, based on the writings of two thirteenth-century Shāfiʿī scholars, emigration is recommended rather than obligatory for those who are sufficiently protected by their clans or by their high rank. In the Algerian context, this would suggest that Muslims protected by their sheer numbers or high status need not emigrate. ʿAbd al-Qādir counters that this precedent applies only to lone converts and not conquered Muslims, and challenges his reader to think of a single people or tribe who have lived under infidel rule and whose clan was able to protect them from coercion and corruption.[60]

---

58 On property, see Jazāʾirī, *Tuḥfat al-zāʾir*, 1:414; much of this discussion is missing from the Moroccan manuscripts on which Ibn ʿAbd al-Karīm based his edition. On performing religious obligations, see Jazāʾirī, *Tuḥfat al-zāʾir*, 1:415 and Ibn ʿAbd al-Karīm, *Ḥukm al-hijra*, 55–56. On treaties, see Jazāʾirī, *Tuḥfat al-zāʾir*, 1:418 and Ibn ʿAbd al-Karīm, *Ḥukm al-hijra*, 59. On the "no *hijra*" tradition, see Jazāʾirī, *Tuḥfat al-zāʾir*, 1:416 and Ibn ʿAbd al-Karīm, *Ḥukm al-hijra*, 56–57; Peters translates a portion of this section in *Islam and Colonialism*, 58–59.

59 Ibn ʿAbd al-Karīm, *Ḥukm al-hijra*, 61–62; this section does not appear in Jazāʾirī's *Tuḥfat al-zāʾir*.

60 Jazāʾirī, *Tuḥfat al-zāʾir*, 1:417–18; Ibn ʿAbd al-Karīm, *Ḥukm al-hijra*, 58–59. The two Shāfiʿī scholars are Muḥyī al-Dīn Abū Zakariyyā Yaḥyā b. Sharaf al-Nawawī (d. 676/1277) and ʿAbd al-Karīm al-Rāfiʿī al-Qazwīnī (d. 624/1227). Elsewhere, ʿAbd al-Qādir repeats Wansharīsī's claim that conquered Muslims share a legal status with lone converts as regards the inviolability of their property (Jazāʾirī, *Tuḥfat al-zāʾir*, 1:418–19; Ibn ʿAbd al-Karīm, *Ḥukm al-hijra*, 62–63). Unlike Wansharīsī, he refers to this reasoning as a legal analogy (*qiyās*) and appears swayed by Ibn al-Ḥājj's distinction between the lone convert and the conquered Muslim with regard to their wives and children.

ʿAbd al-Qādir also responds to a pair of arguments related to *taqiyya*, seemingly the inverse of this strength-in-numbers claim. The first argument, employed by Ibn al-Shāhid, is that Qurʾān 3:28 excuses Muslims who ally with unbelievers as long as they do so as a precaution, in order to protect themselves. ʿAbd al-Qādir contends that this verse was abrogated. He cites as evidence a statement by Muḥammad's Companion Ibn ʿAbbās (d. 68/687), that "there is no *taqiyya* today, because of the expansiveness of the lands of Islam."[61] ʿAbd al-Qādir appears to be misquoting two other early Muslims who explained that *taqiyya*, which was permitted at the beginning of Islam, was no longer necessary because of Islam's strength. This mistake is plausible, given that ʿAbd al-Qādir did not have access to his books; it also reinforces his message that Algerians had ample destinations to choose from if they chose emigration—no doubt including the frontier camp from which he was writing. Elsewhere in *Sword of Religion*, ʿAbd al-Qādir cites an interpretation of Qurʾān 4:97 suggesting that the only valid reason not to emigrate is the lack of an appropriate destination.[62]

Directly after addressing Qurʾān 3:28, ʿAbd al-Qādir rejects Algerians' recourse to Qurʾān 16:106.[63] This verse provides a dispensation for those who are coerced into uttering words of unbelief (as long as their hearts remain steadfast in faith). It is unclear how ʿAbd al-Qādir's opponents applied this verse to the Algerian context. He argues that this dispensation is applicable only to those who were captured by infidels and feared that they would be killed, and states that patient endurance is preferable even under such circumstances. ʿAbd al-Qādir asserts that no true Muslim would remain under infidel rule and commit prohibited acts if he were capable of fleeing instead.

Notably, ʿAbd al-Qādir does not engage Wahrānī in his comments regarding *taqiyya* or coercion. If ʿAbd al-Qādir's opponents had adduced the 1504 Letter as a precedent supportive of dissimulation, he probably would

61 Jazāʾirī, *Tuḥfat al-zāʾir*, 1:416–17; Ibn ʿAbd al-Karīm, *Ḥukm al-hijra*, 57. ʿAbd al-Qādir claims that this statement, transmitted on the authority of ʿIbn Abbās, is included in Bukhārī, *Ṣaḥīḥ al-Bukhārī*, in *Kitāb al-Tafsīr*. I have found no such report. ʿAbd al-Qādir *may be* thinking of a statement that appears in Qurṭubī's *al-Jāmiʿ li-aḥkām al-Qurʾān*, the most prominent Mālikī exegetical work: "Muʿādh b. Jabal and Mujāhid said: '*Taqiyya* [was permitted] at the beginning of Islam, before the Muslims became powerful; as for today, God has strengthened Islam above [the need for] Muslims to fear their enemies.' Ibn ʿAbbās said: '[*Taqiyya*] is speaking with the tongue [things normally prohibited], while one's heart remains steadfast in faith.'" Muḥammad b. Aḥmad al-Anṣārī al-Qurṭubī (d. 671/1273), *al-Jāmiʿ li-aḥkām al-Qurʾān*, ed. Muḥammad Ibrāhīm al-Ḥafnāwī and Maḥmūd Ḥāmid ʿUthmān (Cairo: Dār al-Ḥadīth, 2002), 3:429.

62 Jazāʾirī, *Tuḥfat al-zāʾir*, 1:414. See also Jazāʾirī, *Tuḥfat al-zāʾir*, 1:411 for additional emphasis on the spaciousness of the earth. This section is missing from the manuscripts Ibn ʿAbd al-Karīm edited.

63 Jazāʾirī, *Tuḥfat al-zāʾir*, 1:417; Ibn ʿAbd al-Karīm, *Ḥukm al-hijra*, 57. On the interpretation of Qurʾān 16:106, see Qurṭubī, *al-Jāmiʿ li-aḥkām al-Qurʾān*, 5:526–35.

have refuted it here, or explained why dissimulation was valid for Moriscos yet unacceptable for Algerians. The fact that he never mentions or alludes to the letter, despite the length and breadth of the *Sword of Religion* and despite addressing *taqiyya* explicitly suggests that Wahrānī's advice was not well known or that it did not resonate with either side of the Algerian *hijra* debate.

Finally, the *Sword of Religion* is the most harsh of the extant Algerian writings on *hijra.* In his section on inviolability, ʿAbd al-Qādir cites the opinion of Muḥammad b. ʿAbd al-Karīm al-Maghīlī (d. ca. 909/1503–4), who states that anyone who requests protection from infidels or lives under their rule forfeits his inviolability and should be killed, even if found reading the Qur'ān.[64] Unsurprisingly, ʿAbd al-Qādir rejects the testimony of witnesses and the attestations of judges who live under Christian rule. More surprisingly, he truncates Māzarī's opinion on probity in the process, thereby creating the misleading impression that Māzarī affirmed that the probity of Sicilian judges was compromised on both accounts (residence under infidel rule and appointment by an infidel ruler) and therefore, inadmissible in *dār al-Islām*.[65] Most strikingly, ʿAbd al-Qādir closes his treatise by citing earlier scholars who held that anyone who fights for non-Muslims against Muslims are apostates, as are those who flee from *dār al-Islām* to *dār al-ḥarb*, bring happiness to the infidels, or even wear a European hat.[66] He concludes that those who support the Christians and live under their rule—meaning Algerians who remained under French rule—are gladdened by the Christians' victories over the Muslims, and are indeed apostates. This conclusion complements ʿAbd al-Qādir's opening attacks against the Muslim jurists of Algiers, whom he likens to the wrongdoers mentioned in Qur'ān 6:21. By claiming that the Qur'ānic verses regarding emigration were abrogated, they "invent lies against God," the action associated with injustice in this verse. The way these jurists contradict scholarly consensus and permit the forbidden further indicates their unbelief, according to ʿAbd al-Qādir.[67]

---

64 Jazā'irī, *Tuḥfat al-zā'ir*, 1:419. This reference only appears in Jazā'irī's edition. Maghīlī was born in Tlemcen, studied in Tunis, and settled in the Saharan oasis of Tuwāt, on the trans-Saharan trade route from Tlemcen to Timbuktu. In the 1480s, he was instrumental in the destruction of a synagogue in Tamanṭīṭ (the primary village in the Tuwāt oasis) and the slaughter of much of the town's Jewish population. On him, see John Hunwick, *Sharīʿa in Songhay: The Replies of al-Maghīlī to the Questions of Askia al-Ḥājj Muḥammad* (London: Oxford University Press, 1985); Powers, "al-Wansharīsī," 383–86.

65 Jazā'irī, *Tuḥfat al-zā'ir*, 1:416. On Māzarī's opinion, see chapter 5. It is unlikely that ʿAbd al-Qādir was missing this portion of Māzarī's opinion on probity.

66 Jazā'irī, *Tuḥfat al-zā'ir*, 1:420–22; Ibn ʿAbd al-Karīm, *Ḥukm al-hijra*, 63–65.

67 Jazā'irī, *Tuḥfat al-zā'ir*, 1:413; Ibn ʿAbd al-Karīm, *Ḥukm al-hijra*, 49–50.

Gannūn's Treatise on Living in Enemy Territory

The final text we consider here is *al-Taḥdhīr fī al-iqāma bi-arḍ al-ʿaduww* (*Warning against Residence in the Enemy's Territory*), an undated treatise directed to Algerian Muslims by Fez-based jurist and reformer Muḥammad Gannūn (d. 1302/1885).[68] We have little information about how the text was received in Algeria, but its circulation in Morocco attests to the continued interest of Maghribī scholars in the Algerian response to colonialism.[69] Gannūn's *Warning against Residence* appears to be unsolicited, and in terms of genre, it is more like a treatise against blameworthy innovations than a *fatwā*. Gannūn opens by reminding readers that "Religion is sincere advice," and then explains that a warning against living in enemy territory is the best advice he can offer them.[70]

Like ʿAbd al-Qādir's *Sword of Religion*, *Warning against Residence* presents new concerns and arguments while remaining grounded in the proof texts and legal categories of Wansharīsī's *Asnā al-matājir*. Gannūn's initial sections, which consist primarily of materials that first appear in the *hijra* debate in the colonial context, focus on injustice and blameworthy innovations. Here he shares ʿAbd al-Qādir's opposition to acts such as dressing like or resembling the Christians, behaviors that Gannūn argues are prohibited by the directive in Qurʾān 11:113 not to incline toward those who are unjust. This verse also prohibits interaction with the unjust and approval of their actions. It is well known, Gannūn further asserts, that "anyone who is content with a people's actions is one of them."[71] He challenges his readers to imagine the consequences, therefore, of not just contentedly observing an unjust people, but living among them, seeking refuge with them, courting their favor, and supporting them.

---

68 Abū ʿAbd Allāh Muḥammad b. al-Madanī b. ʿAlī Gannūn (d. 1302/1885) was an outspoken and prolific Mālikī jurist and reformer from Fez. In Arabic, the hard 'g' in "Gannūn" is spelled with a *jīm* or with a modified or unmodified *kāf*, depending on the source. E. Lévi-Provençal, *Les Historiens des Chorfa: Essai sur la Littérature Historique et Biographique au Maroc du XVI*[e] *au XX*[e] *Siècle* (Paris: Maisonneuve et Larose, 2001), 373–74; Kattānī, *Salwat al-anfās*, 2:412–14; Makhlūf, *Shajarat al-nūr*, 1:610; Ziriklī, *al-Aʿlām*, 7:94.

69 At least four manuscripts are extant in Morocco: Moroccan National Library MS 2223D.8, pp. 145–46 (incomplete); Moroccan National Library MS 1079D.6, fols. 77b–82b (dated 1299/1882, titled *al-Naṣīḥa*, and given incorrect folio numbers in the library catalogue); Qarawiyyīn Library MS 1994.5, fols. 31b–33a; Muʾassasat al-Malik ʿAbd al-ʿAzīz Āl Saʿūd (Casablanca) MS 249, entire manuscript. A revised and expanded version of the text was published in 1301/1884 in the margin of another of Gannūn's works: Ibn al-Madanī Gannūn, *al-Tasliya waʾl-salwān li-man ibtalā biʾl-idhāya waʾl-buhtān*, Fez lithograph, 1301/1884. *Al-Taḥdhīr* (*Warning*) is in the margins of pages 122–58, by my count; the lithograph repeats the first eight pages of *al-Tasliya*. All references here are to the lithograph edition.

70 *Al-dīn al-naṣīḥa*, or "Religion is sincere advice," is part of a prominent *ḥadīth*. See, for example, *Ṣaḥīḥ Muslim, Kitāb al-Īmān, bāb bayān anna al-dīn al-naṣīḥa, ḥadīth* 95 (Muslim b. al-Ḥajjāj, *Ṣaḥīḥ Muslim*, 1:74).

71 Gannūn, *al-Taḥdhīr*, in the margin of *al-Tasliya*, 125.

In his next section, Gannūn lists four actions that contribute to a believer's distance from God: fearing an oppressor more than God, ingratiating oneself to the oppressor for worldly sustenance, advising and assisting infidels, and failing to advise Muslims, including failing to prohibit them from wrongdoing. Gannūn also warns that associating with a group engaging in prohibited acts can lead one to adopt their behaviors. This material is based primarily on *al-Dhahab al-Ibrīz* (*Pure Gold*), an early modern Sufi text composed in Fez.[72]

The middle section of *Warning against Residence* is devoted to the obligation to emigrate.[73] Here Gannūn quotes extensively from the *Miʿyār*, acknowledging Wansharīsī's compilation as his source. He reproduces much of *Asnā al-matājir*'s opening sections, including proof texts from the Qurʾān and Ḥadīth, Ibn al-ʿArabī's passage on destinations and his assertion that emigration from *dār al-ḥarb* to *dār al-Islām* will remain an obligation until the day of judgment, and Ibn Rushd al-Jadd's prohibition on travel to *dār al-ḥarb* for trade. Gannūn adds to this material commentary and *ḥadīth*s that support emigration, drawn primarily from a Ḥanafī work of exegesis, Ismāʿīl Ḥaqqī al-Barūsawī's (d. 1137/1724) *Rūḥ al-bayān fī tafsīr al-Qurʾān* (*The Spirit of Elucidation: Exegesis of the Qurʾān*).[74]

In keeping with *Asnā al-matājir*'s categories of analysis, Gannūn then addresses probity and the testimony of judges. Here he departs substantially from the precedents that Wansharīsī cites, most notably by omitting entirely Māzarī's *fatwā* on judges' probity. Instead, Gannūn cites Māzarī's opinion that travel to Sicily for trade is prohibited, even to buy food in times of extreme scarcity, as believers must not be subject to infidel laws. In this *fatwā*, Māzarī stresses that God will provide sustenance, an argument that ʿAbd al-Qādir includes in his *Sword of Religion*. Gannūn adds to these rationales by noting that those traveling to enemy territory risk being humiliated for their religion or being compelled or enticed to abandon Islam.

Just prior to citing Māzarī, Gannūn cites two other jurists in favor of invalidating the testimony of anyone who voluntarily travels to enemy territory. One of these precedents is particularly striking, as it sheds light on a source Wahrānī used in his 1504 Letter:

72 Gannūn refers to his source only as *al-Ibrīz*, but he must mean *al-Dhahab al-Ibrīz min kalām Sayyidī ʿAbd al-ʿAzīz al-Dabbāgh*, composed around 1132/1720 by Aḥmad b. al-Mubārak al-Lamaṭī. See *Pure Gold from the Words of Sayyidī ʿAbd al-ʿAzīz al-Dabbāgh*, trans. John O'Kane and Bernd Radtke (Leiden: Brill, 2007).

73 Gannūn, *al-Taḥdhīr*, in the margin of *al-Tasliya*, 131–37.

74 Ismāʿīl Ḥaqqī b. Muṣṭafā al-Barūsawī al-Ḥanafī, *Rūḥ al-bayān fī tafsīr al-Qurʾān*, ed. ʿAbd al-Laṭīf Ḥasan ʿAbd al-Raḥmān, 10 vols. (Beirut: Dār al-Kutub al-ʿIlmiyya, 2003). This is the Arabic rendering of this Ottoman Turkish scholar's name; see also İsmail Hakkı Bursevi.

> Ibn Nājī said: "When I was the judge of Jerba, it happened that [I received] an attestation from the judge of Pantelleria. He attested, on the basis of his knowledge, to the validity of a document demonstrating a legal right. He requested that I validate his handwriting, but I did not oblige the bearer [of the document] and do this, because they are capable of devising a strategy to leave [Pantelleria]. Occasionally someone who is there leaves but returns to [the island], and thus his legal status becomes that of infidels."[75]

Ibn Nājī is Abū al-Qāsim b. ʿĪsā b. Nājī al-Tanūkhī (d. 839/1435), the Mālikī jurist from Qayrawān whose commentary on Ibn Abī Zayd's *Risāla* is the only legal work that Wahrānī cites.[76] As noted in chapter 6, Wahrānī advised the Moriscos to perform their ablutions and prayers by means of mere gestures if necessary to avoid detection. In support of this advice, Wahrānī cites the portion of Ibn Nājī's commentary that concerns the *ḥadīth*, "Do of it what you are able."[77] Ibn Nājī purportedly explained that Muḥammad's statement concerned *tayammum*, a method of ritual washing with sand, which is allowed when pure water is unavailable. For Wahrānī, this *ḥadīth* and commentary provide authoritative sanction for an even more symbolic form of purification using gestures alone.

While Wahrānī used Ibn Nājī's commentary to sanction modifications to the prayers of Moriscos, Gannūn's treatise reveals that Ibn Nājī's views on Muslims living voluntarily under Christian rule were far from accommodating. In the above passage, Ibn Nājī cites voluntary residence in Christian-ruled Pantelleria as the reason he refused to honor a document certified by the island's Muslim judge. He explains that "they" are capable of emigrating (presumably referring to most or all of the island's Muslim

---

75 Jerba is an island off the southwest coast of Tunisia, while Pantelleria—known as *Qawṣara* in Arabic—is an island located between Sicily and Tunisia. Pantelleria was conquered by the Normans of Sicily in 618/1221.

76 Ibn Nājī, educated in Qayrawān and Tunis, served as judge, preacher, and teacher in several cities before returning to settle in Qayrawān. On him, see ʿAbd al-Wahhāb, *Kitāb al-ʿUmr*, 1:777–83; Ziriklī, *al-Aʿlām*, 5:179; Makhlūf, *Shajarat al-nūr*, 1:352. See also 1:19–22 of the following work, an important biographical dictionary begun by another scholar and completed by Ibn Nājī: ʿAbd al-Raḥmān al-Dabbāgh, Abū al-Qāsim b. Nājī, and Muḥammad al-Kinānī, *Maʿālim al-īmān fī maʿrifat ahl al-Qayrawān* and supplement, ed. ʿAbd al-Majīd al-Khayālī, 5 vols. in 3 (Beirut: Dār al-Kutub al-ʿIlmiyya, 2005).

77 This phrase, *"fa-ʾtū min-hu mā istaṭaʿtum,"* is included in more than one *ḥadīth*. See *Ṣaḥīḥ al-Bukhārī, Kitāb al-Iʿtiṣām biʾl-Kitāb waʾl-Sunna, bāb al-iqtidāʾ bi-sunan rasul Allāh, ḥadīth* 6858 (Bukhārī, *Ṣaḥīḥ al-Bukhārī*, 6:2658); *Ṣaḥīḥ Muslim, Kitāb al-Ḥajj, bāb farḍ al-ḥajj marratan fī al-ʿumr, ḥadīth* 412 (Muslim b. al-Ḥajjāj, *Ṣaḥīḥ Muslim*, 2:975). I have been unable to locate this reference in Ibn Nājī's commentary. See Qāsim b. Nājī, *Sharḥ Ibn Nājī al-Tanūkhī ʿalā matn al-Risāla*, ed. Aḥmad Farīd al-Mazīdī, 2 vols. (Beirut: Dār al-Kutub al-ʿIlmiyya, 2007). In Version A of al-Wahrānī's 1504 Letter, this *ḥadīth* is expanded to mean "perform *tayammum* to the extent you are able." Cantineau, "Lettre du Moufti," 8 (*aljamiado* transcription) and 12 (French translation).

residents). In contrast to Māzarī, who gave Sicilian Muslims the benefit of the doubt by presuming that they resided in Norman Sicily for legitimate reasons, Ibn Nājī appears to presume that Muslim residence in Pantelleria was voluntary and blameworthy.[78] Nonetheless, it is only those who have made their ability to emigrate abundantly clear by successfully leaving the island and then returning that he considers infidels.

What we learn of Ibn Nājī from *Warning against Residence* is important because it supports the argument, presented earlier in this book, that Wahrānī did not intend his 1504 Letter as a refutation of Wansharīsī's two *fatwās* on the obligatory nature of Iberian emigration. If Wahrānī wished to contest the obligation that capable Muslims must perform *hijra* and had to choose a single jurist to cite in his *fatwā*, we would expect him to have chosen a jurist who was lenient on the subject of emigration. Instead, Ibn Nājī and Wansharīsī appear to be of one mind regarding *hijra*. Moreover, Ibn Nājī's unequivocal refusal to honor an attestation from a judge in Pantelleria implies that his views on probity were stricter than those of Wansharīsī.

If Ibn Nājī's comments regarding ablutions were critical to Wahrānī's message, it would make sense for Wahrānī to feature Ibn Nājī's views in a letter intended to challenge the obligation to emigrate. Yet Ibn Nājī's commentary is far from essential to the 1504 Letter; Wahrānī could have cited the relevant *ḥadīth* alone, or in tandem with another jurist's discussion, or he could have omitted a legal reference at this juncture entirely and instead added an authoritative legal precedent elsewhere in the letter. Wahrānī's citation of Ibn Nājī appears to be symbolic, a token reference to a named legal authority, a reference that was meant to reassure the Moriscos of the validity of Wahrānī's advice. We must again conclude that Wahrānī meant his 1504 Letter as an aid to Muslims who were truly oppressed and unable to escape, not as an argument against the obligation to emigrate.

In *Warning against Residence*, Gannūn follows this revealing section on probity with sections on trading, spying, and the inviolability of persons and property. While most of this material is taken from Wansharīsī's *Asnā al-matājir*, he includes one opinion from Zayyātī's *Selected Jewels*, namely, Ibn Zakrī's second *fatwā*, the same one al-Sharīf al-Tilimsānī quotes, according to which any Muslim who aids infidels (physically or financially) in fighting against other Muslims should be fought and killed alongside their enemy allies. Gannūn's *Warning against Residence* concludes with a lengthy theological discussion on predestination and God's forgiveness of sins.[79]

---

78 Ibn Nājī likely shared this presumption with his teacher Ibn ʿArafa (d. 803/1401), who used the term Mudéjar to refer to Muslims in Pantelleria.

79 Gannūn, *al-Taḥdhīr*, in the margin of *al-Tasliya*, 141–59.

The advent of French occupation in the mid nineteenth century prompted Muslim jurists to revisit the Islamic legal obligation to emigrate. The extant texts suggest that *hijra* was an especially attractive doctrine for supporters of ʿAbd al-Qādir's armed resistance to French rule, supporters who hoped to weaken local cooperation with the French and to channel resources toward their own camp. Algerian jurists who did not support mass emigration or condemn those who remained in their homes were put on the defensive, forced to justify the legitimacy of their residence in Islamic legal terms. For both sides, the Maghribī opinions issued in the late fifteenth and early sixteenth centuries in response to the Iberian Christian conquest were the crucial precedents that they used to leverage, qualify, or reject.

The *hijra* debate in colonial Algeria thus offers our first test case as to the long-term importance of the legal texts discussed in the first three parts of this book. While Zayyātī's "jewels" were clearly known to Algerian jurists, only Ibn Zakrī's second *fatwā* is cited more than once by Tasūlī and al-Sharīf al-Tilimsānī. The *fatwās* of Waryāglī, Ibn Barṭāl, and Māwāsī each appear once, while Wansharīsī's Berber *fatwā* does not appear at all—a testament to Wansharīsī's successful replacement of this text with his two more prominent opinions on emigration. Wahrānī's 1504 Letter is also absent from the Algerian debate, despite its potential relevance to Ibn al-Shāhid's discussion of coercion and dissimulation.

Three hundred and fifty years after Wansharīsī composed *Asnā al-matājir* and the Marbella *fatwā*, these two texts clearly dominated the colonial-era discourse on emigration from French-occupied Algeria. Multiple factors account for this dominance. Wansharīsī provided later jurists with a rich array of proof texts and arguments that could be deployed in total (as Ibn Ruwīla and ʿIllaysh did) or could be adapted to fit the colonial context (as in the cases of ʿAbd al-Qādir and Gannūn). Wansharīsī's *Miʿyār* had become widespread and was no longer just an ambitious collection of opinions, rather it had come to represent established Mālikī doctrine.[80] The vivid stories and specific examples captured by Ibn Qaṭiyya's questions and the Marbella response allowed jurists like Ibn al-Ḥaffāf to link his adversaries' behaviors to those described in the text, and thereby make personal examples of them.

Perhaps most importantly, the ultimate fate of the Moriscos and the permanent loss of al-Andalus—the "news of al-Andalus"—seemed to validate Wansharīsī's position and illustrate the consequences of the failure

80 In his first response to ʿAbd al-Qādir, Tasūlī comments that a particular rule has become the Mālikī "school doctrine as [stated] in the *Miʿyār*." See my translation in Hendrickson, "Is al-Andalus Different?," 420.

to emigrate. If Wansharīsī indeed suppressed the Luso-Maghribī context of *Asnā al-matājir* and the Marbella *fatwā* in the hopes that *fatwā*s focused on al-Andalus would become more compelling long-term precedents, his strategy paid off. For colonial-era Algerians, his *fatwā*s were indeed a straightforward and definitive response to the Christian conquest of Iberia. Nostalgia for al-Andalus as a lost paradise had spread throughout the Muslim world, while the Portuguese occupation of Morocco was all but forgotten. Added to this shared memory of a tragic loss, many North Africans were also proud to have descended from Andalusī emigrants—a cultural legacy invoked by Mawlāy ʿAbd al-Raḥmān when he welcomed those first Algerian *muhājirūn* to Morocco.

CHAPTER 8

Mauritania: Challenging Legal Filth

Prelude

As French forces advanced on Bandiagara in April 1893, Aḥmad al-Kabīr faced an increasingly familiar choice for African Muslims: submit to "Christian" rule, flee, or fight. The first was hardly an option for Aḥmad al-Kabīr, the Commander of the Faithful of the dwindling state founded by his father, al-Ḥājj ʿUmar Tal (d. 1864). Therefore, he had to choose between *hijra* or *jihād*.

Both religious imperatives—*hijra* and *jihād*—were integral to the ʿUmarian movement of the 1850s: ʿUmar Tal led five *jihāds* to establish Muslim states in formerly "pagan" parts of West Africa in the eighteenth and nineteenth centuries; and he recruited soldiers and settlers by calling for a *hijra* from the expanding French colony of Senegal, based in Saint-Louis. The resulting state dominated parts of today's Mali in the 1860s, yet had declined by the 1880s and 1890s, when France set about conquering what they called the "Tokolor Empire." Before reaching Aḥmad al-Kabīr's last bastion in Bandiagara, France took Segu, his seat for nearly thirty years, without losing a single soldier.[1]

Faced with certain military defeat if he chose to stay and fight, Aḥmad al-Kabīr's followers convinced him to choose *hijra*. He abandoned Bandiagara, but in May 1893, he nonetheless sent an appeal for military aid to Moroccan sultan Ḥasan I (r. 1873–94):

> And now, O Lieutenant of God on earth, successor to the Prophet for his people, descendant of the chief of the prophets, make haste, make

1 On the ʿUmarian movement and Aḥmad al-Kabīr (also known as Amadu Sheku), see David Robinson, *The Holy War of Umar Tal: The Western Sudan in the Mid-Nineteenth Century* (Oxford: Clarendon Press, 1985); David Robinson, "The Umarian Emigration of the Late Nineteenth Century," *International Journal of African Historical Studies* 20, no. 2 (1987): 245–70; Robinson, *Paths of Accommodation: Muslim Societies and French Colonial Authorities in Senegal and Mauritania, 1880–1920* (Athens: Ohio University Press, 2000), 143–60; Robinson, "Jihad, Hijra, and Hajj in West Africa," in *Just Wars, Holy Wars, and Jihads: Christian, Jewish, and Muslim Encounters and Exchanges*, ed. Sohail H. Hashmi (Oxford: Oxford University Press, 2012), 247–53.

> haste! Your friends have been abandoned, your country is ruined and your subjects are dispersed. Death, captivity and pillage, that is the end which awaits them. The enemy has destroyed mosques, burned Qur'āns, thrown our scientific books into the desert, and has transformed our places of prayer into churches—the church bell has replaced the muezzin. He has kidnapped the daughters of the Shaykh and has forced his sons into his service. The children of Muslims have been divided among the chiefs of the army which has taken the whole country . . . The enemies of your God and the competitors of your ancestors have taken your country. Make them leave . . . do not listen to their lying words.[2]

Aḥmad al-Kabīr's letter connects the European conquests in West Africa to the Christian conquests in al-Andalus and the Maghrib by drawing on a shared literature of lamentation and appeal. While evoking Tāzī's lament for Asilah and the anonymous chronicler's lament for al-Andalus in *Nubdhat al-ʿaṣr*, Aḥmad al-Kabīr's letter strongly resembles the Morisco appeal to the Ottoman sultan. Like the anonymous poet of that appeal, Aḥmad al-Kabīr bitterly recounts a history of deception and defeat at the hands of the Christian enemy. He explains that the French government of Senegal initially honored a peace agreement with the ʿUmarian state (from 1866 to 1878), but they ultimately "violated the conditions of the treaty one after the other." In contrast to Iberian Muslims, who were defeated militarily and then signed a treaty, the ʿUmarians suffered military defeat only after this treaty was broken. They were also beset and betrayed not only by the Christian enemy, but also by fellow Muslims who chose to side with the French. Aḥmad al-Kabīr names the principal cities conquered through the joint "treachery and villainy" of the French and their Muslim allies, then arrives at the heart of his appeal above.

In this passage, Aḥmad al-Kabīr sets aside his caliphal title, and instead presents himself and his people as natural subjects of the Moroccan sultan. He ascribes to Ḥasan I the authority to rule, and responsibility to defend, Muslims and Muslim territory in the western Sudan. Like the anonymous Morisco poet, Aḥmad al-Kabīr cites grievances that place the honor of Islam itself at stake. The imagery of mosques transformed into churches is especially striking, as this did not hold true in Aḥmad al-Kabīr's case;

2 A full English translation of Aḥmad's letter is provided in John Hanson and David Robinson, *After the Jihad: The Reign of Aḥmad al-Kabīr in the Western Sudan* (East Lansing: Michigan State University Press, 1991), 243–48. This excerpt also appears in Robinson, "Umarian Emigration," 254; Robinson, *Paths*, 146; and Robinson, "Jihad," 251–52. Robinson's translation is from a French copy of the letter contained in the Algerian archives (GG ALG 22H 36); the Arabic original has not been found.

here his reliance on past lamentations in crafting his own appeal for aid is transparent.[3]

Notably, in contrast to the Morisco appeal, Aḥmad al-Kabīr's letter was directed to a regional power that had thus far managed to evade European conquest, as there was no longer a powerful, expanding Muslim empire to which he could appeal. While the anonymous poet in al-Andalus flattered Bāyazīd II by praying that God would make him a "king over every nation," Aḥmad al-Kabīr expressed no such hopes for Ḥasan I. Casting his people as Moroccan subjects likely appealed to the sultan's southward ambitions, but ultimately no aid was forthcoming.[4] Instead, France's colonial project advanced northward from Senegal.

The Conquest of Mauritania

In the first decade of the twentieth century, France launched the conquest of what later became Mauritania. By then, all of the West African *jihād* states had disappeared and even the nearly century-old Sokoto caliphate in Nigeria was on the verge being conquered by the British. Following Aḥmad al-Kabīr's death on the road to Sokoto in 1897, many of his followers returned home to accept French rule; of those who survived, many of them joined (in 1903) another major *hijra* movement to escape British rule.

As European competition for the control of African territory intensified, many Muslims in the region began to view submission to Christian rule as inevitable. Finding a favorable "path of accommodation" with the French colonial authorities became an increasingly attractive option, especially for local leaders hoping to retain or enhance their own power through collaboration.[5] These Muslims argued that *jihād* was futile, while *hijra* would only lead to the next site of European conquest. Accordingly, an accommodationist stance refuting both *jihād* and *hijra* is better represented in the Mauritanian debate than in that of the Algerians.

In the hopes of expanding its West African holdings with a minimum of force, France cultivated ties with Muslim leaders willing to make a religious

3 The "Lament for the Fall of Seville" (or *Rathā' al-Andalus*) by Abū al-Baqā' al-Rundī (d. 683/1285) is the most prominent poetic lament composed in response to Christian conquest in the Islamic West. Composed in 665/1267, it was also intended as an implicit appeal for military aid from North Africa. The poem, which includes the complaint that mosques have become churches, likely inspired the later laments and appeals mentioned above. See James Monroe's English translation: Monroe, "Curious Morisco Appeal," 290–92.

4 It is not known if Aḥmad al-Kabīr's letter was received. After his death in 1897 near Sokoto, many of his followers returned home and submitted to French rule. Others continued to Sokoto, many of whom participated in a larger 1903 emigration from British rule. Alfa Hashimi Tal, Aḥmad's cousin, reached Medina where he authored an account of Aḥmad's *hijra*. See Robinson, "Umarian Emigration."

5 The term "paths of accommodation" is taken from David Robinson's book of the same name.

case for voluntary submission. Two key figures stand out in this capacity: Saad Buh (d. 1917) and Sidiyya Baba (d. 1924).[6] These leaders leveraged their extensive networks for the French colonial enterprise, mediated disputes, and composed formal texts advocating submission to French rule. Their texts were meant for wide distribution, as I discuss below. In return for their support, France offered peace, economic incentives, and protection from tribal raids.

This strategy of negotiated collaboration with local leaders was proposed by Xavier Coppolani, who planned the conquest and borders of modern Mauritania at the turn of the twentieth century. Coppolani, raised in French Algeria and fluent in Arabic, combined his considerable knowledge of Islam with experience in the colonial administration of Muslim territories. Before leaving Algeria, he co-authored (with Octave Depont) *Les confréries religieuses musulmanes*, an 1897 study of Sufi brotherhoods sponsored by the governor-general of Algeria, Jules Cambon. Coppolani served from 1898 to 1899 in the French Sudan (now Mali), part of the expanding Federation of French West Africa that also included Senegal, Guinea, and the Ivory Coast.

Coppolani's "pacification" of Mauritania, launched in 1902, met with some initial success in the southwest Trarza region where both Saad Buh and Sidiyya Baba had influence. With their aid, Coppolani identified and courted alliances with "*zāwiya*" tribes, whose primary interests were religious and commercial, and favored them over the dominant "*ḥassan*" tribes engaged in political and military pursuits. In addition to stability and better commercial opportunities, France promised to respect its subjects' Muslim identity and practices. Those making the case for France's religious tolerance pointed to Saint-Louis, the capital of Senegal and now also of Mauritania. Not only was the city's Muslim community free to practice Islam, but they built a new mosque under colonial rule and, from 1857, maintained access to a Muslim tribunal for the adjudication of family matters and property disputes. The colonial administration also handpicked a few loyal and influential religious figures to sponsor on the pilgrimage to Mecca.

Not everyone was convinced by these promises or displays of tolerance, which were accompanied by surveillance and the ever-present threat of military force. Nor did Coppolani's conquest remain peaceful for long. When he met with resistance in the Tagant region, he deployed colonial troops to establish control. Coppolani was assassinated in Tagant in 1905, as he was preparing for his next campaign in the northern Adrar region.

6 As Sidiyya Baba and Saad Buh are relatively well known, I have adopted the common spellings of their names rather than using a transliteration from the Arabic (Saʿd Būh and Sidiyya Bāba).

Mā᾽ al-ʿAynayn al-Qalqamī (d. 1910), whose followers assassinated Coppolani, was the key figure in the armed resistance against colonial expansion in the region.[7] Born in what is now southeastern Mauritania, Mā᾽ al-ʿAynayn was educated in Morocco and performed the pilgrimage prior to establishing a base of operations in the northern third of the western Sahara. A powerful businessman and *shaykh* who led his own ʿAyniyya branch of the Qādiriyya Sufi order, Mā᾽ al-ʿAynayn developed a reputation for performing miracles. He maintained close ties with the Moroccan sultanate, to which he provided slaves and religious guidance. In the late nineteenth century, he directed his earliest armed campaigns against Spanish settlements in Dakhla, in the southern third of the western Sahara. Once Coppolani made inroads into Mauritania's southwestern regions, Mā᾽ al-ʿAynayn shifted his attention to combating the French occupation of Adrar.

Coppolani's assassination buoyed the anticolonial resistance and stalled French expansion for nearly four years. Mā᾽ al-ʿAynayn's sons led the *jihād* against the French and their regional allies until 1909, when France's new governor-general of Mauritania, Colonel Henri Gouraud, subjugated Adrar by force. Mā᾽ al-ʿAynayn, following an unsuccessful attempt to secure material support from Moroccan sultan Mawlāy al-Ḥafiẓ (r. 1908–12), retired to the southern Moroccan town of Tiznīt, where he died in 1910. In 1912, France declared a protectorate over Morocco; in 1920, it secured the modern borders of Mauritania; and in 1934, it put down the last anticolonial revolts there. The Islamic Republic of Mauritania gained independence in 1960.

The Mauritanian *Hijra* Debate

Over four hundred years after Wansharīsī composed *Asnā al-matājir* and the Marbella *fatwā* in the hope of finally settling the issue of *hijra* for conquered Muslims, the debate continued. In the first decades of the twentieth century, Mālikī scholars in Mauritania produced a rich legal literature on the topic, far outstripping the number of texts that have reached us from prior cases. Far from being static or outmoded, the Islamic legal discourse on *hijra* inherited by these modern scholars proved adaptable and relevant to the colonial context. Muslim scholars and *shaykh*s framed French occupation as a Christian conquest of *dār al-Islām*. While introducing novel concerns and forms of argument, they also revisited the core legal issues and proof

7 On Mā᾽ al-ʿAynayn, see: *EI*[2], s.v. "Ma᾽ al-ʿAynayn al-Ḳalḳamī" (H. T. Norris); B. G. Martin, *Muslim Brotherhoods in Nineteenth-Century Africa* (Cambridge: Cambridge University Press, 1976), 125–51; Ibn Ḥabīb Allāh, *al-Ḥaraka al-Iṣlāḥiyya fī bilād Shanqīṭ (Mūrītānīyā) bayn al-istijāba lil-istiʿmār al-Faransī wa-difāʿihi min khilāl baʿḍ al-fatāwā wa᾽l-wathā᾽iq* (Salé: Manshūrāt Mu᾽assasat al-Shaykh Murabbīhi Rabbuh li-Iḥyā᾽ al-Turāth wa᾽l-Tabādul al-Thaqāfī, 2006), 293–319.

texts that had dominated the Ibero-Maghribī and Algerian debates on submission to Christian rule.

At least seventy *fatwās*, letters, treatises, and poems that form part of the Mauritanian debate on submission to Christian rule have now been published. Our largest reference for these texts is also the most recent, namely, *al-Majmūʿa al-kubrā al-shāmila li-fatāwā wa-nawāzil wa-aḥkām ahl gharb wa-junūb gharb al-Ṣaḥrāʾ* (*The Great Comprehensive Collection of Legal Opinions, Cases, and Judgments from the Western and Southwestern Sahara*), a twelve-volume compilation published by Mauritanian historian Yahya ould El-Bara in 2009.[8] *Al-Majmūʿa al-kubrā* contains roughly sixty entries related to *jihād* and *hijra* in the face of colonialism. Another eleven entries pertain to Muslim children's attendance at French schools, a significant issue in the Mauritanian debate. These and other published texts clearly refer to additional letters and treatises on the subject; these are unpublished and privately held.[9]

In this chapter I review in detail select contributions to the Mauritanian *hijra* debate. I summarize additional texts in broad strokes, with particular attention to the relationship of these twentieth-century opinions to their counterparts from the fourteenth, fifteenth, and nineteenth centuries treated earlier in this book. I proceed thematically through three sections: texts supporting accommodation with the French, including those of Sidiyya Baba and Saad Buh; texts advocating *hijra*; and one substantial treatise defending the inviolability of conquered Muslims' property. This last treatise, composed by Muḥammad ʿAbd Allāh b. Zaydān al-Buṣādī (d. 1933 or 1934), is particularly noteworthy for its sustained critique of Wansharīsī's central analogy in *Asnā al-matājir*.

---

8 Yahya ould El-Bara (as Yaḥyā wuld al-Barāʾ), *al-Majmūʿa al-kubrā al-shāmila li-fatāwā wa-nawāzil wa-aḥkām ahl gharb wa-junūb gharb al-Ṣaḥrāʾ*, 12 vols. ([Nouakchott]: Mūlāy al-Ḥasan b. al-Mukhtār b. al-Ḥasan, 2009), esp. 7:2838–3114 (*bāb al-jihād*). These texts are not edited or annotated, but the source library is noted. Biographies of the scholars are provided in volume 2.

9 In addition to those available in *al-Majmūʿa al-kubrā*, Arabic texts relevant to this debate are published in Ibn Ḥabīb Allāh, *al-Ḥaraka al-Iṣlāḥiyya*, 379–412; al-Khalīl al-Naḥwī, *Bilād Shinqīṭ, al-mināra wa'l-Ribāṭ* (Tunis: al-Munaẓẓama al-ʿArabiyya lil-Tarbiyya wa'l-Thaqāfa wa'l-ʿUlūm, 1987), 406–68; and in Ibn al-Shaykh Māmīnā, *al-Shaykh Māʾ al-ʿAynayn: ʿUlamāʾ wa-ʿumarāʾ fī muwājahat al-istʿmār al-Ūrūbbī*, 2nd ed., 2 vols. (Rabat: Manshūrāt Muʾassasat al-Shaykh Murabbīhi Rabbuh li-Iḥyāʾ al-Turāth wa'l-Tanmiya, 2011), 2:473–83. Summaries of these published texts and additional, unpublished texts may be found in Ibn Ḥabīb Allāh, *al-Ḥaraka al-Iṣlāḥiyya*, 357–403; Ibn al-Shaykh Māmīnā, *al-Shaykh Māʾ al-ʿAynayn*, 2:67–106; Ould El-Bara, "Les réponses et les *fatâwâ* des érudits Bidân face à l'occupation colonial française en Mauritanie," in *Colonisations et Héritages Actuels au Sahara et au Sahel: Problèmes conceptuels, état des lieux et nouvelles perspectives de recherche (XVIIIe-XXe siècles)*, ed. Mariella Villasante Cervello (Paris: L'Harmattan, 2007), 127–49; and Ould El-Bara (as Yahya wuld al-Bara), "Les théologiens mauritaniens face au colonialism français: Étude de *fatwa*-s de jurisprudence musulmane," in *Le temps des marabouts: Itinéraires et stratégies islamiques en Afrique occidentale française v. 1880–1960*, ed. David Robinson and Jean-Louis Triaud (Paris: Éditions Karthala, 1997), 85–117.

As the existence of Buṣādī's treatise suggests, Wansharīsī's opinions were central to the Mauritanian debate, but in ways that differ from their role in the Algerian debate. Mauritanian scholars do not appear to have adopted *Asnā al-matājir* or the Marbella *fatwā* in whole, nor are they dependent on the proof texts and arguments set forth in these two texts. In Mauritania, Wansharīsī's material is less influential, and it appears amidst a greater variety of other legal sources than in the Algerian debate. Mauritanian scholars debate with Wansharīsī, contesting not only the continued relevance of this *fatwā*, but also the initial validity of his opinions. And yet, they must still argue with Wansharīsī. This final case study demonstrates that even in the twentieth century, *Asnā al-matājir* and the Marbella *fatwā* were still the Mālikī precedents of record with regard to Muslims living under non-Muslim rule.

Arguments for Accommodation

The most distinctive aspect of the Mauritanian *hijra* debate is the rich set of texts preserved from scholars who argued against *jihād* and *hijra*, in favor of submission to colonial rule. Over a dozen such texts, composed by at least nine scholars, are included in *al-Majmūʿa al-kubrā*.[10] Largely undated, these texts range in genre, and include a French-solicited *fatwā*, a dialogue between two scholars of differing opinions, and unsolicited declarations of "advice" (*naṣīḥa*).

A few characteristics common to these opinions are especially noteworthy. Of the Maghribī opinions treated in the first three parts of this book, only Wansharīsī's *Asnā al-matājir* and Marbella *fatwā* are cited in the Mauritanian debate. Mauritanian scholars clearly found it necessary to refute the applicability of Wansharīsī's opinions to their present context, but were not concerned by Zayyātī's "jewels" and were likely unaware of Wahrānī's 1504 Letter. This neglect of Wahrānī continued, despite the importance of *taqiyya* to these modern scholars' arguments for accommodation. While the Mauritanian opinions were informed by the Algerian *hijra* debate, including Ibn al-Shāhid's appeal to *taqiyya*, they also addressed a distinctive set of concerns. Foremost among these new concerns for accommodationist scholars were the dangers posed by *fitna* and banditry. To illustrate this first body of opinions, I consider the writings of Sidiyya Baba, Saad Buh, and Muḥammad al-Amīn.

10 These figures are approximate because the texts could be counted in a variety of ways. Ould El-Bara assigns an entry number to each element of a back-and-forth exchange, even if contained in a single document, and to each answer to multi-part questions.

Sidiyya Baba's 1903 Fatwā

Sidiyya Baba, a respected Sufi leader and erudite scholar, was instrumental to the French conquest of Mauritania.[11] In the second half of the nineteenth century, increasing political instability in Trarza threatened the impressive commercial and diplomatic network established there by his grandfather, Sidiyya al-Kabīr (d. 1868). Concerned for the continued prosperity of this network, Sidiyya Baba allied with the French as a means to promote stability in southwestern Mauritania and to retain a position of power. He aided Coppolani and subsequently Gouraud in the planning and implementation of their conquest, while advocating submission to French rule in the region.

Sidiyya Baba's 1903 *fatwā* arguing for the advantages of accepting French rule is among the most prominent texts in the Mauritanian *hijra* debate.[12] In contrast to their strategy in Algeria, from the outset of the campaign, French officials decided that a credible *fatwā*, one that articulated (in religious legal terms) the case for accommodation and was issued by an influential local authority, might dampen resistance and discourage emigration. It is likely that Coppolani brought to Mauritania copies of the 1841 *fatwā* obtained by Léon Roches from the Tijāniyya and a copy of the 1893 *fatwā* obtained for Governor-General Jules Cambon from the *muftī*s of Mecca.[13] He likely used these texts to formulate a question for Sidiyya Baba, and may even have provided the responses as well.

The question posed to Sidiyya Baba does not identify the questioner—this was probably a way to deflect attention from the fact that it was the French soliciting his response. Sidiyya Baba is asked if Muslims are required to fight the Christians who have occupied their lands, if these Christians do not hinder the practice of Islam. The questioner notes that the Christians in fact support the religion by appointing judges and organizing the judicial system. He also notes that the Muslims of Mauritania are as powerless as those of the eastern Maghrib (Algeria and Tunisia) to wage an effective *jihād*.

---

11 On Sidiyya Baba, see Robinson, *Paths*, esp. 178–93.

12 This *fatwā* was published first in French translation and later in Arabic. The 1907 French translation, by Edouard Michaux-Bellaire, is based on a document provided to him by a French administrator. It is not an exact match of the Arabic version, which forms part of a document recording several exchanges between Coppolani, Saad Buh and Sidiyya Baba. See Michaux-Bellaire, ed. and trans., "Une fetoua de Cheikh Sidia, Approuvé par Cheikh Saad Bouh ben Mohammed El Fadil ben Mamin, frère de Cheikh Ma El Ainin," *Archives Marocaines* 11 (1907): 129–53; Ibn Ḥabīb Allāh, *al-Ḥaraka al-Iṣlāḥiyya*, 417–21; Wuld al-Barā', *al-Majmūʿa al-kubrā*, 7:2942–45. Robinson's partial English translation of the French version is available online at http://aodl.org/islamicmodernity/sidiyyababa/object/64-247-17/. Verskin provides a full translation, also based on Michaux-Bellaire's French version, in *Oppressed in the Land*, 109–16.

13 On the 1893 *fatwā*, see chapter 7 and Ganān, *Nuṣūṣ siyāsiyya*, 262–64. A French version of the 1893 *fatwā* is included in Xavier Coppolani and Octave Depont, *Les confréries religieuses musulmanes* (Algiers: Adolphe Jourdan, 1897), 34–37.

This 1903 question appears to be a revision of the 1893 Algerian question. The Meccan *muftīs* were offered the same description of the situation, but were asked for a three-part response covering *hijra*, *jihād*, and the status of the conquered territory as *dār al-Islām* or *dār al-ḥarb*, in that order. The singular focus on *jihād* in the question to Sidiyya Baba suggests that, in the Mauritanian context, the French were far more concerned about armed resistance than emigration. They were also keen to counter Māʾ al-ʿAynayn's 1885 treatise (*Hidāyat man ḥāra fī amr al-Naṣārā*, or *Guide for Those Confused About the Matter of the Christians*) advocating *jihād*. Although Māʾ al-ʿAynayn composed this treatise in defense of his raids against the Spanish in Dakhla, many of his legal arguments in support of the individual obligation for Muslims to wage *jihād* against foreign occupation were later applied to Mauritania.[14]

Sidiyya Baba's response is surprisingly direct. In their joint response a decade earlier, and before acknowledging an exemption for those (Algerian) Muslims in question, the Meccan *muftīs* had labored over the obligation to emigrate, citing the Qurʾānic warning that hell will be the refuge of those who shirk this responsibility.[15] By contrast, Sidiyya Baba begins by declaring that the (Mauritanian) Muslims in question must make peace with the Christians. Rather than exhausting themselves in a futile struggle, he states, they must make every effort to live amicably with the Christians.

The body of the *fatwā* addresses *jihād*, *hijra*, and submission to Christian rule. In the first section, Sidiyya Baba devotes most of his attention to demonstrating the legitimacy of a truce with the Christians. His evidence is drawn primarily from the *Mukhtaṣar* of Khalīl b. Isḥāq (d. 776/1374), the most prominent and concise summary of Mālikī law. He spends relatively little time on *jihād*, dismissing it as impossible for Mauritanians. These Muslims are exempt from any obligation to fight, he states, because of their obvious weakness, as well as their lack of unity, funding, and arms. Sidiyya Baba also introduces a new argument, one that recurs in the Mauritanian debate: he states that legal authorities unanimously agree that one must choose the lesser of two harms. While he is clear that *jihād* is the greater harm, he only implies that submission to Christian rule is the lesser one, and thus, is also a harm.[16]

---

14 On Māʾ al-ʿAynayn's treatise, see Ould El-Bara (Wuld al-Barāʾ), "Les réponses," 133–34; Ibn Ḥabīb Allāh, *al-Ḥaraka al-Iṣlāḥiyya*, 357–69. Wuld al-Barāʾ includes this treatise in *al-Majmūʿa al-kubrā*, 7:2889–2905. A scholarly edition is provided in Murabbīhi Rabbuh Māʾ al-ʿAynayn, *al-Shaykh Māʾ al-ʿAynayn wa-maʿrakat al-Dākhila, 1885; maʿa taḥqīq "Hidāyat man ḥāra fī amr al-Naṣārā"* (Rabat: Manshūrāt Muʾassasat al-Shaykh Murabbīhi Rabbuh li-Iḥyāʾ al-Turāth wa'l-Tabādul al-Thaqāfī, 1999), 53–105.

15 Ganān, *Nuṣūṣ siyāsiyya*, 263.

16 In a pro-*hijra* text, Aḥmad b. al-Ḥasan b. Mādi al-Tandaghī explores three possible meanings for a lesser-of-two-evils argument he finds unclear. He may have been responding to Sidiyya

Sidiyya Baba dismisses *hijra* immediately, by arguing that Mauritanians are exempt from the obligation to emigrate because of their inability, and the lack of suitable destinations.[17] As in the first section, here too he offers textual evidence focusing on the exception rather than the rule. He cites Qurʾān 4:98 that exempts those who are weak from the obligation to emigrate, and follows this with excerpts from the exegetical works of ʿAbd Allāh b. ʿUmar al-Bayḍāwī (d. 685/1286), a Shāfiʿī theologian and jurist, and Abū al-Barakāt al-Nasafī (d. 710/1310), a Ḥanafī scholar. Both exegetes interpret the verse as exempting those without the means to travel or knowledge of the routes from the obligation to emigrate.

The final portion of the *fatwā* is astonishing for its praise of Christian rule. Sidiyya Baba first affirms and elaborates on his questioner's positive assessment of the Christians. They do not oppose the practice of Islam, he states, but have, in fact, built mosques and organized the judiciary. Moreover, they have promoted the public welfare by putting an end to thievery and banditry and by fostering peace between warring tribes. In the French version of this *fatwā*, Sidiyya Baba adds that the French are very successful at this, while in the Arabic he adds that the need for such stability in these lawless regions is well known.

This passage is remarkable for its breach of the *muftī*'s classical purview, which is to accept the facts as described in the question and offer an opinion based only on the applicable law. Yet, in relation to the French, Sidiyya Baba further suggests that "Perhaps God (may He be exalted) has sent them as a mercy to His worshipers, and a kindness to them."[18] It is hard to imagine a clearer expression of "contentment with Christian rule," the most grievous offense Wansharīsī and his contemporary peers imagined.

Perhaps unsurprisingly, Sidiyya Baba does not mention any of the late fifteenth-century opinions issued by Wansharīsī or his peers. Instead, he adduces three Qurʾānic verses in support of cooperation with non-Muslim rulers. The first of these, Qurʾān 60:8, states that God does not forbid Muslims from dealing kindly with those who neither fight against them nor turn them out of their homes. The second verse, Qurʾān 3:28, prohibits alliances with unbelievers except as a precaution, in order to guard against some danger; this is the primary proof text for the doctrine of *taqiyya*. The Algerian *muftī* Ibn al-Shāhid had similarly used this verse to justify continued residence in Algiers, while ʿAbd al-Qādir countered that it was

Baba, although it is the greater harm that he finds unclear. See Wuld al-Barāʾ, *al-Majmūʿa al-kubrā*, 7:3024.

17 Michaux-Bellaire, "Une fetoua de Cheikh Sidia," 137–38; Ibn Ḥabīb Allāh, *al-Ḥaraka al-Iṣlāḥiyya*, 419–20.

18 Ibn Ḥabīb Allāh, *al-Ḥaraka al-Iṣlāḥiyya*, 420; Michaux-Bellaire, "Une fetoua de Cheikh Sidia," 138.

abrogated by the expansiveness of the lands of Islam. Sidiyya Baba notes that according to Shāfiʿī exegetes Jalāl al-Dīn al-Suyūṭī (d. 910/1505) and Jalāl al-Dīn Maḥallī (d. 864/1459), Qurʾān 3:28 applies to all areas in which Islam is not powerful. The third verse Sidiyya Baba cites is Qurʾān 12:55, in which Joseph asks the Egyptian pharaoh to appoint him guardian of the storehouses. According to Sidiyya Baba, Nasafī and others interpreted this verse as validation of the acceptance of appointments from unjust leaders. In his treatise, ʿAbd al-Qādir refuted this interpretation of the Joseph story.

These three Qurʾān verses likely indicate a debt to the Algerian *hijra* debate, and also set the agenda for the Mauritanian debate. All three verses recur in the Mauritanian texts, as do Sidiyya Baba's main arguments against *hijra* and *jihād*. It is also worth noting that Sidiyya Baba's overall style of citation in this *fatwā* departs from the Iberian and North African legal texts reviewed earlier, but is typical of Mauritanian opinions. These Mauritanian texts feature a stronger reliance on works of Qurʾānic exegesis and *ḥadīth* commentary than do their Maghribī counterparts, as well as a greater consideration of non-Mālikī sources.

Appended to Sidiyya Baba's *fatwā* is a brief endorsement by Saad Buh, one of Māʾ al-ʿAynayn's younger brothers and a long-time ally of the French in Senegal and Mauritania.[19] Saad Buh indicates his support for Sidiyya Baba, and adds that the Christians are well-supplied with men and resources and have conquered vast territories in the east and west.

Sidiyya Baba's Letters

In addition to his 1903 *fatwā*, Sidiyya Baba composed a number of letters to individuals and groups in West Africa, urging the peaceful acceptance of French rule.[20] Many of these letters were intended for broad distribution. Among the core arguments and proof texts that recur in these letters are the assertion that *jihād* is futile and will lead to Muslim deaths; that Muslims currently under French rule are stable and prosperous; that unjust rule is preferable to lawlessness and banditry; that the Qurʾān verses prohibiting alliances with Christians apply only to religious matters, not worldly affairs; that Qurʾān 60:8 allowing kind dealings is not abrogated; that Qurʾān 3:28 allows for Muslims to forge alliances as a protection against danger; and that Qurʾān 16:106 allows for Muslims to form alliances under coercion, as long as one's heart is firm in faith.

---

19 On Saad Buh, see Robinson, *Paths*, 161–77. For this text, see Michaux-Bellaire, "Une fetoua de Cheikh Sidia," 140; Ibn Ḥabīb Allāh, *al-Ḥaraka al-Iṣlāḥiyya*, 420–21; Wuld al-Barāʾ, *al-Majmūʿa al-kubrā*, 7:2945.

20 Four of these letters appear as entries 2240 to 2243 in Wuld al-Barāʾ, *al-Majmūʿa al-kubrā*, 7:2926–42. An edition of the letter addressed to Sīdī b. Ḥabatt also appears in Ibn Ḥabīb Allāh, *al-Ḥaraka al-Iṣlāḥiyya*, 423–26.

In all four of his letters that are preserved in *al-Majmūʿa al-kubrā*, Sidiyya Baba refutes the obligation to emigrate. Beyond the two exemptions against emigration that he acknowledges in his *fatwā* (i.e., weakness and a lack of suitable destinations), he argues consistently that emigration is not obligatory in the first place, if Muslims can practice their religion and Islam is not threatened. This argument, which is common in Mauritanian texts rejecting *hijra*, is the dominant Shāfiʿī position and is based on Shāfiʿī legal precedents, rather than Mālikī precedents. Sidiyya Baba also revisits the meaning of the *ḥadīth*s stating "no *hijra* after the conquest" and "I am not responsible for any Muslim who lives among the polytheists," in light of his position on practicing one's religion.[21] He argues that the former *ḥadīth* ended the obligation for all Muslims (save those who are persecuted in their religion or who are converts to Islam in *dār al-ḥarb*) to emigrate. As for Muḥammad's declaration in which he distances himself from those who choose to reside among non-Muslims, Sidiyya Baba explains that this only pertains to those who are not secure in the practice of their religion. He even suggests that proclaiming Islam among non-Muslims is more virtuous than performing *hijra*.

In a letter to Sīdī b. Ḥabatt in June 1909, Sidiyya Baba dismisses Wansharīsī's *fatwā*s on emigration by distinguishing between the circumstances addressed in the *Miʿyār* and those of Mauritania.[22] He claims that the Spanish persecuted Muslims because of their religion, and that it was easy for Iberian Muslims to emigrate. They could move to a kingdom within the peninsula with a Muslim sultan and the power to fight in the way of God. Sidiyya Baba appears to have in mind the Naṣrid kingdom of Granada, and was likely unaware of the specifics of the history of the area, that is, that the Naṣrid kingdom lacked power and was months from surrender when Wansharīsī composed *Asnā al-matājir*.

In his letters, as in his *fatwā*, Sidiyya Baba's bold praise of French rule is striking. In this same letter to Sīdī b. Ḥabatt, Sidiyya Baba contrasts the fortunes of the *sūdān* ("blacks," here the Senegalese) with those of the *bīḍān* ("whites," or Arabs/Moors north of the Senegal River). Under French rule, he asserts, Senegal has become a safe and prosperous earthly paradise. Its formerly infidel population is now majority-Muslim and the French facilitate Islamic practices such as the pilgrimage. Sidiyya Baba argues that nothing would benefit the *bīḍān* more than to cease fighting and aspire to

21 These two *ḥadīths* appear in Wansharīsī's *Asnā al-matājir* and are discussed in chapter 5.

22 Ibn Ḥabīb Allāh, *al-Ḥaraka al-Iṣlāḥiyya*, 425–26; Wuld al-Barāʾ, *al-Majmūʿa al-kubrā*, 7:2928. Sīdī Muḥammad b. Aḥmad (Ḥabatt) al-Ghalāwī (d. 1954) is the author of an unpublished (and inaccessible) treatise rejecting residence under French rule, titled *Minārat al-ḥayārā fī ḥukm man ghalaba ʿalā waṭanih al-Naṣārā* (*Beacon for the Confused: The Legal Judgment Concerning Those Whose Homeland the Christians Have Conquered*).

the same conditions. In a letter written in 1921, he laments the lawlessness and perpetual warfare in West Africa prior to French rule and praises them for the lives and money saved by their conquest. We must thank God for this great blessing, he says, and thank France for improving the conditions of Muslims under their rule.[23]

Saad Buh's 1909 Letter to Māʾ al-ʿAynayn

Early in 1909, Saad Buh wrote a letter to his older brother, Māʾ al-ʿAynayn, in which he urges the abandonment of *jihād* and the return to scholarly pursuits.[24] Any further effort to expel the French, advises Saad Buh, would be as futile as attempting to return milk to a cow's teat. The letter, titled *al-Naṣīḥa al-ʿāmma waʾl-khāṣṣa fī al-taḥdhīr min muḥārabat al-Farāniṣa* (*General and Specific Counsel, Cautioning against Combating the French*) was widely distributed, though it did not necessarily reach Māʾ al-ʿAynayn himself.[25] While Saad Buh primarily focuses on refuting legal arguments in favor of *jihād*, his comments on emigration, which appear midway through the letter, are significant.

In the context of condemning the seizure of property belonging to Muslims living under French rule, Saad Buh defends the legitimacy of these Muslims' residence, by differentiating them from the Muslims addressed in Wansharīsī's *fatwās*:

> Yes, there is a response in the *Miʿyār*, in one of the compiler's own writings that he named *Asnā al-matājir* . . . It is a well-researched response containing [several] studies and distinct cases, as should be evident to anyone who examines the *Miʿyār*. Yet the circumstances of the people of al-Andalus are not like the circumstances of these [members] of the *zawāyā* (tribes). Therefore, these [tribes] may not be considered analogous to them. Rather, they are many times weaker [now] and today's Christians are a hundred times stronger than at that time.[26]

This passage is noteworthy, as Saad Buh is not contesting the validity of *Asnā al-matājir*. Like Sidiyya Baba, he agrees that Andalusīs were obligated to emigrate following the Christian conquest of their homelands. What both scholars reject is the applicability of this precedent to Mauritania. The fact

23 Wuld al-Barāʾ, *al-Majmūʿa al-kubrā*, 7:2931–32.

24 Ibn Ḥabīb Allāh, *al-Ḥaraka al-Iṣlāḥiyya*, 427–49; Wuld al-Barāʾ, *al-Majmūʿa al-kubrā*, 7:2914–26. Dedoud Ould Abdallah offers a French translation of this letter in his "Guerre sainte ou sédition blâmable? *Nasiha* de sheikh Sa'd Bu contre le *jihad* de son frère sheikh Ma al-Ainin," in *Le temps des marabouts*, ed. Robinson and Triaud (Paris: Éditions Karthala, 1997), 127–53.

25 Ould Abdallah, "Guerre sainte," 125–26. See also Robinson, *Paths*, 175.

26 Ibn Ḥabīb Allāh, *al-Ḥaraka al-Iṣlāḥiyya*, 439. *Zawāyā*, also spelled *zwaya*, is the plural of *zāwiya*.

that these modern scholars felt the need to refute the continued relevance of Wansharīsī's *fatwās* on emigration four centuries after his death affirms Wansharīsī's success in positioning these opinions as authoritative precedents for later scholars.

To confront the issue of the presumed applicability of *Asnā al-matājir*, Saad Buh was not content to simply assert that the situations of the Mauritanians and Andalusīs were wholly disparate. Instead, he further argues that it would be a violation of Islamic law to apply the same rules to different circumstances. Here Saad Buh appeals to Egyptian Mālikī jurist Shihāb al-Dīn al-Qarāfī (d. 684/1285). In his influential treatise distinguishing between the work of the judge and the *muftī*, Qarāfī states:

> Applying these rulings, which were deduced on the basis of customs, even after those customs have changed, is a violation of the scholarly consensus [on this matter] and [demonstrates] an ignorance of the religion. Rather, for every legal matter that is determined according to customs, its judgment changes as the custom changes, to [a new judgment that] is required by the new custom. This does not constitute a new instance of *ijtihād*, but is, rather, a principle that the scholars have thoroughly examined and concerning which they have come to a consensus. Thus, we are following them in this, and not appealing to a new *ijtihād*.[27]

By citing the former part of this passage, Saad Buh affirms his recognition of *Asnā al-matājir* as appropriate for its time, but implies that Wansharīsī based his opinion on "customs" or prevailing circumstances that do not hold true for Mauritania. A change in prevailing circumstances requires a change in the legal ruling, even if the same general rules apply. Saad Buh's citation of the latter part of this passage reveals his concern to appear faithful to his legal heritage and avoid the impression that he is selectively choosing precedents or acting as a *mujtahid*, deriving new rules at will. The passage allows Saad Buh to argue that setting aside the dominant precedent on *hijra* represents, in this case, faithful adherence to the school's core legal principles.

For Saad Buh and his like-minded peers, the key circumstances that differentiate the Andalusī and Mauritanian cases are the increased power of the Christians (as they referred to the French) in the modern era; the lack of suitable destinations, due to widespread European penetration; banditry; the desert landscape; and Muslims' ability to practice their

27 Ibn Ḥabīb Allāh, *al-Ḥaraka al-Iṣlāḥiyya*, 439. Many editions of Qarāfī's treatise have been published. For this passage, see Qarāfī, *al-Iḥkām fī tamyīz al-fatāwā ʿan al-aḥkām, wa-taṣarrufāt al-qāḍī wa'l-imām*, ed. Aḥmad Farīd al-Mazīdī (Beirut: Dār al-Kutub al-ʿIlmiyya, 2004), 72.

religion under French rule. Saad Buh elaborates on the legal import of this last "custom" with reference to Shāfiʿī authorities, including the prominent jurist Māwardī (d. 450/1058). If Muslims living in infidel territory are able to practice their religion, according to Māwardī, then that territory is part of *dār al-Islām*. If there is hope of winning converts to Islam, then continued residence there may be preferable to migration.[28]

In this letter, Saad Buh thus presents himself as a faithful Mālikī *muqallid*, while simultaneously reaching beyond the confines of his school to adopt a Shāfiʿī position on emigration. This contradiction may explain why he also seems eager to reconcile Wansharīsī's and Māwardī's positions on residence under Christian rule. In fact, Wansharīsī's opinions are not compatible with Māwardī's position that Muslims may reside under non-Muslim rule as long as they can practice their religion. In the Marbella *fatwā*, Wansharīsī explicitly rejects the argument that Muslims can practice their religion without a Muslim ruler, while in *Asnā al-matājir* he argues that the ability to practice one's religion is irrelevant to the obligation to emigrate. Yet for Saad Buh, ignoring Wansharīsī's opinions or rejecting them as invalid probably seemed too bold a departure from the dominant Mālikī precedents. Thus, he dismisses them as applicable to past circumstances, not the present case.

Muḥammad al-Amīn's Defense of Homeland

Not all Mauritanian scholars who urged accommodation with the French were reticent to critique Wansharīsī. Several scholars, Sidiyya Baba included, implicitly contested the validity of Wansharīsī's opinions by rejecting his interpretations of the *ḥadīth*s on "no *hijra* after the conquest [of Mecca]" and "I am not responsible." We also hear from at least one scholar who was born and raised in the colonial era and robustly defends Mauritanians' continued residence in their home country.[29] The jurist Muḥammad al-Amīn b. Muḥammad al-Mukhtār Akhṭūr al-Jaknī (1905–74) composed an undated declaration excusing "those inhabitants of Shinqīṭ [Mauritania] who did not emigrate from this region because it is their homeland, and their families are there."[30] This phrase in Arabic mimics the

28 Ibn Ḥabīb Allāh, *al-Ḥaraka al-Iṣlāḥiyya*, 443. On Māwardī's opinion, see also Khaled Abou El Fadl, "Islamic Law and Muslim Minorities," 150.

29 We also have at least one pro-resistance text by a scholar raised in the colonial era. Jurist al-Mukhtār b. Sīdī b. Aḥmad b. Ablūl (d. 1975) argued in favor of *hijra*, but noted that this is a selfish option, one that saves the emigrants while leaving the territory in Christian hands. It is better to throw off colonialism, he argues, and save the strong and the weak together. See Wuld al-Barāʾ, *al-Majmūʿa al-kubrā*, 7:2854–60, esp. 7:2859.

30 Wuld al-Barāʾ, *al-Majmūʿa al-kubrā*, 7:3041–45. Later in life, Muḥammad al-Amīn appears to have changed his mind concerning his homeland. In 1948, he performed the pilgrimage to Mecca and remained in Saudi Arabia to pursue a teaching career. He died there in 1974. On him, see Wuld al-Barāʾ, *al-Majmūʿa al-kubrā*, 2:178–79.

full title of *Asnā al-matājir* but emphasizes one's "homeland" and does not mention living under Christian rule. Muḥammad al-Amīn repeats many of the familiar arguments justifying residence under French rule, including the legitimacy of alliances concluded by necessity, the lack of suitable destinations for emigration, and the stability brought by Christian rule. He agrees that the "no *hijra*" *ḥadīth* brought an end to mandatory emigration, except in cases in which Muslims are unable to practice their religion. He adds an assertion that the majority of Wansharīsī's proof texts pertain only to the type of *hijra* that was obligatory in early Islam and that was subsequently abrogated by the "no *hijra*" *ḥadīth*. Muḥammad al-Amīn implies that all of *Asnā al-matājir* and the Marbella *fatwā* are suspect as a result of this flawed use of evidence, in which the proof texts for an abrogated *hijra* are used to support a continuing obligation to emigrate.

Arguments for Emigration

Ould El-Bara's great compilation *al-Majmūʿa al-kubrā* contains eleven texts (by my count) by authors who argue for the necessity of performing *hijra* from French-controlled territory. The majority are undated, but appear to post-date and respond to the earliest pro-accommodation texts. Each argument advanced in favor of submission to colonial rule is noted and rebutted. In general, these authors appear to engage an audience that is well acquainted with the doctrine of *hijra*; rather than introducing the case for emigration, they defend a well-known doctrine against specific claims that their situation represents an exception or that the doctrine of *hijra* is entirely irrelevant to colonial Mauritania.

This group of texts includes poems, *fatwās*, letters, named treatises, and declarations. While some merely allude to major precedents and points of debate, others present a rich variety of proof texts in response to each contested issue. Mauritanian scholars in favor of *hijra* make substantial but far from exclusive reference to Wansharīsī's *fatwās*. Wahrānī again does not figure in these texts, despite the jurists' repeated references to *taqiyya*, and there appears to be only one reference to the *fatwās* preserved by Zayyātī. Two texts, one composed by Sīdī al-Mukhtār al-Lamtūnī (d. ca. 1906) and one by Murabbīh Rabbuh (d. 1942) serve to illustrate this side of the Mauritanian debate.

Sīdī al-Mukhtār al-Lamtūnī's Letter to the Scholars

Sīdī al-Mukhtār al-Lamtūnī, a jurist from the Brakna region of southwestern Mauritania, emigrated to Morocco in 1905 as a means of resisting French colonization. Shortly thereafter, he wrote at least two legal texts to fellow scholars who had remained behind, urging them to fight or emigrate. The first, *Irshād al-ḍāl fī wujūb jihād al-Naṣārā wa-ḥurmat al-taʿāmul maʿahum* (*Guide for the Lost: The Obligation to Fight the Christians and the Prohibition of Cooperating with Them*), is unfortunately inaccessible. But the second, a long letter to the author's cousin, has now been published and appears to be a draft of many of the arguments presented in *Irshād al-ḍāl*.[31] The letter is undated, but must have been written between 1905 and 1908, the latest date offered for Sīdī al-Mukhtār's death. He died in Morocco, en route to Mecca for the pilgrimage.

Sīdī al-Mukhtār's opening invocation, "Praise be to God who made the *hijra* obligatory, just like *jihād*," leaves no doubt as to his position. He addresses the letter to his fellow scholars, reminding them at the outset of their responsibility to guide others. When they sin, he warns, their own wrongdoing is compounded by the sins of those they have led astray. Thus, they of all people must not continue to live among the Christians, interact with them, and aid them in the absence of any legitimate necessity.

The two primary themes of Sīdī al-Mukhtār's letter are the establishment of this lack of necessity, and the emphasis on the severity of these scholars' sins (should they continue to mislead others). The letter is organized as a series of rebuttals against the claims advanced by one of Sīdī al-Mukhtār's cousins, who had defended submission to French rule. According to Sīdī al-Mukhtār, the same cousin had acknowledged the prohibitions on residing with Christians and allying with them; yet, he presented reasons, according to which Mauritanians could be considered exempt from this general rule.

Three of the arguments Sīdī al-Mukhtār rejects relate to the feasibility of emigration. In response to his cousin's assertion that those who remained under French rule are incapable of emigrating, Sīdī al-Mukhtār reviews Wansharīsī's discussion of Qurʾān 4:98 and the "weakness" mentioned there. It is false, Sīdī al-Mukhtār asserts, to pretend that all those in question meet this standard for exemption. Many of these same people perform the pilgrimage or travel long distances for trade, making their ability to leave home quite apparent. In response to an unspecified argument regarding women and the poor, Sīdī al-Mukhtār asserts that women have the same obligation to emigrate as men do. His cousin must have argued that these two groups are necessarily too weak to emigrate, and possibly that men must therefore remain as well, to support their families and the less fortunate. Sīdī al-Mukhtār further rejects a claim that Muslims under French rule should remain because there is no use emigrating from a territory in

31 On Sīdī al-Mukhtār b. al-Mukhtār ʿAynayn b. Aḥmad al-Hādī al-Lamtūnī, see Ould El-Bara, "Les réponses," 129 (where his death date is given as 1326/1908); Wuld al-Barāʾ, *al-Majmūʿa al-kubrā*, 2:112 (where his death date is given as 1325/1906). Sīdī al-Mukhtār's letter appears in Wuld al-Barāʾ, *al-Majmūʿa al-kubrā*, 7:3002–3019, and in Ibn al-Shaykh Māmīnā, *al-Shaykh Māʾ al-ʿAynayn*, 2:473–83. The latter version is abbreviated slightly.

which Islam is not upheld because of infidelity, to one in which Islam is not upheld because of lawlessness. In response, Sīdī al-Mukhtār cites Ibn al-ʿArabī's passage on destinations from Wansharīsī's *Asnā al-matājir*, which emphasizes the obligation to leave infidel territory and to seek the best possible alternative, even if that is tyranny.

Sīdī al-Mukhtār also warns against using the concepts of *ḍarūra* (necessity) or *maṣlaḥa* (public interest) too readily or too broadly. Necessity does not make all prohibited things permissible, he argues, nor may an appeal to public interest be used to justify whatever is most convenient from one week to the next. Sīdī al-Mukhtār further argues that the maxim obligating a Muslim to commit the lesser of two evils, when properly applied to the Mauritanian context, requires emigration because harm to one's religion is a greater evil than harm to one's material comfort. Sīdī al-Mukhtār also refutes the notion that it is permissible to sell cows, horses, or leather to the enemy, as such goods empower them against Muslims. He supports these arguments with reference to the writings of ʿIllaysh and Gannūn, both prominent in the Algerian *hijra* debate, and the *Mukhtaṣar* of Khalīl b. Isḥāq.

Only one of the arguments Sīdī al-Mukhtār refutes contests the applicability of *hijra* to the Mauritanian context. His cousin must have claimed that *hijra* to escape religious persecution is the only type of emigration that remains obligatory according to the *ḥadīth* stating "no *hijra* after the conquest [of Mecca]," and that persecution like that suffered in Mecca is absent under colonial rule. To counter this argument, Sīdī al-Mukhtār quotes extensively from *Asnā al-matājir*.[32] He reproduces Ibn Rushd al-Jadd's and Ibn al-ʿArabī's statements that *hijra* remains obligatory until the day of judgment, and that only traveling to the Prophet in Medina ceased to be obligatory upon the conquest of Mecca. He includes Wansharīsī's passage stating that the Qurʾān, Ḥadīth, and scholarly consensus are all unanimous as to the obligation to emigrate from *dār al-ḥarb* to *dār al-Islām*. Finally, Sīdī al-Mukhtār reiterates Ibn Rushd al-Jadd's declaration that only a Muslim whose faith was diseased could be content to live among infidels. This last passage was likely intended to counter the image of Muslims accepting colonial rule under duress, yet with hearts content in faith.

Indeed, the claims (that Mauritanians are exempt from emigration) that Sīdī al-Mukhtār rejects most strenuously and repeatedly are those based on *taqiyya* and coercion. His cousin, like Sidiyya Baba, appears to have argued that Qurʾān 3:28 and 16:106 mean that alliances with infidels are justified

32 While Sīdī al-Mukhtār attributes all of these passages to the *Miʿyār*, he is reading them as found in ʿIllaysh's *Fatḥ al-ʿalī*.

and that normally prohibited actions are permissible as long as Muslims undertake them as a result of coercion or fear, and as long as their hearts remain secure in faith. Specifically, Sīdī al-Mukhtār charges his cousin with alleging that those Muslims who live with the Christians, who aid the enemy by exposing the Muslims' vulnerabilities to them, who bear the Christians' instruments of war and provisions for them on their pack animals, who build churches in which the Christians may fortify themselves, and who turn their children over to be educated by them in such a manner as to aid the enemy against Muslims—that these Muslims are coerced in all of this by the fear of death and the fear of losing their livelihoods.[33]

Sīdī al-Mukhtār's repudiation of these claims is uncompromising. These Muslims have no recourse to the principal of coercion, he notes, because they can and should have emigrated before committing any of these prohibited acts. And they cannot appeal to the doctrine of *taqiyya* unless they fear death, a claim that Sīdī al-Mukhtār clearly considers disingenuous. He states that even if they genuinely feared death—not material discomfort—*taqiyya* nonetheless does not excuse actions that threaten the lives and rights of other Muslims. Chief among these inexcusable actions is espionage, as those residing under French rule cannot help but expose the Muslims' vulnerabilities to the infidel enemy. Sīdī al-Mukhtār does not elaborate on this point, but presumably means that living and working together would allow the French to gather information (i.e., regarding networks, towns, routes, and supplies) that could be exploited to increase their power. For Sīdī al-Mukhtār, no legal dispensation softens or excuses this treachery. These people are not only sinners and traitors, but they also risk incurring the penalty for espionage: death without an opportunity to repent.[34]

Sīdī al-Mukhtār not only rejects each proposed justification for remaining under French rule, but he further warns readers that making these excuses verges on apostasy. Twice he reminds them that neglecting an obligatory act is not nearly as serious as denying the very existence of the obligation. For example, eating carrion is merely prohibited, but to say that carrion is permitted is infidelity; neglecting prayer is not infidelity, but mocking the obligation to pray is.[35] In both instances, Sīdī al-Mukhtār stresses that making a mockery of divine law is apostasy. "Don't you dare, don't you dare, *don't you dare* end up being described in the same way as those [regretful Andalusī emigrants]!" he warns, repeating a dozen of Wansharīsī's derogatory terms for this group.[36] While he does not accuse his contemporaries of the same

33 Wuld al-Barā', *al-Majmūʿa al-kubrā*, 7:3016.

34 This composite summary of Sīdī al-Mukhtār's view on *taqiyya* is taken from Wuld al-Barā', *al-Majmūʿa al-kubrā*, 7:3006–8 and 7:3016.

35 Wuld al-Barā', *al-Majmūʿa al-kubrā*, 7:3003 (carrion) and 7:3006 (prayer).

36 Wuld al-Barā', *al-Majmūʿa al-kubrā*, 7:3011.

explicit public mockery of *hijra* that is ascribed to the Andalusīs in *Asnā al-matājir*, Sīdī al-Mukhtār nonetheless links the two groups. He implies that his peers' baseless claims of exemption approach the denial and mockery of these regretful Andalusīs, and this is tantamount to infidelity.

Sīdī al-Mukhtār repeatedly pleads with his cousin and other peers to return to the right path and join him in performing *hijra*, most powerfully when he raises the spectre of their resemblance to the perilously misguided Andalusīs. He dwells on their case, reproducing Wansharīsī's condemnations of their character and rejections of their claims. In colonial Mauritania, these regretful Andalusī emigrants thus remained a poignant symbol of the willful belittlement of divine law, the privileging of personal whims and material comfort over religion, and contentment with an inverted world order in which infidelity dominates Islam.

Murabbīh Rabbuh's **Fatwā** *on the Obligation to Emigrate*

In 1925, Mā al-ʿAynayn's son Muḥammad al-Muṣṭafā Murabbīh Rabbuh (d. 1942) composed *Ṣawlat al-kārr wa-malja' al-fārr fī taḥrīm al-iqāma maʿa al-kuffār* (*The Attacker's Assault and Retreater's Refuge, on the Prohibition of Residence with the Infidels*).[37] Presented as a *fatwā*, the text purportedly responds to the queries of some travelers who wished to understand the prohibition on residence in infidel territory. Murabbīh Rabbuh focuses primarily on *hijra*, supporting the obligation to emigrate with extensive reference to the writings of Wansharīsī and Tasūlī.

In his introduction, Murabbīh Rabbuh cites two key Qur'ān passages on relationships with infidels. He uses Qur'ān 9:23–24, as interpreted by Shāfiʿī exegete Fakhr al-Dīn al-Rāzī (d. 606/1209), to establish Muslims' obligation to prioritize religion over worldly interests such as commerce, property, and even close familial ties. Murabbīh Rabbuh then cites the latter part of Qur'ān 60:9, most likely in response to Sidiyya Baba's use of Qur'ān 60:8–9. This is the passage in which God allows Muslims to deal kindly with those who do not fight against them in their religion and who do not drive them from their homes. Sidiyya Baba adduced this verse as evidence that formal relations with the French were permissible, because the French were not guilty of these actions. Murabbīh Rabbuh cites the latter part of Qur'ān 60:9, which states that those who ally with such offenders are wrongdoers, as an implicit counter-argument that the French are indeed guilty of fighting Muslims and threatening their religious practices. For Murabbīh Rabbuh, these verses affirm that relations with the French are prohibited and that continuing

37 Ibn Ḥabīb Allāh, *al-Ḥaraka al-Iṣlāḥiyya*, 457–68. This title is a play on *al-karr wa'l-farr*, a battle technique of retreat and counter-attack. This word for retreat, *farr*, also connotes flight and is often the word used for emigration.

these relationships will bring severe consequences. From Rāzī's commentary, Murabbīh Rabbuh further cites an opinion attributed to the Companion Ibn ʿAbbās, according to which those Muslims referred to in Qurʾān 60:9 become polytheists like those with whom they have allied because they are content with polytheism, and contentment with unbelief is unbelief.

Murabbīh Rabbuh's severe tone is consistent with Sīdī al-Mukhtār's letter and with both scholars' extensive reliance on texts composed or cited in the Algerian debate. Early in his *fatwā*, Murabbīh Rabbuh cites Ibn Zakrī's opinion that if Muslims living under infidel rule fight against other Muslims, they should be fought and killed. He also endorses Tasūlī's position that the property of Muslims living under French rule is licit because of their financial support for the enemy. Sīdī al-Mukhtār had supported, unapologetically, the same basic position, although by referring to Wansharīsī's *Asnā al-matājir*, Sīdī al-Mukhtār stated that those who remain under French rule forfeit the inviolability of their property (that is, it becomes legitimate booty for other Muslims).

This position on property was not merely "academic," but reflected one of the most contentious aspects of the fight against colonialism in what became Mauritania. Some elements of the resistance raided and pillaged Muslims living under French rule, justifying their actions with reference to *fatwās* such as these. More than one scholar, including Buṣādī, whose lengthy treatise on property rights is addressed below, condemned this tactic.[38]

In this first portion of his *fatwā*, Murabbīh Rabbuh reproduces much of Tasūlī's section on *hijra* from his first set of answers to ʿAbd al-Qādir. As Tasūlī drew on *Asnā al-matājir*, this section of Murabbīh Rabbuh's *fatwā* contains several elements of Wansharīsī's opinion, including Wansharīsī's discussion of the ability to undertake emigration; the *ḥadīth* reports related to emigration, including the question of their mutual compatibility; the concurrence of evidence from the Qurʾān, Sunna, and scholarly consensus as to the prohibition on living in infidel territory; and the analogy between converts to Islam in *dār al-ḥarb* and conquered Muslims. Quoting directly from *Asnā al-matājir* and acknowledging his source, Murabbīh Rabbuh then reproduces Wansharīsī's sections on the definition of "weakness" as an exemption from the obligation to emigrate and as used in the Qurʾānic verses prohibiting alliances with non-believers, Ibn Rushd al-Jadd's statement that *hijra* remains an obligation until the day of judgment, and on *ḥadīths* supportive of this obligation. Murabbīh Rabbuh ends this section

38 On the issue of pillaging, see Ould El-Bara, "Les réponses," 130–32. Māʾ al-ʿAynayn's letter appears in Arabic in Wuld al-Barāʾ, *al-Majmūʿa al-kubrā*, 7:2914, and in French translation in Ould El-Bara, "Les réponses," 131.

with a passage reiterating that anyone capable of emigrating is obligated to, even if this entails hardship, and condemning those who are capable of emigrating but contentedly remain living with unbelievers.

Murabbīh Rabbuh later addresses several new arguments, including Fakhr al-Dīn al-Rāzī's commentary on Qurʾān 8:74. This verse designates those who fight and emigrate in the way of God to be the true believers. Rāzī explains that if believers who are living in infidel territory might weaken the enemy by leaving, then they must do so, as did the earliest Meccan Muslims who emigrated to Medina. Murabbīh Rabbuh likely introduces this argument to counter two claims made by accommodationist scholars: first, that continued residence might be preferable to *hijra* if infidels may be won over to Islam, and second, that leaving a territory may be prohibited if doing so might contribute to its reversion to *dār al-ḥarb*.

Murabbīh Rabbuh, who clearly held that French-controlled Mauritania had already reverted to *dār al-ḥarb*, reviews the criteria for considering whether a territory is *dār al-Islām* or *dār al-ḥarb*. He notes that Shāfiʿī and Ibn Ḥanbal agreed with Mālik's position that the application of infidel laws renders a territory *dār al-ḥarb*, while Abū Ḥanīfa held that two additional criteria are necessary for a territory to lose its status as *dār al-Islām*: the territory in question must be separated from the rest of *dār al-Islām*, and Muslims and *dhimmī*s must have lost their former protections.[39] Despite this difference of opinion as to territorial status, Murabbīh Rabbuh reminds his readers that all the early scholars agreed that the property of Muslims living in *dār al-ḥarb* may be seized as booty.

This unfriendly reminder precedes a second accusation of apostasy, this time a much more forceful one. Without additional comment, Murabbīh Rabbuh reproduces (approvingly) a passage from Aḥmad al-Sharīf al-Sanūsī's 1912 treatise calling for *jihād* against the Italian colonizers of what is now Libya.[40] In the passage, Sanūsī warns believers against those hypocrites who call themselves Muslims while urging surrender and submission to the enemy. They have traded their religion for worldly interests, he remarks, against the admonition in Qurʾān 2:16. Sanūsī affirms that anyone who supports infidels in fighting against other Muslims is undoubtedly an apostate, and concludes this passage with two rhetorical questions: What kind of unbelief could be greater than working for the degradation of Islam and the glorification of unbelief? Who should be called apostates, if not these very apostates?

39 See Khalid Abou El Fadl, "Islamic Law and Muslim Minorities," 161–62.

40 Ibn Ḥabīb Allāh, *al-Ḥaraka al-Iṣlāḥiyya*, 465–66. On Aḥmad al-Sharīf al-Sanūsī (1876–1923) and his treatise, *Bughyat al-musāʿid fī aḥkām al-mujāhid*, see Knut S. Vikør, "*Jihād*, *ʿilm*, and *taṣawwuf*—Two Justifications of Action from the Idrīsī Tradition," *Studia Islamica* 90 (2000): 153–76, esp. 161–64. Italy's military conquest of Libya took place between 1911 and 1934.

Following this fascinating reference to the contemporary situation in Libya, Murabbīh Rabbuh returns to more familiar precedents from colonial Algeria and the fourteenth- to fifteenth-century Maghrib. He reiterates his position on the property of Muslims living under infidel rule, this time by citing Tasūlī's second response to ʿAbd al-Qādir. From this second response, Murabbīh Rabbuh approvingly cites Waryāglī's position that Muslims who live among infidels, spying and fighting for them, must be fought and their property taken as booty. This is the sole reference to Waryāglī in the Mauritanian debate, and it is indirect; like Tasūlī, Murabbīh Rabbuh does not name Waryāglī and instead attributes this opinion solely to Zayyātī. Murabbīh Rabbuh further reinforces his own position on the property of conquered Muslims by stating that those remaining in *dār al-ḥarb* do not have valid ownership of their property or children; he attributes this opinion to the *Miʿyār* in general, not to Wansharīsī or his *fatwā*s specifically.

The *fatwā* concludes with the Qurʾānic warnings not to obey unbelievers (3:149), not to practice hypocrisy (4:138–39), and not to ally with those who fight Muslims in their religion (60:9). In this second mention of Qurʾān 60:9, Murabbīh Rabbuh draws on the exegetical work *Rūḥ al-bayān* (also cited by Muḥammad Gannūn in the Algerian debate) in which Ismāʿīl Ḥaqqī al-Barūsawī (d. 1724) links this verse directly to Qurʾān 4:97. Verse 60:9 states that those who ally with the prohibited class of non-believers are *ẓālimūn* (wrongdoers or oppressors), while in Qurʾān 4:97 the angels reprimand those found oppressing themselves (*ẓālimī anfusihim*) by not emigrating from the source of their torment. Murabbīh Rabbuh thus ends with another counter to Sidiyya Baba's use of Qurʾān 60:8, while also reinforcing this classic proof text for the obligation to emigrate (Qurʾān 4:97).

The Final Word: Buṣādī's *Fatwā* on Property

Mauritanian scholar Muḥammad ʿAbd Allāh b. Zaydān al-Buṣādī (d. 1933 or 1934)[41] composed one of the most remarkable Mālikī legal texts regarding the obligation to emigrate. Titled *Taḥrīm nahb amwāl al-muʿāhidīn lil-Naṣārā* (*Prohibition on Plundering the Property of Those under Treaty with the Christians*), this lengthy *fatwā* may be the most serious critique

41 On Buṣādī, see Muḥammad ʿAbd Allāh b. Zaydān b. Ghālī al-Buṣādī, *Taḥrīm nahb amwāl al-muʿāhidīn lil-Naṣārā*, ed. Ḥamāh Allāh wuld al-Sālim (Beirut: Dar al-Kutub al-ʿIlmiyya, 2013), 9–26; Ḥamāh Allāh wuld al-Sālim, "Dawr al-ʿulamāʾ al-Shanāqiṭa fī al-thaqāfa biʾl-Mamlaka al-ʿArabiyya al-Saʿūdiyya fī ʿahd al-Malik Saʿūd b. ʿAbd al-ʿAzīz," *Al-Dāra* 4 (2006): 329–30. Buṣādī's death date is inconsistently rendered as either 1933 or 1934, and other sources suggest he died in Mecca. According to Wuld al-Sālim, Buṣādī's unusual tribal *nisba* derives from a six-fingered ancestor who was nicknamed "Abū al-Sādis." This name is subject to variant spellings.

of Wansharīsī's opinions to date.[42] In the course of defending the property rights of conquered Muslims, Buṣādī refutes one of the critical premises of Wansharīsī's *Asnā al-matājir*, which is to consider the legal statuses of conquered Muslims equivalent to that of lone converts to Islam. *Prohibition on Plundering* also represents a middle ground in the Mauritanian *hijra* debate, as Buṣādī encourages emigration while upholding the inviolability of Muslims' property under colonial rule.

Buṣādī, educated in eastern Mauritania, emigrated in response to French expansion. He traveled first to Morocco, where he was received warmly by the king of Morocco. Buṣādī continued eastward in order to perform the *ḥajj*, arriving in Mecca as early as 1905. There he remained for many years, becoming a prominent linguist and legal scholar. After a brief period in the Sudan, he ultimately settled in Cairo, where he taught at al-Azhar until his death. Buṣādī's own *hijra* appears to have preceded the largest collective movement away from colonial Mauritania; in 1908 a *hijra* of 600 families journeyed east, organized by members of the Buṣādī tribe who led the Ghuẓfiyya Sufi order.[43]

Summary of Prohibition on Plundering

Buṣādī's undated *fatwā* is a response to a request to clarify God's legal judgment regarding the property rights of Shinqīṭī Muslims who live in enemy territory. The unnamed questioner may have been Māʾ al-ʿAynayn, who was forced to revisit his own views on this issue in response to a heated debate between scholars and resistance leaders in Mauritania. In his 1885 *Hidāyat man ḥāra fī amr al-Naṣārā* (*Guide for Those Confused about the Matter of the Christians*), Māʾ al-ʿAynayn declared the property of Muslims living in Spanish territory to be licit. In a later directive to his followers in Mauritania he reversed course, and urged them to fight the Christians, but also to respect the property of those Muslims residing amidst the Christians.[44]

---

42 Wuld al-Sālim's book-length critical edition of this *fatwā*, based on a single privately-held manuscript, is noted above. Ould El-Bara (Wuld al-Barāʾ) also includes the text in *al-Majmūʿa al-kubrā* (7:3045–59), based on a different manuscript held by the Mauritanian Institute for Scientific Research. The first edition of this text appeared as appendix E in my dissertation (Hendrickson, "Islamic Obligation," 437–67), based on two manuscripts located in Morocco: Ḥasaniyya Library MS 12438.3, fols. 164a–176b, and Muʾassasat al-Malik ʿAbd al-ʿAzīz Āl Saʿūd MS 440, entire manuscript. Instead of "*Taḥrīm nahb . . .*", the latter is titled *Jawāb ʿan ḥukm Allāh taʿālā fī māl al-Muslimīn min al-Shanājiṭa al-muqīmīn fī arḍ al-ḥarbiyyīn* (*Response regarding the Legal Status of the Property Belonging to Shinqīṭī Muslims Living in Non-Muslim Territory*). My edition remains the most complete, as the Ḥasaniyya manuscript contains significant material not included in the other two editions.

43 On this *hijra* movement, see Wuld al-Sālim, "Dawr al-ʿulamāʾ al-Shanāqiṭa," 326–28.

44 Māʾ al-ʿAynayn's directive appears in Arabic in Wuld al-Barāʾ, *al-Majmūʿa al-kubrā*, 7:2914, and in French translation in Ould El-Bara, "Les réponses," 131.

In his introduction, Buṣādī humbly protests about the difficulty of pronouncing a *fatwā* on such a matter, but explains that he cannot remain silent while the truth is reviled.[45] He presents his text as a counsel to the scholarly community, meant to clarify and remedy. Whether or not we can credit Buṣādī for Māʾ al-ʿAynayn's reversal, *Prohibition on Plundering* provided scholars on both sides of the *hijra* debate with the technical legal case for considering the property of conquered Muslims to be inviolable.

Here I detail that legal case at length, because of its value as a refutation of Wansharīsī's *Asnā al-matājir*, a text so influential that Buṣādī's contemporaries were still basing some of their arguments on this four-century-old document. While Buṣādī was far from the first or only scholar to disagree with Wansharīsī, his text alone clearly and directly dismantles the legal reasoning underpinning *Asnā al-matājir*. This approach is distinct from earlier tactics employed by other scholars, such as relegating the applicability of Wansharīsī's opinions to the past; adopting non-Mālikī positions; arguing that Wansharīsī was working with abrogated proof texts; or favoring alternate interpretations of those same proof texts. Buṣādī argues with Wansharīsī on his own terms, so to speak, by accepting the same proof texts as valid and by adhering only to Mālikī precedents. This direct refutation is important because it demonstrates that the long-term success of Wansharīsī's opinions was not a result of their unassailable legal reasoning.

Toward the beginning of the *fatwā*, Buṣādī establishes the parameters of legitimate scholarly disagreement regarding the property rights of conquered Muslims. The later scholars who have examined this issue agree, he notes, that we have no evidence to suggest that any of the early jurists considered the property of these Muslims to be licit. Although Buṣādī does not state this explicitly, this lack of precedent is presumably explained by the fact that the early jurists only discussed lone converts, not conquered Muslims. Buṣādī further affirms that the later scholars also agree that the property of any Muslim who is incapable of emigrating remains inviolable. Thus, what later scholars have disagreed on is the property rights of Muslims who voluntarily remain in conquered territory.

There are two opinions on this matter, Buṣādī explains. Those who hold the first opinion take the established Mālikī rule for lone converts, which is that their property is licit as long as they remain in *dār al-ḥarb*, and extend that same rule to the case of conquered Muslims. Buṣādī, like ʿAbd

45 Buṣādī's uncommon term for reviling the truth, *taʿyīr al-ḥaqq*, is likely an allusion to the *Miʿyār*, from the same Arabic root word. See Hendrickson, "Islamic Obligation," 438 (my Arabic edition). This sentence is missing from Wuld al-Barāʾ's edition (*al-Majmūʿa al-kubrā*, 7:3045) and appears as *taʿayyun al-ḥaqq* in Wuld al-Sālim's edition (*Taḥrīm nahb amwāl*, 95).

al-Qādir, apparently considers it evident that this opinion is grounded in *qiyās* (analogical reasoning), and he does not address Wansharīsī's avoidance of this term. The second opinion, Buṣādī continues, is that a conquered Muslim's property is inviolable, regardless of any change in the status of his territory. Proponents of the second opinion consider these two cases (that of a conquered Muslim and that of a lone convert in *dār al-ḥarb*) too disparate to be linked through analogical reasoning. Buṣādī laments that the second opinion is the correct one, but has not been properly analyzed.

Indeed, the first opinion so dominated Mālikī thought that Buṣādī devotes considerable attention to justifying his right to revisit this analogy. He notes that later scholars may be more knowledgeable on certain points than earlier scholars, and cautions that arguments must be evaluated on the strength of their evidence, and not simply accepted as the opinions of particular exemplars. Buṣādī asserts that the decision to consider these two cases analogous is one such opinion that must be thoroughly re-evaluated.

To support his primary argument that conquered Muslims' property remains inviolable, Buṣādī devotes the majority of his treatise to refuting the analogy between a conquered Muslim and a lone convert in *dār al-ḥarb* as it has been understood by Wansharīsī and others. In what follows, Buṣādī argues that this analogy is invalid for two reasons: the two cases are in fact disparate, and the rationale offered for this analogy contradicts a clear proof text governing the original case (of the lone convert). To lay the groundwork for this argument, Buṣādī first reiterates the components of *qiyās* and illustrates how they have been applied to the current analogy. He establishes a few preliminary points regarding this analogy, then elaborates each of his two main critiques of it (that the lone convert and conquered Muslim are disparate cases, and that the rationale for this analogy contradicts an established proof text). Following his refutation of this analogy's validity, Buṣādī offers a counter-analogy, one that reinterprets the case of the lone convert to support the inviolability of conquered Muslims' property. In the conclusion to *Prohibition on Plundering*, Buṣādī applies this new rule explicitly to the Mauritanian context.

Buṣādī on Qiyās *and His Opponents' Analogy between Lone Converts and Conquered Muslims*

First, Buṣādī explains that *qiyās* has four components: (1) the *aṣl* (original) case; (2) the *ḥukm* (rule) governing the original case; (3) the *farʿ* (branch), which is a new case in need of a legal judgment; and (4) the *ʿilla* (effective cause), which is the rationale for the rule governing the original case. This rationale must also be present in the new case, to justify extending the rule from the original case to the new case. In the dominant analogy, (1) the *aṣl* is the convert's property and children, who have remained in *dār al-ḥarb* since his conversion; (2) the *ḥukm* is that this property and these children are licit; (3) the *farʿ* is the property and children of a conquered Muslim voluntarily remaining in *dār al-ḥarb*; and (4) the *ʿilla* is the convert's residence in *dār al-ḥarb* and consequent alliance with infidels.

Buṣādī accepts the first two components of this analogy, that the property and children of a convert to Islam in *dār al-ḥarb* are licit. But, he argues, the *ʿilla* has been misidentified and misapplied. Buṣādī first explains the argument of the "analogists," represented by Wansharīsī. He reproduces the section of *Asnā al-matājir* in which Wansharīsī states that the early jurists discussed only the case of lone converts, as one manifestation of the broader case of Muslims in non-Muslim territory, because the case of conquered Muslims had not yet arisen; when the case of conquered Muslims arose after the fall of Sicily and parts of al-Andalus, later jurists agreed that the two cases of converts and conquered Muslims were completely equivalent. Buṣādī notes that Wansharīsī also mentions an alternative view to this position, meaning the opinion of Ibn al-Ḥājj, but Buṣādī states that this opinion has not been properly explored.

Buṣādī argues that aspects of Wansharīsī's explanation are contradictory. He considers the following statement in *Asnā al-matājir* to convey the *ʿilla* in Wansharīsī's analogy: "[the later scholars] saw no difference between the two groups in this regard. This is because the two [groups] are as one with respect to submitting to the enemy, living among them . . ."[46] Yet, Buṣādī protests, how can the *ʿilla* for judging a Muslim's property as licit be submission to infidel rule, if the analogists also assert that submission to non-Muslim rule was nonexistent during the first several centuries of Islam? If submission to the enemy had never before taken place when the early jurists determined the rule for the original case (of lone converts), then it cannot provide the rationale for the first case of this, nor can it be common to the two cases.

Could the analogists have meant that a new kind of submission to the enemy arose after the Christian conquests of Sicily and al-Andalus, not that it arose for the first time in the fifth century (eleventh century CE)? Buṣādī anticipates and rejects this counter-argument by asserting that the two instances of submission are exactly the same. In both cases, a man's identity as a Muslim precedes his voluntary residence in *dār al-ḥarb*. This is obvious in the new case, argues Buṣādī, and is likewise true of the original case. The convert is only a Muslim in non-Muslim territory after his conversion, when he becomes subject to the laws of Islam.

46 See appendix B, 299. Note that Wansharīsī does not explicitly identify an *ʿilla* because he denies using analogical reasoning.

At this point, Buṣādī's insistence that these two cases are analogous is curious, because he seems to deploy the same logic as Wansharīsī. Wansharīsī had claimed that the two cases are one; they are both instances of a Muslim in infidel territory. Wansharīsī argued that it was irrelevant whether this was a result of the person's change in status (the lone convert) or the territory's change in status (the conquered Muslim); this difference was without legal consequence. Yet, the difference in these two scholars' arguments is that Buṣādī only grants that the two scenarios produce a single result with respect to the Muslim's submission to infidel rule. He does not believe that this submission is an effective cause (*ʿilla*) that allows the established legal judgments on converts' property to be extended to conquered Muslims. Thus, he maintains a disparity in the cases with respect to property rights.

Buṣādī concludes his summary of the analogists' position by revisiting Wansharīsī's claims that the early masters only discussed the case of converts and were silent regarding the new case, that of conquered Muslims. Buṣādī's aim is to establish that this analogy, based on the specific *ʿilla* of submission to infidel rule, is his opponents' sole evidence for declaring the property of conquered Muslims to be licit. Buṣādī asserts that once it is established that this analogy (based on this *ʿilla*) is his opponents' only evidence, then there can be no recourse to any other *ʿilla*, nor any appeal to additional evidence, should this *ʿilla* prove to be invalid.

Although Buṣādī affirms the accepted Mālikī position that a lone convert's property (and children) are licit before they are brought to *dār al-Islām*, he reviews a passage from *Asnā al-matājir* in which Wansharīsī differentiates this position from the alternatives.[47] He highlights the two areas of scholarly disagreement found there: is what guarantees the inviolability of a Muslim's property his being Muslim or his residence in *dār al-Islām*, and are *ḥarbī*s (non-Muslim residents of *dār al-ḥarb*)[48] considered to have legally valid ownership of their own possessions (that is, do Muslims grant that they have property rights). Buṣādī's purpose is to establish aspects of the Mālikī position that will aid him in refuting the validity of his opponents' analogy.

On the basis of the passage cited, Buṣādī makes two initial "notes" and establishes three related points. His first note is that power is not a requisite for ownership. An explicit proof text indicates that the property

---

47 The passage in *Asnā al-matājir* that Buṣādī cites includes an excerpt from Ibn al-ʿArabī's *ʿĀriḍat al-aḥwadhī* and commentary by Wansharīsī. See appendix B, 303–5; Wansharīsī, *al-Miʿyār*, 2:127–28; and Hendrickson, "Islamic Obligation," 359–61. For a discussion of this passage in the context of *Asnā al-matājir*, see chapter 5.

48 The term *ḥarbī* is derived from *dār al-ḥarb*. As opposed to *dhimmī*s, who are Jews or Christians living under Muslim rule, *ḥarbī*s are non-Muslims who normally reside in non-Muslim territory (though they might travel outside it). Although the literal meaning of *ḥarb* is war, these terms do not indicate active warfare; they simply indicate territory that is not under Muslim rule (*dār al-ḥarb*) and the non-Muslims who live there (*ḥarbī*s).

of Muslim prisoners of war is inviolable, while Muslims whose property is seized by *ḥarbī*s likewise remain the rightful owners. Thus, the converts' state of infidelity at the time of acquisition, not their powerlessness, must be the rationale for the violability of their property.

In his second note, Buṣādī asserts that while new converts must bring their property to Muslim territory in order to establish legal ownership of it, the continued inviolability of that property is not contingent on these converts' remaining in Muslim territory. He acknowledges that one could interpret statements such as "the guarantor of inviolability is being in Muslim territory," and "the Muslim does not have real ownership if he is among them (non-Muslims in *dār al-ḥarb*)," to mean that continued residence in Muslim territory is required to maintain ownership, and that it would not be sufficient, for example, to make a single trip to establish ownership and then return to *dār al-ḥarb*. Yet the analogists did not interpret these statements from earlier jurists in this way. If the analogists interpreted these statements to mean that continued residence in Muslim territory is required to maintain property rights, then these precedents would apply directly to both converts and conquered Muslims, a possibility that is negated by the analogists' claims that (1) no direct precedent addresses conquered Muslims, and that (2) converts are an earlier case, the rules for which may be extended to the later case of conquered Muslims.

The three points that Buṣādī establishes in relation to this passage on inviolability (from *Asnā al-matājir*) are straightforward. The first, based on a direct statement attributed to Mālik, is that the property of converts only becomes inviolable once it is brought to *dār al-Islām*. The second point is that the early jurists' scholarly disagreement regarding the guarantor of inviolability (territory or religion) pertains specifically to the means by which a person's property initially becomes inviolable after it had been licit (as in the case of the convert). This disagreement (territory or religion) did not address the factors that might cause a loss of inviolability for previously protected property. Buṣādī's third point is that the other scholarly disagreement (do *ḥarbī*s have property rights?) relates only to the property that these *ḥarbī*s obtained while they were infidels (in *dār al-ḥarb*); the property obtained by converts once they had become Muslims was not addressed in this dispute.

Critique 1: The Conquered Muslim and Lone Convert are Disparate Cases

Once these points are established, Buṣādī argues that the rationale specified by the analogists (submission to infidel rule) is invalid. If this submission was a valid *ʿilla* for the rule (i.e., that a Muslim's property is licit) in both of the cases in question, one of two impossible propositions would also have to be true: either (1) a Muslim's submission to infidel rule is what renders that Muslim's property licit in general (regardless of the prior status of the property), or (2) a Muslim's submission to infidel rule renders only his previously inviolable property licit (as in the case of conquered Muslims). The first proposition is not possible because the violability of the convert's property precedes his submission to non-Muslim rule, according to the argument (introduced above) that he was not a Muslim residing in *dār al-ḥarb*, in submission to infidel rule, until his conversion. Because an effect cannot precede a cause, the convert's sudden illegitimate residence cannot be the reason for the pre-existing and ongoing violability of his property.

As for the second proposition, that this illegitimate residence is the *ʿilla* for making previously inviolable property licit: this would work for the new case of conquered Muslims, but it is not possible for the case of the convert. This is because the convert's property is initially licit and remains so until he has transported it to *dār al-Islām*, where he must establish valid ownership of it. Thus, it is rationally impossible, asserts Buṣādī, for a Muslim's residence in enemy territory under infidel rule to be the effective cause that renders his property licit.

Nor is it possible, Buṣādī continues, for residence in *dār al-ḥarb* (as a Muslim who has submitted to infidel rule) to be a legal obstacle (*mānʿ*) that prevents the convert from being granted the property rights that are normally associated with being Muslim. This is because a legal obstacle cannot block something that does not yet exist; the convert cannot lose his property rights because of this residence if he had never established those rights in the first place, as in the case of any convert who has remained in *dār al-ḥarb* (and not traveled to *dār al-Islām* to establish ownership). In the case of the convert, the condition for inviolability is absent, rather than a hindrance to inviolability being present.

Buṣādī ultimately declares that the only possible *ʿilla* explaining the rule for the original case (the convert's property) is the convert's state of unbelief prior to his conversion. This unbelief is only present in the original case, and thus may not serve as a shared *ʿilla* that would allow a jurist to apply the established rule to the new case. The conquered Muslim was at no prior point an unbeliever. While Wansharīsī rejected the argument (advanced by Ibn al-Ḥājj) that the convert's prior state of unbelief distinguished his property rights from those of a conquered Muslim, for Buṣādī that past unbelief is relevant and consequential because it renders these two cases too disparate to support the analogy that he attributes to Wansharīsī (i.e., that the lack of property rights in both cases results from a single, shared cause, which is Muslim submission to infidel rule).

Critique 2: The Analogists' Rationale Contradicts Mālikī Precedent

Once this disparity between these two cases is established, Buṣādī pursues his second primary critique of his opponents' analogy. He argues that the *ʿilla*, that they use to explain why a convert's property is licit (that is, submission to non-Muslim rule) contradicts the established Mālikī rationale for this rule. Buṣādī reiterates Mālik's clear position that *ḥarbī*s (including converts prior to conversion) do not have valid ownership of their property. This lack of true ownership, Buṣādī adds, is the reason that any property acquired prior to conversion is licit. While Mālik's position as described by Wansharīsī and others is that mere conversion does not render the new convert's property inviolable (only bringing it to *dār al-Islām* does this), Buṣādī frames this position differently by adding the following qualification: Mere conversion does not render the convert's property inviolable because it is Muslim territory, not being Muslim, that is the guarantor of inviolability *for property acquired while still an infidel.* By contrast, in Buṣādī's reframing of Mālik's position, property acquired while Muslim, even for a new convert remaining in *dār al-ḥarb*, is immediately inviolable.

Thus, Buṣādī insists that being an infidel at the time of acquisition, rather than being in infidel territory, is what makes property licit. While submission to infidel rule may entail sin and compromise probity, he notes, this sin has no legal effect on the property a convert had before converting. This argument, while seemingly straightforward, requires Buṣādī to furnish evidence distinguishing the convert's existing property from any property he acquires after conversion. The strongest precedent at Buṣādī's disposal is an opinion attributed to an early Mālikī scholar, Abū al-Ḥasan, who held that Mālik's position allowing a convert's property to be seized as booty only applies to property acquired as an infidel. If we recall the problem raised by Waryāglī's *fatwā* (in part 1) of distinguishing Muslims from non-Muslims in enemy territory, this additional distinction between the property owned by a convert to Islam before and after his conversion sounds impractical. How would an invading Muslim soldier know the difference between property that must be respected as inviolable, and property that may be used or taken as booty, especially when that soldier often cannot even establish who is Muslim and who is not? This is a problem that Buṣādī is not only aware of, but that he uses in support of conquered Muslims' property rights later in his treatise (below).

Buṣādī's Counter-Analogy and Defense of Conquered Muslims' Property Rights

At this point in his argument, Buṣādī proposes that a proper analogy between converts and conquered Muslims would prove the opposite of what the analogists have intended. The original legal problem in the analogy (the *aṣl*), he argues, should not be the legal status of (all) property belonging to converts in *dār al-ḥarb*; rather, it should be the legal status of property acquired by converts *after* their conversion to Islam in *dār al-ḥarb*. The rule applied to this case, which is that these new converts' property is inviolable, would then be extended to the case of conquered Muslims. With this counter-analogy, Buṣādī completes what he admits has been a belabored refutation of the *ʿilla* in his opponents' analogy.

Buṣādī then shifts his attention to the undesirable result of his opponents' analogy, which is to render licit the property of conquered Muslims. It is wrong, he argues, to suspend a Muslim's property rights merely because he has committed a sin (in this case, residence in enemy territory). Buṣādī asserts that it is widely acknowledged that only an act of infidelity should render a Muslim's inviolable property licit. He further suggests that it would be impractical to implement a rule allowing property to be seized only from those Muslims who are capable of emigrating. How would these Muslims be distinguished from those who are legitimately exempt from emigrating? If these groups of able and exempt Muslims were commingled, how could the inviolable property be protected and only the licit property be seized?

Buṣādī follows these rhetorical questions with a series of textual precedents meant to bolster the position that conquered Muslims retain their property rights. He first revisits the Barcelona precedent, also cited in *Asnā al-matājir*, that Ibn al-Ḥājj used to distinguish between converts to Islam and those who are born as Muslims.[49] In the relevant passage, Mālik's disciple Ibn al-Qāsim addresses those Muslims who remained in Barcelona after it was conquered in 185/801. Although they sought to protect themselves by fighting for their Christian conquerors against other Muslims, Ibn al-Qāsim states that because they are still Muslim, their property is not licit. For Buṣādī, this explicit and specific text from an early Mālikī authority demonstrates that residence in *dār al-ḥarb* does not change the status of a Muslim's existing, inviolable property.

Implicit in his use of the Barcelona example is Buṣādī's a fortiori argument that if conquered Muslims who fight against other Muslims retain their property rights, so too should Muslims who commit no sin other than continuing to reside in their conquered homelands. He makes this argument explicit in two precedents related to Kharijites and apostates. Buṣādī notes that according to early Mālikīs, Kharijites who attacked other Muslims could be killed in battle, but their property was not to be taken. If Kharijites, whom some jurists do not even consider Muslim, retain the inviolability of their property even when fighting against Muslims, Buṣādī

49 On this passage, see chapter 5 and appendix B.

argues, then surely conquered Muslims retain these rights. As if this were not evidence enough, he continues, scholars such as Mālik and Ibn al-Qāsim supported the continued inviolability of property belonging to apostates. If a man commits apostasy, flees, and fights against Muslims, and even if he does these things for rest of his life, these authorities held that his property remains inviolable until such time as he is asked to repent and return to Islam, and refuses.[50] Buṣādī stresses that if an apostate's property is not made licit, then it does not make sense to declare the property of conquered Muslims licit because they reside in non-Muslim territory.

Perhaps to ensure that this series of comparisons with traitors, sectarians, and apostates does not present conquered Muslims in a negative light, at this juncture Buṣādī reminds his readers that affiliation with non-Muslims is not of one kind, but varies, from behavior that is considered indicative of unbelief to behavior that is recommended. He argues that verses such as Qurʾān 5:51 and 9:23, according to which the allies of unbelievers are considered like unbelievers, were revealed only with regard to those who approve of unbelief and thus may be considered apostates. Those who do not approve of unbelief and do not commit apostasy, but who are friendly to unbelievers and reside among them voluntarily—the actions of this groups are prohibited. Muslims who affiliate with infidel family members, with no harm to Muslims, represent a third group whose actions may be recommended. Buṣādī supports this category in part by citing Qurʾān 60:8, the same verse Sidiyya Baba adduced to permit residence under French rule and that Murabbīh Rabbuh used to argue the opposite of Sidiyya Baba's view (in conjunction with 60:9). Buṣādī's final category is permissible residence for Muslims who are compelled. Here he cites, without elaboration, Qurʾān 3:28, the *taqiyya* verse so often cited by his peers to justify submission to Christian rule.

Buṣādī's Conclusion: Challenging Legal Filth in Mauritania

Buṣādī begins his conclusion to *Prohibition on Plundering* with the final statement in his sustained refutation of his opponents' analogy between converts and conquered Muslims. While Wansharīsī praised his forebears' assimilation of these two cases as being of "of the utmost excellence and beauty," Buṣādī counters that it was in fact "of the utmost corruption and filth."[51] Rather than the two cases being "completely equivalent," Buṣādī considers them to be complete opposites, as follows:

---

50 In general, if a Muslim is accused of apostasy, he must be asked to repent three times before the penalty for apostasy, which is death, may be applied. See *EI*³, s.v. "Apostasy" (Frank Griffel).

51 See appendix B, 299; Hendrickson, "Islamic Obligation," 458.

- In the original case of the convert to Islam residing in *dār al-ḥarb,* the subject of legal judgment is that portion of the convert's property over which he has not established legal ownership (by bringing it to *dār al-Islām*). The rule is that this property is licit, while the rationale (*ʿilla*) for this judgment is the owner's unbelief at the time of acquisition. In the new case (of the conquered Muslims), a legal rule is needed concerning these Muslims' property after the conquest. In contrast to the first case, this is property over which they had already established ownership (prior to the conquest). The rule for this new case is that their property is inviolable, because the owner was Muslim at the time of acquisition.
- In the original case (of the convert), the complication that arises is the owner's conversion to Islam; under the presumption of continuity (*istiṣḥāb*), his property remains licit. In the new case (of the conquered Muslim), the complication that arises is the owner's (sudden) residence in non-Muslim territory; under the same presumption, his property remains inviolable.
- In the original case (of the convert), this property remains licit regardless of whether or not the Muslim's continued residence in *dār al-ḥarb* is willful, while in the new case (of the conquered Muslim), the property of an owner who is exempt from the obligation to emigrate cannot become licit in any circumstance.

The remainder of *Prohibition on Plundering* addresses the implications of Buṣādī's critique for the current situation in Mauritania. He states that the region's people are afflicted by severe crises as well as internal discord and disagreement. They are filled with dread and subject to plunder, banditry, and violence. What if, for the sake of argument, one accepted that a convert in *dār al-ḥarb* and a conquered Muslim were analogous; and claimed that many of these people are obligated to emigrate; and claimed that if they remain, their property will be plundered? In that case, Buṣādī argues, another principle would have to be considered: Any prohibited act that is an offense against God (rather than against other humans) becomes permitted in cases in which one fears for one's life, family, and property. Emigration is such an offense, emphasizes Buṣādī, and no one with any knowledge of these people's conditions could deny their tremendous state of fear, nor claim that they are content to live under Christian rule. Even when some of them have managed to emigrate, they have been met with hostility instead of support and been forced to return home. In support of these arguments, Buṣādī cites the opinions of Ibn Abī Zayd al-Qayrawānī and Burzulī and reproduces part of Māzarī's *fatwā* on Sicilian judges, including his appeal to give these Muslims the benefit of the doubt as to the reasons for their continued residence under Christian rule.

Buṣādī finishes with a scathing rebuke of his fellow jurists. They have grasped at a convenient analogy and applied it indiscriminately and relentlessly, he states, thereby risking the lives and property of fellow Muslims. Despite the warnings of God and the pious ancestors, laments Buṣādī, those unqualified to derive legal rulings from analogy (*qiyās*) have done so and have corrupted the law as a result. Buṣādī supports this rebuke by citing favorably a passage from another of Wansharīsī's *fatwās*, one on reprehensible versus commendable innovations; thus, he uses Wansharīsī's own words against him (and the other analogists). In the cited passage, Wansharīsī condemns the issuance of *fatwās* by those ignorant of the law, as this is an innovation that leads to calamity and the destruction of religion and people. His proof texts include a *ḥadīth* forecasting the issuance of baseless opinions by ignoramuses who err and lead others astray. Wansharīsī also cites the opinion of an earlier scholar who complained that in his time people without knowledge had taken to evaluating sources of disagreement for themselves, picking from among them the opinion, from any school of law, best suited to their interests. These people would take it upon themselves to determine what is prohibited and permitted, misinterpreting and abusing dispensations and deviant opinions, and sometimes even violating scholarly consensus.

Buṣādī's primary purpose in *Prohibition on Plundering* is to defend Mauritanians residing under French rule against theft, violence, and condemnation by their fellow Muslims. To this end, he undermines the legal rationale that justifies such harmful actions, a rationale that he finds at the heart of Wansharīsī's *Asnā al-matājir*. Yet in arguing that Muslims residing under French rule retain their property rights, Buṣādī is not siding with those Mauritanian scholars who argued in favor of submission to French rule, nor are those scholars spared his closing critique. Buṣādī does not name these scholars, but assures readers that he is not partial to lenient opinions that excuse residence under non-Muslim rule. It is absolutely prohibited, he affirms, for those capable of emigrating to remain under the control of those who deny the revelation of the Qurʾān and the prophethood of Muḥammad. Buṣādī closes with a prayer and, in one manuscript of the text, a poem summarizing the *fatwā*.

The Mauritanian *hijra* debate, fascinating in its own right, serves as our second test case for the long-term impact of the Maghribī opinions presented earlier in this book. For Mauritanian jurists, the Algerian case was an added layer in their engagement with those more distant precedents, a prior grappling with French colonization that left a clear mark on their own case. It may not be surprising, then, that the results of this second test case resemble those of the first: we find but a scant trace of Zayyātī's "jewels," Wansharīsī's *fatwās* remain the dominant Mālikī precedents on emigration, and Wahrānī's letter is not mentioned at all.

Beyond confirming this pattern of relationships with precedents, the Mauritanian case offers us a distinct vantage point from which to understand our late fifteenth- and early sixteenth-century opinions. We consider each of them in turn. First, the presence of Zayyātī's "jewels" here is negligible, despite their relevance to aspects of the arguments of Sīdī al-Mukhtār and Murabbīh Rabbuh. As these texts already played little role in the Algerian *hijra* debate, perhaps, by the time of the Mauritanian case in the twentieth century, they had simply faded into obscurity. In their wake, Mauritanian jurists introduced dozens of new sources into the *hijra* debate, focusing in particular on works of Qur'ānic exegesis, *ḥadīth* commentaries, and commentaries on the *Mukhtaṣar Khalīl*, the prominent textbook of Mālikī law.

Of the two reasons offered in chapter 7 for the relative paucity of references to Zayyātī's "jewels" in Algeria, one remains more salient than the other. As the pro-*hijra* jurists in Mauritania were confronted by an array of arguments in favor of submission to French rule, the lack of attention to counter-arguments in the *fatwās* Zayyātī preserved may have been problematic. By contrast, Wansharīsī's refutation of potential counter-arguments and his curatorial work in assembling a wealth of precedents that could be selectively arranged and redeployed made his opinions far more adaptable to new circumstances.

The "news of al-Andalus," meaning the near extinction of Iberian Islam as a result of Christian conquests, was less poignant for Mauritanians, who were at a greater temporal and geographic remove from Iberia than their Algerian counterparts. The pro-*hijra* jurists in Mauritania apparently made no attempt to claim the Morisco period as predictive of French intentions, while their accommodationist opponents dismissed the Iberian context as incomparable and therefore irrelevant to their present reality. Instead, Sidiyya Baba saw French colonialism in Senegal as the most relevant historical precedent by which to understand Muslims' likely fate under Christian rule. Thus, while Wansharīsī's evocation of a tragic Iberian past rendered his *fatwās* more relevant to the Algerian case than Zayyātī's "jewels," this factor is far less salient in the Mauritanian case.

Nonetheless, even the Mauritanians who argued that it was acceptable to reside under French rule agreed with Wansharīsī that Iberian Muslims had been obligated to emigrate. We can expect that the fall of al-Andalus remained a powerful communal memory undergirding the continued prominence of Wansharīsī's *fatwās* even in this remote context. His memorable imagery certainly continued to inspire jurists like Sīdī al-Mukhtār, who implored his cousin not to imitate *Asnā al-matājir*'s ill-fated emigrants.

Yet while Wansharīsī's *fatwās* remained the most influential individual opinions on *hijra* in the case of Mauritania, this case reminds us that their success in achieving such a long-term authoritative status was not inevitable. These opinions were disputed and contested; they did not reflect a univocal, stable Mālikī consensus or "orthodoxy" at the time of composition. Buṣādī's *Prohibition on Plundering*, the Mauritanian pro-accommodation *fatwās*, and Ibn al-Shāhid's *fatwā* all demonstrate that *Asnā al-matājir* and the Marbella *fatwā* rested on questionable legal reasoning and arguable interpretations of the relevant proof texts.

Further, the plethora of accommodationist opinions unique to this case suggest that a few arguments condoning residence under Christian rule stood the test of time. In part 2, we saw that Wansharīsī withheld mention of Ibn Rabīʿ's opponent, but refuted each of that jurist's arguments (the "no *hijra*" *ḥadīth*, the ability to practice Islam, the opportunity to spread Islam, and the protection provided by treaties). In addition to these arguments, Wansharīsī rejected the two claims to exemption illustrated by Ibn Qaṭiyya's questions; namely, the inability to emigrate, and the desirability of assisting weaker Muslims. While we find new arguments against *hijra* in the Mauritanian case, the articulation of most of these old arguments, previously revealed only in refutations to them, helps us to imagine that jurists also voiced these arguments against *hijra* in Wansharīsī's time. The need to defeat such competing alternatives in part explains the length and complexity of Wansharīs's *fatwās*, especially considering his strategic insistence that his work reflects an indisputable scholarly consensus.

That said, there may not have been a jurist like Sidiyya Baba in Wansharīsī's time. Wansharīsī would likely have seen Sidiyya Baba's offenses as greater than those of the contented fishermen and regretful emigrants combined. He not only openly rejected *hijra* and claimed that French-ruled territories were superior in law and order, but actively worked alongside the colonial authorities to propagate this view. He appeared to pray contentedly not only for the continuation of French rule, but also for its expansion. In Sidiyya Baba we have one kind of antithesis to Wansharīsī, a figure who—alongside Buṣādī—places Wahrānī in a new light. Bold and unapologetic, Sidiyya Baba sought to persuade his fellow Muslims to accept French rule voluntarily and without reservations. By contrast, Wahrānī wrote furtively to an oppressed group without access to the three options with which this chapter opened (submit to Muslim life under Christian rule, fight, or flee). Had Wahrānī prioritized open contestation with fellow jurists rather than sympathetic and secretive advice, he might well have endangered the very people he was attempting to serve. A longer, more detailed treatise might have been discovered by the Christian authorities in Granada, to the detriment of the Moriscos, or those same authorities might have been apprised of the text's deliberate circulation in North Africa.

Buṣādī represents a second, very different kind of antithesis to Wansharīsī. Ironically, it was not a figure like Sidiyya Baba who produced a scholarly rebuttal to *Asnā al-matājir*, but a jurist who agreed completely with Wansharīsī regarding the obligation to emigrate, such that he abandoned his homeland and emigrated in the face of French colonialism. Yet Buṣādī also recognized that this choice was impractical for most and that attempts to identify and punish those who remained voluntarily were dubious, harmful, and illegitimate.

Prohibition on Plundering, a treatise the length of *Asnā al-matājir* and the Marbella *fatwā* combined, is also a good example of what a serious refutation involves. While Wahrānī's letter is written as a comforting and practical guide for lay Muslims, with one symbolic citation of an earlier jurist's opinion and a handful of allusions to scriptural proof texts, Buṣādī's text is a substantial and sustained technical critique of the legal reasoning Wansharīsī employs, supplemented with several related arguments grounded in revealed proof texts and the authoritative commentaries of earlier jurists, crafted in a high rhetorical style, and explicitly intended to change the prevailing legal discourse. As important as Wahrānī's letter was for generations of Moriscos, it was was not equal to *Asnā al-matājir* in the scholarly arena.

CONCLUSION

Centering the Maghrib

I will sweep up from Africa, and thus the empire of the one God, the true God Allah, will spread.

First, across Spain. Then, across Europe.

Then, the whole world![1]

These are the words of Almoravid ruler Yūsuf b. Tāshufīn (r. 463–500/1071–1106) in the opening scene of *El Cid*, the 1961 historical epic starring Charlton Heston and Sophia Loren. The year is 1080 according to the voice-over, or rather "one thousand and eighty years after the coming of Christ," a simple rhetorical flourish that grounds the film's worldview in Christian imagery even before we meet our Muslim villain. The sun sets over a beautiful Spanish landscape, featuring a fortress on a grassy hill with a town nestled in the valley below. The narrator tells us that this is the story of Spain's greatest hero, Rodrigo Díaz (d. 1099), known as "El Cid," or "the Lord." He rose above religious hatreds, we are told, to unite both Christians and "Moors" against a common enemy who threatened to destroy their land.

That enemy is Yūsuf, who is "gathering his savage forces" on the northern shores of Africa. The camera pans south to a craggy hill overlooking the Mediterranean, where Yūsuf arrives on horseback to the steady beat of war drums. The drums continue as a black-clad figure dismounts and strides toward the Andalusī *amīr*s kneeling before him. As his face comes into view, we are drawn to Yūsuf's black-rimmed eyes, the rest of his face concealed by a black turban. He comes to a halt, eyes widening, and proclaims "The Prophet has commanded us to rule the world!" Drums still beating, Yūsuf delivers a stern invective, castigating the kneeling figures for their association with poetry, music, and science. "You have become *women*!" he spits with disdain, commanding them to train warriors, to invent war machines, to kill, and to burn. As the music builds to a crescendo, Yūsuf

1 *El Cid*, directed by Anthony Mann, 1961 ([New York]: The Weinstein Company, 2008), DVD.

reveals his plans for world domination, quoted above, and suddenly thrusts one arm toward the camera, fingers bending forward as if to grasp or to choke. His face and eyes lift upward until the frame freezes, fixing Yūsuf in this menacing pose. He then fades away, replaced by a piercing bright light on the opposite shore, seemingly in the shape of a cross.

This scene paints a stark, hierarchical divide between Iberia and its inferior, southern neighbor. Spain is a source of light, a beautiful homeland to be protected; a place of chivalry, honor, and heroes; a Christian land, but one that values religious coexistence; a place of culture and enlightenment, where the arts and sciences flourish. The Maghrib is dark, a harsh African landscape home to a fanatic Muslim villain and his savage followers. They disdain knowledge and culture and degrade women; they are foreign zealots poised to destroy Spain and to impose their barbaric form of Islam over all of Europe—unless defeated.

El Cid's portrayal of the Ibero-Maghribī divide is the caricature that we would expect from a Hollywood production. Yet aspects of this portrayal have been shared by popular as well as academic histories of medieval Iberia.[2] The Almoravids and Almohads have often been depicted as uncivilized fanatics who destroyed a vibrant culture of interreligious tolerance unique to Iberia.[3] In such portrayals, Maghribīs become an important foil by which Iberians, including Andalusī Muslims, may shine more brightly. In other instances, connections between Iberia and the Maghrib are suppressed or relevant Maghribī actors and processes ignored, thereby exaggerating the exceptionalism of medieval Iberia. The Strait of Gibraltar has provided the physical separation that renders these sharp divisions plausible and the modern borders that have made them desirable, for nations that seek to articulate their own distinct histories.

One of my primary goals in *Leaving Iberia* has been to challenge the Ibero-centric approaches dominant in a particular facet of the shared history of Iberia and North Africa: Islamic legal responses to Christian conquest. At their most extreme, scholarly portrayals of Wansharīsī have easily rivaled *El Cid*'s menacing portrait of Yūsuf b. Tāshufīn. Wansharīsī has been a cruel villain gazing across the strait from his perch in North Africa, stretching out the arm of the law to condemn and ultimately destroy a people whose values he disdained and whose challenges he dismissed, good Iberian Muslims whose only fault was their love of Spain. In more tempered portrayals,

2 This congruence was not a coincidence, as Spanish historian Ramón Menéndez Pidal was a primary advisor to the film. See Richard Fletcher, *The Quest for El Cid* (Oxford: Oxford University Press, 1989), 4–5.

3 See Menocal, *Ornament of the World*, 43 and 45. In reality, the Almoravids had no plans to conquer Iberia. They first entered al-Andalus reluctantly and in response to repeated calls for aid from the Muslim *ṭāʾifa* rulers. See Bennison, *Almoravid and Almohad Empires*, esp. 40–48.

Wansharīsī was simply a "rigorist" who interpreted the law strictly with regard to Mudéjars' obligations and legal status. Yet these approaches share a consistent assumption that Wansharīsī's *fatwās* were focused solely on Andalusī Muslims and that they are best understood in conversation with other opinions regarding conquered Iberians or Sicilians.

The central case study of this book, in part 2, shows that these well-known views are better understood in their North African context, as an extension and willful replacement of Maghribī jurists' earlier opinions regarding Portuguese occupation of parts of Morocco. Many of the clues necessary for discovering Wansharīsī's hidden commentary on Maghribī politics were hiding in plain sight, so to speak, obscured only by our overriding interest in Mudéjars. As I show in chapter 4, Wansharīsī is transparent about the Maghribī identity of his questioner (*mustaftī*) and immediate audience, Ibn Qaṭiyya; the Maghrib-based crime and exemplary punishment proposed for *Asnā al-matājir*'s unhappy emigrants; his fear of *fitna* spreading among those exposed to the emigrants; and his patriotic defense of a slandered Maghrib. In chapter 5, the deeper detective work distinguishes Wansharīsī's original contributions to *Asnā al-matājir* and the Marbella *fatwā* from the materials he "borrowed" from Ibn Rabīʿ. These original contributions confirm a textual link to Wansharīsī's Berber *fatwā* and his persistent concern with Muslim submission to Portuguese control in the Maghrib.

Meanwhile, the body of Portuguese-focused Maghribī opinions preserved in Zayyātī's *Selected Jewels* has been overlooked or even suppressed. No sooner did these "jewels" come to light than at least one medieval historian dismissed them as "unlikely," insisting that Muslim submission to Portuguese rule in Morocco was too insignificant for Maghribī jurists to have addressed the topic and therefore, that these opinions must pertain to Iberia, not to the Maghrib.[4]

Regardless of how fascinating or unique we find the course of Muslim history or interreligious relations in Iberia, it is unreasonable to suggest that Maghribī jurists did not think and write about the Maghrib. The historical overview offered in chapter 1 shows that jurists concerned with Muslim sovereignty had plenty to write about in the fifteenth- and early sixteenth-century Maghrib, including the foreign control of Morocco's most important ports, the southward expansion of Christian conquests into North Africa, the launch of Portugal's overseas empire, and the competition between Iberian powers for the rights to "reconquer" Maghribī and other African lands.

And these jurists did write. Despite their relative obscurity, the legal opinions related to Portuguese rule that I have analyzed in chapter 3 are

4 Verskin, *Islamic Law*, 22 and 103–4. See part 1.

nearly as numerous as the *fatwās* scholars have studied for the entire Mudéjar period in Iberia. These texts demonstrate that despite some key differences between the Iberian and Maghribī contexts, Muslim jurists saw that the Christian conquests in these two regions represented the same basic legal problem, to be addressed with reference to a shared set of legal concerns, categories, and proof texts. Beyond their value in improving our understanding of Islamic legal thought on this issue, these opinions also offer us invaluable insights as to the impact of foreign rule on Maghribī warriors, merchants, farmers, fishermen, tribespeople, students, husbands, and wives. Moreover, our knowledge of both Iberian and North African history is enriched by examining these texts, which reveal a deeply interconnected web of peoples, goods, and conquests in the western Mediterranean—both before and after the 1492 fall of Granada so often claimed as the natural fulfillment of the Christian Reconquest.

My second primary aim in *Leaving Iberia* has been to advance a new approach to understanding the construction and maintenance of authoritative precedents in Islamic law. I argue that even seemingly intolerant, reactionary opinions can be well adapted to the present circumstances, and that evaluating the enduring relevance or obscurity of opinions over time helps us to interrogate the factors that make some opinions more compelling than others for later jurists. In order to demonstrate the first point, in chapter 5 I undertook a detailed assessment of Wansharīsī's choices in crafting *Asnā al-matājir* and the Marbella *fatwā*, and reveal the considerable effort he expended in order to maintain the appearance of continuity with accepted doctrine.

Demonstrating the second point has encompassed all five case studies in *Leaving Iberia* and has widened our perspective beyond Iberia and North Africa to include colonial Mauritania. While Zayyātī's "jewels," Wansharīsī's 1491 *fatwās*, and Wahrānī's letter of advice to the Moriscos were all well adapted to their contexts, the Algerian and Mauritanian cases confirm that *Asnā al-matājir* and the Marbella *fatwā* were best positioned to serve as the opinions of record for future Mālikī jurists. I explain the enduring relevance of Wansharīsī's *fatwās* with regard to the questions' dramatic appeal; his strategic and often misleading use of past precedents; the inclusion of these *fatwās* in the *Miʿyār*; and the historic events that reaffirmed Wansharīsī's message for his audiences, especially for Algerians. Far from mechanically applying a fixed set of rules, Wansharīsī exercised considerable discretion in crafting opinions that were responsive to two contexts—those of the Mudéjars and Maghribīs—and had the potential to resonate with future jurists.

Those future jurists were not required or destined to find Wansharīsī's opinions correct or "orthodox," and indeed not all of them did. The Algerian and Mauritanian cases are especially valuable because they preserve alternative Mālikī positions on the obligation to emigrate. While dissenting positions also may have circulated in Wansharīsī's time, these later texts support the conclusion that Wahrānī's 1504 Letter should not be considered a dissenting voice. Algerian and Mauritanian jurists devoted substantial attention to *taqiyya* without alluding to Wahrānī; this suggests that it never circulated among North African jurists or that it was not considered a relevant or edifying precedent—after all, even if Wahrānī had engaged in a serious legal argument or critiqued the obligation to emigrate, the Moriscos' ultimate fate would have rendered his advice a poor precedent. Further, it is in Buṣādī's *Prohibition on Plundering* that we encounter a serious and direct refutation of *Asnā al-matājir*.

It is fitting that we must ultimately turn away from Iberia and look southward in order to find formidable opposition to Wansharīsī. If we return to the comparison between *El Cid*'s villain and the most extreme portrayals of Wansharīsī, this turns out to be a point of real common ground. While the Hollywood Almoravids were fixated on the conquest of Iberia, the historical Almoravids were primarily concerned with controlling and reforming the Muslims of the Maghrib. They did so until defeated by the Almohads, a second Berber empire arising from the south. Like the film caricature of Yūsuf b. Tāshufīn, the exaggerated, villainous version of Wansharīsī circulated his *fatwās* among Iberian Muslims, compelling many to leave, condemning those who stayed, and thereby rendering Iberian Islam too vulnerable to survive. In reality, those *fatwās* may not have crossed the strait, at least in his lifetime; instead they circulated among the Maghribī Muslims whose values and behaviors he most fervently sought to shape. And while Wansharīsī's opinions remain influential to this day, if we follow the Mālikī school's rich intellectual tradition and textual legacy southward we find that Buṣādī's critique reveals that these opinions are not timeless, nor are they seamless. Their excellence or corruption, their beauty or filth, must be continuously renegotiated.

Yet looking southward from Morocco defies scholarly convention. In the introduction to this book, I noted the formation of the Spain-North Africa Project (SNAP) and the call by its executive board for increased research that bridges the Iberia-North Africa divide. Contemporaneous with this development, a series of articles appeared in *Research in African Literatures* and the *Journal of African History* (*JAH*), in which another group of scholars critiqued a well-established divide between the study of North Africa and sub-Saharan Africa.[5] The latter is often considered

5 See Ziad Bentahar, "Continental Drift: The Disjunction of North and Sub-Saharan Africa," *Research in African Literatures* 42, no. 1 (2011): 1–13; Jean-Louis Triaud, "Giving a Name to

Africa "proper," while North Africa is portrayed as a world apart, racially and linguistically distinct from the remainder of the continent and better viewed from Europe or the Middle East as the southwestern shore of the Mediterranean or the western edge of Islamdom. Some of these presumptions are relatively new, such as the French colonial insistence that *Islam noire* (black Islam) is distinct from the Arab Islam of North Africa or the *Islam maure* (Moorish Islam) of West Africa. Other presumptions are quite old, such as the European "civilizational bias" that has, historically, favored the once-Roman northern coast of Africa. To look south from the Maghrib has often been to look down, to lands considered remote not only from the interests and advancements of European societies but also from the "pure" Islam of the Arabs.

Major historical peoples and processes that have connected North Africa to the Sahara and beyond include extensive trade networks (especially the movement of West African gold and slaves into the Mediterranean world); the Almoravid Empire's expansion into Ghana in the late eleventh century; Moroccan expansion into Songhay in the late sixteenth century; a shared tradition of Islamic thought and practice, including traveling scholars and *ḥajj* caravans; direct links between French colonial administrators in Algeria and in Mauritania in the nineteenth and twentieth centuries; and African migration into North Africa and the Mediterranean in the twenty-first century. Just as the SNAP executive board inventoried past scholarship linking Iberia to North Africa, those lamenting the Maghrib's marginalization from African studies also note substantial work by earlier scholars who have indeed bridged the African divide. Curiously, the SNAP executive board's "Unity and Disunity across the Strait of Gibraltar," and Ghislaine Lydon's contribution to the parallel discourse on Africa, "Saharan Oceans and Bridges," open in precisely the same way, with reference to Fernand Braudel's expansive vision of geographic connectivity across the Mediterranean and North Africa—down to and including the Sahara.[6] Yet aside from a shared appeal to the pivotal figure

Islam South of the Sahara: An Adventure in Taxonomy," *Journal of African History* 55 (2014): 3–15; Scott S. Reese, "Islam in Africa/Africans and Islam," *Journal of African History* 55 (2014): 17–26; Benjamin Soares, "The Historiography of Islam in West Africa: An Anthopologist's View," *Journal of African History* 55 (2014): 27–36; Ghislaine Lydon, "Saharan Oceans and Bridges, Barriers and Divides in Africa's Historiographical Landscape," *Journal of African History* 56 (2015): 3–22; and Baz Lecocq, "Distant Shores: A Historiographical View on Trans-Saharan Space," *Journal of African History* 56 (2015): 23–36.

6 Liang, et al., "Unity and Disunity," 1–2; Lydon, "Saharan Oceans," 3–4. See the group of articles noted above for additional references to works linking North Africa to Saharan or sub-Saharan Africa. Of particular note is E. Ann McDougall, "Research in Saharan History," *Journal of African History* 39 (1998): 467–80.

of Braudel, these calls to incorporate North Africa into a broader frame of reference pull in opposing directions.[7]

In *Leaving Iberia* I respond to both of these calls for inclusion, placing the Maghrib in the middle of a Mālikī world that stretches from al-Andalus to West Africa and across northern Africa. More fundamentally, I center this book on the Maghrib by placing Maghribī texts and actors firmly in their North African context, asking first and foremost what they might have meant for Maghribī audiences.

7 The third scholarly trend that must be mentioned here is the recent resurgence of Mediterranean studies. As noted in my introduction, *Leaving Iberia* contributes to this field but also shares what Eric Calderwood describes in *Colonial al-Andalus: Spain and the Making of Modern Moroccan Culture* as a "vexed relationship" with Mediterranean studies (Calderwood, *Colonial al-Andalus*, 23–24). While supportive of this field's focus on cross-cultural interactions and the need to overcome national divides, I share Calderwood's concern that "Mediterranean" is often an asymmetrical category, one that allows southern Europeans to claim intercultural tolerance and encourages northern Africans to emphasize proximity to Europe. Furthermore, while definitions of North Africa occasionally include Mauritania (often as a peripheral appendage to the Maghrib), the current scholarly conception of the Mediterranean, not unlike the Roman one, deemphasizes the Sahara and orients the African littoral northward toward the sea.

APPENDICES

APPENDIX A

Al-Jawāhir al-mukhtāra fīmā waqaftu ʿalayh min al-nawāzil bi-Jibāl Ghumāra[1]

Selected Jewels: Legal Cases I Encountered in the Ghumāra Mountains

Excerpt from the Chapter on *Jihād*

Compiled by ʿAbd al-ʿAzīz b. al-Ḥasan al-Zayyātī (d. 1055/1645)

First *Fatwā* of Ibn Barṭāl[2]

The jurist Abū al-Ḥasan ʿAlī b. ʿAbd Allāh, who I believe is the one known as Ibn Barṭāl[3] (may God have mercy upon him) was asked about some people who have made an agreement with the Christians to the effect that they would pay a tribute to them [the Christians], and they would leave them [the Muslims] be, to reside in their lands. [The Muslims] fall into categories with regard to their [relations] with them. Among them are those who spy on the Muslims and convey information about them to them [the Christians]. There are also those who go trade among them [the Christians]. There are

1 This translation is based on my partial Arabic edition of Zayyātī's chapter on *jihād*, included as appendix D in Hendrickson, "Islamic Obligation," 411–36. My edition, the first of this text, is based primarily on the following three manuscripts: Moroccan National Library MS 1698, 2:1–74 (BNRM); Ḥasaniyya Library MS 5862, 225–67 (Ḥ); and General Library and Archives of Tetouan MS 178, 239–81 (T). These page ranges indicate the entire chapter on *jihād*; the specific range for each *fatwā* is given below. Only the Tetouan manuscript, copied in 1102/1691, bears a date. I have emended the text occasionally based on versions of these *fatwās* that appear in the following sources: Van Koningsveld, Wiegers, and Ryad's unpublished edition of Ibn Rabīʿ's *fatwā*; Wazzānī's two *fatwā* collections; and Tasūlī's unpublished *fatwā* compilation, *al-Jawāhir al-nafīsa fīmā yatakarraru min al-ḥawādith al-gharība* (*Precious Jewels, concerning Difficult and Recurring Cases*), Ḥasaniyya Library, MS 12575 and Tunisian National Library, MS 5354. This appendix follows the order of the texts as they appear in *al-Jawāhir al-mukhtāra*. The titles in italics are my own editorial additions.

2 BNRM, 2:40–41; Ḥ, 247; T, 262. Wazzānī incorporates a part of this *fatwā*, along with the two other *fatwās* by the same jurist found here, into one composite ruling in *al-Nawāzil al-ṣughrā*, 1:419.

3 On Ibn Barṭāl (d. ca. 901/1495), whose name is given most fully in the third of his *fatwās* below, see chapter 3.

those who have started fighting against them [the Muslims], who go forth into battle alongside the Christian soldiers and prevent the Muslims from reaching their enemy. Among them also are those who only pay the tribute, but who do not do any of the other things mentioned here. There is also among them a group whom the enemy has exempted from paying the tribute, including prayer leaders (*ṭalaba*) and callers to prayer (*muʾadhdhinūn*).[4] What is the judgment of God concerning their lives, property, ability to lead prayer, and ability to testify? What [status] applies to each of these groups? [Provide us with] a comprehensive answer.

He answered: The group of people who have concluded this pact with the Christians (may God the exalted destroy them) on the basis that they pay them tribute are a depraved people, disobedient to God, and in violation of the *sunna* [exemplary behavior] of His Prophet.

As for those who keep to their houses, and who do not frequent them [the Christians] for trade or for any other [purpose], but who pay them the tribute: they are disobedient to God on account of their payments to them and their remaining under submission. Thus their testimony is not permissible, nor is their leading of prayer. Nonetheless, their situation is less serious than the situation of those [Muslims] who go to them [the Christians] and make themselves useful for their interests. The status of this category [of Muslims who keep to their houses] is [as follows:] their property is not licit to anyone, nor are their lives violable.

As for those who spy on the Muslims, the commonly accepted view is that [taking] the life of a spy is licit, that he should be killed, and that his killer should be rewarded.

As for those who sell weapons to the Christians and join their army, this category has deviated from the religion and their status is [like] that of the Christians with regard to both lives and property.

As for those who have begun trading among them, they are depraved and they sin more gravely than those who keep to themselves at home.

As for the prayer leaders and callers to prayer who are content to remain subjects of the Christians (*taḥt dhimmat al-Naṣāra*) (may God destroy them), they are vile prayer leaders and callers, whose testimony is not accepted and whose leading of prayer is not permissible. They are greater in sin than the others because they are [exemplars] whose guidance [others] follow. Thus, repentance is obligatory for them after they relocate from those lands that the infidels have conquered. May God grant us success.

End [of the text] from one of the notebooks.

---

4 Here and below (in Wansharīsī's Berber *fatwā*), I translate *ṭalaba*, literally "students," as prayer leaders. In Moroccan usage, a *ṭālib* is not a student, but a religious functionary whose primary duties include leading prayer and teaching Qurʾān memorization.

Fatwā of Waryāglī[5]

The jurist Abū Muḥammad ʿAbd Allāh al-Waryāglī,[6] who I believe is among the jurists of Tangier (may God have mercy upon him) was asked: "What do the masters of right guidance say about our Muslim brothers who are settled in their [own] lands where the laws of the infidels apply to them, [and who live] on land adjacent to Muslims but have not moved from their [own] lands to other lands in Islamic territory, where they would not be subject to the customs and laws of the infidels? Is it permissible for Muslims (may God increase your honor) to shed their blood, capture their women, and take their property? Are their prayers, giving of alms, and fasting during Ramadan valid or not?

He answered: What you mentioned of this vile, contemptible group, whose perceptive faculties God has obscured after [having granted them] vision, and whom He has led astray through the spread of unbelief into their hearts after [having given them] insight, and who are content to live under the impure infidels who do not believe in [God] the Compassionate and who insult our Prophet and master Muḥammad (may the best blessings and purest peace be upon him), upon my life, the likes of this [behavior] could only arise from someone weak in faith, whom God has previously led into error and from whom He has withdrawn. This is in addition to their glorifying the infidels and exposing [the testification] "There is no god but God" to the scorn of those who worship idols; and all of this is by their choice, without compulsion. [The legal assessment] that our masters have chosen with regard to these people, and [that is adopted in] the *fatwā*s our learned masters have issued concerning them, is that it is necessary to kill them and take their property as booty (*fayʾ*), because the land [they are in] is infidel territory and their property is under infidel control, not under their own control. This is because they can take it from them [i.e., the infidels can seize the Muslims' property] whenever they wish, given that the territory is theirs and they have authority over it [the land and everything in it].

Likewise, their [Muslim] wives should be captured and taken from them until they reach Muslim territory, [where] they should be divorced by a judge. These [women] should be prevented from [remarrying] their spouses, and they should be married off [to other men]. It is not permissible for the wives [of these men living among Christians] to remain with them.

Oh questioner, you have committed a serious error by calling them "our Muslim brothers." Rather, they are our enemies and the enemies of the religion (may God frustrate their efforts and block their good fortune). They

5 BNRM, 2:41; Ḥ, 247–48; T, 262–63. Neither Wansharīsī nor Wazzānī include this text in their *fatwā* collections, but Tasūlī includes it in *al-Jāwāhir al-nafīsa*.

6 On Waryāglī (d. 894/1488–9), see chapter 3.

are the brothers and supporters of the infidels (may God strengthen the Muslims against them and enable their swords to [strike] their necks and the necks of the infidels) whose group they have joined and to whose side they have gone. Peace be upon you, oh questioner, but not upon them.

We must answer with a response supported by the texts of the early jurists. The *fatwās* of the later masters will follow this response, God willing; but in this [response] is a [full] explanation and comprehensive [answer]. May God deliver us and you from deviance and error, and allow us to die loving the religion of the Prophet whose teachings are true.

End of [the text] from the aforementioned notebook.

Fatwā of Māwāsī[7]

The *shaykh* and jurist Abū Mahdī ʿĪsā al-Māwāsī[8] (may God have mercy upon him) was asked about some people who were living in their homelands as subjects of the infidel enemy (may God destroy and divide them) even though it would be easy for them to move from these lands, and they have the means to leave them. Is their remaining under subjection to the infidel enemy permissible or not?

Their status with regard to them [the enemy] falls into categories: one category pays to them a tribute but does not frequent them. Another category frequents them for trade but not for any other [purpose]. Another category frequents them and informs them of the Muslims' affairs. Another category goes out [in boats] with them to fish and says to them, "may God prolong this period and this hour" (may God not accept their supplications).

Provide us with a comprehensive explanation of the rule for [each of] these categories.

He answered: As for Muslims' remaining under infidel rule, this is prohibited. Whoever frequents their homes has lost his religion and his [standing in the] world, and is in violation of what his master [Muḥammad] has commanded of him; for it is not permissible for a Muslim to conclude a treaty with the infidel to the effect that he will pay him tribute. This is agreed upon within the Mālikī school, so for whoever does that [lives under infidel rule], his testimony is not accepted, nor is his leading of prayer. This is the rule for the first category; for Islam should be elevated, and [no other religion] should be elevated above it.

---

7 BNRM, 2:41–42; Ḥ, 248; T, 263. Wazzānī records a version of this *fatwā* in *al-Nawāzil al-ṣughrā*, 1:418.

8 On Māwāsī (d. 896/1491), see chapter 3. While the biographical references all record "Māwāsī," some of the manuscript copies of this *fatwā* misspell his name as Māwasī or Māsawī. See Hendrickson, "Islamic Obligation," appendix D.

As for the judgment concerning the second category, which consists of those who frequent their places for trade, they are worse than the first category and their situation is more repugnant.

As for the third category, which consists of those who frequent their places for trade and inform them of the Muslims' affairs, this is the most repugnant of the three groups and the closest in status to that of a spy who points out the Muslims' weaknesses. His informing [the Christians] as to the Muslims' weaknesses is similar [in status] to banditry, the perpetrators of which must be killed in order to prevent the harm and corruption [they cause]. This is the considered view of those who say that the spy must be killed. [Others say] that he should not be killed, but that the ruler (*al-imām*) should determine his punishment and admonishment, or [that] a distinction ought to be made between one who acted in this manner [during] a single lapse [in judgment, as opposed to repeatedly]; this is a well-known point of scholarly disagreement. Also, should his repentance be accepted or not? [As to this question, his case] resembles the religion of the heretic with regard to the concealment of his action—this is [regarding] the one who frequently visits them, who shows the most affection toward them, and informs them of the routes leading to the Muslims' settlements; for this is the most malicious and repugnant group. [This group] is closer to the infidels than to the believers, because love for the infidel and praying for his strength and power over the Muslims are among the signs of unbelief. May God protect us from apostasy and a change of conviction.

End, also from the aforementioned notebook.

Second *Fatwā* of Ibn Barṭāl[9]

The jurist Abū al-Ḥasan ʿAlī b. ʿAbd Allāh b. Barṭāl (may God have mercy upon him) was asked about the judgment concerning some people who are residing in their homelands, while the Christians live in their immediate vicinity. They are of three categories: One category engages in strife and war with the infidels, like the people of Jabal (Mount) Ḥabīb.[10] Another category, when the treaty was concluded with the Christians, [the Christians] gave them a fixed time period [during which the Muslims could remain]. Their intention is not to pay them any monetary tribute, and that if they are asked for it, they will flee to the lands of Islam. What is the judgment concerning their residing in their lands with this intention? There is also a category [of Muslims] whose intention is to reside in their lands and pay tribute to

---

9 BNRM, 2:42; Ḥ, 248; T, 263. Wazzānī combines Ibn Barṭāl's three *fatwās* into one composite ruling in *al-Nawāzil al-ṣughrā*, 1:419.

10 A mountain in northwestern Morocco. Although all three manuscripts read Ḥabīb, this may be an error for Mount Zabīb in the Ghumāra mountain range. See chapter 3, n. 10.

the Christians for as long as the world remains. Clarify for us the judgment concerning these categories.

He answered: The answer to this first horrifying affair that has threatened the pillars of Islam and blotted out the very days and nights, is that the first third consists of those Muslims whose intercession is accepted by [the strength of] their Islam, and from the dust of whose footsteps we must seek a blessing; for they are engaged in a powerful act of devotion to God. I only wish I were with them, so that I could attain a great victory.

As for the second third, who have agreed among themselves that if they are forced to pay a tribute they will flee with their lives, [they] have committed a reprehensible act by residing in a territory in which the infidel has established his control and supremacy. Nonetheless, this third, if they fulfill what they have pledged through their intentions, will be among the saved, God willing; for they will have deceived [the enemy] and escaped.

As for the third third, they have lost their religion and their [standing in this] world, and have violated what their master [Muḥammad] has commanded of them; thus they deserve a severe punishment. There is disagreement as to their punishment, [and this is divided] among five opinions. The commonly accepted one is that which was held by Ibn al-Qāsim and Saḥnūn, which is that they should be killed without being asked to repent (may God protect us from this calamity). While the Muslim's life is inviolable, through this [their intention to reside permanently among infidels] they render their [own] lives licit.[11]

Likewise, it is not permissible for a Muslim to buy and sell [goods] with the Christians, as through this they [the Christians] are made stronger against the Muslims. The people in these lands should have patiently endured their affliction [rather than trading with the Christians] until God provided an effective end to [the situation].

End, from the aforementioned notebook.[12]

11 The punishment Ibn Barṭāl describes here, for a group that pays tribute to Christians and remains under their authority, is inconsistent with his first and third *fatwās*. In both of his other answers, death without repentance is reserved for spies, while Muslims paying tribute without additional offenses lose their probity but not their inviolability. This second *fatwā* thus shows some textual corruption. It is likely that Ibn Barṭāl was asked only two questions: one resulting in his first *fatwā*, and one resulting in an additional question-and-answer exchange that has survived in two different versions, the second and third *fatwās* attributed to Ibn Barṭāl here.

12 In between Ibn Barṭāl's second and third *fatwās*, Zayyātī offers excerpts from the *fatwā* collection of Abū al-Qāsim al-Burzulī (d. 841/1438) and from the opinion of Ibn Rabīʿ (d. 719/1319). BNRM, 2:42–43; Ḥ, 248–49, T, 263–64; Burzulī, 2:22–23. I omit these excerpts here; they are included in Hendrickson, "Islamic Obligation," appendix C (translation) and appendix D (edition).

Third *Fatwā* of Ibn Barṭāl[13]

The jurist Abū al-Ḥasan ʿAlī b. ʿAbd Allāh b. ʿAlī al-Aghṣāwī, who I believe is the one known as Ibn Barṭāl (may God have mercy upon him) was asked about some people whose lands are close to the Christians. Their status with respect to their residence in [these lands] falls into categories: One group lives in a state of discord with the Christians and cultivates [the land] at the edges of those regions under treaty; [their cultivation is] a form of theft, as the enemy does not know the borders of the territory or the location of their cultivation.

Another category signed a treaty, but their intention is that they will not pay any tribute. [This is] because the Christians delayed their payment until the month of October, at which point they must pay them [the tribute]; so they have resolved to themselves that they will reside in their lands until that time. Then if the Muslims aid them, they will be the first in [waging] *jihād*; or, if they do not aid them, [in that case] they will relocate to [join] them [i.e., they will move to Muslim territory]. What is the judgment of God concerning those who are in this category?

Another category signed a treaty, and their intention is to reside [there] permanently as well as to pay the tribute. What is the judgment of God concerning [those who live] in the manner described?

Another issue: A man from Asilah (may God the exalted return it to Islam) came to owe a debt to a man, after which the enemy captured him [the debtor]. He has property here. Can the creditor retrieve his debt from this property, or should the man be ransomed first? Clarify this for us.

He answered: The answer to this horrifying affair that has threatened the pillars of Islam and blotted out the very days and nights is that the [first] third who remain in a state of war with the enemy and [in a state] of preparation for *jihād* against them, and who lie in wait to attack them—they are the Muslims whose intercession is accepted because of [the strength of] their Islam, and from the dust of whose footsteps we must seek a blessing; for they are engaged in the greatest act of devotion to God. I only wish I were with them, so that I could attain a great victory.

As for the second third, who reside with the intention that if the enemy pressures them to pay the tribute, they will flee; they have committed a reprehensible act by residing in a territory in which the infidel has established his control, supremacy, and dominance over [the Muslims'] families and property. Nonetheless, this third, if they fulfill what they have pledged through their intentions, they will be among the saved, if

13 BNRM, 2:43–45(a); Ḥ, 249; T, 264. BNRM MS 1698 repeats page numbers 45 and 46; this *fatwā* ends on the first instance of page 45, which I refer to as 45(a). Wazzānī combines Ibn Barṭāl's three *fatwās* into one composite ruling in *al-Nawāzil al-ṣughrā*, 1:419.

God the exalted wills; [this is] if they refuse to pay them the tribute on the first instance [it is imposed], for they will have deceived [the enemy] and escaped.

As for the third third, they are a truly vile third, because they have lost their religion and their [standing in this] world, and have violated what their master [Muḥammad] has commanded of them; for it is not permissible for a Muslim to conclude a treaty with the infidels which stipulates that he must pay them a tribute; [this is] by agreement within the school of Mālik. Thus anyone who does this has been disobedient to God the exalted and has contravened His messenger (may God bless him and grant him salvation). What is obligatory upon you and upon our masters[14] who reside there is to inform this third of their error and to rebuke, as much as they can, those among this third who have power and authority. Then if they disobey, they should be renounced; and it will not be permissible for you to act as their guardians or executors, nor for you to witness for them, nor to pray the funeral prayer for their dead, nor to attend to their [legal] affairs, unless they turn back from their sinful action and their contemptible depravity.

You had informed us in your question before this[15] that the third category contains groups who convey news of the Muslims to the Christians, inform them as to their weaknesses, and work with them in matters damaging to the Muslims; this group deserves a severe punishment. There is disagreement as to their punishment, [and it is divided] among five opinions. The commonly accepted one is that which was held by Ibn al-Qāsim and Saḥnūn, which is that the punishment for whoever does this is death, without his being asked to repent (may God protect us from this great calamity). While the Muslim's life is inviolable, through this [informing against Muslims] he makes his [own] life licit.

You also had informed us that they pay tribute to the Christians, they trade with them, and they bring to them things from which they can benefit. We answered you, saying that it is not permissible for a Muslim to bring to the Christians anything that strengthens them against the Muslims, nor is it permissible for him to sell to them, or to buy from them, in a place where he is humiliated by them, such as in your lands. Islam should be elevated, and [no other religion] should be elevated above it. The people in these lands should have been patient in their religion until they had completely despaired of

---

14 This expression, *sādātinā*, meaning "our masters" or "gentlemen" is likely used here as a plural of *sīdī*, a standard Moroccan form of address indicating respect.

15 While Ibn Barṭāl appears to refer to another three-part question, his answer makes it clear that he has in mind here a question analogous to the one posed in his first *fatwā*. It is possible that his second and third *fatwās* were both copies, each partially corrupted, of his second attempt to answer his questioner. The questioner must have sent the five-part question initially, then followed up with a three-part question prior to receiving Ibn Barṭāl's first answer.

any hoped-for assistance. This is because [their land] is adjacent to Muslim territory, and especially as ʿImād al-Marīnī is still active, his victory is anticipated, he is strongly intent on freeing his lands, he is courageous and determined, pained and distressed by this grievous injury.[16] God is asked to release his bonds, to eliminate the harmful consequences of his deeds, to repair his condition, and to make fortunate his era. We also ask Him to reconcile His servants and to restore those of His lands that have fallen.

We answered you prior to this, immediately upon the arrival of your question, and sent it [the response] to you, but its arrival was not immediate.

The answer to the last issue is that the creditor should establish before the judge the debt owed to him. If there is no judge [he should do this] before a group of the area's notaries. Once he has established this [debt], he should retrieve his due, which should be paid from the prisoner's property. The judge, or group of notaries in his absence, should assume responsibility for this. The payment of the debt should not be delayed in order to pay ransom. Indeed, if the prisoner had set aside for himself a specified amount of money [from which to ransom himself], that money is part of the rest of his debts. If his money can cover all of his debts, they should all be paid; if not, specific parties should be paid according to the amount of the debts.

End, from the aforementioned notebook, which states that it was transmitted from the handwriting of the person who transmitted it from the hand [of the author].

16 This passage, unique to Ibn Barṭāl's third *fatwā*, is corrupted and appears to be out of place. The three manuscripts of *al-Jawāhir al-mukhtāra* (*Selected Jewels*) show greater variation than usual in this section; see my Arabic edition, noted above, for details. All three manuscripts of *al-Jawāhir al-mukhtāra* and the Tunisian National Library manuscript of *al-Jawāhir al-nafīsa* (fol. 241b) read "ʿImād al-Marīnī," while the Ḥasaniyya manuscript of *al-Jawāhir al-nafīsa* (page 238) records a blank instead of "ʿImād," indicating a particular problem with this name or word. In my edition, I emend this name to read ʿUthmān al-Marīnī. In this case, the passage would refer to Marīnid sultan Abū Saʿīd ʿUthmān III (r. 800–823/1398–1420), who was in power when Portugal captured Ceuta in 1415. Part of a legal response to that earlier occupation might have been inserted into Ibn Barṭāl's response as an anachronistic element. It is also possible that both ʿImād and al-Marīnī are corruptions and this passage indeed belongs to Ibn Barṭāl, but refers to another ruler or military commander. The event described here—a population fleeing in advance of the enemy rather than waiting for Muslim armies to arrive—fits well with late fifteenth- and early sixteenth-century Morocco.

Wansharīsī's Berber *Fatwā*[17]

The master jurist and *ḥāfiẓ*[18] of his age, Abū al-ʿAbbās Aḥmad b. Yaḥyā al-Wansharīsī (may God have mercy upon him) was asked about a group of Berbers who were residing in their homelands under submission to the infidel enemy, despite having the means to leave these lands:

Is their residence there permitted, or not? With respect to [their relations] with the enemy, they fall into categories: Some of them reside in their homeland but do not go to them, either for trade or any other [purpose]. Others go to them for the purpose of trade, but for no other [reason]. Yet others go to them for the purpose of trade and in order to inform them of the Muslims' affairs. And yet others fish with them, inform them regarding the Muslims' lands, go to them with their legal disputes, and say to them: "May God prolong your time."

Master, what is the legal assessment regarding Muslim property seized by the infidel enemy? May it be purchased from them, or not? A prayer leader (*ṭālib*) has been going to them in order to recover books from their possession through purchase.

Clarify this for us. May you be rewarded, and peace be upon you.

He answered: The substance of this question, encompassing all its variations, comes down to several questions. The first is residence in *arḍ al-ḥarb* (the land of war) and submission to infidel rule. The second is going to them for trade and to inform [them] of the Muslims' weaknesses. The third is fishing with them, using their courts, and praying for their continuance. These [latter] two questions are like two variations of the first question, which acts as a general category under which they are subsumed. The fourth [question] is the legal assessment regarding what may be recovered of the Muslims' property.

As for the first [question], its answer (and God, may He be glorified, grants success by His grace in determining what is right) is that submission to infidel rule and residence in *dār al-ḥarb*, despite the ability to move from there and to distance [oneself] from this, is prohibited; it is not permissible [even] for one instant or one hour of one day. The prescribed, imperative obligation is to emigrate from infidel areas, to move away from them to *dār al-Islām* where their [infidel] laws do not apply.

---

17 BNRM, 2:45(a)–2:45(b); Ḥ, 249–51; T, 264–66. Note that BNRM MS 1698 repeats page numbers 45–46; Wansharīsī's *fatwā* begins on the first instance of page 45, which I refer to as 45(a), continues through the first instance of page 46, and ends on the second instance of page 45, which I refer to as 45(b). Wazzānī includes an abbreviated version of this *fatwā* in *al-Miʿyār al-jadīd*, 3:28–31. Etty Terem includes an analysis and partial translation of Wazzānī's version in Terem, *New Texts, Old Practices*, 94–100. On the sources for Wansharīsī's biography, see chapter 3.

18 A *ḥāfiẓ* is someone who has memorized the Qurʾān.

The Book, the Sunna and the consensus of the jurists are all evidence for this [obligation]. As for the Book: In His words, may He be exalted: "Those whom the angels take in death while they are wronging themselves, the angels will say to them: 'In what circumstances were you?' They will say, "We were abased in the earth." The angels will say, "Was God's earth not spacious enough for you to have migrated therein?" Hell will be the refuge for such men—a wretched end! Except for the weak among men, women, and children, who are unable to devise a plan and are not guided to a way; as for these, perhaps God will pardon them. God is Most Clement, Oft Forgiving."[19]

Those who are not guided to a way that they might turn toward [in order to emigrate], who, if they set forth, will perish; for them, it is hoped that God will forgive them—that is, for their residence, because they [remain] among the polytheists.

As for the Sunna: There are the words of [Muḥammad] (may God bless him and grant him peace): "I am not responsible for any Muslim who lives among the polytheists."[20]

The master jurists have reached a consensus on this.

Thus, if by virtue of the Book, the Sunna, and the consensus of the master jurists, it is obligatory for those who have converted to Islam in non-Muslim territory to emigrate from there and to join the territory of the Muslims; and not to settle or remain among them, in order that they [the converts] not be subject to their laws; then surely it is even more proper and worthy that [emigration] is obligatory with respect to those who are originally Muslim.

Mālik (may God have mercy upon him) deemed it reprehensible for anyone to live in a land where the pious ancestors were derided, so how [could it be permissible for anyone to live] in a land where he would be subject to Satan's rule and God's wrath, where the Trinity is invoked and idols are worshiped? Only a soul whose creed is repulsive and whose faith is diseased could settle upon this desire [to live among infidels].[21]

The master jurists have stipulated that if he does not find a means of freeing himself from the infidels' ropes other than by expending what money he has, we have made this [expenditure] an added obligation upon him. If he does not do this, his inviolability is compromised, his testimony is inadmissible, and he has no right to a share in the booty or divisible spoils of war.

19 Qur'ān 4:97–99.

20 For the full *ḥadīth* and citation, see the translation of *Asnā al-matājir* in appendix B.

21 The preceding two paragraphs are drawn largely from Ibn Rushd al-Jadd (d. 520/1126), *al-Muqaddimāt al-mumahhidāt*, 2:153.

For this reason, [scholars in] the *madhhab* have disagreed as to the status of the Mudéjars' property: Is its status that of the territory, and therefore like enemy property? Or is it still under their possession?

According to one scholar, interacting with them [Mudéjars] is not permissible, nor is greeting them, similar to those with heretical beliefs (*ahl al-ahwāʾ*).

The judge Abū al-Walīd al-Bājī[22] (may God have mercy upon him) stipulated that if a Muslim who lives in *dār al-ḥarb* despite the ability to leave is killed unintentionally, no blood money is owed [to his family] on his account.

Adherents of the [Mālikī] *madhhab* have also stipulated a refusal to accept the written attestations (*mukhāṭabāt*) of the Mudéjars, such as the judges of the Mudéjars of Valencia, Tortosa, Pantelleria, and Majorca. They explained this by the fact that a condition for accepting a judge [i.e., accepting his written documents as valid] is the validity of his appointment, by someone demonstrably entitled to appoint him.[23]

As for those who go to them for trade, mundane aims, and the accumulation of worldly ephemera, this is the first of two variations on the second question according to our refinement [of the questions]. It represents the entirety of the second question in the original [*istiftāʾ*], and is also one of two variations of the third question in that [original *istiftāʾ*]. He[24] (may God have mercy upon him) stipulated that this [entry for trade] entails a loss of legal probity, which invalidates their leading of prayer and offering of testimony. This is because it is not permitted for anyone to enter infidel territory, for any other reason than to ransom Muslim prisoners.

It is obligatory upon the leaders of the Muslims and upon the community (may God provide for and assist them) to prevent entry into *dār al-ḥarb* for trade, and to place observation posts along the route for this [purpose], such that no one finds a way [to enter]. This is especially [necessary] if it is feared that something will be brought to them for use in their wars (something that [would increase their] power over the Muslims and whose sale to [the enemy] is prohibited).

22 Abū al-Walīd al-Bājī (d. 474/1081), an Andalusī judge and jurist. Makhlūf, *Shajarat al-nūr*, 1:178.

23 In *Asnā al-matājir*, Wansharīsī attributes this view to Ibn ʿArafa (d. 803/1401) specifically, rather than to "adherents of the *madhhab*" in general. Verskin erroneously considers this paragraph a continuation of the views that Wansharīsī attributes to Abū al-Walīd al-Bājī. Verskin, "The Evolution of the Mālikī Jurists' Attitudes to the Mudéjar Leadership," *Der Islam* 90, no. 1 (2013): 44.

24 Wansharīsī is unclear about who he is referring to here, but he likely means to attribute this opinion to Mālik.

[Saḥnūn] states in the *Mudawwana*:[25] Mālik strongly disliked travel to non-Muslim territory for the purpose of trade. He said: "The polytheists' laws will apply to them; and instruments of war must not be sold to the inhabitants of non-Muslim territory (*al-ḥarbiyyīn*), including horses, weapons, saddles, and anything else that strengthens them in war, including copper, furnishings, and the like.

In *al-Wāḍiḥa*, according to Muṭarrif and Ibn al-Mājishūn:[26] If we have a truce with the polytheists there is no harm in selling them food, but it is disliked to sell them horses, weapons, iron, copper, furnishings, leather, and anything else used in war. In the absence of a truce, it is not permitted to sell them food or anything else that may be a strength to them in their territory.

In *al-Muqaddimāt*,[27] it is not permissible to sell to them anything they might make use of in their wars, including horses, weapons, or iron; nor anything that might be used to intimidate [those fighting for] Islam during battle, such as banners, or any garments they would wear during their wars, thereby displaying themselves proudly before Islam. Copper is likewise [prohibited], as they fashion drums from it, thus using it to intimidate the Muslims. Likewise it is not permissible to sell them Christian slaves, because they may act as guides against the Muslims, an [exploitable] weakness against them. Only those goods may be sold to them which they will not use to strengthen themselves in war, or to intimidate [Muslims] during battle; with respect to clothing, only what protects against heat and cold, no more; with respect to food, only what one cannot subsist on, such as oil, salt, and the like.

As for the second of the two variations on the second question, which concerns those going to the [enemy] in order to guide them against the Muslims and inform them of [the Muslims'] weaknesses: according to Ibn al-Qāsim and Saḥnūn, it is obligatory to kill those deficient, contemptible Muslims whose [guilt as to spying] has been proven with sufficient, irrefutable evidence; their repentance is not accepted. Saḥnūn stated that no blood money is owed to their inheritors, as in the case of a criminal or illegitimate rebel.

It has also been said that [spies] should be given an exemplary whipping, imprisoned for a long time, and exiled beyond enemy territory. Saḥnūn transmitted this opinion, from some of our fellow [Mālikīs]. It has also been

25 ʿAbd al-Salām Saḥnūn b. Saʿīd (d. 240/854) composed the *Mudawwana*, a foundational Mālikī text.

26 ʿAbd al-Mālik b. Ḥabīb al-Sulamī (d. 238/853) was an Andalusī Mālikī jurist who composed *al-Wāḍiḥa fī al-fiqh wa'l-sunan*, a foundational Mālikī text. Muṭarrif b. ʿAbd Allāh b. Muṭarrif (d. 220/835) and ʿAbd al-Mālik b. ʿAbd al-ʿAzīz b. al-Mājishūn (d. 212/827 or 214/829) were both Medinan students of Mālik.

27 This work is Ibn Rushd al-Jadd's *al-Muqaddimāt al-mumahhidāt*, noted above.

held that [spies] should be killed unless they repent; this was the view of Ibn Wahb.[28] Ibn al-Mājishūn, held another opinion: If the [offense] was an unexpected lapse and the [informant] is thought to be ignorant [of his actions], and there is no recurrence on his part, and he is not among those who bring harm to Islam, then he should be given a severe punishment and beaten; but if he is accustomed to [spying], then he should be killed. Others have held that [an informant] should be killed unless he is excused as a result of his ignorance. Another view is that the *imām* should form an independent judgment on the matter—this is the view narrated by ʿUtbī and Lakhmī.[29] [Mālikīs have discussed] this issue in detail; it would be [too] lengthy for us to present it [all here].

As for the first two variations on the third question, [as set forth in] our refinement [of the original question], which concerns those who fish with them and take their legal disputes to their courts—this is the fourth group according to the categories in the [original] question: the legal assessment for these [acts] is the loss of probity [for the offender]; these [acts] are tremendously reprehensible, and they come close to [being] prohibited because of the humiliation they bring to the glory of Islam and its people. Islam must grow and not decline, it must dominate and not be dominated by others.

As for the third [variation] on the third question, which concerns praying for the cursed infidels (may God do away with them), to remain and for their period be prolonged: it is evident that this is a sign of the supplicant's apostasy and deviation from right belief, and of the corruption of his heart and of his convictions. [This is] because this [prayer] indicates contentment with unbelief; and contentment with unbelief is unbelief. Shaykh Abū al-Ḥasan al-Ashʿarī (may God be pleased with him) put the desire for unbelief on a par with unbelief, such as the construction of churches in which to engage in infidelity, or the killing of a prophet despite believing in the validity of his message, in order to do away with his legal code. According to Qarāfī,[30] delaying someone who comes to you to convert also constitutes [a desire to further infidelity], because you advise him to delay [conversion to] Islam, and the desire to prolong infidelity, meaning the desire for its continuation, is infidelity.

A legal issue arose during Shihāb al-Dīn al-Qarāfī's days (may God have mercy upon him) that illustrates this [principle]. One man said of another,

---

28 ʿAbd Allāh b. Wahb (d. 197/813) was one of Mālik's Egyptian students.

29 Abū ʿAbd Allāh Muḥammad al-ʿUtbī (d. 254 or 255/868–9), an Andalusī Mālikī jurist from Córdoba, wrote the *Mustakhraja*, also known as the *ʿUtbiyya*. Abū al-Ḥasan ʿAlī b. Muḥammad al-Ribʿī al-Lakhmī (d. 478/1085–6) was a prominent Mālikī jurist in Ifrīqiyā.

30 Shihāb al-Dīn Aḥmad b. Idrīs al-Qarāfī (d. 684/1285) was a prominent Egyptian Mālikī scholar.

"May God make him die as an infidel!" The shaykh Sharaf al-Dīn al-Karkhī issued a *fatwā* [confirming] this [first] man's infidelity, on account of the desire for infidelity implied by [his statement].

This [desire for infidelity] is even clearer and more obvious in this case of yours. The best case for these deviants is for one to go to great lengths to beat them, and apply the utmost effort to punishing them, such that they repent. [This should be done] just as [the caliph] ʿUmar (may God have mercy upon him) beat Ṣabīgh, whose conviction was suspect, until he said: "Oh Commander of the Muslims, if you wanted to heal me, you have cured my illness; and if you wanted to kill me, finish me off." So he let him go.

As for the fourth question, which concerns purchasing what they possess of the Muslims' property: what is the legal assessment of this? His [Wansharīsī's] answer: [Saḥnūn] states in the *Mudawwana*—and there is a similar [statement] in the *ʿUtbiyya*, transmitted from Ibn al-Qāsim, but this wording is from the *Mudawwana*:

> If you entered *dār al-ḥarb* under an agreement of safe passage and bought a Muslim's slave from a *ḥarbī* [a non-Muslim resident of *dār al-ḥarb*] who had taken him prisoner, or to whom the slave had escaped, or if the *ḥarbī* offers him to you as a gift and you repay him, then his [former Muslim] master has the right to take him [back] after paying you whatever price or goods you conveyed [to the *ḥarbī*]. If you did not repay your donor [for the slave], his [original] owner may take him without [paying] anything.

Shaykh Abū ʿUmar and Ibn al-Ḥājib pointed to a summary of the legal assessments for this issue. In his words [i.e., those of Ibn al-Ḥājib]:[31]

> By agreement [of the Mālikī scholars], when someone compensates [a *ḥarbī*] in *dār al-ḥarb* for the property of a Muslim or *dhimmī*, the [original] owner is entitled to take back [that property] for the price [paid in compensation] . . .[32]
>
> If [the property] was recovered without cost, [the owner] may take it back without cost. If the person who recovered the property [then] sold it [to someone other than the original owner], the [sale] stands, but the [original] owner is entitled to the profit, if there is any.

---

31 The following passage appears, with slight differences, in Jamāl al-Dīn b. al-Ḥājib, *Jāmiʿ al-ummahāt*, ed. Abū ʿAbd al-Raḥmān al-Akhḍar al-Akhḍarī, 2nd ed. (Damascus: al-Yamāma lil-Ṭibāʿa wa'l-Nashr wa'l-Tawzīʿ, 2004), 253.

32 My ellipsis indicates Wansharīsī's omission of the following sentence from Ibn al-Ḥājib: "In the case of retaking property that has been recovered without cost from a thief, there are two opinions." See Ibn al-Ḥājib, *Jāmiʿ al-ummahāt*, 253.

> In assessing the possession rights for [this recovered] property, Lakhmī applied the legal assessment for booty, but other [jurists] applied the legal assessment for a gift that is [then] sold. There are two views regarding this [latter position]: the commonly accepted opinion is that [the one who recovered the property from a *ḥarbī*] is akin to one who pays compensation for [that property, and thus is entitled to sell it]. It is also held that [when the original owner] buys back [his property from a third party] for a price, he may demand that full price—but no more—from the person who was given the property without cost [and then sold it].

Whereas we stated that the [original property] owner may retake it for the [same] price, the seller should be trusted [as to that price] as long as there is no evidence that he is lying. The owner takes back [his property] in exchange for its value on the day of its purchase, in the place where he [the seller] bought it. If [these details] are unknown, then [the value should be determined] according to the nearest place [of business]. If the [original owner] accuses [the seller of deceit], the buyer [who is now selling the property] is believed if he gives his oath, if [the price he quoted] approximates [the market rate]; if not, the owner [is believed] if the price [he named] approximates [the market rate]; if not, [the price] is determined by the value of the property [according to the market rate]. If [either of them] refuses [an oath], the other one is believed instead of him, even if [the price he claimed] does not approximate [the market rate].

The legal assessment of entering [*dār al-ḥarb*] in order to recover books and goods is in this sense the same, so there is no sense in devoting a separate discussion [to this case]. To be sure, the prayer leader who enters [*dār al-ḥarb*] for this particular purpose should begin by recovering what books he can, proceeding from the most to the least important. The most important books to be rescued are: the Book of God, even if its rescuer is not in a state of purity, followed by the *ḥadīth* of the messenger of God (may God bless him and grant him peace) followed by works of law (*fiqh*), followed by the two *uṣūls* [i.e., *uṣūl al-fiqh* (jurisprudence) and *uṣūl al-dīn* (theology)], followed by Arabic, linguistics, medicine, and first-rate exegetical works, especially Ibn ʿAṭiyya's exegesis; as well as books on the "readings" of the Qurʾān.

End, from the aforementioned notebook. Most of the *responsa* that I have copied from the aforementioned notebook contain mistakes, so whoever finds another copy, let him correct what is corrupted here (may God reward him).[33]

---

33 In *al-Jawāhir al-mukhtāra*, Wansharīsī's *fatwā* is followed by an opinion by Fāsī jurist Abū al-ʿAbbās Aḥmad al-Abbār al-Fāsī, known as Ḥamdun (d. 1071/1660–1) regarding the obligation of a Mālikī Muslim to emigrate from territory inhabited by a non-Sunnī (presumably, Kharijite) group of Muslims (BNRM, 2:45(b)–46(b); Ḥ, 251–52; T, 266–67). See notes above

Fatwā of Bijā'ī[34]

I want to record a question and answer from another scholar, because of its agreement with the meaning of the preceding [opinions]. The ascetic jurist Sīdī Aḥmad al-Bijā'ī[35] (may God be pleased with him) wrote to the most learned scholar and jurist Sīdī Aḥmad b. al-Ḥājj al-Bayḍāwī (may God have mercy upon him) [in response to] a question.[36] This is his [Bayḍāwī's] text:

Praise be to God, my master (*sīdī*), may God be pleased with you, prolong your good health by His grace, and grant Muslims enjoyment through your continuance. Your answer [is requested] regarding a locality teeming with evildoers and oppressors, where unlawful acts and taxes are widespread, where Muslims are debased and infidels glorified, where tyrants hold themselves high but the learned humble themselves, and where Muslims must pay taxes on all purchased goods. The matter is particularly problematic for those seeking guidance. None of the [region's] virtuous men [will openly] condemn reprehensible [acts], whether out of fear for themselves or the mockery that results, I do not know. A person who has been compelled to study with the scholars of the aforementioned region thus fears for himself because of the [same problems] recorded above.

May God grant you honor. Is it permissible for him to remain in that region, despite not having the ability to correct the [inhabitants'] reprehensible behaviors, other than slightly—and in this manner he would be imitating his master? And is it permissible for him to buy some of the taxed goods, if he is compelled to do so, and he would be safe from falling into places of peril? Or is it necessary for him to move away from that region to another one, because [the shepherd] who pastures [his flock too] close to the sanctuary is on the verge of crossing into it?[37] Clarify for us this matter, for one compelled and in need of [the answer] for his own sake. May you be rewarded.

The text of the answer: Praise be to God. It is necessary for the true believer who sincerely cares for himself to flee with his religion from corruptions and to settle only in a place where exemplary practices are upheld. He must only acquire the religious knowledge he needs from someone who

---

regarding the page numbers for BNRM 1698. A short, unidentified excerpt on the categories of *hijra* follows (BNRM, 2:46(b)–47; Ḥ, 252, T, 267), prior to Bijā'ī's *fatwā*. Versions of both appear in Wazzānī's *al-Mi'yār al-jadīd*, 3:36–39.

34 BNRM, 2:47–48; Ḥ, 252; T, 267. Wazzānī includes a version of this *fatwā* in *al-Mi'yār al-jadīd*, 3:39–41, but mistakenly records the *muftī*'s name as Aḥmad al-Jāyy.

35 On Bijā'ī (d. ca. 901/1495), see chapter 3. In manuscript (Ḥ), Zayyātī records Lajā'ī instead of Bijā'ī.

36 In Zayyātī's introduction, Bijā'ī appears to be the *mustaftī*. My added text in brackets shows that he is actually the *muftī*, as Ibn 'Askar makes clear (*Dawḥat al-nāshir*, 114–15). Rather than Bayḍāwī, Ibn 'Askar attributes the question to another Abū al-'Abbās al-Bijā'ī; I have not located either possible *mustaftī* in the relevant biographical dictionaries.

37 The questioner is referring to a prominent *ḥadīth* preserved in Bukhārī and Muslim and featured as *ḥadīth* number six in Nawawī's *Forty Ḥadīth*. The report emphasizes the need to avoid any questionable actions.

exhibits the signs of fear and humility. He should seek [this knowledge] in [all] the regions and quarters of the earth, by evidence of [the Qur'ānic verse]: "Was God's earth not spacious enough for you to have migrated therein?"[38] This [obligation to migrate is conditional on his] ability [to travel] and the presence of what he desires in another place.

If he lacks these [conditions] as the routes are difficult for him and he has found no virtuous and agreeable place [to go], nor a sincere and rightly guided teacher, then let him remain in that place, persevering in graceful patience. He may be [considered] one of "the weak among men, women, and children, who are unable to devise a plan and are not guided to a way,"[39] [and are thus exempt from the obligation to emigrate.] Let him also pray like those who prayed when they had found no supporter or helper in religion, "Lord, rescue us from this town whose people are oppressors! By your grace, give us a protector and give us a helper."[40]

He should gather what knowledge he needs from anyone who promotes himself as a teacher, for "many a man bears knowledge to those more knowledgeable than he," "the sick person might be cured with an infidel doctor's medicine," and "God might further the religion even through a sinful man."[41] Of goods, he should buy what food and clothing he requires, taking care to not live recklessly but to grant pious caution its due. In this, he must exercise his own discretion (*ijtihād*) and judiciousness. He should avoid buying [goods] from those who have unjustly seized them as taxes, buying [instead] what remains in the hands of the [original] owner. The man must be careful to adhere to established laws and recorded legal precedents and to remain within the bounds of necessity. He must not allow himself too many "permitted" whims, let alone give in to prohibited actions. If he limits himself to his needs, his religion will not be adversely affected; for if [all] the world was a putrid corpse, [even] that would be a permitted source of sustenance for the believer.[42]

End of the necessary part, from the aforementioned notebook.[43]

---

38 Qur'ān 4:97.

39 Qur'ān 4:98.

40 Qur'ān 4:75.

41 The first of these three sayings is attested in Muttaqī's *ḥadīth* collection, *Kanz al-ʿummāl*, no. 29375. See ʿAlāʾ al-Dīn ʿAlī al-Muttaqī al-Hindī (d. 975/1567), *Kanz al-ʿummal fī sunan al-aqwāl wa'l-afʿāl*, ed. Bakrī Ḥayyānī and Ṣafwat al-Ṣaqqāʾ, 18 vols., 5th ed. (Beirut: Muʾassasat al-Risāla, 1985), 10:258. The third saying appears in at least four *ḥadīths*. See, for example, *Ṣaḥīḥ Muslim, Kitāb al-Īmān, bāb ghilaẓ taḥrīm qatl al-insān nafsah . . .*, *ḥadīth* 178 (Muslim b. al-Ḥajjāj, *Ṣaḥīḥ Muslim*, 1:105–6); *Ṣaḥīḥ al-Bukhārī, Kitāb al-Maghāzī, bāb ghazwat Khaybar*, *ḥadīth* 3967 (Bukhārī, *Ṣaḥīḥ al-Bukhārī*, 4:1540). I have not found a reference to the second saying.

42 Bijāʾī's last analogy is a variation on a weak *ḥadīth* in which the world's only sustenance is the spilt blood of a slaughtered animal (not a putrid corpse). Blood, like carrion, is normally prohibited, but becomes permitted in times of necessity.

43 Three short *fatwās* on *hijra* by Abū al-Ḥasan ʿAlī b. ʿUthmān al-Zawāwī (d. 815/1412–3) follow Bijāʾī's *fatwā* (BNRM, 2:48; Ḥ, 252–53; T, 267–68); all three manuscript copies record

First *Fatwā* of Ibn Zakrī[44]

The *imām* Abū al-ʿAbbās Aḥmad b. Muḥammad b. Zakrī (may God have mercy upon him) was asked a question, of which this is the text:

Master (may God be pleased with you and aid you with that which he has entrusted you) what is your view regarding a certain *sharīf* who is undertaking command of the *jihād* now in the Far Maghrib [modern-day Morocco], in the environs of Ceuta and its sister [cities]? Are his actions legally permissible today, considering that the sultan of these lands has signed a peace treaty with the polytheists, and the place in which the *sharīf* is [active] is located within this sultan's area of governance? It is understood that this treaty was signed only after the enemy's complete acquaintance with the Muslims' weaknesses, that they seized the aforementioned lands with the utmost force in terms of soldiers and weaponry, and that the public treasury is in good shape. Are the *sharīf*'s actions permitted given this understanding, or not?

It is also understood that the aforementioned treaty has a duration exceeding twenty years. Is this legitimate, or not?

He answered: If the man leading the *jihād* is safe, and his party is safe from danger at the hands of those who would prevent him from combating the enemy, then fighting the infidels is permissible provided that he believes the enemy to be fighting Muslims elsewhere, other than the aforementioned *sharīf*'s locality.

As for the existing treaty, it is not valid because of its provisions strengthening the enemy and weakening Muslims in this period, and because the limit for a treaty concluded between Muslims and their enemies is two or three years. God grants success in determining what is right, by His grace and blessing.

End, from one of the notebooks.

Second *Fatwā* of Ibn Zakrī[45]

He was also asked: What do you say concerning the tribes of the Far Maghrib, near Ceuta, Tangier, Asilah, and al-Qaṣr [al-Ṣaghīr] that have intermingled their affairs with [those of] the Christians? Such friendship has developed between them that when the Muslims plan a raid, these Maghribī tribes inform the Christians and the Muslims find them nothing

---

his name incorrectly as Zarwālī. Versions of all three *fatwā*s appear in Wazzānī's *al-Miʿyār al-jadīd*, 3:41–42. Although Zawāwī lived in Bijāya, these texts appear to be concerned with Iberian Muslims.

44 BNRM, 2:48–49; Ḥ, 253; T, 268. Wazzānī includes a version of this *fatwā* in *al-Miʿyār al-jadīd*, 3:42–3. On Ibn Zakrī (d. 899–900/1493–4), see chapter 3.

45 BNRM, 2:49; Ḥ, 253; T, 268. Wazzānī includes a version of this *fatwā*, but omits all city names, in *al-Nawāzil al-ṣughrā*, 1:419.

if not watchful and prepared. It is understood that the Muslims must pass through these tribes' lands in order to fight these Christians, and often the tribes fight the Muslims alongside the Christians. What is God's legal assessment with regard to their lives, property, women, and children? Should they be exiled from these lands or not? If they refuse exile except through fighting, may they be fought, or not?

He answered: The description of the aforementioned group necessitates fighting them and killing them like the infidels with whom they have allied. Whoever allies with the infidels is one of them.[46] And God knows best.

End, from the aforementioned notebook.

46 This is a reference to Qurʾān 5:51.

APPENDIX B

Asnā al-matājir fī bayān aḥkām man ghalaba ʿalā waṭanih al-Naṣārā wa-lam yuhājir, wa-mā yatarattabu ʿalayh min al-ʿuqūbāt waʾl-zawājir[1]

The Most Noble Commerce: An Exposition of the Legal Rulings Governing One Whose Homeland Has Been Conquered by the Christians and Who Has Not Emigrated, and the Punishments and Admonishments Accruing to Him[2]

by Aḥmad Abū al-ʿAbbās Aḥmad b. Yaḥyā al-Wansharīsī (d. 914/1508)

---

1 Wansharīsī offers this title in the *fatwā*'s colophon. My translations of *Asnā al-matājir* and the Marbella *fatwā* are based primarily on Aḥmad Najīb's 2006 critical edition of these texts. I also consulted the modern Rabat edition, the Fez lithograph, Ḥusayn Muʾnis's edition, and the El Escorial manuscript of *Asnā al-matājir*, all noted in chapter 4. **Text marked in bold** indicates material that Wansharīsī quotes or paraphrases closely, without acknowledgment, from the *fatwā* by Ibn Rabīʿ (d. 719/1319) discussed in chapters 4 and 5. I am grateful to Sjoerd van Koningsveld, Gerard Wiegers, and Umar Ryad for sharing with me their unpublished edition of this important text. On the basis of Ibn Rabīʿ's *fatwā*, I have agreed occasionally with the Rabat edition of *Asnā al-matājir* against Najīb's edition; other considerations on the basis of Ibn Rabīʿ's *fatwā* are noted below. References to Wansharīsī's *Miʿyār* are to the Rabat edition, as throughout this book; I refer to Najīb and Muʾnis rather than to Wansharīsī when using their editions, and I make special note of references to the Fez lithograph or El Escorial manuscript. These translations are based primarily on the original versions included in my 2009 dissertation, which were based solely on the Arabic texts. In revising the text, I have consulted the new and newly-accessible translations noted in chapter 4, and agreed, occasionally, with their stylistic choices. Here I note only important disagreements with, or debts to, these other versions.

2 This title follows a conventional two-part format for medieval Islamic works, in which a memorable phrase that will serve as the work's title of reference precedes a descriptive title; the two parts rhyme and are normally separated by the preposition *fī* ("about"). The first part of the title, often with flowery imagery related to gardens or embroidery, bears no relationship to the contents of the work. Verskin follows Asmal in positing that "*Asnā al-matājir*" refers to the excellent deal that emigrants make when they give up worldly comfort to perform *hijra*. It should be interpreted instead as referring to Wansharīsī's work—an excellent commodity that provides the reader with a full account of the legal consequences for those who have *not* migrated. Asmal, "Muslims under Non-Muslim Rule," 150; Verskin, *Islamic Law* 14. On titles, see Alfonso Carmona González, "La Estructura del Titulo en los Libros Árabes Medievales," *Estudios Románicos* 4 (1989): 181–89.

The Question[3]

The honorable master jurist, the accomplished preacher, the enduring virtuous exemplar, the pure sum of excellence, the man most admired for his moral rectitude, Abū ʿAbd Allāh b. Qaṭiyya[4] (may God perpetuate his noble achievement and reputation) sent me the following text:

"Praise be to God alone. Your answer [is requested], my master (may God be pleased with you and [may He] benefit the Muslims by means of your life) regarding a legal case that has arisen (*nāzila*).[5] This [concerns] a group among those Andalusīs who emigrated from al-Andalus, who left behind their houses, property, orchards, vineyards, and other types of immovable property; who spent in addition to this a large sum of their available money, and who escaped from under the rule of the infidel community; and who allege that they fled for the sake of God, taking with them [only] their religion, their lives, their families, their offspring, and whatever money they had left, or that some of them had left; and who (praise be to God the exalted) settled in the land of Islam (*dār al-Islām*), in obedience to God and His Prophet and under the authority of Muslim rule.[6]

"After having reached the land of Islam they regretted their emigration (*hijra*). They became angry and alleged that they found their condition difficult and impoverished. They alleged that they did not find in the land of Islam, which is this land of the Maghrib (may God preserve it, safeguard its lands, and aid its ruler), any kindness, ease, or support, nor did they find sufficient security with respect to their ability to move throughout the region. They made this clear in a variety of ugly statements that demonstrated their weakness in religion, their lack of true certainty in their beliefs, and the fact that their emigration was not for God and His messenger as alleged. Rather, it was only for worldly gain[7] that they hoped to attain immediately upon their arrival, in convenient accordance with their desires. When they found that [emigration to the Maghrib] was not amenable to their interests, they

3 These section headings are my own editorial additions, partly inspired by those of Muʾnis.

4 On this jurist's name and identity, see chapter 4.

5 *Nāzila*, literally "occurrence," is a technical term for a legal case that arises and occasions an *istiftāʾ*, or request for a *fatwā*. Collections of *fatwās* are also commonly referred to as *nawāzil*.

6 *Ḥukm al-dhimma al-Muslima. Dhimma*, meaning custody or guardianship and most often associated with the "protected" status of Christians and Jews under Muslim rule, is used throughout the *fatwā* as a term for both Muslim and non-Muslim rule. It may be an error in some cases for *umma* (community). I have translated *ḥukm al-dhimma* and *dhimma* in all cases simply as "rule."

7 *Li-dunyā yuṣībūnahā*. This language appears in a popular *ḥadīth*. See *Ṣaḥīḥ al-Bukhārī, Kitāb Badʾ al-waḥy, bāb kayfa kāna badʾ al-waḥy . . .* , *ḥadīth* no. 1 (Bukhārī, *Ṣaḥīḥ al-Bukhārī*, 1:3). This *ḥadīth* states that actions are rewarded according to their intentions; those who emigrate for God and His messenger are thus rewarded, whereas a *hijra* motivated by worldly gain or marriage is assessed accordingly.

openly derided the land of Islam and its state of affairs, cursing and defaming that which had prompted their emigration. They openly praised the land of unbelief (*dār al-kufr*) and its inhabitants, and (openly expressed) regret at having left it.

"It is [even] occasionally reported that one of them, in rejecting emigration to the land of Islam, which is this land (may God protect it), said, 'Emigrate from there to here? Rather, it is from here to there that emigration should be required!' And that another of them said, 'If the ruler of Castile came to these parts, we would go to him requesting that he send us back there,' meaning to the land of unbelief. [It is reported] also that some of them are looking for any kind of scheme[8] by which they may return to the land of unbelief, thereby reverting, by any means possible, to [living] under infidel rule.[9]

"What manner of sin, diminished religious standing, and loss of credibility accrues to them for this? Are they committing the very act of disobedience [to God] from which they were fleeing, if they persist in this behavior without repenting and returning to God (may He be exalted)? What of those among them who—God forbid!—return to the land of unbelief after having reached the land of Islam? Is it obligatory to punish those among them who have been witnessed making these statements, or the likes of them? Or should there be no [punishment] until they have been admonished and warned concerning this matter? Then whoever repents to God (may He be exalted) would be left alone, with the hope that his repentance would be accepted, and [only] those who persist in this [behavior] would be punished?

Or, should they all be ignored, leaving each one to whatever he has chosen? [Should we assume] that for those God establishes contentedly in the land of Islam, their intention is valid and God (glory be to Him) will reward them for it, while whoever chooses to return to the land of unbelief and resume [submission] to infidel rule invites God's wrath? [In this case] should those who malign the land of Islam, whether explicitly or implicitly, be left alone without lament?

---

8 Asmal and Verskin interpret *ḥīla*, scheme, in the technical sense of a legal stratagem that would satisfy the letter, but not the spirit, of Islamic law. The rest of the question suggests (i.e., "by any means possible") that these emigrants were not concerned with the legitimacy of their actions in the eyes of Muslim jurists, and that the ordinary sense of a "scheme" applies. Asmal, "Muslims under Non-Muslim Rule," 152; Verskin, *Islamic Law*, 15.

9 Najīb chooses a variant from a single manuscript here that reads *al-milla al-kāfira*, against the other three editions (Rabat, Fez lithograph, and Mu'nis) that all read *al-dhimma al-kāfira*.

"Clarify for us, by means of a comprehensive, general,[10] explicit, and sufficient statement, the judgment of God (may He be exalted) concerning all of this. Is it a condition of [the obligation to] emigrate that no one has to emigrate other than to a standard of living guaranteed to be in accordance with his desires, immediately upon arrival and in whatever region of the Islamic world he has alighted? Or is this not a condition? Instead, is emigration obligatory from the land of unbelief to the land of Islam [no matter if] that entails sweetness or bitterness, abundance or poverty, or hardship or ease, with regard to conditions in this world? Surely its purpose is the protection of religion, family, and offspring, for example, and escape from the infidel community's rule to that of the Muslim community, and to whatever God wills by way of sweetness or bitterness, poverty or wealth, and so on, with respect to worldly conditions. May God (glory be to Him) reward you [for your efforts], may a noble peace support your elevated station, and may the mercy and blessings of God (may He be exalted) be upon you."

The Answer—Introduction

I answered him with the following text:

Praise be to God alone, and after Him may blessings and peace be upon our master and lord, Muḥammad.

The answer to what you have asked (and it is God, glory be to Him, who grants success by His grace) is that emigration from the land of unbelief to the land of Islam remains an obligation until the day of judgment. The same applies to emigration from a land in which sin and falsehood are the result of oppression or corruption (*fitna*).[11] The messenger of God (may God bless him and grant him peace) said, "The time will soon come when a Muslim's best property will be sheep, which he will drive to mountaintops and to areas of rainfall, fleeing with his religion from corruption (*fitnas*)." This [*ḥadīth*] is recorded by Bukhārī, by [Mālik in] the *Muwaṭṭa*ʾ, by Abū Dāwūd,

10 *Mujarrad* literally means "abstract," "peeled bare," or "disengaged." In law, *tajrīd* often refers to an opinion in which a *muftī* offers only a concise answer, omitting a detailed presentation of his legal reasoning or proof texts. Concision is not what Ibn Qaṭiyya has in mind, though, nor is it what Wansharīsī provides. Instead, Ibn Qaṭiyya is requesting that Wansharīsī provide an answer that transcends the specific case at hand by identifying and explaining the legal rules that are generally applicable to such cases as this.

11 *Fitna* may refer to any type of communal discord, from civil war to the presence of corrupting elements in society.

and by Nisāʾī.[12] Ashhab[13] narrated from Mālik,[14] "No one should reside in a place where anything other than the truth prevails." [Ibn al-ʿArabī][15] stated in *al-ʿĀriḍa*:[16]

> If one were to object, "What if no place can be found other than one like that [where truth does not prevail]?" We would respond that one should choose the least sinful place. For example, if a region contains unbelief,[17] then a region containing injustice is better than that. Or if a region contains justice along with the forbidden (*al-ḥarām*), then a region containing injustice along with the permitted (*al-ḥalāl*) is better than that for residence.[18] Or, if there are transgressions of God's rights in one region, that is preferable to a region with transgressions against

12 See *Ṣaḥīḥ al-Bukhārī, Kitāb al-Īmān, bāb min al-dīn al-firār min al-fitan, ḥadīth* 19 (Bukhārī, *Ṣaḥīḥ al-Bukhārī*, 1:15); *al-Muwaṭṭaʾ*, *Kitāb al-Jāmiʿ*, *bāb mā jāʾa fī amr al-ghanam*, *ḥadīth* 2735, in Mālik b. Anās, *Kitāb al-Muwaṭṭaʾ: Riwāyat Yaḥyā b. Yaḥyā al-Laythī* (Rabat: Manshūrāt al-Majlis al-ʿIlmī al-Aʿlā, 2019), 4:1510–11; *Sunan al-Nasāʾī, Kitāb al-Īmān waʾl-sharāʾiʿ, bāb al-firār biʾl-dīn min al-fitan, ḥadīth* 5080, in Aḥmad b. Shuʿayb al-Nasāʾī, *Kitāb al-Mujtabā, al-maʿrūf bi-: Al-Sunan al-ṣughrā*, ed. Markaz al-Buḥūth wa-Taqniyat al-Maʿlūmāt (Cairo: Dār al-Taʾṣīl, 2012), 7:562; *Sunan Abī Dāwūd, Kitāb al-Fitan, bāb mā yurakhkhaṣu fīhi al-badāwa min al-fitna, ḥadīth* 4267 (Abū Dāwūd, *Sunan Abī Dāwūd*, 6:323). This *ḥadīth* appears in additional chapters of *Ṣaḥīḥ al-Bukhārī* and in other collections.

13 Ashhab b. ʿAbd al-ʿAzīz al-Qaysī (d. 204/819), an Egyptian student of Mālik. *EI³*, s.v. "Ashhab" (Jonathan Brockopp).

14 Mālik b. Anas (d. 179/795), eponymous founder of the Mālikī school of law. *EI²*, s.v. "Mālik b. Anas" (J. Schacht).

15 Abū Bakr Muḥammad b. ʿAbd Allāh b. Muḥammad, known as Ibn al-ʿArabī (d. 543/1148), a prominent Mālikī jurist from Seville. *EI²*, s.v. "Ibn al-ʿArabī" (J. Robson); Mashannī, *Ibn al-ʿArabī*, 13–40.

16 Ibn al-ʿArabī, *ʿĀriḍat al-aḥwadhī bi-sharḥ Ṣaḥīḥ al-Tirmidhī*, ed. Jamāl Marʿashlī, 13 vols. in 8 (Beirut: Dar al-Kutub al-ʿIlmiyya, 1997). This work is often referred to as *al-ʿĀriḍa*. Although Wansharīsī introduces the following passage as a quote from *ʿĀriḍat al-aḥwadhī*, and I have offset the text as such, at this point, Wansharīsī had been using Ibn al-ʿArabī's language for a full paragraph, from "emigration from the land of unbelief." *ʿĀriḍat al-aḥwadhī*, 7:66 (volume 7 is in the fourth physical volume).

17 The Rabat edition of the *Miʿyār* reads *kibr* ("arrogance"), instead of *kufr* ("unbelief"). While *kibr* may also mean an arrogant lack of belief in God, this is a typographical error in the Rabat edition; the Fez lithograph as well as the manuscripts consulted by Muʾnis and Najīb read *kufr*.

18 In the Fez (2:92) and Rabat (2:121) editions of this *fatwā*, which Najīb follows here (44), it is not clear which land is the preferable one for residence in the first two of these three propositions: *mithl an yakūn balad fīhi kufr wa-balad fīhi jawr khayr minhu, aw balad fīhi ʿadl wa-ḥarām wa-balad fīhi jawr wa-ḥalāl khayr minhu lil-maqām*. In the El Escorial manuscript followed by Muʾnis ("Asnā al-matājir," 23) each pair of choices is linked by *fa-balad*, not *wa-balad*, making it clear that the second choice in each case is the one considered preferable for residence. This reading (*fa-balad*) also appears in *ʿĀriḍat al-aḥwadhī* (7:66).

men.[19] This model supports what he [Ashhab] narrated.[20] ʿUmar b. ʿAbd al-ʿAzīz[21] (may God be pleased with him) has said, "So-and-so is in Medina, so-and-so is in Mecca, so-and-so is in Yemen, and so-and-so is in Syria; by God, the earth is filled with injustice and oppression."[22]

Evidence from the Qurʾān

This obligation to emigrate does not lapse for those whose fortresses and lands have been overtaken by tyrants (may God curse them), except in a situation of total incapacity [to emigrate] by any means.[23] Neither homeland nor wealth [are considered], for all such [concerns] are invalid in the eyes of the Law. **God (may He be exalted) said: "Except for the weak among men, women, and children, who are unable to devise a plan and are not shown a way; as for these, perhaps God will pardon them. God is Most Clement, Oft Forgiving."[24] This weakness that characterizes those who are forgiven is not the same weakness that is offered as an excuse at the beginning of the verse.[25] This [latter type of weakness] is**

---

19 In the third proposition, it is clear grammatically that the first case is preferable to the second: *aw balad fīhi maʿāṣī fī ḥuqūq Allāh, fa-huwa awlā min balad fīhi maʿāṣī fī maẓālim al-ʿibād.* Muʾnis suggests emending the text of this third proposition to read that the first region is more suitable *for emigration from it,* which would allow the structure of this proposition to parallel that of the first two ("Asnā al-matājir," 23). Such an emendation is unwarranted, as the meaning is sound as is; many jurists consider the "rights of men" (man's duties to other people) to take precedence over the "rights of God" (man's duties toward God).

20 Muʾnis and Najīb suggest something is missing here, and Wansharīsī himself may have been confused. In this passage, as presented here, "he" must refer to Ashhab. The point must be that his pro-emigration narration is valid and applicable even if the earth has precious few regions in which truth prevails; people are still required to choose the lesser of two evils, with infidelity being the greatest "evil." The closing quote by ʿUmar b. ʿAbd al-ʿAzīz is used to acknowledge that injustice (as opposed to infidelity) is often unavoidable. Elsewhere in the *Miʿyār*, Wansharīsī quotes this same passage from *ʿĀriḍat al-aḥwadhī*, but emends it such that "his narration" refers not to Ashhab but to the *ḥadīth* around which Ibn al-ʿArabī's original discussion revolves (*ʿĀriḍat al-aḥwadhī*, 7:65–66; *al-Miʿyār*, 2:440). The "No *hijra* after the conquest" *ḥadīth* is discussed below. The overall point remains the same in both readings.

21 ʿUmar b. ʿAbd al-ʿAzīz (d. 101/720), Umayyad caliph (r. 99–101/717–20). *EI*², s.v. "ʿUmar (II) b. ʿAbd al-ʿAzīz" (P. M. Cobb).

22 As Muʾnis notes, ʿUmar b. ʿAbd al-ʿAzīz is referring here to Umayyad-appointed governors.

23 Instead of *illā bi-taṣawwur al-ʿajz ʿanhā* (except in a situation of incapacity), Muḥammad ʿInān's summary translation of this passage reads *wa-lā yutaṣawwaru al-ʿajz ʿanhā* (and no situation of incapacity can be imagined). This reading, which is not supported by the critical editions, does not fit the context. ʿInān, *Nihāyat al-Andalus wa-tārīkh al-ʿArab al-mutanaṣṣirīn*, 3rd ed. (Cairo: Maṭbaʿat Lajnat al-Taʾlīf waʾl-Tarjama waʾl-Nashr, 1966), 61.

24 Qurʾān 4:98–99.

25 By "the beginning of the verse," Wansharīsī actually means the previous verse, Qurʾān 4:97: "Those whom the angels take in death while they are wronging themselves, the angels will say to them: 'In what circumstances were you?' They will say, 'We were abased in the earth.' The angels will say, 'Was God's earth not spacious enough for you to have migrated therein?' Hell will be the refuge for such men—a wretched end!" By the "latter part" of the verse (below), he means Qurʾān 4:98 and 4:99, which he quotes here.

the claim by those who wronged themselves: "We were abased in the earth." God (may He be exalted) certainly did not accept their claim as excusing them [from their obligation], for He indicated that they were capable of emigrating by some means. Through His words, "As for these, perhaps God will pardon them," He offered forgiveness for the type of weakness that renders one incapable of devising a plan or being shown a way. "Perhaps" on the part of God indicates a necessary occurrence [not a probability]. The weak man who is punished at the beginning of the verse is the one who is capable [of emigrating] by some means, while the weak man who is forgiven in the latter part of the verse is the one who is incapable [of doing so] by any means.

If someone afflicted with this residence is incapable of fleeing with his religion or finding a way to do so; and no scheme appears to him, nor any power at all to devise such a scheme; or if he is disabled, captive, or the like; or if he is very sick or very weak; then it is hoped that he will be forgiven, and he assumes the same [legal status] as someone who is forced to utter words of unbelief. Nonetheless, he must maintain a steadfast intention that, if he were to have the power or ability, then he would emigrate. Accompanying this intention must be a sincere resolve to emigrate the moment that he gains the power to do so. As for someone who is capable [of emigrating], be that by any possible means or scheme, he is not excused [of the obligation to do so]. He wrongs himself if he remains, according to what is contained in the relevant Qur'ānic verses and *aḥadīth.*

God (may He be exalted) said: "Oh you who believe! Take not My enemy and your enemy as allies. Do you show them affection when they have rejected the truth that has come to you . . . [driving out the Messenger and yourselves because you believe in God, your Lord? If you have come forth to strive in My way and to seek My pleasure (do not show them affection). Do you show them affection in secret, when I am most aware of what you hide and what you reveal?] Whoever among you does this has strayed from the straight path" [Qur'ān 60:1].[26]

God (may He be exalted) said, "Oh you who believe! Take not as intimates those outside your ranks; they will constantly strive to corrupt you. They desire suffering for you. Hatred is revealed by their mouths, but what their breasts conceal is greater. We have made plain to you the signs, if you will understand" [Qur'ān 3:118].

He (may He be exalted) said, "Let not the believers take unbelievers for their allies in preference to believers. Whoever does this has no

26 I have supplied in brackets the portion of the verse (here and below) that is represented in the text only by the shorthand phrase *ilā qawlih* ("up until He says . . .").

connection with God, unless you but guard yourselves against them as a precaution. God bids you beware only of Himself, and unto God is the return" [Qur'ān 3:28].

He (may He be exalted) said, "Incline not toward the unjust, or the Fire will seize you. You have no protectors apart from God—and then you will not be helped" [Qur'ān 11:113].

He (may He be exalted) said, "Give to the hypocrites the grievous tidings that for them there is a painful punishment. Those who take as allies unbelievers instead of believers, do they seek glory among them? Verily all glory belongs to God. [He has already revealed to you in the Book: when you hear people denying and ridiculing God's revelation, do not sit with them unless they take up a different subject, or else you yourselves will become like them. Indeed, God will gather all the hypocrites and disbelievers together in Hell. The [hypocrites] watch you, and if God grants you victory, they say: "Were we not with you?" But if the unbelievers have some success, they say [to them] "Did we not gain an advantage over you, and protect you from the believers?" God will judge between you on the day of Resurrection], and God will not grant the unbelievers any way against the believers" [Qur'ān 4:138–41].

He (may He be exalted) said, "Oh you who believe! Do not take for allies unbelievers instead of believers. Do you wish to give God a clear warrant against you?" [Qur'ān 4:144].

He (may He be exalted) said, "Oh you who believe! Take not the Jews and Christians as allies; they are the allies of each other. Whoever among you allies himself with them is one of them. Verily God does not guide the unjust" [Qur'ān 5:51].

He (may He be exalted) said, "Oh you who believe! Take not as allies those of them who were given the scripture before you, and the unbelievers who make of your religion a mockery and a sport; but fear God if you are indeed believers. When you call to prayer, they make of it a mockery and sport, because they are a people who do not understand" [Qur'ān 5:57–58].

He (may He be exalted) said, "Your true ally is God, and His messenger, and those who believe—those who establish the prayers and pay the alms, and who are bowed in worship. Whoever turns to God and His messenger, and to those who believe—for the party of God, they are the victors" [Qur'ān 5:55–56].

He (may He be exalted) said, "Those whom the angels take in death while they are wronging themselves, the angels will say to them: 'In what circumstances were you?' They will say, 'We were abased in the earth.' The angels will say, 'Was God's earth not spacious enough

for you to have migrated therein?' Hell will be the refuge for such men—a wretched end! Except for the weak among men, women, and children, who are unable to devise a plan and are not guided to a way; as for these, perhaps God will pardon them. God is Most Clement, Oft Forgiving" [Qur'ān 4:97–99].

He (may He be exalted) said, "You see many of them allying with those who do not believe. Evil is what they have sent forward for themselves; God is angered against them and they will abide in torment. Had they only believed in God, in the Prophet, and in what has been revealed to him, they would not have taken them as allies. But many of them are transgressors" [Qur'ān 5:80–81].

Those who are "wronging themselves" in the preceding verses are none other than those who fail to emigrate despite having the ability to do so, as is indicated by the words of God (may He be exalted): "Was God's earth not spacious enough for you to have migrated therein?" [Qur'ān 4:97]. **Indeed, their wronging of themselves consists of their failure [to have emigrated], which meant residing with the unbelievers and increasing their numbers. There is an admonition in His words, "whom the angels take in death" which is that those rebuked and punished for this are only those who die while persisting in this residence [among unbelievers]. As for those who repent and emigrate [before] death overtakes them: even if [they are still] on the road, "those whom the angels take in death" does not include them. It is hoped that their repentance will be accepted, and that they will not die while wronging themselves. This [conclusion] too is indicated by the words of God (may He be exalted): "Whoever goes forth from his home as an emigrant in the way of God and His messenger, [and whom death then overtakes, his reward from God is sure.] For God is Most Forgiving, Most Merciful"** [Qur'ān 4:100].

All of these Qur'ānic verses—or most of them, aside from His words "You see many of them allying with those who do not believe . . ." [Qur'ān 5:80–81]—are **clear texts prohibiting alliances** with unbelievers.[27] As for the words of God (may He be exalted), "Take not the Jews and Christians as allies; they are the allies of each other. Whoever among you allies himself with them is one of them. Verily God does not guide the unjust" [Qur'ān 5:51]: [This verse indicates that] no pending doubt remains as to this prohibition. These words of God (may He be exalted) are similarly [comprehensive]: "Oh you who believe! Take not as allies those of them who

27 Wansharīsī makes a distinction between the clear command "Take not as allies . . ." that appears in many of the verses cited, and this verse, which only implies a prohibition by describing the wrongdoing of a particular group.

were given the scripture before you, and the unbelievers who make of your religion a mockery and a sport; but fear God if you are indeed believers" [Qurʾān 5:57].[28]

The repetition of verses to this effect, and their conformity to a single consistent theme, confirms the prohibition [of alliance with unbelievers] and removes any potential uncertainty[29] concerning it. For if there is a clear text to this effect, and it is confirmed through repetition, then the uncertainty has clearly been removed. Moreover, these Qurʾānic texts, the prophetic *ḥadīths*, and the clear consensus of scholars are all mutually reinforcing with regard to this interdiction. You will not find any [scholar] among those who pray toward Mecca (*ahl al-qibla*) and adhere to the Noble Book who disagrees with this prohibition of residence among unbelievers and of alliance with them. For [God said of the Qurʾān:] "Falsehood cannot approach it from before or behind it. It is a revelation from the Wise, the Praised One" [Qurʾān 41:42].

This is a categorical religious prohibition like the prohibitions against [eating] carrion, blood, and pork, unjustified killing, and similar cases concerning the five universal needs[30] which the leaders of [all] sects and religions have agreed are inviolable. Any [scholar] who contradicts this [prohibition] now, or who wants [to stir up] disagreement as to those who reside with or rely upon [unbelievers], and who therefore permits this residence, considering it a matter of little consequence and making light of the law on this—[any such scholar] will have deviated from the religion and parted from the Muslim community. **He is defeated with [evidence] that no Muslim can defend [himself] against, and he is preceded by [scholarly] consensus, which must not be contradicted** and the course of which must not be violated.

The Precedent of Converts to Islam in *Dār al-Ḥarb*

The leader of the jurists, the judge Abū al-Walīd b. Rushd[31] (may God have mercy upon him) stated in his *Muqaddimāt*, at the beginning of the chapter covering trade in the land of war (*arḍ al-ḥarb*):

28 These two verses are similar, in that both specifically include people of the book, Jews and Christians, in addition to the generic category of "unbelievers."

29 *Rāfiʿ lil-iḥtimāl al-mutaṭarriq ilayh* more literally implies the removal of any loopholes or weaknesses in the case for this prohibition, loopholes that might have rendered it probable rather than certain, or qualified rather than absolute.

30 These universal human needs are the protection of religion, life, reason, progeny, and wealth.

31 Abū al-Walīd Muḥammad b. Aḥmad b. Aḥmad b. Rushd al-Jadd (d. 520/1126), a prominent Mālikī jurist from Córdoba and the grandfather ("*al-jadd*") of the Ibn Rushd known as Averroes.

> The obligation to emigrate has not lapsed; rather, emigration remains obligatory until the day of judgment. By consensus of the Muslim [scholars], anyone who converts to Islam in non-Muslim territory is obligated not to reside there, where he would be subject to the laws of the polytheists. He must emigrate from there and establish himself in Muslim territory,[32] where he would be subject to their [Islamic] laws.[33]

The messenger of God (may God bless him and grant him peace) said, "I am not responsible for any Muslim who lives among the polytheists."[34]

Nonetheless, this obligation to emigrate does not prohibit an emigrant from returning to his homeland, should it revert to a land of belief and Islam. [By contrast], a return to Mecca was forbidden for those Companions of God's messenger (may God bless him and grant him) who were Emigrants [from Mecca to Medina].[35] God reserved this [prohibition] for them because of the merit it entailed.

[Ibn Rushd al-Jadd] said:

> If by virtue of the Book, the Sunna, and the consensus of the community, it is obligatory for anyone who converts to Islam in non-Muslim territory to emigrate from there and to establish himself in Muslim territory; and not to settle or remain among the polytheists, to ensure that he is not subject to their laws; how, then, could it be permissible for anyone to enter their territory, where he would be subject to their laws, whether [regulating] trade or anything else?
>
> Mālik (may God have mercy upon him) deemed it reprehensible for anyone to live in a land where the pious ancestors were derided. How, then, [could anyone live] in a land where the Merciful One is denied, and where idols are worshiped instead? Only the soul of a Muslim whose faith is diseased could be at ease with this.[36]

If you were to say:

"What follows from the discussion of the *Muqaddimāt*'s author, and [from] other early jurists, is a case in which [conversion to Islam] is newly added to [an ongoing state of] residence among polytheists. [In contrast], the case in question is one in which [a state of] residence [in non-Muslim

32 The Arabic here and below (*ʿalā man aslama bi-dār al-ḥarb . . . an yalḥaqa bi-dār al-Muslimīn*) means literally to "join" Muslim territory, but the intended meaning is to establish residence, or "to establish a physical presence" in modern immigration parlance.

33 Ibn Rushd al-Jadd, *al-Muqaddimāt al-mumahhidāt*, 2:153.

34 See the full *ḥadīth* and citation below.

35 The Emigrants (Muhājirūn) were a group of Muḥammad's earliest Companions (Ṣaḥāba) who emigrated from Mecca to Medina with him. There they joined the Helpers (Anṣār), the earliest Companions in Medina.

36 Ibn Rushd al-Jadd, *al-Muqaddimāt al-mumahhidāt*, 2:153.

territory] is newly added to an original state of Islam [i.e., being Muslim]. There is a vast difference between these two cases, so it is not appropriate to use [the first case] as the evidence [by which to judge] the present case in need of a ruling."

I would say:

The early jurists' deliberations [on this issue] simply related to those who fail to emigrate in general. They exemplified this [failure] using one of its manifestations, which is [the case of] someone who converts to Islam in non-Muslim territory and remains there. This [case presently] in question is a second manifestation [of this same failure]. It is no different from the first [case], the one used as an example, except with respect to residence [in non-Muslim territory] being a new addition in particular.

In the first case, the one used as an example by the [early jurists], [conversion to] Islam is newly added to residence [in non-Muslim territory]. In the second case, the one now in question and [the one] that should be assimilated[37] to the [first case], [that same] residence is newly added to Islam. The difference as to which [status] is newly added is a superficial one, and it should be disregarded in any call to restrict this rule entirely to [the first case].

The rightly guided masters who preceded [us], whom [we] emulate, devoted their discussions to the case of someone who has converted to Islam without emigrating (*man aslama wa-lam yuhājir*) only **because submission to polytheist rule[38] was nonexistent in the beginning** and early period **of Islam. [This submission] only arose**, it has been said, **after centuries had passed, and after the master jurists (*mujtahids*) of the great cities had all died out.[39] It is for this reason—without a doubt—that none of them turned their attention to the legal rules [pertaining to this second case].**

Then, when submission to Christian rule appeared this time from the fifth century AH [/eleventh century] onwards—**when the**

37 Here and below, Wansharīsī (following Ibn Rabīʿ) uses variations of the verb *alḥaqa,* meaning "to join" or "to link." When used to refer to legal rules and cases, I translate this term as "assimilate" (or in this instance, "assimilated" for *mulḥaqa*). This conveys more of the intended meaning than "to join" or "to liken"; the jurists here have determined that a new legal case, one that initially appeared to be different from an existing case, was in fact the same. The new case is then made to conform to the existing case and the two are joined as one.

38 *Al-muwālāt al-shirkiyya.* Variants of this phrase (*al-muwālāt al-kufrāniyya, al-muwālāt al-Naṣrāniyya*) are used throughout to mean submission to non-Muslim rule. The use of *muwālāt* (alliance), from the same root as *awliyāʾ* (allies), links the submission described in these passages to the Qurʾānic verses cited earlier, which prohibit Muslims from allying with non-Muslims.

39 This likely refers to the eponymous founders of the law schools and their earliest disciples.

accursed **Christians** (may God destroy them) **seized the island of Sicily and some regions in al-Andalus**—[at that point] **some of the jurists**[40] **were questioned about this, and they were asked about the legal judgments pertaining to those who commit [this act of submission]. They answered that they [i.e., conquered Muslims] are subject to the same rules as are those who convert to Islam but who do not emigrate. They assimilated those** [conquered Muslims] in question, about whose legal status [the early jurists were] silent, **to them [i.e., the converts]. [These jurists] considered the two groups to be equal in terms of the legal rules pertaining to their property and children—they saw no difference between the two groups in this regard. This is because the two [groups] are as one with respect to submitting to the enemy, living among them, interacting and** associating with them, being indistinguishable from them, **abandoning** their obligation to **emigrate**, [failing] to flee **from them, and so on. [They are on par with respect to] every condition that necessitates these rules**—[rules] that had not been articulated [yet] with regard to the case whose status was being questioned.

[These later jurists] (may God have mercy upon them) **thus assimilated the legal rules on which they [i.e., the early jurists] had been silent,** and which pertain to those [Muslims] about whom they had been silent, **to the legal rules that they had elaborated**, [that] pertain to those [converts]. **Thus, the later jurists' independent reasoning (*ijtihād*) in this matter consisted merely of assimilating the unarticulated [case] to the one that had been addressed, which in substance was completely equivalent to [the unaddressed case].**

[This answer] from [the later jurists] (may God have mercy upon them) reflects judicious speculation, a cautious use of independent reasoning, and a trust placed in adhering to [the opinions of] the rightly guided **masters who preceded [us], whom [we] emulate.** Therefore, it was of the utmost excellence and beauty.

Evidence from the *Ḥadīth*

As for the evidence from the Sunna that this residence [in non-Muslim territory] is prohibited, here is what al-Tirmidhī includes [in his collection]:

> **The Prophet (may God bless him and grant him peace) sent a raiding party to Khathʿam. Some people sought protection by prostrating, but they were killed quickly. This [news] reached the Prophet (may God bless him and grant him peace) whereupon**

40 Ibn Rabīʿ specifies that these were Maghribī jurists.

he ordered that one-half of the blood money be paid to them. He said: "I am not responsible for any Muslim who lives among the polytheists." They said: "Why, Oh Messenger of God?" He said, "Their fires should not be visible to one another."[41]

From the same chapter [of al-Tirmidhī]: "The Prophet (may God bless him and grant him peace) said: 'Do not live among the polytheists or associate with them. Whoever lives among them or associates with them, is one of them.'"[42]

The explicit stipulation in these two traditions (*ḥadīths*) as to the intended meaning is such that it should be obvious to anyone with sound judgment and a correct approach to evaluating evidence. They are both proven to be among the "good" traditions [*ḥasān*] included in the six compilations of *ḥadīth* around which the core of Islam revolves.[43]

They said:[44] **'There is nothing that contradicts [these reports]—no abrogating [texts], no [evidence] that restricts their applicability to specific cases, and no other such [evidence that might qualify their applicability]. No Muslim disagrees as to what these two [traditions] stipulate. This [alone] is sufficient for using these two [traditions] as evidence [in legal reasoning]—and this is in addition to the corroboration and attestations we find for these two verses in the clear texts of the Book and in the principles of the law.**

In *Sunan Abī Dāwūd*, there is a tradition related on the authority of Muʿāwiya,[45] who said: "I heard the Messenger of God (may God bless him and grant him peace) say: 'The duty to emigrate will not cease until repentance ceases; and repentance will not cease until the sun rises in the West.'"[46]

---

41 *Sunan al-Tirmidhī, Abwāb al-Siyar, bāb mā jāʾa fī karāhiyyat al-muqām bayna aẓhur al-mushrikīn, ḥadīth* 1709 (Tirmidhī, *Sunan al-Tirmidhī*, 2:601); *Sunan Abī Dāwūd, Kitāb al-Jihād, bāb al-nahy ʿan qatl man iʿtaṣama biʾl-sujūd, ḥadīth* 2645 (Abū Dāwūd, *Sunan Abī Dāwūd*, 4:280–83); *Nasāʾī* (*Kitāb al-Sunan al-Kubrā*), *Kitāb al-Qasāma, bāb al-qawd bi-ghayr ḥadīda, ḥadīth* 6956 (Nasāʾī, *Kitāb al-Sunan al-Kubrā*, 6:347–48). Ibn al-ʿArabī discusses this *ḥadīth* in *ʿĀriḍat al-Aḥwadhī*, 7:78–79.

42 *Sunan al-Tirmidhī, Abwāb al-Siyar, bāb mā jāʾa fī karāhiyyat al-muqām bayna aẓhur al-mushrikīn, ḥadīth* 1710 (Tirmidhī, *Sunan al-Tirmidhī*, 2:602); *Sunan Abī Dāwūd, Kitāb al-Jihād, bāb fī al-iqāma bi-arḍ al-shirk, ḥadīth* 2787 (Abū Dāwūd, *Sunan Abī Dāwūd*, 4:413–14).

43 Traditions classified as *ḥasan* ("good"), are considered reliable transmissions originating from Muḥammad. Only *ṣaḥīḥ* ("sound") reports are given a higher rating. An overview of *ḥadīth* collections and terminology may be found in Jonathan A.C. Brown, *Hadith: Muhammad's Legacy in the Medieval and Modern World* (Oxford: Oneworld, 2009).

44 It is unclear who "they" are. Asmal suggests that "they" are the *ḥadīth* compilers or authors of *ḥadīth* commentaries. Asmal, "Muslims under Non-Muslim Rule," 160 n. 3.

45 ʿAbd Allāh b. Muʿāwiya (d. 130/747–8). *EI*[2], s.v. "ʿAbd Allāh b. Muʿāwiya" (K.V. Zetterstéen).

46 *Sunan Abī Dāwūd, Kitāb al-Jihād, bāb fī al-hijra, hal inqaṭaʿat?, ḥadīth* 2479 (Abū Dāwūd, *Sunan Abī Dāwūd*, 4:136). Note that according to another *ḥadīth*, the sun rising from the West will be one of the signs of the day of judgment.

In this [same chapter] is a tradition narrated on the authority of Ibn ʿAbbās. He stated: "The Messenger of God (may God bless him and grant him peace) said on the day of the conquest of Mecca: 'There is no *hijra* after the conquest; but there [remains the obligation of] *jihād*, and of [correct] intention; so if you are summoned to battle, then go forth.'"[47]

Abū Sulaymān al-Khaṭṭābī[48] said:

> At the beginning of Islam, emigration was recommended, not obligatory, in accordance with the words of God (may He be exalted): "Whoever emigrates in the way of God will find much refuge and abundance in the earth" [Qurʾān 4:100]. This [verse] was revealed when the suffering inflicted on the Muslims by the polytheists in Mecca became severe. Subsequently, upon the departure of the Prophet (may God bless him and grant him peace) for Medina, emigration became obligatory for Muslims. They were ordered to move to his city in order to be with him, so that they could cooperate and show solidarity if anything serious befell them, and in order to learn and study deeply the affairs of their religion.
>
> Fear of the Qurāysh, who were the people of Mecca, had become great in that time. Then, once Mecca was conquered and submitted in obedience, this meaning [of emigration, to be with the Prophet himself] came to an end. The obligatory nature of emigration was lifted, and its status returned to that of a recommended or desirable duty.
>
> These, therefore, are two different *hijras*. Of the two, the one that has ceased is the obligatory one. The one that remains is the recommended one. This is how the two traditions may be reconciled, although there is also a disparity between their chains of transmission. The chain of transmission for the tradition reported by Ibn ʿAbbās is sound, with an uninterrupted chain of narrators leading back to Muḥammad (*muttaṣil ṣaḥīḥ*), while the chain of transmission [for the tradition reported by] Muʿāwiya is contested.

I say:[49] These two *hijras* that are addressed in the traditions [reported by] Muʿāwiya and Ibn ʿAbbās are the two *hijras* which ceased to be

---

47 *Ṣaḥīḥ al-Bukhārī, Kitāb al-Jihād waʾl-siyar, bāb faḍl al-jihād waʾl-siyar, ḥadīth* 2631 (Bukhārī, *Ṣaḥīḥ al-Bukhārī*, 3:1025); *Ṣaḥīḥ al-Bukhārī, Kitāb al-Jihād waʾl-siyar, bāb wujūb al-nafīr . . . , ḥadīth* 2670 (Bukhārī, *Ṣaḥīḥ al-Bukhārī*, 3:1040); *Ṣaḥīḥ Muslim, Kitāb al-Imāra, bāb al-mubāyaʿa baʿd fatḥ Makka . . . , ḥadīth* 86 (Muslim b. al-Ḥajjāj, *Ṣaḥīḥ Muslim*, 3:1488); *Sunan al-Tirmidhī, Abwāb al-Siyar, bāb mā jāʾa fī al-hijra, ḥadīth* 1693 (Tirmidhī, *Sunan al-Tirmidhī*, 2:595).

48 Ḥamd (or Aḥmad) b. Muḥammad b. Ibrāhīm b. Khaṭṭāb al-Bustī, known as Abū Sulaymān al-Khaṭṭābī (d. 386/996 or 388/998) was a well-traveled jurist and traditionist who was born and died in Bust (modern-day Afghanistan). *EI*², s.v. "Al-Khaṭṭābī" (Editors).

49 Although Wansharīsī attributes this next paragraph to himself, he has only lightly adapted a passage from Ibn al-ʿArabī, *ʿĀriḍat al-aḥwadhī*, 7:66.

obligatory upon the conquest of Mecca.[50] The first *hijra* is that which is motivated by fear for one's religion and life, like the *hijra* of the Prophet (may God bless him and grant him peace) and of his Meccan Companions. This [*hijra*] was an obligation for them,[51] without which [their] faith would not have been complete. The second [*hijra*] consisted of emigrating to the Prophet (may God bless him and grant him peace) in his land, where he had settled. Those who went to him pledged their allegiance [to him] on the basis of their *hijra*, while others pledged their allegiance on the basis of Islam.

As for emigration from the land of unbelief, it is obligatory until the day of judgment. Ibn al-ʿArabī stated in *al-Aḥkām*:[52]

> Travel may be divided into six categories. The first is emigration, which is leaving the land of war (*dār al-ḥarb*) for the land of Islam (*dār al-Islām*). This was an obligation in the days of the Prophet (may God bless him and grant him peace) and this *hijra* remains obligatory until the day of judgment. The [*hijra*] that ceased with the conquest [of Mecca] was that of traveling to the Prophet (may God bless him and grant him peace) wherever he was. [Thus, it is obligatory for anyone who converts to Islam in the land of war to depart for the land of Islam].[53] If he remains in the land of war he commits an act of disobedience and his status is disputed.

(You may) consider the remaining categories of emigration in [Ibn al-ʿArabī's *al-Aḥkām*].

---

50 In this excerpt, Wansharīsī must mean the two *hijras* that are addressed by Khaṭṭābī, not the two *hijras* described in these *ḥadīth* reports. It would not make sense to argue that the enduring *hijra* in the tradition narrated on the authority of Muʿāwiya came to an end with the conquest of Mecca. In the passage Wansharīsī adapts from Ibn al-ʿArabī, the latter is addressing only the "no *hijra*" *ḥadīth*.

51 Najīb's edition (67) reads "to him," as does the Rabat edition (2:126). "To them" makes more sense here and is the variant that appears in Muʾnis's edition (34) and in Ibn al-ʿArabī.

52 The following passage appears in Ibn al-ʿArabī's *Aḥkām al-Qurʾān*, a work of exegesis covering five hundred verses of the Qurʾān deemed to have legal import. Ibn al-ʿArabī, *Aḥkām al-Qurʾān*, ed. Riḍā Faraj al-Hamāmī (Beirut: al-Maktaba al-ʿAṣriyya, 2003), 1:496.

53 Wansharīsī omits this sentence, but I have included it in order to render this excerpt from Ibn al-ʿArabī more intelligible (*al-Aḥkām*, 1:496). The rest of this passage in *Asnā al-matājir* differs slightly from Ibn al-ʿArabī's text. Most notably, while *hijra* is indeed the first category of "movement on the earth" (i.e., travel) in *al-Aḥkām*, Ibn al-ʿArabī considers *hijra* by itself, and divides it, not all travel, into six categories. His categories of travel are far more numerous.

Inviolability of Muslims' Lives and Property

Ibn al-ʿArabī also stated in *al-ʿĀriḍa*:[54]

> At first, God prohibited Muslims from residing among polytheists in Mecca and obligated them to join the Prophet in Medina. When God granted [the Muslims] victory over Mecca, the *hijra* lapsed but the prohibition on residence among polytheists remained.
>
> As for those [people of Khathʿam] who sought protection by prostrating , it was not [the case] that they converted to Islam and then [chose to] remain among the polytheists; instead, their appeal for inviolability was made only at that moment. Yes, [it is true] that according to the consensus of the scholars, it is not permissible to kill one who hastens to Islam when he sees the sword at his head. Yet they were killed for one of two reasons: either because prostration does not grant inviolability, and inviolability is instead attained only by pronouncing the two parts of the testimony of faith;[55] or, because those who killed them did not know that [prostration] rendered their lives inviolable. This [latter possibility] is the correct [one]. For when Khālid[56] rushed to kill the Banū Jadhīma, they declared: "We have converted, we have converted! (*ṣabaʾnā*)" They did not know that it is best to declare, "We have converted to Islam (*aslamnā*)!" He therefore killed them, but the Prophet (may God bless him and grant him peace) then paid blood money to [their families to compensate] for Khālid's error. [Damages resulting from] the ruler's errors and those of his agents are [payable] from the treasury.

[Ibn al-ʿArabī] said:

> This indicates that it is not a condition of [conversion to] Islam to state specifically "There is no god but God, and Muḥammad is the messenger of God"[57] . . . [Muḥammad] paid half of the blood money [to the people of Khathʿam] only in the interests of peace and the public good. He paid the people of Jadhīma twice as much [i.e., full blood money][58]

54 Ibn al-ʿArabī, *ʿĀriḍat al-aḥwadhī*, 7:79.

55 The *shahādatayn*, that is, "I testify that there is no god but God, and that Muḥammad is the messenger of God."

56 Sayf al-Dīn Khālid b. al-Walīd (d. 21/642), one of early Islam's most prominent military commanders.

57 In the elided sentence that follows, Ibn al-ʿArabī states that if someone says he is Muslim, this should suffice to give him the legal status of being Muslim.

58 Ibn al-ʿArabī reads *mithla dhālika* (the same amount), while Wansharīsī reads *mithlay dhālika* (twice as much). The two cases differ in that the people of Khathʿam engaged in battle and the religious status of those prostrating was unclear to the Muslim forces. The people of Jadhīma had converted prior to Khālid's arrival and they laid down their arms when they saw his forces.

in accordance with what was required by the circumstances of each person, based on his word.[59]

The scholars have differed as to the status of one who converts to Islam but remains in the land of war (*dār al-ḥarb*).[60] What if he is then killed, or his family is captured and his property taken? Mālik held that his life is protected, but that anyone may take his property until he establishes [legal] ownership of it within Muslim territory.[61] [Other scholars] held that [the convert] maintains legal ownership of his property and family; Shāfiʿī held this view.[62]

This issue is accepted as being among the issues upon which scholars disagree. [In this case, their disagreement] is based on [two questions]: **Do [non-Muslim] residents of enemy territory (*ḥarbīs*) possess valid ownership? Is it Islam or [Muslim] territory that guarantees [a Muslim's] inviolability?**[63]

Those who are of the opinion that he [the *ḥarbī*] possesses valid ownership hold to the words [of Muḥammad] (may God bless him and grant him peace): "Has ʿAqīl left us any house?"[64] **And to [Muḥammad's] words (may God bless him and grant him peace): "I was ordered to fight people until they proclaim 'There is no god but God.' Once they proclaim this, they have protected their lives and property from me, except by [legal] right to them."**[65] **[Muḥammad] thus treated lives and property equally and linked them [both] to [the converts] using a possessive grammatical**

59 After Khālid's return, Muḥammad sent ʿAlī to speak with the people of Jadhīma and to compensate them for lost lives and damaged property. On the Jadhīma incident, see Muḥammad Ibn Isḥāq, *The Life of Muḥammad*, trans. A. Guillaume (Oxford: Oxford University Press, 2003), 561–65.

60 Abou El Fadl provides a useful overview of Islamic legal opinions on this issue. See Abou El Fadl, "Islamic Law and Muslim Minorities," 165–69.

61 Here Ibn al-ʿArabī notes that Abū Ḥanīfa also held this position.

62 The Rabat edition of the *Miʿyār* (2:127) mistakenly reads *innahu yajūz mālahu*, whereas *ʿĀriḍat al-aḥwadhī* (7:79) reads *yaḥūz*. The former reading would mean that according to some, Mālik considered the convert's property to be licit—but this would be redundant with the preceding sentence.

63 Ibn al-ʿArabī's original passage includes neither this second question, nor the *ḥadīth* regarding *ʿAqīl*. These appear to be Ibn Rabīʿ's additions.

64 *Ṣaḥīḥ al-Bukhārī, Kitāb al-Maghāzī, bāb ayna rakaza al-nabī* . . . , *ḥadīth* 4032 (Bukhārī, *Ṣaḥīḥ al-Bukhārī*, 4:1560); *Ṣaḥīḥ Muslim, Kitāb al-Ḥajj, bāb al-nuzūl bi-Makka* . . . , *ḥadīth* 440 (Muslim b. al-Ḥajjāj, *Ṣaḥīḥ Muslim*, 2:984–85). Abbreviated here, this *ḥadīth* reinforces the rule that Muslims and non-Muslims may not inherit from one other. Because this rule implies that non-Muslims have property rights, this *ḥadīth* also supports the position that non-Muslims, including those in enemy territory, have legal ownership of their possessions.

65 *Ṣaḥīḥ al-Bukhārī, Kitāb al-Zakāt, bāb wujūb al-zakāt, ḥadīth* 1335 (Bukhārī, *Ṣaḥīḥ al-Bukhārī*, 2:507); *Ṣaḥīḥ al-Bukhārī, Kitāb al-Jihād wa'l-siyar, bāb duʿā' al-nabī ilā al-Islām* . . . , *ḥadīth* 2786 (Bukhārī, *Ṣaḥīḥ al-Bukhārī*, 3:1077–78); *Ṣaḥīḥ Muslim, Kitāb al-Īmān, bāb al-amr bi-qitāl al-nās* . . . , *ḥadīths* 32–33 (Muslim b. al-Ḥajjāj, *Ṣaḥīḥ Muslim*, 1:51–52).

construction; the possessive construction necessarily indicates ownership. He [Muḥammad] then stated that if any of them converts to Islam, he is inviolable; this [statement] necessarily indicates that no one has any right [to act] against him.[66]

Those [scholars] who ascribe his property to him [the convert] further hold to these words of [Muḥammad] (may God bless him and grant him peace): "Whoever converts to Islam while in possession of something, that remains his [lawful property],"[67] **and to his statement (may God bless him and grant him peace): "The property of any Muslim is only made licit by his own consent."**[68]

By contrast, Mālik, Abū Ḥanīfa, and those who agree with them hold that [being in Muslim] territory is the only guarantor of inviolability. This means that as long as a Muslim does not establish possession of his property and offspring within Muslim territory, anything seized in infidel territory constitutes booty (*fay'*) for the Muslims. It is as if, for them [these scholars], infidels have no [legal] ownership—instead, their property and offspring are licit to any Muslim capable of [seizing] them, just as their lives [are not protected]. [In this view] if someone converts to Islam but does not establish possession of either [his] property or [his] offspring in Muslim territory—then it is as if he has no property or offspring. Indeed, it is as though ownership [of these things] belongs to the infidels, just as the territory belongs to them, and a Muslim's ownership is not valid as long as he remains in their midst.[69]

Ibn al-ʿArabī [this should read: Mālik] also stated: **"The guarantor of inviolability for** the **Muslim's life is Islam, and for his property, [being**

66 In Ibn al-ʿArabī, this passage reads: "He then stated that they [i.e., the lives and property] were protected, and that this necessarily indicates that no one had a right to them." Ibn al-ʿArabī, *ʿĀriḍat al-aḥwadhī*, 7:79.

67 *Al-Sunan al-Kubrā* (*Sunan al-Bayhaqī al-Kubrā*), *Kitāb al-Siyar, bāb man aslama ʿala shayʾ fa-huwa la-hu, ḥadīth* 18259. Abū Bakr Aḥmad al-Bayhaqī, *al-Sunan al-Kubrā*, ed. Muḥammad ʿAbd al-Qādir ʿAṭā (Beirut: Dār al-Kutub al-ʿIlmiyya, 2003), 9:191–92.

68 *Al-Sunan al-Kubrā* (*Sunan al-Bayhaqī al-Kubrā*), *Kitāb al-Ghaṣb, bāb man ghaṣaba lawḥan . . . , ḥadīth* 11545 (Bayhaqī, *al-Sunan al-Kubrā*, 6:166).

69 These last two analogies are somewhat contradictory: non-Muslims either own nothing, or everything in their territory. The position Wansharīsī is characterizing may be explained as follows: the property, families, and lives of unbelievers outside of Muslim territory are not protected; they are licit to Muslims within the bounds of the rules governing warfare. When an unbeliever converts to Islam, that conversion does not change the legal status of his property and family, which remain liable to capture by raiding parties of Muslims from *dār al-Islām*. The legal status of all property in non-Muslim territory is the same, because it is the territory that is the determining factor in the status of property and family. In order to change the status of his property and enjoy the legal protections normally afforded to other Muslims, a convert must bring that property to Muslim territory.

in Muslim] territory."[70] Shāfiʿī said: "The guarantor of inviolability for both of them is Islam."[71] Abū Ḥanīfa said: "The guarantor of inviolability whose [violation] obliges monetary compensation is [Muslim] territory in both cases [i.e., of life and property], while the one [whose violation] results in the assessment of sin is Islam."[72] This means that if a convert to Islam does not emigrate and is killed [unlawfully], atonement is required in Abū Ḥanīfa's view, but blood money or retaliation is not.[73] If he had emigrated, then atonement would be required and [in addition], the blood money would be incumbent on his [the killer's] kin.

Accordingly, it is said that for Mālik and Shāfiʿī, his [the convert's] life is protected. For Abū Ḥanīfa, his accidental killing requires only atonement, and not blood money, as a specific exception to the general rule.

This [latter opinion] accords with the evident meaning [of the Qur'ān] as interpreted by the exegetes. They cite as evidence for this [opinion] His words (may He be exalted): "As for those who believed but did not emigrate, you owe them no loyalty until they emigrate" [Qur'ān 8:72], **and His words (may He be exalted): ". . . If he belonged to a people hostile to you, and was a believer, then (the penance is) to set free a believing slave"** [Qur'ān 4:92]. **He [God] does not mention blood money [in these verses].[74] [The exegetes] said: What "believer" means [in this latter verse] is none other than the Muslim who fails to emigrate, because he is a believer [living] among an enemy people.**

70 Wansharīsī has erred in attributing this statement to Ibn al-ʿArabī. In copying from Ibn Rabīʿ's text, Wansharīsī rearranged and partially confused his predecessors' presentation of various scholars' views regarding the life, property, and family of converts to Islam in non-Muslim territory. Ibn Rabīʿ attributes this statement to Mālik, not Ibn al-ʿArabī. Furthermore, this statement, which does not appear in Ibn al-ʿArabī's published works, is not an accurate characterization of his views. As becomes clear, he agreed with Shāfiʿī's position.

71 For a more detailed discussion of Shāfiʿī's position, see Najīb, ed., *Asnā al-matājir*, 75, n. 3.

72 In the first clause, Wansharīsī reads *al-ʿāṣim al-muqawwima*, likely a mistake. My translation follows Ibn Rabīʿ, whose text reads *al-ʿāṣim al-mugharrima*; the parallel term in the second clause is *al-ʿāṣim al-muʾaththama*. This distinction appears to be an effort to make sense of inviolability in a way that is consistent with Qur'ān 4:92. This verse requires both blood money and atonement for the accidental killing of believers in general, but requires only atonement for the accidental killing of Muslims who reside in enemy territory. See Ibn al-ʿArabī, *al-Aḥkām*, 1:490–91.

73 The act of atonement specified in Qur'ān 4:92 is the freeing of a Muslim slave, as noted below. In his commentary on this verse, Ibn al-ʿArabī speculates as to why blood money would not be required in the case of Muslims killed in enemy territory. If the convert has no Muslim relatives, the money would go to non-Muslims in enemy territory, potentially strengthening them in war against Muslims. See Ibn al-ʿArabī, *al-Aḥkām* (1:490–91) and *ʿĀriḍat al-aḥwadhī* (7:79).

74 This is the portion of Qur'ān 4:92, noted above, that addresses the accidental killing of believers who reside in enemy territory. The same verse also addresses accidental killing of believers in general, and believers whose community shares a covenant with Muslims. In both of these latter cases, blood money is required.

He is thus one of them, according to His words (may He be exalted): "Whoever among you allies himself with them is one of them" [Qurʾān 5:51]. **Therefore, he is a believer from an enemy people.**

When He mentions blood money at the beginning of this verse [Qurʾān 4:92] **in regard to [the killing of] believers in general, and [again] at the end of the verse, with regard to believers whose communities are under a treaty and covenant with us (that is, the *dhimmīs*) [Christians and Jews under Muslim rule], and [when] He does not mention it in regard to these believers in the enemy's midst, He has indicated that [the payment of blood money] is annulled [in this case] and that He has required atonement alone, as a specific exception to the general rule. This is the rule regarding the legal status of his life [i.e., the Muslim convert residing in enemy territory].**

Ibn al-ʿArabī said:[75]

> It was in Khurāsān that this issue was of great importance.[76] The Mālikīs did not encounter it, nor did the ʿIrāqī masters know of it. So how would Maghribī jurists who follow previously established doctrines (*muqallids*) [know how to respond]?[77]
>
> Abū Ḥanīfa's followers support their opinion that [Muslim] territory is what grants inviolability with the argument that only fortresses and citadels [are effective] in guarding, preserving [lives and property], and warding off [danger]. [They argue] also that if an infidel came to our territory, his life and property would be protected. Thus, [this issue] comes to resemble [the status of] property: If it has been left lying in the road [and is taken], the punishment of amputating a thief's hand does not follow in this [event]; but if it has been secured in its place of safekeeping, then amputation is warranted.

---

75 I have not been able to locate the following passage in Ibn al-ʿArabī's works.

76 Khurāsān, "the land of sunrise" refers broadly to the lands east of western Persia, including Central Asia and Afghanistan, as well as to a specific region of northeastern Persia. The term is analogous to the Maghrib, "the place where the sun sets," which can refer broadly to the western lands of Islam, to North Africa, or in modern times, to Morocco specifically. *EI*², s.v. "Khurāsān" (C.E. Bosworth).

77 As Khurāsān and the Maghrib represent opposite ends of the Islamic world, Ibn al-ʿArabī appears to be emphasizing his peers' geographical and temporal distance from any developed legal discourse or precedent regarding Muslims living in non-Muslim territory. It should be noted that we cannot be certain what specific "issue" Ibn al-ʿArabī has been discussing up to this point, as the source text has not been identified. Based on the material that follows, though, it is reasonable to assume that he is referring to the legal status of the lives and property of Muslims living in non-Muslim territory. Ibn al-ʿArabī may be overstating the case; while the Mālikīs lacked a systematic legal discourse on this issue, they were not without precedents regarding Muslims' inviolability while in *dār al-ḥarb*. On Mālikī responses to Muslims who stayed in Barcelona after its conquest in 185/801, see Abou El Fadl, "Islamic Law and Muslim Minorities," 169; Molénat, "Le problème," 396–97; Wansharīsī, *al-Miʿyār*, 2:129–30.

Shāfiʿī supports his opinion with the words of the Prophet (may God bless him and grant him peace): "I was ordered to fight people until they proclaim 'There is no god but God.' Once they proclaim this, they have protected their lives and their property from me, except by [legal] right to it."[78] For this [text] stipulates that it is only the profession of Islam that grants inviolability of person and property. Even if a Muslim were to enter *dār al-ḥarb*, his life and property would [remain] inviolable. [The legal status of the] territory is of no relevance.

As for the opinions of our fellow [Mālikīs] (that Islam provides inviolability for one's life but not for children or property) and of Abū Ḥanīfa's followers (that only fortresses protect and preserve): this is nonsense, as it pertains to a tangible protection that may be gained by any infidel or rebel [behind physical walls]. The law pays no account to this [physical protection, in determining inviolability]. [Scholarly] discussion should concern only what is legally relevant.

Do you not see that Muslim rebels and infidels may protect themselves in fortresses, but the lives and property of both [groups] remain licit? In one case, [infidels' lives are licit] unconditionally, and in the other case [rebels' lives are licit] on the condition that they persist rather than desist, that they persevere and grow stronger. In contrast, property is made inviolable only through the owner's protection, by virtue of having it with him in a place of safekeeping.

I say [Wansharīsī]: **Ashhab and Saḥnūn**[79] **shared Shāfiʿī's opinion, which is also the choice of Abū Bakr b. al-ʿArabī,** according to what his discussion [just] now indicates. **Abū Ḥanīfa and Aṣbagh b. al-Faraj**[80] **shared the opinion of Mālik, which Ibn Rushd** [al-Jadd] **also chose,** and which is the commonly accepted view (*al-mashhūr*) attributed to Mālik (may God have mercy upon him). **The source of disagreement [between these two groups] is** as mentioned previously.[81]

The renowned jurist and judge Abū ʿAbd Allāh b. al-Ḥājj[82] and other later jurists addressed the property of this Muslim in question—[who became a] resident of *dār al-ḥarb* [when] he did not leave following the tyrant's conquest of [his homeland]—in the context of the above debate among the

78 See above for the sources of this *ḥadīth*.

79 ʿAbd al-Salām Saḥnūn b. Saʿīd (d. 240/854) wrote *al-Mudawwana*, one of the Mālikī school's foundational texts. *EI*², s.v. "Saḥnūn" (M. Talbi).

80 Aṣbagh b. al-Faraj b. al-Saʿīd al-Nāfiʿ (d. 225/840), a prominent Egyptian Mālikī student of Ibn al-Qāsim.

81 That is, whether or not *ḥarbīs* can possess valid ownership, and whether it is being Muslim or being in Muslim territory that provides inviolability for lives and possessions.

82 Abū ʿAbd Allāh Muḥammad b. Aḥmad, known as Ibn al-Ḥājj (d. 529/1134), a judge in Córdoba. Ziriklī, *al-Aʿlām*, 5:317.

master jurists of the great cities regarding the property of someone who converts to Islam but continues to reside in *dār al-ḥarb*. **After linking these related rules and treating them as equivalents**, Ibn al-Ḥājj subsequently distinguished [between the two cases]. [The distinction] is that the convert's property was licit prior to his conversion to Islam, in contrast to the property of the **[conquered] Muslim**. For **[the conquered Muslim's] ownership never ceased; at no prior point had unbelief rendered his property and children licit for the Muslims, even for a day. Therefore, no one has a [lawful] means to claim either of them. [According to Ibn al-Ḥājj] this is the preponderant (*rājiḥ*) opinion in this debate. It is clear from reason and examination and so evident, upon consideration of the above source of disagreement, as to be lost on no one.**

[Ibn al-Ḥājj] supports this distinction with another text, a case addressed in the *Samāʿ Yaḥyā*,[83] in the chapter on *jihād*. The passage is as follows:[84]

> I asked him [i.e., Yaḥyā b. Yaḥyā asked Ibn al-Qāsim[85]] about those Muslims from Barcelona who failed to move away from them [their Christian conquerors] after [the expiry of] the one-year period set for their departure on the day [the city] was conquered.[86] [These Barcelonans] subsequently made raids against the Muslims in order to protect themselves, because they feared being killed if they were defeated [by Muslims retaking the city].

---

83 Abū Muḥammad Yaḥyā b. Yaḥyā al-Laythī (d. 234/848), a Córdoban jurist, is credited with the introduction of Mālik's *Muwaṭṭaʾ* in al-Andalus. The *Samāʿ Yaḥyā* refers to Yaḥyā's recension of the *Muwaṭṭaʾ*, which became the canonical version of this text in the Islamic West (there were several other transmissions). *EI*², s.v. "Yaḥyā b. Yaḥyā al-Laythī" (Maribel Fierro).

84 The following passage is taken from the *Mustakhraja* of Abū ʿAbd Allāh Muḥammad b. Aḥmad al-ʿUtbī (d. 254 or 255/868–9), also known as the *ʿUtbiyya*. ʿUtbī, an Andalusī jurist originally from Córdoba, compiled this legal work after studying with Yaḥyā b. Yaḥyā, Saḥnūn, and other major transmitters of Mālikī doctrine. No longer extant as an independent text, the entire *ʿUtbiyya* is preserved in Ibn Rushd al-Jadd's commentary on this text, *al-Bayān wa'l-Taḥṣīl*. Ibn Rushd al-Jadd (d. 520/1126), *al-Bayān wa'l-taḥṣīl wa'l-sharḥ wa'l-tawjīḥ wa'l-taʿlīl fī masāʾil al-Mustakhraja*, ed. Muḥammad Ḥajjī, et al., 2nd ed. (Beirut: Dār al-Gharb al-Islāmī, 1988), 3:41–42. Ibn Abī Zayd al-Qayrawānī (d. 386/996) drew heavily from ʿUtbī's work; this same passage appears in his *al-Nawādir wa'l-ziyādāt ʿalā mā fī al-Mudawwana min ghayrihā min al-ummuhāt*, ed. ʿAbd al Fattāḥ Muḥammad al-Ḥulw, et al. (Beirut: Dār al-Gharb al-Islāmī, 1999), 3:352.

85 Ibn Rushd al-Jadd leaves Yaḥyā b. Yaḥyā's interlocutor ambiguous in *al-Bayān wa'l-taḥṣīl*. Asmal and Verskin choose Ibn Nāfiʿ (d. 186/802–3), who appears to be one possibility. Yet Ibn Abī Zayd al-Qayrawānī identifies Ibn al-Qāsim as Yaḥyā's interlocutor in *al-Nawādir wa'l-ziyādāt*, noted above. ʿAbd al-Raḥmān b. al-Qāsim al-ʿUtaqī (d. 191/806–7), known as Ibn al-Qāsim, was the most prominent Egyptian disciple of Mālik. On this passage, see also Ana Fernández Félix, *Cuestiones Legales del Islam Temprano: La ʿUtbiyya y el Proceso de Formación de la Sociedad Islámica Andalusí* (Madrid: Consejo Superior de Investigaciones Científicas, 2003), 427–28.

86 Barcelona was conquered in 185/801.

> [Ibn al-Qāsim] said: I do not see his status as any different from that of the bandit or rebel (*al-muḥārib*) who steals from Muslims in *dār al-Islām*; this is because he remains in the religion of Islam. If he is caught, his case is referred to the ruler, who judges his case in the same way he would judge those involved in corruption and rebellion.[87] As for his property, I do not deem it permissible for anyone to take it.

> The relevant part of the [passage] ends [here].[88]
> Ibn Rushd [al-Jadd] [commented on this passage as follows]:

> [Ibn al-Qāsim's] opinion—that by raiding Muslims, they occupy the position of bandits or rebels (*muḥāribīn*)—is correct. There is no disagreement on this point. This is because the judgment regarding a Muslim who engages in banditry or rebellion is the same regardless of whether his banditry occurs in Muslim territory or infidel territory.

> As for [Ibn al-Qāsim's] opinion regarding his property—that it is not permitted for anyone to take—is in clear contradiction to Mālik's opinion in the *Mudawwana*. In the case of someone who converts to Islam in enemy territory, after which Muslims invade that territory and capture his family and property, [Mālik's opinion] was that all of this is [legitimate] booty. For he did not distinguish in this matter between the army's capturing [a convert's] property and child before or after his departure [for Muslim territory].[89]

I [Wansharīsī] say:

Ibn Rushd [al-Jadd]'s commentary evidently calls for considering the preponderant opinion [on this issue to be] a different opinion from the one that his contemporary and fellow townsman, the judge Abū ʿAbd Allāh b. al-Ḥājj, held to be the preponderant one concerning the property and children of those in question. Thus, consider this matter.

Some of the senior jurists who have examined [this issue] consider it evident that the judgments pertaining to [new converts'] persons, children, and property [also] apply to those residing among hostile Christians.

87 On the comparison between Muslims in *dār al-ḥarb* and rebels, see Abou El Fadl, "Islamic Law and Muslim Minorities," 169.

88 This passage continues as follows: "[Ibn al-Qāsim] said: If he was forced and commanded to do what he did, and was unable to disobey his commander out of fear for his life, then I do not see that he is a rebel, nor that he should be killed if he is captured. Nor is he punished, if it is clear that he was commanded to do this and feared for his life." Ibn Rushd al-Jadd, *al-Bayān*, 3:42; Ibn Abī Zayd, *al-Nawādir*, 3:352. Molénat argues that Wansharīsī omits the end of this passage because he does not agree with it. While this may be true, Wansharīsī also may be maintaining a focus here on the inviolability of property and children for converts and conquered Muslims. See Molénat, "Le problème," 397, 399.

89 Wansharīsī, *al-Miʿyār*, 2:130; Ibn Rushd al-Jadd, *al-Bayān*, 3:42.

[What those judgments are may vary] in accordance with the scholarly disagreement noted above and the determination of preponderance that has been set forth.[90] Thereafter, if they fight us alongside their allies, the opinion that their lives are licit must become the preponderant one at that point. If they support [their allies] materially in their battle against us, the opinion that their property is licit must become preponderant. Capturing their children [already] has been determined to be the preponderant opinion, in order to free them from their control and to raise them among Muslims, safe from religious corruption and protected from the sin of abandoning emigration.

Andalusī Emigrants: Worldly Punishment

The question mentions the regret and resentment that have overtaken some of those who emigrated from the land of war to the land of Islam; [regret and resentment] that resulted from the poverty and lack of subsistence that they claim [should have excused them from the obligation to emigrate]. From the perspective of the noble law, this is an invalid claim and an unsound delusion. Only someone of weak conviction—or rather, someone who is devoid of sense and religion—would be deluded by this reasoning, consider it [legally relevant], or make it a focus of his concern. How could one imagine that this reasoning constitutes an argument for nullifying the obligation to emigrate from *dār al-ḥarb*? While the lands of Islam (may God exalt His word) is a spacious domain for the strong and the weak, the rich and the poor?[91] **God has made these lands expansive so that** those afflicted by this infidel attack and Christian strike against their **religion, family, and offspring might take refuge therein.**

A large group among the greatest and most noble **Companions** [of Muḥammad] (may God be pleased with them) **emigrated** to Abyssinia, **fleeing with their religion** from the torment of the polytheists, the people of Mecca. Among this noble delegation were Jaʿfar b. Abī Ṭālib, Abū Salama b. ʿAbd al-Asad, ʿUthmān b. ʿAffān, and Abū ʿUbayda b. al-Jarrāḥ—[even though] the conditions in Abyssinia were not known.[92] Others emigrated

90 This point may be clarified as follows: the conquered Muslim should be considered analogous in status to the convert to Islam in enemy territory. Once this is determined, the existing disagreements regarding the status of the convert's property (licit or not), based on the underlying points of dispute (do *ḥarbīs* truly own anything, and is it Islam or Muslim territory that provides inviolability), apply also to conquered Muslims. A jurist may argue legitimately for or against the inviolability of the property of these Muslims, for example, by adopting the opinions of Ibn Rushd al-Jadd (licit) or Ibn al-Ḥājj (inviolable).

91 *Al-thaqīl wa'l-khafīf* means literally "the heavy and the light." According to Najīb, exegetes gloss this phrase with such opposing pairs as "the rich and the poor" or "the young and the old." Najīb, ed., *Asnā al-matājir*, 85.

92 Najīb includes biographical references for each of these Companions (*Asnā al-matājir*, 85–86).

elsewhere, **relinquishing their homes, property, children, and elders; they [these emigrants] disowned, fought, and made war on them [the polytheists in Mecca], holding fast to their religion and renouncing their worldly concerns.**

So how [could anyone abandon emigration] for some ephemeral worldly good, when relinquishing and renouncing it would have no adverse effect on his ability to make a living among Muslims, and no impact on the bounty available to those seeking sustenance?[93] [This is] especially [true] in this devout Maghribī region (may God preserve it, increase its honor and nobility, and protect it from the vicissitudes of fortune and sorrow, from its center to its frontier), for its soil is among the most fertile on God's earth, and its lands among the most spacious in length and breadth, especially the city of Fez and its jurisdiction, its districts, and the regions surrounding it in every direction.

If indeed this delusion is established, and its holder lacks—God forbid—discernment, sound reason, and understanding, then he has furnished a sign and proof of his vile and contemptible character. [He has done this] by **giving greater weight to a despicable,** ephemeral **worldly goal than to a pious action rewarded in the hereafter. This determination of preference, this giving preponderance [to worldly aims] is a great wrong; whoever adopts this preference and falls into this belief has gone astray and is lost.**

This man who was deceived in his bargaining, who regretted his emigration from a land in which the trinity is invoked, church bells are rung, Satan is worshiped and the Merciful is renounced—did he not realize that **a person has only his religion, by which to attain his eternal salvation and his happiness in the hereafter, and in the service which he should exert his precious life, to say nothing of his wealth?**

God (may He be exalted) said: "Oh you who believe! Let not your wealth nor your children divert you from the remembrance of God. Those who do this, they are the losers" (Qur'ān 63:9). **He (may He be exalted) also said: "Your wealth and your children are only a temptation; but with God is a mighty wage"** (Qur'ān 64:15).

Among the greatest and most honorable benefits of wealth, for those with discernment, **is spending it in the way of God, in seeking His pleasure. How could anyone plunge obstinately into submission**

93 This sentence makes more sense in Ibn Rabīʿ's *fatwā*, where the *istiftāʾ* concerns a group of Muslims who remained under Christian rule for the sake of their properties. Wansharīsī has copied this sentiment into *Asnā al-matājir* even though the regretful emigrants in this context abandoned their properties and claimed difficulty in supporting themselves in the Maghrib. He is arguing that their claims must be false and their expectations of worldly comfort remain too high.

to the enemy for its sake? [How could he] rush to hurl and throw himself [toward them], when God (may He be exalted) had said: "You see those in whose hearts is sickness, vying with one another in hastening to them, saying 'We fear lest a misfortune befall us . . .'" (Qur'ān 5:52)?[94] **The misfortune in this [present] case is the loss of ownership over immovable property, so [this man] may be described as sick of heart and weak of faith. If he had been strong in religion and correct in conviction, if had he trusted in God (may He be exalted) relying and depending upon Him, then he would never have neglected the principle of trust in God (*tawakkul*). [Yet he did so], despite the elevated standing [of this principle], its abundant fruits, and the testament it provides as to the soundness of faith and depth of conviction.**

Once this is established, **there must be no dispensation of any kind,** for any of those whom you mentioned, either in returning [to Iberia] or in neglecting to perform the *hijra*. **None of them is excused [from this obligation], no matter what he must do to fulfill it, whether through burdensome toil or delicate strategy; rather, [he must pursue] whatever means of escape he can find** from the noose of the infidel. Where he does not find a tribe to defend him or protectors to guard him, and he is content [nonetheless] to remain in a place detrimental to religion, where it is prohibited to manifest Muslim practices, then he has strayed from the religion and joined the ranks of the heretics (*mulḥidīn*).

It is obligatory to flee from a land conquered by an idolatrous and depraved people to the land of faith and security. **For this reason, upon making excuses [for not migrating, those previously mentioned] were countered by His words in response: "Was God's earth not spacious enough for you to have migrated therein? Hell will be the refuge for such men—a wretched end!** (Qur'ān 4:97). **This means that wherever the emigrant turns, even if he is weak, he will find the earth spacious and limitless. Thus, there is no manner of excuse for anyone who is capable [of emigrating], even if this involves hardship with regard to devising a strategy or carrying one out,** or in making a living, or experiencing poverty. **Only the truly weak, who are fundamentally incapable [of emigrating are excused], those who can devise no means and are not guided to a path.**

[As for] anyone who hastens to flee the land of perdition for the land of the pious, his rush to depart is a clear sign in the current world of what his status will be in the hereafter. This is because triumph and success are

94 The preceding verse warns against taking Jews and Christians as allies, making clear that in this verse, the reference is to Muslims hastening to join non-Muslims.

anticipated for whomever virtuous deeds are made easy; but perdition and loss are feared for whomever evil deeds are easy. May God make us and you among those for whom prosperity is made easy, and who benefit from remembrance [of Him].

[As for] the ugly language, the cursing of the land of Islam (*dār al-Islām*), the desire to return to the land of polytheism and idols, and other detestable monstrosities which could only be uttered by the depraved, that you report coming from those emigrants—disgrace is required for them in this world and the next, and they must be lowered to the worst of positions. It is obligatory for whomever God has empowered in the land and enabled to prosper to seize these people. He must inflict upon them a severe penalty and an intense, exemplary punishment, through beating and imprisonment, so that they do not transgress the bounds of God. This is because their corrupting ideas (*fitna*) are more severely damaging than the trials of hunger, fear, or the taking of people and property.[95] This is because whoever perishes from the latter [elicits] the mercy of God (may He be exalted) and His most generous forgiveness, while someone whose religion has perished [incurs] the condemnation of God and His greatest anger. Fondness for submission to **polytheist rule, living among Christians,** the determination to **reject emigration, [the] reliance upon infidels,** contentment with **paying them the poll tax (*jizya*), renouncing the honor of Islam, [the] obedience to the *imām* (ruler), and allegiance to the sultan, [contentment with] the Christian sultan's triumph over, and degradation of, [Islamic power and honor]**—[these are] serious, perilous abominations, mortal blows that verge on unbelief (*kufr*)—may God protect us.

As for the loss of legal credibility (*jurḥa*) for anyone who remains [in enemy territory], returns after emigrating, or who desires to return, and with regard to their disqualification from holding any of the religious offices requiring complete integrity—judging, witnessing, and leading prayer—this matter is beyond doubt, obvious to anyone with the slightest grasp of substantive law and legal issues. Just as their testimony should not be accepted, nor should the attestations of their judges.[96]

95 As noted above, *fitna* may refer to any of several types of communal discord, from civil war to the presence of corrupting elements in society. Wansharīsī uses *fitna* twice in this sentence, once for the corrupting ideas spread by the emigrants and once for the trials or temptations brought about by hunger, fear, and loss. He employs the same contrast between the *fitna*s of corruption and hunger elsewhere in the *Miʿyār*, in a passage condemning those who mislead themselves and others by presuming greater knowledge of the law than is their right (*al-Miʿyār*, 2:503).

96 *Khiṭāb ḥukkāmhum* here refers to the written communications that judges send to one another attesting, for example, to the validity of legal documents that will be used in other jurisdictions.

Mudéjar Judges and Māzarī

Ibn ʿArafa[97] (may God have mercy upon him) said: "The acceptance of a judge's attestation is conditional upon the validity of his appointment by someone who is demonstrably entitled to appoint him. This [condition] is a precaution against [having to accept] the statements of the Mudéjar judges—such as the judges of the Muslims of Valencia, Tortosa, Pantelleria,[98] and so on—when received by us [in Ifrīqiyā]."[99]

Imām Abū ʿAbd Allāh al-Māzarī[100] (may God have mercy upon him) was asked in his time about rulings from the judge of Sicily, as well as [the testimony] of their professional witnesses. Should these be accepted [in Ifrīqiyā] or not—considering the necessity [of these offices],[101] and that it is not known whether their residence there under the infidels is by compulsion or by choice?[102]

He answered:

> Two factors might impugn this [judgment or testimony]. The first implicates the judge and his pronouncements, in terms of his integrity—for remaining in *dār al-ḥarb* under infidel command is not permitted. The second [factor] concerns [the legitimacy of] his appointment, because the judge is appointed by the infidels.

---

97 Abū ʿAbd Allāh Muḥammad b. Muḥammad b. ʿArafa al-Warghamiyya, known as Ibn ʿArafa (d. 803/1401), was *imām*, *khaṭīb*, and *muftī* of the Great Mosque of Tunis.

98 *Qawṣara*, misprinted as "Mawṣara" in the Rabat edition of *Asnā al-matājir*, is Pantelleria, an island between Sicily and Tunisia. The Muslim inhabitants acquired Mudéjar status in 618/1221 when the Almohad governor of Tunis signed a treaty giving control of the island to Emperor Frederick II of Sicily. See *EI*[2], s.v. "Ḳawṣara" (M. Talbi) and Henri Bresc, "Pantelleria entre l'Islam et la Chretiente," *Les Cahiers de Tunisie* 19, nos. 75–76 (1971): 105–27.

99 Significantly, Ibn ʿArafa uses the term *ahl al-dajn* for Mudéjar. Wansharīsī repeats this quotation in a later section of the *Miʿyār* treating Andalusī and Maghribī conventions for one judge's acceptance of another judge's written communications. Wansharīsī, *al-Miʿyār*, 10:60–76, esp. 10:66.

100 Abū ʿAbd Allāh Muḥammad b. ʿAlī b. ʿUmar al-Māzarī (d. 536/1141), known as Imām al-Māzarī. See chapter 5 for biographical sources.

101 Each community is obligated to fulfill the collective duty of having a judge. See Muhammad Khalid Masud, Rudolph Peters, and David S. Powers, "Qāḍīs and their Courts: An Historical Survey," in *Dispensing Justice in Islam: Qadis and their Judgments*, ed. Masud, et al. (Leiden: Brill, 2006), 19.

102 Abdel-Majid Turki has published an Arabic edition, French translation, and short study of Māzarī's *fatwā*, based primarily on a version of the *fatwā* found in H.H. ʿAbd al-Wahhāb's biography of Māzarī. See Turki, "Consultation"; Abdel Majid Turki, *Qaḍāyā thaqāfiyya min tārīkh al-gharb al-Islāmī: nuṣūs wa-dirāsāt* (Beirut: Dār al-Gharb al-Islāmī, 1988), 61–80; Ḥasan Ḥusnī ʿAbd al-Wahhāb, *al-Imām al-Māzarī* (Tunis: Dār al-Kutub al-Sharqiyya, 1955), 87–89. Wansharīsī's citation of this *fatwā* in *Asnā al-matājir* is abridged (2:133–34), but he produces a longer version elsewhere in *al-Miʿyār* (10:107–9). This *fatwā* also appears in Māzarī, *Fatāwā al-Māzarī*, ed. al-Ṭāhir al-Maʿmūrī, 365–66. Najīb's edition of *Asnā al-matājir* notes the differences between Wansharīsī's citation of Māzarī's *fatwā* in *Asnā al-matājir* and what he calls the original version of Māzarī's *fatwā*, by which he means the one edited by ʿAbd al-Wahhāb. Najīb, ed., *Asnā al-matājir*, 93–101.

As for the first [factor], there is a principle [that should be] relied upon in this and similar cases, which is to give the benefit of the doubt to Muslims and to presume their innocence.[103] One should not turn away from this principle toward false suspicions and baseless imaginings. For example, one should accept [the probity] of someone who appears to be upright, even though it is possible for that person, in reality, to have committed a major sin in secret—unless evidence could be furnished proving his complete innocence [even in private]. This possibility [of private sin] should be disregarded and the judgment should be based on what is evident. [What is apparent] has preponderance unless indicators appear that would necessitate a departure from this [presumption of] probity. At that point, [judgment] must be suspended until some [evidence] arises that would necessitate withdrawing this presumption of probity. Thereafter, the judgment [as to his probity] remains whatever is most likely.

A judgment is derived from specifically defined evidence, so that [judgment] should be operative, whereas probity is based on unrestricted evidence and thus should not be considered [operative here].[104] I have written a section about this in *Sharḥ al-Burhān*.[105] I mention the approaches of Abū al-Maʿālī and myself, when we discussed the disagreements and discord that occurred among the Companions (may God be pleased with all of them).

---

103 *Taḥsīn al-ẓann bi'l-Muslimīn wa-mubāʿadat al-maʿāsī* means, more literally, to think well of Muslims and distance them from sinful acts.

104 *Wa'l-ḥukm huwa mustafād min qarā'in maḥṣūra fa-yuʿmalu ʿalayhā, wa-qarā'in al-ʿadāla ma'khūdha min amr muṭlaq fa-tulghā*. Māzarī's point is that a judicial decision regarding the judge's own probity should be based on the same considerations informing other court judgments, where the apparent meaning of any applicable evidence is given preponderance. A thorough determination of one's overall probity, however, would be a more subjective affair governed by less specific standards. That prospect is therefore set aside in favor of the more defined, practicable standards for the validity of a judgment (*ḥukm*) issued by a court judge. Here Māzarī is invoking a general principle of *uṣūl al-fiqh* regarding the interpretation of absolute (*muṭlaq*) and restricted (*muqayyad*) language in the sources of the law; on this distinction, see Mohammad Hashim Kamali, *Principles of Islamic Jurisprudence*, 3rd ed. (Cambridge: Islamic Texts Society, 2003), 155–58. This passage in *Asnā al-matājir* has confounded its editors. The Rabat edition of the *Miʿyār* records the final word as *fa-tulghā*, as above, but the editors note a variant in one manuscript copy, which reads *mutlaqā*, "received" (Wansharīsī, *al-Miʿyār*, 2:133). Mu'nis records *salafī mutlaqā* without explanation (Mu'nis, "Asnā al-matājir," 47), while Maʿmūrī records *mutlaqā*, also without explanation (Maʿmūrī, *Fatāwā al-Māzarī*, 365). Turki chooses *salafī mutlaqā* in a footnote to his French translation of Māzarī's *fatwā*, but he does not translate the passage because it does not appear in his version of this text (Turki, "Consultation," 702). Najīb chooses *fa-tulghā*, notes the variants, and states that the expression is difficult (95). I find *fa-tulghā* convincing because it preserves the parallelism of the sentence: one thing is restricted and operative; the other is absolute and inoperative.

105 Māzarī is referring to his commentary on Juwaynī's (d. 478/1085) *al-Burhān*, a work of jurisprudence (*uṣūl al-fiqh*). See Māzarī, *Īḍāḥ al-Maḥṣūl min Burhān al-uṣūl*, ed. ʿAmmār al-Ṭālibī (Dār al-Gharb al-Islāmī, 2001).

If this [judge's] residence in non-Muslim territory is by compulsion, then there is no doubt that it does not compromise his probity.[106] This is also the case if his reason [for voluntary residence] is valid. For example, his residence in non-Muslim territory might be in hopes of guiding the infidels [to Islam] or delivering them from some error.[107] Bāqillānī[108] made this point. Similarly, Mālik's followers endorsed the permissibility of entering [non-Muslim territory] in order to redeem captives.[109] If he lives [there] voluntarily out of willful ignorance [of the law] and without providing an explanation, then this compromises his probity. [Jurists] in the [Mālikī] school disagreed as to rejecting the testimony of someone who voluntarily enters [non-Muslim territory] for the purpose of trade. They disagree even more vehemently in interpreting the *Mudawwana* on this [point].

Therefore, the legal principle should be to excuse those [Muslims] who appear to be upright and whose reasons for residence [in non-Muslim territory] are uncertain. This is because most of the preceding possibilities [for why they would remain] support excusing them. These should not be rejected in favor of just one possibility unless the evidence supports [that one possibility, which is that] their residence was voluntary rather than for a [legitimate] reason.

As for the second [factor which may compromise the judge's probity], which is the infidel's appointment of judges, notaries, trustees, and others, in order to prevent people from [wronging] one another—this is obligatory, to the point that one follower of our [Mālikī] school has claimed this to be rationally imperative, even if the infidel's appointment of this judge should be invalid.[110] Moreover, if the [appointment] is at the request of the people, and his administering to them is by necessity, then this does not compromise his authority or

106 In Turki's Arabic edition, the next sentence is as follows: "This is also the case if his [residence] was voluntary and he is ignorant of the rule or convinced of the permissibility [of such residence]. For his obligation to grasp this particular knowledge is not so great that his failure to do so would compromise his integrity." Turki, "Consultation," 702.

107 In Turki's edition, the hope of freeing the territory from infidel rule and returning it to Islamic control is added here. Turki, "Consultation," 702.

108 Bāqillānī (d. 403/1013) was a prominent Ashʿarī theologian and Mālikī jurist. See *EI*[2], s.v. "Al-Bāḳillānī" (R.J. McCarthy).

109 In Turki's edition, this additional text follows: "This is also the case if his reason [for staying] was an error—of which there are innumerable possibilities, just as there are countless dubious arguments among scholars of *uṣūl al-fiqh*. Often what is an error for one scholar is correct for another, in accordance with the view that only one scholar is truly correct but the others are excused [for any errors reached through diligent, qualified effort]." Turki, "Consultation," 703.

110 In Turki's edition, an additional sentence follows: "In the *Mudawwana*, the scholars in a given region take the place of the sultan in his absence, for fear of a lapse in judicial affairs." Turki, "Consultation," 703. This sentence appears below in Wansharīsī.

the enforcement of his judgments. It is just as though a Muslim sultan had appointed him.[111]

In the chapter on oaths [in the *Mudawwana*], in the case of someone who swears, "Your rights will be fulfilled" within an allotted time, [it is noted that] the scholars of a given region take the place of the sultan in his absence, for fear of a lapse in judicial affairs. According to Muṭarrif and Ibn al-Mājishūn,[112] if someone rebels against the ruler and conquers a land, and then appoints an upright judge, the [judge's] rulings should be enforced.

I [Wansharīsī] say: The *shaykh*s of al-Andalus issued a *fatwā* on the status of those living under the authority of the rebel heretic ʿUmar b. Ḥafṣūn. [It said] that their testimony is not permitted, nor are the attestations of their judges accepted.[113]

[Scholars] have disagreed on the acceptance of a judicial appointment from an unjust ruler. In *Riyāḍ al-nufūs fī ṭabaqāt ʿulamāʾ [al-Qayrawān wa-] Ifrīqiyā* [*The Garden of Souls: Generations of the Scholars of Qayrawān and Ifrīqiyā*], by Abū Muḥammad b. ʿAbd Allāh al-Mālikī,[114] Saḥnūn said:

Abū Muḥammad ʿAbd Allāh b. Farrūkh[115] and Ibn Ghānim,[116] the judge of Ifrīqiyā, had a disagreement. Both were among those who narrated from Mālik (may God be pleased with him). Ibn Farrūkh said: "A judge must not assume the judgeship if an unjust commander (*amīr*) appoints him," while Ibn Ghānim said: "It is permissible for him to take office even if the commander is unjust." So they wrote with this [issue] to Mālik, and Mālik said: "Al-Fārisī is correct," meaning Ibn al-Farrūkh, "and the one who claims to be Arab is mistaken," meaning Ibn Ghānim."[117]

---

111 In Turki's edition, this sentence reads: "Therefore, the infidel's appointment of this upright judge, either because of the need for this [office], or to meet the needs of the subjects, does not compromise his authority, and his judgments are enforced, just as though a Muslim sultan had appointed him. It is God who guides to the true path." Turki, "Consultation," 703–4. Turki's edition ends here.

112 Muṭarrif b. ʿAbd Allāh (d. 220/835) and Ibn al-Mājishūn (d. 212/827 or 214/829) were early disciples of Mālik in Medina.

113 Beginning in 267/880, ʿUmar b. Ḥafṣūn (d. 305/918) led an unsuccessful rebellion against the Umayyads of Córdoba. Wansharīsī devotes a lengthy discussion to this case in his chapter on judging, witnessing, and oaths. Wansharīsī, *al-Miʿyār*, 10:109–12.

114 This work has been published: ʿAbd Allāh b. Muḥammad al-Mālikī (d. ca. 360/970), *Riyāḍ al-nufūs fī ṭabaqāt ʿulamāʾ al-Qayrawān wa-Ifrīqiyā wa-zuhhādihim wa-nussākihim wa-siyar min akhbārihim wa-faḍāʾilihim wa-awṣāfihim*, ed. Bashīr al-Bakkūsh and Muḥammad al-ʿArūsī al-Maṭwī, 2nd ed., 2 vols. (Beirut: Dār al-Gharb al-Islāmī, 1994).

115 Abū Muḥammad ʿAbd Allāh b. Farrūkh al-Fārisī (d. 176/792–3) traveled east from Qayrawān to study with Mālik. Mālikī, *Riyād al-nufūs*, 1:176–87.

116 Abū ʿAbd al-Raḥmān ʿAbd Allāh b. ʿUmar b. Ghānim (d. 190/806), an early Mālikī jurist, studied with Mālik and served as judge in Ifrīqiyā. Mālikī, *Riyāḍ al-nufūs*, 1:215–29.

117 Fārisī is Ibn Farrūkh's *nisba* but is also used here to mean "the Persian" in contrast to Ibn Ghanīm, who is chided for his weaker grasp of the law despite having the presumed advantage of being Arab. See Mālikī, *Riyāḍ al-nufūs*, 1:178–79. Wansharīsī's version is slightly abridged.

Ibn ʿArafa said: "[If a judge accepted] an appointment made by a usurper against the ruler, they [Mālikīs] did not consider [the judge's] acceptance to be an impairment [of his probity], for fear of suspending judicial affairs."

Andalusī Emigrants: The Hereafter

[The preceding has addressed] the worldly judgments pertaining to [Muslims living in non-Muslim territory]. **As for [the judgment concerning] the hereafter that pertains to those who spend their entire lives,** exhausting their youth and old age living among them [non-Muslims] and under their authority, **and who do not emigrate, or who emigrate but then return to the land of unbelief (*waṭn al-kufr*), and who persist in committing this major act of disobedience [to God] up until their deaths** (may God protect us) **according to tradition (the *sunna*) and the majority of scholars, they will be punished with a severe torment. Yet they will not suffer eternally, based on [these scholars'] correct belief as to the [eventual] cessation of punishment for those who have committed major sins, and their release through** the **intercession of** our lord, Prophet, and master **Muḥammad**, the elect, the chosen (may God bless him and grant him peace). [This is] **according to what is recorded in sound reports.**[118]

The **evidence for this** [cessation of punishment] is **His words** (may He be exalted and glorified): "**God does not forgive that a partner should be ascribed to Him; but he forgives anything else, to whom He pleases**" [Qurʾān 4:48]. **And His words: "Say: 'Oh my servants who have transgressed against themselves! Do not despair of God's mercy. Surely God forgives all sins; for He is the Forgiving, the Merciful'"** [Qurʾān 39:53]. **And His words: "Verily your Lord is the Lord of forgiveness to mankind, for all their wrongdoing"** [Qurʾān 13:6].

Nonetheless, the words of God (may He be exalted): "Whoever among you allies himself with them is one of them," [Qurʾān 5:51] **and the statements of Muḥammad (peace be upon him) "I am not responsible for any Muslim** who lives among the polytheists" and "Whoever lives among them or associates with them, is one of them" are very severe toward them.

The statement, "Emigrate from there to here?" that you relate from [that emigrant] who is feeble in mind and religion, is a model of contempt and mockery. [As for] the other fool's statement, "If the ruler of Castile came to these parts, we would go to him . . . ," his talk is offensive and his words repugnant. The ugliness of expression contained in the statements

118 For examples of *ḥadīths* on Muḥammad's intercessory role, including for those who have committed major sins, see Najīb, ed., *Asnā al-matājir*, 102.

of each of them will be obvious to your Honor, just as it will be obvious what censure and severe reproach each of them deserve for this. For no one would utter such a thing, nor deem it permissible, except someone who had disgraced himself and lost (may God protect us) his senses; and who desires to repeal that which is authentic in both transmission and meaning, as to whose prohibition no one has disagreed in the entire Islamic world, from where the sun rises to where it sets. [He desires to repeal this] as a result of selfish interests which are illegitimate in the view of the law and are complete nonsense.[119] These delusional interests could only proceed from a heart seized by Satan, who has made it forget the sweetness of faith and its location among the lands [i.e., in Muslim territory].

Whoever commits and is ensnared in this [behavior] has hastened disgrace for his wicked soul, [disgrace which is] guaranteed in this world and the next. Yet in terms of [his] disobedience, sin, injurious conduct, vileness, odiousness, distance from God, diminished [religious standing], blameworthy [status], and [his being] deserving of the greatest condemnation, he does not equal someone who abandons emigration completely, by submitting to the enemy and by living among those who are far [from God]. This is because the extent of what has issued from these two wicked men [who have made the above statements] is a firm resolve (*ʿazm*), that is, planning and preparing oneself for action, while neither of them has yet undertaken that action.[120]

Our Ashʿarī masters disagreed as to the assessment of blame for [intentions]. The master Abū ʿAbd Allāh al-Māzarī (may God have mercy upon him) transmitted from many [previous masters, the principle] that [resolve] should not be assessed blame directly, because of the apparent meaning of [Muḥammad's] words (peace by upon him): "God has forgiven my community for whatever thoughts occur to them."[121] The judge Abū

---

119 *Lā ra's lahā wa-lā dhanab*, literally, which have neither head nor tail.

120 Two misprints in the Rabat edition (uncorrected in the Beirut edition), which render these last two paragraphs particularly difficult to understand, are indicative of the errors to be found throughout this edition. In the two examples given above of statements made by the emigrants, the Rabat edition introduces the second statement as "*qawluhu al-safīh al-ākhar*," or "his other foolish statement," as though only one emigrant is under discussion (the correct reading is "*qawl al-safīh al-ākhar*," "the statement of the other fool"). In the second paragraph, the Rabat edition reads "*illā innahu yusāwī*," or "yet he is equal to," omitting the "*lā*" which should negate this statement. The effect is to render the non-emigrant and the one who desires to return to non-Muslim territory equal to one another in sin. The two wicked men in the last sentence would then have to refer to these two, the non-emigrant and the would-be return emigrant, who both would have resolved to do something but would not have done it yet. Wansharīsī, *al-Miʿyār*, 2:135.

121 *Ṣaḥīḥ al-Bukhārī, Kitāb al-Ṭalāq, bāb al-ṭalāq fī al-ighlāq . . .*, *ḥadīth* 4967 (Bukhārī, *Ṣaḥīḥ al-Bukhārī*, 5:2020); *Ṣaḥīḥ Muslim, Kitāb al-Īmān, bāb tajāwuz Allāh ʿan ḥadīth al-nafs . . .*, *ḥadīth* 201 (Muslim b. al-Ḥajjāj, *Ṣaḥīḥ Muslim*, 1:116). The *ḥadīth* continues, "as long as they are not acted upon or uttered." For Māzarī's commentary on this and other *aḥadīth* in *Ṣaḥīḥ*

Bakr al-Bāqillānī held that [thoughts] are assessed blame, and provided as evidence this *ḥadīth*: "If two Muslims align their swords against one another, the slayer and the slain both go to hellfire. It was said, 'Oh messenger of God! This is for the slayer, but what of the slain?' He said: 'He intended to kill his companion.'"[122] Thus, his sin was on the basis of his intention. [Bāqillānī] was answered that coming face to face and unsheathing [their] swords are actions, and this is the intention referred to [in this case].

[Al-Qāḍī 'Iyāḍ] stated in the *Ikmāl*:[123]

> Most of the early jurists, theologians, and *ḥadīth* scholars held the same position as that of Bāqillānī because of the large number of traditions indicating the assessment of blame for actions of the heart. They interpreted those traditions that suggest the lack of assessment as pertaining to [mere] consideration (*hamm*), [as opposed to firm resolve, *ʿazm*]. Thawrī[124] was asked: "Might we be held accountable for an intention (*himma*)?" He said: "[Only] if it is a firm resolve (*ʿazm*)." Yet the [early scholars also] said: "Only the sin of the intention is assessed, because that is an act of disobedience; but the sin of the intended act is not assessed, because it has not been carried out. If it is carried out, a second sin is recorded; but if it is averted, one good act is recorded, according to the *ḥadīth*: "Indeed, he abandoned it for My sake."[125]
>
> Muḥyī al-Dīn al-Nawawī[126] said: "The assessment of blame for resolve is the evident meaning offered by the texts. For example, the words of [God] (may He be exalted): "Those who love that scandal should be spread concerning those who believe . . ." [Qur'ān 24:19][127] and "Avoid suspicion as much as possible, for suspicion in some cases is a sin" [Qur'ān 49:12]. The community (*umma*) has agreed

---

Muslim, see Māzarī, *al-Muʿlim bi-fawāʾid Muslim*, ed. Muḥammad al-Shādhilī al-Nayfar, 2nd ed. (Dār al-Gharb al-Islāmī, 1992), 2:208–9.

122 *Ṣaḥīḥ al-Bukhārī, Kitāb al-Īmān, bāb wa-in ṭāʾifatān min al-muʾminīn . . .*, *ḥadīth* 31 (Bukhārī, *Ṣaḥīḥ al-Bukhārī*, 1:20); *Ṣaḥīḥ Muslim, Kitāb al-Fitan wa-ashrāṭ al-sāʿa, bāb idhā tawājaha al-Muslimān bi-ṣayfayhimā*, *ḥadīth* 14 (Muslim b. al-Ḥajjāj, *Ṣaḥīḥ Muslim*, 4:2213–14).

123 The Andalusī judge Abū al-Faḍl 'Iyāḍ b. Mūsā b. 'Iyāḍ al-Yaḥṣubī, known as Qāḍī 'Iyāḍ (d. 544/1149) composed *Ikmāl al-Muʿlim bi-fawāʾid Muslim*, a continuation of Māzarī's *al-Muʿlim bi-fawāʾid Muslim*. Both works comment on the traditions contained in the *Ṣaḥīḥ Muslim*.

124 Abū ʿAbd Allāh Sufyān al-Thawrī (d. 161/778).

125 Muslim, *Ṣaḥīḥ Muslim, Kitāb al-Īmān, bāb idhā hamma al-ʿabd . . .*, *ḥadīth* 205 (Muslim b. al-Ḥajjāj, *Ṣaḥīḥ Muslim*, 1:117). In this *ḥadīth*, the angels inform God that a man intends to commit a sin. God orders one sin recorded against him if he commits the act, and one good deed recorded if he desists, because he desists for the sake of God.

126 Muḥyī al-Dīn Abū Zakariyyā Yaḥyā b. Sharaf al-Nawawī (d. 676/1277) was a prominent Shafiʿī jurist.

127 This verse continues: ". . . they will have a grievous punishment in this world and in the hereafter; God knows, and you do not know."

by consensus on the prohibition of envy, contempt of people, and the desire to do prohibited things to them.[128]

This argument is countered by the fact that the "firm resolve" regarding which there is disagreement is [the type] that is externally manifest, such as fornication or wine drinking. As for [the type] that is not externally manifest, like beliefs and such impurities of the soul as envy and the like, these [latter] types are not the source of disagreement. This is because their prohibition concerns them [directly]; this [direct prohibition] occasioned the legal obligation [to avoid envy, etc.]. Therefore, [this obligation] should not be justified on the basis of the consensus that has been concluded in its regard.

Conclusion

Let this be the end of what is written in response to the useful question posed by the honorable jurist, the accomplished preacher, the enduring virtuous exemplar, the pure sum of excellence, the master Abū ʿAbd Allāh b. Qaṭiyya (may God perpetuate his noble achievement and reputation). It is desirable to give this response a title, and so it is called ***Asnā al-matājir fī bayān aḥkām man ghalaba ʿalā waṭanih al-Naṣārā wa-lam yuhājir, wa-mā yatarattabu ʿalayh min al-ʿuqūbāt wa-l'zawājir*** (*The Most Noble Commerce: An Exposition of the Legal Rulings Governing One Whose Homeland Has Been Conquered by the Christians and Who Has Not Emigrated, and the Punishments and Admonishments Accruing to Him*).

By God, I ask that [this response] be of benefit, and that [my] reward multiply on its account. This was composed and written by the lowly worshiper and seeker of forgiveness, the insignificant servant submitted to God's will, Aḥmad b. Yaḥyā b. ʿAlī al-Wansharīsī, may God grant him success. Its composition was completed on Sunday, the nineteenth day of the sacred month of Dhū al-Qaʿda in the year 896 [23 September 1491], may God make His benevolence known to us.

128 See ʿIyāḍ b. Mūsā, *Sharḥ Ṣaḥīḥ Muslim lil-Qāḍī ʿIyāḍ, al-musammā Ikmāl al-Muʿlim bi-fawāʾid Muslim*, ed. Yaḥyā Ismāʿīl (Mansoura: Dār al-Wafāʾ lil-Ṭibāʿa waʾl-Nashr waʾl-Tawzīʿ, 1998), 1:423–27.

APPENDIX C

The Marbella *Fatwā*

by Aḥmad Abū al-ʿAbbās Aḥmad b. Yaḥyā al-Wansharīsī (d. 914/1508)

The Question[1]

The aforementioned jurist Abū ʿAbd Allāh also wrote to me with the following text:

"Praise be to God, and may blessings and peace be upon the messenger of God. Your answer [is requested], master (may God be pleased with you and [may He] bring benefit to Muslims through your life) regarding a case. This [concerns] a man from Marbella who is known for his virtue and piety, and who, when the people from his area emigrated, stayed behind in order to search for his brother who had gone missing while fighting the enemy in enemy territory (*dār al-ḥarb*). He searched for any news of him up until now, but did not find him and has lost hope. So he wanted to emigrate but another reason arose [that caused him to remain behind], namely, that he is a spokesman and support for the subject Muslims (*al-Muslimīn al-dhimmiyyīn*) where he resides, as well as for those like them who live in the neighboring areas of western al-Andalus. When difficult situations arise for them with the [Christians], he speaks with the Christian officials,[2] argues on their behalf, and saves many of them from serious predicaments. Most of them are incapable of taking on this [role] for them; in fact, if he emigrated they would hardly be able to find his equal in this skill. Great harm would befall them in his absence, if they were to lose him.

"Is residing with them under infidel rule permitted for him, on account of the benefit (*maṣlaḥa*) his residence entails for those unfortunate [Muslim] *dhimmīs*, even though he is capable of emigration anytime he wishes? Or is this [residence] not permitted for him, as they also have no dispensation

1 On my methodology in translating this text from the available editions, see appendix B, first note. Prior translations are noted in chapter 4; only substantial disagreements in translation are noted below.

2 While *ḥukkām* might normally be translated as judges, I have opted for officials here. Ibn Qaṭiyya is likely referring to judges and government officials of various types and levels of authority.

for their [residence] there subject to infidel laws, especially considering that they have been granted permission to emigrate and that most of them are capable of doing so whenever they wish? Presuming that this were permitted to him, would he thus also be granted a dispensation to pray in his garments [as they are], in accordance with whatever ability he has [to keep them pure]? For they [his garments] generally would not be free from major ritual impurities (*najāsa*) as a result of his frequent interactions with the Christians, his dealings with them, and his sleeping and arising in their homes while serving these subject Muslims in the manner stated?

"Clarify for us the judgment of God as to all of this. [May you be] rewarded and praised, if God (may He be exalted) wills, may an abundant peace support your lofty station, and may the mercy and blessings of God (may He be exalted) be upon you."

The Answer

I responded with the following text:

Praise be to God alone (may He be exalted). The answer (and it is God the exalted who grants success by His grace) is that our one almighty God placed the poll tax (*jizya*) and abasement[3] around the necks of the cursed infidels, as chains and shackles which they must drag about across the lands and in the major cities and towns, demonstrating the power of Islam and honoring its chosen prophet. Thus any Muslim (may God protect and provide for them) who attempts to invert these chains and fetters [by placing them] on his [own] neck has contravened God and His messenger and exposed himself to the anger of the Almighty, the Omnipotent; he deserves for God to throw him into the fire along with them. For "God has decreed: 'I shall certainly conquer, I and My messengers.' Verily God is Strong, Almighty."[4]

It is thus obligatory upon every believer who believes in God and the last day to strive to preserve the fundamentals of faith by maintaining distance and fleeing from residence among the enemies of the Merciful One's beloved [Prophet]. The attempt to justify the [continued] residence of the aforementioned virtuous man on the basis of the purpose suggested—

3 *Al-jizya wa'l-ṣaghār*. In the Rabat edition of the *Miʿyār* (2:137) and in Muʾnis's edition ("Asnā al-matājir," 56), *khizya* (disgrace) appears in place of *jizya*, although the Rabat editors note *jizya* as a variant found in one of the manuscripts consulted. Najīb favors *jizya* but does not explain his choice (*Asnā al-matājir*, 113). Paired synonyms are common in Arabic, and many copyists were apparently happy to pair *al-khizya* with *al-ṣaghār*, but *jizya* is a far more compelling reading. This passage clearly refers to Qurʾān 9:29: "Fight such of those who have been given the Book who do not believe in God or in the last day, and who do not forbid what God and his messenger have forbidden, and who do not follow the religion of truth, until they pay the *jizya* and are abased (*hattā yuʿṭū al-jizya ʿan yad wa-hum ṣāghirūn*)."

4 Qurʾān 58:21.

interpreting between the tyrant and the disobedient Mudéjars under his authority—does not negate the obligation to emigrate. Nor would anyone imagine that the legally inconsequential circumstances recorded in the question contradict the rule that [*hijra*] is obligatory, except for one who would feign ignorance of, or [genuinely] disregard, the inversion of the natural order; and who has no skill in the methods of the law. For living with infidels, without [their being] subject tributaries (*ahl al-dhimma*), is not permitted or allowed for even one hour of one day because of the pollution, the filth, and the religious and worldly corruptions to which this gives rise, throughout their lives.

Among them [these corruptions]:[5] The purpose of the law is for **the word of Islam and the testimony of truth to be established as predominant, triumphant over all others, far removed from belittlement and from being dominated by the banner of unbelief. Living among them under humiliation and abasement necessarily requires that this sublime, exalted, noble word should be lowly rather than elevated, and belittled rather than honored. It should suffice for you [to know of only] this violation of the principles of the law and the fundamentals [of the religion], and [that there are] those who endure it patiently all of their lives in the absence of either necessity or compulsion.**

Also among them [these violations]: Proper **fulfillment of the required prayers, which are second only to the two testimonies of faith with respect to their virtue and glorification [of God], and their [need to be] declared openly and visibly, cannot be realized—cannot even be conceived of—unless [these prayers] are fully visible, exalted, and free from from belittlement and contempt. Yet living among infidels and closely associating with the depraved entails exposing [prayer] to neglect, belittlement, mockery, and sport. God (may He be exalted) said: "When you call to prayer they take it in mockery and sport; That is because they are a people who do not understand."[6] This violation should also suffice for you [to understand the obligation to emigrate].**

Also among them [these violations]: **Almsgiving. It is obvious to anyone with discernment and an enlightened mind that the collection of alms by the Muslim ruler (*imām*) is a pillar of Islam and a rite of humankind. [It is likewise obvious] that where there is no Muslim ruler, there must be no collection, because its requisite condition is**

5 What follows is a list of Islamic legal principles and practices that Mudéjars violate or fail to fulfill, according to Ibn Rabīʿ and Wansharīsī. Each item in the list begins with "among them" (*wa-min-hā*). In Ibn Rabīʿ's text, "among these violations" is clearly intended in each instance. Wansharīsī has rearranged the text such that his first instance must mean "among these corruptions," a reference to the language he uses in his original opening to this answer.

6 Qurʾān 5:58.

not met; there can be no *zakāt* because there is no [legitimate ruler] entitled to [collect] it. Therefore, this is one of the pillars of Islam that is destroyed because of this submission to infidel rule. As for [alms] being collected by one who would use them against the Muslims, it is further obvious what contradictions this would entail, of all the acts of worship ordained by law.

Also among them [these violations is]: **Fasting during Ramadan, which is obviously an individual obligation, as well as the alms payment due by the end of the month (*zakāt al-abdān*).**[7] **The sighting of the new moon is a prerequisite for [determining] the beginning and end [of the Ramadan fast]. In most cases this sighting may only be established by the testimony of a witness, and that testimony may only be offered before Muslim rulers or their deputies. Where there is no Muslim ruler, there can be no deputy, and therefore no witness testimony.**[8] **Therefore, in terms of legal practice, the beginning and end of the month would be uncertain in that case.**

Also among them [these violations]: **The pilgrimage to the house [of God]. The pilgrimage [is one of these violations], even if [this obligation] has lapsed for [these Muslims] because of a lack of ability,** as they are [nonetheless] commissioned with its performance.[9]

---

7 Individual obligations must be fulfilled by every Muslim who meets the relevant criteria (such as reaching maturity), as opposed to collective obligations (such as appointing a judge or serving in the army), which must be met only by a sufficient number of people in the community. *Zakāt al-abdān*, more commonly referred to as *zakāt al-fiṭr* or *ṣadaqat al-fiṭr* is the name for the obligatory alms Muslims must contribute to the poor prior to the beginning of the ʿĪd prayer, which takes place the morning after the last day of fasting (on the first day of ʿĪd al-Fiṭr). It is included here because, like the fasting itself, it is a time-specific obligation whose validity depends upon correct knowledge of the beginning and ending of the month. Several translators have misinterpreted this phrase.

8 The editors of the Rabat edition of the *Miʿyār*, Muʾnis, and Najīb all note a gap in the text here between the words "*shahādat*" and "*al-shahr*." Ibn Rabīʿ's text reveals that the missing word is "*yakūnu*," such that the end of this sentence and the beginning of the next one read: ". . . *fa-lā shahādat, fa-yakūnu al-shahr idh dhāka mashkūk* . . ."

9 Both Ibn Rabīʿ and Wansharīsī list the pilgrimage to Mecca (the *ḥajj*) among the core religious obligations that Mudéjars fail to fulfill by living under non-Muslim rule, even though they both also acknowledge that this obligation is not currently in effect for the Mudéjars. The obligation to perform the pilgrimage is conditional upon the ability to do so; both jurists acknowledge that Mudéjars do not meet this condition of ability, and so are not obligated to perform the pilgrimage. Wansharīsī's addition, in plain text, clarifies that they are still in a general sense commissioned with this obligation, which would come into effect were they to gain the ability to perform the *ḥajj*. What both jurists seem to imply is that even if the Mudéjars are not violating an obligation that is currently incumbent upon them by neglecting the *ḥajj*, they might nonetheless bear responsibility for remaining in that position of inability. The point is not pressed, most likely because contemporaries of both jurists were issuing *fatwās* exempting Maghribī and Andalusī Muslims in *dār al-Islām* from the obligation to perform the pilgrimage, on the basis of a general lack of ability to do so (see Hendrickson, "Prohibiting the Pilgrimage"). This passage in *Asnā al-matājir* has proven confusing for translators; Muʾnis ("Asnā al-matājir," 58–59) and others have assumed something must be missing from the text.

Fighting (*jihād*) to elevate the word of truth and eliminate unbelief **is also a fundamental Islamic practice. It is a collective obligation when the need arises, [as is] especially [the case] in the places of residence referred to in the question, as well as in the neighboring areas. If they are [neglecting this obligation, in the absence of] any constraint that necessarily and completely prevents them from fulfilling it, then they are equal to those who resolve to abandon [*jihād* willfully], not out of necessity; and those who resolve that they would abandon [*jihād*] without any need to do so are equivalent to those who abandon it freely and deliberately.**[10] **Or [if they are not neglecting *jihād*,] they are daring to pursue the opposite [of *jihād*] by supporting their [Christian] allies against the Muslims, either physically or financially, at which point they have become enemy combatants (*ḥarbiyyīn*) along with the polytheists. This contradiction [of the fundamentals of Islam] and clear error should also suffice for you.**

This account has made plain the deficiency of their prayers, fasting, almsgiving, and *jihād*; their failure to elevate the word of God and the testimony of truth; and their disregard for honoring, glorifying, and raising [the word of God] far above the belittlement of the infidels and the mockery of the depraved. How could any jurist hesitate, or any pious person have doubts, regarding the prohibition of this residence [under Christian rule], considering that it is accompanied by the violation of all these honorable and noble Islamic principles, and by all that entails? And [how could anyone doubt this prohibition] considering all that is associated with living in subjection, which is generally inseparable from worldly inferiority and the suffering of disgrace and humiliation? [This subjected status][11] moreover violates the Muslims' established honor and their elevated standing, and invites contempt for and oppression of the religion.

[This residence under Christian rule entails] additional matters that make one's ears ring. Among them are degradation, contempt, and humiliation, [despite Muḥammad's] having said (may peace be upon him): "A Muslim must not degrade himself,"[12] **and "The upper hand is better**

10 Wansharīsī omits too much of Ibn Rabīʿ's text to intelligibly convey the intended meaning here. Van Koningsveld, Wiegers, and Ryad suggest emending Wansharīsī's text so that it reads as follows: "*thumma, hum immā [tārikūhu min ghayr] ḍarūra māniʿa minhu ʿalā al-iṭlāq, [fa-hum] kaʾl-ʿāzim ʿalā tarkihi min ghayr ḍarūra* . . ." The full passage in Ibn Rabīʿ's text is more elaborate; for a summary, see van Koningsveld and Wiegers, "Islamic Statute," 26–27.

11 This pronoun (*huwa*) is ambiguous in Wansharīsī's text, but in Ibn Rabīʿ's *fatwā* it clearly refers to the situation of Muslims living under non-Muslim rule.

12 *Sunan al-Tirmidhī, Abwāb al-Fitan, bāb* 58 (no name), *ḥadīth* 2419 (Tirmidhī, *Sunan al-Tirmidhī*, 3:327); *Sunan Ibn Māja, Kitāb al-Fitan, bāb qawlih taʿālā* . . . , *ḥadīth* 4016, in Muḥammad b. Yazīd al-Qazwīnī Ibn Māja (d. 273/887 or 275/889), *Sunan al-Ḥāfiẓ Abī Abd Allāh Muḥammad b. Yazīd al-Qazwīnī Ibn Māja*, ed. Muḥammad Fuʾād ʿAbd al-Bāqī (Beirut: Dār Iḥyāʾ al-Kutub al-ʿArabiyya, n.d.), 2:1331–32.

than the lower hand."[13] Also among them are belittlement and ridicule, which no one of sufficient manliness would tolerate unnecessarily.

Also among them are insults and injury to one's honor and often to one's person and property. It is clear what this entails with regard to [following] the *sunna* and [preserving] one's manliness. Also among them are becoming immersed in witnessing reprehensible acts, exposure to [repeated] contact with impurities, and eating forbidden and doubtful [foods].

Also among them are many situations that must be anticipated fearfully during this residence [under Christian rule]. These include the [Christian] king's violation of the treaty and [increased] control over lives, families, children, and property. It has been reported that ʿUmar b. ʿAbd al-ʿAzīz[14] prohibited settlement in the Andalusī peninsula even though at that time it was a frontier station (*ribāṭ*) whose merit was well-known. Despite the strength and dominance of the Muslims, and the abundant numbers and supplies at their disposal, the reigning caliph (whose virtue, piety, righteousness, and consideration for his subjects was agreed upon) forbade this [settlement] for fear of endangerment. So what would become of someone who casts himself, his family, and his children by their own hands [into harm's way] [15] when [it is] they [who] possess strength, dominance, large numbers, and an abundance of supplies—[simply] relying on their fidelity to the treaty concluded in accordance with their laws?

We do not accept their testimony [as legally valid] with regard to themselves, let alone with regard to ourselves! So how could we rely on their alleged fidelity, considering the anticipated [violations] that have [already] occurred as well as the incidents that are attested to by anyone who has studied and examined reports from the inhabited regions?[16]

Also among these [fears] is the fear for one's life, family, children, and property on account of their evildoers, fools, **and murderers; this is the case even if one assumes that their lords and kings are faithful [to their treaties]. This [fear] is likewise attested to by [their current] practice and confirmed by [actual] events.**

13 *Ṣaḥīḥ al-Bukhārī, Kitāb al-Zakāt, bāb lā ṣadaqa illā ʿan ẓahri ghinan, ḥadīths* 1361–62 (Bukhārī, *Ṣaḥīḥ al-Bukhārī*, 2:518–19); *Ṣaḥīḥ Muslim, Kitāb al-Zakāt, bāb bayān anna al-yad . . . , ḥadīths* 95–97 (Muslim b. al-Ḥajjāj, *Ṣaḥīḥ Muslim*, 2:717–18). Some narrations of this *ḥadīth* specify that the upper hand is that of the giver to charity and the lower hand is that of the beggar or receiver.

14 ʿUmar b. ʿAbd al-ʿAzīz was an Umayyad caliph (r. 99–101/717–20).

15 This likely refers to Qurʾān 2:195, which instructs believers not to cast themselves by their own hands into destruction.

16 On the historical events likely referred to here, see van Koningsveld and Wiegers, "Islamic Statute," 35–38.

Also among these is the fear of religious corruption (*al-fitna fī al-dīn*). Even supposing that intelligent adults could protect [themselves] against this [danger], who would protect the minors, the foolish, and the vulnerable among women if the enemy's lords and devils approach them?

Also among these fears is corruption through sexual relations and marriages [between Muslim women and Christian men].[17] How often will a man who has a wife, daughter, or beautiful female relative [be able to] protect [her] against some lowlife among the enemy dogs and infidel pigs[18] **acquainting himself with her, then deluding her as to herself and misleading her as to her religion, and overpowering her [until] she submits to him, and apostasy and religious corruption [then] come between her and her guardian?** This would resemble what happened to the daughter-in-law of al-Muʿtamid b. ʿAbbād[19] and whatever children she had (may God protect us from misfortune and the malicious joy of our enemies).

Also among these fears is the spread of their practices, language, dress, and reprehensible customs, over a length of years, to those residing among them—as happened to the people of Ávila[20] and others, who lost the Arabic language completely. When the Arabic language is lost entirely, its [related] acts of worship are also lost. Let it suffice for you [also, to mention their] neglect of all the spoken acts of worship, in all their number and abundant merit.

Also among these fears is [their] taking control of property by instituting heavy assessments and unjust fines. These would lead to a complete claim on [the Mudéjars'] property by ensnaring it in infidel taxes (*al-ḍarāʾib al-kufriyya*), **either all at once, in the guise of some**

---

17 This phrase is *al-fitna ʿalā al-abḍāʿ waʾl-furūj*; both terms may refer more literally to genitals, while *al-abḍāʿ* may also refer to marriages.

18 This phrase is *kilāb al-aʿdāʾ wa-khanāzīr al-buʿadāʾ*. *Al-buʿadāʾ* means distant or far removed from God; I have replaced it with "infidel," which is equivalent to the intended meaning. This insertion of a rhyming adjective is an example of Wansharīsī's stylistic modifications to Ibn Rabīʿ's text.

19 Al-Muʿtamid ʿalā Allāh Muḥammad b. ʿAbbād (r. 461–84/1069–91) was the last ʿAbbādid ruler of the Kingdom (*ṭāʾifa*) of Seville. His dynasty was brought to an end by the Almoravids, whom he had called for aid against Alfonso VI, King of Castile and León. His daughter-in-law, known as "Mora Zayda," was the wife of his son Maʾmūn, who governed Córdoba until his death in battle in 484/1091. She is said to have fled to Castile, become Alfonso's mistress, converted to Christianity, and borne him a son, Sancho. For a recent account of her story, see Simon Barton, *Conquerors, Brides, and Concubines: Interfaith Relations and Social Power in Medieval Iberia* (Philadelphia: University of Pennsylvania Press, 2015), 123–27, and the references contained therein.

20 Muʾnis identified this town, spelled Ābulla in the text, as Ávila. The town was conquered by Muslims in 145/762 and permanently lost to Christian rule in 481/1088. Van Koningsveld and Wiegers suggest the name could also refer to a number of small villages called Ayelo in Valencia. Muʾnis, "Asnā al-matājir," 62; van Koningsveld and Wiegers, "Islamic Statute," 28–29 n. 44. As Harvey has pointed out, the situation in Ávila was not so dire as Wansharīsī believed (*Islamic Spain*, 62–63); reference via Asmal, "Muslims under Non-Muslim Rule," 180–81 n. 2.

temporary necessity, or through [successive] payments. **Or it may be that this [seizure] is based on a combination of excuses and interpretations as to which no appeal or dispute is possible with them, even if [the excuses] are extremely weak, and the flimsiness and corruption [of their interpretations] is extremely clear.**[21] **The [Mudéjars] do not protest this [situation] for fear that this would stir up the forces of hatred [against them], become a reason for the treaty to be broken, and [thus lead to] the appropriation of their lives, families, and children. The reality attests to this, for anyone who studies it; indeed, this has occurred quite often in the place referred to in the question, [as it has] in other places, on more than one occasion.**

These ongoing and anticipated corruptions **have confirmed the prohibition of this residence [under non-Muslim rule] and the ban on [this form of]** living together that deviates from all that is right. **Through their various, mutually reinforcing considerations, they all convey a single concept. Indeed, because of the strength and clarity of this prohibition, the master jurists extended this judgment from its original [case] to other [cases]. The master jurist of Medina (*dār al-hijra*), Abū ʿAbd Allāh Mālik b. Anas (may God be pleased with him) said: "The [Qurʾānic] verses on *hijra* establish that every Muslim must depart from regions in which traditions are altered and the truth is not operative," to say nothing of departing and escaping from infidel territory** and the lands of the depraved. God forbid that a virtuous community upholding His unity should rely upon those who believe in the trinity, and be content to reside among the impure and filthy while exalting and glorifying Him.

Thus there is no room for the aforementioned virtuous man to reside in the place mentioned for the stated motive. Nor can there be any dispensation for him or for his companions as to the impurities and filth that beset their garments and bodies. This is because forgiveness for this [state of impurity] is conditional upon its being very difficult to guard against it and protect oneself; but no such difficulty [may be claimed in this case] considering their voluntary choice of residence and deviant course of action.

God (may He be exalted) knows best, and is the grantor of success. With greetings to whoever examines this among those who testify "there is no god but God," this was composed by the poor, lowly worshiper and seeker of forgiveness, who desires blessings for those who consider this [*fatwā*] and make use of it; the insignificant servant of God, Aḥmad b. Yaḥyā b. Muḥammad b. ʿAlī al-Wansharīsī (may God grant him success).

---

21 As van Koningsveld and Wiegers point out ("Islamic Statute," 29), this passage most likely refers to unfavorable interpretations of the treaties governing various Mudéjar communities.

CHRONOLOGY

Date	North and West Africa	Iberia and Sicily
711		Muslim armies enter the Iberian Peninsula
756		ʿAbd al-Raḥmān I establishes a new Umayyad emirate based in Córdoba (following the Abbasid defeat of the Umayyad Caliphate in Damascus in 750)
801		Muslim Barcelona is conquered by King Louis of Aquitaine, son of Charlemagne
827–902		The Aghlabids, based in Ifrīqiyā, begin the Muslim conquest of Sicily
929–1031		Umayyad caliphate in Córdoba
ca. 1031–1091		*Ṭāʾifa* period of Muslim rule in Iberia
1055	The Almoravids establish their first capital at Sijilmassa	
1061–1091		Norman conquest of Muslim Sicily
1085		King Alfonso VI of Castile conquers Toledo; beginning of the Mudéjar period
1086		Almoravid ruler Yūsuf b. Tāshufīn enters al-Andalus at the request of al-Muʿtamid, *amīr* of Seville; Almoravids defeat Alfonso VI at the Battle of Zallaqa, then return to North Africa

Date	North and West Africa	Iberia and Sicily
1091		The Almoravids defeat most of the Muslim Iberian kingdoms
1094		El Cid takes Valencia from the Almoravids, rules the city until his death in 1099
1120s	Beginning of the Almohad movement in southern Morocco	
1141	Death of Māzarī, who composed an undated *fatwā* on Muslim judges in Christian Sicily	
1146		The Almohads take control of Muslim Iberia from the Almoravids
1212		Christian kingdoms defeat the Almohads at the Battle of Las Navas de Tolosa
1230–1248	The Marīnid dynasty defeats the Almohads in Meknes (1246) and Fez (1248)	Ferdinand III of Castile conquers Córdoba, Valencia, and Seville; Ibn al-Aḥmar, founder of the Naṣrid dynasty, rules Granada as a vassal of Castile
1267		Abū al-Baqāʾ al-Rundī composes "Lament for the Fall of Seville"
1269	The Marīnids defeat the last Almohad caliph and capture Marrakesh	
1291		Castile and Aragon sign the treaty of Monteagudo, dividing North Africa into prospective zones of conquest
Late 13th or early 14th century		Ibn Rabīʿ (d. 719/1319), in Málaga, composes the *fatwā* later used by Wansharīsī
1397	Ibn Miqlāsh, in Oran, composes his *fatwā* regarding Muslims who remain in Iberia	
1408		Death of Granadan *muftī* Ḥaffār, who composed an undated *fatwā* on emigration

Date	North and West Africa	Iberia and Sicily
1415	Portuguese conquest of Ceuta (Sabta)	
1420	Assassination of Marīnid sultan Abū Saʿīd ʿUthmān III; Abū Zakariyyāʾ Yaḥyā I assumes power as the first Waṭṭāsid regent	
1436		Pope Eugenius IV grants Portugal conquest rights in Africa in the crusading bull *Reg Regnum*
1437	The Waṭṭāsids defend Tangier against the Portuguese	
ca. 1450s	Maghribī port cities including Salé, Anfa (Casablanca), Safi, and Azemmour begin to sign commercial treaties with Portugal	
1458	Portuguese conquest of al-Qaṣr al-Ṣaghīr (Alcácer-Ceguer)	
1459	ʿAbd al-Ḥaqq II, the last Marīnid sultan, reestablishes direct Marīnid rule	
1460	Safi allies with Portugal; a Portuguese attack on Tangier is defeated	
1465	ʿAbd al-Ḥaqq II is assassinated in Fez, ending the Marīnid dynasty; Muḥammad al-ʿImrānī al-Jūṭī establishes Idrīsid rule in Fez	
1468–1469	Portugal destroys Anfa; Wansharīsī flees Tlemcen to settle in Fez	Isabella of Castile marries Ferdinand II of Aragon (1469)
1470s	Idrīsid *sharīf* ʿAlī b. Rashīd founds Chefchaouen as a center of resistance against the Portuguese	

Date	North and West Africa	Iberia and Sicily
1471	Portugal conquers Asilah and Tangier; Afonso V commissions the Pastrana tapestries and adopts a new regnal title; Afonso V and Muḥammad al-Shaykh al-Waṭṭāsī sign a twenty-year Luso-Maghribī peace treaty	
1472	Muḥammad al-Shaykh overthrows Jūṭī to become the first independent Waṭṭāsid ruler	
1473	Portugal occupes al-ʿArāʾish (Larache)	
1474		Isabella becomes Queen of Castile
1477–1478	Castile constructs the fortress of Santa Cruz de la Mar Pequeña, on the African coast opposite the Canary Islands	Establishment of the Inquisition in Spain (1478)
1479		Ferdinand becomes King of Aragon; Portugal and Castile sign the Treaty of Alcáçovas
1482		Isabella and Ferdinand begin the decade-long conquest of the Naṣrid kingdom of Granada
1485		Castilian conquest of Marbella
1486	Azemmour allies with Portugal	
1487		Christian conquest of Málaga; Boabdil (Muḥammad XII) appeals for Mamluk and Ottoman aid
1488	Safi allies with Portugal	
Mid to late 1480s	Likely composition of the *fatwās* by Ibn Barṭāl, Māwāsī, Wansharīsī, Bijāʾī, Waryāglī, and Ibn Zakrī that address Portuguese occupation of parts of the Maghrib	

Date	North and West Africa	Iberia and Sicily
1489	João II and Muḥammad al-Shaykh agree to extend the 1471 Luso-Waṭṭāsid peace treaty (set to expire in 1491) by ten years; Portugal halts construction of Graciosa, a fortress on the Lukkus River near al-ʿArāʾish (Larache)	
1491	Wansharīsī composes *Asnā al-matājir* (on 22 September) and the Marbella *fatwā* in Fez	Isabella, Ferdinand, and Boabdil sign the Capitulations of Granada on November 25
1492		Isabella and Ferdinand take control of Granada in January, thereby ending Muslim rule in Iberia; that spring, they issue an edict expelling Jews from Castile and Aragon; death of Granadan chief judge Mawwāq, who composed an undated *fatwā* requiring emigration
1494		Portugal and Spain sign the Treaty of Tordesillas; Isabella and Ferdinand secure the crusading bull *Redemptor Noster* in support of their conquests in Africa
1495		Isabella and Ferdinand secure the crusading bull *Ineffabilis et Summi* in support of their conquests in Africa
1496	Castile completes its conquest of the Canary Islands	Pope Alexander V bestows the title of "Catholic Monarchs" on Ferdinand and Isabella
1497	Spain conquers Melilla; Massa signs a treaty with Portugal	Manuel I expels Jews and Muslims from Portugal and secures a papal bull, *Ineffabilis et Summi*, which sanctions Portuguese conquests in Africa
1498		Jews are expelled from Navarre; Granada is divided into a Christian zone and a Muslim zone, the Albaicín

Date	North and West Africa	Iberia and Sicily
1499–1500		Cardinal Francisco Jiménez de Cisneros, Archbishop of Toledo, arrives in Granada; Muslims in the Albaicín revolt; the Capitulations of Granada are annulled; Granadan Muslims are required to convert to Christianity; Moriscos send an appeal to Mamluk Egypt
1500–1501		Muslim revolts in the Alpujarras and elsewhere are violently suppressed; Muslims are forcibly converted to Christianity in Castile
1501		Unconverted Muslims are expelled from the former Kingdom of Granada; an anonymous poet composes the Morisco Appeal to the Ottoman sultan Bāyazīd II
ca. late 1501 to late 1504	An anonymous veteran of the War for Granada composes *Akhbār al-ʿaṣr fī inqiḍāʾ dawlat Banī Naṣr* (*The News from the Period: The End of the Naṣrid Dynasty*), in Fez	
1502		A royal decree requires all Muslims in Castile and León to convert to Christianity or emigrate; emigration is made nearly impossible
1504	Wahrānī, in Fez, composes his "Letter" to the Moriscos	Death of Isabella
1505	Portuguese merchant João de Sequeira builds Santa Cruz do Cabo de Gué, a fortress near Agadir	
1506	Portugal begins construction of Castelo Real, a fortress at Mogador, or modern-day Essaouira	

Date	North and West Africa	Iberia and Sicily
1508	Portugal occupies Safi; Spain conquers Peñón de Vélez de la Gomera, a small island off Badis on Morocco's Mediterranean coast; Wansharīsī dies in Fez	
1509	Spain conquers Oran (Wahrān), in modern-day Algeria	Portugal and Spain sign the Treaty of Sintra
1510	Spain conquers Algiers and Bijāya (Bougie), both in modern Algeria; Muḥammad al-Qā'im founds the Sa'dian dynasty in southern Morocco; Portugal withdraws from Mogador	
1511	Spain conquers Tripoli, in modern Libya; death of Wahrānī	
1513	Portugul acquires the fortress of Santa Cruz at Agadir and conquers Azemmour (Azamor)	
1514	Portugal begins construction of a fortress at Mazagan (Mazagão; modern-day El Jadida); Waṭṭāsids forcefully evacuate towns near Safi and Azemmour	
1515	The Waṭṭāsids block Portugal's attempt to establish a new fortress at the mouth of the Sebou River, São João da Mamora (Maʿmūra, modern-day Mehdia)	The Castilian edict requiring conversion to Christianity is extended to Navarre
1516	Yaḥyā-u-Taʿfuft invested as Portugal's *alcaide dos mouros* for the Dukkāla region (he is assassinated in 1518)	Death of Ferdinand
1519		Earliest date for copy V of Wahrānī's letter
1520–1522	Drought, famine, and disease in Morocco; death of Moroccan jurist Musfir, who composed an undated *fatwā* regarding northern Morocco	Muslims are forcibly baptized in Aragon

Date	North and West Africa	Iberia and Sicily
1524–1525	The Saʿdians defeat the last Hintātī ruler to take control of Marrakesh; they also expel the Spanish from Santa Cruz de la Mar Pequeña	
1525	Algeria is incorporated into the Ottoman Empire; Portugal abandons a newly-built fortress at Aguz, at the mouth of the Tensift River (south of Safi)	Charles V, Emperor of the Holy Roman Empire and King of Spain (1516–56), decrees that Muslims in Catalonia, Aragon, and Valencia must choose conversion or expulsion
1527	The Waṭṭāsids fail to assert sovereignty over Marrakesh	
1536	The Saʿdians defeat the Waṭṭāsids at the Battle of Abū ʿAqba (Būʿaqba); Waṭṭāsid sultan Abū al-ʿAbbās recognizes Saʿdian sovereignty over southern Morocco	
1537	The Saʿdians and the Portuguese agree to a four-year truce	
1538	The Waṭṭāsids and the Portuguese sign the Treaty of Fez, which recognizes Portuguese authority in northern Morocco; Waṭṭāsid sultan Abū al-ʿAbbās voids the treaty in 1543	
1541	The Saʿdians defeat Portuguese forces at Agadir; Portugal withdraws from Agadir, Safi, and Azemmour; beginning of Portuguese contraction in the Maghrib	
1545	Death of Moroccan jurist Ibn Hārūn, who composed a *fatwā* concerning marriage, conversion, and apostasy in northern Morocco	

Date	North and West Africa	Iberia and Sicily
1549–1554	The Saʿdian dynasty defeats the Waṭṭāsids in Fez; Muḥammad al-Shaykh becomes the first Saʿdian sultan to rule a unified Morocco	
1563		Copy M of Wahrānī's letter
1568–1570		Second Alpujarras Rebellion; the Muslims of Granada are forcibly relocated
1574	Tunisia is incorporated into the Ottoman Empire	
1578	King Sebastião I is killed at the Battle of Wādī al-Makhāzin (the Battle of Three Kings) in al-Qaṣr al-Kabīr (Alcácer Kebir); this is Portugal's last major military defeat in North Africa	
1580	Portugal is incorporated into the Spanish Crown (until 1640)	
1594–1599		The Lead Books are discovered in a hillside near Granada
1609		Copy A of Wahrānī's letter
1609–1614		The Moriscos are expelled from Iberia
1615 and 1622		A cache of Arabic books is discovered in Pastrana (in New Castile)
1633		Marcos Dobelio produces copy X of Wahrānī's letter
1638		Dobelio composes *Nuevo descubrimiento de la falsedad del metal*, in which he argues that the Lead Books are a Morisco forgery
1640	Portugal regains independence from Spain; Spain retains Ceuta	
1645	Death of ʿAbd al-ʿAzīz al-Zayyātī, compiler of *al-Jawāhir al-mukhtāra* (*Selected Jewels*)	

Date	North and West Africa	Iberia and Sicily
1659	The ʿAlawī dynasty assumes power in Morocco	
1769	Portugal withdraws from Mazagan (Mazagão), the last Portuguese holding in Morocco	
1792	Spain withdraws from Oran	
1830	France conquers Ottoman Algiers; the ʿAlawī sultan of Morocco, Mawlāy ʿAbd al-Raḥmān accepts an oath of allegiance from the residents of Tlemcen	
1831	France occupies Oran; Mawlāy ʿAbd al-Raḥmān coordinates a *jihād* against the French, but fails to retake Oran	
1832	Mawlāy ʿAbd al-Raḥmān withdraws his governor from western Algeria; Muḥyī al-Dīn, leader of the Qādiriyya Sufi order, delegates military authority to his son ʿAbd al-Qādir al-Jazāʾirī	
1834	Mawlāy ʿAbd al-Raḥmān recognizes ʿAbd al-Qādir as his deputy in the province of Oran; ʿAbd al-Qādir signs the Desmichels Treaty with the governor of Oran	
1835–1836	The Dawāʾir and Zmāla tribes side with the French; ʿAbd al-Qādir resumes hostilities; France gains control of Mascara and Tlemcen	
ca. 1830–1836	Ibn al-Shāhid composes his letter defending Muslim residence in Algiers	

Date	North and West Africa	Iberia and Sicily
ca. 1835–1843	Ibn Ruwīla, advisor to ʿAbd al-Qādir, composes his letter critiquing the Mālikī *muftī* in French Algiers, Muṣṭafā b. al-Kabābṭī; ʿAlī b. al-Ḥaffāf later adds a commentary	
1837	Tasūlī, chief judge of Fez, composes a five-part treatise in response to ʿAbd al-Qādir's questions on *jihād*; ʿAbd al-Qādir signs the Treaty of Tafna with the French	
ca. 1837–1839	Egyptian Mālikī jurist Muḥammad ʿIllaysh issues a *fatwā* at ʿAbd al-Qādir's request	
1839	ʿAbd al-Qādir resumes active *jihād* against the French, who launch their systematic conquest of Algeria; ʿAbd al-Qādir sends a second *fatwā* request to Fez	
1840	Tasūlī and ʿAbd al-Hādī al-ʿAlawī, the chief judge of Fez, respond to ʿAbd al-Qādir; this is Tasūlī's second response	
1841	Al-Sharīf al-Tilimsānī, preacher of the Great Mosque of Taza, issues a *fatwā* at ʿAbd al-Qādir's request; Léon Roches obtains a *fatwā* from the Tijāniyya Sufi order on behalf of French Governor-General Bugeaud	
1843	ʿAbd al-Qādir composes his treatise on *hijra*, *Ḥusām al-dīn* (*The Sword of Religion*)	
1847	ʿAbd al-Qādir surrenders to the French	
1857	France completes the conquest of Algeria	
1883	ʿAbd al-Qādir dies in Damascus	

Date	North and West Africa	Iberia and Sicily
1885	Mauritanian resistance leader Māʾ al-ʿAynayn al-Qalqamī authors a treatise advocating *jihād* against Spanish occupation of Dakhla (southern Morocco); death of Fez-based jurist and reformer Muḥammad Gannūn, who wrote an undated treatise warning Algerians against residence under French rule	
1893	Jules Cambon, governor-general of Algeria, obtains a *fatwā* from the *muftīs* of Mecca; Aḥmad al-Kabīr, defeated leader of the ʿUmarian state (in modern-day Mali) appeals to Moroccan sultan Ḥasan I for aid	
1897	French administrators Xavier Coppolani and Octave Depont publish *Les confréries religieuses musulmanes*	
1902	Coppolani launches the "pacification" of Mauritania	
1903	Sufi leader Sidiyya Baba writes a *fatwā* in support of French rule in Mauritania	
ca. 1904	Mauritanian jurist Buṣādī (d. 1933 or 1934) emigrates in response to French colonization, and composes his (undated) treatise-length *fatwā* defending the property rights of conquered Muslims	
1905	Coppolani is assassinated in Tagant by followers of Māʾ al-ʿAynayn; jurist Sīdī al-Mukhtār al-Lamtūnī emigrates from Mauritania to Morocco, where he composes his texts encouraging *hijra*	

Date	North and West Africa	Iberia and Sicily
1909	French forces subjugate the Adrar region of what is now Mauritania; Saad Buh writes a letter urging Māʾ al-ʿAynayn to abandon *jihād*; Sidiyya Baba composes his response to Sīdī b. Ḥabatt	
1910	Māʾ al-ʿAynayn dies in Tiznit, in southern Morocco	
1912	France declares a protectorate in Morocco; Spain establishes a protectorate in northern Morocco; al-Sanūsī composes a treatise advocating *jihād* against Italian colonization in what is now Libya	
1921	Sidiyya Baba composes a letter praising French rule	
1925	Murabbīh Rabbuh composes his *fatwā* in support of the obligation to emigrate	
1932	France completes the colonization of Mauritania	
1934	Italy completes the colonization of Libya (begun in 1911)	
1948	Muḥammad al-Amīn, author of an undated letter defending residence in French Mauritania, emigrates to Saudi Arabia	
1956	Morocco gains independence, ending the French and Spanish protectorates	
1960	Mauritania and Tunisia gain independence from France	
1962	Algeria gains independence from France	

GLOSSARY

Al-Andalus	Islamic Iberia; Arabic term for the portion of the Iberian Peninsula under Muslim rule
alcaide dos mouros	"Leader (*qāʾid*) of the Moors," a regional Muslim governor serving Portuguese interests
aljamiado	Spanish (or Romance vernaculars) written in a modified Arabic script
amīr	Commander; the title *amīr al-muʾminīn* means "Commander of the Faithful"
Andalusī	An inhabitant or native of al-Andalus
arḍ al-ḥarb	Land of war; see *dār al-ḥarb*
aṣl	Original; in analogical reasoning, this is the technical legal term for an original case, for which there is an established legal rule
Asnā al-matājir	Short form of Wansharīsī's 1491 *fatwā*, *Asnā al-matājir fī bayān aḥkām man ghalaba ʿalā waṭanih al-Naṣārā wa-lam yuhājir, wa-mā yatarattabu ʿalayh min al-ʿuqūbāt waʾl-zawājir* (*The Most Noble Commerce: An Exposition of the Legal Rulings Governing One Whose Homeland Has Been Conquered by the Christians and Who Has Not Emigrated, and the Punishments and Admonishments Accruing to Him*)
awliyāʾ	Allies
Berbers	Umbrella term for the indigenous peoples of North Africa, who form distinct tribal confederations such as the Ṣanhāja, Zanāta, and Maṣmūda. This term, used by Wansharīsī and his contemporaries, is now increasingly being replaced by Amazigh
convivencia	Coexistence; normally used to refer to interreligious coexistence in medieval Iberia and sometimes used to connote a uniquely harmonious multi-confessional society
dār al-Islām	The land of Islam; Muslim-ruled territory
dār al-ḥarb	The land of war; territory ruled by non-Muslims
dār al-kufr	The land of unbelief; occasionally used as a synonym for *dār al-ḥarb*, the land of war
dhimmīs	Jews and Christians living under Muslim rule as tributaries; also appears as "protected peoples" or *ahl al-dhimma*
elches	European Christian converts to Islam, also termed *ʿulūj* or "renegades"

*far*ʿ	Branch; in analogical reasoning, the technical legal term for a new case for which a legal judgment is needed
Fāsī	An inhabitant or native of Fez (in modern-day Morocco)
fatwā	A non-binding legal opinion issued by a qualifed jurist in response to a question posed by an individual, court, or government representative
fiqh	Islamic jurisprudence, literally, "understanding"
fitna	Corruption, communal discord, or the spread of corrupting ideas
*ghurabā*ʾ	Exiles or strangers
ḥadīth (pl. *aḥādīth*)	An individual report (or "tradition") regarding an action or statement attributed to the Prophet Muḥammad; when capitalized as "the Ḥadīth," the term refers to the collective body of preserved reports that serve as the second primary source of Islamic law and ethics, after the Qurʾān
ḥajj	The Muslim pilgrimage to Mecca
ḥarbī	A non-Muslim resident of *dār al-ḥarb*; as opposed to *dhimmī*s, who are Jews or Christians living under Muslim rule, *ḥarbī*s are non-Muslims who normally reside in non-Muslim territory (though they might travel outside it)
hijra	Emigration; in this book, *hijra* may refer to an act of emigration or to the Islamic legal doctrine that Muslims have an obligation to emigrate from *dār al-ḥarb* to *dār al-Islām*. When capitalized as Hijra, this term refers to the 622 emigration of the Prophet Muḥammad and his followers from Mecca to Medina, in order to escape persecution; the Islamic calendar dates from the year of this foundational event
ḥukm	Legal rule (for example, that an action is permitted or prohibited); in analogical reasoning, this is the existing legal rule governing the original case, that is extended to the new case
Ifrīqiyā	The territory roughly corresponding to modern-day Tunisia
ijtihād	The exertion of independent, intellectual effort in order to derive legal rules from the sources of Islamic law
ʿilla	Effective cause; in analogical reasoning, this is the rationale for the rule governing the original case; this rationale must also be present in the new case, to justify extending the rule from the original case to the new case
*istiftā*ʾ	The question component of a *fatwā*; the request for a legal opinion that is posed to a qualified jurist by a person, court, or government official
imām	In lowercase, this term usually refers to a ruler or prayer leader; when capitalized, Imām is a Sunnī Muslim epithet honoring a master jurist or may indicate the highest religious authority in Shīʿī Islam
"jewels"	Short form of reference for those legal opinions Zayyātī includes in his *fatwā* compilation, *Selected Jewels*

jihād	War, normally sanctioned by a Muslim ruler and fought against non-Muslims
jizya	The annual poll tax paid by adult Jews and Christians living under Muslim rule
kāfir (pl. *kuffār*)	Infidel or unbeliever
khaṭīb	Preacher who offers the Friday *khuṭba* (sermon) in a mosque
madhhab	School of Islamic law, in the sense of an intellectual tradition with shared authorites, doctrines, and methods of legal reasoning (a *madrasa* is a physical school)
al-Maghrib al-aqṣā	The Far Maghrib, or western portion of North Africa that corresponds to modern-day Morocco
Maghrib	North Africa; *al-Maghrib* in Arabic may refer to Morocco specifically, or to northern Africa more broadly (see North Africa below)
Maghribī	An inhabitant or native of North Africa; of, or pertaining to, North Africa
Mālikī	The school of Islamic law that is named after Mālik b. Anās (d. 179/795) and was dominant in al-Andalus; it remains dominant in North and West Africa. The term also means "of, or pertaining to, the Mālikī school of law," as when referring to an adherent of the Mālikī school
al-Miʿyār	Short form for *al-Miʿyār al-muʿrib waʾl-jāmiʿ al-mughrib ʿan fatāwī ahl Ifrīqiyā waʾl-Andalus waʾl-Maghrib* (*The Clear Standard and Extraordinary Collection of the Legal Opinions of the Scholars of Ifrīqiyā, al-Andalus, and the Maghrib*), the most prominent Mālikī *fatwā* compilation. Compiled by Aḥmad al-Wansharīsī (d. 914/1508), it contains at least 5,000 *fatwās* issued between 1000 and 1500 CE by hundreds of *muftīs* in North Africa and al-Andalus
Morisco	Iberian Muslims forcibly converted to Christianity and their descendants, who were nominally Christian but professed Islam in private; also called crypto-Muslims
mouros de paz	Portuguese term for "peaceful Moors," Muslims who cooperated with Portuguese authorities
Mudéjars	Muslims living under Christian rule in Iberia, who were permitted to practice Islam; in Arabic, they are *ahl al-dajn* or *al-Muslimūn al-dhimmiyyūn*, "Muslim *dhimmīs*"
muftī	A Muslim jurist capable of issuing *fatwās*
muhājirūn	Emigrants; when capitalized as Muhājirūn, this term refers to the early Muslims who emigrated from Mecca to Medina with Muḥammad
muḥāribūn	Illegitimate rebels or brigands
mujāhid	Warrior; a fighter engaged in *jihād*
mujtahid	A Muslim jurist capable of *ijtihād*

muqallid	"Follower"; a Muslim jurist who is not capable of *ijtihād* and is expected to practice *taqlīd* (to apply received doctrines)
mustaftī	The person or party who poses a question (an *istiftāʾ*) to a jurist in order to obtain a *fatwā* (legal opinion)
North Africa	Northern Africa, excluding Egypt. This term normally refers to Morocco, Algeria, Tunisia, and Libya; Mauritania is occasionally included
North West Africa	The region covered by this book, including the Maghrib and Mauritania. "North Africa" renders Mauritania too peripheral, "North and West Africa" suggests more complete coverage of West Africa than is provided, and "northwest Africa," while accurate, insufficiently signals the book's core emphasis on North Africa
pragmática	Royal decree
Prohibition on Plundering	Short form of the title for Mauritanian jurist Buṣādī's (d. 1933 or 1934) *fatwā*, *Taḥrīm nahb amwāl al-muʿāhidīn lil-Naṣārā* (*Prohibition on Plundering the Property of Those under Treaty with the Christians*)
qāḍī	Judge
qaṣīda	A genre of formal Arabic verse
qiyās	Technical legal term for analogical reasoning, a form of legal reasoning used to extend to new cases rules that have been established on the basis of clear scriptural proof texts
Reconquest	In modern usage, a term that refers to the centuries-long series of conquests by Iberian Christian kingdoms of Muslim-ruled territories in Iberia, a process seen to have culminated in the 1492 conquest of Granada; also called the *reconquista* or fall of al-Andalus. Formerly, the notion of *reconquista* also extended to North Africa. The term is problematic because of its irredentist implication that later Christian Iberian kindgoms were the rightful political heirs of formerly Visigothic territories
Sepharad	Hebrew term for the Iberian Peninsula; origin of the term "Sephardic" for Jews of Iberian descent
Selected Jewels	Short form of the title for ʿAbd al-ʿAzīz al-Zayyātī's (d. 1055/1645) *fatwā* compilation, *al-Jawāhir al-mukhtāra fīmā waqaftu ʿalayh min al-nawāzil bi-Jibāl Ghumāra* (*Selected Jewels: Legal Cases I Encountered in the Ghumāra Mountains*)
sharīf (pl. *shurafāʾ*)	A "noble" whose family claims descent from the Prophet Muḥammad; sometimes spelled *cherif* or *chorfa* (plural)
sunna	The exemplary behavior of the Prophet Muḥammad
Sword of Religion	Short title for ʿAbd al-Qādir's January 1843 treatise titled *Ḥusām al-dīn li-qaṭʿ shabah al-murtaddīn* (*The Sword of Religion that Severs [Muslims'] Resemblance to Apostates*)

ṭāʾifa	"Party," used to refer to the small Muslim kingdoms of eleventh-century Iberia; the "*ṭāʾifa* period" followed the disintegration of the Ummayad caliphate of Córdoba
taqiyya	A doctrine allowing precautionary dissimulation of one's religious views in the face of danger
taqlīd	Islamic legal term referring to the emulation and application of received doctrines
tayammum	A method of ritual washing with sand, which is allowed when pure water is unavailable for the ablutions that precede prayer
The News	Short title for *Akhbār al-ʿaṣr fī inqiḍāʾ dawlat Banī Naṣr* (*The News from the Period: The End of the Naṣrid Dynasty*), an anonymous, eyewitness chronicle of the 1482–92 War for Granada composed in Fez ca. 1501–4
ʿulamāʾ	Arabic term for scholars
ʿulūj	Arabic term for European Christian converts to Islam (singular: *ʿilj*), also termed *elches* or "renegades"
West Africa	In current usage, a group of sixteen countries in western Africa; under colonial rule, French West Africa expanded inland from Saint-Louis in Senegal to eventually include eight territories governed from Dakar: Mauritania, Senegal, French Sudan (now Mali), French Guinea (now Guinea), Ivory Coast, Upper Volta (now Burkina Faso), Dahomey (now Benin), and Niger

LIBRARIES AND ARCHIVES CONSULTED

Algeria

The Algerian National Library, Algiers (al-Maktaba al-Waṭaniyya al-Jazāʾiriyya, La Bibliothèque Nationale d'Algérie)

Egypt

Bibliotheca Alexandrina, Alexandria (Maktabat al-Iskandariyya)

The Egyptian National Library and Archives, Cairo (Dār al-Kutub waʾl-Wathāʾiq al-Qawmiyya)

France

Archives Nationales d'Outre Mer, Aix-en-Provence

Bibliothèque Méjanes, Aix-en-Provence

Morocco

The ʿAllāl al-Fāsī Institute, Rabat (Muʾassasat ʿAllāl al-Fāsī)

The Dāwūdiyya Library, Tetouan (al-Khizāna al-Dāwūdiyya)

The General Library and Archives, Tetouan (al-Maktaba al-ʿĀmma waʾl-Maḥfuẓāt bi-Tiṭwān, La Bibliothèque Générale et Archives de Tétouan)

The Ḥasaniyya Library, Rabat (al-Khizāna al-Ḥasanīya, La Bibliothèque Ḥasaniyya; also known as the Royal Library, al-Maktaba al-Malakiyya or La Bibliothèque Royale)

The Ibn Sūda Library, Fez (Maktabat Ibn Sūda)

The King ʿAbd al-ʿAzīz Āl Saʿūd Foundation, Casablanca (Muʾassasat al-Malik ʿAbd al-ʿAzīz Āl Saʿūd lil-Dirāsāt al-Islāmiyya waʾl-ʿUlūm al-Insāniyya, Fondation du Roi Abdul Aziz Al Saoud pour les Etudes Islamiques et les Sciences Humaines)

The Moroccan National Library, Rabat (al-Maktaba al-Waṭaniyya lil-Mamlaka al-Maghribiyya or La Bibliothèque Nationale du Royaume du Maroc)

The Library of the Great Mosque of Meknes (Khizānat al-Jāmiʿ al-Kabīr bi-Miknās)

The Ṣbīḥī Library, Salé (al-Khizana al-ʿIlmiyya al-Ṣubayḥiyya bi-Salā)

Tetouan-Asmir Association for Cultural, Social, Economic, and Athletic Development, Tetouan (Jamʿiyyat Tiṭwān Asmīr lil-Tanmiya al-Thaqāfiyya waʾl-Ijtimāʿiyya waʾl-Iqtiṣādiyya waʾl-Riyāḍiyya)

The Qarawiyyīn Library, Fez (Khizānat al-Qarawiyyīn)

Spain

The National Library of Spain, Madrid (Biblioteca Nacional de España)

Royal Library of the Monastery of El Escorial, San Lorenzo de El Escorial (Real Biblioteca del Monasterio de San Lorenzo de El Escorial)

Tunisia

The Tunisian National Library, Tunis (al-Maktaba al-Waṭaniyya al-Tūnisiyya, La Bibliothèque Nationale du Tunisie)

National Archives of Tunisia (al-Arshīf al-Waṭanī al-Tūnisī, Les Archives Nationales de Tunisie)

BIBLIOGRAPHY

Manuscript Sources

Al-Buṣādī, Muḥammad ʿAbd Allāh b. Zaydān (d. 1933 or 1934). *Jawāb ʿan ḥukm Allāh taʿālā fī māl al-Muslimīn min al-Shanājiṭa al-muqīmīn fī arḍ al-ḥarbiyyīn.* Ḥasaniyya Library, Rabat, MS 12438.3; Muʾassasat al-Malik ʿAbd al-ʿAzīz Āl Saʿūd, Casablanca, MS 440.

Gannūn, Muḥammad b. al-Madanī b. ʿAlī (d. 1302/1885). *Al-Taḥdhīr fī al-iqāma bi-ʿarḍ al-ʿaduww.* Moroccan National Library, Rabat, MSS 2223D.8 and 1079D.6; Qarawiyyīn Library, Fez, MS 1994.5; Muʾassasat al-Malik ʿAbd al-ʿAzīz Āl Saʿūd, Casablanca, MS 249. Also printed in the margins of Ibn al-Madanī Gannūn, *al-Tasliya waʾl-salwān li-man ibtalā biʾl-idhāya waʾl-buhtān*, Fez lithograph, 1301/1884.

Ibn Miqlāsh, Abū Zayd ʿAbd al-Raḥmān (fl. 794/1397). *Fatwā.* Biblioteca Nacional de España, Madrid, MS 4950, fols. 226r–231v.

Ibn Ruwayla, Qaddūr b. Muḥammad (d. 1272/1855). *Risāla ilā Muṣṭafā b. al-Kabābṭī, muftī al-Jazāʾir.* Algerian National Library, Algiers, MSS 1304 and 2083.

Ibn Ṭarkāṭ, Abū al-Faḍl or Abū al-Qāsim (d. after 854/1450). *Al-Nawāzil.* Biblioteca Nacional de España, MS 5135, fols. 72v–72r.

ʿIllaysh, Abū ʿAbd Allāh Muḥammad Aḥmad (d. 1299/1882), et al. *Risāla fī wujūb al-jihād waʾl-hijra.* Tunisian National Library, Tunis, MS 2418.

Al-Tasūlī, ʿAlī b. ʿAbd al-Salām (d. 1258/1842). *Al-Jawāhir al-nafīsa fīmā yatakarraru min al-ḥawādith al-gharība.* Ḥasaniyya Library, Rabat, MS 12575; Tunisian National Library, Tunis, MS 5354.

Al-Wahrānī, Ibn Abī Jumʿa (d. 917/1511). [Advice to the Muslims of al-Andalus]. Bibliothèque Méjanes, Aix-en-Provence, MS 1367 (1223), fols. 130r–139r.

Al-Wansharīsī, Abū al-ʿAbbās Aḥmad b. Yaḥyā (d. 914/1508). *Asnā al-matājir fī bayān aḥkām man ghalaba ʿalā waṭanih al-Naṣārā wa-lam yuhājir, wa-mā yatarattabu ʿalayh min al-ʿuqūbāt waʾl-zawājir.* Real Biblioteca del Monasterio de San Lorenzo de El Escorial, MS 1758; Muʾassasat al-Malik ʿAbd al-ʿAzīz Āl Saʿūd, Casablanca, MS 10–164.

Al-Zayyātī, ʿAbd al-ʿAzīz b. al-Ḥasan (d. 1055/1645). *Al-Jawāhir al-mukhtāra fīmā waqaftu ʿalayh min al-nawāzil bi-Jibāl Ghumāra.* General Library and Archives, Tetouan, MS 178; Moroccan National Library, Rabat, MS 1698D; Ḥasaniyya Library, Rabat, MS 5862.

Published Sources

ʿAbd al-Qādir, Nūr al-Dīn. *Ṣafaḥāt min tārīkh madīnat al-Jazāʾir min aqdam ʿuṣūrihā ilā intihāʾ al-ʿahd al-Turkī*. [Algiers]: n.p., 1965.

ʿAbd al-Wahhāb, Ḥasan Ḥusnī. *Kitāb al-ʿUmr fī al-muṣannafāt waʾl-muʾallifīn al-Tūnisiyyīn*. Edited and expanded by Muḥammad al-ʿArūsī al-Maṭwī and Bashīr al-Bakkūsh. 2 vols. Beirut: Dār al-Gharb al-Islāmī, 1990.

———. *Al-Imām al-Māzarī*. Tunis: Dār al-Kutub al-Sharqiyya, 1955.

Abdel Haleem, M.A.S. (Muhammad), trans. *The Qurʾan: A New Translation*. Reprint edition with corrections. Oxford: Oxford University Press, 2010.

Abou El Fadl, Khaled. "Islamic Law and Muslim Minorities: The Juristic Discourse on Muslim Minorities from the Second/Eighth to the Eleventh/Seventeenth Centuries." *Islamic Law and Society* 1, no. 2 (1994): 141–87.

Abū Dāwūd, Sulaymān al-Azdī al-Sijistānī (d. 275/889). *Sunan Abī Dāwūd*. Edited by Shuʿayb al-Arnaʾūṭ and Muḥammad Kāmil Qurrah Balalī. 6 vols. Damascus: Dār al-Risāla al-ʿĀlamiyya, 2009.

Abun-Nasr, Jamil. *The Tijaniyya: A Sufi Order in the Modern World*. New York: Oxford University Press, 1965.

Al-ʿAbdūsī, ʿAbd Allāh (d. 849/1446). *Ajwibat al-ʿAbdūsī*. Edited by Hishām al-Muḥammadī. Rabat: Wizārat al-Awqāf waʾl-Shuʾūn al-Islāmiyya, 2015.

Adil, Sabahat. "Memorializing al-Maqqarī: The Life, Work, and Worlds of a Muslim Scholar." PhD Dissertation, University of Chicago, 2015.

Al-ʿĀfiyya, ʿAbd al-Qādir. "Al-Hijra min al-Firdaus al-Mafqūd wa-fatwā wa-taʿlīq." *Al-Manāhil* 3, no. 4 (1975): 316–28.

L'Africain, Jean-Léon (Al-Ḥasan al-Wazzān). *Description de l'Afrique*. Edited and translated by E. Épaulard, et al. Revised ed. 2 vols. Paris, Adrien-Maisonneuve, 1956.

Agrama, Hussein Ali. "Ethics, Tradition, Authority: Toward an Anthropology of the Fatwa," *American Ethnologist*, 37, no. 1 (2010): 2–18.

Aidi, Hisham. "The Interference of al-Andalus: Spain, Islam, and the West." *Social Text* 24, no. 2 (2006): 67–88.

Akasoy, Anna. "*Convivencia* and Its Discontents: Interfaith Life in al-Andalus." *International Journal of Middle East Studies* 42 (2010): 489–99.

Alonso Acero, Beatriz. *España y el Norte de África en los Siglos XVI y XVII*. Madrid: Editorial Síntesis, 2017.

Amar, Emile. "La pierre de touche des Fétwas de Aḥmad al-Wanscharîsî: Choix de consultations des faqîhs du Maghreb traduites ou analysées par E. Amar." *Archives Marocaines* 12 (1908): 1–522 and 13 (1909): 1–536. Reprinted by Kraus Reprint, Nendeln/Liechtenstein, 1974 and 1980.

Anonymous. *Akhbār al-ʿaṣr fī inqiḍāʾ dawlat Banī Naṣr*. Edited by Ḥusayn Muʾnis. Cairo: Al-Zahrāʾ lil-Iʿlām al-ʿArabī, 1991.

Anonymous. *Ākhir ayyām Gharnāṭa: Nubdhat al-ʿaṣr fī akhbār mulūk Banī Naṣr*. Edited by Muḥammad Riḍwān al-Dāya. 2nd ed. Beirut: Dār al-Fikr al-Muʿāṣir, 2002.

Anonymous. *Fragmento de la época sobre noticias de los Reyes Nazaritas o Capitulación de Granada y Emigración de los Andaluces a Marruecos*. Arabic edition of *Nubdhat al-ʿaṣr fī akhbār mulūk Banī Naṣr* by Alfredo Bustani.

Translated by D. Carlos Quirós. Larache: Artes Gráficas Bosca, 1940. Edition only republished as Anonymous, *Nubdhat al-ʿaṣr fī akhbār mulūk Banī Naṣr*, ed. Alfredo Bustani (London: Alwarrak Publishing, 2017).

Anonymous. *Al-Ḥadīqa al-mustaqilla al-naḍra fī al-fatāwā al-ṣādira ʿan ʿulamāʾ al-ḥaḍra*. Edited by Jalāl ʿAlī al-Qadhdhāfī al-Juhānī. Beirut: Dār Ibn Ḥazm, 2003.

Al-ʿAwaayishah, Husayn bin ʿAwdah al-ʿAwaayishah, ed. *A Conclusive Study on the Issue of Hijra and Separating from the Polytheists*. Translated by Abu Maryam Ismaʿeel Alarcon. N.p., NY: Al-Ibaanah Book Publishing, 2006.

Arberry, A.J. (Arthur John), trans. *The Koran Interpreted*. 1955. Reprint, New York: Touchstone, 1996.

Asmal, Aboobaker M. "Muslims under Non-Muslim Rule: The *Fiqhi* (Legal) Views of Ibn Nujaym and al-Wansharisi." PhD dissertation, University of Manchester, 1998.

Aṭwī, Ghaniya. *al-Jawāhir al-mukhtāra mimmā waqaftu ʿalayh min al-nawāzil bi-jibāl Ghumāra*. MA thesis, University of Constantine 2, Algeria, 2013.

Ballan, Mohamad. "Between Castilian *Reconquista* and Ottoman *Jihād*: An Analysis of the 1501 Hispano-Muslim *Qaṣīda* to Bayezid II." MA thesis, University of Chicago, 2010.

Barton, Simon. *Conquerors, Brides, and Concubines: Interfaith Relations and Social Power in Medieval Iberia*. Philadelphia: University of Pennsylvania Press, 2015.

Al-Barūsawī, Ismāʿīl Ḥaqqī b. Muṣṭafā al-Ḥanafī. *Rūḥ al-bayān fī tafsīr al-Qurʾān*. Edited by ʿAbd al-Laṭīf Ḥasan ʿAbd al-Raḥmān. 10 vols. Beirut: Dār al-Kutub al-ʿIlmiyya, 2003.

Al-Bayḍāwī, Abū Yaʿlā, ed. *Asnā al-matājir fī bayān aḥkām man ghalaba ʿalā waṭanih al-Naṣārā wa lam yuhājir, wa-mā yatarattabu ʿalayh min al-ʿuqūbāt waʾl-zawājir*. By Abū al-ʿAbbās Aḥmad b. Yaḥyā al-Wansharīsī. N.p., 2005.

Al-Bayhaqī, Abū Bakr Aḥmad b. al-Ḥusayn (d. 458/1066). *Al-Sunan al-Kubrā*. Edited by Muḥammad ʿAbd al-Qādir ʿAṭā. 3rd ed. 11 vols. Beirut: Dār al-Kutub al-ʿIlmiyya, 2003.

Benchekroun, Mohamed B. A. *La vie intellectuelle marocaine sous les Mérinides et les Waṭṭāsides*. Rabat: n.p., 1974.

Bennison, Amira. *The Almoravid and Almohad Empires*. The Edinburgh History of the Islamic Empires. Edinburgh: Edinburgh University Press, 2016.

———. *Jihad and its Interpretations in Pre-Colonial Morocco: State-Society Relations during the French Conquest of Algeria*. London: RoutledgeCurzon, 2002.

———. "Liminal States: Morocco and the Iberian Frontier between the Twelfth and Nineteenth Centuries." In *North Africa, Islam and the Mediterranean World: From the Almoravids to the Algerian War*, edited by Julia Clancy-Smith, 11–28. London: Frank Cass, 2001.

Bentahar, Ziad. "Continental Drift: The Disjunction of North and Sub-Saharan Africa." *Research in African Literatures* 42, no. 1 (2011): 1–13.

Bernabé-Pons, Luis F. "*Taqiyya, niyya* y el islam de los moriscos." *Al-Qanṭara* 34, no. 2 (2013): 491–527.

Brann, Ross. "Andalusi 'Exceptionalism.'" In *A Sea of Languages: Rethinking the Arabic Role in Medieval Literary History*, edited by Suzanne Conklin Akbari and Karla Mallette, 119–34. Toronto: University of Toronto Press, 2013.

Bresc, Henri. "Pantelleria entre l'Islam et la Chretiente." *Les Cahiers de Tunisie* 19, nos. 75–76 (1971): 105–27.

Brower, Benjamin Claude. "The Amîr 'Abd al-Qâdir and the 'Good War' in Algeria, 1832–1847." *Studia Islamica* 106 (2011): 169–95.

Brown, Jonathan A.C. *Hadith: Muhammad's Legacy in the Medieval and Modern World*. Oxford: Oneworld, 2009.

Al-Bukhārī, Muḥammad b. Ismāʿīl (d. 256/870). *Ṣaḥīḥ al-Bukhārī*. Edited by Muṣṭafā al-Bughā. 5th ed. 7 vols. Damascus: Dār Ibn Kathīr, 1993.

Al-Būkhuṣaybī, Abū Bakr. *Aḍwāʾ ʿalā Ibn Yaggabsh al-Tāzī*. Casablanca: Maṭbaʿat al-Najāḥ al-Jadīda, 1976.

Al-Burzulī, Abū al-Qāsim b. Aḥmad al-Balawī al-Qayrawānī (d. 841/1438). *Fatāwā al-Burzulī: Jāmiʿ masāʾil al-aḥkām li-mā nazala min al-qaḍāyā biʾl-muftīn waʾl-ḥukkām*. Edited by Muḥammad al-Ḥabīb al-Hīla. 7 vols. Beirut: Dār al-Gharb al-Islāmī, 2002.

Al-Buṣādī, Muḥammad ʿAbd Allāh b. Zaydān (d. 1933 or 1934). *Taḥrīm nahb amwāl al-muʿāhidīn lil-Naṣārā*. Edited by Ḥamāh Allāh wuld al-Sālim. Beirut: Dar al-Kutub al-ʿIlmiyya, 2013.

Būsharb, Aḥmad. *Dukkāla waʾl-istiʿmār al-Burtughālī ilā sanat ikhlāʾ Āsafī wa-Āzammūr, 1481–1541*. Casablanca: Dār al-Thaqāfa, 1984.

Buzineb, Hossain. "Respuestas de Jurisconsultos Maghrebies en Torno a la Inmigración de Musulmanes Hispánicos." *Hespéris Tamuda* 16–17 (1988–89): 53–67.

Calder, Norman. *Islamic Jurisprudence in the Classical Era*. Edited by Colin Imber. Cambridge: Cambridge University Press, 2010.

Calderwood, Eric. *Colonial al-Andalus: Spain and the Making of Modern Moroccan Culture*. Cambridge: Belknap Press, 2018.

Calero Secall, M. Isabel. "Una aproximación al studio de las fatwas granadinas: Los temas de las fatwas de Ibn Sirāŷ en los Nawāzil de Ibn Ṭarkāṭ." In *Homenaje a Prof. Darío Cabanelas Rodrígeuz, O.F.M., Con Motivo de su LXX Aniversario*, 1:189–202. Granada: Universidad de Granada, 1987.

Cantineau, Jean. "Lettre du Moufti d'Oran aux Musulmans d'Andalousie," *Journal Asiatique*, 210 (1927): 1–17.

Cardaillac, Louis. *Morisques et Chrétiens: Un affrontement polemique (1492–1640)*. 2nd ed. Zaghouan, Tunisia: Centre d'Études et de Recherches Ottomanes, Morisques, de Documentation et d'Information, 1995. First published 1977 by Klincksieck, Paris.

Carmona González, Alfonso. "La Estructura del Título en los Libros Árabes Medievales." *Estudios Románicos* 4 (1989): 181–89.

Catlos, Brian. *Muslims of Medieval Latin Christendom, c. 1050–1614*. Cambridge: Cambridge University Press, 2014.

Cenival, Pierre de., ed. *Les Sources Inédites de L'Histoire du Maroc. Première Série—Dynastie Saʿdienne, Archives et Bibliothèques de Portugal*. Vol. 1, *Juillet 1486–Avril 1516*. Paris: Paul Geuthner, 1934. Published online by the Centro de História d'Aquém e d'Além-Mar, http://www.cham.fcsh.unl.pt/ext/portugalemarrocos/portugalemarrocos.html.

Cheddadi, Abdelkhalek. "Émigrer ou rester? Le dilemma des morisques entre les fatwas et les contraintes du vécu." *Cahiers de la Méditerranée* 79 (2009): 2–17.

Christelow, Allan. *Algerians without Borders: The Making of a Global Frontier Society*. Gainesville: University Press of Florida, 2012.

Clancy-Smith, Julia. *Mediterraneans: North Africa and Europe in an Age of Migration, c. 1800–1900*. Berkeley: University of California Press, 2012.

Coleman, David. *Creating Christian Granada: Society and Religious Culture in an Old-World Frontier City, 1492–1600*. Ithaca, NY: Cornell University Press, 2003.

Cook, Weston, Jr. *The Hundred Years War for Morocco: Gunpowder and the Military Revolution in the Early Modern Muslim World*. Boulder: Westview Press, 1994.

Coppolani, Xavier, and Octave Depont. *Les confréries religieuses musulmanes*. Algiers: Adolphe Jourdan, 1897.

Cornell, Vincent. *Realm of the Saint: Power and Authority in Moroccan Sufism*. Austin: University of Texas Press, 1998.

———. "Socioeconomic Dimensions of Reconquista and Jihad in Morocco: Portuguese Dukkala and the Saʿdid Sus, 1450–1557." *International Journal of Middle East Studies* 22 (1990): 379–418.

Crone, Patricia. "The First-Century Concept of Hijra." *Arabica* 41, no. 3 (1994): 352–87.

Al-Dabbāgh, ʿAbd al-Raḥmān, Abū al-Qāsim b. Nājī, and Muḥammad al-Kinānī. *Maʿālim al-īmān fī maʿrifat ahl al-Qayrawān* and supplement. Edited by ʿAbd al-Majīd al-Khayālī. 5 vols. in 3. Beirut: Dār al-Kutub al-ʿIlmiyya, 2005.

Dachraoui, Farhat. "Integration ou exclusion des minorités religieuses: La concepcion islamique traditionnelle." In *L'expulsió dels moriscos: conseqüències en el món Islàmic i el món cristià*, 195–203. Barcelona: Generalitat de Catalunya, 1994.

Danziger, Raphael. *Abd al-Qadir and the Algerians: Resistance to the French and Internal Consolidation*. New York: Holmes & Meier, 1977.

Dāwūd, Muḥammad. *Mukhtaṣar Tārīkh Tiṭwān*. Tetouan: Maʿhad Mawlāy al-Ḥasan, 1953.

Devereux, Andrew W. *The Other Side of Empire: Just War in the Mediterranean and the Rise of Early Modern Spain*. Ithaca: Cornell University Press, 2020.

———. "North Africa in Early Modern Spanish Political Thought," *Journal of Spanish Cultural Studies* 12, no. 3 (2011): 275–91.

Disney, A. R. *A History of Portugal and the Portuguese Empire, Volume Two: The Portuguese Empire*. Cambridge: Cambridge University Press, 2009.

Doubleday, Simon R. and David Coleman, eds. *In the Light of Medieval Spain: Islam, the West, and the Relevance of the Past*. New York: Palgrave, 2008.

Echevarría Arsuaga, Ana. "De Cadí a Alcalde Mayor: La Élite Judicial Mudéjar en el Siglo XV (II)." *Al-Qanṭara* 24, no. 2 (2003): 273–90.

———. "De Cadí a Alcalde Mayor: La Élite Judicial Mudéjar en el Siglo XV (I)." *Al-Qanṭara* 24, no. 1 (2003): 139–68.

El Cid. Directed by Anthony Mann. 1961. [New York]: Weinstein Company, 2008. DVD.

Encyclopaedia of Islam, Second Edition (*EI*^{2}). Edited by P. Bearman, Th. Bianquis, C.E. Bosworth, E. van Donzel, and W.P. Heinrichs. 12 vols. Leiden: Brill, 1954–2005. Online Edition: https://referenceworks.brillonline.com/browse/encyclopaedia-of-islam-2.

Encyclopaedia of Islam, THREE (*EI*[3]). Edited by Kate Fleet, Gudrun Krämer, Denis Matringe, John Nawas, and Everett Rowson. Leiden: Brill, 2007-. Online Edition: https://referenceworks.brillonline.com/browse/encyclopaedia-of-islam-3.

Epalza, Míkel de. "La voz official de los musulmanes hispanos mudéjares y moriscos, a sus autoridades cristianas: cuatro textos, en árabe, en castellano y en catalán-valenciano." *Sharq al-Andalus* 12 (1995): 279–97.

———. "L'Identité onomastique et linguistique des morisques." In *Actes du II symposium international du C.I.E.M. sur religion, identité et sources documentaries sur les morisques andalous*, edited by Abdeljelil Temimi, 269–79. Tunis: Institut Supérieur de Documentation, 1984.

Fadel, Mohammad. "Reply." *Al-ʿUsur al-Wusta* 9, no. 1 (1997): 21.

———. "Rules, Judicial Discretion, and the Rule of Law in Naṣrid Granada: An Analysis of *al-Ḥadīqa al-mustaqilla al-naḍra fī al-fatāwā al-ṣādira ʿan ʿulamāʾ al-ḥaḍra*." In *Islamic Law: Theory and Practice*, edited by R. Gleave and E. Kermeli, 49–86. London: I.B. Tauris, 1997.

———. "The Social Logic of *Taqlīd* and the Rise of the *Mukhtaṣar*." *Islamic Law and Society* 3, no. 2 (1996): 193–233.

Fancy, Hussein. *The Mercenary Mediterranean: Sovereignty, Religion, and Violence in the Medieval Crown of Aragon*. Chicago: University of Chicago Press, 2016.

Fernández Félix, Ana. *Cuestiones Legales del Islam Temprano: La ʿUtbiyya y el Proceso de Formación de la Sociedad Islámica Andalusí*. Madrid: Consejo Superior de Investigaciones Científicas, 2003.

Fierro, Maribel. *The Almohad Revolution: Politics and Religion in the Islamic West during the Twelfth-Thirteenth Centuries*. Farnham: Ashgate, 2013.

———. "Alfonso X 'The Wise': The Last Almohad Caliph?" *Medieval Encounters* 15, no. 2 (2009): 175–98.

———. "La Emigración en el Islam: Conceptos Antiguos, Nuevos Problemas." *Awrāq* 12 (1991): 11–41.

Fletcher, Richard. *The Quest for El Cid*. Oxford: Oxford University Press, 1989.

———. "Reconquest and Crusade in Spain c. 1050–1150." *Transactions of the Royal Historical Society, Fifth Series* 37 (1987): 31–47.

Fundación Carlos de Amberes. *The Invention of Glory: Afonso V and the Pastrana Tapestries*. Madrid: Ediciones El Viso, [2011].

Galán Sánchez, Ángel and Rafael Peinado Santaella. *La repoblación de la costa malagueña: Los repartimientos de Marbella y Estepona*. Málaga: Centrode Ediciones de la Diputación de Málaga, 2007.

Ganān, Jamāl. *Nuṣūṣ siyāsiyya Jazāʾiriyya fī al-qarn al-tāsiʿ ʿashar, 1830–1914*. Algiers: Dīwān al-Maṭbūʿāt al-Jāmiʿiyya, 2009.

García-Arenal, Mercedes. *La Diaspora des Andalousiens*. L'Encylopédie de la Méditerranée 13. Aix-en-Provence, France: Édisud, 2003.

———. "The Revolution of Fās in 869/1465 and the Death of Sultan ʿAbd al-Ḥaqq al-Marīnī," *Bulletin of the School of Oriental and African Studies* 41, no. 1 (1978): 43–66.

García-Arenal, Mercedes, and Fernando Rodríguez Mediano. *The Orient in Spain: Converted Muslims, the Forged Lead Books of Granada, and the Rise of Orientalism*. Translated by Consuelo López-Morillas. Leiden: Brill, 2013.

———. "Los Libros de los Moriscos Eruditos Orientales." *Al-Qanṭara* 31, no. 2 (2010): 611–46.

García Fitz, Francisco. *La Reconquista*. Granada: University of Granada, 2010.

García Sanjuán, Alejandro. "Rejecting al-Andalus, Exalting the Reconquista: Historical Memory in Contemporary Spain." *Journal of Medieval Iberian Studies* 10, no. 1 (2018): 127–45.

———. *Till God Inherits the Earth: Islamic Pious Endowments in al-Andalus, 9–15th Centuries*. Leiden: Brill, 2007.

———. "Del *Dār al-Islām* al *Dār al-Ḥarb*: La Cuestión Mudéjar y La Legalidad Islámica." In *Actas del I Congreso de Historia de Carmona: Edad Media*, 177–87. Carmona: Diputacion de Sevilla, 1997.

Gardner, Robert, Carrie Gardner, and Jeremy Morrison. *Cities of Light: The Rise and Fall of Islamic Spain*. [Potomac Falls, VA]: Unity Productions Foundation and Gardner Films, 2007. DVD, 116 min.

Gerber, Haim. *Islamic Law and Culture, 1600–1840*. Leiden: Brill, 1999.

———. *State, Society, and Law in Islam: Ottoman Law in Comparative Perspective*. Albany: State University of New York Press, 1994.

Glick, Thomas. "Convivencia: An Introductory Note." In *Convivencia: Jews, Muslims, and Christians in Medieval Spain*, edited by Vivian Mann, Thomas Glick, and Jerrilynn Dodds, 1–9. New York: George Braziller, 1992.

———. *Islamic and Christian Spain in the Early Middle Ages: Comparative Perspectives on Social and Cultural Formation*. Leiden: Brill, 1979.

Al-Ḥafnāwī, Muḥammad. *Taʿrīf al-Khalaf bi-rijāl al-salaf*. Edited by Muḥammad Abū al-Ajfān and ʿUthmān Baṭṭīkh. Beirut: Muʾassasat al-Risāla, 1982.

Ḥajjī, Muḥammad. *Al-Ḥaraka al-fikriyya biʾl-Maghrib fī ʿahd al-Saʿdiyyīn*. 2 vols. Rabat: Dār al-Maghrib lil-Taʾlīf waʾl-Tarjama waʾl-Nashr, 1977–78.

Ḥajjī, Muḥammad, ed. *Mawsūʿat aʿlām al-Maghrib*. 10 vols. Beirut: Dār al-Gharb al-Islāmī, 1996.

———, ed. *Alf sana min al-wafayāt*. Rabat: Maṭbūʿāt Dār al-Maghrib lil-Taʾlīf waʾl-Tarjama waʾl-Nashr, 1976.

Hallaq, Wael. *Authority, Continuity, and Change in Islamic Law*. Cambridge: Cambridge University Press, 2001.

———. "Ifta' and Ijtihad in Sunni Legal Theory: A Developmental Account." In *Islamic Legal Interpretation: Muftis and Their Fatwas*, edited by Masud, et al., 33–43. Cambridge: Harvard University Press, 1996.

———. "From *Fatwās* to *Furūʿ*: Growth and Change in Islamic Substantive Law." *Islamic Law and Society* 1, no. 1 (1994): 29–65.

———. "Murder in Cordoba: *Ijtihâd, Iftâ'*, and the Evolution of Substantive Law in Medieval Islam." *Acta Orientalia* 55 (1994): 55–83.

———. "Was the Gate of Ijtihad Closed?" *International Journal of Middle East Studies* 16 (1984): 3–41.

Hanson, John and David Robinson. *After the Jihad: The Reign of Aḥmad al-Kabīr in the Western Sudan*. African Historical Sources 2. East Lansing: Michigan State University Press, 1991.

Harvey, Leonard Patrick. *Muslims in Spain, 1500 to 1614*. Chicago: University of Chicago Press, 2005.

———. "Chronicling the Fall of Nasrid Granada: *Kitāb nubdhat al-ʿaṣr fī akbār mulūk Banī Naṣr.*" In *Historical Literature in Medieval Iberia*, edited by Alan Deyermond, 105–14. London: Department of Hispanic Studies, Queen Mary and Westfield College, 1996.

———. "The Political, Social, and Cultural History of the Moriscos." In *The Legacy of Muslim Spain*, edited by Salma Khadra Jayyusi, 2nd ed., 2 vols., 1:201–234. Handbook of Oriental Studies: The Near and Middle East, 12. Leiden: Brill, 1994.

———. *Islamic Spain, 1250 to 1500.* Chicago: University of Chicago Press, 1990.

———. "Crypto-Islam in Sixteenth-Century Spain." In *Actas del Primer Congreso de Estudios Árabes e Islámicos, Córdoba, 1962*, edited by F.M. Pareja, 163–78. Madrid: Comité Permanente del Congreso de Estudios Árabes e Islámicos, 1964.

Hendrickson, Jocelyn. "Prohibiting the Pilgrimage: Politics and Fiction in Mālikī *Fatwās.*" *Islamic Law and Society* 23, no. 3 (2016): 161–238.

———. "Is al-Andalus Different? Continuity as Contested, Constructed, and Performed across Three Mālikī Fatwās." *Islamic Law and Society* 20, no. 4 (2013): 371–424.

———. "Muslim Legal Responses to Portuguese Occupation in Late Fifteenth-Century North Africa." *Journal of Spanish Cultural Studies* 12, no. 3 (2011): 309–25.

———. "The Islamic Obligation to Emigrate: Al-Wansharīsī's *Asnā al-matājir* Reconsidered." PhD dissertation, Emory University, 2009.

———. "A Guide to Arabic Manuscript Libraries in Morocco, with Notes on Tunisia, Algeria, Egypt, and Spain." *MELA Notes: Journal of Middle Eastern Librarianship* 81 (2008): 15–88.

Hendrickson, Jocelyn, and Sabahat Adil. "A Guide to Arabic Manuscript Libraries in Morocco: Further Developments." *MELA Notes: Journal of Middle Eastern Librarianship* 86 (2013): 1–19.

Hershenzon, Daniel. *The Captive Sea: Slavery, Communication, and Commerce in Early Modern Spain and the Mediterranean.* Philadelphia: University of Pennsylvania Press, 2018.

———. "Traveling Libraries: The Arabic Manuscripts of Muley Zidan and the Escorial Library." *Journal of Early Modern History* 18 (2014): 535–58.

Hess, Andrew C. *The Forgotten Frontier: A History of the Sixteenth-Century Ibero-African Frontier.* Chicago: University of Chicago Press, 1978.

Huntington, Samuel. *The Clash of Civilizations and the Remaking of World Order.* New York: Simon & Schuster, 1996.

———. "The Clash of Civilizations?" *Foreign Affairs* 72, no. 3 (1993): 22–49.

Hunwick, John O. *Sharīʿa in Songhay: The Replies of al-Maghīlī to the Questions of Askia al-Ḥājj Muḥammad.* London: Oxford University Press, 1985.

Husain, Adnan A. "Introduction: Approaching Islam and the Religious Cultures of the Medieval and Early Modern Mediterranean." In *A Faithful Sea: Religious Cultures of the Mediterranean, 1200–1700*, edited by Adnan Husain and K.E. Fleming, 1–26. Oxford: Oneworld, 2007.

Ibn ʿAbd al-Karīm, Muḥammad. *Ḥukm al-hijra min khilāl thalāth rasāʾil Jazāʾiriyya.* Algiers: al-Sharika al-Waṭaniyya lil-Nashr waʾl-Tawzīʿ, 1981.

Ibn al-ʿArabī, *Aḥkām al-Qurʾān*. Edited by Riḍā Faraj al-Hamāmī. Beirut: al-Maktaba al-ʿAṣriyya, 2003.

———. *ʿĀriḍat al-aḥwadhī bi-sharḥ Ṣaḥīḥ al-Tirmidhī*. Edited by Jamāl Marʿashlī. 13 vols. in 8. Beirut: Dar al-Kutub al-ʿIlmiyya, 1997.

Ibn ʿAskar, Muḥammad b. ʿAlī (d. 986/1578). *Dawḥat al-nāshir li-maḥāsin man kāna bi'l-Maghrib min mashāyikh al-qarn al-ʿāshir*. Edited by Muḥammad Ḥajjī. 3rd ed. Casablanca: Manshūrāt Markaz al-Tūrāth al-Thaqāfī al-Maghribī, 2003.

Ibn Ḥabīb Allāh, Muḥammad Yaḥyā. *Al-Ḥaraka al-Iṣlāḥiyya fī bilād Shanqīṭ (Mūrītānīyā) bayn al-istijāba lil-istiʿmār al-Faransī wa-difāʿih min khilāl baʿḍ al-fatāwā wa'l-wathāʾiq*. Salé: Manshūrāt Muʾassasat al-Shaykh Murabbīhi Rabbuh li-Iḥyāʾ al-Turāth wa'l-Tabādul al-Thaqāfī, 2006.

Ibn Farḥūn, Ibrāhīm b. ʿAlī (d. 799/1397). *Al-Dībāj al-mudhahhab fī maʿrifat aʿyān ʿulamāʾ al-madhhab*. Edited by Maʾmūn b. Muḥyī al-Dīn al-Jannān. Beirut: Dār al-Kutub al-ʿIlmiyya, 1996.

Ibn Hajar al-ʿAsqalānī (d. 852/1449). *Al-Durar al-kāmina fī aʿyān al-miʾa al-thāmina*. Edited by ʿAbd al-Wārith Muḥammad ʿAlī. 4 vols. in 2. Beirut: Dār al-Kutub al-ʿIlmiyya, 1997.

Ibn al-Ḥājib, Jamāl al-Dīn (d. 646/1248–9). *Jāmiʿ al-ummahāt*. Edited by Abū ʿAbd al-Raḥmān al-Akhḍar al-Akhḍarī. 2nd ed. Damascus: Al-Yamāma lil-Ṭibāʿa wa'l-Nashr wa'l-Tawzīʿ, 2004.

Ibn al-Ḥājj al-Sulamī, Muḥammad al-Ṭālib (d. 1857). *Riyāḍ al-ward fīmā intamā ilayh hādhā al-jawhar al-fard*. Edited by Jaʿfar b. al-Ḥājj al-Sulamī. Vol. 1. Damascus: Maṭbaʿat al-Kātib al-ʿArabī, 1993.

Ibn Isḥāq, Muḥammad. *The Life of Muḥammad*. Translated by A. Guillaume. Oxford: Oxford University Press, 2003.

Ibn al-Khaṭīb, Lisān al-Dīn (d. 776/1374). *Al-Iḥāṭa fī akhbār Gharnāṭa*. Edited by Yūsuf ʿAlī Ṭawīl. 4 vols. Beirut: Dār al-Kutub al-ʿIlmiyya, 2003.

Ibn Nājī, Qāsim. *Sharḥ Ibn Nājī al-Tanūkhī ʿalā matn al-Risāla*. Edited by Aḥmad Farīd al-Mazīdī. 2 vols. Beirut: Dār al-Kutub al-ʿIlmiyya, 2007.

Ibn al-Qāḍī al-Miknāsī, Aḥmad (d. 1025/1616). *Durrat al-ḥijāl fī ghurrat asmāʾ al-rijāl*. Edited by Muṣṭafā ʿAbd al-Qādir ʿAṭāʾ. Beirut: Dār al-Kutub al-ʿIlmiyya, 2002.

———. *Jadhwat al-iqtibās fī dhikr man ḥalla min al-aʿlām madīnat Fās*. 2 vols. Rabat: Dār al-Manṣūr lil-Ṭibāʿa wa'l-Wirāqa, 1973–74.

Ibn Rushd al-Jadd, Abū al-Walīd Muḥammad b. Aḥmad (d. 520/1126). *Al-Bayān wa'l-taḥṣīl wa'l-sharḥ wa'l-tawjīh wa'l-taʿlīl fī masāʾil al-Mustakhraja*. Edited by Muḥammad Ḥajjī, et al. 2nd ed. 20 vols. in 19. Beirut: Dār al-Gharb al-Islāmī, 1988.

———. *Al-Muqaddimāt al-mumahhidāt li-bayān mā iqtaḍathu rusūm al-Mudawwana min al-aḥkām al-sharʿiyyāt wa'l-taḥṣīlāt al-muḥkamāt li-ummahāt masāʾilihā al-mushkilāt*. Edited by Saʿīd Aḥmad Aʿrāb. 3 vols. Beirut: Dār al-Gharb al-Islāmī, 1988.

———. *Fatāwā Ibn Rushd*. Edited by al-Mukhtār b. al-Ṭāhir al-Talīlī. 3 vols. Beirut: Dār al-Gharb al-Islāmī, 1987.

Ibn al-Shaykh Māmīnā, al-Ṭālib Akhyār [Al-Ṭālib Akhyār b. Muḥammad al-Amīn]. *Al-Shaykh Māʾ al-ʿAynayn: ʿUlamāʾ wa-ʿumarāʾ fī muwājahat al-istiʿmār al-Ūrubbī*. 2nd ed. 2 vols. Rabat: Manshūrāt Muʾassasat al-Shaykh Murabbīhi Rabbuh li-Iḥyāʾ al-Turāth wa'l-Tanmiya, 2011.

Ibn Tuhāmī, Muṣṭafā. *Sīrat al-Amīr ʿAbd al-Qādir*. Edited by Yaḥyā BuʿAzīz. Beirut: Dār al-Gharb al-Islāmī, 1995.

Idris, Hady Roger. *La Berbérie Orientale sous les Zīrīds: Xe-XIIe siècles*. 2 vols. Paris: Adrien-Maisonneuve, 1962.

ʿIllaysh, Abū ʿAbd Allāh Muḥammad b. Aḥmad (d. 1299/1882). *Fatḥ al-ʿalī al-mālik fī al-fatwā ʿalā madhhab al-Imām Mālik*. 2 vols. Cairo: Muṣṭafā al-Bābī al-Ḥalabī, 1958.

ʿInān. *Nihāyat al-Andalus wa-tārīkh al-ʿArab al-mutanaṣṣirīn*. 3rd ed. Cairo: Maṭbaʿat Lajnat al-Taʾlīf waʾl-Tarjama waʾl-Nashr, 1966.

ʿIyāḍ b. Mūsā (d. 544/1149). *Sharḥ Ṣaḥīḥ Muslim lil-Qāḍī ʿIyāḍ, al-musammā Ikmāl al-Muʿlim bi-fawāʾid Muslim*. Edited by Yaḥyā Ismāʿīl. Mansoura: Dār al-Wafāʾ lil-Ṭibāʿa waʾl-Nashr waʾl-Tawzīʿ, 1998.

Jackson, Sherman. *Islamic Law and the State: The Constitutional Jurisprudence of Shihāb al-Dīn al-Qarāfī*. Leiden: Brill, 1996.

Al-Jazāʾirī, Muḥammad b. al-Amīr ʿAbd al-Qādir. *Tuḥfat al-zāʾir fī tārīkh al-Jazāʾir waʾl-Amīr ʿAbd al-Qādir*. Edited by Mamduḥ Ḥaqqī. 2nd ed. 2 vols. Beirut: Dār al-Yaqaẓa al-ʿArabiyya, 1964.

Al-Jīlālī, ʿAbd al-Raḥmān b. Muḥammad. *Tārīkh al-Jazāʾir al-ʿāmm*. 7th ed. 4 vols. Algiers: Dīwān al-Maṭbūʿāt al-Jāmiʿiyya, 1994.

Johansen, Baber. *Contingency in a Sacred Law: Legal and Ethical Norms in the Muslim* Fiqh. Leiden: Brill, 1999.

Kaḥḥāla, ʿUmar Riḍā. *Muʿjam al-muʾallifīn*. 4 vols. Beirut: Muʾassasat al-Risāla, 1993.

Kamali, Mohammad Hashim. *Principles of Islamic Jurisprudence*. 3rd ed. Cambridge: Islamic Texts Society, 2003.

Al-Kattānī, Muḥammad b. Jaʿfar (d. ca. 1346/1927). *Salwat al-anfās wa-muḥādathat al-akyās bi-man uqbira min al-ʿulamāʾ waʾl-ṣulaḥāʾ bi-Fās*. Edited by ʿAbd Allāh al-Kāmil al-Kattānī, et al. 3 vols. Casablanca: Dār al-Thaqāfa, 2004.

Koningsveld, Pieter Sjoerd van. "Andalusian-Arabic Manuscripts from Christian Spain: A Comparative Intercultural Approach." *Israel Oriental Studies* 12 (1992): 75–110.

Koningsveld, Pieter Sjoerd van, and Gerard A. Wiegers. "Marcos Dobelio's Polemics against the Authenticity of the Granadan Lead Books in Light of the Original Arabic Sources." In *Polemical Encounters: Christians, Jews, and Muslims in Iberia and Beyond*, edited by Mercedes García-Arenal and Gerard Wiegers, 203–68. University Park, PA: Pennsylvania State University Press, 2019.

———. "An Appeal of the Moriscos to the Mamluk Sultan and Its Counterpart to the Ottoman Court: Textual Analysis, Context, and Wider Historical Background." *Al-Qanṭara* 20, no. 1 (1999): 161–89.

———. "The Islamic Statute of the Mudejars in the Light of a New Source." *Al-Qanṭara* 17, no. 1 (1996): 19–58.

———. Introduction, translation, and Arabic text to "Islam in Spain during the Early Sixteenth Century: The Views of the Four Chief Judges in Cairo." In *Poetry, Politics and Polemics: Cultural Transfer between the Iberian Peninsula and North Africa*, edited by Otto Zwartjes, et al., 133–52. Orientations 4. Amsterdam: Rodopi, 1996.

Kugle, Scott. *Rebel Between Spirit and Law: Ahmad Zarruq, Sainthood, and Authority in Islam*. Bloomington: Indiana University Press, 2006.

Kulp-Hill, Kathleen, trans. "Tales of Marian Miracles." In *Medieval Iberia: Readings from Christian, Muslim, and Jewish Sources*, edited by Olivia Remie Constable, 358–68. 2nd ed. Philadelphia: University of Pennsylvania Press, 2012.

Kurzman, Charles. "Introduction: The Modernist Islamic Movement." In *Modernist Islam, 1840–1940: A Sourcebook*, edited by Charles Kurzman, 3–27. Oxford: Oxford University Press, 2002.

Ladero Quesada, Miguel Angel. "Mudéjares y Repobladores en el Reino de Granada (1485–1501)." *Cuadernos de Historia Moderna* 13 (1992): 47–71.

Lagardère, Vincent. *Histoire et Société en Occident Musulman au Moyen Âge: Analyse du Miʿyār d'al-Wanšarīsī*. Madrid: Consejo Superior de Investigaciones Científicas, 1995.

Al-Lamaṭī, Aḥmad b. al-Mubārak. *Pure Gold from the Words of Sayyidī ʿAbd al-ʿAzīz al-Dabbāgh*. Translated by John O'Kane and Bernd Radtke. Leiden: Brill, 2007.

Lecocq, Baz. "Distant Shores: A Historiographic View on Trans-Saharan Space." *Journal of African History* 56 (2015): 23–36.

León-Portilla, Miguel, ed. and introd. *The Broken Spears: The Aztec Account of the Conquest of Mexico*. Translated by Lysander Kemp. Expanded ed. Boston: Beacon Press, 2006.

León-Portilla, Miguel. "A Reply to John F. Schwaller." *Americas* 66, no. 2 (2009): 252–54.

Lewis, Bernard. "The Roots of Muslim Rage." *Atlantic Monthly* 266, no. 3 (Sept 1990): 47–60.

Lévi-Provençal, Évariste. *Les Historiens des Chorfa: Essai sur la Littérature Historique et Biographique au Maroc du XVIe au XXe Siècle*. Paris: Maisonneuve et Larose, 2001.

Liang, Yuen-Gen, Abigail Krasner Balbale, Andrew Devereux, and Camilo Gómez-Rivas. "Unity and Disunity across the Strait of Gibraltar." *Medieval Encounters* 19, nos. 1–2 (2013): 1–40.

Longás, Pedro. *Vida religiosa de los moriscos*. Madrid: E. Maestre, 1915.

López-Baralt, Luce. *Islam in Spanish Literature from the Middle Ages to the Present*. Translated by Andrew Hurley. Leiden: Brill, 1992.

López de Coca Castañer, José Enrique. "Mamelucos, otomanos y caída del reino de Granada." *En la España Medieval* 25 (2008): 229–58.

López y López, Angel Custodio, and Fernando Nicolás Velázquez Basanta. "Ajbār al-ʿAṣr." In *Biblioteca de al-Andalus*, edited by Jorge Lirola Delgado and José Miguel Puerta Vílchez, 1:55–57. 7 vols and 2 appendix vols. Almería: Fundación Ibn Tufayl de Estudios Árabes, 2004–13.

———. "Nubdat al-ʾAṣr." In *Biblioteca de al-Andalus*, edited by Jorge Lirola Delgado and José Miguel Puerta Vílchez, 6:621–22. 7 vols and 2 appendix vols. Almería: Fundación Ibn Tufayl de Estudios Árabes, 2004–13.

Lydon, Ghislaine. "Saharan Oceans and Bridges, Barriers and Divides in Africa's Historiographical Landscape." *Journal of African History* 56 (2015): 3–22.

Māʾ al-ʿAynayn, Murabbīhi Rabbuh. *Al-Shaykh Māʾ al-ʿAynayn wa-maʿrakat al-Dākhila, 1885; maʿa taḥqīq "Hidāyat man ḥāra fī amr al-Naṣārā."* Rabat: Manshūrāt Muʾassasat al-Shaykh Murabbīhi Rabbuh li-Iḥyāʾ al-Turāth wa'l-Tabādul al-Thaqāfī, 1999.

Maíllo Salgado, Felipe. "Del Islam residual mudejar." In *España, al-Andalus, Sefarad: Síntesis y nuevas perspectivas*, 129–40. Salamanca: Universidad de Salamanca, 1988.

———. "Consideraciones acerca de una fatwà de al-Wanšarīšī." *Studia Historica* 3, no. 2 (1985): 181–191.

Makhlūf, Muḥammad b. Muḥammad (d. ca. 1340/1921). *Shajarat al-nūr al-zakiyya fī ṭabaqāt al-Mālikiyya*. Edited by ʿAbd al-Majīd Khayālī. 2 vols. Beirut: Dār al-Kutub al-ʿIlmiyya, 2003.

Mālik b. Anas (d. 179/795). *Kitāb al-Muwaṭṭaʾ: Riwāyat Yaḥyā b. Yaḥyā al-Laythī*. 2nd ed. 4 vols. Rabat: Manshūrāt al-Majlis al-ʿIlmī al-Aʿlā, 2019.

Al-Maqqarī al-Tilimsānī, Shihāb al-Dīn Aḥmad b. Muḥammad (d. 1041/1632). *Nafḥ al-ṭīb min ghuṣn al-Andalus al-raṭīb*. Edited by Maryam Qāsim Ṭawīl and Yūsuf ʿAlī Ṭawīl. 11 vols. Beirut: Dār al-Kutub al-ʿIlmiyya, 1995.

———. *Azhār al-riyāḍ fī akhbār ʿIyāḍ*. Edited by Muṣṭafā al-Saqqā, Ibrāhīm al-Ibyārī, and ʿAbd al-Ḥafīẓ Shalabī. 5 vols. 1939. Reprint, [Rabat]: Ṣundūq Iḥyāʾ al-Turāth al-Islāmī, 1978.

Al-Mālikī, ʿAbd Allāh b. Muḥammad (d. ca. 360/970). *Riyāḍ al-nufūs fī ṭabaqāt ʿulamāʾ al-Qayrawān wa-Ifrīqiyā wa-zuhhādihim wa-nussākihim wa-siyar min akhbārihim wa-faḍāʾilihim wa-awṣāfihim*. Edited by Bashīr al-Bakkūsh and Muḥammad al-ʿArūsī al-Maṭwī, 2nd ed. 2 vols. Beirut: Dār al-Gharb al-Islāmī, 1994.

Al-Manūnī, Muḥammad. *Maẓāhir yaqẓat al-Maghrib al-ḥadīth*. 2nd ed. 2 vols. Beirut: Dār al-Gharb al-Islāmī, 1985.

Manzano, Miguel. "La Península Ibérica y el Norte de África en los Inicios del bajo Medievo: Relaciones políticas y apuntes historiográficos." In *711–1616: De Árabes a Moriscos: Una Parte de la Historia de España*, ed. M. Fierro, J. Martos, J. P. Monferrer, and M. J. Viguera, 67–86. Córdoba: Al-Babtain Foundation, 2012.

Marín, Manuela. "Des migrations forcées: Les ʿUlema d'Al-Andalus face à la conquête chrétienne." In *L'Occident musulman et l'Occident chrétien au Moyen Âge*, edited by Mohammed Hammam, 43–59. Rabat: Faculté des Lettres, 1995.

———. "*Shūra* et *ahl al-Shūra* dans al-Andalus." *Studia Islamica* 62 (1985): 25–51.

Martin, B. G. *Muslim Brotherhoods in Nineteenth-Century Africa*. Cambridge: Cambridge University Press, 1976.

Al-Mashannī, Muṣṭafā Ibrāhīm. *Ibn al-ʿArabī al-Mālikī al-Ishbīlī (468–543 AH) wa-tafsīruh Aḥkām al-Qurʾān*. Jordan: Dār ʿAmmār, 1990.

Masud, Muhammad Khalid. "The Obligation to Migrate: The Doctrine of *Hijra* in Islamic Law." In *Muslim Travellers: Pilgrimage, Migration, and the Religious Imagination*, edited by Dale F. Eickelman and James Piscatori, 29–49. Berkeley: University of California Press, 1990.

———. "*Adab al-Muftī*: The Muslim Understanding of [the] Values, Characteristics, and Role of a *Muftī*." In *Moral Conduct and Authority: The Place of* Adab *in South Asian Islam*, edited by Barbara Daly Metcalf, 124–45. Berkeley: University of California Press, 1984

Masud, Muhammad Khalid, Brinkley Messick, and David S. Powers. "Muftis, Fatwas, and Islamic Legal Interpretation." In *Islamic Legal Interpretation: Muftis and Their Fatwas*, edited by Masud, et al., 3–32. Cambridge: Harvard University Press, 1996.

Masud, Muhammad Khalid, Rudolph Peters, and David S. Powers. "Qāḍīs and their Courts: An Historical Survey." In *Dispensing Justice in Islam: Qadis and their Judgments*, edited by Masud, et al., 1–44. Leiden: Brill, 2006.

Matar, Nabil. *Europe Through Arab Eyes, 1578–1727.* New York: Columbia University Press, 2009.

Al-Māzarī, Abū ʿAbd Allāh Muḥammad b. ʿAlī b. ʿUmar (d. 536/1141). *Īḍāḥ al-Maḥṣūl min Burhān al-uṣūl.* Edited by ʿAmmār al-Ṭālibī. Beirut: Dār al-Gharb al-Islāmī, 2001.

———. *Fatāwā al-Māzarī.* Edited by al-Ṭāhir al-Maʿmūrī. Tunis: Al-Dār al-Tūnisiyya lil-Nashr, 1994.

———. *Al-Muʿlim bi-fawāʾid Muslim.* Edited by Muḥammad al-Shādhilī al-Nayfar. 2nd ed. Beirut: Dār al-Gharb al-Islāmī, 1992.

McDougall, Ann E. "Research in Saharan History." *Journal of African History* 39 (1998): 467–80.

Meier, Fritz. "Über die umstrittene Pflicht des Muslims, bei nichtmuslimischer Besetzung seines Landes auszuwandern." *Der Islam* 68 (1991): 65–86.

Menocal, María Rosa. *The Ornament of the World: How Muslims, Jews, and Christians Created a Culture of Tolerance in Medieval Spain.* Boston: Back Bay Books, 2002.

Messick, Brinkley. *The Calligraphic State: Textual Domination and History in a Muslim Society.* Berkeley: University of California Press, 1993.

Meyerson, Mark D. *The Muslims of Valencia in the Age of Fernando and Isabel: Between Coexistence and Crusade.* Berkeley: University of California Press, 1991.

Mezzine, Mohammed [Muḥammad Mazīn]. "Jihād au pays Jbala (XVIème et XVIIème siècles): Effervescence et regulation." In *Jbala: histoire et société: études sur le Maroc du Nord-ouest*, edited by Ahmed Zouggari, et al., 61–87. Paris: Editions du CNRS, 1991.

———. "Les relations entre les places occupées et les localités de la region de Fès aux XViéme et XVIiéme siècles, a partir de documents locaux inédits: Les Nawāzil." In *Relaciones de la Peninsula Ibérica con el Magreb, siglos XIII-XVI: Actas del coloquio celebrado en Madrid, 17–18 de diciembre de 1987*, edited by Mercedes García-Arenal and Maria Viguera, 539–60. Madrid: Consejo Superior de Investigaciones Científicas, 1988.

Michaux-Bellaire, Edouard, ed. and trans. "Une fetoua de Cheikh Sidia, Approuvé par Cheikh Saad Bouh ben Mohammed El Fadil ben Mamin, frère de Cheikh Ma El Ainin." *Archives Marocaines* 11 (1907): 129–53.

Miller, Kathryn A. *Guardians of Islam: Religious Authority and Muslim Communities in Late Medieval Spain.* New York: Columbia University Press, 2008.

———. "Muslim Minorities and the Obligation to Emigrate to Islamic Territory: Two *Fatwās* from Fifteenth Century Granada." *Islamic Law and Society* 7, no. 2 (2000): 256–88.

Molénat, Jean-Pierre. "Le manuscript *aljamiado* Méjannes 1367 (1223): Un itinéraire entre l'Aragon et la Provence." In *Tercera Primavera del Manuscrito Andalusi: Viajes y viajeros*, edited by Mostafa Ammadi, 99–105. Casablanca: Universidad Hassan II, Facultad de Letras y Ciencias Humanas, 2011.

———. "Le problème de la permanence des musulmans dans les territoires conquis par les chrétiens, du point de vue de la loi islamique." *Arabica* 48, no. 3 (2001): 392–400.

Molina López, Emilio. "Algunas consideraciones sobre los emigrados andalusies." In *Homenaje al prof. Darío Cabanelas Rodríguez, O.F.M., con motivo de su LXX aniversario*, 419–32. Granada: Universidad de Granada, 1987.

Monroe, James T., trans. "Lament for the Fall of Seville." In *Medieval Iberia: Readings from Christian, Muslim, and Jewish Sources*, edited by Olivia Remie Constable, 290–92. 2nd ed. Philadelphia: University of Pennsylvania Press, 2012.

———. "A Curious Morisco Appeal to the Ottoman Empire." *Al-Andalus* 31, nos. 1–2 (1966): 281–303.

Montes Romero-Camacho, Isabel. "Judíos y Mudéjares." *Medievalismo* 13/14 (2004): 241–74.

Muʾnis, Ḥusayn, ed and introd. *Asnā al-matājir fī bayān aḥkām man ghalaba ʿalā waṭanih al-Naṣārā wa-lam yuhājir, wa-mā yatarattabu ʿalayh min al-ʿuqūbāt waʾl-zawājir*. By Aḥmad b. Yaḥyā al-Wansharīsī. Al-Ẓāhir [Cairo]: Maktabat al-Thaqāfa al-Dīniyya, 1996. Originally published in *Revista del Instituto Egipcio de Estudios Islámicos en Madrid* 5 (1957): 1–63 (also numbered 129–91).

———. *Miṣr wa-risālatuhā*. Cairo: Dār al-Maʿārif, 1956.

Muslim b. al-Ḥajjāj, al-Qushayrī al-Nīsābūrī (d. 261/875). *Ṣaḥīḥ Muslim*. Edited by Muḥammad Fuʾād ʿAbd al-Bāqī. 5 vols. Beirut: Dār Iḥyāʾ al-Kutub al-ʿArabiyya, 1991.

Al-Muttaqī al-Hindī, ʿAlāʾ al-Dīn ʿAlī (d. 975/1567). *Kanz al-ʿummāl fī sunan al-aqwāl waʾl-afʿāl*. Edited by Bakrī Ḥayyānī and Ṣafwat al-Ṣaqqāʾ. 18 vols. 5th ed. Beirut: Muʾassasat al-Risāla, 1985.

Al-Naḥwī, al-Khalīl. *Bilād Shinqīṭ, al-mināra waʾl-Ribāṭ*. Tunis: Al-Munaẓẓama al-ʿArabiyya lil-Tarbiya waʾl-Thaqāfa waʾl-ʿUlūm, 1987.

Najīb, Aḥmad, ed. *Asnā al-matājir fī bayān aḥkām man ghalaba ʿalā waṭanih al-Naṣārā wa-lam yuhājir, wa-mā yatarattabu ʿalayh min al-ʿuqūbāt waʾl-zawājir*. By Aḥmad b. Yaḥyā al-Wansharīsī. N.p.: Al-Markaz al-Iʿlāmī lil-Dirāsāt waʾl-Nashr, 2006.

Al-Nasāʾī, Aḥmad b. Shuʿayb (d. 303/915). *Kitāb al-Mujtabā, al-maʿrūf bi-: Al-Sunan al-ṣughrā*. Edited by Markaz al-Buḥūth wa-Taqniyat al-Maʿlūmāt. 9 vols. Diwān al-Ḥadīth al-Nabawī 5. Cairo: Dār al-Taʾṣīl, 2012.

———. *Kitāb al-Sunan al-kubrā*. Edited by Ḥasan ʿAbd al-Munʿim Shalabī and Shuʿayb al-Arnaʾūṭ. Introduction by ʿAbd Allāh b. ʿAbd al-Muḥsin al-Turkī. 12 vols. Beirut: Muʾassasat al-Risāla, 2001.

Al-Nāṣirī al-Salāwī, Aḥmad b. Khālid (d. 1897). *Kitāb al-Istiqṣā li-akhbār duwal al-Maghrib al-Aqṣā*. Edited by Muḥammad Ḥajjī, Ibrahīm Bū Ṭālib, and Aḥmad al-Tawfīq. 9 vols. Casablanca: Manshūrāt Wizārat al-Thaqāfa waʾl-Ittiṣāl, 2001.

Newitt, Malyn, ed. *The Portuguese in West Africa, 1415–1670: A Documentary History*. Cambridge: Cambridge University Press, 2010.

Nirenberg, David. *Communities of Violence: Persecution of Minorities in the Middle Ages*. Princeton: Princeton University Press, 1996.

Novikoff, Alex. "Between Tolerance and Intolerance in Medieval Spain: An Historiographic Enigma." *Medieval Encounters* 11, nos. 1–2 (2005): 7–36.

Al-Nubāhī al-Andalusī, Ibn al-Ḥasan (d. after 792/1390). *Tārīkh quḍāt al-Andalus* or *al-Marqaba al-ʿulyā fī man yastaḥiqq al-qaḍāʾ waʾl-futyā*. Edited by Maryam Qāsim Ṭawīl. Beirut: Dār al-Kutub al-ʿIlmiyya, 1995.

Nuwayhiḍ, ʿĀdil. *Muʿjam aʿlām al-Jazāʾir min ṣadr al-Islām ḥattā muntaṣaf al-qarn al-ʿishrīn*. Beirut: Manshūrāt al-Maktab al-Tijārī lil-Ṭibāʿa waʾl-Nashr waʾl-Tawzīʿ, 1971.

O'Banion, Patrick J. "'They Will Know Our Hearts': Practicing the Art of Dissimulation on the Islamic Periphery." *Journal of Early Modern History* 20 (2016): 193–217.

O'Callaghan, Joseph. *The Last Crusade in the West: Castile and the Conquest of Granada*. Philadelphia: University of Pennsylvania Press, 2014.

Ould Abdallah, Dedoud. "Guerre sainte ou sédition blâmable? *Nasiha* de sheikh Saʿd Bu contre le *jihad* de son frère sheikh Ma al-Ainin." In *Le temps des marabouts: Itinéraires et stratégies islamiques en Afrique occidentale française v. 1880–1960*, edited by David Robinson and Jean-Louis Triaud, 119–54. Paris: Éditions Karthala, 1997.

Ould El-Bara, Yahya. "Les réponses et les *fatâwâ* des érudits Bidân face à l'occupation colonial française en Mauritanie." In *Colonisations et Héritages Actuels au Sahara et au Sahel: Problèmes conceptuels, état des lieux et nouvelles perspectives de recherche (XVIIIe-XXe siècles)*, edited by Mariella Villasante Cervello, 123–54. 2 vols. Paris: L'Harmattan, 2007.

———. *See also* Wuld al-Bara, Yahya *and* Wuld al-Barāʾ, Yaḥyā.

Perlmutter, Amos. *Egypt: The Praetorian State*. New Brunswick, NJ: Transaction Books, 1974.

Peters, Rudolph. *Islam and Colonialism: The Doctrine of Jihad in Modern History*. The Hague: Mouton Publishers, 1979.

Pickthall, M. M. (Muhammad Marmaduke), trans. *The Meaning of the Glorious Qur'an*. 1930. Revised and edited by Arafat K. Al-Ashi. Beltsville, MD: Amana Publications, 2002.

Powers, David S. "Aḥmad al-Wansharīsī (d. 914/1509)." In *Islamic Legal Thought: A Compendium of Muslim Jurists*, edited by Oussama Arabi, David S. Powers, and Susan A. Spectorsky, 375–99. Leiden: Brill, 2013.

———. *Law, Society, and Culture in the Maghrib, 1300–1500*. Cambridge: Cambridge University Press, 2002.

———. "*Fatwās* as Sources for Legal and Social History: A Dispute over Endowment Revenues from Fourteenth-Century Fez." *Al-Qanṭara* 11, no. 2 (1990): 295–341.

Al-Qādirī, Muḥammad b. al-Ṭayyib (d. 1187/1773). *Nashr al-Mathānī li-ahl al-qarn al-ḥādī ʿashar waʾl-thānī*. Edited by Muḥammad Ḥajjī and Aḥmad al-Tawfīq. 4 vols. Rabat: Dār al-Maghrib lil-Taʾlīf waʾl-Tarjama waʾl-Nashr, 1977–82.

Al-Qarāfī, Badr al-Dīn (d. 946/1533). *Tawshīḥ al-Dībāj wa-ḥilyat al-ibtihāj*. Edited by Aḥmad al-Shatīwī. Beirut: Dār al-Gharb al-Islāmī, 1983.

Al-Qarāfī, Shihāb al-Dīn Aḥmad b. Idrīs (d. 684/1285). *Al-Iḥkām fī tamyīz al-fatāwā ʿan al-aḥkām, wa-taṣarrufāt al-qāḍī waʾl-imām*. Edited by Aḥmad Farīd al-Mazīdī. Beirut: Dār al-Kutub al-ʿIlmiyya, 2004.

Al-Qayrawānī, Ibn Abī Zayd (d. 386/996). *Al-Nawādir waʾl-ziyādāt ʿalā mā fī al-Mudawwana min ghayrihā min al-ummahāt*. Edited by ʿAbd al Fattāḥ Muḥammad al-Ḥulw, et al. Beirut: Dār al-Gharb al-Islāmī, 1999.

Al-Qurṭubī, Muḥammad b. Aḥmad al-Anṣārī (d. 671/1273). *Al-Jāmiʿ li-aḥkām al-Qurʾān*. Edited by Muḥammad Ibrahīm al-Ḥafnāwī and Maḥmūd Ḥāmid ʿUthmān. 10 vols. Cairo: Dār al-Ḥadīth, 2002.

Racine, Matthew. *A Most Opulent Iliad: Expansion, Confrontation & Cooperation on the Southern Moroccan Frontier, 1505–1542*. San Diego: Lake George Press, 2012.

———. "Service and Honor in Sixteenth-Century Portuguese North Africa: Yahya-u-Taʿfuft and Portuguese Noble Culture." *Sixteenth Century Journal* 32, no. 1 (2001): 67–90.

Razūq, Muḥammad. *Al-Andalusiyyūn wa-hijrātuhum ilā al-Maghrib khilāl al-qarnayn 16–17*. Rabat: Ifrīqiyā al-Sharq, 1998.

Reese, Scott S. "Islam in Africa/Africans and Islam." *Journal of African History* 55 (2014): 17–26.

Robinson, David. "Jihad, *Hijra*, and Hajj in West Africa." In *Just Wars, Holy Wars, and Jihads: Christian, Jewish, and Muslim Encounters and Exchanges*, edited by Sohail H. Hashmi, 246–62. Oxford: Oxford University Press, 2012.

———. *Paths of Accommodation: Muslim Societies and French Colonial Authorities in Senegal and Mauritania, 1880–1920*. Athens: Ohio University Press, 2000.

———. "The Umarian Emigration of the Late Nineteenth Century." *International Journal of African Historical Studies* 20, no. 2 (1987): 245–70.

———. *The Holy War of Umar Tal: The Western Sudan in the Mid-Nineteenth Century*. Oxford: Clarendon Press, 1985.

Roches, Léon. *Dix ans à travers l'Islam: 1834–1844*. New ed. Paris: Librairie Académique Didier, n.d.

Rosa-Rodríguez, María del Mar. "Simulation and Dissimulation: Religious Hybridity in a Morisco Fatwa." *Medieval Encounters* 16 (2010): 143–80.

Rosenberger, Bernard. "Yaḥyā u Tāʿfuft (1506–1518): des amibitions déçues," *Hespéris-Tamuda* 31 (1993): 21–59.

Rosenthal, Franz. "The Stranger in Medieval Islam." *Arabica* 44 (1997): 35–75.

Rouighi, Ramzi. *The Making of a Mediterranean Emirate: Ifrīqiyā and Its Andalusis, 1200–1400*. Philadelphia: University of Pennsylvania Press, 2011.

Rubiera Mata, María Jesús. "Los moriscos como criptomusulmanes y la taqiyya." In *Mudéjares y moriscos: cambios sociales y culturales: Actas del IX Simposio Internacional de Mudejarismo*, 537–47. Teruel, Spain: Centro de Estudios Mudéjares, 2004.

Sabbagh, Leila. "La Religion des Moriscos entre Deux Fatwas." In *Les Morisques et leur Temps: Table Ronde Internationale, 4–7 Juillet 1981, Montpellier*, 45–56. Paris: Éditions due Centre Nationale de la Recherche Scientifique, 1983.

Saʿd Allāh, Abū al-Qāsim. *Abḥāth wa-ārāʾ fī tārīkh al-Jazāʾir*. 4th ed. 5 vols. Beirut: Dār al-Gharb al-Islāmī, 2005.

———. *Tārīkh al-Jazāʾir al-thaqāfī min al-qarn al-ʿashir ilā al-rābiʿ ʿāshar al-Hijrī (16–20 m.)*. 2nd ed. 2 vols. Algiers: Al-Muʾassasat al-Waṭaniyya lil-Kutub, 1985.

Schacht, Joseph. *An Introduction to Islamic Law*. Oxford: Clarendon Press, 1964.

Schwaller, John F. "Broken Spears or Broken Bones: Evolution of the Most Famous Line in Nahuatl." *Americas* 66, no. 2 (2009): 241–52.

Schwartz, Stuart B.. ed. and introd. *Victors and Vanquished: Spanish and Nahua Views of the Conquest of Mexico*. Boston: Bedford/St. Martin's, 2000.

Secord, Davis. "Muslims in Norman Sicily: The Evidence of Imām al-Māzarī's Fatwās." *Mediterranean Studies*, 16, no. 1 (2007): 46–66.

Serrano Ruano, Delfina. "Ibn Rushd al-Jadd (d. 520/1126)." In *Islamic Legal Thought*, edited by Oussama Arabi, et. al., 295–322. Leiden: Brill, 2013.

Shatzmiller, Maya. "On Fatwas and Social History." *Al-ʿUsur al-Wusta* 9, no. 1 (1997): 20–21.

Skovgaard-Petersen, Jakob. *Defining Islam for the Egyptian State: Muftīs and Fatwas of the Dār al-Iftā*. Leiden: Brill, 1997.

Soares, Benjamin. "The Historiography of Islam in West Africa: An Anthropologist's View." *Journal of African Studies* 55 (2014): 27–36.

Soifer, Maya. "Beyond *convivencia*: Critical Reflections on the Historiography of Interfaith Relations in Christian Spain." *Journal of Medieval Iberian Studies* 1, no. 1 (2009): 19–35.

Soyer, François. *The Persecution of the Jews and Muslims of Portugal: King Manuel I and the End of Religious Tolerance (1496–7)*. Leiden: Brill, 2011.

———. "King Manuel I and the Expulsion of the Castilian *Conversos* and Muslims from Portugal in 1497: New Perspectives," *Cadernos de Estudos Sefarditas* 8 (2008): 33–62.

Stearns, Justin. "Representing and Remembering al-Andalus: Some Historical Considerations Regarding the End of Time and the Making of Nostalgia." *Medieval Encounters* 15, no. 2–4 (2009): 355–74.

Stewart, Devin. "Dissimulation in Sunni Islam and Morisco *Taqiyya*," *Al-Qanṭara* 34, no. 2 (2013): 439–90.

———. "The Identity of 'The *Muftī* of Oran,' Abū l-ʿAbbās Aḥmad b. Abī Jumʿah al-Maghrāwī al-Wahrānī (d. 917/1511)." *Al-Qanṭara* 27, no. 2 (2006): 265–301.

Suberbiola Martínez, Jesús. "Primeros Encabezamientos del Reino de Granada: El Secretario Real, Hernando de Zafra, y Las Rentas De Los Mudéjares de Ronda, Marbella y la Garbía." *Baetica: Estudios de Arte, Geografía e Historia* 30 (2007): 249–83.

Szpiech, Ryan. "Conversion as a Historiographical Problem: The Case of Zoraya/ Isabel de Solís." In *Contesting Inter-Religious Conversion in the Medieval World*, edited by Yaniv Fox and Yosi Yisraeli, 24–38. New York: Routledge, 2016.

Al-Tasūlī, ʿAlī b. ʿAbd al-Salām (d. 1258/1842). *Ajwibat al-Tasūlī ʿan masāʾil al-amīr ʿAbd al-Qādir fī al-jihād*. Edited by ʿAbd al-Laṭīf Ṣāliḥ. Beirut: Dār al-Gharb al-Islāmī, 1996.

———. *Traduction de la fetoua du faqîh Sîdi ʿAlī Et Tsouli, contenant le <<Souâl>> du Hâdj ʿAbdelqâder ben Mahi Ed Din et la réponse*. Translated by E. Michaux-Bellaire. *Archives Marocaines* 11 (1907): 116–28, 395–454; *Archives Marocaines* 15 (1909): 158–84.

Terem, Etty. *New Texts, Old Practices: Islamic Reform in Modern Morocco*. Stanford: Stanford University Press, 2014.

Al-Tinbuktī, Aḥmad Bābā (d. 1036/1637). *Nayl al-ibtihāj bi-taṭrīz al-Dībāj*. Edited by ʿAlī ʿUmar. 2 vols. Cairo: Maktabat al-Thaqāfa al-Dīniyya, 2004.

———. *Kifāyat al-muḥtāj li-maʿrifat man laysa fī al-Dībāj*. Edited by Muḥammad Muṭīʿ. 2 vols. Rabat: Wizārat al-Awqāf waʾl-Shuʾūn al-Islāmiyya, 2000.

Al-Tirmidhī, Muḥammad b. ʿĪsā (d. 279/892). *Sunan al-Tirmidhī wa-huwa al-Jāmiʿ al-kabīr*. Edited by Markaz al-Buḥūth wa-Taqniyat al-Maʿlūmāt. 2nd ed. 5 vols. Diwān al-Ḥadīth al-Nabawī 4. Cairo: Dār al-Taʾṣīl, 2016.

Triaud, Jean-Louis. "Giving a Name to Islam South of the Sahara: An Adventure in Taxonomy." *Journal of African History* 55 (2014): 3–15.

Turki, Abdel-Majid. "Pour ou contre la légalité du séjour des musulmans en territoire reconquis par les chrétiens: Justification doctrinale et réalité historique." In *Religionsgespräche im Mittelalter*, edited by Bernard Lewis and Friedrich Niewöhner, 305–23. Wiesbaden: Harrassowitz, 1992.

———. "Consultation juridique d'al-Imam al-Mazari sur le cas des musulmans vivant en Sicile sous l'autorité des Normands." *Mélanges de l'Université Saint-Joseph* 50 (1984): 691–704. Republished in Arabic as "Fatwā al-Imām al-Māzarī fī al-Muslimīn al-muqīmīn bi-Ṣiqilliyya fī ḥamāyat al-Nurmān." In Abdel-Majid Turki, *Qaḍāyā thaqāfiyya min tārīkh al-gharb al-Islāmī: nuṣūṣ wa-dirāsāt*, 61–80. Beirut: Dār al-Gharb al-Islāmī, 1988.

Udovitch, Abraham L. "Muslims and Jews in the World of Frederic II: Boundaries and Communication." *Princeton Papers in Near Eastern Studies* 2 (1993): 83–104.

Umar, Muhammad S. *Islam and Colonialism: Intellectual Responses of Northern Nigeria to British Colonial Rule*. Leiden: Brill, 2006.

———. "Islamic Discourses on European Visitors to Sokoto Caliphate in the Nineteenth Century," *Studia Islamica* 95 (2002): 135–59.

Velázquez Basanta, Fernando Nicolás. "La relación histórica sobre las postrimerías del Reino de Granada, según Aḥmad al-Maqqarī (s. XVII)." In *El Epílogo del Islam Andalusí: La Granada del Siglo XV*, edited by Celia del Moral, 481–554. Granada: Universidad de Granada, 2002.

Verskin, Alan. *Islamic Law and the Crisis of the Reconquista: The Debate on the Status of Muslim Communities in Christendom*. Leiden: Brill, 2015.

———. *Oppressed in the Land? Fatwās on Muslims Living under Non-Muslim Rule from the Middle Ages to the Present*. Princeton: Markus Wiener, 2013.

———. "The Evolution of the Mālikī Jurists' Attitudes to the Mudéjar Leadership." *Der Islam* 90, no. 1 (2013): 44–64.

Vidal Castro, Francisco. "El Miʿyār de al-Wanšarīsī (m. 914/1508). II: Contenido." *Miscelánea de Estudios Árabes y Hebráicos* 44, no. 1 (1995): 213–46.

———. "El Miʿyār de al-Wanšarīsī (m. 914/1508). I: Fuentes, manuscritos, ediciones, traducciones." *Miscelánea de Estudios Árabes y Hebráicos* 42–43, no. 1 (1993–94): 317–61.

———. "ʿAbd al-Wāhid al-Wansharīsī (m. 1549): Adul, cadí y muftí de Fez." In *Homee a la Profesora Elena Pezzi*, edited by Antonio Escobedo Rodríguez, 141–57. Granada: Universidad de Granada, 1992.

———. "Las obras de Aḥmad al-Wanšarīsī (m. 914/1508). Inventario analítico." *Anaquel de Estudios Árabes* 3 (1992): 73–112.

———. "Aḥmad al-Wanšarīsī (m. 914/1508): Principales aspectos de su vida." *Al-Qanṭara* 12, no. 2 (1991): 315–52.

Vikør, Knut S. "*Jihād*, *ʿilm*, and *taṣawwuf*—Two Justifications of Action from the Idrīsī Tradition." *Studia Islamica* 90 (2000): 153–76.

Vincent, B. "Vers sur la conquête d'Alger." *Journal Asiatique* (December 1839): 503–7.

Al-Wansharīsī, Abū al-ʿAbbās Aḥmad b. Yaḥyā (d. 914/1508). *Īḍāḥ al-Masālik ilā qawāʿid al-Imām Mālik*. Edited by Al-Ṣādiq b. ʿAbd al-Raḥmān al-Ghiryānī. Beirut: Dār Ibn Ḥazm, 2006.

———. *Al-Miʿyār al-muʿrib waʾl-jāmiʿ al-mughrib ʿan fatāwī ahl Ifrīqiyā waʾl-Andalus waʾl-Maghrib*. Edited by Muḥammad Ḥajjī, et al. 13 vols. Rabat: Wizārat al-Awqāf waʾl-Shuʾūn al-Islāmiyya, 1981–83. Lithograph edition: Edited by Ibn al-ʿAbbās al-Būʿazzāwī, et al. 12 vols. Fez, 1897–98.

Al-Wazzānī, Abū ʿĪsā Muḥammad al-Mahdī (d. 1342/1923). *Al-Nawāzil al-jadīda al-kubrā fīmā li-ahl Fās wa-ghayrihim min al-badw waʾl-qurā, al-musammā bi-: Al-Miʿyār al-jadīd al-jāmiʿ al-muʿrib ʿan fatāwī al-mutaʾakhkhirīn min ʿulamāʾ al-Maghrib*. Edited by ʿUmar b. ʿAbbād. 12 vols. [Rabat]: Wizārat al-Awqāf waʾl-Shuʾūn al-Islāmiyya, 1996–2000.

———. *Al-Nawāzil al-ṣughrā, al-musammā: Al-Minaḥ al-sāmiya fī al-nawāzil al-fiqhiyya*. Edited by Wizārat al-Awqāf waʾl-Shuʾūn al-Islāmiyya. 4 vols. [Rabat]: Wizārat al-Awqāf waʾl-Shuʾūn al-Islāmiyya, 1992–93.

Wiegers, Gerard. *Islamic Literature in Spanish and Aljamiado: Yça of Segovia (fl. 1450), His Antecedents and Successors*. Leiden: Brill, 1994.

Wilson, M. Brett. "The Failure of Nomenclature: The Concept of 'Orthodoxy' in the Study of Islam." *Comparative Islamic Studies* 3, no. 2 (2007): 169–94.

Woerner-Powell, Tom. *Another Road to Damascus: An Integrative Approach to* ʿAbd al-Qādir *al-Jazāʾirī (1808–1883)*. Berlin: De Gruyter, 2017.

Wuld al-Bara, Yahya. "Les théologiens mauritaniens face au colonialisme français: Étude de *fatwa*-s de jurisprudence musulmane." In *Le temps des marabouts: Itinéraires et stratégies islamiques en Afrique occidentale française v. 1880–1960*, edited by David Robinson and Jean-Louis Triaud, 85–117. Paris: Éditions Karthala, 1997.

———. *See also* Ould El-Bara, Yahya *and* Wuld al-Barāʾ, Yaḥyā.

Wuld al-Barāʾ, Yaḥyā. *Al-Majmūʿa al-kubrā al-shāmila li-fatāwā wa-nawāzil wa-aḥkām ahl gharb wa-junūb gharb al-Ṣaḥrāʾ*. 12 vols. [Nouakchott]: Mūlāy al-Ḥasan b. al-Mukhtār b. al-Ḥasan, 2009.

———. *See also* Ould El-Bara, Yahya, *and* Wuld al-Bara, Yahya.

Wuld al-Sālim, Ḥamāh Allāh. "Dawr al-ʿulamāʾ al-Shanāqiṭa fī al-thaqāfa biʾl-Mamlaka al-ʿArabiyya al-Saʿūdiyya fī ʿahd al-Malik Saʿūd b. ʿAbd al-ʿAzīz." *Al-Dāra* 4 (2006): 317–43.

Al-Yūbī, Laḥsan. *Al-Fatāwā al-fiqhiyya fī ahamm al-qaḍāyā min ʿahd al-Saʿdiyyīn ilā mā qabl al-ḥimāya*. [Rabat]: Wizārat al-Awqāf waʾl-Shuʾūn al-Islāmiyya, 1998.

Yūsuf ʿAlī, ʿAbdullah, trans. *The Meaning of the Holy Qur'an*. 11th edition, revised. Beltsville, MD: Amana Publications, 2004.

Al-Ziriklī, Khayr al-Dīn. *Al-Aʿlām: qāmūs tarājim li-ashhar al-rijāl waʾl-nisāʾ min al-ʿarab waʾl-mustaʿribīn waʾl-mustashriqīn*. 8 vols. 14th ed. Beirut: Dār al-ʿIlm lil-Malāyīn, 1999.

Al-Ẓufayrī, Maryam Muḥammad Ṣāliḥ. *Muṣṭalaḥāt al-madhāhib al-fiqhiyya wa-asrār al-fiqh al-marmūz fī al-aʿlām waʾl-kutub waʾl-ārāʾ waʾl-tarjīḥāt*. Beirut: Dār Ibn Ḥazm, 2002.

Index of Subjects and Terms

Qur'ān Citations

Index of *Ḥadīths*